OBJECT-ORIENTED METHODS

The Addison-Wesley Object Technology Series

Grady Booch, Ivar Jacobson, and James Rumbaugh, Series Editors

For more information check out the series web site [http://www.aw.com/cseng/otseries/].

Component Software Series

Clemens Szyperski, Series Editor

For more information check out the series web site [http://www.aw.com/cseng/cbdseries/].

OBJECT-ORIENTED METHODS

Principles & Practice

Third Edition

Ian Graham TriReme International Ltd.

with Alan O'Callaghan, De Montfort University
and Alan Cameron Wills, TriReme International Ltd.

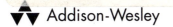 Addison-Wesley

An imprint of **Pearson Education**

Harlow, England · London · New York · Reading, Massachusetts · San Francisco
Toronto · Don Mills, Ontario · Sydney · Tokyo · Singapore · Hong Kong · Seoul
Taipei · Cape Town · Madrid · Mexico City · Amsterdam · Munich · Paris · Milan

PEARSON EDUCATION LIMITED

Head Office:
Edinburgh Gate
Harlow CM20 2JE
Tel: +44 (0)1279 623623
Fax: +44 (0)1279 431059

London Office:
128 Long Acre
London WC2E 9AN
Tel: +44 (0)20 7447 2000
Fax: +44 (0)20 7240 5771
Website: www.aw.com/cseng/

First published in Great Britain in 1991

ISBN 0-201-61913-X

British Library Cataloguing in Publication Data
A CIP catalogue record for this book can be obtained from the British Library.

Library of Congress Cataloging in Publication Data
Applied for.

The programs in this book have been included for their instructional value. The publisher does not
offer any warranties or representations in respect of their fitness for a particular purpose, nor does the
publisher accept any liability for any loss or damage arising from their use.

Many of the designations used by manufacturers and sellers to distinguish their products are claimed
as trademarks. Pearson Education Limited has made every attempt to supply trademark information
about manufacturers and their products mentioned in this book. A list of trademark designations and
their owners appears on page xxi.

10 9 8 7 6 5 4 3 2

Typeset by the author
Printed and bound in Great Britain by Biddles Ltd, Guildford and King's Lynn

The Publishers' policy is to use paper manufactured from sustainable forests

This book is dedicated to my son, Robert Graham Miller.

BRIEF CONTENTS

PREFACE TO
THE THIRD EDITION

He threw down his book, stretched his legs towards the embers in the grate, and clasped his hands at the back of his head, in that agreeable afterglow of excitement when thought lapses from examination of a specific object into a suffusive sense of its connexions with all the rest of our existence.

George Eliot (*Middlemarch*)

When the first edition of this book appeared in 1991, there was a great deal of excitement and interest in object-oriented techniques in the IT industry and in academia, with public seminars held almost weekly. New journals and regular conferences were being established, and the membership of special interest groups was growing rapidly. By the time the second edition came out interest had peaked and many commercial organizations had already had their first experiences of the technology for better or worse. Still the fuss continues and, while the languages have stabilized a little, the furore over methods and life-cycle issues has, if anything intensified even further – even though the emergence of the Unified Modelling Language (UML) has largely settled disputes over notation. Current concern now focuses on cross-enterprise application integration and component-based development. Since the second edition appeared the field of object technology (OT) has, perhaps, trebled in its size and scope: published work and topics covered. It was a daunting prospect to begin to expand this volume, whose original aim had been to provide a comprehensive survey, without making the book excessively large. On the other hand the character of many of the new developments has been that of variations on themes that were around in 1994: the popularity of Jim Coplien's C++ idioms was the first inkling of the huge explosion of interest in design patterns; early object request brokers based on the Object Management Group (OMG) architecture model have matured and been put into production; new, better object-oriented programming languages have emerged; object-oriented databases are now in everyday commercial use – though still on a limited scale. Beside all this there has been a complete shake-out in the area of analysis and design methods. *Plus ça change, plus c'est la même chose.* The result has had to be a very substantial rewrite.

SUBJECT MATTER

This book is essentially a survey of the whole area of object technology. It covers object-oriented programming, object-oriented design, object-oriented analysis, object-oriented databases and concerns several related technologies. There is a number of good books on object technology covering specific languages and methods. More general coverage is provided in these books only incidentally. They give a high level overview of the philosophy and benefits of object-orientation in general but trouble the reader with a great deal of material specifically about programming and are dependent on the syntax of particular languages. At the other extreme there are now some very good 'management surveys' available, but these are not generally of sufficient technical depth for practitioners or students. The reader seeking a reasonably detailed understanding of those aspects of object-orientation not related to programming has to turn to the research literature, conference proceedings, massive monographs or collections of highly technical papers. If such a reader wants to gain a general understanding of the whole field rapidly or evaluate the future rôle of object technology, there are few coherent and comprehensive sources. My aims are therefore to address a gap in the literature in the following ways.

- Providing a single source, comprehensive, language-independent introduction covering all aspects of object technology from the perspectives of both the developer and management.
- Placing much more emphasis on the viewpoint of the conceptual modeller, compared to that of the programmer or designer; and upon the practical issues surrounding the use of object-oriented techniques in commercial environments.
- Propagating the view that object-orientation, artificial intelligence and data modelling together (rather than separately) are required to address the central issues of IT.
- Providing an introduction to and evaluation of object-oriented languages, middleware, databases and methods; and relating them each to conventional technology. In particular, providing the first concise explanation of the powerful Catalysis™ method for component-based development (D'Souza and Wills, 1999).
- Attempting to explode some of the myths surrounding object technology while retaining a genuinely optimistic evaluation of its practical use.
- Supplying sufficient depth and reference material to guide students and practitioners entering the field.

The further objective of this book, which it shares with both previous editions, is to state in a clear manner the answers to the following questions.

- What are object-oriented methods?
- What are the benefits, pitfalls and likely costs?
- What languages, methods and tools are available, and how may they be evaluated?
- What has to be done to get started with adoption?

- What is the rôle of object-oriented analysis and design methods?
- How does one capture requirements for OO systems?
- How can object-orientation be managed?
- What special skills are required?
- What are the links to other areas of Information Technology (IT)?
- What are suitable applications?

Incidentally to the above aims the book exposes some of my own original work on object-oriented conceptual modelling using the idea of rulesets, requirements engineering and development process – collectively referred to as SOMA (Semantic Object Modelling Approach). I have interwoven SOMA with Catalysis and used the UML notation throughout the chapters on method. In reading this material the reader should be aware of the distinctive feature of my approach, which interprets object modelling as a general form of knowledge representation, rather than just a way to describe computer programs.

MAJOR CHANGES IN THE THIRD EDITION

This edition is a very substantial revision and extension of the Second Edition, reflecting major changes in the field since the first two editions. The rapid acceptance of object technology since I wrote the first edition has astounded me along with even the most fervent propagandists for it. The rapid changes in the technology which have occurred during the past three years or so are less surprising. Not only have the products changed and the number of methods grown, but the conclusions that a practitioner or, indeed, a careful observer can draw are quite different from what they were in 1991 or 1994. One of the most significant changes has been the acceptance, by the industry at large, of the OMG and their publication of various standards for object technology. On the other hand there is much that has not changed. Thus, while the objective of the book remains the same, the means of achieving it must be substantially different. This edition brings all the definitional material up to date and into conformity with newly emerging standards. It modernizes the descriptions of products and methods available and draws new conclusions based on the new facts.

The major changes are as follows. Chapter 1 has been modified slightly to reflect greater clarity and standardization of terminology than was present in the industry when the book was first written. It has benefited from what I hope are better, more mature pedagogical techniques that I have developed in the course of lecturing about and teaching the subject to many people. A new Chapter 4 on middleware and migration strategies has been included, with more material on OMG standards. The material on object-oriented databases in Chapter 5 has been completely updated to reflect new and increasingly mature products in this area. The biggest change is to the material on object-oriented analysis and design and their management. The survey of the 50 or more methods that were around six years ago has been relegated to an appendix, which will be of chiefly historical interest. The book now uses UML throughout and Chapters 6 and 7 describe best practice for object-oriented analysis and design, based mainly on the insights of Catalysis and SOMA. A new appendix summarizes the UML notation. Chapter 7 is new and covers software architecture, patterns and component-based development. Chapter 8 describes the SOMA approach to requirements engineering in detail. Chapter 9, on management, is substantially reorganized for greater clarity of exposition and to give a far more definite prescription of the recommended development process. It now includes guidance on user interface design. All other chapters and Appendix A have undergone slight revision and improvement to reflect new developments in the field and correct any errors which remained in the Second Edition and which I was aware of.

I have added exercises at the end of most chapters to assist the substantial number of educational users of whom I became gradually aware over recent years. Selected answers can be found on the TriReme web site; where I know the answers, that is. The Bibliography is substantially expanded, to reflect the general growth in the volume of the literature as well as the new material in this edition, and the Glossary has been updated and improved.

Despite these drastic changes the essential purpose of the book remains unchanged and I hope it is merely a more comprehensive, detailed, up-to-date and accurate survey of object-oriented methods than it would have been without the alterations.

INTENDED READERSHIP   The book is intended to be accessible to readers who do not have deep specialist knowledge of theoretical computer science or advanced mathematics, but at the same time it attempts to treat the important issues accurately and in depth. It provides advice on how best to exploit object technology in practice.

The primary audience I had in mind for earlier editions was the IT and DP profession; software engineers and, generally, people who work with computers whether in user organizations, consultancies, universities or manufacturers. Although this is still the case with this edition, it has become clear that the book now has a loyal following in universities where the book is often used as a text for introductory undergraduate courses in object technology within an information technology or software engineering curriculum, perhaps complementing another course on object-oriented programming. It will therefore be of interest to teachers of Computer Science, Business Systems Analysis and possibly Artificial Intelligence. Researchers will be interested in the book as a survey and for the original contributions. They may also find some of the commentary scattered through the book thought provoking or even controversial. Managers and project planners will read it to gain an understanding of how the technology will affect their business practices and to be able to plan more effectively for change. Consultants, project managers, systems analysts and designers will read it to evaluate and stay abreast of the technology and, I hope, use the techniques explained in their day-to-day work. Programmers will read it to broaden their horizons in this area.

The material in this book, as it evolved, has been presented to very many audiences at various conferences, public seminars and in-house training courses.

READING MAP

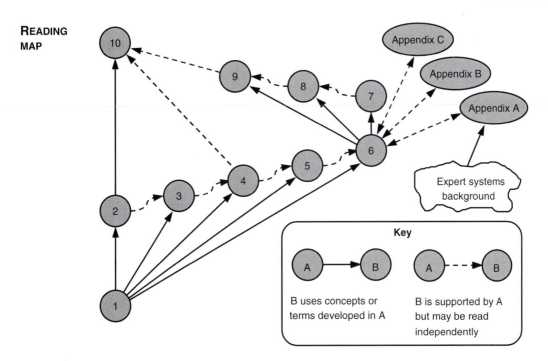

There are a number of optional reading paths through the material presented in this book. The two prime routes through the text are illustrated in the reading map. Managers and those wishing for a high level view of the subject may take the high road through Chapters 1, 2 and 10. Project managers might also include Chapter 9. People interested in analysis methods must take the low road, as Chapters 6–8 build on all previous chapters. However, Chapter 1 should be read even by people familiar with object-oriented programming since it introduces terminology which may differ from that of other works, stressing – as I have indicated – a conceptual modelling viewpoint. Specialist topics and significant digressions are indicated by the diversion icon shown to the left of this paragraph (which is not a digression).

I hope the book tells a story if read sequentially. There are certainly some key themes to look out for. These are the differentiation of the viewpoints of the system designer from the conceptual modeller, the need for object-orientation to absorb techniques and ideas from other areas of computing and the need to add semantic richness to the more well-understood benefits of object-orientation: reusability and extensibility.

A NOTE ON LANGUAGE AND SPELLING

Since many of us are prone to strong opinions on language and spelling, and since some of my habitual usage has attracted comment from some referees of this and previous editions of this work, I feel that it is worthwhile clarifying the principles that I have applied in this respect in this text. Also, the conventions of spelling and the rules of transformational syntax vary between English, American English and other 'Englishes'.

The principle behind the spelling is etymological. Thus many words ending -IZE are spelt that way (as is the American fashion), rather than the more usual modern English -ISE, when the Greek or Latin original indicates that the former is correct. This has to be largely based on guesswork, since I have never formally learnt any foreign languages other than Chinese and German. However, I have discovered that a useful rule of thumb is to ask whether there can be an -IZATION. If not, as with ADVERTISE, CIRCUMCISE or DEVISE, then the S is correct. The only exception I know of (and the only one in the *Concise Oxford*) is IMPROVISATION. CONNEXION is spelt with an X for similar etymological reasons. However, when words from foreign languages or quotations are used the original spelling is retained. Thus, CONNECTIONISM is used for the school of thought on neural nets, due to its American origin. Latin and other imported words are consistently italicized. All such words are to be found in a good English dictionary. Bold characters are used for **definitions** and italics for *emphasis*. Small capitals are used for the names of 'patterns' and for terms we wish to discuss (as in this paragraph).

The word DATA is the plural of DATUM and is used as such throughout. I fail to see why writers on Computing should get away with their almost universal error of treating DATA as a singular when writers in no other discipline do so. This is nothing to do with the differences between American and English, as a brief glance at books on Geography, Statistics, Medicine, Management and so on from both sides of the Atlantic will soon demonstrate. Words with two dictionary definitions such as BIMONTHLY and BILLION are proscribed.

The word METHODS is used in three different ways in this book:

- methods for doing software engineering in general (in the title);
- particular methods for doing software engineering and modelling (as with the Catalysis and SOMA methods); and
- methods (programs) implementing the behaviour of objects.

I have resisted the non-word METHODOLOGIES on the same grounds that I would reject Physicses, or Chemistries. The OED has it that Methodology (and the capitalization is necessary) is 'the science of method' and Chambers adds 'within a science or discipline'. The plural could only be used if there had been a 'paradigm shift' in the sense of Thomas Kuhn (a solecism in itself[1]) in our perception of the way of doing things. Since many people believe that object technology is such a paradigm shift, we could correctly write the sentence: 'There is a difference between the Structured and the Object-Oriented Methodologies.'; meaning that the whole approach to computer science has altered. It is pure barbarism to write: 'There is a difference between the Yourdon and Jackson methodologies.' I try to avoid words like PARADIGM too.

---

[1]PARADIGM really means a model or especially typical example.

Sexist assumptions in writing – as in life – should be avoided. My preference is for a plural personal pronoun or s/he (pronounced 'she') instead of the ugly and intrusive 'he or she'. However, I distinguish between sexual and grammatical gender; so that MAN is merely short for MANKIND and means the same as HUMANITY. Thus the term MAN-DAY is to be taken generically; the gender being grammatical rather than sexual. Otherwise, the French would have to start saying 'le ou la personne' (people are feminine in most European languages) and the English speaker would be obliged to use WOPERSON for WOMAN. Political correctness is achieved by overthrowing evils, not by tinkering with language.

Split infinitives are usually avoided, based on personal preference and my belief that readability is enhanced when adverbs appear late in sentences. No attempt to write in short, journalistic sentences has been made, except where clarity so dictates. I have tried to employ the *correct* word, rather than a word that everybody will know. Particularly obscure (to my referees) words, or words where the dictionary would not be adequate due to nuance, have been added to the glossary or defined in a footnote. The dictionaries used were the *Oxford English Dictionary (Compact Edition)* (OED) and *Chambers English Dictionary*. A certain number of words that are not in the dictionary are inevitable in a book on a technical subject of this kind. An example is WORKSTATION, as opposed to WORK STATION. The latter seems distinctly wrong in the context of a local computer, where the emphasis is on its capability rather than its location. I have taken such liberties fairly thoughtfully though. Language, after all, is a living thing.

These are the theoretical principles applied. In practice there may be several grammatical and spelling errors.

ACKNOW-LEDGEMENTS Although it contains much original material, this book is largely a survey of other people's work and could not have been written without that work. I would like to acknowledge the contribution of these other authors. Also, many of the ideas contained are the result of personal interaction between the author and a number of his colleagues, clients and friends.

Special thanks are due to Akmal Chaudri for his contribution to Chapter 5. The remarks of several anonymous referees were very helpful too. Alan O'Callaghan of De Montfort University co-wrote Chapter 7. Alan Cameron Wills co-wrote Chapters 6 and 7. The latter deserves special mention: many of the figures in these chapters were copied from his original artwork as contained in TriReme's UML and Catalysis course material. Alan is still teaching me a great deal about the subject and I acknowledge a great debt to him for this and his encouragement during the preparation of this text. This should not be taken to mean that either of my co-authors agrees with all the assertions I make or stances I adopt. The responsibility for any errors that remain in the text is entirely mine.

With the long history of this text, there is not space to acknowledge the nature of every individual contribution to this and earlier editions. I want, however, to thank all the following people and organizations for their help: Mark Addison, Nigel Backhurst, Sav Bhoja, Steve Birkbeck, Julia Bischof, Grady Booch, Franco Civello,

Dave Clark, Alistair Cockburn, Graham Collins, Larry Constantine, Cos Constantinou, John Cresswell, Robin Crewe, John Daniels, Sally Davies, Malcomb Dick, Faramarz Farhoodi, Armando Ferreira, Don Firesmith, Martin Fowler, Florence Froidevaux, Stuart Frost, Tim Gee, Thomas Grotehen, Brian Henderson-Sellers, Kevlin Henney, Chris Harris-Jones, Benedict Heal, Tim Lamb, David Harvey, Jane Hillston, Michael Jackson, Margaret James, Peter Jones, Fiona Kinnear, David Lee, Chris Lees, Mark Lewis, Nick Lukic, Margaret Lyall, Neil Maiden, Sonia Math, Clive Menhinick, Sally Mortimore, Derek Pearce, Colin Prosser, Rob Radmore, Al-Noor Ramji, Dan Rawsthorne, David Redmond-Pyle, Elaine Richardson, René Schwarb, Richard Seed, Tony Simons, Richard Smith, Gail Swaffield, John Taylor, Brian Thal, Ulrika Thyssen, Richard Walker, Rose Watson, John Welch, David Welton, Kerry Williams, Benoit Xhenseval, Jennifer Yates, Marcus Zemp, BIS Applied Systems, BIS Banking Systems, Chase Manhattan Bank, De Montfort University, Eric Leach Marketing, Equitable Life, Swiss Bank Corporation (now UBS), TriReme International and the Expert Systems, OOPS and Requirements Engineering Specialist Groups of the British Computer Society. All the staff at Pearson Education demonstrated their usual splendid professionalism and especial thanks are due to my editor, Alison Birtwell.

Thanks go too to the various audiences who endured my seminars and classes during the period when these ideas were being developed and refined and who provided valuable feedback, and occasionally – and most usefully – asked hard questions. I would also like to thank the thousands of people scattered throughout the world, living and dead, whose labour, by hand or by brain, created the word processing system I am now using. Without it no edition of this book would ever have been written.

Lastly, it's about time that I came clean and acknowledged the contribution of The Grove: the hostelry where much of all my books has been written and corrected. It is a Victorian pub with an interior that deserves to be listed and nearly always empty enough to guarantee me a table to work at; which is perhaps why some of the locals – who come from all walks of life from car mechanics to criminologists – call it The Grave. The other writers that rely on it tend to refer to The Balham Reading Rooms instead; to my knowledge at least two books on the culture of the Solomon islands, one novel and a song (The Ballad of Ken Livingstone – copies on request) also had their origins there. It also provides an occasional venue for me to join the resident Wandle Delta String Band and inflict my bodhrán playing on the public. See you there!

Ian Graham
Balham, November 2000
(ian@trireme.com)

CONTENTS

Trademark notice

Action Technologies Workbench™ is a trademark of Action Technologies Inc.; Actor™ is a trademark of Symantec; Adabas™, Adabas Entire™, Natural™, Natural Expert™ and Tamino™ are trademarks of Software AG; Aion™, COOL™, DataBlades™, Ingres™, Jasmine™, Paradigm Plus™, Process Engineer™, Process Continuum™ and Team*work*™ are trademarks of Computer Associates Inc.; Apple®, Lisa™, MacApp™ and Macintosh™ are trademarks of Apple Computer Inc.; ART™ is a trademark of Inference Corp.; Astoria™ is a trademark of Xerox Inc.; Biztalk™, COM™, COM+™, DCOM™, SOAP™, Internet Explorer™, Microsoft Windows™, Access™, PowerPoint™, MS Project™, MFC™, MSMQ™, MTS™, Visio™, Excel™, Intellisense™, OLE™, Visual Basic™, Visual Studio™ and Microsoft Office™ are trademarks of Microsoft Inc.; Caché™ is a trademark of InterSystems Corp.; Catalysis™ is a European trademark of TriReme International Ltd. and a US service mark of Computer Associates Inc.; Cognos™ is a trademark of Cognos Inc.; CORBA Plus™ is a trademark of Ventel; CORBA® and IIOP® are registered trademarks and OMG™, Object Management Group™, ORB™, Object Request Broker™, OMG Interface Definition Language™, IDL™, CORBAservices™, CORBAfacilities™, Unified Modeling Language™, UML™, XMI™, MOF™ and the UML Cube logo are trademarks of the OMG.; DAIS™ is a trademark of PeerLogic; DCE™, DEPOT/J™, IRIS™, NewWave™, TeamFusion™, ObjectIQ™ and Odapter™ are trademarks of Hewlett-Packard Inc.; Delphi™ and Visibroker™ are trademarks of Inprise Inc.; Eiffel™ and Melting Ice™ are trademarks of Interactive Software Engineering Corporation; Ellipse™ is a trademark of Cooperative Solutions Inc.; Encina™ is a trademark of Transarc Corp.; ES/KERNEL™ and TPBroker™ are trademarks of Hitachi; ETX™ is a trademark of Tibco Inc.; eXcelon™ and ObjectStore™ are trademarks of Object Design International; Forté™, Forté Conductor™, Forté Fusion™ and SynerJ are trademarks of Sun Microsystems; G-Base™ and G-Logis™ are trademarks of Graphael; Gemstone™ is a trademark of Gemstone Inc.; Genera™ and Statice™ are trademarks of Symbolics Inc.; Goldworks™ is a trademark of Gold Hill Computers Inc.; IBM™, AS/400™, OS/400™, CICS™, Component Broker™, DB2™, ENVY™, IMS™, Lotus123™, Lotus Notes™, San Francisco™, System-R™, Taligent™, Visual Age™ and Websphere™ are trademarks of International Business Machines Inc.; Iceberg™, Tuxedo™ and Weblogic™, are trademarks of BEA Systems; Illustra™, Informix™ and Informix Universal Server™ are trademarks of Unisys; Itasca™ is a trademark of Itasca Inc.; Java™. EJB™, Enterprise Java Beans™, Java Beans™ are trademarks of Sun Microsystems Inc.; Kappa™, KEE™ are trademarks of Intellicorp Inc.; Lingo™ and Rekursiv™ are trademarks of Linn Technologies Ltd.; Mjølner™ is a trademark of Mjølner Informatics; NetGateway™, Sybase™ and Transact SQL™ are trademarks of Sybase Inc.; Netscape™, Netscape Navigator™ are trademarks of Netscape Inc.; NeWI™ is a trademark of SSA Inc.; Nexpert Object™ is a trademark of Neuron Data; NeXT™, NeXtStep™ and OpenSTEP™ are trademarks of NeXT Corp.; O^2™ is a trademark of Unidata; Objective-C™ is a trademark of Stepstone Corp.; Objectivity/DB™ is a trademark of Objectivity Inc.; Objectory™, Rational Unified Process, RUP, Rose and Requisite Pro™ are trademarks of Rational Inc.; ObjectStore™ is a trademark of Object Design International; ObjectWorks™ is a trademark of ParcPlace Systems; Ontos™ is a trademark of Ontos Inc.; Oracle®, CASE*METHOD™, Express™, are trademarks of Oracle Inc.; Orbix™ is a trademark of Iona Technologies Plc; ORDB™ and UniSQL™ are trademarks of Cincom Inc.; POET™, POET Content Management System™ and Viewsoft™ are trademarks of Poet Software GmbH; PowerBuilder™ and Sybase™ are trademarks of Sybase Inc.; ProcessWise™ and REVEAL™ aretrademarks of ICL Ltd.; Select™ is a trademark of Princeton Softech; Simula™ is a trademark of Simula AS; Software through Pictures™ is a trademark of Aionix Inc.; SOMATiK™ and Leonardo™ are trademarks of Bezant Ltd.; Syntropy ™is a trademark of Syntropy Ltd.; System Architect™ is a trademark of Popkin Software; Tandem Nonstop™, PDP-11™ and VAX™ are trademarks of Compaq Inc.; Telescript™ is a trademark of General Magic Inc.; WordPerfect™ is a trademark of Corel Inc. Together™ and TogetherJ™ are trademarks of Together Inc.; TOP END™ is a trademark of NCR; UNIFACE™ is a trademark of Compuware Inc.; Universal Server™ is a trademark of Informix Inc.; UNIX™ is a trademark of AT&T; Versant™ is a trademark of Versant Object Technologies; Vision™ is a trademark of Innovative Systems Techniques; XShell™ is a trademark of Expersoft Inc.; ZIM™ is a trademark of Zanthe.

1

Basic concepts

My object all sublime
I shall achieve in time –

W.S. Gilbert (*The Mikado*)

In the 1990s it became the case that use of the adjectival phrase OBJECT-ORIENTED was almost synonymous with modernity, goodness and worth in information technology circles. At the end of that period the word COMPONENT began to replace OBJECT, though with little change in the content of the remarks made – at least by journalists. Since we may, even now, be vulnerable to exaggeration of the benefits of this technology, it is desirable to achieve a more balanced view. This book will, firstly, state the case for object-orientation and component-based development in theoretically pure terms but, secondly, show how applications of these abstract ideas can contribute to real, practical advances in building useful computer systems. The approach will be independent of any particular programming language, and will avoid the syntactic niceties in favour of a high level evaluation of the business and technical issues which arise in selecting a suitable development environment and approach. In dealing with things object-oriented we must also realize that we are entering an area that, even now that some standards exist, is not well bounded and where research is still incomplete. We shall be forced to consider many other areas of current concern such as software architecture, distributed open systems, databases, CASE technology, expert systems, and much more. Occasionally, we will enter relatively uncharted territory.

The key benefits usually promised by purveyors of object-orientation are reusability and extensibility. That is, object-oriented systems are to be assembled from pre-written components with minimal effort and the assembled system will be easy to extend without any need to tinker with the reused components. We will examine both these benefits, and the extent to which object-oriented systems can actually live up to them, in detail, in the next chapter.

The phrase OBJECT-ORIENTED METHODS as used in this book refers to more than just object-oriented programming. It connotes a whole philosophy of systems development encompassing programming, knowledge elicitation, requirements analysis, business modelling, system design, database design and many more related

1

issues. The emphasis throughout this book is going to be on this philosophy and how it can be used to address the issues that arise in constructing information systems. Benefits such as reusability and extensibility, for example, are not restricted to the reuse or extension of chunks of code. Potentially, designs and analysis documents can be stored in libraries and reused or extended over and over again, provided of course that potential users have a means to find out about their existence easily.

As I have indicated, OBJECT-ORIENTED has become an extremely overloaded term. To help clarify the issues, in this book we will distinguish between 'object-oriented', 'component-oriented', 'object-based' and 'class-based' programming, design and analysis. We will see in later chapters that few commercial systems live up to the pure concept of object-orientation and that even those that do may have other disadvantages. Nevertheless, object-oriented systems do have a rôle, and it is important to ask not so much whether a system or language is object-oriented or not, but *how* it is object-oriented and in what way it delivers the associated benefits.

This chapter introduces the basic concepts and terminology of object-oriented methods. We begin with a short historical introduction. The motivation for and benefits of object-oriented methods and programming will be dealt with in Chapter 2.

1.1 Historical background

The rise of object-orientation reflects and recapitulates the history of computing as a whole. The earliest work in computing, going back to the late 1940s, concerned itself exclusively with what we now think of as programming. Only later did a conscious concern with design and analysis as separate issues arise. Similarly, it is object-oriented programming that first attracted attention, and only latterly did object-oriented design and, more recently, object-oriented analysis become major areas of endeavour. In this work we thus must start with object-oriented programming before moving on to the design and analysis issues, although the latter will be our more major concern.

Although Ten Dyke and Kunz (1989) have claimed that the designers of the Minuteman missile used rudimentary object-oriented techniques as early as 1957, the history of object-oriented programming really starts with the development of the Simula language in Norway in 1967 – based on ALGOL and the earlier discrete event simulation language Simula 1 – and continues through the 1970s with the development of the Smalltalk language, which almost makes a fetish of the notion of an object. Intermediate influential languages include Alphard (Wulf *et al.*, 1976) and CLU (Liskov *et al.*, 1977). Remarkably, the object-oriented language Simula pre-dates any of the notions of structured programming. Since then there have been very many languages which have been inspired by these developments and have laid claim to the appellation 'object-oriented'.

Simulation modelling is a particularly hard problem for conventional, third-generation language programmers. It requires the programmer to adapt the functional flow of control that is normal in such languages to a control flow which is more naturally described in terms of complex objects which change state and influence events from moment to moment. In object-oriented programming, this functional flow is replaced by message passing between objects which causes changes in object state. Thus object-oriented programming is an extremely natural approach since the structure of the programs directly reflects the structure of the problem. Furthermore, it is usually clear in simulation problems what the objects are: cars in a street; machines on a production line. They are usually 'real-world' rather than abstract objects and easy to identify as such. Sadly this is not always as true for commercial applications, as we shall see.

SMALLTALK AND GUIs The term OBJECT-ORIENTED finally came into the language with the advent of the programming language Smalltalk. Smalltalk was largely developed at the Xerox research centre at Palo Alto, PARC, but it has its origins not only in Simula itself but in the doctoral work of Alan Kay at Utah University which, as Rentsch (1982) records, was based on a vision of a small but ubiquitous personal computer capable of handling any kind of information management problem and capable of being used by all kinds of people. The earliest version of this was the Flex machine which, at PARC, became known as the Dynabook. Smalltalk was essentially the software component of the Dynabook and was heavily influenced by both Simula's notion of classes and inheritance and Lisp's structural features[1]. Smalltalk combined the class notion from Simula with a lot of the functional abstraction flavour of Lisp although, as languages, Smalltalk and Lisp are quite different.

The next phase, roughly the 1980s, showed an explosion of interest in the user interface (UI). The best known commercial pioneers, Xerox and later Apple, brought the world the ubiquitous WIMP[2] interface and many of the ideas in Smalltalk are strongly tied to these developments. On the one hand, object-oriented programming supported the development of such interfaces – notably in the case of the Apple Lisa and Macintosh – while on the other the style of object-oriented languages was heavily influenced by the WIMP metaphor. The most obvious effect of this is the plentiful existence of library objects for interface development, compared to a certain paucity in other areas. One of the contributory reasons for the success of object-oriented programming was the sheer complexity of these interfaces and the concomitant high cost of building them. Without the inherent reusability of object-oriented code it has been suggested that these interfaces could not have been built on such a wide scale. It has been estimated, for example, that the Apple Lisa,

---

[1] Lisp stands for LISt Processing. It is the language originally developed by John McCarthy around 1958 which became the language of choice for much early work in artificial intelligence.

[2] WIMP stands for Windows, Icons, Menus (sometimes Mice) and Pointers and refers to a style of Graphical User Interface (GUI) which makes use of them.

the precursor of the Macintosh, represents over 200 man-years of effort, much of which is accounted for by the development of the interface. The influence of the WIMP style was sufficiently pervasive that all workstations were gradually fitted out with WIMP front-ends such as Microsoft Windows or the like during this period. The drive towards standardized, open systems based on UNIX was also much concerned with the UI aspects where the battle between OpenLook, OSF Motif and the like was, for a time, seen as a crucial determinant of market success. In this sense object-orientation had already firmly left its mark on the world we live in by about 1993.

INFLUENCE FROM AI

Also, from the mid-1970s and later, there was considerable cross-fertilization between object-oriented programming and artificial intelligence (AI) research and development, leading to several useful extensions of AI languages, most principally Lisp. Thus we have languages such as Lisp with Flavors, Loops and CLOS (Common Lisp Object System). AI programming environments, themselves often Lisp extensions, such as KEE and ART had their design heavily influenced by object-oriented ideas. These systems were strongly affected by theories of knowledge representation based around semantic networks and frames. These representations express knowledge about real-world objects and concepts in the form of networks of stereotyped objects that can inherit features from more general ones. Thus the main contribution of this input to object-orientation was the sophistication of its theories about inheritance. Object-oriented methods have still to absorb these lessons fully. AI languages will be discussed further in Chapter 3.

Another stream of research in the AI world, together with research into concurrent computing, led to the notion of *actors*. Actor systems (Agha, 1986), like blackboard systems (*see* Englemore and Morgan, 1988), attempt to model pools of co-operating workers or experts. An actor is a more anthropomorphic notion than an object and has defined responsibilities, needs and knowledge about collaborators. Actor languages were usually directed at real-time and concurrent applications. A related modern notion is that of intelligent agents. It is also worth noting that modern component-based development environments such as COM+ require that components know about their collaborators too. We will have more to say about these matters in Chapters 6 and 7.

NEW LANGUAGES

User interface development poses no significant data management problems compared to commercial applications. Due to the fact that they cut their teeth on simulation and user interface design problems rather than, say, database management, there were performance problems associated with early object-oriented languages when applied to other types of application. This led to the development of new languages such as Eiffel and to extensions of existing, efficient conventional languages such as Ada, C and PASCAL. This focus also meant that object-oriented programming languages often failed to provide facilities for dealing with persistent objects, concurrency, and so on. The development of object-oriented database systems was one response to this problem. These are discussed at length in Chapter

5. Various object-oriented and object-based programming languages are surveyed in Chapter 3.

The demands of many users and in particular of financially important users like the United States of America Department of Defense (DoD) often force computer industry suppliers to change course. The demands of the DoD throughout the 1960s and 70s were consistently for three main things: an engineering approach to software development practice which found its expression in the so-called 'structured' methods, reusable software components (modularity) and open systems. The various system development methods adopted by many major IT suppliers represent a response to the first demand which reached something of a climax with the late 1980s furore over CASE tools. UNIX, X/Windows and Ada were all in some way responses to the DoD's demand that systems be 'open systems', which is to say that whatever software and hardware components we use we should expect to be able to make those systems inter-work with minimum effort. Ada also has the character of a language designed to improve modularity. We will be exploring the extent to which Ada is object-oriented later. More importantly we will be asking whether it, with object-oriented programming in general, contributes anything to these three key issues. Object-oriented programming also addresses a key DoD requirement implicit in the ones mentioned above. It promises to enable system developers to assemble systems from reusable components, thus addressing modularity and software engineering in one go. With the advent of various kinds of message-oriented middleware and message broker products supporting standards such as CORBA (see Chapter 4) the interoperability promise is extended even further, notably to genuinely distributed systems.

As object-oriented programming began to mature, interest shifted to object-oriented design methods and to object-oriented analysis or specification. The benefits of reusability and extensibility can be applied to designs and specifications as well as to code. Biggerstaff and Richter (1989), Prieto-Diaz and Freeman (1987) and Sommerville (1989) have all argued, in a more general software engineering context, that the higher the level of reuse the greater the benefit. Important questions arise in this area, such as whether an object-oriented design must be implemented in an object-oriented language or whether current design methods are in fact tied to specific languages.

NEW DATABASES AND CASE

By the early 1990s, just as relational databases were beginning to become respectable, if not required, technology in commercial environments, we saw the major vendors introducing various 'post-relational' extensions to their products having their origins in fields such as expert systems, functional programming and, latterly, object-oriented programming. Object-oriented and semi-object-oriented databases emerged as commercial products and the theoretical side of object-orientation had to take on concerns with such typically database issues as how to deal efficiently with persistent objects, caching, and object versioning. We may interpret this development as part of the regularization of object-oriented notions that took place in this period. It also raised a number of issues concerning the relative efficiency of declarative relational query languages compared with approaches based on object-identity. It is almost ironic, in the light of this history, that the latter property is possessed not only by object-oriented databases but also by the early network and hierarchical systems. Recently it has become clear that there is a fundamental split between two approaches: pure object-oriented databases and hybrid object-relational databases. In fact there are two standards for query languages based on this dichotomy: OQL and SQL3 respectively. Chapter 5 will take a closer look at database theory, object-oriented databases and these issues.

Computer aided software engineering (CASE) has become increasingly important in the development of commercial systems. It is variously regarded with enthusiasm or scepticism. The emergence of a number of object-oriented analysis and design methods and CASE tools supporting them forces us to ask whether there is any advantage to be gained through their use. Chapters 6 to 8 deal with object-oriented analysis and design techniques. CASE tools supporting these methods are also surveyed in Chapters 6 and 7.

DISTRIBUTED SYSTEMS AND THE WEB

With the advent of the 1990s came both the increased pressures on business to develop new software, as outlined above, and the availability of cheaper and much more powerful computers. This led to a ripening of the field and to a range of applications beyond GUIs and AI. Distributed and client-server computing became both possible and important and object technology was the basis of much development, especially with the appearance of so-called three-tier client-server systems, although relational databases played and continue to play an important rôle. The new applications and better hardware meant that mainstream organizations adopted object-oriented programming and now wanted proper attention paid to object-oriented design and (next) analysis. Object-oriented databases also matured during this decade and are now beginning to be used commercially. The appearance and popularization of the world wide web eventually provided the problem that this solution had been looking for. Since the web was to present multiple media – text, graphics, sound, video – relational databases could no longer be relied upon to deliver the performance required for applications that needed to store and retrieve complex structures. Also, the natural style of programming to handle these media was object-oriented. The first widely known web-aware language therefore was a fully object-oriented language: Java. Companies operating busy web sites, such as Microsoft and IBM, were forced to use object-oriented databases, such as Versant and ObjectStore, to provide the replication, version control, speed and resilience they needed. Network computing, thin clients and agents, now cry out for an encompassing theoretical framework and software engineering method. Object technology offers the best hope yet. We will see throughout this work the development of this solution.

ANALYSIS AND DESIGN

Concern also shifted from design to analysis from the start of the 1990s. The first book with the title *Object-Oriented Systems Analysis* was produced by Shlaer and Mellor in 1988. Like Booch's original paper it did not present a genuinely object-oriented method, but concentrated entirely on the exposition of extended entity-relationship models, based on an essentially relational view of the problem and ignoring the behavioural aspects of objects. Shlaer and Mellor published a second volume in 1992 that argued that behaviour should be modelled using conventional state-transition diagrams. In the meanwhile, Peter Coad had incorporated behavioural ideas into a simple but object-oriented method (Coad and Yourdon, 1990, 1991). This was followed by an explosion of interest in and publications on object-oriented analysis and design.

More recently, concern shifted to standards. Object technology can only succeed against the inertia of existing practice if users can achieve the confidence in moving to it that they require from a move to open systems. If object-oriented applications are all mutually incompatible, if object-oriented databases cannot inter-work with each other and with relational databases and if there are no standard notations and terms for object-oriented analysis there is little hope of this. The chief protagonist in the standards area has been an organization called the Object Management Group (OMG). The OMG is a very large group of influential companies (around 700) committed to establishing broad agreement between vendors on both the terminology of object-orientation and on interface standards. This level of co-operation has been seen rarely in the computer industry. Meetings of the OMG Technical Committee rotate between Europe, the USA and the Far East, helping to ensure an international base. The OMG is committed to the fast production of published standards, faster anyway than the official standards bodies can operate, and has already published several standards ranging from several versions of the widely used Common Object Request Broker Architecture (CORBA), a layered architecture for interoperation of distributed object-oriented applications, analogous in some ways to the ISO seven-layer model for networks, to a standardized definition of the notion of a currency. The first version of CORBA defined the basis for products that could hide the complexities of RPC-based distribution strategies. The CORBA 2 standard allowed object request brokers from different vendors to interoperate with each other and CORBA 3 added a scripting language and support for asynchronous messaging for guaranteed message delivery. It also introduced the CORBA Component Model, which is similar to Enterprise Java Beans (EJB) – these are server-side components as discussed further in Chapter 7. Several suppliers offer Object Request Broker (ORB) products compliant with the CORBA standards. Only a few OMG standards have been made official (by the ISO) but they nevertheless have extremely wide acceptance. However, a competing set of popular *de facto* standards has emerged from the Microsoft camp under the labels Active X, COM+ and DCOM. These architecture models, CORBA and DCOM are discussed further in Chapter 4. The OMG also adopted UML as a standard notation for object-oriented design, based on the merged notations of Booch, Jacobson and OMT. These developments are discussed in detail in Chapter 6 and Appendix B.

COMPONENTS At the time of writing the most recent preoccupations of those concerned with object technology have been component-based development (CBD), patterns, the standardization of notation for object-oriented analysis and design, the development process and architecture. These issues are discussed in Chapters 6 and 9. As the technology has entered the mainstream migration strategy has been increasingly important for adopters, as have e-commerce, the web and middleware. These issues are explored in Chapters 4 and 5.

Thus the latest phase of the history of object-orientation is characterized by a shift of emphasis from programming to design and analysis and by an awareness of the issues of distributed systems and standards. Furthermore, attention has shifted to applications where large computations or complex data manipulations are required; thus the emergence of object-oriented databases. Practically all commercially sold software is now produced using object-oriented methods. In user organizations, many current, medium-scale software development projects and quite a few large and mission-critical ones already use object-oriented programming and methods. Chapters 6 to 9 will examine object-oriented software engineering in depth. Chapter 10 describes several applications of object-oriented programming and its approach. Table 1.1 summarizes our brief history of the first three decades of OT.

Table 1.1 Three decades of object-oriented methods.

Phase I: 1971–80 *The Age of Invention*	Phase II: 1981–90 *The Age of Confusion*	Phase III: 1991–2000 *The Age of Ripening*
Discrete event simulation Simula Kay: FLEX machine PARC: Dynabook Smalltalk	WIMP interfaces Xerox & Apple Lisp extensions AI environments New languages: Eiffel, C++, ...	Focus on analysis, design, architecture & business models Commercial applications Distributed & web systems Object-oriented databases Standards, patterns, Java, components, migration

Object-oriented methods are now a firmly established part of software development culture, though still ignored by many mainframe development shops. With increased emphasis on distributed systems the object metaphor appears to be the most natural one to adopt, given its emphasis on encapsulation and message passing. Increasing concern over maintenance costs may well lead to the recognition that reusability is *the* key issue in programming, design and analysis. However, it is all too easy to be beguiled by object-oriented propaganda. Only a few commercial projects which have used object-oriented techniques have yet resulted in any significant amount of reusable code, though some have reported such benefits as discussed in Chapter 2. However, the emerging market for components does seem to be delivering genuine reuse on quite a large scale. Most experts believe that successful CBD will require a heightened focus on software architecture and an enhanced emphasis on object modelling. Furthermore, as the panic over the Year 2000 problem passes into history, larger organizations will be getting back to basics and installing sound software engineering processes. In view of such developments we could hazard that one could characterize the first decade of the twenty-first century as the age of architecture and process maturity and extend Table 1.1 with the column in Table 1.2.

Table 1.2 The immediate future of object-oriented methods.

Phase IV – 2001~10
The Age of Architecture and Process Maturity
Focus on architecture & patterns (micro architecture)
Mature OO development processes
Distributed systems everywhere
Migration to component-based systems and wrapped legacy systems
Component-based development delivers real reuse
Increased attention to business modelling and requirements engineering
Shifted emphasis from C++ to Java and other safer languages

In my view, what is required in the immediate future is not only better, purer, more efficient object-oriented languages alone but better methods for object-oriented software engineering and requirements engineering. Efficient hybrid languages such as C++, with associated UI toolkits such as Microsoft Visual Studio already exist, as do many useful low level object libraries. Without methods and tools to make these libraries usable on a commercial basis the approach is seriously compromised. I firmly believe that this is an important pre-condition for the wide acceptance of the object-oriented approach. UML will form the basis for much of this work, but it must evolve to meet real business needs. Better methods for requirements engineering will be needed too. The methods and process models that address this issue will be discussed in Chapters 8 and 9, where we emphasize earlier testing than has been common. Of course, the most useful library components will have to be developed during real projects. The benefits and potential pitfalls of object-orientation are analysed in Chapter 2 after this chapter has equipped the reader with the necessary terminology and concepts.

Object technology has undergone a regularization, like that experienced by expert systems and rule-based techniques. Object-oriented methods are now as much a part of the general toolkit of the software developer as 4GLs, databases, graphics software and so on. However, there is still room for object technology to absorb further ideas from human factors, data modelling, artificial intelligence and other areas of computing. Research continues in this area. However, taken as a whole, object-oriented programming can be regarded as a mature discipline worthy of regular use by commercial organizations. The technologies of object-oriented databases and object request brokers too can be viewed as relatively mature, as we shall see later in this chapter. However, if there is a worry about maturity then it is still in the methods area that this is most true. To understand why, we must understand the basic principles of object-orientation.

⊟ 1.2 What are object-oriented methods?

As I have repeatedly emphasized, the phrase OBJECT-ORIENTED METHODS refers to several things, as do the terms OBJECT-ORIENTED (OO) and OBJECT TECHNOLOGY (OT) themselves. In particular, the phrase refers to object-oriented programming, design, analysis and databases, in fact to a whole philosophy of systems development and knowledge representation based on a powerful metaphor.

Historically, as I have indicated in the foregoing, interest began with object-oriented programming and only more recently was there great interest in these other issues. From a managerial point of view the programming issues are perhaps the least interesting, but in order to understand the basic concepts and terminology, we will have to start with a review of object-oriented programming and its associated terminology with the aim of leaving it rapidly behind. In the sequel, and especially in Chapters 6 and 7, which cover methods, CASE tools and related issues, and in Chapter 9 we will see how these basic concepts can be applied throughout the system development life cycle and indeed as a method of analysis for organizations. In other words, we shall proceed from the concrete concerns of programming to the abstract ones of design and analysis and then back to the concrete in a treatment of the managerial issues. Object-oriented development encompasses much of what is now called component-based development although, strictly speaking, one can build components without using object-oriented programming; the end-products just look like objects when they're finished. We deal with this in Chapter 7. For me, object technology is about much more than programming and even design. It provides an extremely general metaphor for knowledge representation that can be applied to business modelling as well as systems. Chapters 6 to 8 explore this further.

The next section introduces the terminology of object-oriented methods. The Glossary summarizes this terminology as well as including definitions of some other possibly unfamiliar terms. The reader should be aware that different authors sometimes use these terms in subtly different ways. This is not altogether surprising in a still emerging subject. Fortunately, some standard terminology has emerged thanks largely to the efforts of the Object Management Group, and the remainder of this text will refer to these standard terms. The terms used in this book represent, I hope, the emerging consensus, but also reflect the view that areas like business process modelling, artificial intelligence, semantic data modelling, knowledge management and object-orientation must converge.

⊟ 1.3 Basic terminology and ideas

As we will see in the next chapter, changes to data structures account for around

16% of IT spending. In order to understand the basics of OT let us try to understand why this is so for conventional computer systems and see how OT helps to reduce the burden if properly applied. In doing so we will begin to grasp the meaning of the fundamental terms.

Being based on the so-called Von Neumann architecture of the underlying hardware, a conventional computer system can be regarded as a set of functions or processes together with a separate collection of data; whether stored in memory or on disk does not matter. This static architectural model is illustrated in Figure 1.1 which also indicates that, when the system runs, the dynamics may be regarded as some function, f(1), reading some data, A, transforming them and writing to B. Then some other function, f(2), reads some data, perhaps the same data, does whatever it does and writes data to C. Such overlapping data access gives rise to complex concurrency and integrity problems but these can be solved well by using a database management system. The question that I ask you to consider before reading on is: what must be done when part of the data structure has to change?

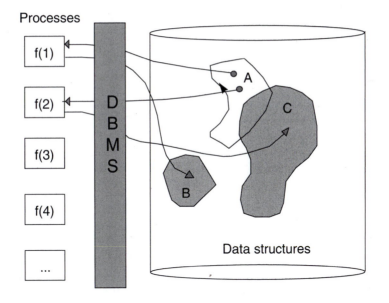

Figure 1.1 The architecture of a conventional computer system.

Considering this from the point of view of a maintenance programmer, the only conclusion that one can come to is that every single function must be checked to see if it may be destabilized by the change. Good documentation can help with this but is rarely available in practice. Part of the reason for this is that good documentation for this task would itself consist in an object-oriented description of the system and is unlikely to be divorced from an object-oriented implementation or at least design.

Furthermore, every function that is changed to reflect the new structure may have side effects in other parts of the system. Perhaps this accounts for the extraordinarily high costs of maintenance.

Figure 1.2 illustrates a completely different architectural approach to systems. Here, all the data that a function needs to access are encapsulated with it in packages called *objects* and in such a way that the functions of no other object may access these data. Using a simile suggested by Steve Cook, these objects may be regarded as eggs. The yolk is their data structure, the white consists of the functions that access these data and the shell represents the signature of the publicly visible operations. The shell interface hides the implementation of both the functions and the data structures. Now suppose again that a data structure is changed in the egg 'shelled' for maintenance in Figure 1.2. Now the maintenance programmer need only check the white of this particular egg for the impact of the change; maintenance is localized. If the implementation changes, no other object can possibly be affected. This is **encapsulation**: data and processes are **combined** and **hidden** behind an interface.

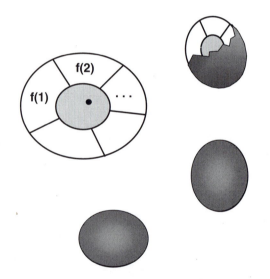

Figure 1.2 The architecture of an object-oriented system.

As it stands, there is a problem with this model. Suppose that every object contains a function that needs the same datum. In that case the potential for data duplication is staggering and the approach would be quite impracticable. The solution is to permit the objects to send messages to each other. In this way object X may need data A but not encapsulate them. Provided that X stores in its yolk the identity of another object, Y, that does contain the required data, it may send a message requesting the data or even some transformed version of them. This is depicted in Figure 1.3, where the small sperm-like dot represents the identity of a target object and the arrows show the outward direction of the message. This, in a nutshell, is 50% of the idea behind object technology. The other 50% involves allowing the objects to be classified and related to each other in other ways. Notice that with this approach the maintenance problem is localized and thus greatly simplified. When a data structure changes, the maintainer need only check the functions in the albumen that encapsulates it. There can be no effect elsewhere in the system unless the shell is cracked or deformed; that is, if the interface changes. Thus, while we may claim to have reduced the maintenance problem by orders of magnitude, we now have to work very hard to ensure that we produce correct, complete and stable interfaces for our objects. This implies that sound analysis and design are even more worthwhile and necessary than they were for conventional systems. This extra effort is worthwhile because object technology leads to some very significant benefits. The curious thing is that this principle of encapsulation has been regularly ignored by the creators of object-oriented analysis methods, as we shall see later.

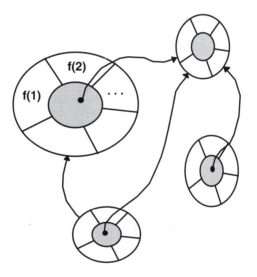

Figure 1.3 Message passing eliminates data duplication.

With these basic ideas clearly understood, we can lay bare the jargon of object-oriented methods. Object-oriented software engineering is usually characterized by the following terms and concepts.

OBJECTS The basic units of construction, be it for conceptualization, design or programming, are **objects**: instances organized into classes with common **features**. These features can be of three kinds.

■ **Attributes**, such as size, position or colour, representing associations with other objects and the state of the object itself.

- Procedures or services that the object can perform, such as move or stretch. These are called **operations** or **methods**.

- Rules that specify how the other features of the object are related or under what conditions the object is viable. These are sometimes called **invariants**.

Strictly speaking, methods are the functions that implement operations and operations are the abstract specifications of methods. In the purist orthodoxy of object-oriented programming the attributes are not visible to other objects, but we will see below and in Chapter 6 that this condition can be relaxed and that the relaxation has important benefits. This idea of bundling the functions up with the data is closely related to the notion of a data type in ordinary programming languages, wherein 3 is an instance of the 'type' integer, and integers are characterized by just one attribute (their value) but by several allowable arithmetic operations. Real numbers are characterized by similar operations, but the actual implementation of multiplication for a floating point number is quite different from that for integers. Similarly we can treat more complex objects, such as employees of the sort normally found in data models, by specifying their attributes and methods. METHOD is the original terminology of Smalltalk and this specialized usage has nothing to do with the other usage: object-oriented methods. The latter refers to the system development methods dealt with in detail in Chapters 6 to 8. Here a **method** is defined as a procedure or function that alters the state of an object or causes the object to send a message. The description or signature of a method is called an **operation**. Operations define which messages an object is able to process successfully.

A **class**, in the sense used in object-oriented programming, is a collection of objects which share common attributes and methods. To emphasize this we usually name classes in the plural in this book. A class may be regarded as a template for creating instances. An object **type** is the specification of a class and a class is the implementation of a type. Object types represent ideas (the *intension* of a class) rather than collections (the *extension*) and are thus named in the singular. The attributes and methods of an object type are often referred to as its **features** or **responsibilities**. An attribute represents a responsibility for knowing something and a method a responsibility for doing something.

Objects should, as far as possible, be based on the real-world entities and concepts of the application or domain. Objects can be either classes or instances, although some authorities and standards such as UML use the term OBJECT synonymously with INSTANCE. I object to this usage since there is scope for confusion when two words are used for the same thing and, as Berard (1993) has also observed, in some languages a class itself can be an instance of some higher level class or metaclass. Throughout this book I shall use the term OBJECT, as if it were slang, to mean either a class or an instance. The precise term will be used where the difference matters. The term OBJECT can be given a precise meaning as 'anything with identity', but we will defer this point until Chapter 5 where it becomes central.

IDENTITY   At the level of conceptual modelling, objects, whether types, classes or instances, have unique identities throughout their lives. This distinguishes object-oriented models from, say, relational ones. It will be particularly important when we come to deal with object-oriented databases. At the programming language level it can be argued that classes do not have identity, but this discussion will be avoided for the time being.

ENCAPSU-LATION   The data structures and method implementation details of an object are hidden from other objects in the system. The only way to access an object's state is to send it a message that causes one of its methods to execute. Strictly speaking, the attributes are shorthand for access methods that get and set values. In other words, the attributes provide the vocabulary with which one can discuss the externally visible behaviour of an object. This makes object types equivalent to abstract data types in programming, broadly speaking. However, to specify an object fully, one must also include assertions in its interface, as we discuss later. Some of the methods of an object may also be hidden behind the interface: the **private** methods. The interface is best regarded as a public declaration of the **responsibilities** of the object. Attributes may be regarded as *responsibilities for knowing* and operations as *responsibilities for doing*. Another way of thinking about this is to say that the public interface defines the *questions we can ask* of an object and the *instructions we can give* to an object. Thinking about objects in this way is sometimes called 'anthropomorphizing' an object – treating it as an intelligent homunculus in the machine, able to hold a conversation with others and reason about its own capabilities. This turns out to be a very good way to think about objects during requirements elicitation and systems analysis.

MESSAGES   Objects, classes and their instances, communicate by message passing. This eliminates much data duplication and ensures that changes to data structures and routines encapsulated within objects do not propagate their effects to other parts of the system. Messages are usually implemented as function calls. Messages always return data to the sending object. An object can only send a message to another if it stores that object's identity. This may be regarded as a weakness of the object-oriented metaphor when it is necessary to broadcast messages to many objects, though we will see later that there are ways round the problem.

INHERITANCE   The reason that inheritance is important can be derived from our boiled egg simile. We agreed that maintenance could be localized and thus reduced because changes to the implementation were hidden from other objects by the interface. Therefore to get this benefit we assumed that the interface never changed. However, we do not live in an ideal world. People – even developers – make mistakes. Requirements do change. So the interface is bound to change and we could be even worse off than with conventional development, because of the newness of the technology. The answer is to legislate against making changes to interfaces and insist that modification be made by introducing subclasses that extend or possibly override the features of existing objects. Any deviation from this régime must be regarded as a major architectural rewrite of a system. This rule implies that our classes must be designed for extension and reinforces the need for sound object-oriented analysis and design even further. Instances (usually) inherit all and only the features of the classes they belong to. This is called **classification**, but it is also possible in an object-oriented system to allow classes to inherit features from more general superclasses. In this case inherited features can be overridden and extra features added to deal with exceptions. Inheritance implements the ideas of **specialization** and **generalization** and represents a special case of a structural interrelationship between a group of classes. Inheritance is only one of the conceptual structures with which we organize the world; but it is a particularly important one and its importance corresponds to the importance of the verb *to be* in language. We will examine other key structures, such as composition (corresponding to the verb *to have*), later.

POLY-MORPHISM

The ability to use the same expression to denote different operations is referred to as polymorphism. This occurs where + is used to signify real or integer addition and when the message 'add 1' is sent to a bank account and a list of reminder notes: the same message should produce quite different results. Polymorphism represents the ability of an abstraction to share features. Polymorphism is often implemented by *dynamic binding*. Inheritance is a special kind of polymorphism that characterizes object-oriented systems. Some authorities claim that polymorphism is *the* central idea in object-oriented systems, but there are non-object-oriented metaphors which take this point further, as exemplified in languages such as ML or Miranda.

SUBSTITUT-ABILITY

To obtain the benefits of reusable software one should be able to substitute subclasses for their parent classes. For example, when a new subclass of People is created to represent French people then any message that was previously understood by People should be understood by the new subclass. This implies certain design restrictions which often violate common sense at the conceptual modelling level: such as making polygons a subclass of rectangles. This will be discussed further in Chapters 6 and 9.

DELEGATION: CLASSLESS INHERITANCE

Object technology is **class-oriented** in the sense that instances derive their features from classes which in turn may derive their features from more abstract ones up through a hierarchy or network of classes. Another way to achieve the benefits of the object-oriented approach is to use a classless approach where each object is regarded as a prototype in the following sense. Every object is an instance that is regarded as typical. Other instances may be created by making slight variations to the features of an existing one. Thus, the typical dog has four legs and is called Fido or Rover. There are several instances of dogs with different names all derived from the pattern or prototype provided by Fido. My friend's dog Spock lost a leg in an accident. Spock thus was thoroughly Fido-like except in having three legs.

Languages that support this model of inheritance such as SELF (Ungar and Smith, 1987) are known as **prototype languages** and are said to support **classless inheritance** or **delegation**. AI frames and scripts can be regarded in this way as prototypes although they may also use class-based inheritance. **Actor systems** also use the idea of delegation. They allow objects to delegate to other objects the permission to perform operations on their behalf. Actor languages are usually very low level languages compared to object-oriented programming languages.

IN A NUTSHELL

Summarizing, the data structures and implementation details of an object are hidden from other objects in the system. The only way to access an object's state is to send a message that causes one of the methods to execute. The interface is best regarded as a public declaration of the *responsibilities* of the object. To abstract from all this, object-orientation in a programming language, system design or computer system is characterized by two key features, which are glorified by two impressive words:

- Encapsulation
- Inheritance

As with all dichotomies, encapsulation and inheritance are not cleanly separated; there is a tension and opposition between these abstractions. Inheritance can violate reuse because subobjects may have privileged access to the implementation of their superobjects' methods. Thus, some terms, such as polymorphism, come up under both headings and even inheritance can be viewed as a form of abstraction. The areas of overlap and the dialectic between abstraction and inheritance are examined in Section 1.3.3. Other authors prefer the term 'abstraction' to our 'encapsulation' to convey the general concept. I find myself using the terms interchangeably, and do not really have a strong view on which is the better one.[3] Both words conceal a number of important concepts. The point to remember is that encapsulation is merely one way of supporting the principle of information hiding.

The following two subsections examine these two fundamental principles in order to clarify their meaning and establish terminology for later use.

1.3.1 Abstractions and encapsulation

Abstraction, which is a key software engineering skill, encompasses various issues and can be difficult to grasp at first. It is often said to be *the* critical skill of the object-oriented designer. The meaning given by the Oxford English Dictionary (OED) closest to the meaning intended here is: 'the act of separating in thought'. A closer definition might be: 'representing the essential features of something without including background or inessential detail'. Closely associated with this notion of abstraction is the idea that abstractions should be complete in that they should encapsulate *all* the essential properties of a thing. In object-oriented programming

---

[3] For a finer distinction see Berard (1993).

terms this means that objects should abstract and encapsulate both data and processes. Things are apprehended not only through their properties but through their behaviour: *by their ways shall ye know them.* An abstraction is encapsulated if it consists of an interface visible to the outside world and an implementation hidden behind it. The interface can be regarded either as the public 'face' of a class or as something separate from it which defines what the class will implement.

One important difference between the interfaces, types and classes of object technology and conventional types is that the former are not fully specified by the attributes and operations (the *signature* of the type). Object interfaces may also include **assertions**: statements about the signature. A typical assertion is a pre-condition or post-condition on a method or a class invariant. This will be very significant when we study object-oriented analysis and design in Chapter 6, but will be ignored for the present.

An **abstract data type** (ADT) is an abstraction, similar to a class, that describes a set of objects in terms of an encapsulated or hidden data structure and operations on that structure. Abstract data types, as opposed to primitive data types like Integer, may be defined by a user in constructing an application rather than by the designer of the underlying language. It may be noted that this idea of abstract data types bears a strong resemblance to the notion of entity type as used in data modelling methods. This is not accidental and is the basis for much of what I have to say about object-oriented analysis in Chapter 6. However, the key difference between ADTs or classes in object-oriented programming and entity types is that ADTs include methods. For example, an ADT representing lengths expressed in imperial units would include methods for adding feet and inches.

Figure 1.4(a) describes a class called Employees together with some of its defining attributes and methods. Once defined, this abstraction is available to the programmer in a very direct and facile manner. Figure 1.4(b) shows the same type using an older object-oriented notation, in which the instance variables are suppressed. In this book the UML notation of Figure 1.4(a) will be used.

From the programmer's point of view there is a difference between classes and types, because the type information only gives a specification of an object; the class it belongs to may only be determined at run time. The difference is that classes describe specifications that may be shared among collections of instances or other classes, not just among instances. From the analyst's point of view, however, classes and types are effectively the same thing.

As indicated above, in object-oriented programming it is normal to regard only instances as having unique identity, which reflects the reality of run-time instantiation in a computer system. I think this is an error outside of the context of programming and regard classes also as having unique identity. After all, there is only one class of Apples in the conceptual world. In this book, an **object** is anything with unique identity. It can be a concrete individual, real or invented, or a concept, abstract or concrete. This contrasts with many books and papers where 'object' is used as a synonym for 'instance'. I think that if we are to speak about OBJECT TECHNOLOGY then 'object' should be a general term within that domain. In this way we could think of 'object' as merely an abbreviated form for 'object type' when a class is intended.

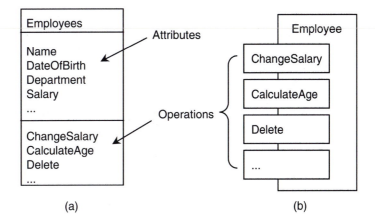

(a)   (b)

Figure 1.4 (a) A class that captures the notion of an employee expressed in UML notation; **(b)** the Employee object type in another common notation with the accessors suppressed.

Abstract classes may not have instances; they exist only to provide general concepts that will be used by their subclasses. When the distinction between a class and an instance is important the term object should not be used. **Concrete classes** can have instances.

An object has two aspects; an internal and an external aspect. The internal aspect describes the state, implementation and instantiation of the object. The external view, in the pure object-oriented style, shows only the names of its methods and the types of their parameters; what the object can do, as in Figure 1.4(b). I have fudged this pure view a little here by showing the object's attributes as in Figure 1.4(a). To return to purity, we can justify this by identifying these attributes not with internal state but with standard methods that permit access and update. However, it is convenient to talk about the attributes directly when no confusion can arise. In many books and articles on object-oriented programming this point is insisted on very strongly. However, the examples given are usually very low level programming abstractions such as sets, bags, collections, stacks and so on. For example, a stack is described as a data structure with four methods: push, pop, top and empty. That is to say that a stack is an ordered list of things that can be added to and taken away from at one end only and can report the value held at that end. Access to the stack data is only via these methods and there is no need to describe the implementation which might be as a linked list or as an array with an associated stack pointer. Stack has no visible attributes, although TOP and EMPTY could be regarded as such.

For commercial systems the objects are far more complex and it is impossible to think of abstract concepts like employees or invoices without comprehending their attributes. Purists may continue to think of attributes as identified with two standard methods per attribute A; get A and set A.

Instances of objects (or strictly of classes or 'object types') are analogous to records in a database. They comprise concrete data having the properties of the object. All instances of an object have the same set of attributes and methods. This may not be true for more general classes because class inheritance includes the potential for specializations of classes to delete or acquire extra attributes and methods. For example, a stack is a special case of a list but has no methods for concatenation. Another example might be a pet fish which inherits the attributes of fish in general but additionally has an owner.

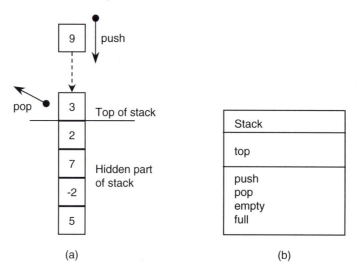

(a)   (b)

Figure 1.5 (a) Physical representation of a particular stack of integers; **(b)** the protocol of a stack object type in UML.

The attributes of an instance are sometimes referred to as **instance variables** and those of a class as **class variables**. Class variables are shared by *all* instances of the class. For example, the number of instances of a class is a suitable candidate for a class variable. We also distinguish **class methods** from **instance methods**. Again, calculating a total or average across all instances of a class would be a class method.

Under the general heading of abstraction we encounter many seemingly abstruse technical terms such as encapsulation, polymorphism and genericity. Let us look at the meaning of some of these terms. In doing so we will uncover more of the general features of the object-oriented style.

Encapsulation, which supports the principle of **information hiding**, refers to the practice of including within an object everything it needs, and furthermore doing this in such a way that no other object need ever be aware of this internal structure. Thus, in the example in Figure 1.4 the details of the ChangeSalary algorithm may be hidden inside the Employees object in such a way that other objects or even users are unable to access the details. Similarly certain data, such as salaries, may be private to an object. The implementation of data storage should always be private to the object. It is not necessary to know whether the salary is stored as packed decimal, floating point or integer to access or change it. The same applies to methods; their implementation details should be private to the object and only their behaviour visible to other objects. As well as their identity, objects may have internal state but it is not directly accessible. One consequence of this principle is that clients of the object are not exposed to danger when its implementation is changed as long as the interface is not also changed. The hidden or encapsulated parts of an object are its **private implementation**; the visible attributes and methods are said to be its **public interface**.

Berard (1993) castigates me, along with practically every other author on the subject incidentally, for confusing the concepts of abstraction, encapsulation and information hiding, as indeed I have done deliberately in this book. Information hiding (Parnas, 1972) is the principle that modules should conceal design decisions concerning themselves from each other. Berard defines abstraction as the process by which we decide what information should be visible and what hidden. Encapsulation is merely the packaging strategy used to implement these decisions. He points out that information hiding is not necessarily good and certainly is not an idea unique to object-oriented programming. While I accept these somewhat pedantic distinctions I remain convinced that to blur them in an introductory text of this nature will serve not to confuse but to clarify.

BINDING STRATEGIES

In programming, the ability to determine an object's class at run time and allocate its storage is referred to as **dynamic binding**. In statically bound languages the compiler allocates storage to objects and their type determines their class uniquely. Because this book is not principally concerned with programming we will routinely blur this distinction between classes and types. However, it will be important to remember that a class is not just a set. A class has members and operations whereas a set only has members. Dynamic binding is to be contrasted with **early** or **static binding**, when the allocation of types is carried out by a compiler. Dynamic binding is also known as **late binding**. Dynamic binding is the programming technique that is usually used to implement polymorphism in object-oriented programming languages. As usual there is a trade-off between the flexibility and speed that comes with dynamic binding and the performance of statically bound systems.

Figure 1.6 shows ways in which dynamic binding and polymorphism can be implemented.

MESSAGES AGAIN

Data are obtained from an object in object-oriented systems in one way and one way only; by sending the object a **message**. A message consists of an address (which object or objects to send it to) and an instruction, consisting of a method name and zero or more parameters.

If the addressee contains a method for which the instruction makes sense then an answer is returned to the sending object. Thus I can send the integer object 3 the message 'add 5' and expect the answer '8' to come back. If I were to send the message 'report salary' to the employee named Erica, I might get back either that very information or something like 'You are not authorized to see Erica's salary' as the hidden procedure may involve an access to some security tables. If the addressee does not contain a method which can process the message then a standard error message is returned. For example, such an error would result if the message CalculateAge were sent to 3, an instance of type Integer. If the language is compiled then the compilation should pick up errors of this kind before this situation can arise. Recall that the methods encapsulated within an object define exactly which messages that object is able to process successfully. The set of messages an object can respond sensibly to is sometimes called its **protocol**. The message's name is sometimes called its **selector**. A message may be interpreted in different ways by different receivers that decide exactly what will happen.

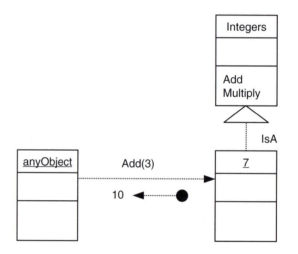

Figure 1.6 (a) The message Add(3) is sent to the integer 7, which inherits the addition procedure from the class integer.

In strongly statically-typed programming languages the compiler can ensure that objects cannot receive illegal messages. Dynamic binding implies that objects must each take on the responsibility for protecting themselves against such messages. Note that messages arrive at the interface of an object whereas it is the hidden implementation that dispatches messages.

When classes are regarded as components we often split the protocol up into, possibly overlapping, sets of messages called **interfaces**. Normally, however, we think of the complete set of messages as the interface.

SET
ABSTRACTION Thus the terms encapsulation, data abstraction and information hiding all refer to much the same thing. However, some authorities distinguish between mere information hiding and what is known as 'set abstraction'. Set abstraction refers to the notion that concrete instances are regarded as objects belonging to a set with properties defined separately and inheriting those properties. For example, Fred is an instance of a man and he has brown eyes, but he inherits most of his properties from the abstract set of Men, including the attribute 'colour of eyes'.

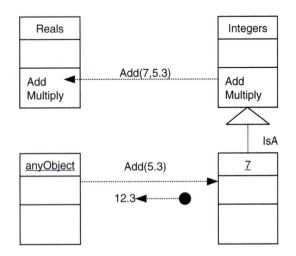

Figure 1.6 (b) The message Add(5.3) cannot be handled by Integer, so the routine is collected from Real. This is called **forwarding**.

Another feature of objects is that they have unique identification for their entire lifetime. Object identity gives rise to some severe problems and some great benefits in database systems. This is discussed further in Chapter 5.

MORE ON
POLY-
MORPHISM Other terms often encountered are **polymorphism, overloading** and **operator overloading**, which refer to the ability to use the same symbol for different purposes when the context is clear. For example, sending the message 'add 5' to an integer and to a real number actually invokes quite different procedures but it is convenient to use the same notation '+' for both purposes; it aids understanding and makes the language easier to learn and remember. Similarly 'delete' may be required to do different things to different objects, especially if some integrity checking must be performed prior to deletion of a database record. Formally, polymorphism – having many forms – means the ability of a variable or function to take different forms at run time, or more specifically the ability to refer to instances of various classes. Overloading is the special case where two different operations merely share the same name, such as the operation 'open' applied to files or to windows.

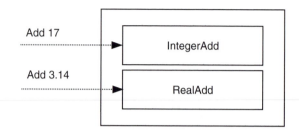

Figure 1.7 Operator overloading (*ad hoc* polymorphism) applied to addition.

In point of fact, Smalltalk cheats slightly with its notion of polymorphism. The pure concept is better exemplified in functional languages, such as ML, where functions are permitted to have arguments of different types. While the understanding of polymorphism presented above will be adequate for the purposes of this text, there is a large theoretical literature on the subject in which many fine distinctions are made.

Table 1.3 Wegner's classification of types of polymorphism.

Ad hoc polymorphism	Universal polymorphism
overloading	parametric polymorphism
coercion	inclusion polymorphism

Cardelli and Wegner (1985) distinguish several kinds of polymorphism. At the highest level the distinction is made between *ad hoc* and universal polymorphism. *Ad hoc* polymorphism refers to using the same symbol for semantically unrelated operations. Operator overloading fits into this category if, for example, we use the symbol + for addition of integers and matrices. Another kind of *ad hoc* polymorphism, called coercion, allows operations to work on input of mixed type, as when adding an integer to a real. Universal polymorphism splits into parametric and inclusion (or inheritance) polymorphism, the latter of which is dealt with in Section 1.3.2. Parametric polymorphism refers to the ability to substitute arguments from a range of types into a function call. It may, for our present purposes, be safely confused with genericity. The types of polymorphism are summarized in Table 1.3.

GENERICITY   **Genericity** is the ability to define parametrized modules and is found in many languages that support encapsulation such as Ada. An example of a generic type is a list where the list could be a list of names, a list of integers or a list of something specific like names of employees. The actual type is only determined by context. In languages such as Ada, Modula-2 and even ALGOL, it refers to the ability to define parametrized modules. Usually the parameters are types. Generic messages allow the creation of reusable components and frameworks by removing the dependency of the calling routine on what is called.

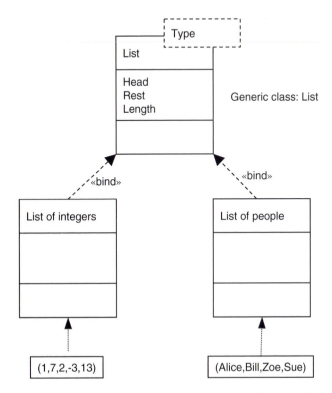

Figure 1.8 Using genericity to simulate inheritance for the generic class 'list'.

Genericity and inheritance may be viewed as *alternative* techniques for providing extensible and reusable modules, but genericity is far more limited in practice as we will see later. It is nevertheless a very useful feature to have in a programming language because genuinely reusable components should apply to more than one type. For example, a searching or sorting engine that only worked on numbers would be pretty useless.

IDENTIFYING OBJECTS The outstanding issue is how to identify objects in a real application. This issue is one that provokes deep philosophical debate and often much confusion. An Empiricist view maintains that objects are out there just waiting to be perceived, and an extreme version holds that this is easy to do. In fact, the OED has it that an object is something 'thrown before the mind'. A Phenomenologist view, on the contrary, recognizes that perception is an active, creative process and that objects come both from our consciousness and from the world through a dialectical process. An even richer view suggests that real-world abstractions are a reflection of social relations and human productive processes as well as having an objective basis in the real world. We will be returning to this thorny issue in later chapters. For now, we merely state that objects may be apprehended by an analyst familiar with an application in many different ways and that choosing the 'best' representation is a fundamental contribution that human intelligence always makes to computer systems.

Some objects correspond directly to real-world objects such as employees, but others such as stacks correspond to invented abstractions. Abstractions sum up the relevant divisions of the domain. What is relevant may depend on the application, but this will compromise the reusability of the abstraction and so the designer should try to think of abstractions with as wide an applicability as possible. On the other hand, care should be taken not to compromise efficiency with absurdly and gratuitously general objects. Thus, when defining the **Employees** class we do not include 'planet of origin' among its attributes nor knowledge of galactic credits in the salary payment routines, although some future systems designer may yet exist to regret our decision. What such a designer would have to do is use the concept of inheritance, to which we now turn.

As we shall see in the next chapter, one reason for emphasizing abstraction and encapsulation is to deliver code and specifications which are reusable. Using an object via its specification as an abstract type or class means that if its internal aspect undergoes modification, other parts of the system will not be affected. Equally, if other system objects have their implementation changed this object should not be affected. The only problem is that the interface must not change. Getting hold of the 'right' abstractions is therefore very important, which is why we place great emphasis on object-oriented analysis in this text.

1.3.2 Inheritance

The second characteristic feature of an object-oriented system is the way it deals with the structural and semantic relationships between instances and classes (or types) and eliminates the redundancy of storing the same datum or procedure more often than necessary. The key notion is that of an inheritance, generalization or classification structure.

In object-oriented programming, a class can create instances of itself in memory. These instances 'inherit' exactly all the features of the class: its methods and attributes. The class is said to **classify** its instances, and the IsA relationship between an instance and its class is called the classification relationship. An instance can be a member of only one class; in other words, **multiple classification** is disallowed. Also disallowed is **dynamic classification**: the ability of an instance to change its class at run time. It is also possible for classes to inherit all the features of more general classes. In Figure 1.9 we can see an example in which the classes of **Cars** and **Cycles** are specializations (subclasses) of the class of **Vehicles**. Note the small isosceles triangle or arrowhead, which is the UML symbol for the A Kind Of (AKO) relationship. This example shows **single inheritance**: each class has at most one generalization. We shall see later that some languages permit **multiple inheritance**, where a class can have more than one generalization (superclass). Such structures are properly called **generalization** structures. When we consider structures that involve both classes and instances – both generalization and classification – we will speak of **inheritance structures**. Whereas instances inherit *exactly* the features of their class, subclasses can add features; so that if we create a subclass of Cycles called MotorizedCycles we would add some new features such as FuelType. Furthermore, in some languages features can be overridden. Of course, overriding gets rid of substitutability and so is disallowed in some languages and design approaches that value this property.

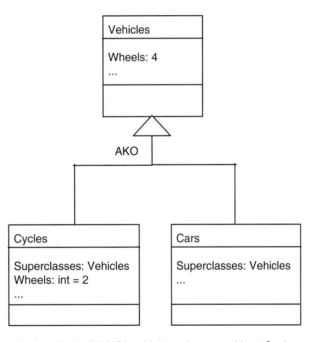

Figure 1.9 A cycle is a kind of (AKO) vehicle as is a car. Here Cycles overrides the inherited default value for Wheels. Cars and Cycles, and possibly other classes, are subclasses of Vehicles.

If an object has a type then it can be thought of as an instance of a class. For example, Fido is an instance of the class of dogs. We can go further and notice that a dog is a special case of a mammal, a mammal is a kind of vertebrate, and so on; eventually reconstructing the entire Linnaean order. Formally, we include among the attributes of each instance a special attribute (or *slot* in the AI literature where objects are often called *frames*) called the **IsA** slot. This attribute contains the name of the class to which the instance belongs; its parent in the hierarchy. Even classes may have parents and our convention here is to call the special attribute **AKO** (A Kind Of). The AKO attribute contains a list of the superclasses that generalize the class in question. The advantage of formalizing this observation in this way is that lower level classes and objects may inherit shared properties and methods, eliminating the need to store them in every instance. For example, the attribute BirthDate is shared by all subtypes of **Person**, so we need not have mentioned it explicitly for **Employee** if we had included (AKO: Person) in the type specification.

Inherited methods can be **overridden** in certain circumstances. An example would be the `Delete` method inherited by **Employees** from the general class **Objects** which carries methods for most routine operations with objects of all types. If some security or authorization checking is to be maintained we may wish a special method for deletion to override the standard one. Although overriding destroys substitutability, this price is often worth paying in order to get much more natural and comprehensible models.

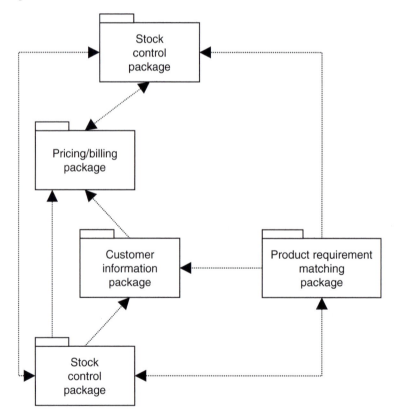

Figure 1.10 The high level structure of SACIS.

Whereas the ideas of abstraction dealt with in the last section are largely derived from work in programming language theory and practice, the ideas of inheritance have their roots in the study of artificial intelligence (AI), where semantic networks (Quillian, 1967) and frames (Minsky, 1981) are techniques for representing knowledge about stereotypical concepts and objects, and the relationship between more general and more specialized concepts is handled through the inheritance of properties and procedures. Concepts of inheritance have also been current in data modelling, where the notion of entity subtypes is widely used. In AI all things are possible: frames are allowed to break encapsulation, multiple and dynamic classification are possible and default values can be inherited right down the inheritance structure. Bassett (1997) argues that frame-based systems are far more likely to deliver reuse than conventional object-oriented ones. Normally, in object-oriented programming work, objects inherit methods and attributes from their superior classes, but they do not inherit the values of attributes. An instance inherits merely the ability to have a certain type of value. In AI and in some database applications, on the other hand, the ability to inherit values is supported. Let me illustrate this by introducing an example to which we will return occasionally throughout this book.

AARDVARK IS FOR FUN   Aardvark Leisure Products is a company that retails toys and leisure goods to the general public. It is in the process of constructing a stock and customer information system that goes under the acronym SACIS. Aardvark wants to be first in more ways than its position in the telephone directory, so it has decided to take an object-oriented approach to the development of SACIS. It is also committed to making the system easy to use, so that customers and shop staff can use it in sales situations. This means that the user interface will be very important and that a certain amount of intelligence must be built in so that the system can give help in matching products to customer needs. Thus, SACIS will be an expert object-oriented database system.

Consider some classes needed in SACIS. They must at least include People, Customers, Adults, Children, StockItems, SportsItems, Toys, Shops, Employees and perhaps Suppliers. Both Toys and SportsItems are kinds of StockItem. Suppose that there is also a class called Frisbees and that F123 is a particular frisbee. StockItems has a class method called 'report stock level' that is inherited by Toys and Frisbees. If we send the message 'report stock level' to Frisbees the inherited method looks in the StockLevel attribute and returns a number representing the number of frisbees in stock. It clearly makes no sense to send this message to F123; the method is overridden. Individual instances can deal with messages. In this case the message 'delete' might be sent to F123 when it is sold, or better for future customer support reasons, it could be sent the message 'mark yourself as sold' with the purchaser's identifier as a parameter. F123, in conventional object-oriented programming, inherits all the attributes of Frisbees but not their values. Similarly, Frisbees inherits the attributes of Toys. In an AI system we would allow inheritance of values, in particular of default values. Here is why. Toys has the attribute 'safe for children' and it is reasonable to assume that most toys are thus safe. Thus, by default, this attribute may be set to have the value 'yes'. I think it is useful for both the class Frisbees and the instance F123 to inherit this value so that the customer can enquire unequivocally 'is this one safe?' and receive the unequivocal answer 'yes'. F124 which is a customized frisbee with chains attached to the perimeter would have the value overridden. In languages such as Smalltalk and C++ all this has to be done in the application. In AI systems some of the work is done for you.

Classification structures of this type implement partial inclusion polymorphism. That is messages sent to Toys will be understood by Frisbees and F123 unless overridden.

COMPOSITION AND AGGREGATION Not all structural relationships have the semantics of inheritance, however, and practical object-oriented languages need to be able to deal with situations involving compositional structures. In addition to the inheritance, generalization or kind-of structure, we will consider here another kind of structure: the **composition**, **aggregation** or **a-part-of** (APO) structure. The most typical case is a parts explosion for an object such as a car which is composed of a body, wheels and engine. In turn the wheel may be composed of axle, spokes, rim and tyre.

The diamond notation for aggregation in Figure 1.11 will be further explained in Chapter 6. Ambiguous phrases like 'has a' are to be avoided at all costs. Other associative structures, such as ownership, liking, debt or even analogy, could be modelled in a similar way. As we will see in Chapter 6, these are better treated as associations.

MULTIPLE INHERITANCE Returning to the inheritance semantics, we have to take note of the case where an object or class may have two or more parents. A good example is a guppy which, as a typical pet fish, is an exemplar of both the class of Fish and the class of Pets. A guppy should inherit the properties of both classes. This ability is referred to as multiple inheritance. The difficulty with multiple inheritance is that on rare occasion the properties inherited from two (or more) parents may be directly or partially contradictory. For example, oversimplifying slightly, a fish lives in the sea and a pet lives in the owner's home, so where does a guppy live? There are many solutions to this problem in practical implementations. The most usual is to allow the system to report such a conflict to the user and ask for a value for the offending attribute. Alternatively, some systems allow the designer to write a procedure to resolve such conflicts automatically. There have even been suggestions for combining the answers into a composite or compromise solution; see for example the treatment given in Appendix A. Other suggestions include maximizing scepticism and assuming the values are unknown (Horty *et al.*, 1990).

Two types of conflict are possible: name conflict and value conflict. The literature on object-oriented programming usually deals only with name conflict, whereas the artificial intelligence literature tends to deal more fully with value conflict as intended in the previous paragraph. Value conflict occurs when an attribute inherits two different values from parent classes. These might be default values if the object is itself a class, or actual instance values where instance level inheritance (IsA) is supported. Name conflict occurs when two parent classes contain different attributes or methods with the same name. Name conflicts usually arise in relation to method inheritance and Wegner (1987) lists the following seven conflict strategies used in the Flavors system.

- Call the most specific method.
- Call all methods in their order of precedence or in reverse order.
- Execute the first method to return a non-null value.
- Execute all methods and return a list of their results.
- Compute the sum of all returned values.
- Call all *before* demons, then call all *after* demons.
- Use the second argument to select one method or a subset of methods.

We will return to the issue of conflict strategies in Chapter 6. The notion of demons will be explained later in the text. Roughly, a demon is a procedure which fires when a datum changes and the terms *before* and *after* refer to whether the procedure fires at the beginning of a change or when it is completed; rather like pre- and post-conditions.

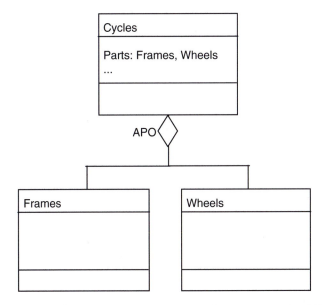

Figure 1.11 A composition hierarchy showing that Cycles are made of Frames and Wheels (and possibly other components). APO stands for A Part Of.

A different way to avoid some of the dangers of multiple inheritance is to separate the inheritance of interfaces from the inheritance of implementation, as exemplified in the Java language. This is discussed in Chapter 3.

RÔLES   Multiple inheritance and the absence of dynamic classification both raise an issue that we have fudged up to now: that of rôles. In Figure 1.4 we pretended that **Employees** was a class. This would be valid in a payroll system but generally the status of being employed is something that may come and go. In other words, **Employees** represents a **rôle** and not a class. Because instances cannot change their class in object-oriented programming languages, Anne Arbeiter cannot migrate from **Students** to **Employees**, or from **Employees** to **WelfareClaimants** for that matter. To retain Anne's identity we should make her an instance of **People** and give this class an instance attribute to store employment status. Alternatively, we can model the rôle as a class and use the STATE or VISITOR design patterns (see Chapter 7) to migrate the instance from one class to another. The greatest danger with modelling rôles as classes is that it can lead to over-complex and often huge multiple inheritance structures.

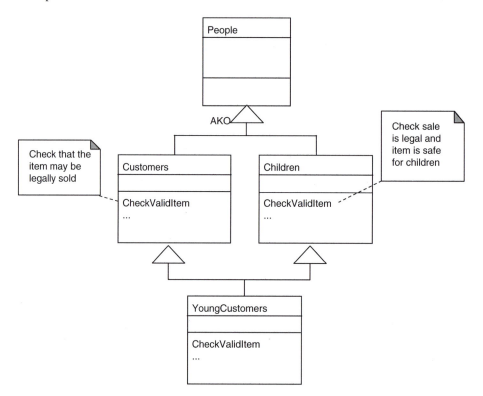

Figure 1.12 Multiple Inheritance in SACIS.

AARDVARK NEVER KILLED ANYBODY In SACIS, an example of the need for multiple inheritance might arise with the class YoungCustomer which must inherit the properties and behaviour of both Customer and Child. Note that some children may not yet be customers and that some customers are adults. YoungCustomer inherits properties and methods from Child, which ensure that they are not sold dangerous items, and these must override the more lax conditions inherited from Customer. This again shows the need for conflict resolution strategies in systems which support multiple inheritance. An example where the strategy is even more complicated arises in the case of items, such as bicycles, which are both toys and sports items. Typically a toy is a low cost item with a short life expectation and no maintenance programme. Sports gear, on the other hand, is often costly and in need of regular maintenance.

Note in Figure 1.12 that CheckValidItem is a different operation for Customer and for Child, because the former checks for a legal item and the latter for a safe and legal item.

As we have seen, the classical object-oriented programming view has it that classes inherit methods and attributes (the ability to have a value of a certain type) whereas in artificial intelligence the instances may actually inherit values. In this book we shall sometimes prefer the latter view. This means we are better able to deal with semantic notions, such as defaults. It also posits the distinction between AKO and IsA relationships. Inheritance of features by a class is treated as an AKO (A Kind Of) relationship and inheritance by instances as an IsA relationship. The distinction may be viewed as analogous to the difference between inclusion and membership in set theory. Recall that object-oriented programming forbids multiple classification. Figure 1.13 illustrates the naturalness of both multiple inheritance and multiple classification.

Inheritance delivers extensibility. A new kind of object can be added without the need to rewrite existing code. Thus, our hypothetical employee from Ganymede (a moon of Jupiter) could be accommodated by a new class AlienEmployees inheriting the properties and methods of Employees but adding extra features and overriding others. Inheritance thus ensures that functions are only ever coded once.

1.3.3 Encapsulation, inheritance and object-orientation

The astute reader will have noticed that Section 1.3.1 could not avoid references to inheritance ahead of time. Annoying as this may be, it shows clearly how closely the two concepts of encapsulation and inheritance are interwoven. The connexion is mediated by concepts such as polymorphism, overriding, object identity and message passing.

Inheritance is often viewed as merely a special case of polymorphism, but the concept is so rich and natural that I think this view does not do it justice. As long as we are dealing with programming languages then this type-theoretic view is sound and useful. In the context of specification and design it is more limited. Value inheritance, as discussed above, does not fit neatly into this view.

One of the key benefits claimed for object-oriented approaches is reusability, as we shall see in the next chapter. However, it is necessary to be extremely cautious about this claim. Certainly, abstraction delivers reusability but it is also true, as Snyder (1987), Szyperski (1998) and others have argued, that inheritance or delegation can both compromise this objective. The reason for this is that inheritance sometimes exposes implementation details to an object's clients. Also, the hierarchy itself may be exposed so that changes to it cannot be safely made. For example, if a stack is defined as a special case of the class 'list' it may inherit the implementation of the 'head' operation as its method for 'top' and merely exclude the irrelevant operations such as 'length'. If the implementation of stack is changed to a more efficient direct one there is a danger that its clients may depend on the old implementation as a special kind of list. This problem becomes even more severe when multiple inheritance is permitted. Fortunately, as Snyder shows, careful design procedures can get round this difficulty. Page-Jones (1992) designates this problem 'polymorphism connascence'. On the other hand, inheritance is partly responsible for the possibility of reuse since without inheritance it is unlikely that many classes could be reused exactly as defined.

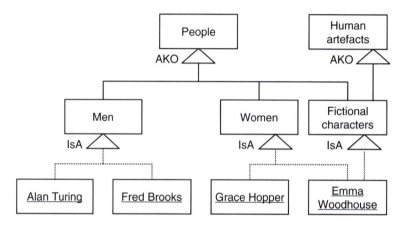

Figure 1.13 AKO and IsA links in a classification structure.

The use of complex inheritance schemes certainly complicates a system and may compromise reusability. The compensatory benefit of extensibility is further enhanced by the capture of the structural semantics of the application. The more complex a system is, the more difficult it is to maintain, and the more semantically rich it is, the more specific and therefore less reusable its components will be. However, there are some applications where a simple solution is a bad solution. Using complex inheritance schemes may then be justified. Applications in AI and expert systems where such schemes have been developed are typical of such applications. As expert systems techniques find their way into conventional systems this issue will have to be faced by more and more analysts and designers. For example, in SACIS the problem of matching product to client is seen as requiring an expert systems solution.

MORE DEFINITIONS

Before closing this section on basic terminology we need a few more miscellaneous definitions.

A key concept of object-orientation is that of **self-recursion** or self-reference. This means that objects can send messages to their own methods recursively; or send messages to themselves. In Smalltalk the reserved word 'self' is used to refer to the instance on behalf of which an operation is being executed, rather than the class which contains the definition of the operation. This means that the operation is bound to the object only at run time. Another way of looking at it is that an object must know its own unique identity, and be able store itself as the value of one of its own attributes. For example, in the class of employees the attribute 'ManagedBy:' for the instance 'J.Smith' may contain the value 'J.Smith', if J. Smith happens to be the managing director of Aardvark. In fact, every object must contain a reference to any object to which it may send messages, unless it is passed such a reference as a parameter.

Thus, an object-oriented system for programming, design or analysis will be expected to provide facilities for representing encapsulation and inheritance in the manner outlined above and contain a notion of object identity and self. For each object one has to declare which internal data – aspects of its state – it may alter explicitly. Its external powers are completely circumscribed by message passing.

Now we can define **object-based** programming as that style of programming supporting encapsulation and object identity; that is, methods and attributes are hidden within and private to objects and these objects have unique identifiers. There is little or no support for classes in the sense that set abstraction is not supported. In other words, objects do not belong to abstract classes which have a separate identity. Further, there is no support for inheritance. Ada is a typical object-based language.

Class-based languages, such as CLU, include the notion of set abstraction at the instance/class level but do not support inheritance between abstract classes which may have no concrete instances. Class-based systems include all the features of object-based ones; they inherit them.

Object-oriented systems are defined by inheriting the features of both object-based and class-based systems and additionally having full inheritance between classes and classes; that is, both instances and classes inherit the methods and attributes of the class(es) to which they belong. Some object-oriented systems permit instances to inherit the values of attributes set at the class level. Object-oriented systems also support self-recursion.

Component-based systems are (tautologically) systems built using components. A component is an executable unit of independent production, acquisition and deployment; that is, a unit of composition with contractually specified interfaces and explicit context dependencies. The interfaces usually conform to a standard interface definition language. A component plays a part in a composition and corresponds to a class or a collection of several classes.

This equips us with all the necessary terminology to begin to look at the practical advantages and pitfalls of the object-oriented approach, before dealing with some specific languages and asking how well they match up to the theoretical ideal presented above. The Glossary may be used as a terminological *aide-mémoire* and the reader may wish to note that acronyms are expanded in the Subject Index.

⊟ 1.4 Summary

In this chapter I have introduced most of the basic terminology of object-oriented methods and programming. We have also begun to discuss the technology in its historical and commercial context, looking at whence it came and the key concerns of software engineering that it addresses:

- ensuring the reusability and extensibility of modules;
- industrializing the software development process;
- making systems with open interfaces which can share resources;
- capturing more of the meaning of a specification.

An object-oriented language or system supports two characteristic features: encapsulation and inheritance.

Abstraction is the process of identifying relevant objects in the application and ignoring the irrelevant background. Abstraction delivers reusability and information hiding through encapsulation. Encapsulation consists in hiding the implementation of objects and declaring publicly the specification of their behaviour through a set of attributes and operations. The data structures and methods that implement these are private to the object.

Object types or classes are similar to data types and to entity types with encapsulated methods. Data and methods are encapsulated and hidden by objects. Classes may have concrete instances. The term *object* means either a class or an instance in this book.

Inheritance is the ability to deal with generalization and specialization or classification. Subclasses inherit attributes and methods from their superclasses and may add others of their own or override those inherited. In most object-oriented programming languages, instances inherit all and only the properties of their class. Multiple inheritance occurs when a class is a subclass of more than one class. Inheritance delivers extensibility, but can compromise reusability. Multiple inheritance is powerful but introduces additional problems and so should be used parsimoniously.

Objects communicate only by message passing. Polymorphism or overloading increase readability and programmer productivity but may lead to slower performance.

```
object-based     = encapsulation  + object identity
class-based       = object-based   + set abstraction
object-oriented   = class-based    + inheritance  + self-recursion
component-based   = object-oriented + outbound interfaces
```

1.5 Bibliographical notes

The seminal works on object-oriented programming are probably (Dahl and Nygaard, 1966), (Kay and Goldberg, 1977), (Ingalls, 1978) and (Goldberg and Robson, 1983).

A number of good introductory texts on object-oriented programming and its benefits, though not on object-oriented methods in general, exist. The best in my opinion is (Meyer, 1988), whose main aim is describing the language Eiffel but which also has a good high level introduction to object-orientation in general. In the second edition of his book Meyer (1997) presents an up-to-date version of the same ideas together with a much more complete coverage of the entire field of methods. However, it is now a very large and somewhat daunting work. Another excellent book of the same type is (Cox and Novobilski, 1991), which sets out to describe the language Objective C, but has a good high level introduction to object-oriented concepts and is highly readable and recommended. Neither book contains much material on object-oriented analysis or databases, but Meyer has interesting things to say about object-oriented design. (Booch, 1991) is a first-rate introduction to object-oriented programming, concepts and design. The best management level introductions to object technology to appear are by Taylor (1997) and Meyer (1995).

Those readers who wish to delve deeper may explore the huge volume of research papers, some of which are listed in the Bibliography. Two old but useful and accessible collections are (Shriver and Wegner, 1987) and (Kim and Lochovsky, 1989). Both contain a deal of very technical and academic material. (Mandrioli and Meyer, 1992) is representative of more recent collections of this type. (Blair *et al.*, 1991) combines several good introductory papers. (Zamir, 1999) is a wide-ranging collection of articles on all aspects of object-oriented methods. The proceedings of the annual OOPSLA and TOOLS conferences are always a useful insight into the state of the art.

Two journals are worthy of mention as sources of application and theoretical information. They are the *Journal of Object-Oriented Programming* (JOOP) and the Chapman and Hall journal *Object-Oriented Systems*, which provides more theoretical material.

The distinction between object-based, class-based and object-oriented systems was originally made by Wegner in an article to be found in the volume referred to above (Shriver and Wegner, 1987).

I regard objects as being either classes or instances whereas most contemporary texts identify objects with instances. I have not chosen to violate this convention lightly in this text as, I hope, the remainder of this book will show.

1.6 Exercises

1. Choose **two** characteristic features of OO:
    a) Polymorphism
    d) Abstraction
    g) Information hiding
    b) Inheritance
    e) Encapsulation
    h) Object identity
    c) Reusability
    f) Genericity
    i) Dynamic binding

2. Which artificial intelligence concept is closest to the idea of an object?
    a) Slot
    c) Knowledge base
    e) Facet
    b) Inference engine
    d) Frame
    f) Rule

3. What is the difference between the following (one sentence each)?
    a) an instance and a class
    e) a class and a component
    b) a data type and a class
    f) dynamic binding and polymorphism
    c) a class and a rôle
    g) genericity and inheritance
    d) an object type and an entity type
    h) inheritance and classification

4. Justify including attributes in class descriptions.

5. Distinguish the pure OO style of inheritance from the approach found in AI systems by discussing how they support or don't support the following concepts:
    a) dynamic classification
    e) value inheritance
    b) dynamic specialization
    f) overriding
    c) multiple inheritance
    g) substitutability
    d) multiple classification

6. Define object identity.

7. Define and give examples of a:
    a) class attribute/method;
    b) instance attribute/method.

8. What is multiple inheritance? When should it be used?

9. 'Multiple inheritance is thoroughly dangerous; it should be banned. Even single inheritance should be removed from our languages and methods.' Discuss.

10. 'Object technology is dead. It has been replaced by component-based development.' Discuss.

11. Draw inheritance and composition structure diagrams for the classes mentioned in the discussions of SACIS in this chapter.

2

The benefits of object-oriented programming and methods

The only end of writing is to enable the readers
better to enjoy life or better to endure it.

Dr Johnson (Review of Soame Jenyns' *The*
Enquiry into the Nature and Origin of Evil)

This chapter examines the benefits usually claimed for object-oriented and component-oriented methods and the extent to which they are attainable for commercial system developers and users. It also points out some actual or potential limitations, problems and pitfalls associated with the technology. Lastly, we will examine some reported results from actual projects.

Modern software development organizations, whether they be internal IT departments, consultancies or software houses, have adopted object technology for a number of commercial reasons. The promises of higher programmer productivity, quality and interoperability resulting from reuse have been important drivers, although the holy grail of reuse has often proved elusive in practice. Faster speed to market, through the use of rapid development and because of reuse, has also contributed and, here, there have been notable successes at many companies. Greater traceability to business requirements is important in an environment where increased flexibility to changing requirements must be accommodated, and this will be a key theme of this work. However, the most important benefit of object technology is, in my opinion, the lower maintenance burden that it should support if utilized properly.

Amid repeated claims that reuse is a major benefit of object technology we must remind ourselves that reuse is not unique to object-oriented approaches. For many years function libraries provided solid reuse in conventional COBOL and

FORTRAN environments. However, it is known that conventional top-down decomposition leads to application-specific modules that are unlikely to be reusable. Encapsulation and inheritance help to maximize reuse potential but they do not guarantee that the benefit will be achieved. Success requires changes to both the organization and the development process itself. It also requires a clear understanding of the basic principles and the determination to succeed; reuse is a deferred benefit and it is not free.

Since the 1970s studies have shown that software maintenance is by far and away the biggest cost faced by IT organizations, with many experts estimating maintenance cost as up to 95% of the data processing budget and that changes to requirements account for approximately 43% of change requests. This is natural and, I think, unavoidable and it is the prime reason why I advocate rapid application development; systems can be evolved easily. Shaving even 1% off these figures world-wide would amount to savings measured in thousands of millions of dollars.

As Taylor (1992a, 1997) has pointed out, the commercial drivers towards more flexible and robust computer systems are largely predicated on the increasing rates of change to the environment to which businesses are subjected. The pace of change in technology, society and competition continues unabated. The increasingly global nature of a company's operations exacerbates this; multiple currencies, regulations and languages must be dealt with routinely. Decentralization and distribution of businesses imply a greater need for distributed computer systems, as does the greater empowerment of front line staff in terms of decision taking. Increased competition encourages a focus on product quality and the desire to produce a product customized to the needs of individual customers – but while still retaining the economies of scale associated with mass production.

Work by Alan O'Callaghan and his students at De Montfort University and British Telecom (Graham and O'Callaghan, 1997) reinforces these conclusions, suggesting that accelerating competition enforces the need for flexibility, reduced time-to-market and the necessity of driving up the productivity of both users and developers. Object technology offers the only known approach to computing that can tackle flexibility and productivity simultaneously, as I have argued elsewhere (Graham, 1995). O'Callaghan divides the drivers into business and technical categories. The business drivers are: that 'enabling' component architecture is needed to give competitive edge; that overheads must be reduced by building a shared understanding of requirements and systems among users and developers; and that software infrastructure must be driven by business needs. Notice that the call here is not just for object technology but for better requirements engineering and rapid application development practices. The technical drivers are bottom-up and include increasingly cheap computing power, maturing object-oriented tools, the emergence of architectural standards such as CORBA (Common Object Request Broker Architecture) and the appearance of internet, intranet and Java-based applications. The barriers to the adoption of this technology were found to be as follows. There is widespread scepticism in the business community because much of object technology has matured invisibly within apparently non-OO applications;

e.g. IIOP (Internet Inter-ORB Protocol) in web browsers and the use of object-oriented databases to power busy web sites. It was found that mainly 'risk absorbing' organizations had made large investments in object technology (OT); i.e. those with large R&D budgets, those operating in risk intensive sectors such as Finance or Telecommunications and those small enough to be highly flexible in their approach to business. On top of all this the major barrier has been the existence of huge, mission-critical legacy systems.

2.1 The benefits

Object-oriented methods in general, and object-oriented programming in particular, proffer several benefits to the designer and user of software. These benefits are of much the same general character as those offered by structured programming and design, but go much further in some directions and, in doing so, lead to the questioning of many of the basic assumptions of the structured methods school of thought.

Anticipating our analysis but drawing on the remarks made in the last chapter about information hiding and inheritance, the principal benefits are as follows.

- Maintenance is localized and thus is less costly and error-prone, even in the face of changing requirements, provided that the inheritance structure does not have to be rewritten.
- Object technology addresses the trade-off between quality and productivity. Well-designed object-oriented systems are the basis for systems to be assembled largely from reusable components, leading to higher productivity. Reusing existing classes that have been tested in the field on earlier projects leads to systems which are of higher quality, meet business requirements better and contain fewer bugs. This is probably the most publicized benefit of object technology.
- Object-oriented programming, and inheritance in particular, makes it possible to define clearly and use modules that are functionally incomplete and then allow their extension without upsetting the operation of other modules or their clients. This makes systems more flexible, more easily extensible and less costly to maintain.
- Object-orientation is a tool for managing complexity, leading to increased scalability. Partitioning systems on the basis of objects helps with the problem of scalability. There is no reason why effort should increase exponentially with project size and complexity as is the case with conventional systems.
- In the same way, the partitioning of work in a project has a natural basis and should be easier. Analysis and design by partitioning a domain into objects corresponding to a solution-oriented view of their real-world counterparts is

often more natural than a top-down functional decomposition.

- Prototyping and evolutionary delivery are better supported, thus reducing time-to-market and requirements drift.
- The message passing metaphor means that interface descriptions between modules and external and legacy systems become much easier.
- There is greater seamlessness in passing from conceptual modelling, through analysis and design to coding. Objects can be used for all stages of modelling and there is a greater chance that the coded objects will correspond to something in the vocabulary of users: opening the possibility of shared understanding between developers and their clients.
- Object-oriented systems are potentially capable of capturing far more of the meaning of an application; its semantics. Since object-oriented methods are mainly concerned with modelling systems they can be used to carry out scenario modelling and facilitate changes within the business. This property leads to greater reversibility in the end product and enhances the possibility of reverse engineering systems and of tracing features back to requirements.
- Information hiding through encapsulation helps to build secure systems.
- Formal specification methods can be made to blend with object-oriented design to some extent. I will have more to say on this in Chapter 6.
- Some applications have defeated other approaches and object technology seems to be the only way to build them efficiently. Examples are graphical user interfaces, distributed systems, agent-based systems and workflow systems.

Software production or software engineering is concerned *inter alia* with the manufacture of high quality systems for a reasonable outlay of effort, and thus cost. Attempts to attack the issue of software quality have come from innovations in programming languages and from several structured approaches to system development. When there are claims that up to 80% of the cost of a system is accounted for by software costs, and that even skilled programmers have been generally unable to produce resilient, correct code, then something is seriously amiss. Structured methods, 4GLs, CASE tools, prototyping techniques, database systems and code generators all represent attacks on this problem. The extent to which structured methods succeeded was questioned in a report from Butler Cox in 1990 that showed that the users of, for example, structured design were actually impairing both their productivity and the quality of the end-product. A more recent Butler Cox (now CSC Research) report confirmed and refined these findings. In really complex applications some authorities have claimed that the use of 4GLs can degrade productivity too, due mainly to the restrictiveness of very high level languages and the need to switch to and from 3GL coding.

The impetus to structured methods came largely from the realization that many systems were either not finished, not used or were delivered with major errors. Figure 2.1 shows the fate of a selection of US defence projects in the 1970s. It must be remembered that these systems were mainly mainframe systems written in languages such as COBOL and it is probably impossible to make a fair comparison with systems developed with modern tools. However, the point that something was wrong cannot be avoided. More recent reports from the Standish Group in 1995 and 1997 only serve to confirm these findings, estimating that some 59% of US projects are cancelled or overrun their budgets.

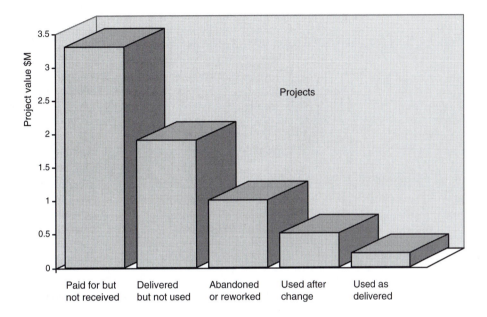

Figure 2.1 The fate of US defence projects according to US government statistics (Source: Connell and Shafer (1989))

Lietz and Swanson (1979) take up the same issue in a slightly different way and analyse the reasons for maintenance requests in a survey of nearly 500 major projects as shown in Figure 2.2. The significance of this breakdown is that most change requests are, where they are not a result of incorrect specification, unavoidable. The 'changes in user requirements' heading may, of course, be partly a surrogate for inadequate specification, but also reflects the dynamic character of modern business. In a changing world, software systems must be adaptable, and this is precisely the point addressed by the ability of object-oriented systems to be extensible and modular. Second only to these types of changes come changes in data structures, and here encapsulation offers the greatest promise as a technique for making systems resilient to changes in implementation. When, for example, British Telecom change the format for London telephone numbers, as they periodically do, software written in an object-oriented style suffers less from such a change since the internal implementation of 'phone_no' is hidden and the only changes that occur should be within this object; other parts of systems not needing major changes.

Similarly, all of the year 2000 date bug problems would have been avoided had all programs called upon date objects: the implementation of 4- instead of 2-digit year fields would have been transparent to client programs. Of course there are always limitations to these benefits. Suppose, for example, that one's printed stationery was not physically wide enough to take the new codes and that the printing machinery was not capable (physically) of printing smaller typefaces.

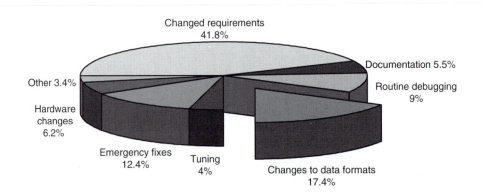

Figure 2.2 Breakdown of maintenance costs.

Another point to be made about the need for constant change relates to the way *ad hoc* or panic changes are made. Emergency fixes in conventional code often produce unexpected effects. In object-oriented systems this may still happen but, I claim, will do so less often and in a way that is eminently more traceable since the changes are either encapsulated within an object, affecting its internal implementation and visible only through the interface, or as a result of different routing of messages.

Prototyping is, I believe, an important tool for obtaining correct specifications. This is discussed in detail in Chapter 9, where we will deal with the management of systems development. Properly controlled, prototyping can be used within conventional software developments but, when combined with object-oriented methods, offers additional benefits. Object-oriented programming languages, such as Smalltalk, are good prototyping languages and the existence of reusable code modules in languages like Java supports faster prototype construction just as it does faster final system development. When prototyping is used as a specification tool this synergy applies to object-oriented designs and specifications as well as to programming languages.

The point mentioned above about emergency fixes points, in my view, to a major problem with code generators. The idea of CASE tools which generate code and ensure adequate compatible documentation of all developments is that all changes are made in a systematic manner. If the duty programmer on the night shift is faced with an emergency then often the only choice is to reach in and manipulate the source code directly; there just isn't time to go through the rigmarole of altering the diagrammatic models and documentation. As time goes on, therefore, the specification inevitably moves out of line with the code and changes become harder and harder. Advocates of code generators usually respond that this is a managerial issue and that such changes should be outlawed. Real life, however, dictates that users will not tolerate their systems being unavailable for hours or days while such laudable procedures are followed. Object-oriented systems address this question by making it much easier to trace emergency fixes, so that they can be 'reverse engineered' into the specification later. While we are on the subject of CASE tools, another problem worth mentioning is a common difficulty faced by managers of very large projects using them. CASE tools of the 'code generating' sort require that most effort is spent in the analysis and architectural design stages. This leaves little time in the project plan for fixing errors that arise when the code is tested. Most project managers are not prepared to take the risk of finding that, at the very end of the project, they have to extend deadlines to deal with potentially huge unforeseen problems. The author has seen several projects abandon CASE because of this fear factor. An object-oriented CASE tool that generates code certainly suffers from the same problem, but the enforced modularity supplied by encapsulation means that modules can often be tested independently and early on in the project, giving an opportunity for a confident assessment of the cost of last-minute code fixes.

Top-down decomposition has long been advocated as a cure for many of our design ills, although I suspect that its original proponents never really intended it as a device to guide design but advocated it as a method of *describing* systems, for which it indeed is very useful. Object-oriented methods are not top-down. They recognize that real systems often do not have a top. What, for example, is the single top level function of an operating system? Work partitioning is accomplished by packaging objects not by breaking tasks down into smaller and smaller components; an activity that is nearly always highly application specific and therefore leads to non-reusable modules. Within an object, of course, functional decomposition can still be used to specify a method or refine a use case.

QUALITY According to Meyer (1988, 1995), Sommerville (1989) and several other authorities, the quality of a software system is to be evaluated according to several criteria. We may arguably consider the following 13 quality issues as a comprehensive list.

- *Correctness.* Programs should meet their specification correctly.
- *Resilience and reliability (robustness).* Programs should be robust even in abnormal conditions.
- *Maintainability and extensibility.* Programs should be easy to evolve and extend as requirements alter.
- *Reusability and generality.* Programs should be built of reusable modules.
- *Interoperability.* Programs should be readily compatible with other systems; they should be 'open systems'.
- *Efficiency.*
- *Portability.* Programs should be portable across hardware and operating

systems.
- *Verifiability.*
- *Security.* Data, knowledge and even functions may require selective and effective concealment.
- *Integrity.* Systems need protection against inconsistent updates.
- *Friendliness.* Systems must be easy to use for a majority of users without becoming inappropriately verbose.
- *Describability.* It must be possible to create and maintain documentation.
- *Understandability.*

Object-orientation contributes to many of these objectives, although some individual object-oriented languages may score poorly in terms of efficiency, understandability, robustness or portability. In particular, the advantages most often put forward in favour of object-oriented systems are the inherent reusability of the objects, the extensibility of object-oriented systems and the fact that formal methods of specification may be made to blend with the object-oriented approach.

Reusable code has long been a goal of systems designers. There has been limited success with reusable functions in the form of libraries of commonly used mathematical and statistical functions, but even these are often difficult to use because of the need to know a great deal about the validation of entries in long parameter lists. As far as data are concerned the picture has been uniformly black outside of the field of package software. Part of the reason for this has been the popular insistence on top-down decomposition which, in striving for a decomposition of a problem into chunks small enough for an individual to program in a short time, tends to make these chunks highly dependent on the way the decomposition itself is done. Top-down functional decompositions are by their very nature application specific. As a result the resultant modules are often not of any general applicability, and programmers constantly reinvent the same solutions in different contexts.

Some industry commentators have observed that reuse, if widely applied, could save up to 20% of development costs and that even a 1% saving gives massive competitive advantage. Other estimates claim that 70% of programmers' efforts are devoted to the maintenance of existing code and that 80% of this effort is spent on corrections rather than enhancements. The United States DoD estimate that corrections cost ten times as much as new developments. Thus anything that contributes to better specification or to reusability must be high on the agenda for the software industry.

Object-oriented design contributes significantly to the issues of reusability, maintainability and interoperability by employing three main techniques: bottom-up design, encapsulation and inheritance.

A bottom-up approach to design significantly improves the potential for reuse of modules. A particularly obvious and simple example for most programmers is the way dates are handled. If it is determined in advance that some system will need to make use of dates or calculate with them, then it may be worthwhile stepping back from the immediate requirements of the system in hand to ask if it would be beneficial to provide a generic set of date routines usable by all future systems. Thus, if the present system has no need to calculate the date on which Easter falls, it may still be worth including at least hooks for this function in the interface, if not a full implementation. A functional decomposition would not identify any need for this and might result in a routine where calculating public holidays involved a major change. It is encapsulation, or information hiding, that makes bottom-up design possible.

The second technique is encapsulation itself. Modules implemented in an object-oriented style are accessed purely via their interface and the programmer need only be aware of this interface, which is equivalent to a specification of the function of the module. Its implementation is hidden and irrelevant to its use in the system. Information hiding can also contribute to security. A simple set of interfaces (i.e. they are small, explicit and there are few of them) contributes to interoperability and to friendliness. In fact one of the earliest widespread applications of object-oriented programming was in the area of user interface design, as we saw in Chapter 1.

Inheritance, genericity or other forms of polymorphism make exception handling easier and improve the extensibility of systems. In a system with inheritance, functions can be added by adding child objects that inherit their parents' specification and implementation, but still behave differently in the key areas relevant to them. In this way incremental changes become a great deal more easy to conceive and implement. As was remarked in the last chapter, inheritance, if not used with care, can compromise abstraction and make systems unduly complex. On the other hand the benefit of extensibility is closely tied to that of reuse. A module that is not extensible may have a very limited range of applications in which it may be reused.

Correctness and robustness are addressed by formal specification and prototyping methods, which will be discussed later (see Chapters 6 and 7) and which can be harmonized with object-oriented methods. If, and it is a big 'if', modules are well constructed with reuse in mind they are likely to be more robust. Every time they are used they are *a fortiori*[1] tested as well.

Maintainability, reusability and verifiability are all supported by the simultaneously 'open' and 'closed' nature of object-oriented systems. Meyer's 'open-closed' principle states that reusable systems should be both open, in the sense that they are easy to extend, and closed, in the sense that they are ready to use. An example of code that does not satisfy this principle can be found in almost any system which utilizes computed goto or case statements in a conventional language. Consider, for example, the following code fragment concerned with error handling in a C-like language.

```
Switch (n)
{case 1: error = 49;
```

---

[1] with stronger reason

```
      print("Warning - Error 49");continue;
case 2: error = 71;
      print("Execution halting due to Error 71");break;
case 3:
      break;
}
```

This code suffers from a complete lack of reusability and extensibility. Furthermore, it would be extremely difficult to document more concisely than the code itself. In order to add a new case – or handle a new error – the programmer would have to take the module off-line, make the changes and recompile. Thus, the system is not closed – it cannot be used 'as is' while the changes are made and indeed there is no guarantee that the handling of the existing functions will not be affected by some slip of the programmer. It is not open in that extensions involve changing existing code at the implementation level in order to add the new functions. Systems that employ inheritance, including object-oriented ones, do satisfy the open/closed principle. There are even object-oriented languages that permit changes to modules while the system is actually running.

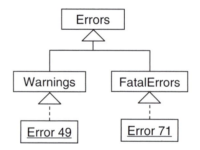

Figure 2.3 Object-oriented error trapping.

The prime technique of object-oriented programming used to provide extensibility is inheritance. If we had approached the same error trapping problem with an object-oriented point of view we would have reasoned that errors had a structure, as illustrated in Figure 2.3. In this simple case they break down into fatal errors and warnings. Both types of error inherit the attributes and methods of errors in general, and individual errors may be regarded as instances of the appropriate subclass. To add a new error, or more importantly a new type of error, we need only create a new class and a new object and specify its class. So, if we discovered a new type of error that was neither a warning nor fatal, we could make a new subclass of error describing its special features. The way existing errors are handled cannot be affected and the only compilation necessary is that of the new class.

Of course this is a trivial and unrealistic example, but it demonstrates the main point: that inheritance supports the construction of extensible systems. A more realistic example is illustrated in Figure 2.4. Here a system developer may have written some code for the common features of all bank accounts, such as methods for printing statements, and dealt with the special features of deposit and current ('checking' in American) accounts in subclasses; deposit accounts for example need to compute interest. Now when an interest bearing current account is introduced it is easy to add a new class, as a subclass of either deposit accounts or of current accounts. Alternatively, multiple inheritance could be used to inherit features from both as indicated by the addition of the grey generalization arrow.

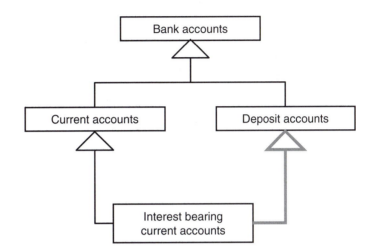

Figure 2.4 Classification structure for bank accounts.

Both object-oriented and functional programming offer the programmer the opportunity to write open-closed systems. This is not the place to describe functional programming, but I will deal with it peripherally in the next chapter.

This apparently self-contradictory open-closed principle contributes to software maintenance, project management and especially to change control in a profound manner. It is what enables eXtreme Programming (Beck, 2000). Systems must be open because designers rarely foresee all the uses or effects of a module when it is being developed; new features may thus need to be added later. However, systems that are not closed off and released to users are of no use whatever. Open-closed systems imply an explicit recognition of change control procedures from the very beginning of development. Evolutionary development and object-oriented programming should both be viewed in the light of this observation and will be something of an implicit theme in much of the remainder of this book.

There is a combinatorially large number of ways to do a functional decomposition. The way it is done is thus likely to be highly application specific. Taking a bottom-up approach based on the metaphor of objects is likely to result in better reusability. However, this is not the easiest option. In the days when database suppliers were not thoughtful enough to provide dates as built-in primitive data types, we had to write our own date arithmetic routines. I recall writing one, and thinking myself very far-sighted in incorporating an algorithm for finding the date when Easter fell. The specification of this algorithm is published in The Book of Common Prayer. It enabled, in those days, the computation of the dates of all UK public holidays. The trouble was, with the benefit of hindsight, that I omitted to put in routines for Ramadan, Yom Kippur and the Chinese new year. The lesson here is that programming bottom up, with reuse in mind, is very costly indeed, and that completely reusable code would be infinitely expensive. The solution to this dilemma is to use a combination of bottom-up and top-down approaches and to code only those functions where a potential for reuse can be foreseen. The idea of pluggable frameworks introduced by Catalysis (D'Souza and Wills, 1999) addresses this very question. Catalysis recommends that potential variation points should be identified and dealt with by calling separate routines. Such a pure bottom-up approach is, in practice, very difficult to adopt because of the cost of calls to objects and the unpredictability of what may vary. An object-oriented system's extensibility guarantees that unforeseen functions can be added later, but there is a cost. This idea is discussed further in Chapter 7. Object-oriented programming increases programmer productivity. The danger is that it increases it too much, and that programmers introduce unnecessary functions.

Cox (1986) had the vision of what he called Software Integrated Circuits (Software ICs), the simile being with hardware that is literally assembled from standard components in most cases, just as are cars, radios and refrigerators. The same idea is now routinely referred to as component-based development (CBD). The economic benefits of this approach are well known. So why has it proved untenable and an elusive goal for software systems? Firstly, it is largely the case that the non-package software systems that represent the majority of systems, unlike most manufactured goods, are not mass produced; there is but one end-product. Thus, the economies of scale associated with mass production are unavailable, and project sponsors are often unwilling to invest extra effort in developing anything not immediately cost justified by the task in hand. Secondly, the prevalence in the recent past of methods of top-down decomposition has led to division of labour based on an application-specific decomposition of problems. This has meant that the boundaries of modules have been defined in a way that depends on the decomposition, which in turn depends on the functional characteristics of the specific application, rather than a natural decomposition based on objects in the world: objects which would be bounded in the same way in many applications and therefore be reusable. Object-oriented methods address the latter point in avoiding the over-zealous application of the top-down philosophy. If they are to address the first point then project managers and sponsors both need to be re-educated somewhat. Project planning and costing need to be done on the basis of future as well as current projects. The problem here is that, in a society increasingly concerned with short-term, and increasingly short-term, profits, it is nearly always easier to justify projects on an individual basis. Because of this economic reality, it is sadly likely that reusable modules will be created more by luck than by judgement, and techniques that encourage 'willy-nilly' reusability are possibly the only ones that will work. The object-oriented methods described in this book have this character, in that reusability is actually easier to deliver with object-oriented methods and may add little or nothing to overall costs, although the initial development cost of a reusable module may be far, far higher than that of an application-specific module; up to ten times higher according to extreme estimates. There is always a small chance that the object-oriented style will produce reusable modules at no extra cost. This will occur when the objects are chosen well; that is, chosen to correspond to genuine, universal objects in the application domain.

MODULARITY The importance of modularity has long been emphasized in the writings of software theoreticians. Parnas (1972) introduced the notion of using modules for information hiding. Meyer (1988) lays down five criteria and five principles for modularity. These criteria he names as:

1. Decomposability
2. Composability
3. Understandability
4. Continuity
5. Protection

Decomposability refers to the software engineering and project management requirement that systems be decomposable into manageable chunks so that they can be changed more easily and so that individuals or teams can be assigned coherent work packages. The technique of top-down decomposition achieves this on the basis of a single top-level function. It is compromised by the possible non-existence of a genuine 'top' in, for example, a system such as an operating system. It is also possible to define modules with very complex interfaces to each other in this way. Object-oriented decomposition is based on a bottom-up approach and the principles of information hiding and simple interfaces.

Decomposability is strongly related to decentralization. Decentralization helps to simplify code by eliminating hidden dependencies. The latter causes large code changes to follow on from relatively small design changes. If each module in a system needs only to know about its own implementation rather than that of its servers then its code can be more readily extended internally. Design changes are thus isolated and do not automatically affect the rest of the system.

Composability refers to the property of modules to be freely combined even in systems for which they were not developed. This is fundamental to software reuse and again is supported by the principle of information hiding. Functional decomposition, as I have said, can be used to support decomposition but it has nothing to offer to aid composability. One of the strikingly unique features of the object-oriented approach is that it supports both composability and decomposability. Composability is related to the notion of extensibility, which refers to being able to add functions to a system without radical surgery. Composability and extensibility are supported by the object-oriented principles of small interfaces (see below) and especially, as we have seen, by inheritance. This argument presupposes that we are working within one language. The question arises, however, whether it is possible to compose systems from objects written in different languages. We look at this issue in Chapter 4. Top-down decomposition can certainly deliver decomposability, but it cannot deliver composability except in very special circumstances.

Understandability helps people to comprehend a system by looking at its parts prior to gaining an understanding of the whole. This is a valid principle even though the whole may exhibit emergent properties not shown by its parts, since it assists learning and maintenance if treated with proper caution. Object-oriented systems are understandable in this way to the extent that it is not necessary to trace their message passing behaviour in detail in order to understand what they do.

Continuity in a system implies both that small changes made to it will only result in small changes in its behaviour, and that small changes in the specification will require changes in only a few modules. The latter point is the one directly addressed by object-oriented methods. Once again it is inheritance and simple interfaces that deliver this benefit.

The criterion of modular **protection** insists that exception and error conditions either remain confined to the module in which they occur or propagate to only a few other closely related modules. For example, the practice in database systems of incorporating validation checks within entity descriptions supports protection, in that data may not be entered incorrectly by virtue of a property of the module into which they are being entered.

The principles required to ensure these criteria for modularity are observed are identified by Meyer as these five:

1. Linguistic modular units
2. Few interfaces
3. Small interfaces
4. Explicit interfaces
5. Information hiding

I have referred to these principles in the discussion of Meyer's five criteria above. The phrase **linguistic modular units** refers to the need for a correspondence between the modules of a system and the primitive data types or syntactic units provided by the language or method used to describe the problem. Abstract data types in particular support this principle and it, in turn, contributes to decomposability, composability and protection. For example, the use of floating point primitives in most programming languages supports their reuse in widely varying programs, and user defined types extend this benefit to other modules. Many modern software products have obtained benefits in limited applications through the application of this principle. Databases deal with whole records and tables as primitives and financial modelling and on-line analytic processing (OLAP) systems with rows and columns. This makes certain applications much easier to develop, combine and test.

By **few interfaces** we mean that each module should communicate with as few others as possible. I have already alluded to the difficulty of tracing complex message passing. The few interfaces principle contributes to both continuity and protection. It may be implemented in topologically different ways. A good analogy is a local area network where we may regard each workstation and server as objects communicating by message passing. Such a network may be implemented either as a centralized star, or as a ring in which communication is accomplished by only neighbouring nodes being allowed to communicate, although messages may be passed on in relay. Of course real networks do not work like this but the metaphor is applicable to the structure of objects within a system. A network in which every node is connected to every other one violates the principle and would evidently be difficult to maintain and change.

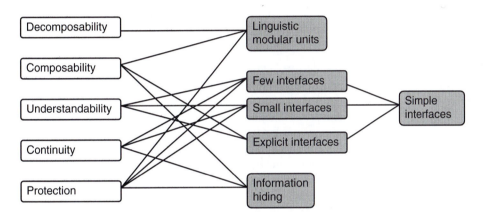

Figure 2.5 The relationship between Meyer's five criteria and principles.

The principle of **small interfaces** states that the interfaces should pass as little data as possible. Again the continuity and protection criteria are addressed by this principle.

The need for **explicit interfaces** arises from the need to use objects via their specification rather than their implementation so that in composition and decomposition the inter-module connexions are known clearly. Continuity is also addressed in that knock-on effects may be seen from the specification of modules. Data sharing may contribute to storage efficiency, but may compromise this principle if not stated clearly in the interfaces between modules.

The last three principles may be combined as the principle of **simple interfaces**. In general object-oriented systems should be written so that all communication with objects is via their interfaces (or specifications) rather than their implementations, and these interfaces should be as simple as possible: few, small and explicit. It is this combined principle to which we shall constantly refer in this book.

The principle of simple interfaces provides the basis for hoping that the criterion of composability can be met by systems written with multiple object-oriented languages. If this principle is not adhered to, such composability is likely to be a vain hope.

The principle of **information hiding** is central. It says that modules may hide the design decisions used in their construction. In the terminology of object-oriented methods this means that modules are used via their specifications, not their implementations. All information, whether concerning data or function, about a module is encapsulated within it and, unless specifically declared public, hidden from other modules. Thus, when the implementation of a module is changed its clients need not be, since they only deal with the interface.

The principles given above apply not only to programming but to designs and specifications as well. We will meet these issues in detail in Chapters 6 and 7. For now, it is only necessary to state that the benefits of object-oriented design and analysis are the central themes of this book. Many of my remarks on object-oriented programming languages in the next chapter are merely laying the groundwork for this view.

OTHER BENEFITS

Another key benefit of the object-oriented approach is that it enables far better management of complexity, as is emphasized by Booch (1993). The problems modelled by computer systems, the systems themselves and the management of the development process are all inherently complex processes. An abstraction of the key elements of the problem domain and a decomposition into objects and inheritance, aggregation and usage structures based on real-world objects and concepts helps with the management of complexity in several ways. First, the system and the problem are in close correspondence, so that the cognitive insights of everyday life can be mapped onto the solution. Second, encapsulation divides the problem up into coherent chunks small and simple enough for us to understand them as a whole. Third, object-orientation provides several ways to model structure and meaning: inheritance structures and so on. Lastly, the reusability and extensibility of object-oriented systems mean that complex systems may be assembled from simple ones, and that complex systems can evolve incrementally in simple steps into even more complex ones.

The pressure for more 'open' and distributed systems highlights both the benefits of and the need for object-oriented methods. Interoperability, modularity, extensibility, simple interfaces and information hiding are intimately related in the contribution they make to the development of truly open systems. Open systems are to be thought of as those which do not tie buyers or developers to particular suppliers of hardware, systems software or networks. To guarantee this ideal state of affairs, future systems will need to interoperate; that is they must communicate and share resources. Although there are many other considerations, it is natural to think of each system within a distributed open system as an object composed of objects. Each such system needs to communicate not only with other whole systems, but with their components. The object-oriented approach supports this idea by making the interfaces that need to be defined small, explicit and few in number. Specifying communication protocols which depend only on the defined interface – not the implementation – is possibly the only way we yet know of to make open systems work. It is thus no surprise that many of the companies seriously committed to open systems have invested heavily in object-oriented technology. This point has also been taken up by the proponents of the idea of object request brokers which make it possible for objects or whole systems to co-operate across networks. The Object Management Group's CORBA, discussed in Chapter 4, is a standard for such products.

A basic prerequisite for software reuse is a component library or software repository. Many CASE tools recognize this but fail to address the openness of the repository or the need for its components to satisfy the principles of linguistic modular units, simple interfaces or information hiding. The benefits of object-oriented programming and methods will be better realized when open code and/or specification libraries are widely available commercially. The development of such libraries, the basis for software repositories, is an urgent task for the software industry. These libraries will be all the better for being based on real systems developments as part of commercial projects. Several commercial repository products from companies such as Adaptive, Oracle and Unisys exist, but they are mainly focused on storing metadata and file interchange standards.

MORE AARDVARK

The aims of Aardvark, in building SACIS, are:

- to construct a system that will be both a database and enquiry system;
- to be capable of changing and being extended with the business;
- to be able to support both conventional and expert systems components;
- to offer the option of distributed installation;
- not to lock Aardvark into any manufacturer's products;
- to have all rule-based and semantic components stored in explicit form rather than hidden in the code or normalized design; and
- to offer the possibility of using modules developed for SACIS in future systems developments.

At the outset, although it seems that an object-oriented solution is the only one even potentially capable of meeting all these requirements, the IT manager is not convinced that there is a development system that will actually do the job. What should she do? Aardvark's consultants have recommended the following cautious approach. First, the specification and business analysis should be constructed using object-oriented techniques. This means that implementation in an object-oriented programming language will be straightforward if a suitable one can be found by the end of the analysis stage but, if not, the system can still be implemented in a conventional language. The benefits of having a specification with extensible and reusable components remain. In view of the uncertainty surrounding the final development platform, the specification is to use throwaway prototyping for which it is natural to use an object-oriented language. Smalltalk was considered, but due to existing skills and because the prototype might still evolve into the full system, it was eventually decided to use a mixture of Java and C++ with suitable libraries, including a suite of Java expert system classes. HTML will be used to provide reports through a browser at remote locations and XML to support communication with existing package solutions and legacy systems. The developers will receive basic training in object-oriented concepts and in Java, to help overcome any residual prejudices from their days working with C. The project will be started with a three-day, facilitated requirements workshop. While the specification is being further elaborated, Aardvark is investigating options for the database components. We will follow this development in subsequent chapters. Aardvark's caution is justified because object-orientation is not without drawbacks. In the next section we examine some of them.

2.2 Some problems and pitfalls

Caution is needed in assessing the benefits of any technology. Object-oriented methods are not a panacea and there is a profound need to state the areas where the claimed benefits may not be delivered, along with a need to identify those which may only be delivered in certain circumstances. I have claimed software reuse, for example, as a key benefit. In fact, reusable data structures have proved an elusive goal even where object-oriented methods have been used. One of the reasons for this is that designing reusable modules actually adds to the cost of a project and there is always a temptation to get the job in hand done as quickly as possible even at the expense of future reusability. I have already remarked on the economic short-termism which seems to characterize post-industrial society especially in periods of high interest rates. In such a milieu, it is extremely difficult to make a case for extra investment in reusability, and although object-oriented methods make reusable systems *less* costly they do not remove all extra costs. The extra costs can only be justified in terms of future reuse savings which are discounted back to present-day prices. This may prove to be a serious impediment to the delivery of this promised and much vaunted benefit. The author once conducted an informal survey of colleagues who have carried out object-oriented projects by asking them what reusable components emerged from their projects. In a straw poll of about six projects, only one didn't remark to the effect: 'Oh! We really didn't have the time to sort that one out. No, nothing really emerged that we would ever use again.' However, and against this, several staggering successes with reuse are reported in the next section. Furthermore, component-based development is changing the picture rapidly, as dicussed in Chapter 7. Here it will be seen that reuse must be planned and managed, with specific components being built for architectural reuse.

Another problem I have already alluded to is the lack of commercially available object libraries. Without such libraries of classes and components, developed in anger on real projects, the true benefit of reuse cannot be delivered in volume. On the other hand in the absence of such libraries, why should any company take up the technology? It seems that we are caught on the horns of a dilemma. Unless pioneering companies take considerable risks, possibly motivated by benefits other than reuse, useful component libraries will not emerge and the technology will not mature. The success of commercially developed reusable components depends on the willingness of project sponsors and investors to allow for the extra cost of their development, and to be prepared to recover investments over a longer period. In Chapters 6 to 9 we will look at the issue of higher level reuse: the reuse of designs and specifications. Here too, good libraries and good tools to navigate these libraries will be needed.

If libraries are to be useful we must find ways of navigating through their volume and complexity. Even when useful object libraries, and classification and navigation techniques for them, are developed and become widely available, another problem still has to be faced. How are developers going to know that a particular library contains just the object they need in this particular case? Here is a potentially huge information overload difficulty. People just cannot be expected to know what is in every library and it is inconceivable that every library could contain all, or even most, of the objects that a typical developer is likely to need. Several solutions to this problem are possible. Service companies may act as information brokers. Expert systems containing the information may be developed and sold commercially. Group work and techniques for the classification of objects will be needed. High level languages will be needed to describe the interactions among objects in the library. Widespread use of libraries may never go beyond those restricted to programming and interface level objects such as those that already exist. It is even conceivable that a successful vendor might be able to create one big product with most of the useful classes created by others, but this seems a very remote possibility. Reuse across domain boundaries will only work if domain-neutral classes can be constructed.

I suspect that vertical, industry-specific libraries will emerge as the property of product and consultancy companies and used in contract developments. One obstacle to this happening is the fact that these companies, at least the consultancies, have been traditionally reluctant to make this kind of investment, although there are already some offerings in the Finance sector and the OMG has proposed building other standards for services in selected vertical industry sectors.

The management of large component libraries for object-oriented programming is still a significant unsolved problem. Two chief ways of organizing such libraries have been explored. The classes in the library can be organized hierarchically which permits browsers to be used. Alternatively, retrieval can be accomplished by storing keywords with the classes in the manner of a conventional information retrieval system. It turns out that neither approach is ideal and the current thinking is that a combined approach is best, but there are still no sufficiently mature commercial software products to assist with this severe problem and manual methods are in use at most sites.

The problem of emergency fixes, which I referred to above, is yet another serious obstacle to the widespread adoption of object-oriented techniques. The reusability of an object may be seriously compromised if a zealous programmer fixes a bug in it in an improper or incautious way. *The best laid schemes o' mice an' men gang aft a-gley.* Configuration management systems can be used to alleviate this problem partially, but, as with CASE code generators, it is not always possible to enforce managerial controls strictly in the hurly-burly of real system operation.

We also need to develop protocols for change and version control for systems of complex objects with multiple interconnexions. Work on formal specification of object interfaces is required so that composability languages can be developed to allow library modules to be configured to meet a specification. There has been interest in building tools that can estimate the impact of a changed interface on other objects in a system (Hood *et al.*, 1987).

Most object-oriented programming languages do not support the notion of persistent objects; that is objects which, stored on disk, persist unchanged between executions. Thus, data and object management is not well supported by object-oriented programming. The emergence of object-oriented databases addresses this deficiency, but there is still a wide gulf between the object-oriented programming and database communities. Indeed, some purists, such as Wegner, have claimed that persistent objects defy the basic philosophy of object-orientation. A programming style that cannot tolerate persistence, however, is merely doomed in my opinion. Object-oriented databases will be dealt with in detail in Chapter 5.

The efficiency of some object-oriented programming languages with their support for dynamic binding and garbage collection (see Chapter 3) is in doubt. For applications, perhaps embedded or real-time applications, where efficiency or sheer scale is of major concern these languages are simply not a viable proposition, although a few small-scale, real-time applications have been written in such languages. Hybrid languages, on the other hand, may be more efficient but they often compromise object-oriented principles and benefits. A similar paradox in the field of expert systems, which at one time were often written in the similarly inefficient language Lisp, has now been effectively resolved by the emergence of mature hybrid development systems. Such a maturation of object-oriented programming environments is necessary before the benefits of object-oriented programming can become widely realized.

As pointed out in Chapter 1, inheritance compromises reuse unless fairly strict procedures are adhered to. Thus, inheritance-free approaches, as proposed by some advocates of component-based development and others, have a distinct place in the armoury of the software developer.

I have emphasized the benefit of the reduction of maintenance costs arising from sound object-oriented design and programming. Even here there are dangers waiting to trap the unwary. Validating and verifying an object requires tests that go well beyond its boundary; the whole of all related inheritance structures must be looked at too. This implies that OO methods must test their products more rigorously and earlier.

Reusing parts of applications still requires a large helping of creativity. It requires developers to separate the functionality of different domains from that of applications built to model them. This is something that we can never provide an exhaustive set of rules for, automate or de-skill. A bad programmer can produce unusable – never mind unreusable – systems just as easily in an object-oriented language as in any other. As the old adage has it: real programmers write FORTRAN, and can do so in *any* language.

Inheritance structures are only one form of semantics. As we will see in subsequent chapters, other forms include client-server relationships, association and composition structures, cardinality constraints, business rules and control rules. It is my contention that including any semantic information in a system potentially compromises the reusability of its components. The reason is that the more you say about something, the more specific you are, the more you have related it to its context. On the other hand, a non-specific object will be a poor model of a real-world object, which is always perceived and used in a context. The trade-off between reuse and semantics must become an important concern of component designers, analysts and programmers. In certain applications, such as graphical user interfaces where the objects themselves are largely computational artefacts, the context is tightly circumscribed and this problem arises less sharply. In general commercial systems, and even in simulation problems, this is not so.

I have commented that sometimes it becomes necessary to trace the behaviour of a system, in order to debug it, by tracing the passage of messages from one object to another. This tracing of message passing behaviour in understanding or debugging a system can be enormously difficult and remains, in my view, a very serious defect of object-oriented systems. One envisages future generations of software engineers criticising their counterparts of today for 'spaghetti message passing structures' or some such.

The field is still developing, though the pace has slowed a little, and some current languages (even Java!) may still be superseded by newer ones. For example, full support for multiple inheritance is not available yet in any single system in the sense that it was defined in the preceding chapter. That is, no system in wide commercial use supports class and instance level inheritance of methods, attributes and attribute values with explicit, user-defined rules for conflict resolution. Nor are there object-oriented languages that support dynamic or multiple classification. Support for multiple inheritance and genericity is not available yet in popular languages like Java. I think this is a deficiency and that there will be new or extended languages that address it. From the point of view of someone building a large system in an object-oriented programming language this possibility must be worrying, since the organization will ill be able to afford to switch languages mid-stream. Fortunately, this problem does not apply to object-oriented analysis or design.

I have emphasized the benefits arising from simple interfaces and information hiding. I have claimed that when a module's implementation changes, its clients will not be affected. There are, however, circumstances when this euphoria is ill justified. Suppose, for example, that the change is so large or profound that the interface itself changes. For example, suppose that we have lived comfortably with the notion of 'employee' and that all our systems and databases contain a uniform interface to employee objects. Now workers' self-government, or slavery, or some completely different social system is introduced. Surely our notion of the interface of the employee object must undergo radical change. What are we to make of employees who receive no salary, for example – or shareholders who take no profit?

Function libraries, especially in scientific programming, have been quite successful as a reuse strategy but are often considered hard to use because of the need to remember long parameter lists, or 'common blocks' in FORTRAN, and to understand the inner working of the functions in some cases. It remains to be seen whether this will be posterity's judgement on object libraries. For the reasons given in the previous section, I think not.

The principal additional costs in adopting object technology are the investment in new hardware, software and methods that may be required, the costs of the essential training and re-education of both developers and management and the extra costs of developing reusable components and managing libraries. This point is explored further in Chapter 9.

It is also the case that reusable components may cost a great deal more to write than conventional estimates would indicate; Jacobson *et al.* (1992) estimate over ten times as much, and most experience indicates a factor of at least six. For some applications, such as GUI development or Finance, class libraries or application frameworks can be purchased commercially. This at least removes the cost of component development, but few domains receive this treatment at present. Having written or bought a suite of classes, the problems do not end. Managing component libraries is difficult and costly. As we will see, defining and managing business object libraries and component versioning also remain problems without a known general solution, though progress is being made.

One of the most difficult problems to face up to is the organizational and cultural changes that must follow the adoption of object technology if it is to be fully beneficial. We are used to rewarding analysts and programmers according to the amount of code they produce (scaled according to the language generation they work with of course) rather than the amount of other people's code they reuse. This implies a change in the reward structure that may well be resisted. Furthermore, project managers are paid to make projects come in on time and not to write code for the benefit of subsequent projects. This too could be a big shock and some workers have suggested that class development should be totally separated from application building. However, this is often impractical and not always feasible since so many development ideas come from direct involvement with users.

The final problem with object technology I want to raise arises from the view taken by its more extreme proponents that it is the last word in software engineering; the so-called silver bullet. Major investments in OT may be impeded by the more sensible view that it will eventually be succeeded by an even more powerful metaphor, just as relational databases – once also the last word – are now being superseded in some application areas by newer approaches (see Chapter 5). An indication that improvements over and above OT are possible is given by the emergence of new metaphors based on research languages like BETA (see Section 3.6.1). Fortunately, it appears that such developments will incorporate, rather than displace, the object-oriented metaphor, so that investments made now should be secure against technological change.

2.3 Case studies

In this section we will examine very briefly some of the benefits that have been reported by users of object technology.

Perhaps the oldest and best known case of the large-scale, beneficial application of object technology is the one at Brooklyn Union Gas where a customer management system consisting of 1.5 million lines of PL/1 was replaced by a system written using an object-oriented pre-processor. The new system was very large, with 850 on-line users, a 100 gigabyte database and 10,000 code modules. The benefits reported included a 40% reduction in code size due mainly to reuse, low maintenance costs (12 people in the team), trouble-free installation and above all great flexibility and extensibility. These benefits were not free. The developers had to invent their own object-oriented development methods and standards as these were not available in the development period from 1987 to 1990; traditional methods were found seriously wanting.

Another early application where striking benefits were noted was a maintenance management system developed for General Motors. This system helped the company schedule repairs and maintain the parts inventory. The old system consisted of 265,000 lines of PL/1, took 12.5 man-years to develop and used 13.6 Mbytes of mainframe memory when running. A replacement was written in Smalltalk 80 in less than a man-year and consisted of only 22,000 lines of code and used a mere 1.1 Mbytes of memory. Remarkably, the performance of the two systems was roughly the same and the overall productivity gain was estimated at 14:1. Admittedly, building a system for the second time is nearly always easier to do, but the ratio is still very impressive.

Although I have argued that reuse is a hard benefit to achieve, compared to extensibility, some companies have been able to realize it. Petroleum Information supplies geographic data to the oil and gas industry. They built a geographic information system (*Sorcerer's Apprentice*) using CLOS and reported a figure of 80% for code reuse. This led in turn to much shorter development times and to the developers tackling problems that would have previously been thought intractable.

Other large-scale applications include many front-office trading systems written in Banking. Objective C under NeXtStep was used at Swiss Bank Corporation in the early 1990s, when it was shown that measured programmer productivity increased by 50% in three consecutive years (Graham, 1994e).

Harmon and Taylor (1993) describe 20 of the 225 case studies entered for the 1992 *Object World* competition for the most beneficial use of object technology.

These include an accounts and administration system for the Southern California Gas Company, an OOA simulator for Boeing and a software engineering environment for a hospital. These awards continue to be made and are reported in the proceedings of the *Object World* series of conferences.

More recently, conventional systems have been re-engineered rapidly and successfully using object-oriented programming and associated methods such as Beck's extreme programming (XP) (Beck, 2000). I, and many of my colleagues, have been involved in many succesful OO projects to the extent that their success has become commonplace and unremarkable. However, this is not to say that there have not been many failures, and it is notable that many of these have led organizations who adopted C++ and related methods in the early 1990s to back off from object technology.

The themes that emerge from these experiences are that reuse is achievable, though more than a good object-oriented programming language is required to achieve it. What is required is the determination to succeed, good project management, sound methods, attention to the problems of education, training and change management and a modicum of luck. Given these factors reuse is attainable but only at a cost. Reusable code naturally takes a little longer to write and test. However, the immediate benefits that arise from extensibility often push reuse into second place as a consideration. Extensibility is one of the key characteristics that businesses require from systems. Thus, even if reuse is not an option you may still gain greatly from object-oriented methods.

Despite a large number of successes, it is still the case that the majority of organizations have not been able to benefit from massive reuse. The reasons are largely economic and managerial rather than to do with the technology itself. We will look at them in Chapter 9.

2.4 Adoption strategies

The danger with new technologies is that people are either too enthusiastic and unrealistic in their expectations or too pessimistic and obstructive. In the first case they plunge into them with gay abandon and often discredit the technology if not actually damaging their own careers. In the second, the Luddites are overtaken by companies that take the best aspects of the technology and use it for competitive edge.

The example that springs to mind to support this view is the example of expert systems. In the early 1980s, as expert systems emerged from the AI research labs, there was enormous media hype, much of it ill-informed, but a lot taken directly from the propaganda put out by professors of AI, who should have known better, but who had research grants to win. Thus, we had a relatively immature technology with modest real capabilities and a market expectation of systems which would, in the words of Herb Simon (1965), be 'capable of performing any task that a man could perform within 20 years'. This is the formula for failure: immature technology + unrealistic expectations.

I will caricature the process of failure in a parable. The Data Processing manager of a large corporation in 1983, say, became excited by the possibilities of expert systems, having read about them in the press. The R&D expert was asked to investigate. The preliminary investigation showed that benefits could be obtained and it was decided to run a pilot project. So far so good, but now things began to go wrong. The DP manager – let's call him Abe S. Traction, wondering whom he could spare for this task, began to survey the corporate horizon. Lo, there was the OR department. Now they hadn't done anything useful for years (OR had been discredited in the late 1960s through a process similar to the one I am parodying here). So Abe went to see the head of OR who, happy to be needed, offered to help. Whom could he spare? Well, those guys in department C weren't doing anything right now, so, Bob's your uncle, the expert systems section was created. The new department was given a minuscule budget and told to find a suitable problem for expert systems, buy a couple of shells to play with and report back. As time went on they were directed away from any application that was in any way significant to the business: 'What if it goes wrong? People will notice.' When they did find an application – probably concerned with the help desk – the solution didn't work very well, but that didn't matter because nobody significant noticed. However, after five or six attempts Abe had had enough and decided that expert systems were a load of hype – he actually used a slightly different word, but that need not detain us here. In this company, and in the world at large, unrealistic expectations gave way to pessimism, and the so-called AI winter commenced in the late 1980s. Expert systems are actually now a mature, powerful and useful technology and many companies are gaining benefits; but they are the companies with very different DP managers from Mr Traction.

I hope you will see by now that I am constructing a simile between expert systems and object-orientation. The latter is still a fairly new technology which is widely believed to be the solution to many IT ills. How should companies wanting to explore object-oriented systems proceed? The answer is simple: don't do what Abe did. Here are some guidelines.

- Choose the people you can least afford to spare for the development team. Object-oriented methods, just as expert systems, need good people, not left-overs from the corporate elephant's graveyard.
- Choose a business-critical application to test the methods on, but allow time for false starts. By all means choose a small application, but make sure it will be noticed, fail or succeed.
- Allocate a budget in proportion to the importance of the application. This implies carrying out proper cost and business justification exercises.
- Set clear objectives for the project team; not just technical objectives but business objectives.
- Establish clear senior user management commitment to the project. Keep users involved throughout and report back lessons learnt.

From the supplier's point of view there are some general lessons to be drawn from my simile. They apply to nearly all new technologies. When new technology is first developed it has low capability and is largely unknown to the market. Gradually, through its lifetime, this capability will increase until some saturation level is reached or its potentialities are exhausted. However, the reputation that the technology acquires represents its perceived value and may be driven up by hype out of all proportion to its real capability. This is illustrated by the curves in Figure 2.4.

Eventually, as the hype fades and early users try out the technology, gloom sets in. It is discovered that there are problems and the exaggerated claims of both suppliers and journalists are debunked. At this point expectations fall to the level of the initial real capability. However, in the meantime the capability of the technology has improved and the two curves cross over at point Q in the diagram. Now, price is based on exchange-value, which is based on demand, which is in turn based on expectations and not on use-value or capability. Thus, buyers in the period between points P and Q have been paying a premium for the technology. After the cross-over they may purchase at a discount until normality is restored at point R.

The only difficulty in using this model is estimating where one is on the expectation curve. The technical press is a good indicator of expectation and experts in the technology will usually be able to estimate its real capability. At the time of writing (mid-2000) I believe that we are well into the Q–R range. This applies to object-oriented programming, object-oriented methods and object-oriented databases about equally, though object-oriented programming is slightly more advanced than the other two areas and the situation with CBD is less advanced. Since it takes about two years for an organization to understand and adopt a new approach fully, now is the time for users to adopt object technology: while discounts are still available.

Market trends that are evident from my experience are upward and changing in character. In 1990 user organizations were attending awareness briefings and gathering information. By 1991 a vendor's OT capability had become important in winning bids for more general work in computing but only a few mission-critical projects using it had begun. The market for training courses in object-oriented programming and methods began to mature in 1992 and advanced users were completing their first pilot projects. In 1993 OT was beginning to be used on the first large-scale, mission-critical projects in the mainstream of data processing; and a very small number of advanced users had completely switched to object-oriented development for new systems while continuing to maintain conventional legacy systems pending migration. One head of IT for such an organization, Swiss Bank Corporation, claimed (*Computing,* 19 November 1993) that the chief motivation was rapid development because systems that came in over budget might detract from performance by 8% while those that came in late would affect the bottom line by over 30%. OT contributes to rapid development in several ways but principally through reuse and extensibility. A comprehensive approach to object-oriented rapid application development is presented in Chapters 6 to 9. By 1997 OT had become a mainstream approach for most IT organizations and nearly every supplier, though full migration was stalled for many by the efforts needed to deal with the year 2000 date problem and the Euro. The early years of the 21st century will almost certainly see nearly universal adoption.

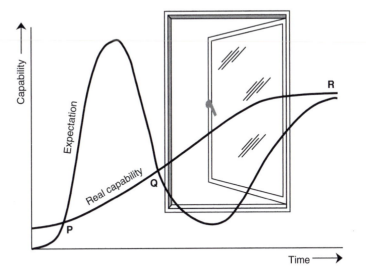

Figure 2.6 The window of opportunity for new technologies.

Management must fully appreciate the benefits, pitfalls and consequences of adopting OT. Many organizations adopting OT have special needs and a customized training programme is often best. Mentoring has been highly successful as a means of knowledge transfer. This means that an experienced object technologist works with a development team offering guidance and practical help.

The danger is to see OT as merely the next 'silver bullet'. We should view it with circumspection but I still believe that most modern companies will be unable to ignore it in the coming years insofar as it remains distinguishable at all from that activity which I like to call 'building computer systems'.

Perhaps the key question facing managers concerns getting from where they are now with a legacy of conventional, difficult to maintain but essential systems to where they want to be with object technology. This is the question of migration strategy and it is the subject of the Section 4.4.

Before an organization can contemplate migrating to object technology it must first review where it is currently in terms of the classes of tools, products, methods and languages in use. It is often helpful to convince COBOL programmers that many of the concepts of object technology are already familiar and that many of the principles of object-oriented design are already known to them under the heading of 'good software engineering practice': principles such as modularity, information hiding, low coupling, and so on. This helps them to accept any required changes far more readily. It is worth pointing out that a traditional module can be viewed as a set of interface functions with a shared data structure.

Organizations migrating to object technology must understand that there is some good news and some bad news due. The good news concerns better usability, rapid development, easier re-engineering, the ability to deal with more complex systems, higher reuse levels and greater flexibility. The semantic richness of object models makes specifications more reversible and supports rapid application development directly. Extensibility gives immediate benefits. Sound object-oriented analysis helps to deliver the benefits of OT much earlier in the life cycle. Reuse can slash development costs and some organizations have doubled productivity annually over several years because of this. The bad news is that reuse is not free and its successful adoption may involve major cultural changes and high levels of investment. Organizations migrating to object technology will have to implement major changes in the reward structures, with reuse specialists being rewarded quite differently from developers and developers being rewarded for speed and quality more explicitly. Key personnel will have to be taken away from the maintenance of important legacy systems in order to bring sufficient business knowledge to new, object-oriented developments. Every manager in the organization will have to be completely re-educated in the new approach, otherwise we shall merely recreate the nightmares of the waterfall model and the structured perspective with object-oriented tools. This requires clear, positive leadership and immense clarity and single-mindedness about the benefits and the risks inherent in object technology.

The range of applications of OT is almost endless. Object-oriented systems analysis produces semantically rich models and helps to support business re-engineering projects.

The computing industry requires object technology to solve the problems of satisfying users in increasingly adaptable businesses in a productive manner. The key to successful migration is the adoption of a comprehensive approach to object technology throughout the systems development life cycle, from early requirements capture to implementation. The true justification for object-orientation is the production of flexible, friendly and robust systems. It helps us to tackle the maintenance problem through more correct specification based on prototyping in semantically rich languages, and through easier extensibility based on inheritance and the pluggability of component-based design. It helps us with the development of new systems because we can build those systems from reusable components which encapsulate the state and behaviour of abstractions based on stable objects in the real world of an application or enterprise. It helps us build systems which are more secure, by exploiting further the encapsulation of the state of objects. It helps us build friendly, ready-to-hand, flexible user interfaces. It supports a very high level of modular (reusable) design and easy extensibility of function. Although these ideal benefits may sometimes be limited, as with the tension between abstraction and inheritance discussed in the first chapter, the justification remains convincing for companies who want to survive the corporate rat race.

All this adds up to a very strong requirement on industry to adopt object-oriented methods cautiously but quite wholeheartedly. Object-oriented methods have reached the stage where the window of opportunity is wide open.

⊟ 2.5 Summary

This chapter has concentrated on the tangible benefits arising from the use of object-oriented programming and to a lesser extent, object-oriented methods in general. The benefits of the latter, object-oriented analysis and design, are more fully explored in Chapters 6 and 7. We take a closer look at the particular benefits of object-oriented databases in Chapter 5. We have also noted certain disadvantages of the object-oriented approach.

The benefits may be summarized in the formula:

encapsulation + inheritance + identity ⇒ reusability + extensibility + semantic richness

Reuse, extensibility and other object-oriented benefits apply to designs and specifications as well as to programming.

Top-down decomposition can lead to application-specific modules and compromise reuse. The bottom-up approach and the principle of information hiding maximize reuse potential. Encapsulation delivers reuse.

Polymorphism and inheritance make handling variation and exceptions easier and therefore lead to more extensible systems. The open-closed principle is supported by inheritance. Inheritance delivers extensibility but may compromise reuse.

Semantic richness is provided by inheritance and other natural structures, together with constraints and rules concerning the meaning of objects in context. This also compromises reuse and must be carefully managed.

Meyer's five criteria for, and five principles of, object-oriented design were explained.

Other benefits identified in this chapter include the following.

- Maintenance is localized and thus is less costly and error-prone.
- Higher productivity and quality at the same time.
- Inheritance leads to more flexible, more easily extensible systems with lower maintenance costs.
- Object-orientation is a tool for managing complexity. Partitioning systems on the basis of objects helps with the problem of scalability.
- Partitioning of work has a natural basis and should be easier.
- Prototyping and evolutionary delivery are better supported.
- Interface descriptions between external and legacy systems become easier.
- Greater seamlessness in passing from conceptual modelling to code.
- OO models capable of capturing more of the meaning of an application.
- Encapsulation helps to build secure systems.
- Formal specification methods can be used where appropriate.
- For some applications there is no sensible alternative to object technology.

The benefits we claim are not unqualified and there are a number of pitfalls in the object-oriented approach. These include:

- Tight project deadlines may mean that reusability is not delivered.
- Libraries must be developed and knowledge about them disseminated.
- The field is developing rapidly and current languages may still be superseded. For example, full support for multiple inheritance and genericity is not available yet in popular languages like Java.
- A mature component market has yet to be firmly established.
- When inheritance or other semantic constructs are used, strict controls are necessary if reuse is not to be compromised.
- Issues such as persistence, concurrency and performance have still to await the benefit of consensus.
- Messaging topology is important and it is quite possible to write bad object-oriented systems.
- Reusable components may cost a great deal more to write than conventional estimates would indicate.
- Managing component libraries is difficult and costly.
- Culture change is necessary and everyone hates it.
- There are unavoidable costs associated with training and re-education.
- Object technology may not be the last word in software engineering.

Several commercial users have reported real benefits, including reduced code size and maintenance, high levels of reuse and good extensibility. There is a widespread belief that the approach scales up better than traditional approaches but little empirical proof of this yet. A small number of quite large projects do support this belief in scalability. Managerial and economic problems still limit the benefits of reuse to a minority of organizations.

When beginning to use object-oriented methods, use the best people and tools. Set a realistic budget, get management commitment and choose small, but business-critical, applications. The window of opportunity for object-oriented methods is wide open.

2.6 Bibliographical notes

The clearest exposition of the business motivation for and the benefits of object technology as a whole is to be found in Taylor (1997). He also provides a large amount of valuable case study material. Further case studies may be found in Harmon and Taylor (1993) and the proceedings of the several object-oriented conference series: *TOOLS, OOPSLA, Object Expo* and *Object World*.

Bertrand Meyer's excellent books (1995, 1997) contain a particularly clear exposition of the reasons for and benefits of an object-oriented approach to programming and design, although they concentrate on Meyer's own language,

Eiffel, in explaining the concepts. I have borrowed from them extensively in this chapter and recommend the serious student of object-oriented programming to read both of them. Cox and Novobilski (1991) also provide an extremely down to earth assessment of the benefits of object-oriented programming and concentrate on the issue of software reuse. Most books on object-oriented analysis and design offer a study of the general benefits of object technology but the list is too long to give here.

Bassett (1997) criticizes object technology's failure to deliver large-scale reuse and offers an alternative approach. Szyperski (1998) also attacks the limitations of conventional approaches to object technology and suggests that the problems are that classes have been at too small a scale for reuse and that inheritance has been used inappropriately.

⊟ 2.7 Exercises

1. What is the essential difference between object-oriented and conventional systems?
   a) OO is more reusable   d) Changes to data structures are localized
   b) OO uses inheritance   e) OO systems reduce development costs
   c) OO is more fashionable

2. Name up to eight benefits of object technology in general.

3. Name up to four pitfalls of object technology in general.

4. Describe an OO project known to you and elaborate the benefits it derived from using object technology and any problems that arose. Alternatively, describe a conventional project and discuss how OT could have helped and/or hindered.

3

Object-oriented and object-based programming languages

Language is the dress of thought.
Dr Johnson (*Lives of the English Poets*)

Chapter 1 gave a fairly informal introduction to the main concepts behind object-oriented programming and methods. In dealing with programming languages, this chapter introduces a little more in the way of technicalities and rigour. Although this is not intended to be primarily a book on object-oriented programming languages, their importance in the development of object-oriented ideas means that it is obligatory to give at least a brief treatment. We shall, however, be largely concerned with future directions in software development and the languages presented in this chapter will be discussed from the point of view of their likely commercial adoption.

There are well over 100 object-oriented and object-based programming languages. Naturally, there is not the space to even mention all of them here. Readers wishing to learn an object-oriented programming language are directed to the many good books offering such tuition mentioned in the bibliographical notes at the end of this chapter.

⊟ 3.1   Object-oriented languages

It is probably impossible to give a complete, watertight definition of what a truly object-oriented language is. However, we know from Chapter 1 that object-oriented at least means class-based plus inheritance and self-reference. This section deals with languages which fit this mould and which most people would agree are object-oriented. Scholastic arguments about whether languages are 'truly' object-oriented are particularly sterile, especially in view of the fact that there is no formal theory as with logic or functional programming. Until such a theory appears there can be no object-oriented equivalent of, for example, Codd's twelve rules for relational databases (Codd, 1985).

3.1.1 Simula

Simula, formerly Simula 67, was probably the first language to introduce the notions of classes and inheritance into general purpose programming. Its origin in 1967 (Dahl and Nygaard, 1966; Dahl *et al.*, 1968) was based on earlier work on a specialized language, Simula 1, for discrete event simulation and this influenced many of its features. Simula 1 and its descendants were all, in turn, strongly influenced by Algol with its notion of program blocks.

Simula came out of work on discrete event simulation and operational research dating back to 1949, when Nygaard was working on the design of nuclear reactors. The differential equations involved in such problems were too hard for even numerical solution, so alternative techniques had to be developed from first principles. A successful technique is to simulate a world which moves (transforms its state) in discrete steps corresponding to time intervals. With such simulations, which can be run and re-run on a computer, the effects of different parameters can be observed rather than calculated. This is analogous to the use of spreadsheets for business 'what if' analysis. However, the languages available in the 1960s were not particularly suited for simulation. Whereas the abstractions of conventional languages like FORTRAN attempted to describe processes in the computer, Simula, with its abstractions, essayed to describe real-world processes.

The seminal simulation problem involved objects which were neutrons and absorbent rods in a nuclear reactor. A more readily understandable example is the simulation of traffic passing through a complex intersection which involves random arrival rates, saturation flow rates, traffic light settings and queuing. The vehicles are generated and tracked through the system as it passes through discrete time steps, rather like time-lapse photography, and the behaviour can be observed, at each time step, in terms of queue lengths, delay times, junction locking and similar features. It is also possible to observe global phenomena such as stability or convergence to a stable state. The system, once constructed, can be tested under different assumptions on such variables as volume, signal linking or cycle times.

Simula, which still has many active users, is a programming language with a built-in notion of classes and hierarchical inheritance. Multiple inheritance is not supported. Information hiding is accomplished by 'protecting' a feature, which in effect prevents it from being inherited downwards. Polymorphism in the form of overloading is supported. Type checking can be carried out either statically at compile time, for efficiency, or at run time if a feature is declared 'virtual'. The system needs to perform garbage collection from time to time while running. That is it has to reclaim the memory occupied by instances which were assigned but are no longer being used. This, in common with most other object-oriented languages, is a feature which militates against run-time efficiency, but, as we have seen, the main application influence behind Simula came from problems of simulation where performance is seldom the key issue. Simula has a library of special classes that contain most of the primitives required for discrete event simulation; in most other object-oriented languages these would have to be written. Another consequence of Simula's simulation background is that it has a set of unique features addressed to supporting applications where concurrency is important; 'coroutines' can be invoked and left to run while the main process continues uninterrupted until it needs the results from the coroutine.

The emphasis is on processes rather than data but Simula is responsible for many of the ideas which informed its descendants, especially those of classes, instances and inheritance. The idea of abstraction is implicit, but notions like message passing had to wait for the arrival on the scene of Smalltalk. The developers of Simula went on to develop a new language BETA (Kristensen *et al.*, 1987), which is an object-oriented language that also includes the features of functional and constraint-based programming and is further described in Section 3.6.1. The same group was responsible for a strongly typed, object-oriented formal specification language called ABEL (Dahl, 1987).

Table 3.1 Simula features.

Type checking/binding	Late or early
Polymorphism	Yes
Information hiding	Yes
Concurrency	Yes
Inheritance	Yes
Multiple inheritance	No
Garbage collection	Yes
Persistence	No
Genericity	No
Object libraries	Simulation

3.1.2 Smalltalk and its dialects

To this day the language which is widely considered as the purest representation of the object-oriented ideal is Smalltalk, which existed in two dialects: Smalltalk 80 and Smalltalk V (not a Roman numeral, and pronounced 'vee' for Virtual) until their companies merged. Smalltalk came about as a result of work by Alan Kay, Adele Goldberg, Daniel Ingalls, and others at Xerox PARC throughout the 1970s. In fact Smalltalk is not just a language but a complete programming environment, with editors, class hierarchy browsers and many of the features of a 4GL. It was Smalltalk which established clearly the idea of message passing as the main and only way that objects could communicate. Influenced by Simula, its designers took the notion of objects to an extreme and declared that everything should be an object, including classes themselves. In Smalltalk even the humble integer is an object. Because of this decision there is a need to deal with classes of classes, metaclasses, and some authorities have commented that the rather odd notion of metaclass in Smalltalk tends to make the language difficult to understand, at least for beginners. Also, treating numbers as objects is all very well for consistency, but it is not necessarily very efficient and is puzzlingly strange to most programmers used to other languages. Smalltalk is not a strongly typed language so that errors, that arise, for example, when an object receives a message it cannot deal with are processed entirely at run time. It also needs to garbage collect and all binding is done only at run time. All these characteristics mean that Smalltalk is by no means a fast language in execution terms. It makes up for this by being an excellent environment for development, especially prototyping, and is perhaps best known for its iconic or WIMP interface.

Thus the work on Smalltalk not only introduced the term OBJECT-ORIENTED into the language, but was largely responsible for the ideas behind the distinctive graphical user interfaces to be found in many modern systems from the Apple Lisa onwards. Perhaps the ease with which such interfaces are built in Smalltalk was responsible for the early predominance of graphical interfaces among the applications of object-oriented programming and the fact that few object libraries aimed at other applications were available.

It has been estimated that the Lisa project consumed over 200 man-years of effort. Clearly, a company such as Apple cannot afford to expend this much resource every time a new machine is released. The benefit of reusable software is therefore not merely a benefit but a necessity in such applications.

One important and influential notion introduced by Smalltalk is the notion of metaclasses. A metaclass, in ordinary parlance, is merely a class of classes, which cannot be instantiated, and represents therefore an abstract concept from which more concrete concepts may inherit. In Smalltalk, the above notion is called an abstract class and a metaclass is defined as a template for class construction; something that can create classes. This is almost certainly a result of the influence of Lisp on the language, and makes it possible to describe the language within the language and indeed to extend and change the structure of the language. In Smalltalk each class is the sole instance of its metaclass and a metaclass is created when the class is. Each metaclass is an instance of the class **Metaclass** and subclasses of the class **Class**. The class methods are actually stored in the metaclass. The language has no built-in types (other than 'object') and some commentators regard classes as user-defined types. This reflects another strong influence from Lisp and functional programming on the language.

Smalltalk has no built-in control structure; any such structure must be built from message passing. For example, enclosing an expression in square brackets – called a 'block' – defers evaluation of the expression. Most control structures are implemented as messages to objects which take blocks as arguments.

Smalltalk only supports single inheritance, and applications requiring multiple inheritance have to be designed in a possibly unnatural way to overcome this limitation. According to Meyer (1988) this often involves much code duplication and makes heavy use of dynamic binding.

Change control is an important issue in classic Smalltalk environments since programmers can, in principle, modify each other's work. The Smalltalk browser supports good communication amongst the team and other change control tools are provided. One key weakness here is Smalltalk's lack of any notion of persistent objects. Another is its essentially single-user character. The ENVY development environment was a partial answer to this deficiency. ENVY provided a shared code repository that provides editions, versions and releases of classes, methods and associated persistent objects. This makes multi-programmer projects feasible by enabling configuration management in a distributed environment. The alternative, before such products emerged, had been file-oriented check-in/check-out systems that were clumsy to use. The ENVY developers went on to develop IBM's Visual Age for Smalltalk, a new compiler which builds in many of the same ideas as well as including a powerful visual programming environment.

Although Smalltalk is a comprehensive, productive environment for programmers, garbage collection, dynamic binding and the lavish graphical user interface all make heavy demands on hardware. Also, Smalltalk is a complete environment which – prior to CORBA – could not readily inter-work with other languages, so that it could not be easily integrated with existing code. These were two of the main factors that impeded its acceptance.

The advantages of Smalltalk are:

- its conceptual uniformity in making everything an object;
- a superb run-time environment including symbolic debuggers, browsers and full access to the class hierarchy;
- dynamic binding supports polymorphism therefore great flexibility;
- automatic memory management;
- it is easier to understand and tune the overall design than in conventional languages;
- the fact that it is very hard not to write in an object-oriented style, making Smalltalk an excellent pedagogical tool. That is, it can be used to teach the key concepts, so that programmers get into the habit of writing in an object-

oriented style even in languages such as C++ where the style is not enforced.

The disadvantages include:

- efficiency and memory requirements;
- no support for persistent objects;
- messaging errors can only be detected at run time.

Since Smalltalk there have been many attempts to produce object-oriented languages which attempt, at the risk of compromising Smalltalk's purity and consistency, to overcome efficiency problems and maintain the key benefits of object-oriented programming. These attempts fall into a number of different categories and must be evaluated along a number of different axes. First, there is a split between languages which emphasize abstraction at the expense of inheritance or *vice versa*. Next, there is a split between languages descended from the artificial intelligence tradition and those which emanate from the cogitations of computer language specialists. Finally, we have a three-way split between logic programmers, functional programmers and the rest. A large section of the conventional programming camp has taken the route of extending existing languages with object-oriented features. It is to these that we now briefly turn.

Table 3.2 Smalltalk features.

Type checking/binding	Late
Polymorphism	Yes
Information hiding	Yes
Concurrency	Poor
Inheritance	Yes
Multiple inheritance	No
Garbage collection	Yes
Persistence	No
Genericity	No
Object libraries	Several

3.1.3 C extensions

One approach to efficient object-oriented programming that has been popular is to extend an existing language to include object-oriented features. C is an example of an efficient base language that has been extended in this way. There are essentially two ways in which this can be done, exemplified by the languages Objective-C and C++. Objective-C (Cox, 1986; Cox and Novobilski, 1991) extends vanilla C by including one additional data type in the form of a C structure within a function library with, in essence, the functionality of Smalltalk. AT&T's C++ (Stroustrup, 1986; 1997) on the other hand actually changes the C compiler and extends the syntax with a new primitive data type for classes.

OBJECTIVE-C

Objective-C is a language based on ordinary C with a library offering much of the functionality of Smalltalk's language elements. It introduces a new data type, object identifier, and a new operation, message passing, and is a strict superset of C. Objective-C originally operated as a pre-processor which transformed statements into a form acceptable to the ordinary C compiler. It is now a *bona fide* compiler in most environments.

Cox's terminology differs from that of Smalltalk. Storage is managed by 'factory' objects, which represent classes and are created at compile time. Factory objects all have a method called 'new' which creates instances of their class at run time, by responding to a message of the form:

```
thisObject = [Object new]
```

Such objects encapsulate methods and state variables which are inherited by instances. The instances encapsulate state values and have a unique identifier. Inheritance may be overridden by the existence of a variable or method with the same name in the instance or subclass. Multiple inheritance of classes is not supported, but can be implemented by the programmer. However, Objective-C introduced the idea of 'protocols': interfaces that classes may inherit, without inheriting their implementations. This idea was taken up by the designers of Java under the name 'interfaces'. Multiple interface inheritance is supported in this way.

Objective-C is supplied with a number of built-in classes such as those for objects, arrays, collections, sequences, sets, and so on. Class libraries are also available. It was bundled with the NeXT machine as standard and has been used for some of the biggest object-oriented programs ever written. Nowadays the OpenStep environment runs on several machines and effectively offers a huge class library for Objective-C programmers. Objective-C is not widely used outside this environment.

Table 3.3 Objective-C features.

Type checking/binding	Late (default) or early
Polymorphism	Yes
Information hiding	Yes
Concurrency	Poor
Inheritance	Yes
Multiple inheritance	Interfaces only – protocols
Garbage collection	Yes
Persistence	No
Genericity	No
Object libraries	A few + OpenStep

C++

C++ is an upward compatible extension of the C language itself rather than a new language. The principal change is the introduction of a new genuine primitive data type 'class'. It has no high level data types or primitives and relies, as with C, on libraries to provide such extensions. Thus, new types are defined in the language itself. The main inspirations for the language came from C (and its noble ancestor BCPL) and from Simula. C++ is designed with both portability and efficiency in mind. In fact it was certain weaknesses in Simula 67, in terms of efficiency, which led to its development. It also emphasizes the goal of being able to incorporate the large quantity of existing C code. Thus, although it is much harder to do so by accident than in C, in C++ the programmer can violate the data protection and typing rules and data may then be accessed in inconsistent ways. C++ is a compromise between the object-oriented ideal and pragmatism.

C++ supports abstraction, inheritance, self-reference and dynamic binding. Both static and dynamic typing are supported. The type system, unlike Smalltalk's, is not organized as a single rooted tree structure but as a collection of relatively small trees. Therefore C++ tends to encourage broad and shallow class structures compared with the narrow and deep structure enforced by Smalltalk, where everything is a subclass of Object. This observation may be of some use in determining application suitability.

Class declarations are divided into public, protected and private parts. In a class, the private data and methods are available only to the object's own methods, while the public ones are available to any other object or function. Methods in C++ are called 'member functions'. Message passing corresponds to function calls. Instance variables ('private member variables' in the terminology) store data. Data can be stored at the class level, in a limited way, by allocating store when the program is loaded. Thus, such data are fixed for all instances of the class.

One novel feature of C++ is the ability to give a function or class access privileges to the private parts of several classes of which it is not a member. This is done by declaring the function to be a 'friend' of these classes. This can be used to simplify the description of an operation on two types. For example, if we wish to define multiplication of vectors by matrices, defining multiplication as a friend of these classes allows their implementation to be accessed. Friend functions need an extra argument to point at the object to which the operation is applied. Friends support the facility of being able to call C++ functions from normal C programs. This feature needs to be handled with great care if encapsulation is not to be compromised.

As with Smalltalk, the same name can be used for different methods. Thus for example, multiplication of integers or matrices can use the same symbol. The reader will recall from Chapter 1 that this facility is called 'operator overloading'; a form of *ad hoc* polymorphism.

Inheritance is implemented though the definition of subclasses. In C++ subclasses are referred to as 'derived classes'. Derived classes inherit as public all the public properties of the base class in terms of which they are defined. Complete hierarchies are possible since a base class may itself be a derived class. Inherited methods may be overridden. Multiple inheritance is fully supported and a full exception handling mechanism is provided using the try/throw/catch model.

By default, binding is established at compile time as in a conventional language either as a global variable, or one scoped within a program block. Alternatively the object can be created in the free store and created and destroyed under program control. With these techniques, the types of the arguments of a function must be known at compile time. Dynamic binding is implemented by 'virtual functions' and interfaces (or deferred inheritance) by 'pure virtual functions' defined – but not implemented – in a base class, which can be redefined in derived classes. In this way the types of arguments can be determined at the time a function is applied.

C++ has no automatic garbage collection. Any such feature would have to be implemented by the programmer or provided by an environment with suitable code libraries. However, there are now several add-on garbage collectors for the language (*cf.* ftp://parcftp.xerox.com/pub/gc/gc.html). C++ templates were a late addition to the language. They provide support for unconstrained genericity but have been criticized as leading to code bloat and slow compilation. There is a standard template library (the STL) available for all compilers (Glass and Schuchert, 1996). The assert macro allows for some formal checks to be made during debugging in addition to the try/throw/catch checks. However, C++ does not have the strength of the assertions of Eiffel.

Whilst it is possible to use C++ as an object-oriented programming language, it is equally possible to ignore or misuse all (or some) of its object-oriented features. A particularly sobering statistic is that, of the very many C++ programs in existence within AT&T in 1989, it was estimated that less than 1 in 10 contained even a single class statement. Although understanding of OO has arguably improved since then, this perhaps suggests that C++ programmers, migrating from C, should be forced to do a stint of Smalltalk, Java or Eiffel programming (perhaps prototyping the projected C++ implementation) where they may lose some of their more deeply ingrained habits and will be forced to think in terms of objects. It also suggests a need for sound object-oriented design and analysis methods.

The language now exists in a number of different versions, some of which are open source or public domain – the Gnu compiler for example – on a wide range of machines.

As I have remarked, C++ is a compromise, but it is a sensible compromise. It gives low level control over the hardware when required and the benefits of object-oriented programming when required – and enforced. The worse things that can be said about C++ are, first, that it is a very difficult language to use well and, second, that many programmers continue to use it as simply a 'better' C. In some ways it is really more suitable as a systems programming language than as one for application development: a machine-independent assembler! Despite this it is one of the most successful object-oriented programming languages in commercial applications on workstations and PCs, and looked likely to remain so for the foreseeable future until the emergence of Java. There are many large projects involving C++ with hundreds of staff, thousands of classes and millions of lines of code. Its long-term success is predicated on the performance issues that have dogged early Java applications and the further development of good quality, component libraries.

The advantages of C++ are:

- it is possible to do anything at any level of the operating system;
- it is probably the fastest object-oriented language extant;
- there are many C++ programmers on the market.

The disadvantages include:

- lack of automatic memory management (garbage collection) and the prevalent use of pointers make it very difficult to guarantee run-time safety;
- it is extremely difficult to learn to be a *good* C++ programmer.

The specific strengths of C++ are, as Stroustrup (2000) succinctly puts it: 'for applications that have a systems programming component, systems with demanding time or space requirements, and those that span several technical cultures or application areas. In such systems, more simple, less efficient and more specialized languages become liabilities'.

Table 3.4 C++ features.

Type checking/binding	Late or early (default)
Polymorphism	Yes
Information hiding	Yes
Concurrency	Poor
Inheritance	Yes
Multiple inheritance	Yes
Garbage collection	No
Persistence	No
Genericity	Yes – templates
Object libraries	Very many

3.1.4 Eiffel

Eiffel (Meyer, 1990) is a purpose-written object-oriented language that consciously attempts to address the issues of correctness, robustness, portability and efficiency. Its design was influenced by COBOL, Ada and Simula. Unlike Smalltalk and Objective-C, in Eiffel classes are not objects because Eiffel identifies classes with modules. This enables static typing to help eliminate run-time errors and improve efficiency.

A class describes the implementation of an abstract data type. It is defined at compile time and can create instances of the type (objects) at run time. The terminology differs from that of other languages in that methods are called 'routines'. Classes encapsulate both routines and attributes which are referred to collectively as 'features'. Features may be private or public (exported) in the same way as in Java, C++ or Ada.

An important feature of Eiffel is the ability to specify the formal properties that an object's operations must obey by writing 'assertions'. Assertions may express pre-conditions, post-conditions on methods or invariants on the class. Pre-conditions force a check whenever a method is called, post-conditions are guaranteed to be true when the method terminates or returns values and invariants are always true once an object is created or a method called. These features are provided to help towards the goal of producing proofs of correctness and reflects Meyer's background in software engineering and formal methods. This sort of feature can be added to Smalltalk with a little effort, as was shown in the Fresco project at Manchester University (Wills, 1991). Eiffel can be regarded as a design language as well as a programming language. The design is implemented as a set of high level classes and the methods are filled in later. This reduces the risk of errors when translating formal design notations into code. It is small and easy to learn but comes with a comprehensive programming environment and a superb class library. It has influenced nearly all advanced object-oriented methods greatly, especially in respect of assertions.

Applications are compiled into C for efficiency and portability. Importantly for efficiency, garbage collection is optional. When it is used, Eiffel garbage collects incrementally using a novel algorithm.

Assertions permit Eiffel to incorporate exception handling features. A violation can cause a message to fail or may invoke a 'rescue' procedure contained in the offending method. Assertions may be viewed as a formal contract between a server and its clients. For efficiency the assertion mechanism can be switched off during final compilation.

As in Ada there is a notion of generic classes – classes with parameters representing types – without the performance overhead imposed by C++ templates and with support for constrained genericity. Multiple inheritance is supported but inheritance conflicts are not dealt with because attributes or methods inherited from two parents must be renamed in the descendant. Note that in all the languages dealt with so far the values of attributes are not inherited, only the ability to have a value. Inclusion polymorphism is supported by allowing type checking to authorize more specific objects but not more general ones. In Eiffel, the notion of deferred classes allows inherited methods to be overridden.

Eiffel now contains a simple concurrency mechanism based on the addition of a single keyword: separate. Another invaluable feature of the environment is its Melting Ice technology. This means that one can think of source code as a liquid that is 'frozen' when compiled. With most languages a module must be completely defrosted before it can be changed, refrozen and linked to other modules. With Eiffel you only need to melt the lines that need changing. These can then be tested as interpreted code running alongside all the still frozen elements of the system. Eiffel developers rely heavily on the use of multiple inheritance to deliver genuinely reusable components (Meyer, 1994).

Although Eiffel appears to be ahead of its time and an important extension of the concepts of object-oriented programming, its early versions received some bad press as a system for commercial developments. At the ECOOP'89 conference it was suggested (Cook, 1989) that Eiffel was not type safe, although this is contested through an appeal to the existence of compiler errors. Leathers (1990) reports that the 4GL supplier, Cognos, abandoned a key redevelopment using Eiffel because of both performance problems due to an early version of Eiffel and a certain lack of surrounding tools (browsers, etc.) but, more importantly, because of the errors made in managing the unfamiliar technology. Some important lessons to which Leathers points are lack of staff experienced in object-oriented product development, lack of management understanding of the technology and failure to apply conventional project management disciplines. The most important observation to emerge from this experience was that prototyping is essential. A throwaway prototype, as a first phase to the project, would have enabled more rational decisions to have been taken concerning the final development. In Chapter 9 we will take up the issue of prototyping and its management in detail. More recently the Chicago Board of Trade has successfuly adopted Eiffel for its core trading systems.

Newer developments include new, much better releases of the original proprietary compiler and the fact that the language is now in the public domain with a number of very good third-party compilers becoming available. Many of us regard Eiffel as the best existing object-oriented language yet it has not enjoyed wide adoption despite many individual project successes. It is now seriously threatened by the popularity of Java even though it has several advantages over the latter. The Eiffel 'agent' mechanism introduces ideas from functional languages, like Lisp and Miranda, into what is basically a statically typed language, thus providing additional flexibility to the prototyper or extreme programmer. Note that this usage of the word 'agent' has nothing to do with the intelligent or mobile agents discussed in Chapters 8 and 10.

Table 3.5 Eiffel features.

Type checking/binding	Early (default)
Polymorphism	Yes
Information hiding	Yes
Concurrency	Yes
Inheritance	Yes
Multiple inheritance	Yes
Garbage collection	Yes
Persistence	Some support
Genericity	Yes
Object libraries	Available from ISE Inc.

3.1.5 Java

When Java appeared it took the industry by storm. There were several reasons for this.

- It was a web-enabled language with support for security and concurrency so that small Java programs could be delivered as *applets* to run in a browser such as Internet Explorer or Netscape Navigator.
- Fully fledged applications could also be written.
- Its syntax resembled C++ but it was a pure object-oriented language, had automatic memory management and discouraged the use of pointers; thereby being much safer.
- It was put in the public domain but supported by a powerful vendor: Sun.

Java compiles into pseudo-code (p-code or byte code) which needs a virtual machine to interpret – on the model of the much older USCD-Pascal (Nori *et al.*, 1991). The Java virtual machine is available on nearly every platform. This makes development virtually machine independent and gives universal portability, but at the cost of poor performance. For this reason native compilers soon emerged for many platforms. Additionally there are just-in-time (JIT) compilers that convert byte code to native code the first time an applet is run. Subsequently execution is much faster. New compilation techniques are undergoing rapid change at the time of writing and the reader is advised to consult the specialist literature on this. Machine independence is further enhanced by the provision of an abstract windows toolkit as a package of platform-independent widget classes: originally the Java Abstract Windows Toolkit (AWT), now the Swing libraries.

Java had its origins in the Oak language that was designed to run on embedded chips in devices such as microwave ovens and cameras; so it had to be small. However, standard Java is not so small when one considers the need to import many classes from the packages supplied with the language before anything sensible can be done; the standard packages (.io, .lang and .util) contain about 350 methods. Packages provide a level of organization above that of classes. To make sensible use of Java, the programmer must become familiar with the many standard libraries that make up the environment.

As a language, Java was influenced heavily by Objective-C and thereby Smalltalk despite its purely syntactic resemblance to C++. Primitive data types are not objects but they can be made into (immutable) classes if you wish. Java separates the notion of class from that of interface and attempts to overcome the dangers of multiple inheritance by only allowing it for interfaces. This can be annoying because one has to write an implementation for things that appear to be inherited. I much prefer the approach taken in Eiffel, where all I have to do is tell a class that it is a subclass of both serializable and printable to make it so; without writing any code. There are three versions: standard, enterprise and micro. The later is for use on embedded processors in the spirit of Oak.

Exception handling is similar to C++'s try/throw/catch but much more rigorous.

Good style is for every class to implement the Throwable interface and declare what exceptions it throws. Concurrency is handled by declaring lightweight threads which communicate through side effects and synchronization protocols.

Java Beans are components: collections of classes and the resources they need. They are similar to OLE or Active X controls but cannot be containers for other controls. They are intended to be used mainly for the provision of custom GUI widgets. Enterprise Java Beans (EJB) – part of the enterprise version – are server-side components and represent a much more complicated approach that will be discussed in Chapter 7. These and support for XML make the language suitable for application servers.

Table 3.6 Java features.

Type checking/binding	Early
Polymorphism	Yes
Information hiding	Yes
Concurrency	Threads
Inheritance	Single for classes
Multiple inheritance	Interfaces only
Garbage collection	Yes
Persistence	via JDBC
Genericity	No
Object libraries	Beans

Java comes with its own object request broker technology: RMI (remote method invocation). This allows applications to call methods executing in other Java applications across a network. It also incorporated a CORBA-compliant, language-independent broker since version 2. Object request brokers are discussed in Chapter 4. It also contains classes for managing interaction with relational databases: JDBC and for foundational graphics.

The security model of Version 1 of Java bluntly prevented applets accessing the hard disk. Version 2 introduced a more flexible model using certificates.

3.1.6 Object-COBOL

The Codasyl standards committee began to lay the basis for an object-oriented version of COBOL in the early 1990s, under pressure from user groups advocating open systems and stressing the importance of software reuse as projects get larger. Certainly, Object-COBOL of some sort was then urgently needed by users who wanted the benefits of reuse and extensibility while needing to protect a huge investment in existing code; an estimated 70,000 million lines of code, world-wide. However, the finished product, COBOL-97, took so long to emerge and be standardized that many of these organizations had already shifted to C++, Smalltalk or to object-based languages like Visual Basic by the time it did. Nevertheless,

Object-COBOL remains important for a few large mainframe shops, although less than might have been expected. Two or three COBOL-97 compilers are now established, with the most prominent suppliers – Computer Associates (CA), Hitachi, IBM, Realia and MicroFocus – being early to market.

Object-COBOL provides the following features:

- user defined types based on COBOL record structures;
- encapsulation;
- classes as templates for abstract data types;
- classification (instantiation by loading a program);
- message passing as program calls via the USING verb;
- inheritance using the COPY verb;
- polymorphism using multiple entry points and the READ statement;
- the ability to use objects written in other languages;
- garbage collection for single objects using the CANCEL verb;
- upward compatibility from COBOL;
- better support for prototyping.

Although it is unlikely that really leading-edge applications will be written in COBOL, the emergence of Object-COBOL will be welcomed by some traditional development shops. The maturity of a programming style is to be recognized when it is applied to the mundane, not the esoteric.

3.2 Other languages with object-oriented features

There are a number of languages which, while they do not have the purity of Smalltalk, do have object-oriented features. Generally speaking these emphasize either abstraction or inheritance. Languages such as Ada 83, Modula-2 and perhaps even Object Pascal fall into the former category. Several products with an artificial intelligence genealogy fall into the latter, and we often hear the term FRAME-BASED in that case. We deal with the latter in Section 3.4.

Languages such as Ada 83, and to a lesser extent Modula-2, exemplify languages where data abstraction and the benefit of reuse are the key concepts. As discussed in Chapter 1, such languages are referred to as object-based.

In Ada 83, and similar object-based languages, packages are not first-class objects in that they may not be passed as parameters. This means that Ada does not fully support data abstraction. It does, however, support operator overloading and provides garbage collection as an option.

Ada 83 has no direct support for inheritance but generic packages can be used to implement a limited form. Although subtypes and derived types can be defined by restriction, Ada cannot extend existing types by adding new attributes and methods. This leads to the need for code duplication and seriously limits any extensibility benefits. The latter benefits are also compromised by the enforced early binding of this language. Ada emphasizes early binding and strong typing for efficiency and safety.

Ada, due largely to DoD fiat, became the language of choice for most defence-related work in the USA. It failed to penetrate commercial developments significantly. One common and major criticism of Ada has nothing to do with its lack of object-orientation. It is a very rich language and its critics claim, with some justification, that this makes it very difficult to learn and use well, due to the sheer number of primitive statements. This also makes it compare poorly with lean languages like C in terms of the compiler's space requirements.

The latest version Ada 95 offers object-oriented constructs such as class hierarchies, (single) inheritance, dynamic binding, method overriding at both class and instance levels in addition to standard Ada features. Ada 95 also supports rapid prototyping better than Ada 83 and is equipped with automatic trace facilities.

Object Pascal (Apple) was a successor to a language called Clascal, which was used to develop some of the Apple Lisa and Macintosh interface. It is essentially a simple superset of Pascal. Objects are Pascal records encapsulating procedures and functions. Object Pascal supports only single inheritance and does not offer garbage collection as a built-in feature. Inprise's Delphi incorporates an object-oriented Pascal that is an extension of Pascal with many object-oriented features but lacking any multiple inheritance facilities. Ultimately, the Pascal extensions will only be attractive to organizations that already have a heavy investment in Pascal code and wish to move to object-oriented programming. There are now versions of Delphi that use Java or C++ instead.

Table 3.7 ADA features.

Type checking/binding	Early (Late for record types in Ada 95)
Polymorphism	Yes
Information hiding	Yes
Concurrency	Difficult
Inheritance	Yes – since Ada 95
Multiple inheritance	No
Garbage collection	No
Persistence	No
Genericity	Yes
Object libraries	Not many

CLU was an advanced language developed at MIT in the late 1970s (Liskov *et al.*, 1977). Its central unit of abstraction is the 'cluster', a concept identical to a Simula class. In contrast with the Algol-like nature of Simula, procedures and data structures may not be defined outside of a cluster in CLU. CLU coexists with a separate class-based formal specification language designed for it. The design method calls for the description of the algebra of each data type's operations and supports genericity. Inheritance between classes and their instance is supported but not inheritance between metaclasses and their subclasses.

Another object-oriented programming language Lingo, developed at Strathclyde University, formed the basis of the Linn Rekursiv machine (Harland, 1988; Pountain, 1988) which, along with the NeXT machine, probably represented the first generation of object-oriented computers. IBM and Apple created a company called Taligent to produce an object-oriented machine and operating system with a broadly similar profile to the NeXT that, it was hoped, would have greater compatibility with other systems and standards. The project broadly failed for a number of commercial and technical reasons. Taligent's CommonPoint provided over 100 frameworks composed of around 4,000 classes and 53,000 methods. This could have been compared to, say, the Windows 3.0 API with only 1,500 callable features. This complex architecture together with the foibles of the C++ object model was widely blamed for the collapse of the venture (e.g. Szyperski, 1998).

A claim could also be made for the operating systems of the IBM System 38 and AS/400 machines as a zero[th] generation, since object-oriented ideas clearly influenced their design. Once again, 'object-based' is probably the right term for such developments.

3.3 Functional and applicative languages

Some authors have emphasized the distinction between object-oriented and value-oriented programming. MacLennan (1982) points out that values (such as the number 17) are applicative and read-only; they are timeless abstractions. Objects, i.e. instances, exist in time and can be created, destroyed, copied, shared and updated. Values are referentially transparent; whatever refers to them will always be using the same value. In part, this implies a major criticism of the approach taken in Smalltalk, where everything is an object. The failure to make a proper distinction leads to several dangers. Data structures unwittingly shared may be updated erroneously, or there is a potentially costly duplication overhead. Given all the advantages of applicative or value-oriented programming, why should we need objects at all?

Firstly, simulation of the world in a computer system is vastly simplified if the data structures used correspond to real-world entities. Files are objects and cannot be described by algebras. Variables in ordinary programming languages are objects, identified and differentiated by their locations regardless of their current values. A value is said to belong to a type whereas an object belongs to a class. The essential difference is that two objects with the same description may be different objects, whereas there cannot be two values with the same description. For example, there can only be one integer with the value 17, but there may be two identical copies of the Mona Lisa. That the converse is not true can be seen by considering the two objects with different descriptions, the morning and evening stars, represented by the same physical object, the planet Venus. Many languages obfuscate this issue. For example, files in Pascal may not be assigned to or used in expressions, even though they are declared in the same manner as other types. Programmers simulating systems must deal with 'state' and changes of state, they must deal with time and (at least in artificial intelligence) with possible worlds. Applicative programming is not designed for this but for dealing with timeless mathematical abstractions.

What is needed, then, is a clear distinction between values and objects and a language that supports the distinction and allows the most appropriate models (values or objects) to be used.

Functional programming is a style exemplified by languages based on formal logic and mathematics such as Lisp or ML. Conventional programs work by assigning values to variables which represent storage locations in memory. Any prior value stored in that location is overwritten and lost forever, unless steps have been taken previously. Applicative languages such as Lisp do not use this destructive assignment process. Applicative, as opposed to imperative, programming does not permit assignments or side effects. In practice this means that the processor has to do some garbage collection periodically to get rid of values no longer required in order to save on storage. Another common feature is 'lazy evaluation' whereby values are not computed until a function requires them. Such languages are based on function application and composition and depend on a logical system known as 'lambda calculus' which will be described below. Applicative programming becomes functional programming when it maintains 'referential transparency', which is to say that every expression or variable has the same value within a given scope; all variables are local. This implies that we can always substitute an expression with one of equal value without altering the value of the whole expression. This property is useful in theorem proving and database enquiry where rewriting expressions and substitution are fundamental operations. Although this scoping rule is reminiscent of object-oriented languages, functional programming does not allow objects to have state.

A procedural language instructs a computer how to carry out a particular task. A non-procedural one tells it only what to do, not how to do it. Consider the following database enquiry which asks how many employees are working in each department, and in those groups, what the total and average salaries are.

```
SELECT  DNAME, JOB, SUM(SAL), COUNT(*), AVG(SAL)
FROM    EMPLOYEE, DEPARTMENT
WHERE   EMPLOYEE.DEPTNO = DEPARTMENT.DEPTNO
GROUP BY     DNAME, JOB
```

This query in fact produces correct output but the results need not concern us here. The language is SQL. Notice that nowhere is the computer told how to answer the question. This would involve obtaining a list of employees, sorting it by department and job and then computing the count and average and total salaries. Finally, department name must be substituted for department number in the output. That would be a fairly complicated procedure involving reading records and saving intermediate results at each stage. The non-procedural language SQL, based on relational calculus which we will cover in Chapter 5, makes all this unnecessary. In actual implementations of SQL there are built-in functions which introduce an element of procedurality. Purity is a rare boon.

The term declarative is a slightly more general one than non-procedural, because it includes purely descriptive languages. It is more to do with the way data are represented than with any particular programming style. The opposite of a declarative language is usually referred to as an imperative one, but this usage is falling back under the onslaught of the snappier but less euphonic 'non-procedural'. The language Prolog also has a declarative and non-procedural style (although the present of a cut (!) operation enables it to be used in a clumsy procedural style as well). Let us now turn to the logics which make such languages possible.

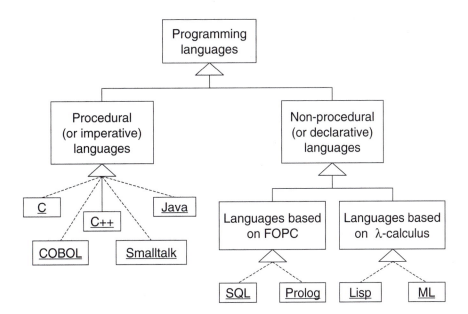

Figure 3.1 A classification structure for programming languages

Both Prolog and SQL are based on the first order predicate calculus, a form of mathematical logic, with SQL being based on a smaller subset and thus being less expressive. Such languages are commonly called logic programming languages only when they are as expressive as Prolog. Functional languages are based on another logical system, the lambda calculus, and are not usually referred to as logic programming languages, even though they are rooted firmly in logic.

There are a number of distinct benefits usually associated with functional programming languages, including:

- their formal basis;
- the fact that they are easy to extend by adding extra, reusable functions;
- the uniform programming metaphor, whereby everything is a function;

- the fact that higher order constructs (functions of functions) are easy to express; and
- their support for polymorphic types (as in ML) or a completely type free style (as in Lisp).

Diversion

The remainder of this section on functional programming is slightly more advanced than the rest of the chapter and may be omitted by people with an aversion for mathematical notation. Understanding it in detail is not a prerequisite for understanding the rest of the book.

The lambda-calculus originated in the 1930s and was principally due to Alonzo Church. His original motivation was to provide a foundation for all of mathematics based on rules; that is, the idea of a function being a process of passing from argument to value rather than Dirichlet's more modern notion of functions as graphs (subsets of relations). It is possible to think of such functions or rules as being given by natural language sentences applied to arguments (also expressed in words), or as computer programs that may be applied to other computer programs or structures. In both cases the language is type free, which is to say that there is no distinction between the sort of objects that constitute a function and those which can be its possible arguments. In particular, a function can be applied to itself. Self-recursion is thus supported. The axiom of foundation makes this impossible in ordinary set theory and the logic which it models; FOPC[1]. Church's original theory was shown to be inconsistent by the discovery of the Kleene-Rosser paradox, but he managed to salvage a consistent sub-theory which forms the basis of current research and of a number of programming languages, the most prominent of which has been Lisp which first originated in about 1956 (McCarthy, 1960).

In Lisp, which stands for LISt Processing, as with the lambda-calculus there is no distinction between program and data, both of which are expressed as hierarchically structured lists.

The lambda-calculus represents a class of partial functions – i.e. functions not defined on their entire domain – defined on the integers which turn out to be the recursive functions, and these are equivalent to the Turing computable functions. Based on this equivalence, the Church-Turing hypothesis states that the ordinary, intuitive notion of a function that can be computed by a terminating algorithm is equivalent to the notion of a recursive function. Thus the interest of computer scientists in this subject is not surprising. Church soon discovered that the lambda-calculus was undecidable. The problem concerned whether the terms of the lambda-calculus have a normal form; in the language of Turing machines these are functions that have no unpleasant infinite loops, and are equivalent to Turing's 'satisfactory' machines.

In order to achieve completeness Church introduced the abstraction operator 'lambda' which lets us create or 'abstract' a function from terms of the language. Thus, (lambda *x.M*)*a* is the function that is equal to the result of substituting *a* for all

---

[1] First Order Predicate Calculus.

occurrences of x and applying the function M. For example, we can make a function of one argument as follows.

$$g = (\text{lambda } x.2^*x+3)$$

So that $g(1)=5$, $g(2)=7$, $g(3)=9$, and so on. Additionally, the lambda-calculus supports an operation based on a term which takes the values 'true' and 'false' which permits conditional expressions to be included in function definitions. For example,

$$g = (\text{lambda } x.\text{if } x>5 \text{ then } f(x) \text{ else } -f(x))$$

Function abstraction and application are the primitive operations of this logic. The operator lambda extends the type of the language in a universal way which is analogous to the way that introducing inverse elements x^{-1} extends the language of elementary group theory, or negative numbers extends that of natural number arithmetic. However, Curry showed that lambda is not absolutely necessary, although it is intuitively appealing in a mathematical context. Modern dialects of Lisp have begun increasingly to drop the explicit lambda notation, but it is still implicitly present as is apparent from the care that has to be taken with variable bindings in difficult programs.

Formally, the language (of lambda calculus) is defined as follows:

- The alphabet consists of variables $x,y,z,...$ together with symbols for reduction $\rightarrow$, equality = and abstraction λ (lambda). The terms are defined recursively as follows:
- Variables are terms
- Application of two terms yields a term
- If M is a term and x is a variable then (lambda xM) is a term

The well-formed formulae are defined by saying that if M and N are terms, $M\rightarrow N$ and $M = N$ are formulae. The reduction, equality and abstraction operators are defined by requiring that they satisfy certain axiom schemes.

A variable is **free** if it is not in the scope of a lambda x and **bound** otherwise. In this way lambda is analogous to the universal quantifier of predicate logic or the definite integral of school calculus.

All of the many dialects of the Lisp language rest on the lambda-calculus. Lisp is in some ways a very low level language resting on very few primitives which can be thought of as specifying a virtual machine. The most fundamental primitives are CAR, CDR (pronounced coo'der), ATOM and LAMBDA (or PROG). The only primitive data type is the list. A list consists of a head and a tail (physically a pointer to the head of another list). CAR returns the head as an atom and CDR the tail as a list – modern terminology usually refers to 'head' and 'rest'. Thus, the head of the list (apples, bananas, carrots) is (apples) and the rest is (bananas, carrots). Atoms refer to values in store and are the raw material from which lists are built. CONS constructs new lists by adding a new head to a list. There are, in addition, several control structures and arithmetic and relational operators. Like C and PASCAL, Lisp is a recursive language.

Logic programming as exemplified by the various dialects of Prolog is based on a particular form of mathematical logic known as the first order predicate calculus (FOPC). The term 'first order' is important. It represents the idea that the logic cannot deal directly with statements about statements but only with statements about objects of primitive (atomic) type. Although it can be shown mathematically that first order systems can express higher order notions, this expression is often otiose and extremely unnatural. Functional programming may also be regarded as a form of logic programming but the underlying logic is a different one; the lambda calculus described above. The interesting point about both kinds of logic programming is that they are based on a formal theory whereas object-oriented programming is only based on a metaphor; there is absolutely no formal theory. This means that it is very difficult to prove anything about object-oriented applications. There have been continuing attempts to remedy this apparent defect. EQLog (Goguen and Meseguer, 1986) and its sister language OBJ2 (Futatsugi et al., 1985) are based on yet another kind of logic – equational logic – and OBJ2 sets out consciously to seek a unified formal basis for logic and object-oriented programming (Goguen and Meseguer, 1987). FUN (Cardelli and Wegner, 1985) represents another such attempt. We take up some of these research efforts in Section 3.6.2. However, my feeling is that the lack of a formal theory is not only not an encumbrance to commercial developments but actually may be a positive benefit, as we shall see in the remainder of this book and especially in the chapter on databases. Other important functional languages include ML (Milner, 1978), Hope (Burstall et al., 1980) and Miranda (Turner, 1985).

In the research literature there have been a number of attempts to unify object-oriented programming with functional programming, and indeed with logic programming. One of the basic difficulties here is that logic programming based on FOPC seems to be fundamentally incompatible with object identity, although abstraction and inheritance can be modelled readily.

One of the most long-lived and popular functional programming languages, however, is Lisp. In the next section we turn to the various object-oriented extensions of Lisp.

3.4 AI-based systems

The treatment of AI-based, object-oriented developments in this section is divided in two. The section treats first of Lisp extensions and then of modern expert systems development environments, which are not all based on Lisp.

3.4.1 Lisp extensions

For many years Lisp was the main language for academic research in artificial intelligence. Lisp provides much of what is needed for the implementation of an object-oriented language in the Smalltalk style. It has garbage collection, dynamic binding, editors, debuggers and a uniform typeless style. There are also large numbers of reusable functions available, some in the public domain. Therefore it is natural that there have been several object-oriented extensions of Lisp.

The artificial intelligence influence shows chiefly in the inheritance systems of some Lisp extensions, where not only attributes but their values can be inherited, multiple inheritance is usually supported and demons, or event-driven processes, are supported. Demons (or triggers in the database literature) are operations that are attached to data structures and which fire when the structure is accessed. Thus, there are 'if needed' and 'if updated' demons. These two are sometimes called backward and forward chaining demons respectively. We also find them described as 'when needed' and so on in some systems. These operations are usually attached not to objects, but to the attributes of objects. This can be viewed as making such attributes into separate objects in their own right or as breaking the principles of encapsulation, according to whether you are an opponent or a supporter of this kind of system. The key point about this approach, as I will argue, is that it captures much more of the semantics of an application.

The standard now for Lisp extensions is CLOS, the Common Lisp Object System (Moon, 1989). CLOS is a Lisp extension based on the ideas of generic functions, multiple inheritance and method combination. Metaobjects enable the user to alter the basic structure of the object system itself (Kiczales *et al.*, 1991). It was designed, like Smalltalk, at PARC.

In AI systems, the notion that corresponds most closely to that of an object is a frame. A **frame** is a structural abstraction that tries to capture the idea of a stereotypical object. Frames consist of an extensible list of **slots** which are equivalent to attributes, or class variables. Slots may contain both state and process description, and methods are attached to a particular slot. Slots containing state may also have **facets** (in addition to 'value'), which are methods for determining search, default values and triggers. In CLOS each object has a unique identifier, and the slots contain pointers to other objects representing the state of the entire object. Every instance belongs to a class, and every class is a type. Slots may be either type restricted or free; that is, they may only be allowed to take values of a specified type, or they may be permitted to take any value whatsoever regardless of type. Generic functions, in Common Lisp, work on objects of several types. Methods, in CLOS, are specified to determine what generic functions do when called with particular arguments. The mapping between a generic function and its corresponding set of methods is part of a mapping between functional and object-oriented programming. Methods are defined by specifying a generic function, conditions under which it applies to objects, parameters, inheritance rules and code.

Methods are of several types. **Accessor** methods give access to, or update, the value facet of a slot. They are the special methods referred to in Chapter 1 which make it possible to talk directly about attributes in an object-oriented environment. This means that the implementation of state is hidden behind standard accessors such as get and put value. This will be an important concept in Chapter 6.

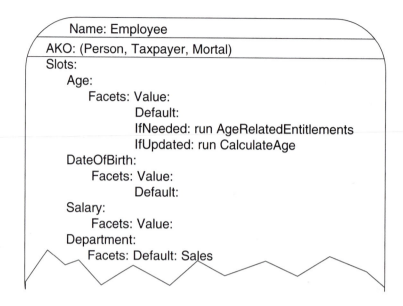

Figure 3.2 Part of a frame (not necessarily a CLOS frame) for Employee. Note that each slot has facets for its value, default value, and if-updated and if-needed demons. The if-updated demons are procedures (or rules) which fire whenever the value (or sometimes default) facet changes. The if-needed demon searches for a value to fill the value facet when it is accessed and contains no value at that point in time.

An important difference between CLOS and many object-oriented programming languages is the provision for facets (i.e. sub-slots) other than 'value'. An attribute or slot of an instance may have a value; e.g. the value of BirthDate for Employee 'Ian Graham' may take the value 19480813. Proper classes may have attributes with default values that may be inherited; so that, in Figure 3.2, an employee whose department is unknown may be assumed to be in the sales department. In CLOS, subclasses may add slots, methods and type and initialization conditions to those inherited from superclasses. In this respect CLOS is similar to Smalltalk. The close association between Lisp and artificial intelligence makes it unsurprising that CLOS supports multiple inheritance. Like Flavors, an earlier object-oriented Lisp extension, CLOS inheritance conflicts are resolved by defining an order of precedence in the list of superclasses in a class's definition. This is a flexible system but not as general as the scheme described in Chapter 6 for general object-oriented specification purposes. The class precedence list determines which characteristics of a slot to inherit when name conflicts arise. When more than one method is inherited, CLOS allows methods to co-operate by a complex technique called 'method combination' based on the Flavors notion of 'mixins'. How best to do this is not a fully resolved issue at present, although it represents an important advance over the approach of other object-oriented programming languages. We will return to this issue in Chapter 6 in a context free of particular language considerations. Just as slots may have defaults, there may be default methods, which may be overridden. Backward and forward chaining demons may be specified to simulate pre- and post-conditions, triggers and side effects. CLOS, like Smalltalk, regards everything as an object, including its own language constructs with constructs called meta-objects which provide particularly good facilities for extending the language itself. Like all Lisp systems, CLOS garbage collects, sometimes at inconvenient moments. Dynamic binding is supported using the same mechanism that Lisp uses to allocate storage at run time. Since slot names are encapsulated but not hidden, CLOS classes are not true abstract data types, but this disadvantage can be overcome by good programming disciplines.

CLOS applications as diverse as the production of animated graphics for television commercials, geographic information systems and telephone network control have been written and used.

Table 3.8 CLOS features.

Type checking/binding	Late
Polymorphism	Yes
Information hiding	Yes
Concurrency	Difficult
Inheritance	Yes
Multiple inheritance	Yes
Garbage collection	Yes
Persistence	No
Genericity	Yes
Object libraries	A few

Various object-oriented extensions to Lisp emerged piecemeal within the artificial intelligence community through the 1970s and 80s. LOOPS (Bobrow and Stefik, 1983) , Common LOOPS (Bobrow *et al.*, 1986) developed at Xerox , Flavors, KEE and NewFlavors represent typical such attempts. CLOS represents the standard that synthesizes all these approaches in the Lisp world.

A particularly interesting such extension is CommonObjects, developed by Snyder (1987). This system emphasizes the importance of not allowing inheritance to compromise encapsulation. This is accomplished by preventing the inheritance of attributes; only methods may be inherited. An alternative and, I think, preferable suggestion is to have two distinct inheritance hierarchies for methods and attributes (see Danforth and Tomlinson, 1988) or, better, for interface and implementation, as in Java. The AI notion of inheritance and the Lisp culture tend to oppose this kind of protection and, as we have seen, the protocols for protection suggested by Snyder could be imposed by good programming practice rather than by compilers. This is one of the issues which is unresolved and leads me to suspect that object-oriented programming is still a somewhat immature discipline.

The number of different object-oriented extensions of Lisp is too large for them to be enumerated here, let alone described. They include, in addition to those already mentioned, Ceyx developed at INRIA, Oaklisp (Lang and Perlmutter, 1986) and many more.

As the engineering discipline of expert systems emerged from the academic one of artificial intelligence, a number of higher level programming environments for this kind of work emerged, not all based on Lisp. We now turn to these.

3.4.2 Other AI-based development systems

KEE and ART are Lisp-based expert systems development environments designed originally for specialized workstations. They all support an object-oriented style to some extent. We will take KEE as a surrogate for both. Its main claim to object-orientation derives from the fact that its **units** support attribute and method inheritance and multiple inheritance. Slots in the units contain *facets* which can be used to determine the control régime under which inheritance takes place; for example, to determine whether inheritance takes precedence over defaults or the type of multiple inheritance regime. KEE is not, however, so strong in terms of encapsulation and the user may obtain direct access to the state of a unit from Lisp.

Kappa and Nexpert Object represent attempts to provide similar facilities in a non-LISP environment. The latter is available in class library form. Kappa and Nexpert are written in C rather than Lisp and the main effects of this are in terms of performance. Taking Nexpert as a representative of this type of package, we note first that while multiple inheritance is supported among classes, an object can be an instance of no more than one class. In general these packages have similar features to KEE and ART. Hitachi's ES/KERNEL and Expersoft's XShell are both expert system shells with a strong object-oriented content. The latter is written in C++ and emphasizes distributed implementation. Both products are unusual in offering facilities to incorporate fuzzy logic. ObjectIQ is a Romanized version of ES/KERNEL with these fuzzy facilities removed.

CA's Aion is a rule-based expert systems development environment that supports object-oriented programming too. CA have developed a modelling technique for Aion based on the Catalysis design method and the KADS knowledge engineering approach. Its philosophy is very similar to the ideas of rule-based agent objects which I present in Chapter 6; but methods are divided into inference methods and procedural ones rather than there being a separate concept of a rule encapsulated in an object. However, like most expert systems shells it tends to be rule-centric rather than object-centric.

All the AI-derived systems tend to major on their support for inheritance and be rather deficient in terms of encapsulation. They also offer a semantically rich form of inheritance that differs from the one found in most object-oriented programming languages like Smalltalk. Although C++ permits the inheritance of default values, in some object-oriented languages this is not so. In the frame-based AI systems, values (in particular default values) can be inherited as well as attribute names. This means that dealing with multiple inheritance is a more complex problem, but this merely reflects the general principle that semantically complex systems make tougher demands on programmers and designers. My view is that the AI people have got it right and that this kind of inheritance will eventually have to penetrate the world of object-oriented programming. Object-oriented programmers have a lot to learn from other computing disciplines including AI and, as pointed out by Roger King (1989), from work in the area of semantic data modelling. This will be a recurrent theme in this book.

At present, there are no ideal object-oriented expert systems development tools though there are some very good ones. One reason is the need to implement efficient reasoning algorithms, such as the RETE algorithm, which is easier to do when objects are created as a by-product of processing rules rather than having rules attached to objects in mini expert systems.

Thus, we have seen that, among the vast number of languages claiming to be object-oriented in some way, there are considerable differences of emphasis and function. One is tempted to suspect that the use of the term 'object-oriented' is often motivated as much by marketing considerations as by veracity. In other words it has become fashionable to describe almost any product as object-oriented or component-based in order to make a spurious differentiation from its competitors. Journalists call such usage 'hype'; *caveat emptor*![2]

3.5 Object libraries, application frameworks and OO 4GLs

An object library is a collection of complete, tested, documented, reusable objects, available either as a commercial package or as part of an in-house software library. Object libraries are key to object-oriented developments because without them few reuse benefits can be obtained. Most object-oriented programming languages are delivered with basic, generic object libraries, but these are seldom adequate for productive application development. For that reason there are now many commercially available libraries which can supplement a language, one popular example being the Rogue Wave library.

ObjectWorks from ParcPlace Systems was an early environment which can be based on C++ or Smalltalk. In the C++ version it provides an interface to UNIX, incremental compilation, source level debugging and graphical browsing/editing facilities. It is type safe and supports multiple inheritance, which C++ and Smalltalk didn't always do. In the Smalltalk 80 version it includes a library of over 300 classes and several thousand methods. It runs unchanged across a variety of machines from PCs to UNIX workstations, and is source compatible across this range.

Object libraries for building graphical user interfaces in C++ are now widely available on a commercial basis. There are also libraries integrated with most

---

[2] Let the buyer beware!

development environments such as MFC within Microsoft's Visual Studio. Typically, all these libraries offer classes dealing with relatively low level programming abstractions such as stacks or linked lists, and graphics concepts such as rectangles, buttons or windows. Libraries with classes which will be needed for specific vertical commercial systems developments are beginning to appear, an early example being the San Francisco library from IBM.

There are several object-oriented **application frameworks** for commonly required types of computer system. These frameworks bolster productivity for applications with significant demands for graphical user interface programming, database access and client/server links. They usually offer visual programming and extensive class libraries for windows programming and database interfaces along with the usual low level foundation classes. Sometimes they include report generator classes and other useful tools.

LispWorks is a commercial programming environment for workstations incorporating CLOS. Access to X windows is via an extensible set of 'widget' classes; that is, classes of pre-defined window elements corresponding to the hardware and operating system in question.

Sun's Forté is a repository-based application development environment that includes a genuinely object-oriented 4GL called TOOL. It also has interfaces to relational databases, CORBA and middleware products and a GUI generator. The PCTE-compliant repository is based on ObjectStore. Forté has been used extensively in Enterprise Application Integration (EAI) due to its facility in building wrappers and is currently focused on component-based development. It includes an extensive component library.

Without object libraries object-oriented programming becomes intensely and unnecessarily tedious. One of the strengths of C has always been its ability to include libraries of functions, and adding libraries of objects is a natural continuation of the progress of the language which will probably increase its commercial acceptability. However, there is a negative side to systems that rely heavily on libraries of either sort, as the history of C has indeed demonstrated. That is to say, every inclusion from a proprietary library decreases application portability. This is often not important for one-off applications but is very important for package developments. Furthermore, since one of the main reasons for the use of object-oriented programming is reusability, one is forced to wonder whether this benefit itself is compromised by a lack of portability. System developers should consider this trade-off early in the planning phase of each new project.

A major difficulty with class libraries is the sheer difficulty of knowing what the library contains and what its classes do. It is estimated that it takes a good programmer about a day to become fully conversant with a class. Thus, to become familiar with a typical class library (Smalltalk 80 has about 350 classes in its library) takes over a man-year. Against this it is estimated that the production of a fully tested and debugged class at the right level of granularity takes, on average, about two man-months of effort; about 60 years for a 350 class library. Of course, no program is likely to need every class in the library. These observations point to the need for group work. Teams should meet regularly to review code being developed. The advantage of this is that someone other than the developer may well know of a class which could be used to speed development. Group work techniques should be already familiar to FORTRAN programmers used to working with large function libraries, such as the NAG library of FORTRAN mathematical procedures. They are essential for object-oriented programming.

In the presence of large object libraries change control becomes an especially critical issue. The matter is further complicated by the existence of complex objects that consist of more than one interconnected object. If one of the components changes, how does this affect the whole? Theoretically, in perfectly encapsulated languages, a changed implementation should not have any effect, but if inheritance is allowed this may not be the case and, worse still, we can never really guarantee that the interface of an object may not have to be changed. One way round the problem is suggested by module interconnexion languages, such as DeRemer and Kron's MIL75; meta-languages that make the connexions among objects explicit. To achieve the benefits of software reuse we need a composability language that can be used to specify module interfaces, so that ultimately reusable modules can be configured to meet a specification and the implementation language of each module can be independent. Further, object classification techniques are needed to help programmers understand the libraries they are dealing with. There is thus a profound need for a tool that can estimate the impact of changing an interface – i.e. change prediction (Hood *et al.*, 1987). The general absence of such tools and techniques in the commercial domain is an indicator of the immaturity of object-oriented programming. However, the emergence of such tools may be an index of its maturation. We have already discussed the fact that component management is a difficult and unsolved problem in Chapter 2.

The absence of existing high level class libraries for most commercial applications is a serious obstacle to the widespread adoption of object-oriented programming. Here is a vicious circle: without such libraries development is too costly, and good library modules can only emerge from real projects. Companies wishing to obtain the benefits of object-oriented programming will have to cost-justify projects in terms of long-term reuse, which is especially hard to do in a period of high interest rates. This suggests that the first commercial libraries will be sold by companies that have built systems and wish to recoup some of their development expenditure; and these libraries may, initially, take the form of tailorable application packages.

Buyers of such packages will need further assurance that the quality of the modules is sufficiently high; i.e. that they have been designed and written to support reuse from the outset, and not just sold as a means to recoup development costs.

3.6 Other developments

This section reviews some languages that have been important or influential in the development of ideas. We then look at the feasibility of implementing object-oriented ideas in conventional languages. Most of the topics covered in this section take us slightly away from the common concerns of object-oriented programming so that omitting or skimming the section will not harm the reader's understanding of what follows.

3.6.1 Other languages

TRELLIS   Trellis/Owl (Schaffert, 1986), developed at DEC, was rare in being a strongly typed language and data management system combined. It was strongly influenced by CLU and supported multiple inheritance, concurrency and genericity. It also incorporated a data model. Object-oriented and other types of database are discussed in Chapter 5.

The Trellis Object System was integrated with Rdb under VMS via SQL and included a library of tools for browsing, debugging and programming. It provided garbage collection and persistent objects. It also provided for concurrency using multiple threads of control, multiple inheritance and overriding. Trellis was supplied with source code though DEC did not support it if altered. DEC's attitude to Trellis was reminiscent of their attitude to the OPS-5 rule language, where for many years they built up in-house skills and some large applications in a language not widely used on other hardware. The advantages were that the language was tuned to the environment and very detailed support was available. The disadvantage, for the user at least, was a potential lack of portability.

A number of other so-called 'persistent object' languages are described in (Rosenberg and Koch, 1990). PS-Algol, a persistent version of Algol, is described by Gray *et al.* (1992).

ACTOR   Actor (Whitewater Group, 1989) is an object-oriented language and environment which seems to have been inspired in name only by the actor model (Agha, 1986). It was designed to support developments under Microsoft Windows and contained an extensive class library for this purpose, along with a browser and debugger. The language supports encapsulation, single inheritance, late binding, incremental compilation and garbage collection. Actor was acquired by Symantec in 1992.

There have been a number of suggestions for concurrent object-oriented programming languages and similar ideas very closely related to objects such as actor systems. Just as everything is an object in Smalltalk, everything is an actor in actor systems. Actors have unique permanent identity and current behaviour which may change over time and which determines how the actor will respond to the next message it receives. The behaviour is composed of instance variables, called *acquaintances*, and methods, called its *script*. Acquaintances determine the other actors with which the actor may communicate. An actor with no acquaintances is a candidate for garbage collection. On receipt of a message the current behaviour may replace itself. If it does not have a method to handle the message, the actor may *delegate* to a *proxy*, which is an actor nominated among its acquaintances. This notion is similar to that of a superclass, but the methods are not inherited; that is, no code is copied, all that takes place is message passing. Unlike object-oriented programming, there is a well-defined semantics for actor systems, but actor languages are very low level and difficult to use.

In addition to actor languages, such as Act 3, there are also concurrent versions of pure object-oriented languages, such as ConcurrentSmalltalk (Yokote and Tokoro, 1987), and hybrids such as Orient84/K, which combines the Smalltalk and Prolog styles (Ishikawa and Tokoro, 1987).

Actor languages such as Act 3 and ABCL/1 implement inheritance without using classes, so it is difficult to decide whether they should be called object-oriented or not. In practice, they deliver the same benefits as encapsulation and inheritance and so the distinction is baroque though actor languages tend to be very low level. Actor is an object-oriented language, not an actor language.

BETA AND
MJØLNER

BETA aims to combine the ideas of constraint-oriented logic programming with object-orientation. It was a research project that is now commercially available within a development environment called Mjølner[3] (Knudsen *et al.*, 1994) which is sold by a Danish company, Mjølner Informatics. BETA (Madsen *et al.*, 1993) is based on a more general model than Smalltalk and provides greater conceptual modelling abilities by allowing objects and methods to be detached from classes. It is derived from Simula and appears to be a significant advance over object-oriented programming providing, perhaps, an indication of future directions in languages.

In BETA, objects are regarded as physical, real-world entities. Each has unique identity and may be an aggregate of other objects. A clear distinction is made between being part of something and being a property of something as exemplified by my car having a wheel and having a colour. Unlike Smalltalk, numbers are values and not first-class objects, which overcomes a major objection to Smalltalk. The language's most powerful concept is that of a **pattern**. A pattern could represent a class, a record type, or a procedure; e.g. a car, a log entry or a 20,000 mile service. Patterns can represent almost any phenomenon, such as variables, data structures, coroutines or procedure activations. Objects are instances, not of classes, but of patterns, and patterns participate in inheritance networks. It is interesting that workers in object-oriented analysis have also discovered the usefulness of patterns independently. Coad (1992) suggests looking for repetition in classification and composition structures and Jacobson *et al.* (1992) use inheritance not only for objects but for use cases (see Chapter 6).

BETA has been implemented by Nokia Telecommunications, a Finnish company, on a digital telephone switch. BETA and Mjølner are available in versions

---

[3] Mjølner was Thor's magical hammer. The perfect tool capable of producing thunder.

for the Microsoft, Macintosh and UNIX environments. The latter include a CASE tool for early parts of the life cycle. The tool includes code generation and visual programming facilities and programs are reversible to the diagrams. I will argue in subsequent chapters how important reversibility is for software engineering. No other language known to me seems to offer such support for it. As in Smalltalk, there is a meta-programming feature whereby the environment itself can be altered.

These developments point the way to enhancements of the object-oriented metaphor itself, but at present they have not gained any widespread commercial acceptance and BETA is little used outside Scandinavia. However, I suspect that the good ideas of BETA will begin to penetrate other languages and, even more rapidly, methods.

OTHERS   Oberon was developed by Wirth as a successor to Modula-2. Modula-3 was DEC's equivalent with class-like record types on the model of Ada 95. Sather (Szyperski et al., 1994) was a research language with aims similar to those of Eiffel but with a stronger emphasis on formality and substitutability. The Squeak language (Ersavas, 1999) is an attempt by Alan Kay to get back to the original vision of Smalltalk, which he thinks has been corrupted by commercial concerns. It is basically a new implementation of Smalltalk 80 on top of a virtual machine written in Smalltalk with links to the GemStone object-oriented database.

SUBJECTS   Subject-oriented programming (Harrison and Ossher, 1993) and aspect-oriented
AND ASPECTS programming (Kiczales, 1994) (SOP and AOP) both address a weakness of OOP, which occurs when features cut across the class structure and interfaces change. We know that OOP localizes changes to the data structures or implementation of a program but feature changes have more profound consequences. SOP is derived from the idea of property lists in Lisp. A subject associates state or behaviour with an object identifier. Different subjects can then view the same object as having different behaviour. AOP proposes that developers should code the various 'aspects' of a program, such as security, persistence, accounting or computation, separately. A tool, such as AspectJ (Kiczales and Lopes, 1999), is then required to 'weave' all the aspects together. Component-based development, as discussed in Chapter 7, is also concerned with this issue.

3.6.2 Type theories and object-oriented programming

Up to now object-oriented programming has developed without the guidance of any rigorous mathematical theories of syntax or semantics. Object-oriented programming is a style or metaphor rather than a formal method, but it is a very powerful metaphor indeed. For this reason there have been a number of attempts to provide more rigorous foundations. These attempts divide into explorations intended to unify object-oriented programming with either functional or logic programming, or both, and attempts to supply rigorous type theories (for a survey of these approaches see (Danforth and Tomlinson, 1988)) or even denotational semantics (Cook, 1989).

Functional and logic programming share a feature with object-oriented programming in that they all attempt to divorce the description of computation from its details. They try to model the real-world problem rather than the computational process as in conventional languages like COBOL or FORTRAN. Functional and logic programming are usually based on formal theories of logic that are first order and untyped. Research in this area includes the development of algebraic languages such as OBJ2 (Futatsugi *et al.*, 1985). These efforts are also directed at constructing provably correct compilers. Theories based on algebraic models, such as OBJ2, make a strong distinction between values and operations, whereas those based on higher order logics, such as SOL (Mitchell and Plotkin, 1985), FUN (Cardelli and Wegner, 1985), DL (MacQueen, 1986), Russell (Demers and Donahue, 1979; Hook, 1984) and Poly (Matthews, 1983) allow functions and even types themselves to be treated as arguments (values); in other words as first-class objects. Abadi and Cardelli (1996) attempt to get away from the usual λ-calculus-based approaches and introduce object calculii whose primitive terms are objects.

Type theories for programming languages are useful because they enable compilers to carry out a lot of checking at compile time and thus avoid many run-time errors. Borning and Ingalls (1982) suggest that the type of an object in Smalltalk could be taken to be its nearest superclass. In Emerald (Black *et al.*, 1986) a subtype belongs to a type X if it provides all the operations of X via the same argument list and issues results of the same type.

Substitutability is related to the issue of decideability and the topic becomes even more intricate when multiple threads or distribution is introduced. Layered architectures that permit call-backs further complicate the issue. For an interesting discussion of these issues see Szyperski (1998). This whole area is the subject of much deep and active research and it will be some time before all the disputes are sufficiently resolved to lead to a model acceptable for broad commercial purposes. In the meanwhile we will have to make do with the object-oriented metaphor without the comfort of a universally agreed formal basis. However, the fact that such formal theories are within the grasp of the researchers is encouraging.

I believe that the absence of a formal theory is not an obstacle to the development of commercial applications, except maybe in safety-critical and security-sensitive domains. The reason for my belief is a strong conviction that the real world can never be captured in a single formal theory.

3.6.3 Object-oriented programming in conventional languages

If software development is, as I believe, to be organized according to the sort of object-oriented analysis and design techniques discussed in Chapters 6 to 9, then many users worried about the performance characteristics and difficulty of learning object-oriented languages may consider implementation in a conventional language. Most purists in the field are scathing about this option and it is increasingly unnecessary. However, we consider here whether it is a practical possibility.

Although there are specifically object-oriented (or at least object-based) versions of Pascal, implementing an object-oriented specification in ordinary Pascal is very difficult. This is chiefly due to the language's main strength, its block structured nature. Such a structure emphasizes decomposition by process, and although abstraction features such as enumeration data types are provided, the overall control structure is most naturally functional in nature.

Implementing an object-oriented design in COBOL is, at best, a bizarre prospect. The remarks made in relation to Pascal also apply to COBOL to some extent.

With both FORTRAN and C it is quite possible to implement object-oriented designs, and in fact there is an existence theorem in the sense that Objective-C is implemented in C. However, it is difficult and costly and, in FORTRAN, the lack of dynamic arrays means that assembler extensions will probably be required and some other programming constructs in the language would obstruct such developments.

If, as the saying goes, real programmers write FORTRAN, then the *really* tough guys write assembler. There have even been a few attempts to write assembly language in an object-oriented style. Dorfman (1990) lays down some guidelines for doing this.

In Ada and Modula-2 object-oriented programming is only partially possible unless considerable trouble is taken and extra documentation is usually necessary. They have already been discussed as an object-based rather than object-oriented language, and of course the encapsulation aspects of object-orientation are provided for. Genericity can be used to simulate a limited form of inheritance, but this is not the natural way to proceed.

Rumbaugh *et al.* (1991) give a number of useful heuristics for implementing an object-oriented design in a conventional language. A revised version of these guidelines which I have found useful is as follows.

- Classes are converted to data structures: structs in C; records and packages in Ada; arrays and common blocks in FORTRAN; records in PASCAL.
- Messages are converted to function calls.
- Storage for objects is allocated to global or stack variables.
- Inheritance hierarchies are 'flattened' by making each non-abstract class a structure and re-implementing inherited methods in each one, usually by subroutine calls.
- Polymorphic references are resolved at compile time by identifying the class of each object and at run time by testing each instance or by using select/case statements.
- The associations of the data model are mapped to pointers or implemented as data structures themselves.
- To preserve encapsulation global variables should be avoided (but see above), scoping should be parsimonious and access methods should be used to access fields of different classes. They should not be accessed directly.

The existence of large investments in programs written in conventional languages such as COBOL has to be recognized. An important concept, which can protect this investment during the move to object-oriented programming, is that of 'object wrappers' (Dietrich *et al.*, 1989). It is possible to create 'object wrappers' around existing code which could then be gradually replaced. An object wrapper enables a new, object-oriented part of a system to interact with a conventional chunk by message passing (see Chapter 4 for a discussion of the issues concerning wrappers).

Many commentators, especially the specialists in object-oriented programming, think that implementing an object-oriented design in a conventional language can't be done, or at least is inadvisable. As we remarked above, there is an existence theorem here in the form of Objective-C. Clearly it can be done but it is a question not of possibility but of productivity. After all, we could do object-oriented programming in machine code since that is what all systems, even interpreted ones, end up as. The real question here is how easy it is to produce and maintain the code.

3.7 Selecting an object-oriented language

How then are we to choose a tool or language that will deliver the benefits we seek from object-oriented methods? The answer is complex. First, we must look at the characteristics and requirements of each application and try to choose the tool best suited for the job, as there is no object-oriented panacea. For example, in choosing between C++ and Smalltalk, we might consider whether classification structures discovered during the analysis stage are broad and shallow or narrow and deep. Second, we must ask ourselves seriously about the organizational impact of our choice; will it fit in with other systems standards or be acceptable to existing staff? Much of the motivation for using languages such as Ada or C++ is predicated on the last point. The alternative is to step back from the problem slightly and ask if the benefits can be better obtained through the use of object-oriented analysis and design, deferring the choice of programming language till later or even implementing the design in COBOL, FORTRAN or some 4GL.

As we shall see in the next chapter, the construction of complex GUIs is practically impossible without a language that supports a high level of reuse and extensibility. Thus, organizations contemplating the construction of a GUI should seriously consider adopting an object-oriented programming language for this purpose. Similarly, if the application is simulation of some sort then an object-oriented programming solution is strongly indicated.

Selecting a particular language or set of languages depends on enumerating the known features of the application and predicting what features may be needed in the future. The language features can then be checked off. The difficulty with this approach is that it is almost impossible to guarantee the prediction's accuracy or completeness. This leads to a search for a language with the maximum number of features, to insure against future change. This would be a fairly simple matter if there were a language with *all* desirable features and if some features were not at odds with others. For example, in terms of maximum features, there is no object-oriented language with both comprehensive data abstraction features and totally flexible multiple inheritance. Even the Smalltalk dialects that do support multiple inheritance do not have the flexibility of the AI-derived systems mentioned in the foregoing. In terms of contradictory features, we have seen that there is no language that is 'fully object-oriented' and at the same time capable of high volume, multi-user, real-time performance.

At present, I recommend people to gain experience first by prototyping in a language like Eiffel then, if developing on workstations, to move the same team over to develop the application in something like C++. If a mainframe implementation is called for, I usually advise them to wait and see. The next section gives my view on what they should be waiting for.

Any language selected now runs a risk of being superseded by some as yet unwritten language that is destined to become an industry standard. Here again is a conundrum. Should we wait for this mature technology and then have to begin to learn how to use it, or should we plunge in now, knowing that some of our results may be redundant? I think that companies entering the field now must do so on the basis that what they learn will be more valuable than the programs they write. In that sense selecting an imperfect language may not matter much. The object-oriented metaphor may well prove more important than the final language. The philosophy of this book is that analysis and design for reusability and extensibility will have a lasting value and enable users of the object-oriented metaphor to gain the benefits of mature languages when they arrive.

In subsequent chapters we take up these questions in some detail, looking at object-oriented analysis and design as a separate issue from implementation and going into some depth on object-oriented databases. In the next chapter, for example, we survey the sort of applications that have been typical for object-oriented programming systems and try to determine how to map an application's requirements onto a suitable language.

3.8 Directions and trends

There are two common objections to object-oriented systems usually advanced: they don't scale up, and they are inefficient. Experience shows that big systems can be built. These applications are in varied domains and include maintenance management, real-time train control systems, decision support systems, financial trading systems, hardware diagnostics, CAD and GIS products, customer management systems, systems for tracking container movements around dock areas and a CAT[4] scanner. This latter is an interesting example of an object-oriented system in a safety-critical domain. With conventional systems there seems to be a qualitative change at about 100,000 lines of code where everything gets harder out of all proportion to a small amount of extra functionality. Experience suggests that this just doesn't happen with object-oriented systems. Although this evidence suggests that the above objections are not serious, it is noteworthy that these successes apply to a limited range of application types. The real question is not whether object-oriented programming is inefficient or scalable, but what applications it can be applied to. This question will only be answered on the basis of experience, although, as we have seen, this experience will be coupled with the emergence of new languages with new features and new class libraries and application frameworks.

It has to be admitted that some real-time systems do exhibit insuperable performance problems. Fast real-time systems are feasible though, in certain application areas.

Libraries should be tested on real applications. Some people believe that components should be delivered in binary to support reuse. Particular testing problems arise because of inheritance, since it gives rise to side effects and can expose a class to the implementation of a parent's instance variables. The test harness must automatically test through all the inheritance levels. Such a test harness soon repays its cost on even quite small projects. Testing strategy is summed up by 'try to kill the worst bug first'. Testers should ask themselves: 'If there were such a bug, where would it be?'. Object-oriented programming has demonstrated that it can achieve very good error rates if properly managed; up to twice as good as the industry average. Generally, object-oriented systems just seem to be more reliable.

Another thing that recent experience has shown is that there is real need for project managers to realize that they must train object-oriented programmers properly. It takes about six months to become comfortable with the object-oriented style. The best way to learn is on the job with experienced people, as a sort of journeyman. A common beginner's mistake is designing objects with far too fine a granularity.

It must be realized that the development life cycle for object-oriented systems is fundamentally different as is the structure of project organizations. Object-oriented projects have more in common with mathematical modelling than with traditional business systems projects. The whole feel is that of simulation rather than analysis and design. The waterfall model is no use for this sort of project and prototyping is important. For software reuse, there must be a technical review of every single line of code. This is partly because it is very hard for any programmer to know what is in all the code libraries and also because of this it has been found that group work helps considerably – someone else might know that 'just the class you need' is in such and such a library.

---

[4] Computer Aided Tomography: A CAT scanner is a sort of X-ray scanner that works by focusing on a series of parallel planes.

The two main obstacles to the proliferation of the object-oriented style are performance problems and the habit of trying to apply traditional life-cycle and design techniques.

In the meantime, project managers wishing to make a migration would be well advised to create object wrappers around their existing code which could then be replaced or allowed to wither away. Big companies are now taking up the cudgels lured by the promise of a 24:1 productivity gain. With the steady improvement of hardware, languages like Java have caught on. One project I know of switched from Pascal to Smalltalk and the system actually ran faster because in an object-oriented environment it is possible to gain a better understanding of the whole system and this makes it easier to do global optimization.

For the present, C++ and Java look like becoming the most successful, practical, general purpose object-oriented programming languages.

Object-oriented programming languages are powerful but immature, in the sense that they are acquiring new features rapidly, and new languages are still emerging. For certain applications, such as GUI development and distributed computing, they are absolutely indispensable as we will see in the next chapter.

3.9 Summary

There is a vast range of languages which are connected to the idea of object-orientation. These range from 'pure' object-oriented programming languages like Smalltalk to object-based languages like Visual Basic. No firm classification is appropriate. I have made an *ad hoc* classification as follows, although the following is not intended to be a complete list.

- Pure object-oriented languages
  CLOS
  Component Pascal
  Eiffel
  Java
  Simula
  Smalltalk
  Prolog++ and DLP
- Extended conventional or hybrid OO languages
  C++
  Objective-C
  Object Pascal
  Modula-3 and Ada 95
  Object COBOL
- Extended Lisp and AI environments
  KEE, Joshua and ART
  KBMS and ADS

Nexpert Object and Level 5 Object
ProKappa, Kappa, ObjectIQ and XShell
- Object-based languages
Ellie
Modula-2
PowerBuilder
Visual Basic
- Class-based languages
CLU

Object-oriented designs can be implemented in conventional languages, but it is difficult and many of the benefits may be lost.

Object wrappers can be used to migrate to object-oriented programming and still protect investments in conventional code.

Object-orientation is a metaphor backed by no formal theory, but research work is proceeding on this topic.

Strict waterfall process life cycles are not appropriate for object-oriented programming. Iteration is essential and group work is highly advisable where class libraries are being used. This is further discussed in Chapter 9.

It appeared until recently that C++ would become the most successful, practical, general purpose object-oriented programming language, at least in the world of workstations and down-scaling. Increasingly, interest is turning to Java. The emergence of Object COBOL should have been of critical importance for the future of object-oriented programming in the world of mainframes and commercial systems, but has not proved popular in the event.

Object-oriented programming languages are powerful but still slightly immature, in the sense that they are acquiring new features rapidly, and new languages are still emerging. For many applications they are sufficiently mature for practical purposes and in some cases absolutely indispensable. For others, class libraries will have to be developed as part of flagship projects for major users.

3.10 Bibliographical notes

The original reference on Simula is (Dahl and Nygaard, 1966), but there are several modern introductions now, including (Kirkerud, 1989).

There are also many introductory texts on Smalltalk, including the seminal one by Goldberg and Robson (1983) and many other more recent books too numerous to list. I like (Gray and Mohamed, 1990) as a simple tutorial. One of the most comprehensive tutorials on Smalltalk 80 is by Lalonde and Pugh (1990; 1991). For Macintosh users, (Schmucker, 1986) contains useful guidelines for the use of Object Pascal and MacApp (Apple, 1988), its class library. Another excellent treatment is (Liu, 1996).

Stroustrup (1986) described the original C++ language in detail along with a philosophical justification for its approach. The latest edition is (Stroustrup, 1997). His 1994 *Design and Evolution of C++* has also been influential. Other primers include those by Eckel (1989), Ellis and Stroustrup (1990), Lippman and Lajoie (1998), Mullin (1989), Hansen (1990), Pohl (1994), Pinson and Weiner (1988) and Weiner and Pinson (1990). (Deitel and Deitel, 1994) includes a CD-ROM-based tutorial. (Winder, 1993) is a good, popular text emphasizing the newer features of C++ such as the use of templates; unusually, it does not assume a knowledge of C. Musser and Saini (1996) describe the C++ Standard Template Library (STL). Pohl (1996) summarizes the ANSI C++ standard. (Coplien, 1992) is widely considered the best book for advanced C++ programmers. Cox and Novobilski (1991) provide a general introduction to object-oriented programming illustrated heavily with examples written in Objective-C but comparing it with other languages.

Undoubtedly, the best references on Eiffel are the books by Meyer (1994; 1997) referred to in the last chapter which again provides comparisons with other languages. Meyer also has a lot to say about the difficulties of doing object-oriented programming in conventional languages.

The are countless books on Java. The standard reference is (Gosling *et al.*, 1996). Other notable ones include (Flanagan, 1996), (Lemay and Perkins, 1997) and (Winder, 2000), with my favourite being (Budd, 1998). McGraw (1998) discusses the Java security model in detail.

The principles behind Object-COBOL are discussed by Belcher (1991). Arranga and Coyle (1996) and Topper (1995) provide more comprehensive treatments of the language. McCabe (1992) discusses the object-oriented extension of Prolog and logic programming in general. Eliëns (1992) describes a research language DLP with far more power than Prolog++ that also addresses issues of parallelism. The advanced object-based language Ellie is introduced by Andersen (1992). BETA and Mjølner are succinctly described by Durham (1992).

Booch (1991) gives detailed worked examples of object-oriented designs based around C++, CLOS, Smalltalk, Object Pascal and Ada. These were omitted from his book's second edition.

Tello (1989) deals with some of the artificial intelligence related languages such as Nexpert Object, Goldworks, ART, KEE and LOOPS and CLOS, but is very out of date now.

Tomlinson and Scheevel (1989) and Yonezawa and Tokoro (1987) describe concurrent object-oriented programming and actor languages. A special edition of *Comms. of the ACM* (Meyer, 1993) was devoted to concurrency and object-oriented programming.

Shriver and Wegner (1987) cover some of the more obscure issues in object-oriented programming language theory. (Cardelli and Wegner, 1985) is the classic paper on polymorphism. This paper also includes an exposition of the research language FUN mentioned in Section 3.3.

(Moon, 1989) is an excellent introduction to the ideas behind CLOS, while Snyder (1987) introduces Common Objects. Both papers give important advice on how to use inheritance without compromising abstraction and its main benefit, reusability.

Danforth and Tomlinson (1988) give an excellent and penetrating survey of research into type theories for object-oriented programming languages along with many interesting general comments on object-orientation. Further references on the languages mentioned in Section 3.6.5 will be found in this paper. (Abadi and Cardelli, 1996) is a more recent contribution.

The object-oriented Rekursiv machine is described in an introductory manner in (Harland and Drummond, 1991).

Tom Love's *Object Lessons* (1992) is full of practical experience and commercial wisdom concerning object-oriented programming and its applications.

The *Journal of Object-Oriented Programming* is a useful source of more up-to-date material, with more language specific material being available in *The C++Report*, *The Java Report* and *The Smalltalk Report*.

3.11 Exercises

1. Which programming language is associated with the beginnings of OO?
   a) Algol 68   c) Simula   e) Ada
   b) PL/1   d) Pascal   f) Lisp

2. Which of the following did *not* help with the development of Smalltalk?
   a) Adele Goldberg   c) Bjarne Stroustrup   e) Brad Cox
   b) Alan Kay   d) Dan Ingalls

3. Compare the features of two object-oriented languages known to you.

4. Why did Java succeed so quickly, while Eiffel didn't?

5. What are the major benefits and pitfalls associated with C++?

6. Distinguish between Java Beans and Enterprise Java Beans.

4

Distributed computing, middleware and migration

From each according to his abilities, to each according to his needs!

K. Marx (*Critique of the Gotha Programme*)

The theme of this chapter is sharing: the sharing of both data and functions by different systems and across different platforms and processes. This leads us to the consideration of the technology of distributed systems, client-server computing, object request brokers, message-oriented middleware, distributed databases, knowledge management and workflow systems. We begin also to look at component-based development (CBD) and enterprise application integration (EAI). Distributed systems are composed of nodes that offer services according to their interface definitions to other nodes as and when required. In this chapter, the emphasis is on the practical issues of migrating from centralized, conventional systems to these distributed systems and we must be aware at the outset that some of the components that are to be distributed will remain conventional while others will be built using object-oriented programming. Above all I will emphasize the rôle of object-oriented models as a way of describing and understanding distributed systems. Many modern companies are determined to base their future computer infrastructure on distributed components as far as possible and must therefore construct a sound migration strategy. If there are mainframes, they will be there for specialized applications with high transaction processing requirements or to act as data servers when an existing corporate database or application cannot be replaced economically. Success in the shift to web-based commerce (e-commerce) will mean that these legacy systems must be integrated with new object-oriented code. Many will be connected via XML.

Distributed computing is in some sense a return from the chaos (or freedom) of the PC to the golden (or dark) age of the mainframe. Early computers were single-user machines with low storage capacities. Time-sharing operating systems offered the possibility of using the same hardware architecture to support multiple co-operating users. When wide area networks (WANs) arrived, this co-operation could extend across the planet and still only need a few central points of management and integrity control. Workstations, when they arrived, took us right back to single-user machines where we did our own backups and so on and were once again isolated from other users with whom we might wish to share and co-operate. LANs and the web ended this quarantine but reintroduced all the complexities of operating a mainframe; only now the 'mainframe' is distributed and harder than ever to manage. Nevertheless, on balance, the advantages seem to outweigh the extra complexity. Distributed computing is, in principle, more resilient, fast, flexible, scalable and open, and it is needed to support ever more global and distributed businesses.

In this chapter we consider the basic ideas of distributed systems and explain the notions of distributed object computing. I then introduce the ideas of object request brokers and of message-oriented middleware before considering how a migration strategy can be constructed. In Chapter 10 we will re-examine this in the context of e-commerce.

4.1 Distributed and client-server computing

Distributed systems can be thought of as networked computers that do not share memory as do multiprocessors for example. This means that the nodes must communicate by message passing and immediately indicates that object-oriented models may be appropriate for modelling such systems. Also, objects provide a natural metaphor for combining data and control and are the natural units of distribution. Performance is enhanced by the implicit parallelism involved. Expensive, under-utilized resources such as plotters can be shared to reduce costs. In a well-designed system there may be no single point of failure or it may be possible to duplicate services so that higher availability and greater resilience become possible. Nodes can be added and the system can be reconfigured piecemeal, to reduce costs or facilitate upgrades – rather like component hi-fi systems. These and other advantages must be weighed against the additional overheads of maintaining a complex architecture and the increased difficulty of understanding and describing such complexity. To continue the simile, compact 'hi-fi' systems are much easier to install and use than component hi-fi, though their power, quality and flexibility are vastly lower.

TYPES OF DISTRIBUTED SYSTEM

The operating systems of distributed systems can be **distributed** or **networked** (Tanenbaum and Renesse, 1985). In the former case the operating system is itself distributed over all the nodes in fragments and the network is largely invisible to the user. Networked operating systems give every node a full copy of its own operating system and the network is visible.

We can distinguish three data management strategies for distributed computing: centralized, replicated and partitioned. **Centralized** management involves placing the data at one node and routing all requests there. The advantage of this is that changes need be made only once. The disadvantage is that all accesses result in a message across the network. **Replicated** management makes copies of the data where they are most often needed. This avoids the need for two-phase commits[1] but may lead to a user working with out-of-date data unless complex additional measures are taken. Where read accesses are more common than writes this is a good strategy. **Partitioned** data management stores data across several nodes, usually based on access demand predictions. This necessitates two-phase commits but can be efficient when the partitioning follows some natural division of data ownership in the business. Object-oriented decomposition is even better because not only ownership but conceptual stability drives the decomposition. Nowadays, database vendors offer a choice between two-phase commits and replication as distribution strategies. Sybase was an early example of a relational, distributed database that offered replication.

Apart from the kind of operating system and the details of data management, there are several different kinds of distributed computer architecture and it is easy to become confused among them. **Client-server** computing involves a single server with one or many clients and most of the intelligence is located in the clients. Often the server is a file-store or a database, although the terminology may be used to include print servers. This is a simple form of distribution, with the GUI and business logic usually entangled. **Three-tier** client-server architectures separate the GUI and the business logic, while **n-tier** arrangements make yet finer separations. This is a common architecture for web-based applications wherein some of the business logic can be run on a so-called **thin** client; i.e. as a Java applet running under a web browser. A further level of complexity is the **multi-client/multi-server** system where there may be several servers but the servers may not communicate directly; in other words: nodes cannot be both clients and servers. Several database products support this architecture. The most general case occurs when every process node may be both a client and a server (in general simultaneously) though this is rare at present. This case involves **peer-to-peer** communication between nodes. Nodes may represent processors or task images within a processor. Messages may be split,

---

[1] Two-phase commit only allows a transaction to be committed on all participating machines when they have *all* signified that they have successfully completed the updates concerned. If any node does not respond 'OK' (or times out) after the first phase of update then all nodes are rolled back to their state before the update.

relayed and combined as they pass from node to node. Implementing this kind of system is not without its difficulties.

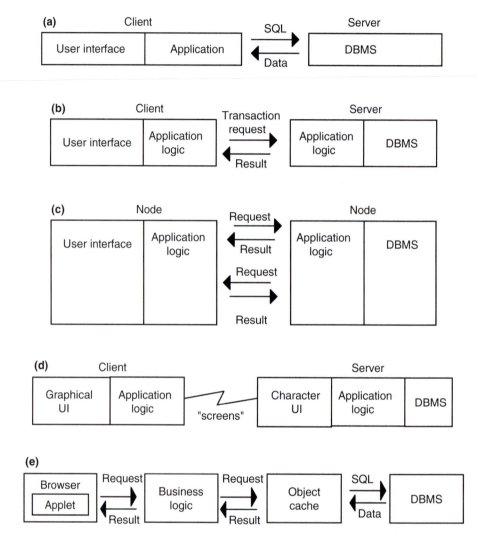

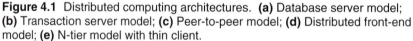

Figure 4.1 Distributed computing architectures. **(a)** Database server model; **(b)** Transaction server model; **(c)** Peer-to-peer model; **(d)** Distributed front-end model; **(e)** N-tier model with thin client.

Another way of viewing the different types of distributed architecture is presented in Figure 4.1. Here, we distinguish five models: the database server model, the transaction server model, the peer-to-peer model, the distributed front-end model and the n-tier model. The database server model offers a limited choice as to where to locate the function of the system while the transaction server model is a more effective way to balance the processing load between nodes and reduce network traffic; data-intensive tasks can be handled by the server and interface manipulation and secondary computation by the client. Further, SQL queries can be pre-compiled to improve performance and there is a central point of maintenance.

The peer-to-peer model is the most flexible and general but the most difficult to program and manage. In applications such as real-time process control, workflow and groupware it is almost mandatory. The distributed front-end model is really only used as a sort of wrapper strategy when there is a legacy mainframe with a character interface based on synchronous terminal protocols such as 3270. Here, the workstation client should be envisaged as re-mapping between its own and the host screen format and transmitting or receiving the results.

The three-tier model is increasingly common but we will see later how it is being supplanted by peer-to-peer and n-tier models based on middleware that hides much of the complexity of such models.

**CLIENT-
SERVER
MODELS**

Client-server computing (CSC) can be defined as the division of processing and data between one or more front-end client machines that run applications and a single back-end server machine which provides a service to each client. This is often taken to mean that the machines are connected by a network and that the clients are workstations running a graphical user interface. More generally, a client-server system can be defined as one in which some element of the computation, user interface or database access is performed by an independent application, as a service to another; possibly on the same machine. In this broader sense all object-oriented systems are client-server systems, though the converse is not true.

Client-server computing, as we have seen, is a special case of distributed computing but does not necessarily involve a distributed database, though it may. One should avoid the temptation to confuse it with terminal emulation on workstations or with purely graphical front-ends. Further, CSC is not a new invention. In the 1970s terminals were often attached to front-end processors (usually small minicomputers) which switched the services of a mainframe application (often a database or modelling system). By the 1980s we were using PCs for terminal emulation and a small amount of the application logic, often concerned with display, had migrated to the PC. CSC became a mature possibility with the advent of multi-tasking PC operating systems so that the user could maintain links with a remote server while running a local application as well.

It is worth noting that resource sharing systems such as file servers are not in the same category as database servers. With a file server, the client application requests a file which is then locked and transferred to the client for processing. If the access is for update, the file may be locked until the client releases control. All the processing is done by the client. With a database manager running on the server, the client issues queries and updates. The server processes these and returns only the result. Processing is shared, network traffic is reduced and locking is minimized.

Most client-server systems are of the database server type. However, there is a range of types, as depicted in Figure 4.2. The division between client and server can occur at any horizontal line in the diagram. Application servers correspond exactly to objects and object wrappers. We could slightly generalize the idea of a database server to that of a domain object server and differentiate it from an application object server. This point of view emphasizes a layered architecture rather than a single division between client and server as in the figure. We then begin to see that object-oriented systems are nothing other than, possibly layered, multi-client/multi-server or peer-to-peer systems. Figure 4.4 suggests six layers; the right number depends on the application. The light grey areas show opportunities for the introduction of extra layers.

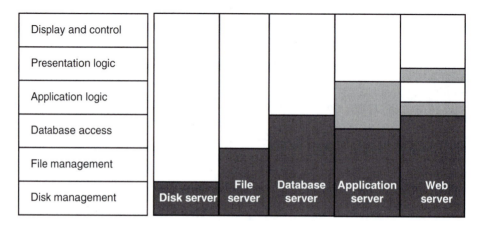

Figure 4.2 Levels of abstraction of client-server systems.

Conventional database tools are often organized around the client-server metaphor. One of the earliest commercial products to do this was Sybase, with more recent versions of Ingres, Oracle and other products working as multi-client/multi-server systems. The original Sybase approach offered each client a single access point to a multi-threaded server. There was one process and each user represented a thread of control within it. This is efficient in terms of memory utilization but cannot be exploited by modern multi-processor machines or parallel processors. The multi-server approach offers each client a single-threaded process of its own and is thus far better able to exploit parallelism even through slightly more hungry for memory. These kinds of tool assume network support and adherence to certain standards. The client and the server applications communicate via an API (such as the Sybase 'Open Client' API), connectivity software (such as 'SQL Connect') and some network protocol (such as TCP/IP, IBM's LU6.2/APPC or Novell's SPX/IPX). With the relational products, what is transmitted through all these filters is usually SQL, but this need not be so for object-oriented databases or other kinds of application. Again, with relational systems, the ones that make use of stored procedures are able to reduce network traffic considerably. This is because whole transactions are not fragmented into separate statements and they may be precompiled to improve performance further. Object-oriented systems, of course, give these benefits automatically, provided that the methods really are stored with the corresponding objects. Multi-client/multi-server systems extend the CSC model to give users heterogeneous access to several servers without the need to know where the services are located.

Stored procedures in relational systems provide not true object-orientation but the possibility of regarding the database server as one huge object; i.e. of creating a wrapper. The difficulty is that the encapsulation is not enforced by the system and the discipline of a robust approach to object-oriented analysis must be enforced by the standards, procedures and QA policies of the organization. It is quite possible for the undisciplined – or badly educated – developer to access the database structure directly using SQL rather than by going through the access routines supplied as stored procedures. One rather unwieldy solution to this problem is for the database administrator to remove all access privileges from all users so that the only access must be via stored procedures; but this also removes most of the advantages of a relational database in terms of being able to perform *ad hoc* associative queries. Two-tier client-server architectures are now regarded as far too inflexible for modern business needs.

CENTRALIZED There is a contradiction between the need to have all applications interoperate with
VERSUS each other and the need to permit each department to work in its own way.
DISTRIBUTED Housekeeping too becomes a more complex task. On the one hand, users may not consider routine backups and disk purges as part of their job but, on the other, nothing is more annoying than when the Information Systems Stasi comes round and erases all those useful little files on your hard disk over the weekend. One possible solution is automated housekeeping but the danger of a totalitarian approach remains.

There are yet other areas where distributed systems increase complexity. In a centralized system the operators and administrators take backups and tune the system. In a distributed one each user must be both operator and administrator. Physical distribution often makes central backups and software release control impractical. Network shared file servers help but they fail to provide a complete answer. A true distributed system implies a distributed operating system that makes the multitude of systems look like one system as far as both its users and administrators are concerned. Such a system must ensure both fault tolerance and parallelism. That is, no single part failing should bring the system down and there must be interconnected units containing both processor and memory. The first requirement implies that the system nodes must share state or, in the present context, that objects must be replicated.

The sheer cost of a simple solution may also increase complexity. Fully interconnected networks are simple but expensive; and thus the need for complex routers and scheduling techniques. Mullender (1989) illustrates this point well by comparing the operating policy of a railway connecting two towns with a track in each direction with one having a single track, possibly plus sidings for passing. This example also illustrates the concept of **latency** in networks, which is too often ignored by designers of distributed systems. At 60mph a single track network (with no sidings) connecting two points 120 miles distant has a latency of 2 hours while the double track railway has a latency of almost zero. Latency in a computer network is the time taken to call another thread of control. High latency networks often have severe clock synchronization problems. Latency is an important concept in the design of any object-oriented system, distributed or not. In that context it refers to delays due to blocking sends.

Early adopters of distributed approaches discovered the hard way that existing structured methods not only contribute little but actually impede progress in many areas. This is because the methods of functional decomposition and the separation of data from processing offer no representational techniques for describing communication between autonomous actors (objects). Thus, there is, in these organizations, a profound need for object-oriented analysis methods to help describe the systems being built. Also, new skills are needed; some specifically to do with distributed computing itself, but more significantly in terms of the different kinds of hardware and software platforms that will be used. The rise of XML re-emphasizes the need to design interface semantics carefully; despite its power, on its own it is not enough to define semantics.

One of the main problems with distributed computing compared to centralized computing is that the software becomes far more complex, and a strategy is required for managing or reducing this complexity. This is where object technology can help by providing tractable modelling techniques based on message passing, class libraries to protect developers from complex APIs, purpose built routers and full-blown object request brokers to simplify location management and inter-process communication even further.

Distributed systems have to be far more complex to prevent problems that just do not arise with conventional systems. If one processor fails while another proceeds, the application may end up in an inconsistent state – leading to the need to be able to roll back portions of an application selectively and intelligently. Imagine what would happen if you posted a cheque to a country whose postal service failed, after you had deleted the money from your account on the assumption that it would be credited to that of the recipient.

There are also problems when two processors access the same data and when the network itself goes awry. Most of us have experienced network errors, which are far more frequent than on standalone machines and consequently increased our save rate during tasks such as word processing. In fact, the trade-off between independent communicating nodes and a single network operating system is strongly reminiscent of the trade-off between planned, integrated, co-operative human societies and rampant individualism; each has its advantages – at least for some members.

Most commercial object-oriented databases offer such support, though their architectures vary greatly in terms of how they handle the sharing of storage and computation between the client and server components. The advantage of this approach is that one can maintain a consistent, fully object-oriented model for the whole application. Also, storage, recovery, transaction management, concurrency and, often, version control are handled automatically by the database. The disadvantage is the potentially large cost of converting existing data and/or applications if the new system is to take advantage of the conceptual model, performance benefits and the possibilities of extending the system using object-oriented programming languages. As Ewald and Roy (1993) point out, where migration in the context of extensive legacy systems is contemplated, the disbenefits can predominate. They remark that existing applications often already have their own methods for instance management, whether as proprietary file management systems or relational database systems. They conclude that object request brokers (ORBs) are often a better solution even though the latter may sacrifice a pure object-oriented style for flexibility. These are flexible precisely because they permit the use of existing applications, packages and other resources within the object-oriented framework. Reuse of such resources, however, is a coarse-grain reuse; sometimes violating the principle of small interfaces. Also, an ORB will not dictate exactly where and how applications should be coupled with pre-existing systems.

LOCATIONAL TRANS-PARENCY Object technology provides a natural way of modelling distributed applications because an object model consists of a set of independent entities, each with its own thread of control, collaborating by message passing; i.e. distributed method invocations. In conventional systems, library interfaces are usually procedural. In distributed systems they are more involved. Just as an object's state is encapsulated, it is easy to see that its location can be 'hidden' in the same way – the location is part of the state. However, some means of finding these objects must be provided. When an object references another (i.e. sends a message) the routing of the message is of no concern to the sender. Providing there is some sort of global address table, the sender should not need to care whether the receiver is even on the same machine. This must be the case for an object-oriented system because objects have unique identity for their lifetimes – regardless of location. In other words the object-oriented model both assumes and implies **locational transparency**.

It is considered axiomatic that distributed computing should offer locational transparency. That is, the user should not need to be aware of the physical location of the services being requested at any time. Even where this is true logically, network delays will sometimes make it only too apparent that requests are being processed remotely. Even finer distinctions become possible when the services are accessed by a mixture of local and wide area networks whose response characteristics are very different. Remote procedure calls (RPCs) violate locational transparency because the client application needs to know where the remote procedure is located to address it. This is sometimes hidden from the user by clever network software such as Sun's NFS and the reusable network services of the OSF's DCE but it remains a problem in principle. The extent to which the services offered by these systems are packaged as objects varies but such packaging, especially of the

API, definitely represents a trend. We will see how distributed object systems overcome this problem in a general way later.

DCE (Distributed Computing Environment) is a software architecture that supports multi-vendor distributed data and process sharing. It protects the user against variations in communications protocols but relies almost entirely on remote procedure calls (RPCs) and is thus rather threatened by the emergence of object request brokers and component models, although some of these use DCE under the covers.

Realizing that locational transparency is possible in principle for object-oriented systems does not lead to the conclusion that implementing such systems is trivial. In fact, a great deal of programming is required to set up the requisite support services and environment, and this involves several technologies as well as networking.

BENEFITS   The benefits most often claimed of distributed computing are that it permits organizations to:

- reduce the incremental cost of meeting the demands of users for increased functionality and access to corporate systems;
- reduce hardware and development costs by allowing the use of tools optimized for particular tasks;
- reduce development times by using existing systems as components;
- reduce hardware costs by utilizing low cost workstations (downsizing) and optimizing the utilization of other hardware (rightsizing);
- increase competitive edge and empower users;
- enable new business models such as e-commerce; and
- ease integration by hiding the complexities of communication between machines and adopting open standards.

Centralized computing offers the advantages of security, economies of scale and easier enforcement of management and accounting disciplines. However, operating costs can be high, systems inflexible, development and maintenance costly and the user has little control – and often limited access. Furthermore, most mainframes are poor calculating machines; so that the users' need to build models of business processes is hard to cater for in this way. This has led to considerable demand for end-user computing and distributed systems but there are still difficulties such as network bottlenecks, failures when not all machines are switched on, costs due to under-utilized CPUs, security breaches, data integrity and file locking delays. New skills are required within many IT organizations and change management is nearly always advisable to ameliorate the level of resistance to change. IT staff need not only their old mainframe skills but skills with PCs, networks and new, complex communication standards and component models. In my view, they will benefit most from an understanding of the principles of OT and, above all, a sound grasp of object-oriented analysis. This too involves, often significant, extra costs in terms of recruitment, consultancy, education and training.

Though distributed architectures usually involve two or more machines, in principle both client and server can reside on the same machine. The distinction is logical as well as physical. Originally, object-oriented programming languages were restricted to only one address space. Objects compiled by different compilers (even in the same language) couldn't communicate with one another, so that class libraries could not be delivered in binary form. Thus technologies such as RPCs, COM and CORBA, arose to tackle the problems of multi-language inter-object messaging. These led on to the emergence of component models and metamodels, including EJB and MOF.

Network nodes can be regarded as abstract data types or objects. However, inheritance and composition links shouldn't cross the network. Associations that span the network should be minimized for reasons of efficiency. Typically, a system layer should be implemented at a single node. In fact, nodes are best regarded as wrapped components.

4.1.1 Network and architectural issues

Distributed systems use more network capacity than centralized ones and it is a common error to underestimate the demand. It is a good idea therefore to involve users – who can often forecast what they want to do, network and operating systems specialists and application builders.

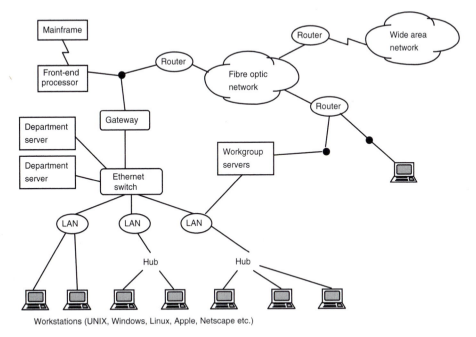

Figure 4.3 A typical network architecture during migration.

These three groups together should be able to produce a reasonable forecast of network loading and avoid the situation where people are taking half an hour to move their gigabyte database across the LAN and, incidentally, preventing anyone else from moving data.

Peer-to-peer communication can be used to build big systems out of relatively small computers. The paradigm for this was DECnet. IBM's APPN protocol and TCP/IP follow the same model, though TCP/IP is more widely supported and less proprietary. It is also the basis for the world wide web.

One of the most urgent questions facing an organization migrating to object technology is that of systems, application and network architecture. It is essential that new and legacy systems must be able to interoperate during the migration period. Often the *status quo* is a goulash of different systems, machines and networks. Figure 4.6 shows a simplified version of a typical architecture of the sort required by the migrating organization.

In the figure, the mainframe may be running all sorts of COBOL, FORTRAN, DB2 or VSAM applications and using proprietary network standards, such as SNA, for connectivity. The key component that must be added to the mainframe is some software that allows clients to interact directly with the mainframe relational database, using SQL, or execute COBOL routines remotely. A second key component is the gateway. This is some special software that would normally run on a dedicated machine and which acts as a bridge between UNIX clients and the mainframe network. Several database vendors can supply suitable software. Routers connect different LAN and WAN technologies and hubs permit point-to-point wiring between workstations. Ethernet switches help to maximize both flexibility and throughput. Various other equipment is needed but this is not a book on network architecture and the simplified view presented here will suffice. In future, object request brokers will simplify the picture considerably and it is this development that we consider next.

4.2 Object request brokers and middleware

The need to co-operate transparently with existing systems, packages and other object-oriented systems across telecommunications and local area networks is our next subject. The requirement is to represent applications and services on a network through a common object schema. This schema consists of objects to represent every service, with all locations and implementations transparent to the user and to other client objects.

Gartner Group define middleware as 'run time system software that directly enables application level interactions among programs in a distributed computing environment' although wags say that it is 'the software that nobody wants to pay for'. In other words, middleware is part of the infrastructure of a distributed computing system. There are several kinds of middleware and several levels of abstraction involved. At the lowest level, message-oriented middleware (MOM), such as IBM's MQ Series or Microsoft's MSMQ, provides asynchronous routing and queuing of messages and guarantees their delivery. MOM provides an intermediate tier in a client-server model. This of course does not ensure that the content of the messages is sensible or, indeed, compatible with the format that the target application expects. For this reason it is common to overlay middleware with a semantic layer, usually based on XML.

One important way in which many packages and applications interoperate transparently is through the Object Management Group's Common Object Request Broker Architecture (CORBA). Increasingly CORBA is being combined with MOM and Transaction Processing monitors. Current exemplars include BEA Systems' integration of the Tuxedo TP monitor with its ObjectBroker CORBA product and Tibco's ETX.

Founded in 1989, the Object Management Group (OMG) is a large group of influential companies committed to establishing broad agreement between vendors on both the terminology of object-orientation and on interface standards – based on existing technology. Companies originally involved in the OMG included Borland, Microsoft, Hewlett-Packard, Data General, AT&T, Unisys, Wang, ICL, Sun, DEC and most of the leading hardware, software and object-oriented suppliers along with several major users such as American Airlines and Boeing. At the time of writing there are around 800 members. Meetings of the OMG Technical Committees rotate between Europe, the USA and the Far East, helping to ensure an international base. The OMG is committed to the fast production of published standards, faster anyway than the official standards bodies can operate, and has published *inter alia* an architecture guide and reference model, the CORBA standard for Object Request Brokers (ORBs), a language-independent component model, a standard notation for object-oriented analysis and design (UML), specifications for standard business objects in vertical markets (e.g. currencies), a metamodel for data warehouses (CWM) and a Meta Object Facility (MOF). Several suppliers offer CORBA-compliant products. The fast growth of the OMG suggests that the industry was aware early of both the potential of object technology and the need for standards.

An ORB is a transparent data highway connecting object-oriented applications and object-oriented front-ends to existing applications. It is analogous to the X500 electronic mail communications standard wherein a requester can issue a request to another application or node without having to have detailed knowledge of its directory services structure. In this way, the ORB removes much of the need for complex RPCs by providing the mechanisms by which objects make and receive requests and responses transparently. It is intended to provide interoperability between applications on different machines in heterogeneous distributed environments and to connect multiple object systems seamlessly. It provides a means of using an abstract description of applications and the relationships between them and provides services for locating and using these applications across multi-vendor networks. Applications need not be written in an object-oriented manner since the ORB effectively provides a wrapper and they can be entire third-party packages. Packages and in-house applications can be reused and combined to deliver brand new cross-platform, distributed business systems. As Ewald and Roy (1993) succinctly put it, ORBs bring the benefit of OT to the world of systems integration.

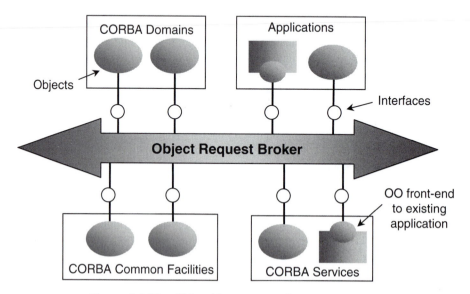

Figure 4.4 The Object Management Group architecture.

Object Request Brokers are products based on the Object Management Group's application architecture, illustrated in Figure 4.4, in which objects are classified as Application Objects, Common Facilities and Object Services. Application Objects are specific to particular end-user applications such as wrapped legacy systems, packages or spreadsheets. Common Facilities are objects which are useful in many contexts such as help facilities, compound document interfaces, browsers, e-mail and so on. Object Services provide basic operations for the logical modelling and physical storage of objects and might include persistence (interfaces to databases), naming, event notification, licensing, security services or transaction monitors. The basic idea is that an application that needs to use the services of some object, whether on the same machine or remote from it, should do so via a broker rather than by using some sort of remote procedure call that would require it to know the location of the server object. The ORB takes care of locating and activating registered remote servers, marshalling requests and responses, handling concurrency and detecting communication failures. Domain services are industry-specific interfaces to common business objects. There are several OMG task forces attempting to define these in sectors such as Transport, Healthcare, Telecomms, e-commerce, Life Sciences and Finance; though the latter is better thought of as dealing with Accounting despite the presence of some retail banks. Facilities reuse or extend Services. Domains reuse or extend Services or Facilities. Applications reuse or extend all these and may have custom extensions.

The OMG also defined a standard for interfaces: its Interface Definition Language (IDL). IDL resembles C++ syntactically but may only be used to define interfaces; it is not a full programming language. In the ORB, a request names an operation and its parameters, which may be object names. The ORB arranges the processing of the request by identifying and running a suitable method and returning the result to the requester.

Object request brokers work by acting on requests from all other types of object. They bind these to objects and route requests to other ORBs for binding. They can be regarded as either communication managers or systems integrators since they either route requests to the correct destination object or understand the syntax and semantics of each request by maintaining an object model, or both. They are a small step towards truly intelligent networks. In future, I anticipate expert systems and machine learning techniques being used to take this development even further.

An ORB makes use of the principles of data abstraction using its object model. In this model the **interface classes** specify the services of the applications known to the broker while the implementation classes represent the object wrapper code. To define an interface class one should specify the class in terms of its superclasses, attributes and operations. An Interface Definition Language (IDL) supports both dynamic and static binding to cater for different performance and extensibility requirements. All location services are handled transparently by the broker. This is handled by implementation classes but CORBA does not include a language for specifying these. Vendors are free to innovate in this area.

ORBs extend the polymorphism of normal object-oriented systems based on features such as inheritance to allow the user to choose, at run time, between different objects that perform the same function. Users can thus select a favourite word processor to perform editing functions based on their skills and preferences, thus maximizing their productivity within an albeit standardized environment. Other common facilities, such as spreadsheets or graphics servers, may be treated in the same flexible but disciplined manner. In this way, ORBs – for all their weaknesses – address some of the fundamental points made about productivity in Chapter 1.

The CORBA standard claims to address five key problems for distributed object systems: integration, interoperation, distribution, reuse and group work. Integration is addressed by providing a standard Interface Definition Language (IDL). Hitherto, the problem of distribution had been solved using very low level RPC programming and every developer, notably those in the banks, invented their own frameworks.

ORBs are closely related to object wrappers since access to an object or package on another system takes place via the broker, which at once defines the protocol in IDL and locates the service. The IDL interface could be to an object-oriented system or it could be to an entire package that is treated as if it were wrapped – provided that the IDL standard is observed by the wrapper.

CORBA Version 1, adopted in 1991, defined IDL as a protocol for inter-object communication. By 1994, Version 2 defined a way for ORBs from different manufacturers to interoperate. The advantage of this in terms of vendor independence is obvious. IIOP is the CORBA Internet Inter-ORB Protocol. It is a lightweight transport protocol that allows heterogeneous ORB products to communicate via TCP/IP; that is to say it consists of a set of message formats. The OMG's General Inter-ORB Protocol (GIOP) defines a way to map IDL interfaces to messages. IIOP converts GIOP messages into TCP/IP, which means that they can be sent over networks or the internet. The Portable Object Adaptor (POA) connects object references with code that provides the services needed, enabling thus portability.

Java has its own, built-in, object request broker: RMI. Java RMI (Remote Method Invocation) is not compliant with CORBA. It allows Java applications to use the services of other Java applications as if they were local, regardless of location. To use a server written in another language the developer must create a proxy in Java on the same server and then use the JNI (Java Native Interface) to connect them. With RMI, Java acts as its own IDL. However, pure Java now also includes IIOP and a separate CORBA-compliant Java IDL.

Microsoft offers a partial alternative to CORBA in the guise of COM and DCOM (Distributed Common Object Model). These developed from OLE (Object Linking and Embedding) which allowed applications to be launched automatically when an item that they had created was accessed in a foreign document. COM assumes the immediate availability of local services but DCOM allows COM to communicate between machines using remote procedure calls. This is a far less elegant and general solution than CORBA but is much easier to implement and therefore popular with developers.

CORBA 2 also added language mappings for Ada, COBOL, C++, Java and Smalltalk and extra features for initialization, transactions, security, abstract interfaces, typeless values and the Dynamic Skeleton Interface (DSI), which allows invoked operations to be selected at run time rather than be hard coded into stubs and skeletons (see below). It allowed objects to be passed by value as well as by reference and, significantly, a COM to CORBA interface.

By 2000, CORBA 3 had added support for firewalls and URLs and some features normally associated with MOM: asynchronous messaging and queuing and real-time features. CORBA 2 had relied entirely on a synchronous model based on RPCs. Version 3.0 also included the CORBA component model (CCM): a model based on Enterprise Java Beans (EJB) but language independent. COM and OLE interoperation is supported; there is a mapping from this CORBA component model to Active X controls and Java beans.

ORBs allow organizations to implement service-based architectures very easily. A good example is the implementation of a volatilities publishing system at a leading wholesale bank. Here traders provide the prices of derivatives for salesmen based on proprietary algorithms and upon the volatility of the underlying instrument prices. Unfortunately, most of the requests for prices from the sales desk do not lead to real, profitable trades. This meant that much valuable time was being wasted. The bank therefore created a system whereby the traders prepared the volatilities and algorithms using their Excel spreadsheets and a library of C++ functions callable from the spreadsheets. The results were then published to a server that could be accessed (via OLE) by other users of Excel or from Java-enabled web browsers across an object request broker. This bank offers many ORB-based services such as this to its internal clients. Another example is its calendar service that enables any user to find out when the various markets around the world are on holiday or closed. This service-based architecture has eliminated much duplication of effort on the part of developers building such functionality into their systems.

The rôle of middleware in software architecture will become increasingly important in the coming period; object request brokers, transaction monitors and message delivery mechanisms all have a crucial rôle to play in the delivery of robust flexible systems. Unfortunately, we operate in a culture where middleware is still often jocularly defined as 'the software that nobody wants to pay for'.

One of the first commercial ORB products to emerge was Hyperdesk's ill-fated DOMS. In fact, the creators of this product were influential in setting up the OMG in the first place. They started building a replacement for Data General's ageing CEO office automation products within that company. HP's NewWave technology was unsuccessfully tried as a basis for this work. In the late 1980s the group was spun off from DG as a separate company and Chris Stone left to form the OMG. Companies such as Sun, HP, DEC and NCR all had ideas on how to solve the distributed office computing problem with objects at this time.

There were two basic approaches, a static approach originating from Sun and HP and a dynamic, but less efficient, one coming from Hyperdesk and DEC. The dynamic model requires a single request building API and a single message unpacking mechanism. In the static model there was one code stub per operation and each request was made by a different subroutine. Each object bound in skeletons specific to each operation. Each skeleton delivered parameters as if the requester were a subroutine. CORBA represents a synthesis of the static and dynamic models of object request brokers and every CORBA-compliant implementation must support both approaches.

A typical, popular CORBA-compliant object request broker is Orbix from Iona Technologies in Eire. Other products among the many available are Ventel's CORBA Plus, IBM's Component Broker, Inprise's Visibroker, Peer Logic's DAIS and BEA's Weblogic Enterprise.

Several ORBs offer interest registration facilities so that broadcast messages can be supported without the need for an explicit blackboard object. The target object is sent a message registering the interest of some other object. When an event occurs in the target object the interested object is sent a message.

Some products use a directory services table structured similarly to that of the X500 E-mail standard. References to distributed objects are obtained from the directory as surrogates that are copied to the task space of the requester. Messages are sent to the surrogate and it relays them to the real object transparently. In fact, the distributed object manager itself is responsible for this. Figure 4.5 illustrates this remote method invocation model.

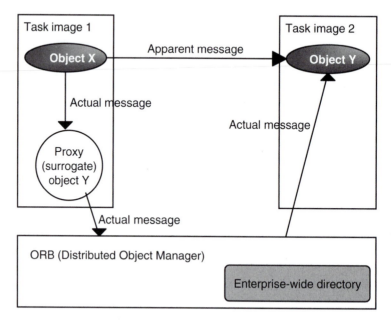

Figure 4.5 Remote method invocation.

IDL is used to define the attributes and operations of interfaces (their signatures). These are compiled into stubs, skeletons and definition files. A stub is a client-side surrogate or proxy object that receives service requests locally (via a generated local function call), marshals the parameters and forwards the message to the real target. A skeleton then receives the invocation, unmarshals the arguments and calls the target methods directly. Skeletons must be filled out with application code.

The term 'marshalling' remained something of a mystery to me until I realized that American speakers call railway goods yards 'marshalling yards'. Thus the image is that of a locomotive sorting and shunting trucks into order, ready for transmission to a new station. By analogy, when the ORB has found a suitable server, it marshals the parameters into a format suitable for transmission. Of course exceptions and error messages may be returned to the stub for relay to the client. Figure 4.6 summarizes the relationships between the various CORBA components discussed so far.

There remain problems that are not directly to do with message passing. These include concurrency, recovery from node failures, optimal object location for efficient access, how objects should be physically distributed when there are conflicting demands from different users and whether and how large objects can be decomposed into their components and distributed. Objects can be divided into active and passive types. Active objects provide services to others, can be copied as surrogates and need concurrency control. A printer might be an active object. Passive objects may be physically distributed when their services are required. A trivial example of a passive object is a number. There are three strategies for determining the location of active objects in this framework:

1. Set the location explicitly.
2. Set the location, statically or dynamically, on the basis of the resources it needs and those available.
3. Allow the requester to set the location dynamically.

This separation of active from passive objects is useful provided that the split can be made or the objects redefined to support it, the processing requirements of active objects can be defined and mapped onto physical hardware and the passive object mapping can be decided upon.

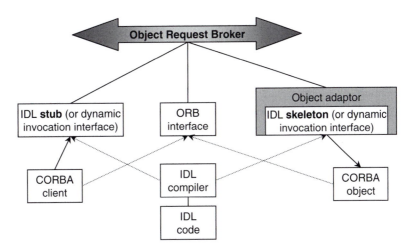

Figure 4.6 CORBA and IDL relationships.

Conformance to standards such as the OMG's CORBA and CORBA Services will allow applications to be portable to multiple platforms. All the object-oriented benefits – reuse, extensibility, localization of maintenance, assembly of applications from 'software integrated circuits' (software ICs), etc. – will then apply in distributed environments. Further, this will provide scalability up to the largest systems imaginable on multi-machine systems implemented under several different distributed architectures. Complex network interfaces and APIs are being replaced by powerful locationally transparent mechanisms that manage messaging, locations and global naming of objects.

Since the acquisition of ObjectBroker from DEC by BEA, another middleware trend has been the integration of ORBs with transaction processing monitors. There are several TP monitors for workstations including Ellipse – Cooperative Solutions Inc., Encina – Transarc Corp., MTS – Microsoft, TOP END – NCR, Tuxedo – part of BEA's Iceberg, and even IBM's CICS. The latter, it is reported, had its internal design heavily influenced by object-oriented ideas taken from Smalltalk and became notorious by winning a Queen's Award for the development team's use of formal specification using Z. Hitachi's TPBroker also combines a high reliability TP monitor with Visibroker, which in any case has its own transaction service. It has been used for such high performance applications as on-line bond trading. I expect that, in the future, the market will close in on a generic class of middleware offering the facilities of both ORBs and MOM with a TP monitor and real-time option. Specific industries will define semantic extensions, probably based on XML, and these may be standardized too.

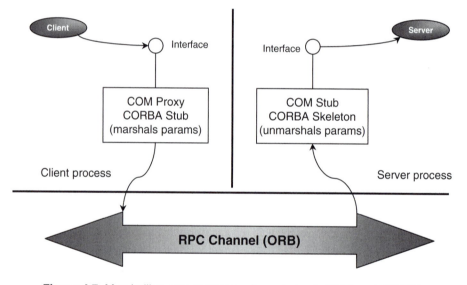

Figure 4.7 Marshalling across process boundaries in COM and CORBA.

ORBs are fundamental to building service-based architectures based on black-box components, because of the implied lack of a single address space.

COM   The main competing standard approach to CORBA comes from Microsoft in the form of COM+, including as it does the proprietary COM, DCOM, MTS and Active X technologies. COM defines a binary standard for interfaces and so should be language independent. CORBA specifies no particular layout in memory and achieves language independence by defining multiple language bindings. However, the COM standard insists that interfaces are built in precisely the same way as C++ virtual function tables, which compromises this aim considerably. The equivalent of the ORB is called the RPC Channel. Stubs are called proxies and CORBA skeletons correspond to COM stubs. In other ways the approaches are very similar, as illustrated in Figure 4.7. For example, COM supports message queuing and event notification via MSMQ. COM also defines its own IDL – not to be confused with the quite different OMG IDL.

COM+ is bundled with Microsoft's Transaction Server (MTS), which compromises it as a true cross-platform standard; partly because this and other extra services are not always supported by COM/CORBA bridges. To remedy this situation Microsoft designed the Simple Object Access Protocol (SOAP) to support component interaction across the web. This allows developers to use any three-tier component architectures on any platform and integrate them.

Distributed computing brings with it problems additional to those of a centralized approach. For example, every user in a different department may work with a different definition of business concepts such as *customers*. A customer could be a company or a person within a company. Is a child a customer when a parent pays but the child chooses? At what point does a prospect become converted to a customer? These questions merely hint at the difficulty. With a centralized system the differences do not matter so much because users can take copies of the data they need and add their own view. The distributed totality is never assembled to reveal any discrepancies. A distributed system therefore means that it becomes necessary for all to agree on definitions, which can be very hard to do. One way that distributed applications can overcome the problems involved is to use XML (eXtensible Markup Language) on top of what ever middleware is in use.

4.2.1 The rôle of XML

XML is an extensible, generalized markup language that can be used to describe data passing between different systems or applications. MOM does not help with locational transparency; you still need to know where the target application lives. Therefore, a router of some sort is needed to go beyond simple point-to-point connectivity. XML is derived from the older SGML (Standard Generalized Markup Language) and is similar to HTML except that data are made self-describing by using a hierarchy of tags, making web pages closer to programs. XML permits message senders to separate content from presentation; so that rather than just saying that a piece of text that we wish to stress is set in bold type, we tag it as <emphasis> and use an XML style sheet to declare that emphasized text is bold – or whatever. For example, in the following fragment we have tags defining the structure of a message (from, to, body), its formatting (italic) and part of its content (customer).

```
<?xml version="1.0"?>
<!DOCTYPE "sales memo">
<from>Suzie Eizus</from>
<to>Eric Cire</to>
<body>We have just received an urgent order from <customer>Imperfect
Palindromes Inc.</customer> please action today.
```

```
...
</body>
```

XML parsers can enforce which tags must be present in a document (its *validity*) by reference to its document type descriptor (DTD). The fact that fields can be optional means that the recipient of an XML message with missing fields can still use the data contained. Thus, if a legacy database holds one definition of a customer, whilst a new system has another, they can still communicate. As a result, one of the chief uses of XML is information exchange between systems with different storage formats for similar information, possibly across platforms. It can be used on top of middleware to create corporate standards for data interchange and to wrap legacy applications. This kind of application has become known as Enterprise Application Integration (EAI). XML also brings the potential of Electronic Data Interchange (EDI) within the budget of far smaller suppliers than was hitherto possible. For such applications, some tags are regarded as metadata.

There as several standards for metadata such as Netscape's Meta Content Framework for describing the content of web sites. In this context one might imagine tags such as: <Geology>, <Shakespeare> or even <useful for wannabe bomb makers>. XML is very flexible and can be used to define new, specialized markup languages for various disciplines. For example, it has been used to define equation editors as well as standard languages for business-to-business e-commerce. It can support multiple languages because of its use of the 16-bit Unicode character set – ASCII had only 7 bits (or 128 characters) originally.[2] XML style sheets are usually written in another extensible language: XSL. There is also an XML user interface definition language (XUL) which uses tree structures to define UI widgets and allows them to be deployed to browsers on the fly.

The self-describing, hierarchical tag structure enables much richer data access possibilities than is normally available in databases, such as context-sensitive queries and navigation. The POET Content Management System provides an example of this kind of application of XML. A related type of application, which I have worked on, is the management of multiple foreign language translations of product labelling or documentation. Here XML allows documents to be treated as composites of smaller sections – right down to standard phrases. Combined with automatic version control, this approach can reduce document creation and maintenance workloads by orders of magnitude. Xerox's Astoria is another product designed specifically for this kind of application. In addition to this kind of initiative there is a group of XML servers, such as ODI's eXcelon and Software AG's Tamino. These products extend OODBs to include an object model based on XML. There are plenty of XML parsers and editing tools on the market; and several are free.

XML is actually rather too flexible. One needs to ensure that messages can map to the constructs of the languages in use while retaining maximal simplicity. One approach is to create an internal standard subset of XML, with defined tags, into which all messages from legacy systems can be converted. Chase Manhattan Bank

---

[2] Of course, an n-bit code permits 2^n characters to be represented.

did this (O'Sullivan, 1999). They needed to connect applications on multiple platforms that used a variety of languages, from COBOL and RPG to C++ and Java. Each system defined a different fixed-length message format. Previously, maintaining multiple point-to-point FTP transfers had been very costly and error-prone. They needed guaranteed delivery and so used IBM's MQ Series MOM product, defining its message formats with XML. This enabled them to define standard message formats for things like trades, with many optional fields – supersetting those of existing formats. Although CORBA was also widely used at Chase, it could no more provide the message transmission format than could MQ Series or notations like ASN.1. None of these were readable by humans either. Chase defined several restrictions that would be built into their parser. These included several 'type safety' rules, such as not allowing message elements to be declared as ANY or EMPTY and insisting that leaf elements declare their type. This is a typical application of XML and similar projects in other banks will lead to inter-industry standard languages of this type. The Open Financial Exchange (www.OFX.net) is a set of standard financial element types representing things like credit card numbers and transaction types. The Open Trading Protocol (www.OTP.org) is another standard for more general electronic trading.

One rather whacky application of XML allows a virtual newsreader's facial image to smile, frown or pout appropriately while speech is synthesized from news text. The expressions are just coded as tags embedded in the text. Her tone of voice is also influenced in this way. This extends the idea of *avatars* – fairly common in chat rooms now but originally predicted in a wonderful science fiction novel (Stephenson, 1992).

Microsoft's Biztalk is a proprietary XML-based server framework that many companies have used as the basis for applications like supply chain integration. Biztalk includes schemata for such business processes as product catalogues, offers and purchasing. It routes messages and can include workflow rules. XMI (XML Metadata Interchange) is an OMG standard that attempts to unify UML, MOF and XML. It uses XML DTDs to describe MOF components and UML models. MOF-compliant models will be interchangeable between XMI-compliant repositories.

XML looks set to be the universal language for self-describing messaging between disparate systems and entire businesses. As long as XML doesn't just mean that even more enterprise programs are able to misunderstand one another successfully!

4.3 Enterprise Application Integration

The 1990s saw many organizations undergoing major changes in technology, principally moving away from systems based on centralized mainframes – usually from a single supplier – to distributed systems. Workstations became desirable platforms for both development and applications due to their increased and more accessible power and the ease of building usable graphical interfaces on them. This was associated with a greater emphasis on rapid response to changing business needs and the use of rapid development. The existence of immovable legacy systems meant that interoperability was a key issue during the migration. Developments in hardware and relational database software also led to increased demand for, and reliance on, distributed architectures. Typically these organizations operated with a goulash of mainframe systems, departmental minis and standalone or networked PCs running word processors, spreadsheet applications and, at the end of that period, browsers. The mainframes ran both relational and non-relational databases and record-oriented applications written in COBOL or Assembler.

As new applications began to appear the first need was for them to access information on the mainframes. This could be accomplished by nightly downloads but the more advanced solution was to build a bridge using open gateway software that could convert between systems such as IMS on the mainframe and Oracle or Sybase on UNIX servers. Often this software was supplied by the relational database vendors themselves, a typical early product being Sybase's NetGateway. In this way, data could be both retrieved and updated rather than merely copied; thus removing the necessity to rebuild terminal data entry screens for new applications. This approach was found to offer considerable locational transparency to users and made database interaction far easier.

One of the complex migration issues that was faced by most organizations was that of network architecture, resilience and management. One organization I worked with viewed its networks as offering a hierarchy of service layers. The highest level enabled users to connect their workstations to various local servers. The next level provided workgroup server support. Both these layers relied chiefly on LAN technology and the workgroup level used matrix switching. The third layer linked the previous two to departmental and database servers using Ethernet switches. Finally, there was a massively complex connectivity layer that supported gateways to the mainframe-based legacy systems, access to WANs and message routing. Security is an important issue in the financial services sector and this company took it very seriously indeed. They adopted the Open Software Foundation's DCE security services standard, Kerberos, within their network management system. Routers were employed to connect different LAN systems such as Ethernet and Token Ring and to provide firewalls between network segments. Within two years their distributed computing architecture enabled this company to construct several complex, business-critical and flexible applications. Typical systems moved trading data from a mainframe network database and combined them with prices from a market data feed. The data were placed in server-based relational systems, validated interactively and then returned to the mainframe and passed simultaneously to local workstations. Other systems provide seamless 'straight-through' links between previously incompatible front and back office systems.

Today EAI is the acronym used for the integration of disparate systems, packages and components into key business processes; i.e. making the different chunks of software within an enterprise work together – ideally as well as if they had been designed as components in the first place. EAI projects therefore need many of the tools we have been discussing: middleware, metadata, message formats, etc.

An organization and its software evolve over a number of years and many point-to-point connectors have been defined between software packages, for specific purposes. The overall system (and therefore the business) is inflexible because the connexions cannot be rearranged without huge effort; the connector definitions are specific to the modules they connect. Some couplings that would be advantageous have never been made. A similar situation arises when legacy systems have evolved in separate departments, or in different subsidiary companies; the move towards e-commerce now demands that they be integrated more closely than before. The solution is to define a set of common connectors – a language that all the components can be adapted to talk. It is then easier to rearrange them. This is not just a matter of choosing a technology such as MOM, CORBA or XML; in addition one must decide upon the protocols and common business model needed. Not is it solely about data integration and warehousing across disparate systems; the functions of the systems must be integrated too.

Competitive pressures, new ways of working and the move to e-commerce imply that there is a need for real-time data and process integrity; overnight downloads and replication are no longer enough. Not only must processes cross organizational boundaries but work may flow across several different companies. All this must be implemented ever more rapidly. Not only must data formats be transformed but business concepts too: converting a 2-digit date to a 4-digit one is a fairly tractable task, but mapping customers that have multiple locations to a system that thinks there can only be one is far harder. Package software is usually too inflexible and incomplete to provide the solution. EAI requires attention to the development of common business standards and a unified technology architecture. It also needs clear, separate interfaces to modules (APIs). Package vendors will claim to supply all this, but – of course – only if you buy most of what you need from them! That route may well lead to next year's legacy integration problem.

In practice, one may have to decide on a core interface technology: standardizing on one of Microsoft COM interfaces, EJBs or CORBA. But even then full consideration has to be given to more than just the technology architecture. Figure 4.8 shows the provenance of various technologies and concepts in relation to architecture.

EAI software products should support event notification, workflow management, rule-based message routing and data transformation. The latter implies that there be tools to define interfaces and data format transforms and a repository to store all this. Vendors that operate in the EAI space include sellers of packages, middleware and wrapping tools, workflow automation tools, database gateways and application servers. Application servers range from integrated e-commerce solutions such as IBM's Websphere and BEA's Weblogic to database caches. There are also vendors of application development tools such as Compuware's UNIFACE and Sun's Forté Fusion. Fusion builds on Forté Conductor – a cross-platform, component-based workflow management and integration system – and the OO

4GLs: TOOL and SynerJ. It uses XML for messaging and XSL for presentation and process rules. Systems are linked through application proxies that talk to native language APIs – such as C, TOOL or XML – via connectors.

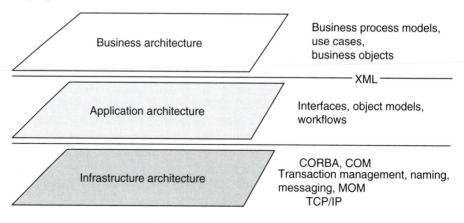

Figure 4.8 Architectural layers.

Introducing the glue that joins up the legacy may of course affect performance and make testing and locating faults harder, but that is the price of increased flexibility in the face of business change

EAI products do not provide an off-the-shelf solution; interfaces, processes and new components will always need to be developed and/or tweaked, and this can be a significant development task. Doing it properly requires honed skills in software architecture and component-based development. In many ways EAI is just a different take on the same set of concerns as CBD, using the same techniques. In CBD, we think of constructing pieces that can be glued together easily; in EAI, we think of adapting existing pieces so that they work together; in practice, most developments are a mixture of the two. We will look at techniques for CBD in Chapter 7 in some detail.

The key technical features in an EAI environment are distribution, connectivity and flexibility. These factors have led away from the waterfall–structured–mainframe mind-set and people have realized that not only are advanced, object-oriented programming environments essential to exploit evolution and describe a parallel, distributed, message-based world, but also they would have to adopt object-oriented analysis and design approaches. Without sound object-oriented analysis and a project management culture that accepts its implications, the distributed solution will soon become even more cumbersome to manage than the mainframes it replaced. The key task for companies engaged in EAI is the definition of such a sound approach.

⊟ 4.4 Migration strategies

Many people and organizations are convinced of the wisdom of shifting their systems development activities towards an object-oriented, component-based development style. This may be because they have seen other companies succeeding in this way or even for that worst of reasons: because OT and CBD are fashionable. Even in the latter, misguided, case these companies may gain from the experience because, even should the project in hand fail, they may gain a better understanding of existing systems and development practices through the construction of an object model. They have several reasons for replacing or extending older systems. For example, a package vendor may see the move to object technology as closely tied to the move to a new platform and, in turn, see this as a way of achieving greater market share. They may wish to compete more effectively by adding value to the existing product with graphical user interfaces, management information system (MIS) features or delivery on distributed platforms. User organizations may wish to take advantage of new standards, friendlier interfaces or opportunities for e-commerce along with the benefits of the move to OT itself that were discussed in Chapter 2. In the latter case it is essential that their e-commerce systems – whether for trading with other businesses, selling to customers or integrating the supply chain – are almost infinitely scalable from the outset, since the number of users is quite unpredictable. Also, there must be total flexibility in the face of requirements that are bound to change rapidly. This implies the flexibility of object technology as well as the need for a sound requirements engineering process: one compatible with both objects and business process change. New e-commerce companies (or subsidiaries) will not face huge legacy integration problems but will have to build up every capability from scratch. One the other hand, they do not face the predictable problems of resistance to changing business practices and culture faced by established companies.

Both vendors and users will be looking to slash maintenance costs, which can account for a huge proportion of the IS budget, and reduce time to market. We have already seen that OT can contribute to both goals if implemented successfully. However, while overnight migration is highly desirable it is seldom possible. Furthermore, gradual migration may take too long for its benefits to be worthwhile. Often the solution is to reuse existing conventional components or entire systems and packages – through EAI. Also, some accounting and ERP package vendors have attempted to 'componentize' their offerings so that one can take modules from competing products and make them interoperate. We will discuss this development separately in Chapter 7 when we deal with component-based development. There are several available options: interoperation, reuse, extension, and gradual or sudden migration. These options are closely related but we will deal with interoperation first.

In this section, we examine various proposed and actual strategies which meet the requirements of organizations facing migration and interoperation problems, emphasizing the concerns of a developer who wants to develop an object-oriented application that needs to use the services provided by applications that incorporate other programming styles such as expert systems, 4GLs, procedural libraries (e.g. the NAG FORTRAN library), parallel processing systems, relational databases or even fuzzy controllers. We must ask what the fundamental issues are in using, designing and building interoperation tools. How do you deal with those critical COBOL or Assembler applications? What is the rôle of object-oriented analysis and component-based design techniques within this kind of migration? Is there a strategy that enables you to metamorphose an existing procedural application into an object-oriented application without disrupting services to the existing users? What is the rôle of EAI tools?

This section will also cover such problems as how to wrap an old application which exists in a large number of different versions. We will also explore the ways in which object-oriented analysis in particular and object technology as a whole can be used as a migration technique.

4.4.1   Interoperation of object-oriented systems with conventional IT

There are a number of scenarios in which an object-oriented application should interoperate with existing non-object-oriented systems. These include:

- the evolutionary migration of an existing system to a future object-oriented implementation where parts of the old system will remain temporarily in use;
- the evolution and integration of enterprise systems which already exist and are important and too large or complex to rewrite at a stroke and where part or all of the old system may continue to exist indefinitely (EAI);
- the need to build on existing package solutions (a second context for EAI);
- the reuse of highly specialized or optimized routines, embedded expert systems and hardware-specific software;
- exploiting the best of existing relational databases for one part of an application in concert with the use of an object-oriented programming language and/or object-oriented databases for another;
- the construction of graphical or browser front-ends to existing systems;
- co-operative processing and blackboard architectures may involve agents which already exist working with newly defined objects;
- the need to co-operate with existing systems across wide and local area networks and the web.

The main issue is how to tackle the migration of a vast system that is almost invariably very costly and tricky to maintain. The first strategy recommended here is to build what I have referred to several times as an OBJECT WRAPPER. Object wrappers can be used to migrate to object-oriented programming and still protect investments in conventional code. The wrapper concept has become part of the folk-lore of object-orientation but, as far as I know, the term was first coined by Wally Dietrich of IBM (Dietrich *et al.*, 1989) though it is also often attributed to Brad Cox and Tom Love, the developers of Objective-C, but in a slightly different context. There are also claims that the usage was in vogue within IBM as early as 1987.

The existence of large investments in COTS (commercial, off-the-shelf) packages and programs written in conventional languages such as Assembler, COBOL, PL/1, FORTRAN and even APL has to be recognized. It must also be allowed that the biggest cost associated with these 'legacy' systems, as Dietrich first called them, is maintenance. Maintenance is costly because, in a conventional system, any change to the data structure requires checking every single function to see if it is affected. As we saw in Chapter 1, this does not occur with object-oriented systems due to the encapsulation of the data structures by the functions that use them. However much we would like to replace these old systems completely, the economics of the matter forbids it on any large scale; there just are not enough development resources. What we must do is build on the existing investment and move gradually to the brave new world of object-orientation and components.

It is possible to create object wrappers around this bulk of existing code, which can then be replaced or allowed to wither away. Building object wrappers can help protect the investment in older systems during the move to object-oriented programming. An object wrapper enables a new, object-oriented part of a system to interact with a conventional chunk by message passing. The wrapper itself can be written in the same language as the original system, COBOL for example, or utilize middleware – as discussed in the previous section. This may represent a very substantial investment, but once it is in place virtually all maintenance activity may cease; at least this is the theory.

Imagine that an existing COBOL system interacts with users through a traditional menu system, each green screen offering about 10 options and with the leaf nodes of the menu tree being normal 'tab, enter and commit' data entry screens. This characterizes a very large number of present-day systems. The wrapper must offer all the functions of the old system as if through the interface of an object, as illustrated by the 'Gradygram' in Figure 4.9 where the small rectangles on the boundary of the wrapper represent its visible operations, which in turn call the old system's functions and thereby access its data too.[3] Effectively, the wrapper is a large object whose methods are the menu options of the old system. The only difference between this new object and the old system is that it will respond to messages from other objects. So far, this gives little in the way of benefits. However, when we either discover a bug, receive a change request or wish to add a new business function the benefits begin; for we do not meddle with the old system at all but create a new set of objects to deliver the new features. As far as the

---

[3]The term GRADYGRAM was coined to stand for the icons with operations indicated by small boxes on the boundary of a rectangle representing the object used by Grady Booch since his work on design for Ada in the 1980s. UML uses them for its module diagrams to this day.

existing users are concerned, they may see no difference when using the old functions; although their calls are being diverted via the wrapper. Wrappers may be small or large, but in the context of interoperation they tend to be of quite coarse granularity. For command-driven systems, the wrapper may be a set of operating system batch files or scripts. It could also be a set of CORBA or COM+ IDL interfaces. If the old system used a form or screen-based interface, the wrapper may consist of code that reads and writes data to the screen. This can be done using a virtual terminal. This is fairly easy to accomplish on machines such as the VAX though it is not always possible with systems such as OS/400 where some specialist software, an object request broker or Java RMI may be required. All new functions or replacements should be dealt with by creating new objects with their own encapsulated data structures and methods. If the services of the old system are needed, these are requested by message passing and the output is decoded by the wrapper and passed to the requester.

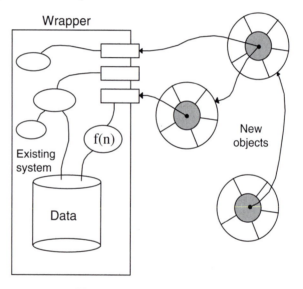

Figure 4.9 Object wrappers.

So much for the propaganda! Implementing wrappers is not as easy as it sounds in several respects. Much of the literature on wrappers is aimed at deriving the necessity of object request brokers. When these are not available, for whatever reason, developers have to face up to the implementation details directly. One such issue concerns granularity. Most of the theoretical arguments and a good deal of the practical experience of object-oriented programmers indicate that small objects are usually more likely to match particular requirements than large ones. Recall the guidelines for object design from Chapter 2: interfaces should be small and simple; no more than about 17 operations per object; and so on. However, with the legacy system, or with large-grain components, we are faced with a *fait accompli*; the system is as it is. There are irreducibly large-grain 'objects' often present in the design of legacy systems. Object request brokers and component models are specifically aimed at dealing with this kind of coarse-grain reuse. The question is whether, without such a broker, we can still gain from the use of a hand-made wrapper. Some developers find that coarse-grain components arise naturally even with new requirements and deduce that object-oriented models are not always appropriate. Brice (1993), for example, found this in the context of geometrical image transformation software. The data structures were straightforward but the processing required pages of equations to describe it and data flow models were found to be the most natural thing to use. Here is a case where home-made wrappers may be beneficial even with greenfield developments.

Component-based development also emphasizes coarse-grain components consisting of many classes implementing several interfaces; so that any component is *a fortiori* usually a wrapper.

This approach to migration is not the only one available. Other options include the use of object request brokers (ORBs) and proceeding in a completely *ad hoc* manner. The *ad hoc* approach is often the correct one, but there are so many ways of approaching a particular problem that few sensible generalizations can be made. The *ad hoc* approach was the only one available until the appearance of ORB products and message-oriented middleware. Now it is very common to use an ORB to implement a wrapper around a legacy system. One leading financial institution, for example, built a straight-through trading system to connect its front and back office systems using objects that effectively comprised self-describing data packets. The result was observed *post facto* to be an application-specific object request broker but the work was completed before any stable commercial CORBA-compliant distributed object management system had come to market. Furthermore, this application went beyond the CORBA specification by using self-describing data, as one would now do using XML.

One of the biggest problems with the concept of object wrappers concerns data management. Using the wrapper is easy until you need to split the storage of data across the old database and some of the new objects.

4.4.2 Data management strategies for wrappers

The object wrapper approach seems ideal at first sight but closer examination reveals some severe data management problems. Where building a wrapper makes it necessary to duplicate or share data across the new and old system components, there are at most four possible strategies:

1. Carry a duplicate live copy of the common data in both parts of the system and keep both copies up to date. The problem with this is that storage requirements could double. Worse still, there are real integrity issues to worry about. It is almost certainly not a viable strategy for either migration or reuse of any commercial-scale system. We will call this the **tandem** or

handshake strategy because it requires constant synchronization of updates and retrievals. It only works when there is little or no overlap between the data of the old and new systems, which is rare.

2. Keep all data in the old system and copy them to the new objects as required. Messages to the old system cause it to handle updates. This is known as the **borrowing** or **download** strategy because data are borrowed temporarily from the wrapper. It is similar to what is done in many existing, conventional MIS applications where data are downloaded nightly from a mainframe to workstations and updates transmitted in batch. A more sophisticated variant of this strategy is common when object-oriented programs are linked to large relational databases. Data from the database are cached in an object-oriented database so that the programmers do not have to concern themselves with the object-to-relational mapping and performance is enhanced (for reasons to be explained in Chapter 5). This variant is the **caching** strategy and application servers often employ it – making the technicalities transparent to programmers.

3. Copy the data to the new objects and allow the old system's data to go out of date. Again there may be integrity problems, and the wrapper may have to send messages as well as receive and respond to them; which greatly increases its complexity. Call this the **take-over** strategy by analogy with a company making a take-over bid for another.

4. Carve out coherent chunks of the database together with related functions. This is difficult and requires a sound method of object-oriented analysis capable of describing the old system as well as the new and/or a translation technique from original systems design documents such as DFDs. On balance, it seems the most promising approach to legacy migration. This is called the **translation** strategy because one must translate the design to an object model. It is easiest to do when the old system was originally written around critical data structures using a technique such as step-wise refinement. These structures and the programs that use them will migrate naturally to the objects of the new system. A refinement of this strategy is to reverse engineer a data model from the existing system and to identify all file access operations in relation to this model using, for example, a CRUD matrix approach. CRUD techniques are often used to organize conventional systems around their data structures. These calls can then be replaced as new objects are constructed around the entities. This improved version of translation can be called **data-centred translation**. Whether it is feasible will depend on the difficulty of obtaining a data model and the complexity of the code in which the database calls are embedded. Reverse engineering tools may prove useful within this strategy and, as Reiss (1991) points out, the most useful tools would contain an understanding of the system semantics.

These strategies may be variously appropriate according to whether we are migrating the system to an object-oriented implementation, reusing its components, extending it or building a better or a distributed front-end. Assuming that our chief aim is to migrate the old system to a new object-oriented one rather than merely to reuse its components, which strategies are feasible? The handshake strategy is flawed for all but the smallest systems, and then there must be little overlap between new and old components. The borrowing strategy may well involve tampering with the old system and is not usually viable for the purposes of system migration unless there is a clean separation between existing functions and new requirements – though it is suitable for enabling legacy reuse. Borrowing does not permit data to move permanently outward across the wrapper boundary. This means that there will come a time when a huge step must be taken all at once to migrate the data out, unless a DBMS has been used for all data accesses. These strategies, as **migration** strategies, do grievous violence to the whole idea of building wrappers. Only the last two strategies promise to be feasible if our intention is to migrate the functions of the old system to a new one, and there are some systems where neither seems to be practical. It is also the case that the type of system, its structure and the quality and type of its documentation will affect the choice of strategy. Dietrich's original application of the wrapper concept was to a solid modelling system of considerable complexity but whose intricacy resided in its code rather than in its data management. Furthermore, his primary concern was with the reuse of the functions of a stable system rather than its reconstruction.

Strategy 4, translation, will work most often, provided that the old system can be decomposed around coherent data sets and if there are, say, some existing DFDs to transform objects from by encapsulating their data stores. If not, one is faced with building a wrapper of much greater complexity using take-over: strategy 3. The latter is a far costlier option.

Critical to all this is the adoption of an architecture-centric approach and the use of patterns and component kits based on sound interface specification techniques. We will see in Chapter 7 how recent advances in object-oriented design such as Catalysis (D'Souza and Wills, 1999; Wills, 2001) contribute significantly.

4.4.3   Practical problems with migration

Another problem arises when the old system exists and is maintained in multiple versions. For example, a commercial package for a particular industry may, over the years, have been adapted for the needs of particular clients. The cost of building a wrapper for each version is usually prohibitive. The wrapper approach will only work if there is a core system common to all the versions, and the modifications will have to be maintained separately in any case until they can be re-implemented. This was the situation on a project that I was involved with where there were around 70 versions of the product customized for particular sites scattered across the globe, with local, dedicated maintenance teams in many cases. Also, the decomposition of the existing system into coherent chunks was exceedingly hard because of the long modification history. The strategy adopted was to model the system using object-oriented analysis and first wrap the core system in such a way that new functionality (an MIS component) could be added using object-oriented methods, leaving the core system much untouched at this stage. The AS400 hardware on which the system had to run, pending a move to UNIX at some future date, did not then support an object-oriented language of any form. Thus, in the short term, the new object-oriented components had to be implemented in a conventional language. To ensure that the new system can be fully object-oriented in the future we had to find a way to minimize the cost of so doing. This led to the use of an object-oriented analysis approach and the conversion of its products to conventional code. It also led to the use of a (now defunct) middleware product, NeWI, that was able to let the developers treat the system as object-oriented while still writing code in C. We also produced an object-oriented description of the existing system to clarify understanding and help carve out separate re-implementable chunks following a translation strategy. It emerged that treating some functions as objects instead of methods was useful. The bulk of the early effort went into designing additional features and their interface, via a wrapper, to the core of the existing system; translation tasks being deferred to the near future. Thus, it proved wise to proceed in steps:

1. build a wrapper to communicate with new object-oriented components using (most probably) the borrowing strategy;
2. perform an object-oriented analysis on the old system;
3. use translation or data-centred translation to migrate;
4. utilize an ORB to implement.

Grass (1991) argues that wrappers work well for mature systems that are essentially frozen, in the context of a requirement to reduce the maintenance burden which she characterizes as 'extremely aggravating' with the panache of understatement. Her main point is that ill-structured legacy systems are costly to understand and wrap. However, even this is worthwhile if the potential maintenance savings are large enough. Like Dietrich's, Grass' principal application (a parser for regular grammars) was complex functionally but not primarily a data-intensive application.

One may conclude that the best approach to migration of legacy systems with significant data management complexity is to build wrappers that support object-oriented front-ends and to build the required new functions within the front-ends. The tandem strategy can be used only when there is little overlap and separate databases will have to be maintained. The exceptions to this are when the existing system already has a coherent data-centred structure that facilitates translation or when the benefits of the migration are large enough to justify the cost of building a very complex wrapper along the lines of the take-over strategy. If there is an existing DBMS this can be wrapped as a whole and maintained for a long time as the wrapped functions are gradually migrated. Then, at some point, one can move all the data at once to an object-oriented database if desired and eliminate the database wrapper. This is a special variant of the translation strategy where the database is one huge 'coherent chunk'. It is probably the ideal option for many organizations already obtaining satisfactory performance from their relational databases.

Having decided to build a wrapper and a new front-end, one needs tools for building them. Some vendors, such as Merant, offer products for wrapping COBOL applications and there are several ORB and middleware tools that address the issue.

A key problem faced by many IT organizations is one I have often heard called the *goulash* problem. It exists where there is a mixture of essentially incompatible hardware and software that somehow has been made to work together over the years. Conceptually it is easy to see that this goulash can be modelled as a system of large components communicating by passing messages with parameters. The wrapper approach is appropriate when just one of these systems is to migrate to an object-oriented platform. Rather than build a wrapper for each old system, which would be expensive to say the least, it is better to wrap the communication system in some way. As we have seen, the most common approach to this problem is to use object request brokers and component-based development. Several Enterprise Application Integration tools are based on middleware together with object-oriented databases and XML technology.

In the product migration project referred to above, it turned out – for the reasons given – that there were no suitable software tools at the outset. Therefore our main tool was our object-oriented analysis approach itself.

We need to deal not only with the evolution of existing systems which are important and too large or complex to rewrite but also with the evolutionary migration of an existing system to a future object-oriented implementation. This implies the need for techniques that will let us reuse components of existing functionally decomposed systems or even entire packages within our new or evolving object-oriented systems. To this issue we now turn.

4.4.4   Reusing existing software components and packages

So far, we have considered the wrapper technique from the point of view of migration. Now we must consider also the problem of reusing existing components when there is no explicit need or intention to re-implement them in an object-oriented style. Dietrich *et alia*'s (1989) work showed in principle how the reuse of highly optimized algorithms or specialized functions could be accomplished using the object wrapper strategy. This can be done by defining application level classes whose methods call subroutines in the old system. The legacy systems can be wrapped in groups or as individual packages, with the latter option offering greater potential for reuse. The more recent efforts of ERP vendors to 'componentize' their offerings reduces the amount of work needed to create wrappers greatly but requires that users upgrade to the latest versions.

There is also a need to build on existing 'package' solutions. Once again a wrapper that calls package subroutines or simulates dialogue at a terminal can be built. The alternative is to modify the packages to export data for manipulation by the new system, but this fails to reuse existing functional components of the old one.

Also, some package vendors may not be prepared to support or even countenance such changes.

Some problems which must be solved in building such a wrapper are identified by Dietrich as follows.

- The designer is not free to choose the best representations for the problem in terms of objects since this is already largely decided within the old system. Here again there is a possibility that the wrappers will represent very coarse-grain objects with limited opportunities for reuse.
- The designer must either expose the old system's functions and interface to the user or protect him from possible changes to the old system. It is very difficult to do both successfully. Generally, one should only allow read accesses to the old system, which tends to preclude the take-over data management strategy.
- Where the old system continues to maintain data, the wrapper must preserve the state of these data when it calls internal routines. This militates against the translation strategy.
- Garbage collection and memory management and compactification (where applicable) must be synchronized between the wrapper and the old system.
- Cross-system invariants, which relate the old and new data sets, must be maintained.
- Building a wrapper often requires very detailed understanding of the old system. This is even more true when migrating but still a significant problem when reusing.

Because access to the internals of package software is seldom available at the required level of detail, the wrapper approach described above will not usually work. A better approach is to regard the package as a fixed object offering definite services, possibly in a distributed environment.

Whereas data-centred translation is the best approach to migration and replacement of existing systems – while borrowing strategies fail to work – where reuse is the main concern, borrowing is a perfectly viable approach. If the existing system or package largely works, for the functions it provides, and can be maintained at an acceptable level of cost (however large that may be), then when new functions are required it may be possible to build them quite separately using an object-oriented approach and communicate with the old system through a wrapper. This wrapper is used to call the services of the old system and give access to its database. New functions are defined as the methods of objects that encapsulate the data they need, insofar as they are new data. When data stored by the old system are required, a message must be sent to the wrapper and the appropriate retrieval routines called; borrowing the needed data. Updates to the existing database are treated similarly – by lending as it were.

It may well turn out that, in the fullness of time, the new object-oriented system will gradually acquire features that replace and duplicate parts of the old system. Data-centred translation then becomes necessary instead of borrowing for the affected parts of the system. Therefore the step-by-step strategy recommended in the last section is indicated for many commercial systems projects.

We may summarize the conclusions of this section so far in Figure 4.10. In this table a 'Y' indicates that a wrapper data strategy may be worth considering for a particular class of problem but not that it is guaranteed to work. An 'N' indicates that it probably will not be suitable. A '?' means: 'It all depends.' The four strategies defined in Section 4.3.2 are compared with four possible reasons for building wrappers: migrating a complex legacy system to a new object-oriented implementation; reusing its components without changing the core system; extending its functionality without changing the core; and building a possibly distributed front-end to provide additional functions. Note that the last three purposes are very similar and the last two have identical Y/N patterns.

	Purpose			
Strategy	*Migration*	*Reuse*	*Extension*	*Front-end*
Handshake	N	N	N	N
Borrowing	N	Y	Y	Y
Take-over	?	N	N	N
Translation	?	N	Y	Y
Data-centred translation	Y	N	Y	Y

Figure 4.10 Suitability of migration strategies for different purposes.

4.4.5 Using object-oriented analysis as a springboard

The burgeoning of interest in object technology in the 1990s led to the widespread use of object-oriented programming languages for software development. With this growth came a realization that structured methods not only failed to support such developments but actually impeded them in many cases. Typical applications where this applies are GUI development, distributed computing, e-commerce and use of object-oriented and object-relational databases. The need for a disciplined approach to such developments led to the development of methods for object-oriented analysis. Another area where there is a need for methods is expert system development, and here object-oriented approaches were strongly indicated by the presence of inheritance structures in frame-based expert systems.

In the case of interoperation between object-oriented and conventional system components we have already seen that it is often necessary to reverse engineer an older system in order to find a description of it in terms of coherent entities. Some technique of object-oriented analysis is clearly required for this, especially if migration to OT is contemplated. Thus, I am suggesting that object-oriented analysis can be used as a fast path to the object-oriented future in the face of interoperability problems and still evolving language technology.

THREE SOURCES OF OBJECTS

There are three distinct ways in which the concept of objects has entered computer science. The programming language community developed the object-oriented perspective from its own concerns with simulation, user interface development and so on. Database theorists in need of abstract models to help model data introduced various semantic data modelling techniques, the best known being that of Chen – the Entity Relationship (ER) model (Chen, 1976). These models dealt with abstract objects and inheritance but focused on the data aspects of entities, ignoring the procedures which entities might be able to perform. The artificial intelligence community went a step further with their concept of frames and allowed entities to have procedures attached to attributes that can be used to search for missing values and cause side effects, but frames are static data structures and offer no specific facilities for specifying the behaviour of entities declaratively. These procedures are often external though linked to the frames and not encapsulated as such. Further, frames are closer in spirit to prototypes than objects. This means that there are no definitional classes with instances that inherit all their features, merely instances that are more or less prototypical of some concept. The solution is to allow classes to be treated as prototype definitions; that is, the instances may not have all of the features of the class as in object-oriented programming. In this way a three-legged, alcoholic dog can be an instance of dogs, which have four legs and drink water from choice. Languages such as SELF (Ungar and Smith, 1987) are based on prototypes rather than classes. Incidentally, this means that if object-oriented analysis techniques are to be truly language independent they must allow the modelling of prototypes by allowing overriding at the instance level. If we permit such relaxations, the object technology movement offers the richest set of means to overcome the obstacles of the semantic data modeller, the knowledge-based systems builder and the programmer alike. Let us take a brief look at each of these perspectives.

SEMANTIC DATA MODELLING

This perspective derived from practical database applications as well as from research efforts. It is at the root of the client-server metaphor and of database triggers and server-embedded business rules. Semantic data modellers use rules and inheritance structures extensively but have not been greatly concerned with the issue of encapsulation. There has been considerable cross-fertilization between this field and object technology. See for example (Gray *et al.*, 1992). The semantic data modelling perspective is concerned only with data and is largely encompassed by the other two.

OOP

The techniques of object-orientation are mainly derived from work on the programming language Smalltalk and its environment, developed at Xerox PARC during the 1970s. There are now many object-oriented languages, including C++, Eiffel and Java. Their developers had various programming-theoretical concerns such as speed, correctness, type safety and denotational expressiveness. As explained in Chapter 1, in the object-oriented style an 'object' is an entity with three features: *unique identity*; *encapsulation* of attributes and methods; and *inheritance*.

Encapsulation means that objects (either classes or their instances) consist of an interface of attributes and methods together with a hidden implementation of their data structures and processes. As we have seen, the key benefits of this approach are that objects are inherently units of reusable code and that systems built from them are extensible using inheritance to add new or exceptional features to a system.

AI

A frame, on the other hand, is usually described as having a set of attributes which themselves can be attached to procedures although these procedures are not usually stored with the object as in object-oriented programming. Interestingly, this is also the approach taken in most object-oriented databases. The difference between frames and objects is the lack of emphasis in the former on the encapsulation of the data and procedures together, hidden behind an interface. Secondly, in AI, the procedures may be regarded as non-procedural rulesets instead of procedural code. Another difference between object-oriented and AI approaches is that AI work has provided very rich methods for dealing with inheritance compared to object technology (OT). Nevertheless, the similarities outweigh the differences, and someone wishing to take advantage of the benefits of object-orientation (i.e. reuse and extensibility) might as well proceed using a Nexpert as a Smalltalk. The advantages are the richer inheritance features and the ability to express relationships as rulesets. The disadvantages are that the level of encapsulation (and thus reuse) is lower and, for some applications such as GUI development or CASE tool construction, existing class libraries or database managers may make the pure object-oriented approach more productive.

4.4.6 Object-oriented analysis and knowledge-based prototyping

Any decent object-oriented analysis approach should be language independent. The disadvantage is that the specification cannot be tested and that the system cannot be delivered and used. The answer to both problems is prototyping. A prototype can be used to agree the specification with users and can even be implemented incrementally, pending a final rewrite in the object-oriented language of choice should performance or some other factor make this desirable. However, what we build as a model in the prototyping language needs to be *reversible* in the sense that it is possible to discover the intentions of the analysts and designers by examining the code. This should also be true of the paper analysis itself, leading to a requirement for a semantically rich analysis language and a readable, declarative, prototyping one.

The two areas of IT where such tools have become available are expert systems and advanced databases; themselves under the influence, it has to be said, of artificial intelligence. Expert systems offer declarative, semantically rich programming languages. Advanced databases allow business rules to be coded as production rules and database triggers. So far, only Illustra and the semantic databases offer anything like this. Even object-oriented databases fall short in this respect. It seems that this situation will change and the database community are certainly aware of the problem. Furthermore, several database workers now accept that business rules should be attached to the entities or objects of the data model. As Andleigh and Gretzinger (1992) put it: 'Clear documentation of the business rules *and which objects each rule is associated with* ensures that the application of the rules is perceived clearly and is well understood by the user before the coding of the rules' (my emphasis).

We may conclude that knowledge-based systems and advanced database products, or perhaps both in concert, can help build reversible prototypes. However, this is best done in conjunction with a machine-independent analysis exercise using a semantically rich and therefore reversible notation.

This was confirmed within my personal experience by the ARIES expert systems project (Butler and Chamberlain, 1988) where we built systems on a workstation with the conscious intention of transporting them to PCs at a later date. At every stage, including prototyping, implementation-independent representations or, more succinctly, paper models were built. Porting then became very easy indeed because we ported not the code but the paper model; the paper model was reversible because it was written in the expressive language of knowledge engineers and not the irreversible products of software engineering.

As expert systems software has advanced and moved closer to object-orientation I have come to regard knowledge-based systems as first-rate prototyping tools in their own right. This is mainly because of their excellent and expressive inheritance features. We are quite happy to see this removed at implementation time to enhance reusability, but for analysis inheritance is indispensable. Knowledge-based systems are also inherently reversible because they express knowledge as rules and objects and not in procedural code or obscure diagrammatic conventions. The use of such an approach to specification and prototyping requires a matching analysis notation and approach so that the expert system prototype can be reversed into a reversible, object-oriented paper model or CASE tool.

One important issue for practitioners is to find analysis and design methods that support the rich features available in existing systems. Another question is: how are we to make immediate use of available technology? One answer is to utilize knowledge-based systems as prototyping tools, basing these developments on a semantically rich analysis and design technique. For the time being we may have to compromise at the implementation stage for performance reasons or even implement in COBOL, but since most of the investment in system building is not implementation, this approach is not only viable but an investment in the future.

4.4.7 Object technology as a migration strategy in itself

Up to now I have been arguing, perhaps rather circuitously, that the key to migration to object technology (OT) lies in the approach taken to analysis and design. We shall be returning to this issue. However, I now want to turn the issue on its head and argue that OT is not an end in itself any more than systems analysis is. The real issues for modern business are how to be both more flexible and more productive and simultaneously to cut costs. This involves many technical and cultural changes and is a hard thing to do right. However, my recent observations lead me to the conclusion that OT itself, together with clear vision and positive leadership, is the answer to this particular corporate maiden's prayer.

We analyse systems to help build them. We computerize businesses to help run them better. Good analysis should lead to better systems. Good systems ought to lead to better businesses. What then is a good system? This of course is highly arguable, but I think few these days can resist the view that good systems are those that are *inter alia* cost-effective, open, flexible, robust, usable and maintainable. How can object technology contribute to these aims? Cost-effectiveness, of course, will be enhanced by reuse and flexibility and maintainability by the use of inheritance and pluggable interfaces; but the other issues are not so directly related to programming with objects. Usable systems are generally regarded these days as having a graphical interface. Of course, it is still possible to build a totally unusable graphical user interface. Perhaps the most important features of all for modern businesses are the costs of operating the computing infrastructure and the costs associated with change in this area. Here the great hope for some time has been distributed computing. Thus, most modern companies would like to move as many applications as possible to such platforms. Unfortunately there are some pretty big difficulties facing them. Their staffs have the wrong training. Distributed computing is far more complex. Few people know the principles of user interface design well enough to produce consistently usable GUIs. And then there is reuse... Even experts in object technology argue about how it can be achieved and managed successfully.

The object-oriented metaphor is capable of describing the distributed nature of systems in a very natural way since message passing is central to both. Furthermore, the fact that object technology offers a way of managing complexity through encapsulation and inheritance means that it at least becomes possible to think about very complex distributed architectures.

Object-oriented tools for GUI development both make it easier and impose a style and consistency that itself contributes to usability. They enhance productivity enormously and can be used to impose standards for user interface design and promote reuse in this area. Similarly, object-oriented tools for expert system construction are beginning to be common, capitalizing on inheritance schemes to reduce the complexity of rule-bases and thus deliver friendlier, more natural dialogues between people and their applications.

It has become clear that experienced COBOL or RPG programmers *can* learn the object-oriented approach and several companies have proved this in practice.

The problems that remain are largely methodological and organizational. Good object-oriented systems analysis is still the key to the methodological aspects in my view. The real nightmare is the organizational issue.

All change management exercises are fraught with peril and the move to object technology is no exception. People often resist change merely because they doubt the benefits will actually accrue to them or their organizations. As Machiavelli

(1961) put it: 'there is nothing more difficult to arrange, more doubtful of success, and more dangerous to carry through than initiating changes'. Those who prospered under the old order and stand to lose will oppose you vigorously, he says, while those who might gain will only provide lukewarm support. The potential gainers are 'generally incredulous, never really trusting new things unless they have tested them by experience'. To win them over, one must demonstrate success early on. Furthermore, one must be sure of not backing the wrong horse. This is the danger of the silver bullet. I wonder how many hours of people's lives have been wasted backing a good technical solution that never survived commercially: the Xerox Sigma, APL, CP/M 86 and perhaps now even the Mac. I worked once in an IT organization that traversed the road to open distributed systems successfully. We achieved this by a positive turn to object technology, by strong leadership and clear vision and by hedging our bets on technology. I do not intend to write a history of that organization's experience. That would take too long and be too specific to be of general use. What I can offer is a distillation of advice.

There is no point in dithering. The aim of the migration strategy should be clearly stated in the form of a mission statement. It has to come from the top. People will accept it or vote with their feet in that case. One might announce that the mainframes are to be replaced within two years or that productivity will be doubled in three; ambitious targets which may not be fully met but which provide direction. These aims should be related to technology so that one might argue that reuse, using objects, is the basis for productivity growth. Next one must select some technology. It is doubtful that one can be sure, in a new field, of what will survive or what will work. Therefore, rather than choosing just one language or one OOA/D method one should choose two or three, giving project managers some leeway to optimize their own performance. Typically the language choice should encompass different programming styles; so that a selection of C++ and Ada would be quite wrong. Different types of project can now be run with what appears to be the most suitable language and lessons learnt by the organization. Similarly, one may give project managers the authority to select from a short-list of object-oriented design methods. The analysis method, however, should not be treated in this way for, if it is, the reuse programme may be endangered. What is required is a sound method that imposes a definite life cycle and guides requirements capture, systems analysis and logical design. In this way, objects can be captured and placed in a repository from the earliest stages of a project. If the method is language independent these objects can be reused regardless of the language used. Think of the dismay that might be caused if a switch of language meant that the reuse library had to be ditched or even substantially redesigned. For those who would answer that wise companies must choose the industry standard UML notation (see Chapter 6) I would agree but remind them that a notation is *not* a method.

The development staff are critical too. The main choice that most organizations will face is that between traditional developers with many years in the business and great experience and newcomers with skills in OT and modern methods. In fact, neither type will do. The newcomers must be used to educate the oldsters and provide mentoring. Obversely, the young Turks must diligently learn about the nature of the business from their predecessors. It is a process that requires a deep and lasting trust between the two groups and establishing such trust is a key management task. Reward schemes that encourage both co-operation among workers and the reuse of other people's objects need to be devised.

Finally, the sponsors of computer developments must be rewarded too. The obvious rewards that can be aimed for are lower costs through reuse and shorter times to market. The quality of the product is thereby enhanced as well. Inheritance means that maintenance cost can be reduced and systems changed more easily in response to business change. Reuse successes lead to funding but are hard to achieve. Most developers expect to get reuse at the code level but this is very difficult to manage and often takes place informally. I believe that a reuse programme should start at the specification level.

4.5   Summary

Object technology makes the sharing by different systems possible. This chapter emphasized the rôle of object-oriented models as a way of describing and understanding distributed systems.

The operating systems of distributed systems can be *distributed* or *networked*. There are three data management strategies for distributed computing: centralized, replicated and partitioned. We examined several kinds of distributed computer architecture: client-server, multi-client/multi-server and peer-to-peer. We distinguished four distribution models: database server, transaction server, peer-to-peer and distributed front-end. The peer-to-peer model is the most general but the most difficult to program and manage. Latency is an important concept in the design of any object-oriented system, distributed or not.

Existing structured methods contribute little and impede progress with distributed systems. Object technology provides a natural way of modelling distributed applications. Network nodes can be regarded as abstract data types or objects. However, inheritance and composition links shouldn't cross the network. Associations that span the network should be minimized for reasons of efficiency. Typically, a system layer should be implemented at a single node. The object-oriented model both assumes and implies locational transparency.

Client-server computing was defined as the division of processing and data between one or more front-end client machines that run applications and a single back-end server machine that provides a service to each client. Client-server computing is a special case of distributed computing. Object-oriented systems are nothing other than, possibly layered, multi-client/multi-server or peer-to-peer systems. N-tier models are more flexible than their two-tier antecedents. RPCs violate locational transparency but this is sometimes hidden from the user by clever network software. Co-operative processing is a special case of distributed computing that offers peer-to-peer communication between servers.

Database tools are often organized around the client-server metaphor. With relational systems, the ones that make use of stored procedures are able to reduce network traffic considerably. The difficulty is that encapsulation is not enforced and the discipline of a robust approach to object-oriented analysis is required. Object-oriented systems give these benefits automatically.

ORBs and other kinds of middleware remove much of the need for complex RPCs. Applications need not be written in an object-oriented manner since the ORB effectively provides a wrapper. ORBs bring the benefits of OT to the world of systems integration. XML is needed to define the meaning of the data included in messages, but is not enough on its own to ensure that disparate systems work well together; for that a common business model is needed too.

The key technical features in this environment are distribution, connectivity and flexibility. These factors have led away from the waterfall–structured–mainframe mind-set to a rapid development, evolutionary, downsized culture. Advanced, object-oriented programming environments are essential to exploit prototyping and describe the parallel, distributed, message-based world. Object-oriented analysis and design approaches are needed. Without sound object-oriented analysis and a project management culture that accepts its implications the distributed solution will soon become even more cumbersome to manage than the mainframes it replaced.

We examined various strategies for organizations facing migration and interoperation problems, emphasizing the concerns of a developer who wants to develop an object-oriented application that needs to use the services provided by applications that incorporate other programming styles. It covered techniques such as object wrappers, object highways and blackboard systems and discussed how to wrap an application that exists in a large number of different versions.

The biggest cost associated with 'legacy' systems is maintenance. However much we would like to replace these old systems completely, the economics of the matter forbids it on any large scale. We must build on the existing investment and move gradually to object technology.

The first strategy recommended was to build object *wrappers*. Building object wrappers helps protect investments in older systems during the move to object-oriented programming. An object wrapper enables a new, object-oriented part of a system to interact with a conventional chunk by message passing. This may represent a substantial investment, but once it is in place virtually all maintenance activity may cease.

Implementing wrappers is not as easy as it sounds in several respects. One issue is granularity. Small objects are usually more reusable than large ones. With legacy systems we are often faced with irreducibly large-grain 'objects' present in the design. Object request brokers are specifically aimed at dealing with this kind of coarse-grain reuse.

The wrapper approach to migration is not the only one available. Other options include the use of object request brokers, object-oriented databases and proceeding in a completely *ad hoc* manner.

One of the biggest problems with the concept of object wrappers concerns data management. Using the wrapper is easy until you need to split the storage of data across the old database and some of the new objects. Four possible strategies for dealing with these problems were defined as follows. The **handshake strategy** involves carrying a duplicate, live copy of the common data in both parts of the system and keeping both copies up to date. It only works well when there is little or no overlap between the data of the old and new systems. The **borrowing strategy** keeps all data in the old system and copies them to the new objects as required. The **take-over strategy** involves copying the data to the new objects and allowing the old system's data to go out of date. There may be integrity problems, and the wrapper may have to send messages as well as receive and respond to them – which greatly increases its complexity. The **translation strategy** carves out coherent chunks of the database together with related functions. This requires a sound method of object-oriented analysis capable of describing the old system as well as the new. It seems the most promising approach to migration on balance. A refinement of this strategy is to reverse engineer a data model from the existing system and to identify all file access operations in relation to this model. These calls can then be replaced as new objects are constructed around the entities. This version of translation is the **data-centred translation** strategy. These strategies may be variously appropriate according to whether we are migrating the system to an object-oriented implementation, reusing its components, extending it or building a better or a distributed front-end.

When the old system exists and is maintained in multiple versions, the wrapper approach will only work if there is a core system common to all the versions. Use a phased approach that builds a wrapper to communicate with new object-oriented components using (most probably) the borrowing strategy. Perform an object-oriented analysis on the old system. Use translation or data-centred translation to migrate.

Having decided to build a wrapper and a new front-end one needs tools for building them. There are no specific products offering wrapper technology for migration at present but there are a number of ORB and GUI tools that may help with reuse. Rather than build a wrapper for each old system it is sometimes better to wrap the communication system in some way. One approach to this problem is to use an object request broker. Many windowing environments now include good, usable GUI class libraries and facilities for developing object wrappers, so that existing, conventional UI code can be utilized. Sometimes the main tool can be the object-oriented analysis approach itself but good CASE tools are then required.

The wrapper technique can be used for migration or for reusing existing components when there is no explicit intention to re-implement them in an object-oriented style. Some problems that must be solved in building such a wrapper were listed. Figure 4.10 summarized the applicability of the four strategies to four migration problems.

We saw that object-oriented analysis could be the main springboard for a company's migration strategy and that object technology was itself a migration strategy. The problems that remain are largely methodological and organizational.

All change management exercises are fraught with peril and the move to object technology is no exception. Management style and the quality of the development staff are critical. Most developers expect to get reuse at the code level but this is very difficult to manage and often takes place informally. A reuse programme should start at the specification level.

🖵 4.6   Bibliographical notes

Mullender (1989) gives an advanced, comprehensive – but slightly dated now – introduction to most of the issues of distributed system development. Daniels and Cook (1993) offer a penetrating discussion of the issues surrounding the sharing of persistent objects together with useful comments on locking strategies and other important related issues.

Andleigh and Gretzinger (1992) provide much useful background information on software engineering, databases and distributed processing. The method is applied in some detail to the design of a distributed financial trading system. Bapat (1994) offers a comprehensive discussion of how to apply object-oriented design to modelling computer networks. Comer (1999) discusses distributed computing at a more technical level, including issues such as network protocols and how RPCs work.

(Agha *et al.*, 1993) is a collection of papers discussing many of the difficult issues related to concurrency in object-oriented systems and the tension between the two areas of research. The September 1993 edition of the *Communications of the ACM* is devoted to concurrent object-oriented programming and contains several important papers. Meyer (1997) also discusses a simple concurrency model in the context of the Eiffel language.

Mowbray and Zahavi (1995) and Otte *et al.* (1996) provide good introductory, though somewhat outdated, treatments of CORBA. Design patterns for CORBA are discussed by Mowbray and Malaveau (1997). The best source of up-to-date information remains the OMG web site (www.omg.org). Hollowell (1993) describes the OMA model in an introductory fashion; the original reference being (Soley, 1990).

Szyperski (1998) provides an excellent survey and critique of component technology as it was in the late 1990s and includes a detailed technical description and comparison of CORBA and COM.

Goldfarb and Prescod (1998) provide a gentle introduction to XML and include many application and product descriptions. There are innumerable other books on

XML and there is a wealth of information on the web. (Bradley, 2000) is a knowledgable introduction to XSL.

Dietrich *et alia*'s (1989) paper is the original source on object wrappers and is well complemented by the analyses of Reiss (1991) and Grass (1991). Some of the panels in the OOPSLA proceedings (Meyrowitz, 1989; 1990) contain useful insights.

4.7   Exercises

1. Discuss the differences and similarities between client-server and object-oriented architectures.

2. Discuss the benefits of centralized *versus* distributed computing and outline the pitfalls of each.

3. What is latency? How does it apply to: (a) network design; (b) architectural design?

4. Define 'middleware'. Give example of different types of products and their uses.

5. Why is locational transparency important?

6. Describe the OMA.

7. What is the difference between CORBA and MOM?

8. Describe a CORBA product in detail.

9. What is the name given to the OMG standard for inter-object communication?
    a) Object Services Architecture
    b) Common Object Request Broker Architecture
    c) Object Interface Definition Standard
    d) None of the above

10. Define the terms: stub, skeleton, proxy, IDL and marshalling.

11. Discuss and contrast the use of XML in e-commerce and one other area such as publishing.

12. Why is having XML and middleware not enough to ensure successful Enterprise Application Integration? Discuss the problems to be expected on a typical EAI project.

13. Enumerate the advantages of XML in contrast with other approaches to EAI.

14. What does the S in XSL stand for?

15. Which concept is said to help with migration to object technology but safeguards investment in existing code?
    a) Coupling   d) Cohesion
    b) Object wrapper   e) Polymorphism
    c) Overloading

16. What is an object wrapper? How could one be implemented?

17. *'Object wrappers are pure idealism. The idea will never work in practice.'* Discuss.

5

Database technology

I have a cat named Trash ... If I were trying to sell him (at least to a computer scientist), I would not stress that he is gentle to humans and is self-sufficient, living mostly on field mice. Rather, I would argue that he is object-oriented.

Roger King (*My Cat is Object-Oriented*)

These days, if you want to sell a software product, you tell the world that it is object or perhaps component oriented. Once upon a time you had to say that it was relational. In this chapter we look at this shift of emphasis, or fashion as the more cynical might put it, and review relational and object-oriented database technology.

The relational database was not inflicted on the commercial world without justification. I was one of the people in the late 1970s and early 1980s who proselytized on behalf of the relational gospel. In the first part of this chapter we will look at the positive reasons for the emergence of the relational approach but also at some of its defects. We will then examine how object-oriented databases address many of these. To make this discussion possible we first have to understand something of the nature and history of databases and data modelling.

All database systems are distinguished from other programs by their ability to manage persistent data and to access very large quantities of these data efficiently and safely. Other common features of database systems, identified by Ullman (1989), include:

- support for an abstract data model;
- support for high level access or query languages;
- support for transaction management in a multi-user environment;
- support for controls on access and data ownership;
- support for data validation and consistency checking;
- support for consistent data recovery from system and hardware failures, which minimizes loss of data.

We will examine only the first two of these issues, and not delve into the remainder which are the proper province of texts on database systems *per se*. Some appropriate references are given in the bibliographical notes at the end of this chapter.

⊟ 5.1 A potted history of data models

If we can skip over that period in computing when we still programmed with plug boards, the beginning of data storage was the sequential file. One read through the file from the beginning until the required datum was matched and then rewound the tape in readiness for the next access. As more sophisticated storage devices such as drums and disks emerged, programming languages were extended to include statements enabling direct access – sometimes called, for some incomprehensible reason, 'random access'. This soon led to the realization that access speeds could be improved by hashing or storing index files.

The existence of indexed files made it possible to conceptualize a structural relationship among these files that would capture some of the structure of the real world or of the application. Since class membership is such an obvious and ubiquitous structural component of the world, the first database products imposed a hierarchical structure among their files. In business systems, this often came about in the form of 'occurrences' of a type; e.g. a company with several addresses. Hierarchical databases such as IMS were both popular and efficient. However, many business relationships did not fit into neat hierarchies and more general networks often emerged from the investigations of systems analysts. This led to the development of network databases exemplified by products such as TOTAL and IDMS and enshrined in the standards of the CODASYL committee. Network systems were nearly as popular and nearly as efficient as their hierarchical forebears. Both types of system, however, depended on fixed pointers and were very difficult to change or extend in response to business reorganization. All these products developed in response to practical requirements and without the benefit of a formal theory; there was no explicitly worked out 'network data model' or 'hierarchical data model'. In this respect object-oriented programming seems to be recapitulating the history of databases as an *ad hoc* technique lacking a formal theory.

The next development was the introduction of the first formal data model, Ted Codd's relational model of data (Codd, 1976). It was based on the first order predicate calculus (FOPC) and, equipped with this theoretical basis, it supported a relationally complete, non-procedural enquiry language. The *de facto* standard now established for data definition and data manipulation, SQL, is loosely based on the relational calculus (one of the possible non-procedural languages). The highly redundant syntax of SQL owes as much to IBM's early language GIS as to the relational calculus, but its great benefit as a standard for enquiry, update and, indeed, communication between databases is well established. This great advantage is supplemented by the flexibility of the relational model and database management systems based upon it. Attributes can be added or removed without the need to reconstruct complex pointer systems, and relational databases make it possible to redefine business systems and organizational structures to better achieve competitive edge in an increasingly international, competitive and complex market.

It was soon realized that the relational model was not the only possible formal data model, and that other models might have certain advantages.

In general terms, a data model is a mathematical formalism consisting of a notation for describing data and data structures (information) and a set of valid operations which are used to manipulate those data, or at least the tokens representing them. The functional model of Shipman (1981) is one of the most successful in theoretical terms, while Chen's Entity-Relational model is one of the most widely used commercially although it lacks a coherent theory about the operations on data. The ideas of the functional model are closely related to ideas of semantic networks in AI and to functional programming. The underlying logic, thus, is closer to the Church-Curry lambda-calculus than to first order predicate calculus. Languages exist which exploit this model; Daplex and Adaplex. In Daplex two entities with the same component values can still be distinguished by having distinct references; they have 'object identity'. This cannot be accomplished in the standard relational model and extensions to the latter have been suggested by Codd and others which introduce unique identifiers for tuples so that an expression can denote a unique object which exists separately from its components. This is related to the idea of 'call by reference' in programming languages, as opposed to 'call by value'.

As with Lisp, the functional approach removes the distinction between data and function (or program) and permits abstract data typing; that is, types are defined implicitly by the operations used. For example, the type List could be defined by the operations CAR, CDR and CONS. New types can be generated by generalization (IsA or AKO) and aggregation, so that entities can be defined and arranged in hierarchies or networks. The functional model thus holds the promise of new developments, especially with the advent of parallel and dataflow hardware architectures when the overhead of non-destructive assignment can be regarded as less important.

Various extended relational models, starting with Chen's Entity-Relationship (ER) model, have been proposed to overcome shortcomings in the relational model. The chief among these shortcomings, in my opinion, was the difficulty of capturing business semantics in relational implementations. It is increasingly realized that semantic models have to attempt to capture functional as well as data semantics. Other suggestions for data models include the binary relational model, where all relations have only two attributes, and Codd's own RM/T (for details of both these models see (Date, 1983)). These were all attempts to deal with widely recognized deficiencies in the relational model. For a long time entity-relationship models were treated as purely analysis and design tools. As we will see, recently there have been several attempts to construct complete DBMSs based on the ER model or even some deductive model capable of incorporating functional semantics (business rules) in the code. For example, the abstract Fact machine, which was based on an extension of the binary relational model, was implemented in the Generis product discussed in Section 5.3 below.

The development of formal data models both led to and was encouraged by the commercial development of relational database management systems (RDBMS). Today nearly all database systems that are not performance critical are being developed as relational systems. Where efficiency is important and the scale is large, as with modern airline reservation systems, the hierarchical and network systems persist alongside new object-oriented database management systems (OODBMS).

There has been a detectable tendency to promote a *post facto* rationalization of the CODASYL work, as though there were a hierarchical or network data model. The functional model turns out to map very well onto the network databases and provides just such a rationalization. It so happens that IsA links and functions correspond closely to the owner-member links and 'sets' of a CODASYL database.

Current interest has now turned to object-oriented database systems and models. Ullman (1989) defines a preliminary object-oriented data model also capable of representing the hierarchical and network databases. Before turning to these later in this chapter, let us examine the relational model and its predecessors in more detail.

5.1.1 Weaknesses of early databases

The early hierarchical and network databases suffered mainly from their inflexibility. In the hierarchical model only certain kinds of structural relationships were expressible; to wit, single inheritance or subtyping. The network systems allowed more general graphs to be constructed, but still it was very hard to change these relationships once the system had been designed. Adding or removing an attribute also often involved a major redesign exercise. In this section we introduce a part of database theory and look briefly at the style of these early approaches.

The simplest non-primitive data structure we can consider is a list, followed closely by lists of lists and the kind of tree-structured lists found in languages like Lisp. Anyone who has written a computer program will have opened a file or stream of data and read through it, record by record, until some condition was satisfied. This is just like looking down a list, or list of lists if the file stores more than one kind of symbol. For example, consider a computerized telephone directory that stores name, address and telephone number for some defined population. If you have the name and address, it is then easy to look up the number. Not so if you have the number and address and want the name. This is because lists or files have logical structure; the structure of being sorted in a particular order. To facilitate our task we would have to read the file in a different order. The telephone book is a list of lists that can be viewed as a table. The situation can be more complicated in that lists of lists of lists, and so on, can arise. For example, our reverse phone book might have the structure shown in Figure 5.1.

There are three extensions in the PR department of ABC Ltd, so we have to include a 'repeating group' consisting of a list of extensions and contact names. A little thought will show that this arrangement has the logical structure of a tree or hierarchy. The use of repeating groups in early databases derived from the restriction to sequential storage devices, such as tape, in early computers.

Phone_No	Company	Dept	No_Of_Exts	Extension	Contact
999-8888	Aardvark	Sales	1	102	S.Jones
777-1234	ABC Ltd	PR	3	110	J.Doe
				111	A.N.Other
				133	E. Codd
123-4567	Blue Inc	Mkting	1	2001	P.C.Plodd

Figure 5.1 A file with a repeating group.

FILE 1

Phone_No	Company	Dept	Dept_Code
999-8888	Aardvark	Sales	17
777-1234	ABC Ltd	PR	23
123-4567	Blue Inc	Mktg	24

FILE 2

Dept_Code	Exten-sion	Contact
17	102	S.Jones
23	110	J.Doe
23	111	A.N.Other
23	133	E.Codd
24	2001	P.C.Plodd

Figure 5.2 Decomposition to eliminate repeating groups.

The next level of complexity occurs when we have more than one file. Given direct access technology, in the above example we do not need to keep the repeating groups in the same file. We can, instead, arrange for the company file records to contain merely logical pointers to the extensions file. The structure is now something like that shown in Figure 5.2.

There are two files with a common field to link them. Logically, this link could be represented differently. It is logically a one-to-many relationship between departments and extensions. An extension cannot be in two departments in this scheme of things, which shows up one major limitation of the hierarchical approach to data structure: the difficulty of dealing with general, many-to-many relationships. More complex hierarchies may easily be envisaged.

The astute reader will detect that I have oversimplified in this example, in that two companies may possess the same department code. The key in the second file should, strictly speaking, be interpreted as a company-department code. However, the idea should still be clear despite this slight abuse of language.

To get a feel for the complexity of the network model, let us suppose that our SACIS database is to contain the information about particular stock items and their suppliers contained in Figure 5.3. The relationship represented is stated as 'for every part there may be many suppliers and for every supplier there may be many parts'. Item i4 has no current supplier. The * indicates the 'many' end of links. The detailed network is shown in the diagram in Figure 5.4.

INo	IName	Description
i1	Marble	½" glass

*

SNo	SName	Location	Price
s1	ABC	London	.30
s2	Aardvark	Paris	.30

INo	IName	Description	
i2	Bat	Willow	

*

SNo	SName	Location	Price
s1	ABC	London	20
s2	Aardvark	Paris	40
s3	Blue	New York	20

INo	IName	Description
i3	Kite	2 string

*

SNo	SNAME	LOCATION	PRICE
s1	ABC	London	40

Ino	IName	Description
i4	Ball	Rubber

Figure 5.3 Data representing the supplied-by relationship.

Notice the ring structure of the links and that there are two ways to retrieve the answer to the query 'Find the description of part i2 made by s2'; either start with the company and look along the pointers for a connector linked to the part, or start with the part and look for the company. It is completely non-trivial to decide which is the most efficient strategy.

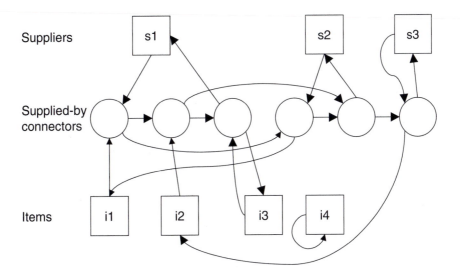

Figure 5.4 Network pointer structure for the supplied-by relationship of Figure 5.3.

Most people seeing a diagram such as that in Figure 5.4 for the first time would surely agree that it looks a frightful mess. The maintenance costs associated with practical network databases seem to bear this view out. However, access via pointers is very efficient.

Relational databases overcome some of the limitations of hierarchical and network systems in terms of flexibility, as we shall see now.

5.1.2 The relational model and how it helps

Due to the commercial importance and theoretical basis of the relational model we must briefly review its main ideas.

The relational model of data was motivated by several aims. Among them were the desire to use formal methods in database design, enquiry and update; the desire to be able to prove the correctness of programs based on non-procedural descriptions; and the urge to meet Occam's razor: that a theory should be as simple as possible while retaining its expressive power. The basic idea is that data are represented as a series of tables or 'flat files'. No repeating groups or implicit hierarchies are to be allowed, and no fixed structural links are to be a part of the database. Logical relationships between the data are constructed at run time or are held in tables themselves. Thus the same type of object is used to represent both entities and relationships. Also these 'cross-reference' tables can be rebuilt without the need to reorganize the basic data. This is a great advantage in databases which model enterprises subject to much organizational change. It is amazing that, even today, many systems development methods still place emphasis on labelling data sets or entities as to whether they are subject to change over time. In a relational database, the assumption is that everything can, in principle, change over time unless some exogenous fiat dictates otherwise. This is typical of the extent to which the relational model has been misunderstood by its proponents as well as its enemies. The chief source of misunderstanding is the confusion between logical and physical data models. The relational model is a logical one. On the other hand there was no real, motivating hierarchical or network model in the logical sense. These are physical designs. In fact, relational database products can be implemented as network databases for efficiency. The logical relational model allows users to view one data structure in many different ways, through so-called user views, and thus one important benefit of relational databases is a higher degree of user acceptance.

HEALTH WARNING   Relational databases have been introduced fairly informally so far. This common practice has often led to misconceptions so we now turn to a slightly more precise development. The reader who already has a thorough understanding of relational theory or who, perhaps, has a broad practical understanding and an aversion to even a little mathematics, may comfortably skip to Section 5.3, or skim the remainder of this section.

Figure 5.5 (a) A 4-ary relation with its four attributes, one primary and one foreign key. Dept is a foreign key because it is the primary key of another relation representing departments.

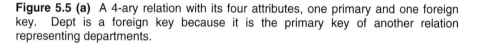

Name	DoB	Salary	Dept
R.L. Stevenson	1/1/1850	10,000	Shipping
C. Dickens	25/12/1812	4,000	Curiosities

Figure 5.5 (b) Some tuples from the Employee relation.

The relational model consists of two intrinsic and two extrinsic parts. The first of the intrinsic parts is a structural part which uses notions of *domains*, *n-ary relations*, *attributes*, *tuples* and *primary* and *foreign keys*. The second is a manipulative part whose main tools are relational algebra and/or calculus and relational assignment. The extrinsic parts include an integrity part in respect of both entities and reference. The fourth component normally considered as within the relational model, although this is not strictly the case, is the design part consisting of the theory of normal forms. We will explain some of this terminology as we go.

A **relation**, mathematically defined, is any subset of a Cartesian product of sets. Given a list of sets $A_1, \dots, A_n$, their Cartesian product is the set of all lists or bags[1] of n elements of the A_i where there can be only one element in the bag from each A_i. Such a bag is called an ordered n-tuple, or just a **tuple**. The relation is sometimes said to be **n-ary** if there are n attributes. Each A_i is called a **domain** when viewed as a set of elements from which an attribute may take its values and an **attribute** when viewed as a label for that set. An equivalent notion is that of a table, and it is this one that is most often used in the context of computers because of the strong physical analogies.

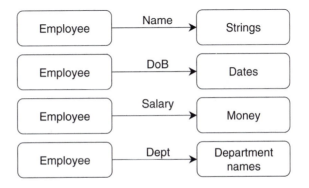

Figure 5.5 (c) The domains of the four attributes.

The next order of structure in a database concerns the relationships between relations. These, of course, are relations themselves. Chen (1976) uses the terminology 'entity-relations' and 'relationship-relations' to distinguish them. We will talk about 'links' as a shorthand; implying no connexion with the links of a CODASYL database. Both kinds of relation must conform to certain integrity constraints. Every entity must have specified at least one primary key set of attributes that uniquely identifies each tuple at any given time. Furthermore, it must be in first normal form; i.e. the attribute values cannot be complex structures (repeating groups, lists, etc.) but must be atomic data types (numbers, strings, etc.). This is no restriction for data processing applications but in list processing, text and image storage and knowledge processing we will see that extensions are going to be needed. The links have two kinds of property, multiplicity and modality. The **multiplicity** (sometimes called **cardinality**) of a link may be one-to-one or many-to-one and the **modality** may be necessary or possible. This level of structure is added

---

[1] A *bag* is a list wherein elements may be repeated, as opposed to a *set* where repetition is not permitted.

to the relational model and is not strictly a part of it. Integrity, multiplicity and modality constraints are usually coded in the application and nearly always in some exogenous procedural language. Thus we will refer to this part of the theory as *extended* relational analysis (ERA).

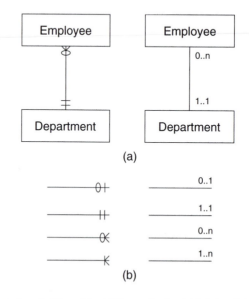

Figure 5.6 ERA notation (left) and its UML equivalent (right). **(a)** example diagrams; **(b)** the four possibilities for association cardinalities.

As Figure 5.6(b) illustrates, there are 16 possible link types connecting two entities or relations. For convenience we show the ERA notation to the left with its UML equivalent to the right. The links are interpreted directionally in such a way that the second modality/multiplicity icon pair is the one read. In the figure we read the outer symbols as multiplicity symbols and the inner ones as modality symbols. The multiplicity symbols are a crow's foot – read as 'many', a bar – read as 'one' and no symbol – read as 'zero'. The zero option is rarely used and is excluded from the 16 possibilities, otherwise there would be 36. The modality symbol for possibility is O – read as 'may be' or sometimes more barbarously 'are optionally'. The symbol for necessity is a bar, 1 – read as 'must be'. Thus, in Figure 5.6(a) we interpret the link from top to bottom by 'for every employee there must be exactly one department', and from bottom to to as ' for every department there may be many employees'. The UML equivalent uses numbers (substituting a * for n) to combine the two idea; so that '0..*' signifies: optionally one to many. The Chen ER notation, discussed later in this chapter, is very similar. Several other data analysis notations with the same semantics exist. For example, the Oracle CASE*METHOD notation

(Barker, 1990), which derives from the Bachman tradition, uses a dotted line to denote possibility.

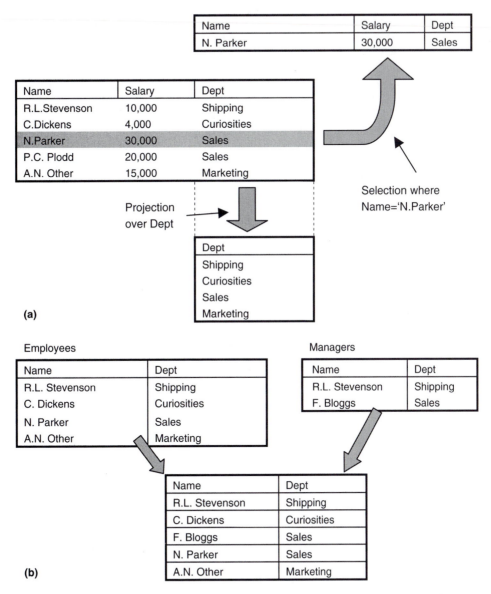

Figure 5.7 Operations of relational algebra. **(a)** selection and projection operations; **(b)** the union of two (compatible) relations.

We will also need the definition of a foreign key; that is, an attribute which is the primary key of some other relation. The integrity rules specify what happens to related relations when a table is subjected to update or deletion operations.

We now turn to the manipulative part of the model; that is, to the means by which queries and update requests can be expressed. There are essentially two methods and various hybrids of them. The two methods are known as the relational calculus and the relational algebra. A manipulation language is said to be *relationally complete* if any possible operation over the database may be prescribed within a single (and *a fortiori* non-procedural) statement of the language. This provides us with an operational definition of a relational calculus. A language permitting all feasible operations over a database to be prescribed, but in more than one statement of the language (and therefore a procedural language), is operationally defined as a relational algebra.

The first method to emerge with Codd's original paper was the relational calculus which is a retrieval and update language based on a subset of the first order predicate calculus. Later, the Berkeley QUEL language used in Ingres was based on it.

In relational calculus, retrieval is done via a tuple-variable which may take values in some given relation. An expression of the tuple calculus is defined recursively as a formula of predicate calculus formed from tuple variables, relational operators, logical operators and quantifiers. In this sense relational calculus is non-procedural. Consider the following statement of predicate calculus:

$$(\exists x,y)(t \in \text{ITEMS}) \land x = \text{INAME} \land y = \text{DESCRIPTION} \land \text{INAME} = \text{'Kite'}$$

This can be regarded as a query which should return the name and description of all items whose name is 'Kite'. Note that the tuple variable, t, is free and the bound variables, x and y, correspond to the attributes. In QUEL the syntax is

```
RANGE OF T IS ITEMS
RETRIEVE(INAME.DESCRIPTION)
WHERE INAME='Kite'
```

A similar syntax permits update operations of arbitrary complexity in this nonprocedural style.

The alternative approach is to regard enquiries and updates as expressed by a sequence of algebraic operations. This is more procedural and comes closer, if not very close, to the physical implementation, since the results will depend on the order of evaluation. In actual implementations, a query optimizer will usually attempt to select the optimal order of evaluation making use of the referential transparency of algebra. Relational algebra is based on four primitive operations: Selection, Projection, Union and Join. These operations are illustrated in Figure 5.7. Selection on a predicate yields those tuples that satisfy the predicate; it corresponds to the comprehension schema of set theory, $\{x: p(x)\}$,[2] and may be thought of as a

---

[2] Read as: the set of all elements, x, such that statement p about x is true.

horizontal subset operation. The corresponding vertical subset operation is just the projection out of the Cartesian product. If two tables have the same attributes, their union may be formed by appending them together and removing any duplicates in the primary key. The join of two relations A and B over a relational operator (or dyadic predicate) p is obtained by building all tuples that are the concatenation of a tuple from A followed by one from B such that p holds for the attribute specified. Duplicates are eliminated here too. The derivative operations such as difference and intersection will not be covered here. This account of relational algebra has been slightly oversimplified for brevity. For the full details the reader may consult (Elmasri and Navathe, 1989) or (Date, 1981). Relational algebra can be regarded as defining the scope for operations such as retrieval, update, view formation, authorization and so on. Purely algebraic languages are extremely rare in practice. Gray (1984) gives a syntax for such a language, ASTRID.

EMPLOYEES

Name	Salary	Dept
R.L. Stevenson	10,000	Shipping
T. Smolett	11,000	Shipping
L. Sterne	9,000	Shipping
I. Graham	13,000	IT
C. Dickens	4,000	Curiosities

MANAGERS

Name	DoB	Dept
R.L. Stevenson	1/1/1850	Shipping
C. Dickens	25/12/1812	Curiosities
N. Parker	13/3/1956	Sales
F. Bloggs	8/11/1977	Sales
A.N. Other	29/2/1948	Marketing

EMP.Name	DoB	Salary	Dept	MAN.Name
C. Dickens	25/12/1812	4,000	Curiosities	C. Dickens

Figure 5.7 (Continued) **(c)** The join of two relations over the predicate: Employee.Dept=Manager.Dept. Note that the tuples with null values are eliminated.

Several hybrid languages based partly on calculus and algebra exist, the most notable being those based on the IBM System-R language, SQL. SQL was partly derived from the motivation to produce a 'structured' language. Later it was found necessary or convenient to add in most of the power of algebra and calculus, so

much so that SQL is a highly redundant and thus inelegant language. However, it
has become the *de facto* industry standard so we will introduce its syntax and use it
in examples.

The query given above, in SQL, would be

```
SELECT INAME,DESCRIPTION
FROM ITEMS
WHERE INAME='Kite'
```

The reader is warned not to confuse this SELECT with the selection of algebra
defined above. This query might be regarded as saying: Project ITEMS over
INAME and DESCRIPTION, and select under the predicate INAME='Kite'.

Note that relational query languages operate on tables, or sets of tuples. A query
always returns a table. Strictly speaking, one should refer to such a language as a
tuple-relational calculus. It is also possible to construct domain-relational calculi,
where variables range over the domains of attributes. In contrast, in the tuple
calculus variables range over tuples. For example, taking the example query about
kites we have been working with up to now, we could express it in a domain calculus
language as follows:

```
RETRIEVE x,y FROM ITEMS(p,'Kite',q,r,y)
```

where the relation schema is:

INo	IName	SNo	Price	Description

and all variables are regarded as free variables. Notice the positional style and the
similarity with IBM's Query By Example. The latter is, in fact, based on the domain
calculus.

We have said that relations must be in first normal form. In fact this condition
sits at the bottom of a hierarchy of normal forms as shown in Figure 5.8, and of
which the most important are the third or Boyce-Codd normal forms. The theory of
normal forms is merely a way of formalizing the common-sense notion of a 'good
design'.

To facilitate the definition of the various normal forms we have to define what it
means to say that one attribute of a relation is functionally dependent on another. An
attribute is **functionally dependent** on another if and only if each value of the
second one uniquely determines the value of the first. In other words, the projection
of the relation onto these two attributes is a function (i.e. a single-valued,
everywhere-defined relation).

Functional dependency is not symmetrical. For example, if the relation is the set
of all points on a parabola, then the y-axis is functionally dependent on the x-axis but
not *vice versa* as illustrated in Figure 5.9. For a more concrete example, in most
company relations, the telephone number will be functionally dependent on the
company number (this assumes no party lines). Date (1981) points out, interestingly
from our present point of view, that a functional dependency is a special form of

integrity constraint; in other words, it is a legality condition relating to the semantics of the situation.

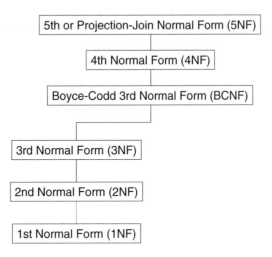

| 5th or Projection-Join Normal Form (5NF) |
| 4th Normal Form (4NF) |
| Boyce-Codd 3rd Normal Form (BCNF) |
| 3rd Normal Form (3NF) |
| 2nd Normal Form (2NF) |
| 1st Normal Form (1NF) |

Figure 5.8 The hierarchy of normal forms.

Functional dependencies express concrete relationships in the real world and require an understanding of the application. Functional dependencies in general cannot be discovered by an automatic process, only by a skilled systems analyst.

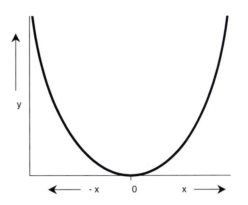

Figure 5.9 The relation on real numbers defined by a parabola ($y=x^2$).

Intuitively, a relation is in (third) normal form if and only if the primary key uniquely identifies a tuple and the other attributes are independent of one another and are all functionally dependent on the key. These attributes are properties or descriptions of an entity. In fact, it has been said that, for a third normal form entity, the value of an attribute depends upon 'the key, the whole key and nothing but the key'.

Formally then, a relation is in **first normal form** if and only if all attributes can take only atomic values; usually numbers or strings, but this actually depends on the underlying logical language. It is in **second normal form** if and only if, in addition, every non-key attribute is functionally dependent on the primary key and on no proper subset of that key. Second normal form designs overcome certain anomalies in respect of the operations of insertion, deletion or modification of tuples. For example, consider the following five relations shown in Figure 5.10.

Relation 1

SNo	Location	Currency	INo	Price
1	London	GBP	1	30
1	London	GBP	2	20
1	London	GBP	3	40
1	London	GBP	4	20
1	London	GBP	5	10
1	London	GBP	6	10
2	Paris	FF	1	30
2	Paris	FF	2	40
3	Paris	FF	2	20
4	London	GBP	2	20
4	London	GBP	4	30
4	London	GBP	5	40

Relation 2

SNo	Location	Curency
1	London	GBP
2	Paris	FF
3	Paris	FF
4	London	GBP
5	New York	USD

Relation 3

SNo	INo	Price
1	1	30
1	2	20
1	3	40
1	4	20
1	5	10
1	6	10
2	1	30
2	2	40
3	2	20
4	2	20
4	4	30
4	5	40

Relation 4

SNo	Location
1	London
2	Paris
3	Paris
4	London
5	New York

Relation 5

Location	Currency
London	GBP
Paris	FF
New York	USD

Figure 5.10 Normalizing relations.

In Relation 1 of Figure 5.10 it is not possible to record the existence of a supplier by its supplier number (SNo) until it supplies an item, unless we allow the key field INo to take null values. Even worse, if the ninth tuple is deleted we lose all the information about supplier 3. This phenomenon is often referred to as 'the connectivity trap'. If we try to amend the location of supplier 1 then all the tuples referring to that supplier must also be amended or the database will become inconsistent, an error that could easily be made in practice. Relation 1 shows our database in first normal form but not in second. Decomposing it into Relations 2 and 3 achieves second normal form and overcomes all these problems. Note, incidentally, that if the layout is conceived of as representing physical storage we may have saved some space on secondary storage too.

The reader should also note the functional dependencies implicit in this database: `Currency` depends on `Location`, which depends on `SNo`, and `Price` depends on both the supplier and the item numbers, which together form the primary key of Relation 1 and separately the primary keys of Relations 2 and 3. We have not, with our new design, overcome all problems. It is not possible to record the currency of a location until a supplier with that location is entered in the database. Similarly if we delete the last tuple of Relation 2 we lose information about dollars. Since this table still contains some redundancy there are update problems that remain also. To recover from these symptoms we note that the functional dependency of `Currency` on `SNo` arises by composing the other dependencies; it is a **transitive dependency**. If we rearrange the database into Relations 3, 4 and 5 we remove all transitive dependencies and thus overcome all the anomalies mentioned.

A relation is in **third normal form** if and only if it is in second normal form and every non-key attribute is non-transitively dependent on the primary key. There is a slightly stronger version of this definition due to Boyce and Codd as follows. A relation is in **Boyce-Codd third normal form** if and only if every attribute on which others depend is a candidate key (i.e. could be the primary key). This definition is not couched in terms of first and second normal forms and is thus slightly more elegant. It can be shown that it implies all the normal forms defined so far, with the possible exception of the first (Ullman, 1981).

Note that the join of Relations 4 and 5 recovers Relation 2 and the join of Relations 2 and 3 recovers Relation 1 without any loss of information in the sense that no spurious tuples are introduced. This need not be the case, although it can be shown that any relation admits such a lossless decomposition. Care must be exercised in database design and manipulation to avoid operations of projection followed by join which lose information in this way. For example, projecting Relation 2 over (SNO,CURRENCY) and (LOCATION,CURRENCY) would give a 'lossy' join over CURRENCY.

To overcome this lossy join problem, and other minor problems, fourth and fifth normal forms have been introduced. Their precise definition is a fairly complex matter and would be out of place in this text. The reader is referred to the works specified in the bibliographical notes to this chapter for these definitions. An informal definition is given in the next paragraph.

It may be useful to provide a crisp summary of the above description of normal forms. First normal form, or 1NF, insists that attribute value entries are 'atomic'; that is, there are no 'repeating groups' or lists and values must be primitive data types rather than pointers. This means that values may **not** represent complex objects with their own structure. Second normal form, or 2NF, says that tuples are uniquely defined by a primary key. Note that this is not the same as unique object identity because two records with the same attribute values but different identity cannot be stored. In relational systems object identity is faked by introducing unique identification fields such as Employee No. The most useful form of 3NF (Boyce-Codd NF) says that every determinant is a candidate key. In other words, every string of attributes that uniquely identifies a tuple could be the key. I like to think of this normal form as a sort of institutionalized common sense, because it is how a seasoned relational designer would write the relations down from the beginning. 4NF helps to avoid redundancy and 5NF prevents what are called lossy joins; that is, if you join two (or more) relations and then decompose to the original form no data are lost.

The theory of normal forms is an aspect of 'bottom-up' design and is complementary to top-down design methods. It is not, strictly, a part of the relational model. The whole theory of integrity is also not a part of the model.

One striking weakness of the usual relational point of view, when it comes to business applications, is the unnatural way in which it handles relations which are directly perceived in multidimensional form. The very best example of this is in the domain of financial modelling and data warehousing. The refusal to recognize as atomic any object of higher type (lists, vectors, etc.) makes the relatively trivial tasks of spreadsheet modelling tortuous within a relational model. The ease of use of such packages as Lotus123, Excel and Oracle's Express derive from the richness of the data structure and its good match with the way in which the problem is generally perceived by humans. In practice, most organizations will store raw data in relational tables and aggregate them in various ways before passing the results to such packages for modelling and decision support applications. This makes it seem as though the relational model is about handling bulk, unrefined data, but this is patently not the case. Some very high level decision support applications do suit the relational organization of data perfectly.

This problem can be addressed partly within the relational model by moving from a tuple calculus to a domain calculus. An example of this approach is to be found in the financial modelling system Oracle Express. The Express system literature refers to the product as supporting a relational data model. This is justified in the sense that the data model is a logical one and that the algebraic operations, such as move, project and so on, are supported. However, the version of the relational model present in these systems differs in important ways from the model described above, thus meeting certain practical needs and pointing to deficiencies in the latter. The enquiry language is based on domain relational calculus.

Express, along with several other post-relational database and decision support systems such as Caché, provides a logical data model to the user that differs from all of the network, hierarchical and relational viewpoints. It is a multidimensional data model; i.e. it is concerned with variables scoped over several dimensions which may be thought of as a hypercube. For example, in a financial model, the dimensions of a pertinent six-dimensional hypercube might be: Time, Balance Sheet Items, Companies, Regions, Products and Currencies. These dimensions need not map into the real line, as in Cartesian geometry, but may themselves be sets. In fact, this data view is simply a transform of the relational model, where instances in a dimension are equivalent to attribute values drawn from a domain.

The benefit of the Express representation lies, of course, in the syntactic ease with which operations over projections of the relations may be expressed. A typical query of this type might be: 'List all the balance sheets of companies in region A'.

Both kinds of relational systems have great strengths. They make changes to the data structure easy and they protect users from complexity with non-procedural enquiry languages which can be optimized automatically. Performance problems have been gradually overcome. After initial resistance, relational databases have now achieved such wide acceptance in industry that most systems planners no longer even consider hierarchical or network solutions, except for the sort of large transaction-intensive applications mentioned already. IBM recommends DB2 even for large applications, and most planners are only faced with the choice between a few relational products such as Informix, Ingres, Oracle or Sybase. The decision criteria are usually only factors such as support, portability or even marketing effort.

5.1.3 Semantic data models and data analysis methods

As has been pointed out already, a data model is a mathematical formalism consisting of a notation for describing data and data structures and a set of valid operations which are used to manipulate those data. Data models also help a designer eliminate redundancy in storage and inconsistencies in the structural design.

There are several extended data models and associated notations including ERA, a notation within the broad Chen tradition, which we have already described. The general term for these richer models is **semantic data models**.

There is a distinction between models based on predicate logic, such as the relational model, which support a declarative access language and a generally declarative style and others. Such models are value-oriented and do not support object identity. The other class of data model may be thought of as object-oriented in the sense that object identity, and usually inheritance, is supported. These 'object-oriented' data models include the implicit models of the old hierarchical and network databases. Ullman (1989) has argued that there is a fundamental trade-off between declarativeness and object identity, and thus object-orientation.

In a model based on relations and only relations, the type of the result of an operation is always the same (a table), so it is a candidate for input to some further operation. Thus operations can be composed easily. In models that support abstract data types this is fundamentally not the case, since object identity introduces type variation and an operation may result in a totally new type. Such a new type may need totally new operations defined on it, although in an object-oriented system it may well inherit them.

Semantic data models started with Abrial's (1974) binary relational model. The schemata of the binary model are essentially semantic networks restricted to classes. Chen's (1976) notation was introduced originally purely as a notation for design. It had quite different goals from the relational model, which attempted to separate the physical and logical description of data and develop powerful non-procedural enquiry languages. Semantic data models were intended to permit the modelling of relationships and integrity. Modern semantic models also include very sophisticated means of dealing with inheritance, composition structures, instantiation, and subtyping. The general idea is to be able to model data at appropriately high and low levels of abstraction and to capture as much meaning as possible.

Smith and Smith (1977) showed that the relational model was insufficiently expressive to capture all of an ER model. Also, pure relational databases cannot support complex objects of any sort, including abstract data types. This is prevented by 1NF. Object-oriented design allows as many types as necessary and permits full inheritance between them. Thus there is an obvious need for object-oriented databases to permit the design to be implemented easily.

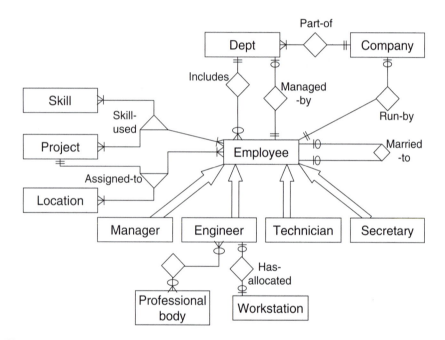

Figure 5.11 A typical EER data model of a personnel and project system, showing binary and ternary relationships and inheritance (the thick arrows).

The most widely used semantic data models are the Entity-Relationship (ER) models. Various ER models arose from attempts to analyse and model data independently of the database software that would be used to implement the design. The principal such models and notations were those due to Chen (1976) and Bachman (1977). ER models have two aims: to classify relations into types and to enforce business rules such as rules for referential integrity. The Chen ER model has only two types; entity-relations and relationship-relations. Schmid and Swenson

(1975) proposed five types, but one is forced to wonder what is special about the number 5. There have been several, semantically richer, extensions of the basic ER model, some of them with similar names. The Extended Entity-Relationship model (EER) introduced by Teorey *et al.* (1986) includes notations which differentiate generalization and subset hierarchies. The Enhanced entity-relationship model (also EER) was introduced by Elmasri and Navathe (1989) with the aim of being a superset of most other ER proposals. To achieve their aims, Teorey *et al.*, and Elmasri and Navathe especially, are forced to introduce classes or abstract types into their EER models much in the manner of object-orientation. It is instructive that these authors seem driven inexorably towards this introduction of classes. Possibly this indicates that the notion of abstract classes with inheritance is canonical; that is, a sort of 'best' way of dealing with higher order notions about entities and concepts in a data modelling context.

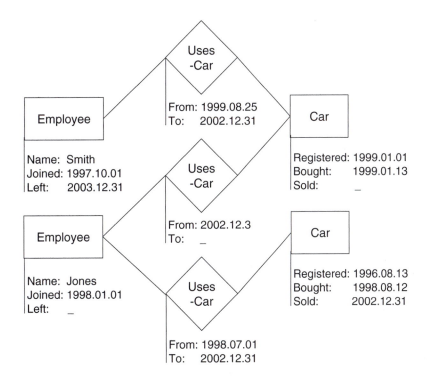

Figure 5.12 Instances of relationships with attributes in an ER model.

Figure 5.11 shows a typical EER notation. Note that the ternary relationships can be factored out by allowing relationships to have attributes corresponding to the third entity. For example, we might create an entity called 'project assignments' with attributes: Employee, Project and Location.

It is worth noting that relationships, in the ER model, can be first-class objects in as much as they can have attributes themselves. Figure 5.12 shows an example where the relationship 'uses-car' may need to store attributes showing the valid range of dates for which a particular car was used by a particular employee.

In fact, there are three ways of representing a relationship in ER models. An object may contain an attribute whose domain is another object representing the relationship, two objects may both contain attributes with each other as domains, or there may be a specific object for the relationship. For example, referring to the data in Figure 5.12, the employee object could instead have a CarUsed attribute, or the Car object have a UsedBy attribute as well. The reason for choosing the third representation is precisely when the relationship itself has several important attributes.

Chen and Bachman style notations are in wide use and their usage permits a variation in notation. One of the most interesting aspects of some versions of the Chen notation is their very explicit way of dealing with the semantics of inheritance and other structures. In particular, subtype relationships may be of four types, denoted as follows:

E/M	—	Exclusive/Mandatory
E/O	—	Exclusive/Optional
I/M	—	Inclusive/Mandatory
I/O	—	Inclusive/Optional

The term 'mandatory' indicates that a member of the supertype must be in one of the subtypes; that is, the subtypes are an exhaustive list or *partition* of the type. The 'exclusive' indicates that each subtype's intersection with the other subtypes is empty. 'Optional' indicates that the list is not exhaustive; there may be more, as yet unidentified, subtypes. 'Inclusive' indicates that the subtypes may overlap. A notation for this is illustrated in Figure 5.13.

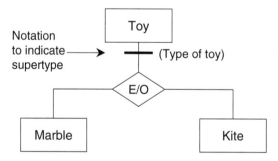

Figure 5.13 Inheritance in a Chen-style ER notation.

The traditional ER models either cannot, or make it extremely difficult to, cope with CAD/CAM database objects such as images, geometric drawings or structure-free text. It is this practical consideration, I believe, that drives data modellers towards object-oriented data models, for much the same reason that database vendors have been forced to introduce object-oriented constructs into their otherwise relational products.

There are two further important observations to make about ER models. In ER models, because not only entities but relationships themselves can have attributes, relationships represent first-class conceptual objects. The second observation is that Chen ER models tend to produce 3NF relations as a matter of course.

There are a number of systems development methods whose data modelling subsystems are largely based on the relational model, such as parts of IE and SSADM, CASE*METHOD, and several extensions to the relational model itself. A significant extension of this type is Codd's RM/T which incorporates null values into the relational algebra and adds some of the abstractions from ER models, including subtypes and multiple inheritance, integrity rules, support for multiplicity and modality constraints and database operations and a distinction between two types of relation. E-relations represent the existence of entities and P-relations their properties. Also, most RDBMS products have been extended in this direction; for example, even MS Access allows one to enforce referential integrity automatically.

There are two broad approaches to semantic data models. The first emphasizes the use of functions or attributes to relate objects, and the second emphasizes the use of type constructors. The first is represented by the Functional Data Model and the second by the various ER models and their extensions. The key difference between the two philosophies is that in the type construction approach relationships are themselves types; first-class objects.

The Functional Data Model (Shipman, 1981) is based on the lambda calculus described briefly in Chapter 3. The primitive concepts are entities and 'functional' relations and their so-called inverses. Functional relations are single-valued relations; many-to-one relations. Inheritance is implemented by function composition. One of the nice things about the logically based functional model is that a formal type theory exists for it. A number of, mainly experimental, systems such as Daplex and Adaplex exist, as we have already seen. We have also seen that CODASYL or network databases can be given a formal foundation based on the functional model. Daplex, according to Gray *et al.* (1992), is suitable for representing objects and is computationally rich but not complete. Completing it takes one in the direction of persistent object languages and object-oriented database management systems.

The Generic Semantic Model (GSM) (Hull and King, 1987) is an attempt to superset most semantic data models, although it was developed primarily for tutorial purposes. SDM is another model proposed by Hammer and McLeod (1978; 1981). In SDM a database is a disjoint set of classes and instances and distinguishes classes from names and values. A value could be an instance of some class or a primitive *name*. It supports inheritance and includes a predicate language for specifying relationships and derived data in the manner of deductive databases. A commercial implementation of SDM called SIM has been produced (Jagannathan *et al.,* 1988).

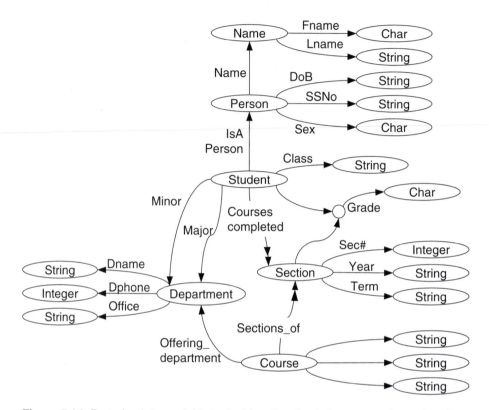

Figure 5.14 Part of a data model in typical functional notation concerning university course enrolments. The ovals are objects (sets) and the labelled arrows represent functions. (After Elmasri and Navathe (1989))

There have been several attempts to build real database systems on the basis of full semantic data models. Adaplex is an early such attempt to do this on top of the functional model by embedding a semantic database language, Daplex, within Ada. The Distributed Data Manager (Chan *et al.*, 1983) is a distributed semantic DBMS based on an extension of Adaplex. Generis is a semantic, or 'deductive', database based on an extended binary relational model. There are also systems called Entity-Relationship databases based on the Chen model and some *ad hoc* extensions to relational database management systems, such as Ingres/Postgres, incorporating features from both semantic models, object-orientation and artificial intelligence. These are discussed later in this chapter with the object-relational database systems such as Oracle and Illustra (aka Informix Universal Server).

Object-oriented models include behavioural abstractions (methods) rather than the purely structural abstractions of data models. They seldom support the rich type constructors of semantic data models, such as the ability to model set-valued functions. Constructed types are arrived at by aggregating attributes, as when we construct the type NAME from STYLE, FORENAME and FAMILY_NAME, or by grouping into sets, as when we construct sets of items of similar type. The inheritance methods associated with the two approaches also tend to be different. Data models, as with AI systems, often allow the inheritance of defaults at the class level, whereas object-oriented models only allow attribute names to be inherited. Also, in data models, inheritance tends to be restricted strictly to subtypes, while, in object-oriented programming, the inheritance of methods can take place between unlike types. For example, textual objects might inherit a 'display_self' method from Geometric_Object, although, in my view, this is bad practice.

King (1989) has emphasized the differences between semantic data models and object-orientation. He says:

> Semantic models focus on the recursive definition of complex objects, and on the inheritance of structural components (aggregations) and relationships. Object-oriented models focus on the definition and inheritance of behavioural capabilities, in the form of operations embedded within types, and also support simpler capabilities for structuring complex objects; but this distinction is not as sharp as it might seem.

However, my interpretation is that there is a strong need for object-oriented databases, and object-oriented methods in general, to absorb the structural modelling features developed by data modellers along with, I think, good ideas from artificial intelligence research and development. In Chapter 6, I will attempt to demonstrate how this can be done at the analysis level. Object-oriented database researchers seem to be pursuing similar goals, and the ORION and Itasca systems discussed later in this chapter provide an example of a project with such goals.

The artificial intelligence, or strictly knowledge-based system, extensions I have in mind are principally to do with the way defaults and inheritance conflicts are handled, but it is also true that rule-based programming has a significant contribution to make to system development. This will be explained more fully in Chapter 6.

For commercial applications, such as SACIS, where there is a strong data modelling element it is beneficial, and even necessary, to build an object-oriented modelling system that incorporates the elements of semantic data models and object-oriented programming. A similar convergence of both object-orientation and semantic data modelling with AI models is also likely to be beneficial because of the richness of the inheritance, grouping and, especially, the metastructural features of the latter, whereby the structure of data may itself be a property of those data. On the other hand the AI frame models have much to learn about encapsulation and pluggability from object-oriented programming and about aggregation and abstraction from data modelling.

Let us now examine why the relational model is not appropriate for such developments.

⊟ 5.2 Weaknesses in the relational model

The great strength of the relational model is its basis in a formal theory; first order predicate logic. This is what makes it possible to have a relationally complete, non-procedural enquiry language such as SQL or QUEL. The logic ensures that certain things about this language can be proved mathematically. Another notable and very real benefit is that the database structure can be easily changed without completely redesigning the database. The other much-vaunted benefit is the rigorous normalization theory that has emerged.

No one, with the possible exception of a few over-zealous and commission-hungry salesmen, claims that the relational model is without difficulties. The difficulties I want to deal with include the difficulty of dealing with recursive queries, problems related to null values, lack of support for abstract data types and, most importantly in my view, severe shortcomings in the representation of data and functional semantics; there is no real support for true business rules. I also want to point out some problems with the theory of normalization. Let us now examine this normalization theory a little more critically, and have a slightly deeper look at the other issues mentioned.

5.2.1 Normalization

There are a number of problems with normalization which are quite obvious to anyone thinking about object-oriented systems. First, normalized relations rarely, if ever, correspond to any object in the real world. The decomposition is driven by considerations of computation or logic, rather than modelled on the structure of the application. This prevents normalized relations being reusable in isolation and prevents any progress towards the assembly of systems from components. Not only do the normalized tables correspond to absolutely nothing in the application, but normalization also hides its semantics completely. One reason for this is that normalization conceals the application knowledge which is represented by functional dependencies among attributes. This means that normalization removes any possibility of full reverse engineering and that the process of normalization is effectively irreversible. For example, in the normalized relations of Figure 5.10, is it possible to tell from them that suppliers set prices in the currency of the state in which their town is located? Clearly not, and the loss of this information, or functional dependency, prevents its recovery. If the rules about currency change (as they did in post-Maastricht Europe) the systems are difficult to redesign.

We have discussed some of the deficiencies of normalized data models. Not everything about normalization is bad. The elimination of redundancy in data storage delivered by 4NF cannot really be faulted in design terms although retrieval efficiency may be affected. In an object-oriented system there is an analogous need for a normalization theory for methods. In fact, encapsulation of methods does provide a sort of normalization automatically. For example, in terms of entities and relationships, if we consider the relationship 'sold to' in SACIS this relationship must ensure (via one of its methods) that the objects related consist of a valid customer and an item which is suitable for that customer. It would be redundant to store these integrity checks in the Customer or StockItem classes. Normalized behaviour requires that they are stored in the SoldTo class, which is the most natural place anyway.

Experienced data modellers instinctively remove many-to-many relationships from their models as part of normalization. This introduces entities which often have no correspondence to things in the real world. In an object-oriented context this seems quite wrong. The usual example given is that of ORDERS and ITEMS which are related in a many-to-many fashion. A new entity called ORDER-LINE is used to resolve the relationship into two one-to-many relationships as shown in Figure 5.15.

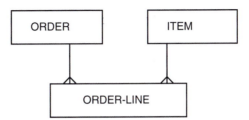

Figure 5.15 Resolving many-to-many relationships.

This strategy is fine when there is a real, physical thing like the printed order line to observe. However, in other cases it is absurd. Consider that a legal regulation may apply to many products and that a product may be subject to many regulations. What is the equivalent of ORDER-LINE? Is it PRODUCT-REGULATION-INCIDENCE? Similarly, cars may be painted many colours and colours applied to different models. What is the equivalent of order-line here? The over-zealous normalization of models is to be carefully avoided in an object-oriented context.

For those who are still worried about update anomalies, it is worth pointing out that these anomalies arise precisely due to the lack of object identity in relational systems where tables and tuples may not correspond to a single object.

5.2.2 Integrity and business rules

Integrity rules are semantic rules which assert that it is incorrect, for example, to delete a supplier reference because that supplier does not supply any part at present. In relational terminology we may state the rules for entity and referential integrity as follows.

Entity integrity: No primary key may include an attribute which may take null as a value.

Referential integrity: If a relation R contains a foreign key whose values are taken from the primary key values of a relation S then every occurrence of the foreign key in R must either match a primary key value in R or be null. R and S may be the same relation.

Note that entity integrity is not the same as object identity because a tuple is identified by its key value, not an unchangeable identity independent of attribute values.

Business rules are rules such as 'if an employee has over five years' service then award an extra day's holiday' or, less crisply, 'long-standing customers who pay regularly deserve special attention'. Business rules relate the attributes of entities.

In most relational systems integrity rules are often coded in each client application, which makes changes very difficult to control. A more recent trend has been to provide facilities in the database server itself to overcome this difficulty. In such 'client-server' database implementations, it is often also possible to store 'triggers' in the server; procedures which update tables automatically when certain data change their values. This gives limited support for business rules, but they are still written in SQL or a procedural extension of SQL which makes understanding and changing them non-trivial. Support for rules of any kind is an extra, not a part of the relational model itself.

5.2.3 Null values

Null values in tuples present a difficulty of interpretation. A null can be taken to mean the logical value 'unknown'. They can mean that a value is just not applicable to particular tuples, or they could merely mean that no values have been supplied yet. Date (1983) suggests disallowing them altogether, but has then to introduce a complex superstructure of new logical operators and defaults. However, null values are a very natural way to deal with incomplete or exceptional data. The difficulty arises because FOPC is a two-valued or Boolean logic; the only values allowed are true or false. Allowing null values immediately means that one must work in a three or four or even infinite valued logic. Thus, against the evident benefits of working within a formal theory, we have to recognize that any such theory imposes limitations which real-world problems soon force us to go beyond.

As with rules, the problem of null values is one of the semantics of the application. The relational model is a purely syntactic model; it contains no intrinsic support for any kind of semantics. Data semantics have to be added on, and there is a huge literature on how to do this in the area of semantic data modelling. Functional semantics are also important. The rules by which a business operates are part of its functional semantics.

5.2.4 Abstract data types and complex objects

First normal form forbids the storage of complex objects, so that abstract data types cannot be dealt with by the relational model. This means that queries over databases which store unstructured BLOBs (Binary Large OBjects), such as those involving structured text, engineering drawings or graphics, may be impossibly slow, since all the structure of a retrieved object must be recovered in the application at run time. It also means that methods cannot be stored ready for use in the database.

Even though relationships can be stored in relational or network databases, they are static; created at the time the database is designed. Furthermore, there is no natural way for relationships to have attributes; they are not first-class objects. The attributes of relationships are useful for such tasks as recording the time span for which a relationship holds, such as when the 'supplies' relationship holds only at certain times of the year. For example, christmas crackers are usually available only between September and December, although sadly this period seems to get longer year by year.

5.2.5 Recursive queries

Another negative effect of 1NF is that it disallows recursive queries; that is, queries about relationships that an entity has with itself. An example of such a relationship is the parenthood relation on the person entity.

Recursive queries were the subject of study at the IBM laboratory in Heidelberg under the umbrella of its ten-year Advanced Information Management (AIM) research project. The researchers reported (Dadam, 1988; Linnemann, 1987) that a short recursive query of the form:

```
SELECT x
FROM   x IN Employees
WHERE  x.Emp_ID = 'W09867'
```

can take as many as 18 lines of SQL to express. The project explored an extension of the relational model where relations can be normalized but do not have to be in 1NF. They call them NF^2 databases. Unnormalized relational models have been applied to office automation by Kitagawa and Kunii (1989). Note that the definition of Boyce-Codd NF does not depend on the definitions of either first or second normal form, so a normalization theory is still possible for such databases.

One way to implement recursive queries is as a search of an inheritance hierarchy. As an example, consider the following query in Adabas Entire, which is discussed in the next section.

```
Find person
 Referencing recursively
  via Child
   person = 'George'
```

This query finds all of George's ancestors. In other words we are searching an inheritance hierarchy upwards, or backwards. Forward, or downward, search is accomplished with the syntax 'Referenced recursively'.

Notice that there is only one relation. All types are stored in the PERSON relation via the explicitly stored relation 'child of' which is stored explicitly since Adabas Entire is an entity-relationship database.

It is worth noting that another consequence of first normal form, and consequently of flat file structures, is that foreign key joins must be performed to reconstruct complex entities in an application. This can be very expensive in terms of processing time.

5.3 Entity-relationship and deductive databases

Apart from genuinely object-oriented databases, which are discussed below, there are several products which address all or some of the problems we have examined. These may be broadly classified as semantic databases. Commercial semantic databases are of four main kinds: entity-relationship databases, deductive databases, extended relational or object-relational databases and functional databases. We will look at examples of the first three of these.

5.3.1 Entity-relationship databases

Adabas Entire was an entity-relationship database wherein the relationships between entities are stored explicitly, rather than being implicit, and are thus recoverable. In fact the Adabas product never insisted on relations being in 1NF, despite the claim that it was a relational database. In fact, you can use Adabas as if it were relational, merely by putting all relations into 1NF. This puts a burden on the database designer to choose the correct path; for NF^2 databases, like all more powerful systems, are more difficult to design. Much more knowledge and understanding are required. However, for complex problems the NF^2 solution is often far more easy to express.

Adabas Entire is directly based on the Chen ER model. Its extra functionality is achieved by a very small extension to the syntax of Natural, the Adabas 4GL and enquiry language. Storing the relationships explicitly not only permits recursive queries, but automatically enforces referential integrity. Typically, ER databases such as Entire have no notion of classes and inheritance, nor do they offer advanced facilities for storing business rules either explicitly or in the server.

To overcome this deficiency, Software AG also developed Natural Expert as an extension to Natural. Natural Expert was sold as a means of incorporating expert systems into Natural applications, but is particularly unusual in that it introduced functional programming (a form of lazy ML in fact) instead of the more usual production rule style. Functional programming when combined with the entity-relationship database could address quite a few of the deficiencies in relational databases alluded to in the foregoing.

The convergence of ER and functional concepts represented by Adabas is also evident in the functional database camp too, where proponents of systems such as Daplex are now regarding a lot of their work as object-oriented. A project exemplifying and illustrating this convergence of ideas and styles is reported in (Gray and Kemp, 1990).

Adabas Entire is by no means the only product in this area. ZIM from Zanthe was another early ER database management system.

5.3.2 Deductive databases

Alongside the development of ER database systems, and mainly influenced by developments in AI and expert systems, a number of systems best described as 'intelligent' or deductive databases have been launched. Many of these systems have all or some of the features of object-oriented databases alongside features more usually found in expert systems. Here we look at just one powerful deductive database, Generis, as a representative of this kind of system.

Generis, formerly called Fact, was a deductive database system based on an extension of the binary relational semantic model first introduced by Abrial (1974), the Generic Relational Model (McInnes, 1988), and rooted in the AI tradition. It supported the explicit storage of facts (A is X), rules (If P then Q), relationships, triggers and complex data structures as well as raw data. It supported classes and multiple inheritance via the assertion of facts of the form: A is a B. It did not contain any significant features for encapsulation, although one 'method' may be encapsulated within certain object types. An extremely powerful query language, IQL, which can fill in missing information in the query using facts stored in the database, made programming very productive. To illustrate, the SQL query:

```
SELECT      EMPLOYEE, SALARY, DEPARTMENT
FROM        EMPLOYMENT, DEPARTMENTS
WHERE       LOCATION='LONDON'
AND         JOB_TITLE='SALESMAN'
AND
EMPLOYMENT.DEPARTMENT=DEPARTMENTS.DEPARTMENT
```

becomes simply:

```
DISPLAY SALARY SALESMAN AND DEPARTMENT FOR LONDON
```

The result is the same, but in Generis the relationships (such as 'works in DEPARTMENT of employee') are retrieved and printed as column headers as illustrated in Figure 5.16.

In other words, the class structure, or the knowledge contained within it, is used to fill in the missing links. Generis also supported recursive queries and had features that made it particularly suitable for intelligent text retrieval applications, and was applied to a number of such applications, particularly in healthcare. Generis was a curious and powerful hybrid formed from relational, object-oriented and expert systems ideas. It extended the relational model with data semantics and supported recursive queries and inheritance, but not abstract data types or full encapsulation. From a practitioner's point of view, one of the most interesting potential applications of such semantically rich languages is specification prototyping. Unfortunately, there are few such products commercially available at present.

EMPLOYEE	works in DEPARTMENT of employee	located in LOCATION of department	Earns SALARY of employee
A.Langham	Sales	London	27000
R.Biter	Production	London	15000

Figure 5.16 Generis standard report format.

There have been several other approaches to deductive databases. Many proceed by adding the power of logic programming to an existing RDBMS, using a language like Prolog as a database extension. Bell *et al.* (1990) offer a study of this approach. Other deductive databases are discussed by Gray *et al.* (1992) and their approach compared to that of object-oriented programming.

5.4 Object-relational databases

So far, in this book, we have seen some advantages offered by object-oriented programming languages, some of the limitations of conventional database management systems in this respect and some suggestions for overcoming them. However, object-oriented programming languages also have their limitations. In particular, languages like Simula, C++ and Smalltalk offer no explicit support for persistent objects; that is, objects which are stored off-line on secondary storage devices and whose state persists from moment to moment and from session to session. Such languages have no effective means for dealing with persistent objects in the manner of a database. It is not possible to send messages to objects stored off-line. The best that can be done in Smalltalk, for example, is to store the entire session image off-line and reload it at the next session. Clearly, this is totally inadequate for any application with large amounts of important stored data; a feature that characterizes practically all commercial applications.

Java, though not a persistent language, does allow classes to implement the standard *serializable* interface, which is some help. Even fully persistent languages do not help with issues such as concurrency, security and recovery. In such languages the programmer must still write extra code to handle them.

The question then is how we may obtain the advantages of an object-oriented approach to systems development and retain the ability to store and manage persistent objects off-line and deal with issues such as concurrency and recovery in as facile a manner as we have come to expect with relational database management systems. Several approaches to resolving this issue have emerged under the banner of object-oriented databases.

There are three reasons why we might consider that an object-oriented database is required: to facilitate a clean interface with an object-oriented programming language, to tackle an application that requires the flexibility of a relational database but for which the performance of the latter is inadequate, or to tackle totally new kinds of application where the message passing metaphor seems particularly appropriate. The remarkable fact is that pure object-oriented databases may be over 100 times faster for the right application and still retain the flexibility of a relational implementation in terms of schema evolution.

The commercial need for fully integrated object-oriented systems has led to the development of a number of systems described as object-oriented database management systems. These were mainly experimental systems for a time, but products such as GemStone, Jasmine, ObjectStore, POET and Versant have now emerged as fully fledged commercial products, with others like Ontos having come and gone. There are also a number of novel database systems with object-oriented features, including deductive and semantic databases, which are not fully fledged object-oriented database systems but share many of their features and benefits. The object-oriented movement even led to a short-lived revival of interest in hierarchical and even network databases. The ER database, Adabas Entire, is ultimately implemented as a network database. Ullman (1988) points out that hierarchical and network databases such as IMS and the CODASYL family do support object identity, although they do not have the other features of the object-oriented model. Their main limitation, inflexibility in the face of schema evolution, is due to the manner in which object identity is implemented as fixed pointers.

	Relational database engine	Object database engine
Relational data model	**SQL Server, Sybase**	**Cincom ORDB**
Object data model	**DB2, Illustra, Oracle**	**GemStone, Itasca, Jasmine, ObjectStore, POET, Versant**

Figure 5.17 Types of object database product.

The key question for systems strategists and planners is whether they should embrace the new object-oriented databases, do nothing or opt for a strategy based on extensions of the relational products. We will attempt to arrive at a solution to this dilemma.

In the mainstream there are basically four types of product available, as illustrated in Figure 5.17.

Clearly, Cincom's ORDB (formerly UniSQL) is in a very special category: offering the flexible query capabilities of a relational product with the efficiencies and semantic richness of an object-oriented one. It will not be considered further here, except to note that it is an intellectual descendant of the Orion object-oriented database discussed later. We begin by discussing object-relational databases

A number of vendors of relational database management systems (RDBMS), under the influence of developments in object-oriented programming and expert systems, have made significant semantic extensions to their products. These object-relational databases now compete for market share with genuine object-oriented databases and will replace RDBMS for many applications.

The relational DBMS Sybase was the first to exhibit novel features of this kind. First, it is based on a client-server architecture whereby the data integrity and business rules may be stored in the server, the database, rather than in each individual application. This has beneficial consequences for maintenance, because when such a rule changes this does not mean that every application must be checked. The rules are implemented as stored procedures and triggers: active or data-driven rules which fire when data are changed. The difficulty is that these rules are written as SQL or procedural code, and are thus not necessarily easy to understand or change; nor can they be stored in a separate layer. The vehicle for this is a non-standard procedural extension of SQL, Transact SQL, which includes control structures, procedures, assignment and other general purpose programming constructs. Sybase thus offers some modest, but important, extensions to the vanilla relational system. Adding stored procedures to database tables is certainly a step closer to object-orientation since data and processes are combined thereby. However, true encapsulation is not achieved since the data may be accessed directly and the tables need not be modelled on domain objects due to normalization. Sybase is not a fully object-relational database.

Ingres, from Version 6, offered similar extensions in the form of a multi-client/multi-server architecture, which is important for performance and distributed database reasons, and support for rules and triggers. However, Ingres went beyond Sybase and other relational systems in offering explicit support for abstract data types, rules, recursive queries and inheritance. Curiously, Sybase and Ingres share common historical roots, in the sense that some of the early workers on Ingres, after a period working on database hardware, wrote Sybase.

It was significant that Ingres decided to disrupt the calm acceptance of the relational model as little as possible, for those companies with large resources committed to the relational approach. The object manager was implemented as a separate layer, but Ingres could still be used as a pure relational database. Ingres also had a knowledge manager, implemented as a separate layer for the same reasons.

The view that object-orientation in databases and commercial systems will be a permanent feature of the software industry was supported by the early appearance of self-appointed standards bodies representing influential players in the market. On the one hand there was the Object Database Management Group (ODMG) and on the other the Committee for Advanced DBMS Function (CADF).

CADF laid the theoretical basis for object-relational databases and the SQL3 query language that they support. It consisted of a group of influential individuals from the database world who published a sort of advanced database manifesto in 1990 (Stonebraker *et al.*, 1990). CADF originally included such figures as Mike Stonebraker and Larry Rowe – the principal architects of Ingres, David Beech – technical adviser at Oracle, one of the designers of IRIS and involved from the early days in the definition of SQL3, Jim Gray – author of Tandem's Nonstop SQL, Phil Bernstein – director of Digital's DBMS laboratory, Bruce Lindset – architect of DB2, and Michael Brodie of GTE, a leading researcher in knowledge-base management systems. The group laid down a number of principles which an advanced database management system ought to meet in the near future. These principles, perhaps analogous to Codd's famous 12 rules for relational systems, include the following.

- Object-oriented databases should have all the facilities of a conventional DBMS, including high volume data management, concurrent multi-user access, high level access languages, simultaneous access to distributed data, support for efficient transaction processing and full recovery and security features.
- Object identity should be supported.
- There should be support for at least one form of inheritance.
- Support for transparent distributed access and update.
- Support for complex objects via encapsulation or abstract data types and classes.
- The provision of computationally rich languages compared to SQL.
- Support for dynamic binding.
- Support for user defined functions.
- Type checking and inference capabilities.
- Effective version and configuration control.

Illustra (now combined with Informix and renamed Informix Universal Server, which is too much of a mouthful to use again here) is the commercial object-relational successor of Ingres and Postgres. It supports all the above-listed object-oriented features on top of a relational storage mechanism and uses SQL3 as its query language. Like Ingres it has a multi-client/multi-server architecture and a fine query optimizer. Methods can (unlike some pure OODBMSs) be stored in the database. User defined types are called DataBlades, which add optimized internal access techniques for such things as time series, images, drawings or web pages. Its other OO features include multiple inheritance, polymorphism and encapsulation. Each record in the database also has an OID, which enables navigational access to be used but, as Taylor (1992) points out, this undermines the mathematical foundations of relational technology. An Illustra OID is value-based, not reference-based, and is simply another candidate key.

Oracle Corporation too began to add object-oriented features to its product. From Version 8 it was an almost fully object-relational database. It too uses SQL3. Both Oracle and Illustra have been optimized to perform faster joins than their predecessors using, mostly, advanced page caching techniques. A notable difference between the two products is that Oracle, unlike Illustra, has no intrinsic support for expert-systems-style production rules. IBM's DB2 Universal Database also supports the CADF manifesto features.

The ODMG group too subscribed to an object-oriented database manifesto (Atkinson *et al.*, 1989) and laid the basis for standards for pure object-oriented databases and the OQL query language for them. The key discriminator between such pure object-oriented databases and the relational hybrids mentioned above is still performance as we shall see below, though this is dependent on application type.

Persistence Software's product range offers a middle ground between object-oriented programming languages and relational databases by mapping language objects onto database tables invisibly and providing caching services to improve performance. The caching approach is proprietary and may be contrasted with that of users who have used commercial object-oriented databases to cache objects stored in relational databases. Persistence interfaces with CORBA and has been used for significant applications by companies such as JP Morgan and Fedex.

Caché from InterSystems represents a slightly different approach to the idea of hybrid object-relational databases by basing itself on a domain-relational or multi-dimensional engine, similar to Oracle Express discussed earlier. It is far easier to map objects to a multi-dimensional engine than to a pure relational one and performance should therefore be better, but there is still an overhead. Caché is aimed specifically at applications characterized by high intensity on-line transaction processing.

5.5 Query languages

Commercial systems, typically, have large amounts of data but the operations performed on them are relatively simple. For this reason the expressive power of most data management languages is very limited. Complex procedures are implemented by recourse to a general purpose language such as COBOL, C or FORTRAN. Databases that have to deal with more complex relationships, such as GIS, VLSI design or CAD, need much greater generality in the access language. This is the significance of the requirement for computationally rich languages; that is, languages which permit any procedural or non-procedural computation to be expressed concisely.

Abstraction in databases means that fewer data have to be retrieved because the server understands more of the semantics of the object rather than regarding it an undifferentiated string of bits (a BLOB) and having to retrieve the whole structure, leaving the application to use its semantic knowledge to extract the relevant data.

Without standards no serious commercial organization will take a technology seriously, except for non-critical applications. The key standards issues for object-oriented databases involve defining what exactly an object model is and defining language extensions for SQL and even standard data management extensions to languages like C++, at least at the level of custom and practice. There are currently two standards for query languages: SQL3 is a complex object-oriented extension of SQL92 supported by the object-relational database vendors and OQL is a simpler language supported by the pure object-oriented database vendors and based on the OMG object model.

The goal of SQL3 is to make evolution more possible. It introduces a notion of type and distinguishes this from tables so that tuples may have a type different from the table that contains them. Subtyping is permitted and one can make new tables of a given type using the syntax:

create object type PartTimers **under** Employees

Non-1NF tables are permitted using tuple-valued attributes. Object identity is supported by having the system generate an uneditable surrogate and foreign keys are superseded by REF types which enables attributes to be typed. Lastly, types can contain function definitions or methods that can be written in the procedural part of SQL3. Attributes can be private or public, as can functions. Beech (1992) claims that SQL3 removes any conflict between the relational model and encapsulation.

SQL3 also supports abstract data types, triggers, recursive queries, quantification and improved security using the Grant and Revoke commands. It is a Turing complete programming language. OQL is part of the ODMG-93 standard (Cattell, 1994). The latter includes also an object definition language based on the OMG's IDL and bindings to object-oriented programming languages such as C++ and Java. OQL has a select/from/where syntax similar to that of SQL92 and is not a full programming language like SQL3. Therefore it is easier to learn. Programming is accomplished in other object-oriented languages for which bindings exist.

As well as supporting OQL, most commercial OODBs are also closely coupled to a particular object-oriented programming language. However, these usually offer APIs for other languages. This means that integrating existing code with the database can be a little more troublesome than need be. We now turn to these pure object-oriented database management systems.

5.6 What is an object-oriented database?

Recall from Chapter 1 that an object-oriented programming language has three key features:

- encapsulation – the ability to deal with complex object interfaces and encapsulate methods and data structures within them;
- inheritance – the ability for objects to participate in networks and share both attributes and methods thereby;
- self or object identity – something we have not paid much attention to until now.

We have seen that the common object-oriented programming languages do not support some basic functions required by a data-intensive application. In particular there is no support in such languages for:

- persistence of objects;
- management of very large amounts of data;
- data and transaction integrity;
- sharing and concurrent multi-user access;
- access or query languages;
- recovery;
- security.

Persistent objects are those which continue to exist after a session terminates. Objects can be created and destroyed in memory by an application or compiler. If some of them are to be persistent, there are two ways to handle their storage. They can be stored in a conventional database. This means that the object is not ready for use; it must be constructed from the files retrieved. If an object-oriented database is used, and the objects stored directly as objects, then a retrieved object is ready for use immediately after retrieval. Persistence is closely related to object identity, because if objects are related via references to unique identifiers, then the relationships among objects persist as well as the objects.

The ability of a system to differentiate objects, throughout their lifetime, according not to their components or attributes, but by a unique identifier, is known as **object identity**. There are three conventional techniques for identifying objects; either by physical locations in memory (pointers), primary keys or user defined identifiers. In a relational system, if the primary key changes then the object (tuple) identity may change too. In such systems identity has to be simulated by surrogates or unique identifiers, such as Supplier_No, but so long as these are not under system control this does not provide a guarantee against violations of identity. An object may be accessed in different ways; bound to different variables. There is no way to determine whether two variables refer to the same object. Using the idea of primary keys is also problematical. Primary keys are not permitted to change. If the key happens to represent a property that can change (are there any that can't?), this can cause severe problems. Furthermore, if we wish to merge two systems which use different keys for the same object, say 'name' and 'employee number' for employees, then the resultant change may break the continuity of identity. Such keys are not usually unique across the whole system, only within relations. For example, if Sam is both an employee and a shareholder in the same company, he may be stored as two entities rather than as one, leading to the possibilities of inconsistency and redundancy. How often have you wondered why you receive the same mail shot three or more times?

There are several ways in which object identity can be implemented. The most common is the use of a system-generated unique identifier. This overcomes the problems mentioned above and is common in both object-oriented databases and languages. The identity of an object will not depend on either its location or its properties, just as an object in the world can have all, or most of, its properties change one by one; but remain the same object throughout. A good example is a river which, in geological time, can change its source, route and contents, but still be the Amazon.

Object identity clarifies and extends the notion of pointers used in hierarchical databases and conventional languages like C. Relationships between objects can make use of a stored identity, or use a value-oriented expression as in SQL. Thus, the object-oriented database approach, in a sense, unifies value-based and identity-based access.

An **object-oriented database** system (or data model) is a database system (or model) – in the sense that it has all the features of databases in general, including access languages, the ability to manage very large amounts of data, persistence, data and transaction integrity, concurrency, security and recovery – which additionally supports encapsulation, inheritance and object identity. Additionally, with a modern object-oriented database, we usually expect some form of versioning system. The latter is largely an historical accident. While relational databases were substantially developed in the days of the standalone minicomputer or mainframe, object-oriented databases emerged in the days of the networked workstation. This meant that these new products were developed within a cultural setting where passing work to colleagues across the network for modification was quite normal. Transactions of this kind are called **long transactions**. They occur frequently in engineering design and document production contexts but not in the sort of applications to which conventional database management has been mostly applied. Traditional databases can only manage short transactions. For example, imagine what happens when the transactions of two Automatic Teller Machine users withdrawing cash collide or reach deadlock. Normally, one of the transactions is aborted and the ATM user must re-key the instruction; irritating perhaps but not disastrous. Now imagine the equivalent situation when two engineers have spent months on their designs and want to commit them to the database simultaneously. If there is a deadlock I suspect that most engineers would feel quite suicidal were their transactions to be aborted and lost. The requirement here is to create a temporary version of the transaction automatically and commit that, rather than merely abort it. Thus, control over versions was seen to be essential and was built into object-oriented database products from the earliest designs.

Objects can store relationships represented as links to other objects, and methods. These relationships are often regarded as objects in their own right and, as such, may have attributes and methods. For example, a usage relationship may be time dependent; so that my use of the office telephone may be restricted to certain times, or zones. In this example, the usage relationship might involve methods concerned with reporting overseas calls to management for certain grades of staff. Thus, object-oriented databases contain much of the functionality of semantic data models although, as we have seen, there are some inheritance features which are not always supported in the object model. Object-oriented databases go beyond semantic models insofar as they capture behavioural abstractions; methods. This means that they can represent and even normalize behaviour.

Conceptually, an object in an object-oriented database stores both attributes, which may themselves be complex objects, and methods together. In an actual implementation, complex objects and method code may not be physically stored with the object identifier, but pointers to the physical location may be stored. It is important that any enquiry language copes with this question of physical storage quite transparently, so that the user or designer of the database application may proceed as though the physical storage were in accordance with the conceptual model. Only a few of the commercial object-oriented databases actually store methods in the database. The majority only store the data structures; methods are dealt with by the run-time system in the conventional manner. Perhaps this justifies the use of the term OBJECT-ORIENTED DATABASE as against the otherwise preferable but never used OBJECTBASE. A consequence of this is that most products are tightly coupled with particular object-oriented programming languages as we will see in Section 5.8.

In object-oriented programming, the emphasis is on behavioural abstraction. As far as structure is concerned, this means that the emphasis is on the inheritance of encapsulated methods. In object-oriented database systems, there is a much stronger requirement to model the structural properties of data and make explicit inheritance and aggregation structures. This kind of structure can arise in several different ways. Objects can be grouped in classes according to their common structural and behavioural properties; this is **classification.** For example, employees and customers can be grouped as people, and people, animals and plants can be grouped as living things. There is no unique way of classifying objects, and real-world objects may be classified as belonging to more than one class. Class inheritance structures (or networks) represent generalization and specialization. Vehicles are generalizations of cars, and specializations of artefacts. Closely related to classification is **association**. Here, concrete instances are grouped into a class according to some property that they share. An example of an association of objects that is not a classification of them might be the set of all things which are red or the set of things which weigh more than one tonne. The distinction, and how to use it in data analysis, will become clearer after you have read Section 6.4.1, where a distinction is made between essential (classificatory) and accidental (associative) objects. Classification sometimes represents a subset relationship and association a membership relationship. Something that is an instance in one application, can be a class in another. For example, in a database of scientific terms, 'hominid' is an instance, while in an anthropological database hominids may have several instances, or indeed subclasses. Objects can be grouped as components of some composite object in two ways; either as a parts structure or as a set of attributes. This is **composition** or **aggregation**. For example, a car is composed of wheels, transmission, body, and so on. We call this notion 'composition structure'. Aggregation structure is more general and includes the possibility of conceptual composition as well as physical composition. For example, a computer is a concept aggregated from concepts including name, operating system, other software, location, access rights, and so on. Note that these components can in turn be aggregates: 'other software' for example. Aggregation of attributes and methods is how objects are formed conceptually in object-oriented programming and design.

It is important to note that inheritance and aggregation networks can interact. An object which is an aggregate of several objects contains (inherits) their attributes and methods. An object that inherits attributes and methods from a supertype also inherits their aggregation structure. This issue does not arise often in object-oriented programming, but in databases it is crucial. The theory of this interaction is not yet fully worked out but the theory of semantic data models has much to offer.

Another kind of structure which is important in the design of complex data management systems is the structure of **usage**, or client-server, relationships between objects. These structures represent the message passing topology of systems and measure the complexity of their control structures. This will be dealt with in Chapter 6.

As we will discuss more fully later, every verb could give rise to an association structure. The ones we have mentioned, to use, to aggregate and to be a kind of, seem to be particularly important. In AI, where semantic nets are used, other structures sometimes emerge, based on relationships like ownership. Attempts to lay down fixed sets of 'conceptual primitives', as for example Schank and Abelson (1977) tried to do within their theory of 'script' objects and Lenat and Guha (1990) with their CYC, have generally failed. I think this reflects a general philosophical issue: the theory of categories. Aristotle gave a set of fixed categories of thought, which were taken up and modified by Kant. The need to revise the set leads us to the observation that these categories are dynamically, socially and historically determined, and cannot be fixed. Human practice determines the canonical ones. In this case, DP practice has further determined that composition, classification and usage are canonical categories or structures. The semantic data models already discussed in this chapter, such as the EER and GSM models, are expressive enough to capture the semantics of classification, aggregation, association and usage, but are weak in behavioural terms. They form the basis for schema descriptions in object-oriented databases. The need for complex, interacting structures of this kind arises because they represent structure in the real world and are part of the semantics of a database application. However, exposing attributes and methods via these structures makes it very hard to enforce the principle of information hiding. An object-oriented database, therefore, is required to do much more with data structures than an object-oriented programming language.

To fill out this loose definition it is important to make a few comparisons between object-oriented and relational databases. First, as Ullman (1989) argues cogently, there is a trade-off between non-procedurality (or non-declarativeness) and object identity. Relational systems offer non-procedural, that is declarative, access languages based on logic which are subject to query optimization. Object-oriented systems are fundamentally navigational and non-declarative in the mode of access via explicitly declared relationships between objects and classification and aggregation structures. However, for the same reason such systems require less optimization, and for enquiries on complex objects can be massively more efficient.

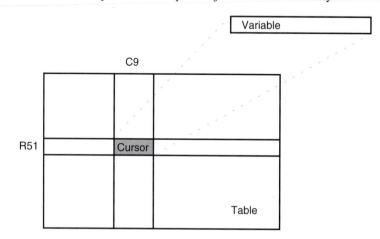

Figure 5.18 The impedance mismatch.

The mismatch between table-oriented languages such as SQL and ordinary record-oriented programming languages means that a separate data manipulation language (DML) is required for access. In a relational system, the unit of currency is the table; every SQL query returns a table. In a conventional programming language the unit of currency is the variable. Database programmers usually have to write code to move a 'cursor' across tables to resolve this problem and map cells to variables and *vice versa*. This **impedance mismatch**,[1] between declarative and procedural styles and between the type systems of the application language and the database, causes a loss of information at the interface and impedes automatic type checking. 4GLs try to overcome these problems, but can only partially do so. In object-oriented database systems there is a match between programming and enquiry languages based on the notion of an object. Computationally rich DMLs can be constructed easily, or the application language can be extended to include the type system of the database. The distinction between the two languages can almost disappear. The Versant object-oriented database system, for example, does all enquiries in extended Java or C++. We will see later (Chapter 6) that this applies to the distinction between languages and methods as well; the language and model

---

[1] So called because an impedance mismatch in an electrical interface prevents optimal power transfer.

impose the method. Resolving the impedance mismatch supports distributed service-based architectures, where more of the semantics is stored in the database. This means that accesses are reduced, and that integrity is better maintained. Also, having a single type system leads to a more natural and uniform data model so that logical database design becomes the same as class library design and no special data analysis methods are needed.

Object-oriented databases do not often need to do joins: the slowest operation that a relational system can ever have to perform. Since objects are stored as coherent wholes, retrieval of an object is a single, simple, although maybe large, operation. In a relational environment, an application derives the structure of the database at run time from disconnected tables, whereas in an object-oriented database the structure is stored directly. So instead of performing joins, the application follows pointers from object to object. This is reminiscent of the structures found in network databases, but object-oriented databases are more flexible in terms of schema evolution. This is because the object metaphor means that data are stored in coherent chunks; often the pointers are restricted within a single file. It also reflects the benefits of encapsulation, because, in a network database, the programmer needs to know whether connexions between record types are implemented as a linked list or as an array of pointers; different commands being used in each case.

Pure relational database management systems (RDBMSs) can store objects, in the form of attributes or tables, but the amount of traffic between an application and such a database is increased because of the need to reassemble objects after retrieval and *vice versa* for storage. Typically, many normalized tables are necessary to represent a real-world object, and this leads to the need for joins to reconstruct coherent objects. This is especially true when the objects are complex ones such as graphical images, documents, balance sheets, etc. This issue of performance is related to the old arguments about network versus relational databases, but now the argument can take place on the level of logical concepts, rather than at a physical level, where empirical results are the only proofs that can be bandied. Typical RDBMSs are optimized for the few large joins which characterize their usual commercial applications. Furthermore, these products have had 20 years of refinement and tuning. This makes them more efficient than current object-oriented databases (OODBs) for constructing accounting and stock control systems and the like. It is the applications that need to carry out many small joins, such as complex bills of materials, the management of structured documents, geographic information systems, e-commerce and CAD, which give them the most trouble. All these applications need to store complex objects and OODBs are usually far more efficient for this kind of work.

In an OODB, integrity constraints can refer to instances, unlike relational systems, where only entity (or class level) constraints may be expressed. In an OODB the semantics of the application, such as functional dependencies, are not hidden in the normalization of tables. Redundancy is dealt with by storing pointers to objects.

Relational systems usually have a limited set of primitive data types, integer, money, date, etc. Some systems support extended types such as text or BLOBs (binary large objects), but these have no accessible internal structure or semantics associated with them. Object-oriented and object-relational databases allow user defined types with semantics attached via the class system. This is what makes it possible to use an object-oriented programming language as both the access language and DML.

In object-oriented programming, there are two ways to define subclasses, by forming unions of types or by defining a subtype explicitly. The second approach is better in database systems because it does not permit *ad hoc* types to be constructed from semantically unrelated types, and it extends naturally to types with encapsulated methods.

The features against which an object-oriented database should be assessed include:

- Platform availability
- Availability and support
- Price and licensing strategy
- Performance
- Multiple inheritance
- Composition structures
- Dynamic schema evolution
- Storage management
- Lock management
- Event notification and communication
- Version management
- Flexible concurrency management
- Group work facilities and versioning
- Query management
- Security and authorization
- User interface and 4GL/visual programming
- External language interfaces and database APIs
- Multimedia support
- Web support

Object-oriented databases are important because they address some key issues for the application of information technology. They promise to deliver the benefits associated with object-oriented programming, reusability and extensibility, and to add the benefits of database systems. In doing so, a wider range of applications can be addressed and the promise of vastly improved performance and storage economy over relational and hybrid systems, while retaining the latter's flexibility, is borne out by many experiences. Perhaps most importantly of all, they promise to deliver the benefits associated with semantically rich languages, in the manner of semantic databases and expert systems. In my opinion, object-oriented databases and their associated 4GLs will find their apotheosis when they are able to combine object-oriented programming, semantic data models and expert systems in one unified framework.

5.7 Benefits of object-oriented databases

The benefits that users are looking for from object-oriented databases mirror those to be obtained with object-oriented programming; reusability, increased modularity and extensibility. Also we would like to think that the flexibility of relational systems can be retained and combined with the efficiency and semantic expressiveness of pointer-based systems.

It is convenient, for exposition, to group the benefits arising from the use of object-oriented databases into three categories as follows: those arising from a need to use an object-oriented programming language or environment; those arising from the enriched semantic capabilities of an object-oriented database; and those arising directly from the capabilities of the object-oriented database design itself.

All the remarks in this section apply equally well to object-relational databases and object-oriented databases proper – except for those relating to performance.

5.7.1 Benefits arising from a need to use object-oriented programming

If an organization has already decided, for reasons which we need not discuss here, that it needs the benefits of object-oriented programming and has to manage persistent data, there are several benefits that accrue from linking the application programming language and environment to an object-oriented database system. These may be summarized as follows:

■ An object-oriented database minimizes the need for paging objects in and out of memory when using object-oriented programming. The other such benefits are those associated with database systems in general, but OODBs are particularly pertinent to sharing, distribution, security and versioning.

■ Object-oriented databases help to close the semantic gap between real-world objects and concepts and their representation in the database. They also attack the impedance mismatch between the application programming language and the DML, which gives the developer less to learn, less to do and a more uniform mode of expressing designs.

5.7.2 Benefits arising from enriched semantic capabilities

These benefits are, principally, as follows:

- It is possible to store both the relationships between objects and the constraints on objects in the server, rather than in the client application. This can have enormous implications for both maintenance and application integrity. A change need only be made once and the possibility of multiple, inconsistent changes is removed, or at least minimized.
- An object-oriented database or model can express whatever the entity-relationship model can express, supersets the hierarchical model, the network model and enriches all of them semantically. The efficiency of hierarchical systems is approached, but dynamic binding of methods and garbage collection can compromise this potential for efficient access.
- There is, at least potentially, support for 'rules' (active objects) in an object-oriented database. All current proposals for this are *ad hoc*, but one can foresee the emergence of a standard protocol for encapsulating rules.
- Object-oriented databases offer the possibility of earlier type checking of *ad hoc* enquiries, compared to relational systems. This is accomplished via the user defined type system, which can be used to reject incorrect types before making an actual database access. The relational compromise is to compile frequently used enquiries in advance, as in Ingres.

In a sense, the semantic capabilities of programming and database systems are an end in themselves. It has long been a goal of software engineering to be able to carry out reverse engineering; that is, to take a piece of executable code and discover enough about its purpose and function to rewrite it in another language or on a different machine, and to do this automatically if possible. As things stand, reverse engineering in this sense is quite impossible. The best that can be done is to re-code small modules individually and that with a lot of manual intervention. Although there are some good automated tools supporting the activity, it still takes a great deal of skill even to do that. The reason for this state of affairs is that programs do not contain, in an explicit form, the semantics contained, say, in a requirements specification. For me then, a benefit, if not the benefit, of the object-oriented approach is that it promises to make reverse engineering possible for the first time. If we can capture the semantics of objects and encode them in explicit, readable form – as rules and classification structures perhaps – then we can recover them and use them to generate new code which need not mimic the physical architecture or module structure of the original system. This is imperative for specification (or throwaway) prototyping.

5.7.3 Benefits of object-oriented databases as such

Object-oriented databases combine the speed of a network database with the flexibility of a relational one. The Sun Cattell benchmark (Cattell and Skeen, 1990) shows typical 100-fold performance improvements for certain kinds of engineering database retrievals and updates. Most object-oriented database products support dynamic schema evolution just as well as any relational system. This means that a whole series of applications which were not amenable to attack with a DBMS can now be tackled straightforwardly. Support for long transactions using persistent locks and for automatic version control makes these products the basis for a new approach to distributed computing. The fact that most products have supported distributed update from the outset is another consequence of their origin in the network and workstation culture. Relational systems only latterly, and after much difficulty, added such capability. Also, the message passing metaphor is a natural one to use to describe distributed systems.

Pure OODBs give generally better performance when complex objects and complex relationships must be dealt with. This is mainly because there is no need to break up large objects for storage in normalized tables and reassemble them at run time via slow join operations. This is especially true in applications involving engineering drawings and complex graphics. Furthermore, the amount of disk space occupied may be far less, because of the need to store many more index files in relational systems. This is the only benefit that does not accrue to the object-relational databases – although careful tuning has vastly reduced the difference for many applications.

The object metaphor supports multi-media applications in a natural way. Objects with the properties of shapes, with temporal behaviour (videos and sound), text and other concepts may all be modelled, and stored, within a unified conceptual scheme.

The benefits of reuse do not need to be restated here. Extensibility is a key benefit that arises directly from the classification structures of an object-oriented database. I would not claim reuse as the key benefit, since complex structures may compromise encapsulation. However, reuse is potentially a key benefit of object-oriented programming languages, and the benefits of a small, smooth interface between an object-oriented language application and an object-oriented database mean that the benefit of reusability can be better delivered in the application itself. OODBs support extensibility since data types can be extended using their inheritance features. New subtypes may be added without the need to restructure existing portions of the database. Aggregation is easier to model and objects can be treated as individuals or as collections within the model.

Mature object-oriented databases may simplify concurrency control and a sound method of query optimization may emerge from current research, but this is still an unresolved issue.

Object-oriented databases give generally better navigational control over queries, because pointers to related objects are stored in objects.

Object-oriented databases have built-in referential integrity and generally richer semantics than other systems. They share these benefits with systems based on the semantic models, and Entity-Relationship and deductive databases. Object identity solves the problem of dangling tuples[2] and means that there is no need for some referential integrity checks, because objects are not referred to but addressed directly. The richer semantics is based on the ability to construct types and encapsulate constraints within objects at any level in the type network, including the possibility of overriding and exception constraints.

Physical clustering of objects on disk is a problem for designers of relational systems. They must ensure that tables which are frequently joined reside on the same device or close to each other in storage, to minimize disk accesses. The only basis for clustering is empirical study of common queries. In object-oriented systems there is a more logical basis for clustering based on class and aggregation hierarchies. Objects that form groups are stored together as composite objects, and, in a well-designed system, classification structures are used as the natural basis of clustering. This is not just an implementational convenience; the clustering reflects the semantics of the application, and therefore it is likely, although not guaranteed, that common queries will refer to nearby physical locations on disk.

Not having a separate DML means that developers have only one language to learn. This is possible because the type systems required in the application and those stored in the database can be made to match. One way of doing this, for example, is to use Java interfaces or C++ classes to extend the type system of the language to include the types that would normally be unique to the DML – such as 'relation' in a relational DML.

The possibility of having class libraries of common database and application-dependent structures helps to speed development. However, it is necessary to beware of the difficulties of awareness and navigation of libraries mentioned in relation to object-oriented programming in previous chapters. Browsers and class librarians are essential tools if this benefit is to be exploited. Here too, group work is an asset.

Although locking is easier to conceptualize in an object-oriented model, because the natural unit of locking is the object, with a single lock on all relevant data rather than multiple locks scattered among unrelated tables, locking has proved a quite severe problem in practical systems. As we shall see, it is easy to lock large hierarchies and so bring the system to its knees in performance terms. Of course, escalation of locks is also possible in relational databases, although it is easier to deal with. Multi-user access is still a problem in object-oriented systems, and purchasers will be wise to ask for concrete demonstrations to allay any doubts in the context of a particular application.

Object-oriented databases map onto distributed architectures well. Sending a message to the encapsulated methods of an object supports a distributed architecture, because it is not necessary to repeat the functionality across many applications. The example used in Chapter 1, where a method for calculating the age of an employee,

---

2 Dangling tuples are tuples which are not represented in all the (normalized) relations which contribute to the representation of an object, and which can thus be lost when a join operation is performed.

or in fact any person, is stored with the object, illustrates this idea. We do not have to copy age routines to several applications, since if they are stored centrally, the danger of the system accidentally evolving several different ways of doing the calculation – say as 'age next birthday' in some places and 'age last birthday' in others – is removed.

I have argued for the ability of computer systems to capture more of the semantics, both data and functional, of an application in explicit form. This theme is expanded upon in Chapter 6.

The object-oriented metaphor is a unified conceptual model covering design, programming and enquiry. The benefits of a unified metaphor are easy to see. It is to be hoped that such a style will lead perhaps to higher productivity and flexibility, but ultimately this will depend on how well programmers understand the metaphor.

5.7.4 Problems with object-oriented databases

As with other aspects of this technology, there are pitfalls as well as benefits. We will consider some of these in this section.

At a purely theoretical level it is a problem that there is no universally accepted object-oriented data model. However, there have been a lot of suggestions in this direction. Ullman (1989) describes a primitive and quite general model. Other excursions include (Beech, 1987), (Lecluse *et al.,* 1988) and (Manola and Dayal, 1986). This disbenefit is not one that should worry the commercial practitioner greatly. As we have seen, the CADF and ODMG models have wide acceptance and may even converge eventually.

Object identity is all very well in theory but real-world objects do not always have accessible unique identities. Not only is it possible for Sam to be stored twice as a shareholder and as an employee in a relational database, if he doesn't volunteer the information that he has an alias (Lord Lucan, say) then our object-oriented database may have two representations of an object that does have unique identity though we cannot find out about it. One way round this is to model only the identity of rôles rather than the objects playing them.

One cannot do query optimization fully in an object-oriented database without compromising the goals of object-orientation, especially the principle of information hiding, because optimization requires looking at the implementation. On the other hand, queries over complex objects are much faster anyway. Object-oriented databases based on the functional model can carry out query optimization, however. Gray *et al.* (1992) show how this can be done in an object-oriented extension of Daplex. Kim (1990) claims that it is likely that only minor changes to existing optimization techniques will be required but admits that it is still essentially a research area.

Yet another problem is the difficulty of modelling relationship types in an object-oriented database. It is also hard to compose operations, because they are not all table-valued as they would be in a relational system; they may return values of any type. The result of an operation may even be of the type of a new ADT with no operations yet defined on it.

Another potential problem arises because of the many different versions of multiple inheritance supported by different database and language products. It seems inevitable that anyone wishing to exploit this aspect of object-oriented technology will need to ensure that the programming language and the database are compatible in this respect.

As with distributed relational databases, distributed object-oriented databases give rise to problems that have yet to be solved. Not only do all the traditional locking and commit strategy issues arise anew, but there are extra problems. For example, no one knows how to guarantee network-wide object identity yet, although progress has been made in the context of component-based development (see Chapter 9). Any system that employs two-phase commits to handle update, as do all current distributed systems, will inevitably be slower than a centralized database. Only parallel implementations can address this problem. Another potentially insuperable problem is that of deciding where to put the data. Practical experience shows that there is very rarely a perfect distribution strategy; one user's need for local storage to perform complex analyses may be contradicted by another's requirement to combine the very same data with others for regular reports.

There are several other unsolved problems concerning concurrency, schema evolution, locking and query optimization. The reader is referred to more technical references such as (Khoshafian and Abnous, 1990), (Kim, 1990), (Gray *et al.*, 1992) and (Zdonik and Maier, 1990), and to other works mentioned in the bibliographical notes at the end of this chapter, for details on these problems and research aimed at overcoming them.

Although the logic of a locking protocol is easier to understand in an object-oriented system it is not obvious that locking can be accomplished efficiently in a multi-user environment. There are very severe locking problems associated with inheritance hierarchies.

Whatever benefits object-oriented technologies may be capable of delivering, design and implementation issues do not go away. For example, the designer still needs to ponder on the construction of indexes, caching, and so on. This needs good, experienced people. It also needs good management. We will look at some of the management issues in Chapter 9.

Object-oriented databases now constitute a mature but still evolving technology. Necessary features from the wish-list are still being added to products. However, the maturation process is proceeding very rapidly. Among the several object-oriented database products dealt with below, some are good for some types of application while some are good for others. If you are using Smalltalk and building a multimedia database, for example, you might consider GemStone. However, for a database extension of a GUI application coded in C++, ObjectStore might be a more natural choice. For a commercial application involving multiple media or complex objects Jasmine or Versant might be better.

5.8 Survey of OODB products

In a short work of this nature we cannot possibly do full justice to all the object-oriented database products in existence. Our main aim will be to discuss the general use of this technology and future prospects, giving an indication of the desiderata for using or avoiding it. As with object-oriented programming languages, however, we cannot avoid a brief survey. We have already described the object-relational databases and now move on to current pure object-oriented products and some of their noble ancestors.

There are three types of object-oriented database product on the market. We have already dealt with the object-relational hybrids. Distinguished mainly by their better performance but, to a lesser extent, also by a lower impedance mismatch are two kinds of pure OODB. Persistent extensions to object-oriented languages, such as ObjectStore, provide a way of dealing with persistence with no impedance mismatch but are usually relatively weak in terms of the facilities of a traditional database **management** system. Proper object-oriented database management systems, such as O₂ and Versant, are better equipped with database management system facilities. For example, O₂ supports a 4GL and Versant has event notification facilities. Presently, both types of product tend to be closely coupled to one object-oriented language (usually C++ or Java) with additional bindings to other languages added on.

5.8.1 Commercial object-oriented databases

GEMSTONE
One of the earliest, and probably the purest, object-oriented database in existence as a commercial product is GemStone (Maier and Stein, 1987; Bretl *et al.,* 1989), which was originally built on top of an extension of Smalltalk called OPAL (Servio Logic, 1989) to deal with persistent objects. Unlike ObjectStore and Versant (see below), which are intimately linked to C++, it was not so closely tied to a particular language and its marketing now emphasizes its Java binding. Thus, although the DML is OPAL, GemStone can be accessed from other languages, including C++. However, the C++ binding does not support multiple inheritance. GemStone is aimed by its vendor mainly at developers building application servers in a three-tier client-server environment. It has been a commercial product longer than any of its competitors and is one of the more mature products.

OPAL has a class library covering a few basic but intricate data structures and supports all of the key object-oriented features; abstraction, inheritance and identity. It is, by default, like Smalltalk, a typeless language. Unlike most common database languages, even primitive operations, such as insert, delete and update, must be declared explicitly for each class defined, which is a nuisance. This reflects the strong encapsulation philosophy behind Smalltalk. Any system based on Smalltalk, with its garbage collection and enforced late binding, must be approached with some scepticism concerning performance issues. Another minor potential problem is that the GemStone access language forms queries and indexes over object attributes. This can be used to violate encapsulation. Attributes and classes can be optionally given a type or **kind** but this does not prevent run-time failures due to polymorphism.

The architecture is based on the client-server model and supports distribution. The Stone is the database server or object manager and is accessed via multiple versions of the Gem, a virtual machine that compiles and runs OPAL methods. The Stone is responsible for garbage collection. GemStone is one of the few products that stores methods in the database. This, and the client-server structure, is what makes it possible to access GemStone from other languages, including C, Pascal, and C++. Because methods can be executed on the server, retrievals over large sets of objects are much more efficient because only the results are returned to the client. Locational transparency and replication are well supported.

Objects cannot be deleted from OPAL except by garbage collection and each object's location is stored in a table. This makes relocation easier. GemStone's locking strategy involves database shadowing for recovery and a combination of optimistic and pessimistic regimes for concurrency control. Each client maintains a shadow of the object table. If concurrency control is pessimistic, applications must obtain explicit locks. Emmerich and Schäfer (1993) show that the optimistic approach may carry an overhead, since longer is required to perform conflict resolution, etc. However, this approach may be more appropriate for design and engineering environments, whilst the pessimistic approach would be more suitable for MIS applications. Optimistic locking, whilst using more CPU than the pessimistic approach, is still practical for MIS applications, due to the ratios between CPU performance and disk speeds on modern machines. Furthermore, read-only queries do not have to acquire any locks and this leads to less contention between updates and read-only transactions. GemStone supports Read, Write and Exclusive locks. Locks are held across transaction boundaries and must be explicitly released. Also, since there is no facility to wait for a lock to be released (by another transaction that may be holding it), no deadlock detection is necessary. Locking is possible for individual objects or collections of heterogeneous objects. However, GemStone does not support locking, copying or manipulating a collection of *interrelated* (composite) objects.

GemStone, in common with most other object-oriented databases, lacks facilities for semantic data modelling, such as aggregation structures, exceptions, rules, constraints, triggers and the like. It also lacks support for many-valued attributes, set-valued relations, one-to-one relations, inverses of relations and keys. Gray *et al.* (1992) discuss this weakness of object-oriented databases at length and present a system called ADAM which addresses some of them.

GemStone is easy to use for Smalltalk programmers. The current instantiation, GemstoneJ 3.0, integrates Java 2, Java Server Pages (JSP),[3] a Java Servlet engine, EJB containers, a CORBA-compliant ORB and a Java-based Transaction Monitor. The product also emphasizes its adherence to the most modern security standards and practices.

VERSANT

Versant, the object-oriented database product from Versant Object Technology, has been one of the more successful object-oriented databases. It uses C++ and Java as the primary access languages, although C and Smalltalk are also available. OQL-compliant SQL is also supported so that existing applications can access the new database. An important feature is event notification, based on instance updates, which assists with inter-process communication and group-work and transaction-centric applications. It is based on a multi-client/multi-server architecture like Ingres and scores very highly on the Cattell benchmark. Multi-threaded, multi-session clients and multi-threaded servers contribute to better performance and scalability. Versant provides gateways to relational systems such as Sybase and Oracle and to others via ODBC and JDBC. Several development tools for GUI development and report writing and bridges to CASE tools exist.

The Versant Fault-Tolerant Server enables round-the-clock availability through asynchronous replication. Dynamic schema evolution means that new types can be added even when the database is live. These features, along with the performance profile of an object-oriented database, make Versant ideal for supporting high-access web sites.

Other features of Versant include good support for composition structures, multiple inheritance and versioning and an extensive class library. Versant's particularly strong transaction management features support co-operative work well. Both optimistic and pessimistic locking strategies are supported and instances can be locked singularly or in groups. A dual caching strategy also adds to performance and scalability. Queries are executed on the server and then transferred to the client cache. CORBA programmers can use object identifiers directly as object references. A legacy access tool was under construction at the time of writing.

Versant has been used as the basis for several busy web sites and for applications in healthcare, telecommunications and financial risk management.

OBJECT STORE

ObjectStore (Attwood, 1991) is yet another successful object-oriented database management system with close ties to C++. Most people regard it as a persistent extension of C++ rather than a database management system *per se*. A native Java interface was added in 1997. Like Versant, performance is very good on the Cattell benchmark and the architecture is multi-client/multi-server to support distribution and scalability. Class libraries are provided to support versioning, configuration management and composition structures. The class library also supports object

---

[3] JSP provides a way of generating dynamic web pages that separate dynamic content from presentation. These are compiled into reusable components: servlets.

indexing and clustering, associative queries, relationship management and iteration over sets. There is a danger that associative queries may violate encapsulation. There is no Object SQL; the idea is that removing the impedance mismatch and providing classes makes programming so easy that there is no need for the complexities of an Object SQL. ObjectStore has, at the time of writing, fewer productivity tools than Jasmine, O_2 or Versant.

Efficiency is addressed by the use of pointer swizzling techniques. Pointer swizzling means that global object references are converted to local memory addresses when an object has been loaded into main memory. Swizzling techniques are used to bring attribute access time down to levels close to that of programming language memory structures. An alternative approach is to partition the object space. Then object identifiers within a single segment need no translation. Static or dynamic clustering of connected objects on disk also helps access efficiency. Some of the things one can do with pointers in ObjectStore, such as pointing at persistent objects directly in virtual memory, seem a little dangerous to me, but power is rarely obtained without risk. This product too has very good versioning, multiple inheritance and transaction management features and would support group work. Its unique approach to persistence allows third-party tools and libraries to be used unmodified. All methods are handled on the client. Like Versant, the product has good support for referential integrity as discussed in Section 5.9.

ObjectStore has been used successfully as an object cache for relational databases, resulting in significant performance gains and removing the impedance mismatch (McCauley, 1999). It is positioned as a high performance, scalable engine for web servers and Object Design offer several web, CORBA and XML productivity tools integrated with the product, including eXcelon: an XML data server that stores and manages legacy data and distributes them across the middle tier. Applications of ObjectStore include network management and application servers front-ending relational products.

O_2

O_2 Technology's O_2 (Bancilhon *et al.*, 1991; Delobel *et al.*, 1995) was developed at GIP Altair and supports multiple object-oriented programming languages and its own 4GL: a superset of C called O_2C. The developers of O_2 pioneered many of the fundamental ideas of object-oriented databases. It comes with a graphical browser, programming environment, debugger and supports OQL. Development is done in interpretative mode during which schema evolution is possible. The final system is compiled and schema evolution halted thereby. O_2 supports class hierarchy indexing and disk clustering and is notable for distinguishing values from objects. For efficiency all object methods are handled by client workstations using a page-server architecture reminiscent of that of ObjectStore. It can store hundreds of gigabytes of data and has been used for many commercial applications. The product was acquired by Unidata in 1997.

JASMINE

Computer Associates' Jasmine was developed at Fujitsu and supports multiple media, complex objects and ODQL (an OQL-compliant query language). It has strong web and animation features and supports multiple inheritance, instance and class methods and attributes and server-side methods. Jasmine has its own visual, object-oriented development environment and class library, Studio, that supports almost completely codeless development. Studio was formerly called JADE. Methods can also be written in C or C++ and there are APIs for HTML, Active X, Java and Smalltalk. Jasmine also integrates with relational databases. Jasmine is interesting because it has a very large vendor behind it, giving a better chance of success outside niche markets such as application server caching.

POET   POET, from Poet Software in Germany, is an object-oriented database that runs on several platforms. It has close coupling to C++ and Java, and was originally a C++ pre-compiler that added persistent classes and other extensions to the language and comes with a graphical browser and query optimizer. Schema evolution and version control are supported. The programmer works in a large, partitioned virtual address space and database access is handled by the system. It has evolved into a powerful object-oriented database management system capable of competing with Versant, O_2 and Jasmine though less language independent. It supports OQL and has a graphical 4GL tool: Viewsoft. One of its unique features is its emphasis on content management and the provision of features like full text search. There are the usual links to relational products.

Ericsson used Poet for the development of an internet telephone 'Penny-2'. A compact embedded Java database meets the ODMG specification for Java Data Objects (JDO). JDO facilitates memory access to and saving of data on all Java platforms, from servers to smartcards. This renders the development of one-off complex software unnecessary. The programmer can now concentrate on writing Java applications. The Poet Content Management Suite extends the basic product to the administration and storage of SGML and XML data. With it the user can reuse separate components, save documents in parallel in different languages and use several current authoring systems. In addition it is possible to edit the data via an internet or intranet. The product has been used for the exchange of catalogue data over the internet. When buyers and distributors contact each other using e-commerce they are able to use, reuse and exchange XML data. Distributors can feed their offers into the system quickly and remain available to help buyers.

OBJECTIVITY   The first major, mainstream hardware manufacturer to endorse a commercial object-oriented database management system was Digital, whose Objectivity/DB (Dick and Swett, 1995) was also originally coupled to C++. It supports distribution, long transactions and versioning. Each object has a structured identifier, since Objectivity/DB uses a hierarchical storage model which at the top level is viewed as a single logical database. This logical database is composed of multiple distributed databases, which are themselves composed of a number of containers. Containers contain pages and objects reside on these pages. The unit of locking is the container, which may consist of individual *hot-spot* objects or groups of thousands of objects. This granularity can be changed dynamically. However, relocating an object requires the allocation of a new OID and the updating of all references, although this is transparent to the user. This is a trade-off against purely logical OIDs, which are slow because hashing is required on access and relationships become essentially the same as a relational indexed join. Special features have been developed to support electrical and mechanical CAD applications.

The papers on the early ORION object-oriented database still contain some of the most profound thinking on the subject to be found anywhere. The ORION research project at MCC concentrated on schema evolution and produced a descriptive semantics and a set of rules which must be followed if a type network is to remain consistent as attributes and methods are added to or removed from a class. These rules are different from those usually adopted in database systems. The schema of an object-oriented database is dynamic and may evolve in the following ways without any need for recompilation.

- Changes to the description of an object: adding, deleting or updating attributes or methods.
- Changes to the objects represented by the system: adding, deleting or changing the identity of an object. Deleting a class usually results in all its subclasses acquiring all the superclasses of the deleted class as parents, rather than themselves being deleted.
- Changes to the structures of the database: adding, deleting or modifying an inheritance, composition, use or associative relationship.

Schema evolution is complicated by the presence of inheritance. If a superclass changes then everything below it in the lattice has to be checked for dependencies. Other structures (composition and use) similarly complicate things. It is important to note that object identity is and must be preserved throughout all schema changes in an object-oriented database. For that reason, it is assumed that schema changes are reasonably gradual. This issue is closely related to that of version control, and most object-oriented databases offer some sort of version control at the instance, class and schema levels. In ENCORE (Elmore *et al.*, 1989), for example, there is a class called History-Bearing-Entity which contains attributes such as previous-version, next-version and member-of-version-set, which can be inherited by any object requiring version control. The version set is an association containing all versions of the object.

Although ORION was inspired largely by Smalltalk, there are a number of important extensions in the model. Multiple inheritance is supported, and there are three built-in methods for conflict resolution: a 'left first' rule is used whereby the first superclass in the list of superclasses is used to inherit the conflicting method or attribute from; the user may specify the choice which the object should make; or the user may specify that the object should inherit both properties and rename one of them. Attributes may have defaults at the class level. We will see the importance of this feature in the next chapter. Even though class level multiple inheritance is supported, an instance is only allowed to belong to one class. Another profound aspect of the ORION work is the recognition that classification (AKO) and composition (APO) structures are often closely coupled, and a semantics for this coupling has been developed. The notation used in ORION to show this coupling is shown in Figure 5.19, where the body of a vehicle is owned by one specific vehicle and cannot exist without it. The AKO links are lines emanating from class attributes that indicate such dependencies. ORION also has a semantics of and a protocol for version control and important ideas on locking. As ORION was a research system there were still problems in such areas as type safety and garbage collection, but the ideas referred to above are, in my opinion, key ones and many have been carried forward into the commercial successor to the ORION prototypes.

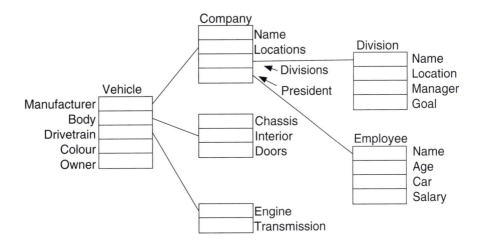

Figure 5.19 ORION class schema (by kind permission of the ACM Press).

In his book on ORION, Kim (1990) argues strongly for the provision of non-procedural enquiry languages for object-oriented databases but does not explore the position held by many others (such as Ullman): that there is a fundamental trade-off between declarativeness and object identity. He justifies this with a mention of research into non-first-normal-form databases. In defining the query model, Kim states that the structure of an object-oriented query 'is basically that of a relational query', and I can't help but wonder whether the truth of this statement depends on the compromises that ORION has made to support a non-procedural approach to queries – joins and all. The strength of the query model, on the other hand, should not be ignored. It is practical and even necessary if object-oriented databases are to become accepted commercially. Kim's discussion offers thoughtful treatment of how both composition (parts) and classification (inheritance) hierarchies or structures affect query processing and optimization.

Itasca is a commercial product based on the ORION research prototypes. Both ORION and Itasca were written in Common Lisp. It shares all of the features of ORION and is unusual in storing and activating methods directly in the database, which makes it possible to embed methods written in any language; currently only Lisp, CLOS, C, C++, Java and FORTRAN. Itasca is based on a distributed multi-client/multi-server architecture and has no centralized name or data server so that there is no single point of failure. Dynamic schema evolution is supported and there are good security, recovery and concurrency services. Authorizations can be inherited, which should reduce the overhead of database administration considerably. Composition structures are well supported and event notification can either be flag-based or message-based. In this way both triggers and workflow applications can be supported. As with Versant, the database can be partitioned into a shared part and various private databases with no need for the user to know where a particular datum is physically stored; Itasca is thus locationally transparent. Class indexing is used to improve performance and, where possible, queries are executed in parallel on different networked machines. Query optimization uses database statistics in a manner reminiscent of the Ingres optimizer. Associative text searches are also possible. The dynamic features of the product make it suitable for applications such as data mining and warehousing, where it occupies a niche market among the other OODBMSs.

The apparent major defects in Itasca are lack of support for encoding business rules and constraints except as methods or triggers, lack of a suite of 4GL development tools and some doubts as to performance. While I suspected that the Lisp implementation limited performance, the supplier assured me once that 'any slowness is due the rich features of the product and not Lisp'.

In a comparative study of object-oriented databases in the context of engineering applications, Ahmed *et al.* (1992) found that Itasca had better feature provision than any other product surveyed and represented the best value for money. They concluded that it had 'very sophisticated features and is relatively easy to use for Lisp programmers, though the Lisp environment incurs some overhead in run-time efficiency'. However, although it has been very influential in terms of their design, Itasca has not achieved the market penetration of the other object-oriented databases we have mentioned so far.

5.8.2 Other influential products and projects

VBASE AND ONTOS
Ontologic's Vbase was one of the first proper object-oriented databases to emerge. It was strongly influenced by CLU, and emphasized strongly typed ADTs. It also attempted to perform as much binding as possible at compile time. Vbase had its own proprietary type definition language, TDL, and used COP (C Object Processor), a proprietary object-oriented extension of C, for access. Its withdrawal from the market and subsequent replacement with a new product, Ontos, pointed up a number of generic issues or problems with first-generation OODBs. First, in the world of commercial databases, SQL was so well established and well understood that introducing a new language such as TDL, however good, was a doomed enterprise. Furthermore, there was no room in the market for yet another object-oriented extension of C, let alone a proprietary one like COP. Second, but even more

significantly, early users of Vbase found that there were severe performance problems due to Vbase's locking mechanism. In any system that supports inheritance this is a potential trouble spot. Suppose, in SACIS, that a particular item belongs to the class ModelCar which, in turn, is a subclass of Toy, Car, StockItem and so on. This item inherits behaviour and data from its superior classes. Suppose now that one of these classes undergoes an update. Surely, everything below it in the hierarchy must be locked. If the updated class is sufficiently general we can soon end up locking effectively the whole database. In a multi-user database this is quite unacceptable. This difficulty was not unique to Vbase and was a problem for several early object-oriented databases. In fact there is a parallel problem in relational systems that support triggers for integrity control, where uncontrolled updates can propagate through the database, locking as they go.

To overcome, or at least limit, these difficulties, Ontologic (renamed Ontos Inc.) released a second generation product, Ontos, again aimed mainly at the engineering and CASE markets. In Ontos, TDL was replaced with an object-oriented extension of SQL, which added object query syntax. COP was replaced by C++. The locking problem was addressed by giving the designer control over the locking strategy, allowing a choice between pessimistic and optimistic protocols. Performance was further enhanced by disk clustering and caching techniques. Better event notification and global deadlock detection, enhanced productivity tools and triggers were also added. A very important feature of Ontos in particular, and this type of product in general, was the provision of support for object version histories and shared transactions. Ontos was one of the more successful early products, in the commercial sense, and was influential. Ontos Inc. claimed over 400 active users world-wide in 1993. However, the company decided thereafter to concentrate on supplying library objects and applications in a Microsoft environment and the product disappeared from sight.

**IRIS,
OPENODB
ODAPTER
AND PCLOS**
IRIS (Fishman *et al.*, 1989) was another system that offered an Object SQL (OSQL). It was developed as an experimental system at Hewlett-Packard, and its data model was based on the functional, rather than a strictly object-oriented, model. It is very relational in style and shows strong Prolog influences. The underlying storage manager was similar to the one used in System R, the precursor to DB2. Natively created objects can be stored in relational databases, including Oracle, Sybase and HP/Allbase. Multiple inheritance is supported and the type of an object can even change at run time. This is a powerful but dangerous facility. Versioning is also supported. In addition to Object SQL, access from Objective-C and Lisp is supported. Support for multimedia databases in IRIS is accomplished via specialized data managers rather than by storing all sorts of objects in a single type system, as with other OODBs. Because the transaction manager of IRIS is based on that of System R the locking of the inheritance hierarchy is a problem. The Itasca approach of having special locking protocols for inheritance networks is far better. A commercial version of IRIS was released under the name Open ODB (Ahad and Dedo, 1992), which was later improved and renamed Odapter. In this product

several language bindings are available, including C++, Smalltalk, Java and CORBA IDL. The C++, Smalltalk and Java interfaces are supported by class libraries that include support for various database operations. A package consisting of the Java client, the Java class builder and the Odapter server is sold as a separate product called DEPOT/J.

PCLOS (Persistent CLOS) was an attempt to build a tightly coupled interface between an object-oriented database (IRIS) and an object-oriented programming language (CLOS).

STATICE

Statice (Symbolics, 1988) was an extension of the Genera programming environment for Symbolics machines and of Common Lisp. It supports the definition of objects with multiple inheritance, object identity and encapsulation of methods. These objects are persistent and sharable. The same reservations about the performance of Lisp-based systems expressed in relation to Itasca apply to Statice, although if you must Lisp, you had best do it on a Symbolics box, which is optimized for the language. Statice was also ported to various UNIX workstations.

OTHERS

On the fringe of the object-oriented database world, there are a few unified object-oriented programming and data manipulation languages such as Vision and DEC's Trellis/Owl. Vision from Innovative Systems Techniques (Insyte) is intended to be simple enough for use by users in the context of financial planning and decision support. Data dependencies in this kind of application rely on time and temporal relationships. To address this kind of problem efficiently Vision adopts a functional style and, although it is not a genuine object-oriented database, this permits the handling of both inheritance and temporal relationships. It uses the notion of prototype objects which blurs any distinction between instances and classes. Vision has been applied in financial applications such as pension fund management.

G-Base was an early object-oriented database developed in France by Graphael and based on Lisp – and came equipped with a closely coupled Prolog-like expert systems development language called G-Logis. It could also be integrated with ART.

ODE (Agrawal and Gehani, 1989) is a research system coupled to C++ in the same manner as ObjectStore. It provides versioning, iteration, query processing, constraints and triggers with timeouts. In ODE a procedural extension of C++ called O++ handles all data manipulations analogously to the way COP in Vbase does so.

LOOM (Kaehler and Krasner, 1983) represents an alternative solution to the problem of making a single user language persistent. It effectively makes the disk drive into a vast virtual memory for Smalltalk. There are several similar products extending Smalltalk.

In addition to the products mentioned above, there have been a number of research systems which influenced later products. Typical such systems were ObServer/ENCORE (Elmore *et al.*, 1989; Zdonik and Wegner, 1985 and 1985a; Skarra and Zdonik, 1986), OOPS (Schlageter *et al.*, 1988) and PDM (Manola and Dayal, 1986). SAMOS was an active object-oriented database produced for research purposes by Klaus Dittrich and his collaborators and the University of Zürich. It continues to be used for this purpose. ObServer was a general purpose object server developed at Brown University. ENCORE (Extensible and Natural Common Object REsource) is its DDL and DML. This system had many of ORION's features and a better transaction manager for supporting group work. These systems were test beds for new ideas and ironing out problems.

A new generation of what Parsaye *et al.* (1989) called 'intelligent' databases also began to emerge in parallel with object-oriented database products. The roots of these developments lay in various attempts to combine database technology with ideas from artificial intelligence and especially expert systems. Some of the early work on Postgres (Stonebraker and Rowe, 1987) – some of which has emerged in Illustra – is situated in this tradition, as were several early attempts to achieve this unification by placing Prolog front-ends on databases to enrich the semantic expressiveness of SQL. The deductive databases mentioned earlier in this chapter also combined work from expert systems and database theory.

At present the only way to achieve expert systems capabilities in a data-intensive application is to use the fairly limited knowledge representation capabilities of systems like Illustra, employ a deductive database or build a loose coupling between a database and an expert system shell of some sort. The problems with such loose couplings arise when there is a large amount of traffic between the application and the database. If, instead of generating database calls in SQL, the shell loads whole segments of the database for processing there are then integrity and concurrency problems. Thus, applications that need knowledge and also need very frequent database access must look towards the emergence of these 'intelligent' databases. Building these couplings involves a great deal of effort and heartache too.

A great deal of work is going on in the tradition of conceptual modelling and functional databases also. Gray *et al.* (1992) describe two systems, P/FDM and ADAM, in this area. A more up-to-date report is available from the University of Aberdeen on request.

5.9 Referential integrity in object databases

The ODMG-93 standard for object-oriented databases uses the term RELATIONSHIP as a synonym for association. We will stick to the term ASSOCIATION here. The standard object model as suggested by ODMG supports one-to-one, one-to-many and many-to-many associations. They are defined as *traversal paths* for each direction of traversal between objects and are declared in the public interface definitions of the objects. An *inverse* clause in both of the traversal path declarations indicates that the traversal paths both apply to the same association. The *inverse* clause ensures that associations maintain referential integrity, which is done by the ODBMS automatically. If the *inverse* clause is omitted, traversal is not possible in the reverse direction.

In ODMG-93, associations are considered types that do not have object identities (OIDs) and that are uniquely identified by the participating instances. The many-to-many association type is composed of two sets of one-to-many associations. These one-to-many associations in turn are defined by sets of one-to-one associations (pointers). There is only a traversal function defined for one direction of traversal of a one-to-many association; i.e. from the single object to the set of related objects. However, the traversal function defined on each of the components' one-to-one associations allows one to go from any element of the set back to the single related instance.

To illustrate how the ODMG-93 standards support referential integrity, I offer the example of ObjectStore, since the inverse association construct of ObjectStore is compliant with the ODMG-93 Standard. I follow the presentation given in the ObjectStore manual (ODI, 1992).

ObjectStore is an object-oriented database programming language and management system that has been sold commercially by Object Design Inc. since 1990. ObjectStore's data model keeps closely to the data model of C++. ObjectStore can be used in three different ways:

- using C programs calling C library functions;
- using C++ programs calling the C++ library functions, with or without generic classes;
- using its C++ extension, the DML, which provides generic classes (based on the C++ templates), query facilities and exception handlers in addition to C++ constructs.

The latter will be the approach considered here with respect to the association integrity maintenance mechanism provided by ObjectStore, although from Version 4 a library interface has been provided for the same purpose.

We will need to know the way ObjectStore defines some of its collection classes. A collection is an object used to group other objects together as ordered or unordered collections that may or may not allow duplicates:

- os_Set: unordered/ no duplicates
- os_Bag: unordered/ duplicates
- os_List: ordered/ duplicates

The collection classes contain member functions to insert, remove and retrieve elements.

In ObjectStore's own C++ extension, associations are represented as data members in the public interface of a class. These links can represent one-to-one, one-to-many, and many-to-many associations. They are implemented as binary associations with pointer-valued or 'collection-of-pointer'-valued data members. The use of a collection type in the **inverse_member** declaration indicates the cardinality of the association.

ObjectStore offers a construct and mechanism to enforce integrity constraints automatically. The data members can be declared inverses of each other (OODM-

Language keyword: **inverse_member**), so that an update to one data member automatically triggers a corresponding update to its 'inverse'.

The integrity constraints underlying the **inverse_member** declaration are quoted here in a slightly modified version to enhance readability:

> If *a* and *b* are inverse data members (representing an association), then, for any two instances *x* and *y* of the two classes, *x* is a value of *a* (which is a data member in the public interface of instance *y*) if and only if *y* is a value of *b* (which is a data member in the public interface of instance *x*).

In a many-to-many association, the value of a data member is a collection type grouping the pointers together. Thus, strictly speaking, every data member is single-valued. Since ObjectStore provides collection classes that allow duplicates (os_List, os_Bag), a more general version of the integrity constraint enforced has to be presented to cover these cases:

> If *a* and *b* are inverse data members (representing an association), then, for any two instances *x* and *y* of the two classes, and for any integer n, *x* occurs n times as a value of *a* (which is a data member in the public interface of instance *y*) if and only if *y* occurs n times as a value of *b* (which is a data member in the public interface of instance *x*).

Table 5.1 Example for many-to-many associations

Class S		Class T	
Instance	inverse association *a*	Instance	inverse association *b*
y	*a.(x, x, z, r)*	*x*	*b.(y, y, s, t)*
s	*a.(x)*	*z*	*b.(y)*
t	*a.(x)*	*r*	*b.(y)*

The **inverse_member** declaration implicitly contains the rule that the integrity constraint quoted above has to be enforced. This is in conformity with my suggestion (Graham *et al.*, 1997a) to impose integrity constraints by encapsulating rules in the class declarations corresponding to the associations represented as pointers with strong semi-inverse rules.

In Figure 5.20, the data members employers (instances of class companies) and employees (instances of class people) are grouped together in collection classes (class os_Set) referring to each other via the **inverse-member** keyword. If an approach other than using ObjectStore's C++ extension (the DML) is chosen, the example above can be expressed in C++ as well. The association concept as such is not supported in C++, but is simulated by the support of automatically generated C++ methods (system pre-defined macros) that implement it. I will not explain this further here.

Integrity constraints are enforced in the following cases:

- establishing a value for an association (if x is established as a value of a for y, y is established as a value of b for x);
- de-establishing a value for an association (if x is de-established as a value of a for y, y is de-established as a value of b for x);
- deletion of an instance (if x is deleted, it is de-established as a value of a for y).

```
class people
{public:
 people *spouse inverse_member spouse;      // 1-1
 os_Set<companies*>employers inverse_member employees;//n-m};

class companies
{public:
 os_Set<people*> employees inverse_member employers; // n-m};
```

Figure 5.20 Using the ObjectStore inverse_member keyword.

Internally, the enforcement of integrity constraints is implemented by a relationship class – embedded in the class – containing the association that encapsulates the pointer (collection-of-pointers) of the data member. If the ObjectStore DML **inverse_member** feature (which is a macro) is not used, the relationship and collection classes in the class library can be used. The implementation of the relationship class entirely hides the inverse maintenance tasks from the code that manipulates the instances of the class containing the association.

An association data member in ObjectStore refers to its 'inverse' in the public interface of the other class. Thus, encapsulation is not compromised.

Integrity is automatically maintained by the ObjectStore DBMS. The **inverse_member** declaration ensures that integrity constraints (which could be regarded as rules or class invariants implicitly contained in the inverse association) are enforced. This seems to be a good exemplar of a solution to the problem of associations that we have discussed: representing associations as mappings that are implemented as pointers and coupled with rules to impose integrity constraints. The same thing can be done in other object-oriented databases such as O_2 (Delobel *et al.*, 1992), although there some code must be written to accomplish this. In either case, encapsulation is not maintained by the implementation, which depends on the global features of the DML rather than on rules encapsulated in the database classes themselves.

Other object-oriented databases such as O_2, Jasmine and Versant model integrity rules in a similar way. In Versant, for example, this is done using its BiLinkVstr keyword in place of ObjectStore's inverse_member, as illustrated in Figure 5.21.

Reuse, considered one of the major advantages of object-orientation, is not threatened either, because – as soon as only one of the classes containing an inverse-member declaration is reused – the DBMS will ensure at compile time that the corresponding class is imported as well. Thus, association information cannot be lost.

```
BiLink_to_BiLink<x,r>::add();          // one-to-one
BiLink_to_BiLinkVstr<x,r>::add();      // many-to-one
BiLinkVstr_to_BiLink<x,r>::add();      // one-to-many
BiLinkVstr_to_BiLinkVstr<x,r>::add()   // many-to-many
```

Figure 5.21 Constructing integrity rules in Versant.

5.10 Applications of object-oriented databases

The applications to which object-oriented databases are best applied are those where relational systems perform poorly or those where the object metaphor is appealing. These include distributed and client-server systems, workflow and group work automation, enterprise integration modelling, multimedia databases, voicemail, geographic information systems (GIS) and product data management. Some complex bill of materials applications may benefit too.

Early, widespread applications of genuinely object-oriented databases were to VLSI design and other CAD applications. Previously, due to the inadequacies of relational systems these applications all had their own purpose-built file systems, which made development costly and sharing of information across systems impossible.

In typical CAD applications, where complex objects representing the design components and the logical relationships between them need to be stored, an object-oriented database helps performance by optimizing the physical location of frequently related data. If the whole design is stored as a single object, this will reduce the number of access operations needed to view or update the design. Computer aided software engineering (CASE) is another area where complex objects and relationships are important.

IBM used GemStone for a complex manufacturing database. POET, O_2, ObjectStore and Versant have been used in telephone network management, CAD, geographic information systems, office automation, airline seat reservation systems, workflow automation, telephone fraud management and financial risk management and real-time trading systems. Other applications have been reported in the areas of computer assisted publishing, materials requirements planning (MRP) and, to a small extent, artificial intelligence.

What all these applications have in common is that they are all concerned with problems that involve very complex objects, and where the relationships among the objects – both in time and in space – are as important as their individual structure. Not only are these objects complex structurally but they also often exhibit complex behaviour. For example, an engineering drawing may be viewed as plan, elevation, side elevation or isometric projection, and these views may be rotated and scaled. Storing behavioural abstractions, the key feature of object-oriented databases, is therefore important in such applications. If there are just complex data types involved then object-relational databases suffice. However, when there are complex networks of such types object-oriented databases come into their own.

The most important application of object-oriented databases at the time of writing is the support of large and busy web sites, an example being the use of Versant to underpin Microsoft's heavily visited site. ObjectStore has also found a successful market in this area and offers an XML data server, eXcelon. POET's Content Management Suite is also an XML server and has been used by General Dynamics in a web-based electronic technical manual. GemStone's product is also focused on the provisional of high integrity application servers.

Versant is the strategic choice of database for the service-based object-oriented architecture of leading investment bank Dresdner Kleinwort Benson. It was also used at Chase Manhattan Bank to deliver a sophisticated volatilities publishing system. The data on volatilities of financial instruments are needed to price complex derivatives, but their structure is complex. Volatilities form a surface or three-dimensional graph, and such structures are not naturally handled by relational systems. Versant gave the required performance and the development team reported that the lack of impedance mismatch substantially reduced their workload.

Some people would argue that the requirement is not for reverse engineering but for correct, zero-defect forward engineering, based on sound analysis and design methods. This argument contains some sense, but still makes the rather idealistic assumption that there will never be circumstances where a company wishes to back out of implementation or analysis decisions.

5.10.1 Distributed databases and full-content retrieval

Object-oriented databases are good at distribution but so are some modern relational products able to work on networks. SQL can be used to connect clients to servers but is usually only used in this way for *ad hoc* queries. More complex applications call for application-dependent code on the server, usually in the form of stored procedures that are not written in the standard part of SQL but in a procedural extension of the language. API standards represented by such products as Sybase's Open Server or Microsoft's rather similar ODBC make it possible, and fairly straightforward, to implement client-server systems in the context of relational databases. The model here is that of a single server. Genuine distributed databases are not yet well supported. Locational transparency, node failure resilience, error handling and latency are all severe practical problems. Non-relational databases can often supply data to relational ones via gateways but the interface to these gateways, and to other relational systems, is usually dependent on a proprietary API of some sort. Standards like ODBC, JDBC and EJB, on the other hand, oblige database vendors to modify their client-end products so that all client applications can talk to any database. However, this only works for single-user workstations and the need for support for multi-user clients is driving some users towards the adoption of object request broker technology.

Khoshafian *et al*. (1992) argue that the solution lies not so much in ORBs but in a combination of object-oriented, relational and rule-based databases that they dub 'intelligent databases'. They also suggest that such databases should incorporate the full-content retrieval capabilities normally associated with library Information Retrieval (IR) systems. The presence of BLOBs or memo fields containing complex information underlines the need for this extension. Furthermore, as databases go beyond the storage of text and numbers to embrace visual and aural media, the indexing and search problem becomes at once more pressing and more complex. Users need to be able to access the content – the meaning – of a stored object without reading it or viewing its content.

IR systems that have to deal with documents whose content changes infrequently can use inverted indexing, concept classification and thesaurus techniques. For more volatile applications, the system's documents may be scanned and their contents compared with a set of keywords or other tokens. Another approach is to build a signature table for each document by hashing keywords into a small numerical signature. This can then be compared against the signature of an arbitrary query. This is a probabilistic approach that does not guarantee that all matching documents will be retrieved or that all those retrieved will match. The best concept indexing systems require people with good knowledge of the subject matter to prepare keyword tables, synonym lists, thesauri and so on. Khoshafian *et al*. (1992) provide a brief but reasonably detailed introduction to the subject of full-content information retrieval systems in the context of general office automation systems and include a discussion of the retrieval of sounds and images as well as text. They also give a reasonable amount of detail on the different technical approaches to data refinement, data capture, parsing and understanding structure, expert-system-based query languages, indexing and compression.

Context is also a problem and IR faces similar problems in this respect to those faced by AI natural language systems. Manual indexing is usually too expensive an option to be worth considering so that some workers have explored automatic indexing systems. Van Rijsbergen (1993) supports the use of statistical techniques and suggests that IR can be regarded as theorem proving with non-Boolean logic. He also refers to the work of Barwise and Devlin on situation theory, which defines a primitive unit of information: the *infon* (Devlin, 1991).

A particularly important application of this theory in the context of this book is its use in retrieving data from a reuse repository. Storing information is a relatively easy problem. The central problem of IR is that of finding the information you require. This has particular significance for object-oriented developers because of the need to retrieve information about class libraries. There have been two basic suggestions. One may organize the references in the form of a hierarchy and use classification to gain access or one may index all class specifications according to keywords and search on them. Neither approach is ideal. Successful reuse of library code objects and specifications can only be achieved through a combination of classification and keyword-based retrieval. Furthermore, it is possible to extend both approaches to encompass uncertainty calculi. For example, the thesaurus of an IR system will often permit the user to ask for a match on a keyword or class specification and then ask that the search be re-computed using a narrowed or broader meaning of the term. Object models can be used in much the same way as Khoshafian's semantic nets to describe the structure and semantics of information and, in one respect, SOMA-extended object models are more powerful. This is because of the incorporation of fuzzy rulesets into objects and fuzzy inheritance. SOMA extended the idea of hierarchical search using four orthogonal structures and permits fuzzy matching on keywords. This is discussed further in Chapter 6 and Appendix A.

5.11 Strategic considerations

Should a company considering the benefits of object-oriented databases go for OQL and a totally object-oriented database product such as Jasmine, Versant, ObjectStore or POET; or should it, rather, choose an extended relational system such as DB2, Illustra or Oracle?

In fact, these are not the only options. Semantic or deductive databases offer many of the advantages of object-oriented systems, and robust commercial products exist and have been used. Companies can also stay with their standard relational products and embed object-oriented constructs in the host language, perhaps using an interface product such as Persistence, although we have seen some of the disadvantages of this approach. They might choose an application-specific embedded database such as in a CAD/CAM system or in a CASE system, as with the Team*work* configuration management system.

However, for most companies the leading question will be the choice between object-relational systems and genuine object-oriented ones. If the latter, they will further distinguish between persistent language extensions, such as ObjectStore, and genuine database **management** systems, such as Jasmine or Versant. As the object-relational products mature the impedance mismatch ceases to be a differentiator since both approaches will now support rapid application development. The key discriminator will be performance and the availability of third-party tools.

In the medium term, I predict that record-oriented DP applications will need to build on existing systems and will go for object-relational solutions. The main reason for this is that the approach protects investment in existing code and staff skills. The issue of migration strategies for organizations was discussed fully in Chapter 4.

Some relational vendors have effectively answered the performance criticism by implementing their products on massively parallel machines but there is no reason why object-oriented products should not be similarly parallelized and speeded up.

On the contrary, the object model is highly suitable for distributed and parallel implementation.

Prospective purchasers of database products should look at what standards the products they are considering support. Relevant standards in this area include the Object Management Group's CORBA, MOF and component standards, Microsoft's MTS, COM+ and ODBC, Sun's EJB and the OQL and SQL3 standards.

You have by now, dear reader, if you have read sequentially, accompanied me through five chapters in which I have warned you that object-oriented languages are still evolving and that object-oriented databases have been rather slow to be adopted. I hope that I have also displayed and conveyed my enthusiasm for this extraordinarily promising technology, since I am convinced that object-orientation and component-based development are here to stay. To use the technology successfully, however, requires new methods of design, analysis, requirements engineering and management. It to these that we now turn.

5.12 Summary

The relational model was the first formal data model. Relational databases based on it were inherently more flexible than earlier, pointer-based, hierarchical and network systems. However, to achieve this flexibility relational databases cannot support object identity, which was a positive feature of earlier systems. Also, pointer-based systems were more efficient. There is a contradiction and consequent trade-off between object identity and non-procedural enquiry capabilities.

A data model is a mathematical formalism consisting of a notation for describing data and data structures (information) and a set of valid operations which are used to manipulate those data. Several more or less formal models emerged after the relational model. The functional model is one of the most successful in theoretical terms, while the Entity-Relational model is one of the most widely used commercially.

The functional model is a formal model which can be used to describe network systems. There are also a number of semantic models and extensions to the relational model which add semantic capabilities. Most important among these are various extended ER models, which support hierarchical and network structures for subtypes, grouping and aggregation.

Object-oriented models include behavioural abstractions (methods) rather than the purely structural abstractions of data models. They seldom support the rich type constructors of semantic data models. The inheritance methods associated with the two approaches also tend to be different. Data models, as with AI systems, often allow the inheritance of defaults at the class level, whereas object-oriented models only allow attribute names to be inherited. Also, in data models, inheritance tends to be restricted strictly to subtypes, while, in object-oriented programming, the inheritance of methods can take place between unlike types.

There is a need for object-oriented databases, and object-oriented methods in general, to absorb the structural modelling features developed by data modellers along with ideas from artificial intelligence. A convergence of both object-orientation and semantic data modelling with AI models is also likely to be beneficial.

Relational databases present difficulties in dealing with recursive queries, null values, abstract data types and the representation of data and functional semantics; there is no real support for business or integrity rules.

Normalization hides and destroys semantics. Normalized relations rarely if ever correspond to any object in the real world and normalization conceals the application knowledge that is represented by functional dependencies among attributes. This means that normalization removes any possibility of full reverse engineering. The process of normalization is effectively irreversible.

There have been several attempts to build real database systems on the basis of full semantic data models.

ER and deductive databases are useful hybrids, capable of addressing many database problems for which the relational systems are unsuitable. Deductive databases are especially useful for specification prototyping.

The object model, now emerging, combines many of the features and benefits of the extended relational, deductive and ER models and pointer-based systems. It also, I will argue, is the location for a convergence of ideas from semantic data modelling, artificial intelligence and object-oriented programming, design and analysis.

Developers now face a choice between pure object-oriented and object-relational systems.

A database management system supports:

- persistence of objects;
- management of very large amounts of data;
- data and transaction integrity;
- sharing and concurrent multi-user access;
- access or query languages;
- recovery;
- security.

An object-oriented database management system combines database facilities with those of object-oriented programming – encapsulation, inheritance and object identity – so that:

Object-oriented database = Database + Object-orientation

Object-oriented databases combine some of the features of semantic data models and object-oriented programming. They should add expert systems features, but often do not. They embody at least two kinds of orthogonal but interacting structures: classification and aggregation structures.

OODBs remove the 'impedance mismatch' between application and enquiry languages. Compared to relational systems, they remove the need to perform expensive joins when objects are used in an application. This makes them potentially much more efficient for applications involving complex objects. OODBs, while much more efficient, retain the flexibility of relational systems. They add support for long transactions and automatic version control. Some offer dynamic schema evolution and support for multimedia and group work.

OODBs have a number of other advantages over RDBMSs, but there are unsolved problems concerning non-procedural enquiry languages, query optimization and locking.

There is a small number of commercial, pure object-oriented database products. These have been mostly applied to applications where complex objects predominate, such as web servers, multimedia databases, geographic information systems and CAD/CAM systems. The main choice now facing users is between these products and object-relational hybrids. Performance, and therefore application type, will be the key discriminant.

There are several ways to achieve benefits, apart from pure object-oriented databases; semantic databases, deductive databases or object-relational databases. The latter offer object-orientation via SQL3 which removes the impedance mismatch but may not address performance issues. This is because key applications of object-oriented databases include those which need to do many small joins to reconstruct complex objects, support distribution and versioning and handle multiple media and co-operative work.

Commercial users should consider object-oriented databases for performance-critical applications, and object-relational systems for record-oriented applications and extensions of existing systems.

Object-oriented database management is a rapidly maturing technology of great significance to information technology in general.

5.13 Bibliographical notes

Ullman's (1981) first text on database theory was the first comprehensive pedagogical introduction and analysis of the relational model, but was superseded as a standard text by (Date, 1981). Ullman's later two-volume text (1989) covers knowledge management and object-orientation, but remains a sound introduction to relational concepts as well. A very readable and comprehensive introduction to all aspects of database theory is the book by Elmasri and Navathe (1989) which also introduces object-oriented databases. All these volumes cover normalization theory thoroughly.

Semantic models are discussed in (Date, 1983), (Elmasri and Navathe, 1989) and (Ullman, 1989). Some important seminal papers on data models are collected in (Zdonik and Maier, 1990).

(Hull and King, 1987) and (Peckham and Maryanski, 1988) are excellent surveys of semantic data modelling techniques, with the former providing a comparison with object-oriented and AI models. (Teorey *et al.*, 1986) is an excellent survey of ER models and introduces one influential extended version and a design method associated with it.

King (1989) discusses the differences between semantic models and object-orientation. Brodie and Mylopoulos (1986) and Brodie, Mylopoulos and Schmidt (1984) cover various issues related to semantic, intelligent and deductive databases, and to combining insights from database theory, artificial intelligence and object-oriented programming.

The Postgres papers (Stonebraker and Rowe, 1987) provide insight into the design decisions involved in extending a relational database with knowledge-based and object-oriented features.

The connexions between semantic data models and object-orientation are discussed fully and profoundly by Gray *et al.* (1992) who give a first-rate introduction to semantic models.

Chaudri and Osmon (1996) surveyed the main commercial ODBMS products both accurately and at a useful level of detail. Two texts specifically about object-oriented databases and well worth consulting are (Gupta and Horowitz, 1991) and (Lausen and Vossen, 1998). Gray *et al.* (1992) present two sets of subject matter. The first is an overview of modern database theory and practice emphasizing the need to incorporate ideas from semantic data modelling and artificial intelligence research into object-oriented databases. The ensuing critique of object-oriented databases descended from the pure object-oriented programming tradition is first rate. The second subject is a report on the rather specialized research of the authors' group into experimental database languages and systems and the construction of a complex protein structure database application. The gloss on this contains important insights of quite general applicability. This book is essential further reading to anyone serious about object-oriented databases. Cattell (1991) includes coverage of the extended relational products. Ahmed *et al.* (1992) provide a comparison of six products from the point of view of engineering applications.

(Kim, Ballou *et al.* 1989) is an introduction to the main features of ORION. It is contained in the excellent collection of papers edited by Kim and Lochovsky (1989) which also includes material on GemStone and a prototype object-oriented database called OZ+ aimed at office automation applications. Kim (1990) is a general text on object-oriented databases but concentrates almost entirely on ORION for examples and may be best regarded as a first-rate introduction to the principles behind Itasca. Another excellent discussion of principles, this time in an O_2 context, is that of Delobel *et al.* (1995).

Winblad *et al.* (1990) give a high level overview of object-oriented databases. Khoshafian and Abnous (1990) provide a deeper discussion, including a treatment of the architectural issues which are not included in this text, which is after all a wide-reaching survey with a focus on methods.

Vbase is described in (Andrews and Harris, 1990), and in (Elmasri and Navathe, 1989) which is also a first-rate textbook on databases in general. Another excellent text on modern database theory, (Ullman, 1989), describes the GemStone language OPAL in detail.

Persistent programming languages are surveyed in (Atkinson and Buneman, 1988) while (Rosenberg and Koch, 1990) gives a glimpse of research in this area. The influential persistent programming language Galileo is described in (Albano *et al.*, 1988).

(Zdonik and Maier, 1990) contains a representative sample of the seminal papers on object-oriented databases, although material on the important topic of schema evolution is omitted. The editors include introductory material that is comprehensive and informed. Interesting material on schema evolution can be found in the papers on ORION, such as (Kim *et al.*, 1989) and (Nguyen and Rieu, 1989) who introduce some AI techniques for automatic propagation of changes and the dynamic classification of instances. Other research papers may be found in (Meersman *et al.*, 1991). (Cardenas and McLeod, 1990) is a collection of seminal papers whose theme is the integration of object-oriented and semantic data models.

As an aside, (Zdonik and Maier, 1990) is part of a series of 'readings in' different areas of computing. They all contain seminal papers on their subjects and, next to the excellent ACM journal *Computing Surveys*, are a good way to become familiar with the broad 'advanced computing' horizon without any risk of vulgarization.

Among several surveys of work on integrated knowledge and database systems (Brodie *et al.*, 1984), (Brodie and Mylopoulos, 1986), (Ullman, 1989) and a number of volumes in the Morgan Kaufmann 'readings in' series edited by Minker, Stonebraker, Mylopoulos and Brodie are worthy of mention. (Parsaye *et al.*, 1989) is an introduction to most of the related technologies and describes a particular model developed by the authors.

JOOP is a good source of current, fairly high level discussions on the topic. The web sites of the various product vendors will be useful for up-to-date product information.

5.14 Exercises

1. In object-oriented databases, what is the name given to the ability of objects to exist after an application program has terminated?
   a) Static binding   c) Two-phase commit
   b) Persistence   d) Object integrity

2. What is the impedance mismatch?

3. How can inheritance be implemented in a relational database?

4. What is the main difference between an object-oriented and object-relational database in practice? Discuss the features of an application that make it suitable for each approach.

5. Describe in detail an object-oriented or object-relational database known to you in the context of an application also known to you.

6. Discuss the problem of locking in relation to databases that support inheritance. What is the difference between optimistic and pessimistic concurrency control?

7. Why can the performance of a pure object-oriented database exceed a relational or object-relational one?

8. What are the advantages and disadvantages of executing methods on the server?

9. Define locational transparency and discuss its importance.

10. Define referential transparency. Why are object-oriented systems (including databases) not referentially transparent? Discuss the consequences of this, including both advantages and disadvantages and giving examples.

6

Object-oriented analysis and design

with Alan Cameron Wills

The will
And high permission of all-ruling heaven
Left him at large to his own dark designs,
That with reiterated crimes he might
Heap on himself damnation.

Milton (*Paradise Lost*)

In this chapter we step back from tools, languages and implementation and treat methods for object-oriented analysis and design in depth. We will focus on the widely used UML notation and upon the principles of modelling. Our treatment is particularly based on Catalysis (D'Souza and Wills, 1999) and SOMA (Graham, 1995). The focus is on best practice and we suggest a set of requirements for a practical analysis and design technique.

This and the next three chapters are the central chapters of this book. Their purpose is to unite several threads which run through other chapters. These themes – of object-oriented programming and its benefits, expert systems and knowledge engineering and data modelling and database management – are united in the requirements for practical, rigorous, object-oriented software engineering.

The strategic problem posed by the maturing technologies of object-oriented programming, databases, middleware and component-based development is addressed by an approach to analysis and design which should permit the phased, gradual exploitation of the benefits of object-orientation at the analysis level, thus laying firm foundations for the exploitation of language and object management technologies. Chapter 7 returns to object-oriented design in the context of component-based development and also covers the important issues of architecture and patterns. Chapter 8 extends our analysis of software specification methods to requirements engineering and business process modelling. Chapter 9 takes up the managerial and life cycle issues raised by object-oriented and component-based development methods.

We introduce and explain the Unified Modelling Language (UML). UML is a standardized notation for object-oriented analysis and design. However, a method is more than a notation. To be an analysis or design method it must include guidelines for using the notation and methodological principles. To be a complete software engineering method it must also include procedures for dealing with matters outside the scope of mere software development: business and requirements modelling, development process, project management, metrics, traceability techniques and reuse management. In this chapter we focus on the notational and analysis and design aspects.

6.1 The history of object-oriented analysis and design methods

The development of computer science as a whole proceeded from an initial concern with programming alone, through increasing interest in design, to concern with analysis methods only latterly. Reflecting this perhaps, interest in object-orientation also began, historically, with language developments. It was only in the 1980s that object-oriented design methods emerged. Object-oriented analysis methods emerged during the 1990s.

Apart from a few fairly obscure AI applications, up until the 1980s object-orientation was largely associated with the development of graphical user interfaces (GUIs) and few other applications became widely known. Up to this period not a word had been mentioned about analysis or design for object-oriented systems. In the 1980s Grady Booch published a paper on how to design for Ada but gave it the prophetic title: *Object-Oriented Design*. Booch was able to extend his ideas to a genuinely object-oriented design method by 1991 in his book with the same title, revised in 1993 (Booch, 1994) [*sic*].

With the 1990s came both increased pressures on business and the availability of cheaper and much more powerful computers. This led to a ripening of the field and to a range of applications beyond GUIs and AI. Distributed, open computing became both possible and important and object technology was the basis of much development, especially with the appearance of n-tier client-server systems and the web, although relational databases played and continue to play an important rôle. The new applications and better hardware meant that mainstream organizations adopted object-oriented programming and now wanted proper attention paid to object-oriented design and (next) analysis. Concern shifted from design to analysis from the start of the 1990s. An object-oriented approach to requirements engineering had to wait even longer.

The first book with the title *Object-Oriented Systems Analysis* was produced by

Shlaer and Mellor in 1988. Like Booch's original paper it did not present a genuinely object-oriented method, but concentrated entirely on the exposition of extended entity-relationship models, based on an essentially relational view of the problem and ignoring the behavioural aspects of objects. Shlaer and Mellor published a second volume in 1992 that argued that behaviour should be modelled using conventional state-transition diagrams and laid the basis of a genuinely OO, albeit data-driven, approach that was to remain influential through its idea of 'translational' modelling, which we will discuss. In the meanwhile, Peter Coad had incorporated behavioural ideas into a simple but object-oriented method (Coad and Yourdon, 1990; 1991). Coad's method was immediately popular because of its simplicity and Booch's because of its direct and comprehensive support for the features of C++, the most popular object-oriented programming language of the period in the commercial world. This was followed by an explosion of interest in and publication on object-oriented analysis and design. Apart from those already mentioned, among the most significant were OMT (Rumbaugh *et al.*, 1991), Martin-Odell (1992), OOSE (Jacobson *et al.*, 1992) and RDD (Wirfs-Brock *et al.*, 1990). OMT was another data-driven method rooted as it was in relational database design, but it quickly became the dominant approach precisely because what most programmers were forced to do at that time was to write C++ programs that talked to relational databases.

OMT (Rumbaugh *et al.*, 1991) copied Coad's approach of adding operations to entity-type descriptions to make class models but used a different notation from all the previous methods. Not only was OMT thoroughly data-driven but it separated processes from data by using data flow diagrams separately from the class diagrams. However, it emphasized what Coad had only hinted at and Shlaer and Mellor were yet to publish: the use of state-transition diagrams to describe the life cycles of instances. It also made a few remarks about the micro development process and offered very useful advice on how to connect object-oriented programs with relational databases. Just as Booch had become popular with C++ programmers because of its ability to model the semantic constructs of that language precisely, so OMT became popular with developers for whom C++ and a relational database were the primary tools.

Two of OMT's chief creators, Blaha and Premerlani (1998), confirm this with the words: 'The OMT object model is essentially an extended Entity-Relationship approach' (p.10). They go on to say, in their presentation of the second-generation version of OMT, that the 'UML authors are addressing programming applications; we are addressing database applications'. Writing in the preface to the same volume, Rumbaugh even makes a virtue out of the relational character of OMT. I feel that a stricter adherence to object-oriented principles and to a responsibility-driven approach is a necessity if the full benefits of the object-oriented metaphor are to be obtained in the context of a fully object-oriented tool-set.

In parallel with the rise of the extended entity-relationship and data-driven methods, Wirfs-Brock and her colleagues were developing a set of responsibility-driven design (RDD) techniques out of experience gained more in the world of

Smalltalk than that of the relational database. The most important contributions of RDD were the extension of the idea of using so-called CRC cards for design and, later, the introduction of the idea of stereotypes. CRC cards showed Classes with their Responsibilities and Collaborations with other objects as a starting point for design. These could then be shuffled and responsibilities reallocated in design workshops. The idea had originated from the work of Beck and Cunningham at Tektronix, where the cards were implemented using a hypertext system. Moving to physical pieces of cardboard enhanced the technique by allowing designers to anthropomorphize their classes and even consider acting out their life cycles – an idea exploited heavily in Chapter 9.

Objectory was a proprietary method that had been around much longer than most object-oriented methods. It originated in the Swedish telecommunications industry and emerged in its object-oriented guise when Jacobson *et al.* (1992) published part of it (OOSE) in book form. The major contribution of this method was the idea that analysis should start with use cases rather than with a class model. The classes were then to be derived from the use cases. The technique marked an important step forward in object-oriented analysis and has been widely adopted, although it is possible to make some fairly severe criticisms of it. Objectory was the first OO method to include a *bona fide*, although partial, development process.

OBA (Object Behaviour Analysis) originated from Smalltalk-dominated work at ParcPlace and also included a process model that was never fully published although some information was made available (Goldberg and Rubin, 1995; Rubin and Goldberg, 1992). One interesting feature of OBA was the use of stereotypical scripts in place of use cases.

Coming from the Eiffel tradition, Waldén and Nerson's (1995) BON (Business Object Notation) emphasized seamlessness and hinted at a proto-process. However, this approach (and indeed its very seamlessness) depended on the adoption of Eiffel as a specification language throughout the process. It made important contributions to the rigour of object-oriented analysis as did Cook and Daniels' (1994) Syntropy. BON improves rigour using the Eiffel idea of class invariants while Syntropy does this and further emphasizes state machines.

MOSES (Henderson-Sellers and Edwards, 1994) was the first OO method to include a full-blown development process, a metrics suite and an approach to reuse management. SOMA (Graham, 1995), which appeared in its mature form roughly contemporaneously with MOSES and was influenced by it, also included all these features, as well as attempting to fuse the best aspects of all the methods published to date and go beyond them; especially in the areas of requirements engineering, process, agent-based systems and rigour.

At the publication of the second edition of this book in 1994, I had counted over 72 methods or fragments of methods. Many of these are surveyed in Appendix B, several in detail. The OO community soon realized that this situation was untenable if the technology was to be used commercially on any significant scale They also realized that most of the methods overlapped considerably. Therefore, various initiatives were launched aimed at merging and standardizing methods.

Thus far, to the eyes of the developer there appeared a veritable soup of object-oriented analysis and design methods and notations. It was an obvious development to try to introduce some kind of unification and the Fusion method (Coleman *et al.*, 1994; Malan *et al.*, 1996) represents one of the first attempts to combine good techniques from other published methods, although some commentators have viewed the collection of techniques as poorly integrated. There is a process associated with Fusion although published descriptions of it appear incomplete compared to the proprietary versions sold by Hewlett-Packard. The modern object-oriented developer had to find a way to pick out the noodles from this rich soup of techniques. Because of this and because there were many similarities between methods it began to be felt by most methodologists that some sort of convergence was in order

The OPEN Consortium was an informal group of about 30 methodologists, with no common commercial affiliation, that wanted to see greater method integration but felt strongly that methods should include a complete process, should be in the public domain, should not be tied to particular tools and should focus strongly on scientific integrity as well as pragmatic issues. The founding members of OPEN were Brian Henderson-Sellers and myself who began to integrate the MOSES and SOMA process models. The result was published as Graham *et al.* (1997b). They were soon joined by Don Firesmith who started work on an integrated notation (OML) with the aim of exhibiting a more pure object-oriented character than the OMT-influenced UML and one that would be easier to learn and remember (Firesmith *et al.*, 1997).

Jim Rumbaugh left GE to join Grady Booch at Rational Inc. These two merged their notations into what became the first version of UML (Booch *et al.*, 1999). Later they were joined by Ivar Jacobson who added elements of his Objectory notation and began the development of the Rational Unified Process (RUP) (*cf.* Chapter 9). UML was submitted to the OMG for standardization and many other methodologists contributed ideas, although the CASE tool vendors have generally resisted both innovations that would cause them to rewrite their tools and simplifications that would make their tools less useful. The OPEN consortium proposed the semantically richer OML which was largely ignored despite many good ideas, probably largely due to its over-complicatedness (Firesmith *at al.*, 1997). Real-time elements were added based on the ROOM method (Selic *et al.*, 1994) and a formal constraint language, OCL, heavily influenced by Syntropy (Cook and Daniels, 1994) introduced. A notation for multiple interfaces to classes was based on Microsoft's work on COM+. Activity diagrams for process modelling were based on the Martin-Odell method. The idea of stereotypes adopted in UML was based on ideas proposed by Rebecca Wirfs-Brock (though much mangled in the first realizations of the standard). The struggle to improve UML continues and we will therefore not assume a completely fixed character for it in this text. Thus were issues of notation largely settled by the end of the 1990s, which has shifted the emphasis to innovation in the field of method and process. Among the most significant contributions to analysis and design methodology, following the naissance of UML, was Catalysis (D'Souza and Wills, 1999) which was the first method to contain specific techniques for component-based development along with coherent guidance on how the UML should be used. My own work showed that objects could be regarded as intelligent agents if rulesets were added to type specifications. This generalized the insistence in other methods (notably BON, Syntropy and Catalysis) that invariants were needed to specify types fully.

Figure 6.1 shows the relationships between several object-oriented methods, languages and notations discussed in this book. See Appendix B for a discussion of these methods and others.

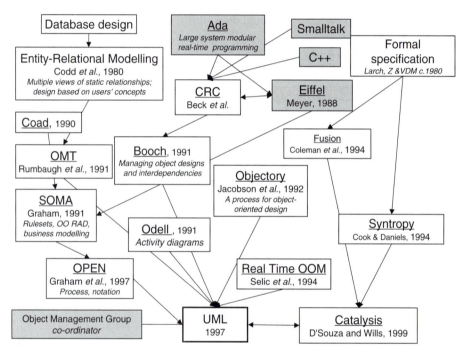

Figure 6.1 Some of the influences on UML.

6.2 Software engineering

Object-oriented methods cover, at least, methods for design and methods for analysis. Sometimes there is an overlap, and it is really only an idealization to say that they are completely separate activities. Ralph Hodgson (1990) argued that the systems development process is one of comprehension, invention and realization whereby a problem domain is first grasped or apprehended as phenomena, concepts, entities, activities, rôles and assertions. This is comprehension and corresponds entirely to analysis. However, understanding the problem domain also entails simultaneously apprehending frameworks, components, computational models and other mental constructs which take account of feasible solution domains. This inventive activity corresponds to the design process. Of course, most conventional thinkers on software engineering will be horrified that I suggest that understanding the answer precedes, to some extent, understanding the problem, but that is precisely what I am saying. All other cognitive processes proceed in this way, and I see no reason why software engineering should be different. These considerations also enter into the realization process where these frameworks and architectural components are mapped onto compilers and hardware. Advocates of evolutionary development have long argued that it is beneficial not to make a rigid separation between analysis, design and implementation. On the other hand, managerial and performance considerations lead to serious questions about the advisability of prototyping in commercial environments. Graham (1991d) suggested a number of ways in which prototyping could be exploited but controlled, an argument which is expanded in Chapter 9. At the root of this debate are ontological and epistemological positions concerning what objects are and how we can apprehend them or know about them. These too are discussed in this chapter.

REUSABLE SPECS.   Biggerstaff and Richter (1989) suggested that less than half of a typical system can be built of reusable software components, and that the only way to obtain more significant gains in productivity and quality is to raise the level of abstraction of the components. Analysis products or specifications are more abstract than designs. Designs are more abstract than code. Abstract artefacts have less detail and less reliance on hardware and other implementation constraints. Thus the benefits of reuse can be obtained earlier in a project, when they are likely to have the greatest impact. However, the less detailed an object is the less meaningful it becomes. Where extensibility or semantic richness is important greater detail may be required, and this may compromise reuse to some extent. This leads us to ask if object-oriented analysis and design techniques exist which can deliver the benefits of reuse and extensibility. In the face of still evolving object-oriented programming and component technology, this question attains even more significance: can we gain these benefits now, pending the appearance of more mature, more stable languages and frameworks? I think we can. However, the subsidiary question of which methods of design and analysis we should use is harder. The popular notation is UML, which was first standardized by the OMG in 1997, but UML is only a notation. We need to add techniques and guidelines to it to arrive at a method.

Software houses and consultancies ought to be particularly interested in reusable and extensible specifications. The reason for this is pecuniary. What the people employed by software houses and consultancies do, to earn their livings, is work with clients to understand their businesses and their requirements and help them produce software solutions to their problems. Having gained all this valuable experience, consultants then go on to the next client and sell what they have learnt, perhaps for a higher fee justified by the extra knowledge. Some firms go further. They try to encapsulate their experience in customizable functional specifications. For example, a firm I worked for, BIS Information Systems, had a product in the 1980s called the 'mortgage model', which was a functional specification of a mortgage application, based on a number of such projects and capable of being tailored to the needs of a particular client. The trouble was, for BIS at least, that the mortgage model could not be sold to greengrocers or washing machine manufacturers, even though some of the entities, such as account, may apply to all these businesses. What is required, then, is a set of reusable specification components that can be assembled into a functional specification suitable for *any* business. Object-oriented analysis, and to a lesser extent design, promises to deliver such a capability, even if the only extant reusable frameworks, such as IBM's San Francisco, are still delivered as code.

To fix terminology, let us begin with a vastly oversimplified picture of the software development process or life cycle. According to this simplified model, development begins with the elicitation of requirements and domain knowledge and ends with testing and subsequent maintenance. Between these extremes occur three major activities: specification and logical modelling (analysis), architectural modelling (design) and implementation (coding and testing). Of course this model permits iteration, prototyping and other deviations, but we need not consider them at this stage. Iterative and evolutionary development, along with the managerial issues it raises, are dealt with in detail in Chapter 9. In real life, despite what the textbooks tell us, specification and design overlap considerably. This seems to be especially true for object-oriented design and analysis because the abstractions of both are modelled on the abstractions of the application, rather than the abstractions appropriate to the world of processors and disks. Design may be divided into logical and physical design, as is well known. In object-oriented design the logical stage is often indistinguishable from parts of object-oriented analysis. One of the major problems encountered with structured analysis and structured design methods is the lack of overlap or smooth transition between the two. This often leads to difficulties in tracing the products of design back to original user requirements or analysis products. The approach adopted in object-oriented analysis and design tends to merge the systems analysis with the process of logical design, although there is still a distinction between requirements elicitation and analysis and between logical and physical design. Nevertheless, object-oriented analysis, design and even programming, through working consistently with a uniform conceptual model of objects throughout the life cycle, at least *promises* to overcome some of the traceability problems associated with systems development. One of the chief reasons for this is the continuum of representation as the object-oriented software engineer moves from analysis through design to programming. In these transitions the unit of currency, as it were, remains the same; it is the object. Analysts, designers and programmers can all use the same representation, notation and metaphor rather than having to use DFDs at one stage, structure charts at the next and so on.

The benefits of object-oriented analysis and design are perhaps obvious to the reader who has absorbed the remarks in earlier chapters, but specifically include:

- required changes are localized and unexpected interactions with other program modules are unlikely;
- inheritance and polymorphism make OO systems more extensible, contributing thus to more rapid development;
- object-based design is suitable for distributed, parallel or sequential implementation;
- objects correspond more closely to the entities in the conceptual worlds of the designer and user, leading to greater seamlessness and traceability;
- shared data areas are encapsulated, reducing the possibility of unexpected modifications or other update anomalies.

Object-oriented analysis and design methods share the following basic steps although the details and the ordering of the steps vary quite a lot:

- find the ways that the system interacts with its environment (use cases);
- identify objects and their attribute and method names;
- establish the relationships between objects;
- establish the interface(s) of each object and exception handling;
- implement and test the objects;
- assemble and test systems.

Analysis is the decomposition of problems into their component parts. In computing it is understood as the process of specification of system structure and function independently of the means of implementation or physical decomposition into modules or components. Analysis was traditionally done top-down using structured analysis, or an equivalent method based on functional decomposition, combined with separate data analysis. Often the high level, strategic, business goal-driven analysis is separated from the systems analysis. Here we are concerned with both. This is possible because object-oriented analysis permits the system to be described in the same terms as the real world; the system abstractions correspond more or less exactly to the business abstractions. In Chapters 8 and 9 this distinction is reintroduced from the viewpoint of requirements engineering and project management, where it is both necessary and convenient.

Object-oriented analysis is analysis, but also contains an element of synthesis. Abstracting user requirements and identifying key domain objects are followed by the assembly of those objects into structures of a form that will support physical design at some later stage. The synthetic aspect intrudes precisely because we are analysing *a system*, in other words imposing a structure on the domain. This is not to say that refinement will not alter the design; a well-decoupled design can be considerably different from a succinct specification model.

As we have seen in Chapter 5, there is a rich theory of semantic data modelling going far beyond the normal use of ER diagrams. This theory encompasses many of the concerns of object-orientation such as inheritance and abstract types. It also illuminates our understanding of relationships or associations between entities. Much of this work has been ignored by workers in object technology and in AI as thoroughly as these two areas have ignored each other.

EARLY OO ANALYSIS METHODS

There are often said to be three primary aspects of a system apart from its identity. These are respectively concerned with: a) data, objects or concepts and their structure; b) architecture or atemporal process; and c) dynamics or system behaviour. We shall refer to these three dimensions as data, process and control. Object-orientation combines two of these aspects – data and process – by encapsulating local behaviour with data. We shall see later that it is also possible to encapsulate control. Thus, an object-oriented analysis can be regarded as a form of syllogism moving from the Particular (classes) through the Individual (instances) to the Universal (control)[1].

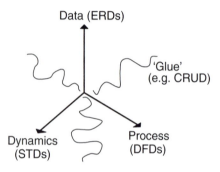

Figure 6.2 Three dimensions of software engineering.

The conventional wisdom in software engineering holds it as self-evident that a system must be described in these three dimensions; those of process, data and dynamics or control. The data dimension corresponds to entity-relationship diagrams (ERDs) or logical data models. The process models are represented by data flow or activity diagrams of one sort or another. Finally, the dynamics is described by either a state transition or entity life history notation. To ensure that these diagrams are consistent, structured methods usually insist that some cross-checking documents are created to 'glue' the model together. For example, to check the consistency of a model between the Entity-Relationship and Data-Flow views, a CRUD matrix might be constructed. CRUD stands for 'Create, Read, Update, Delete'. These letters indicate which processes use which entities and how they are used. This approach creates a potentially enormous overhead in terms of documentation alone. However, it does ensure that all aspects of a system are

---

[1] A syllogism is to be understood here in the original meaning of Aristotle, rather than the vulgar meaning that restricts it to dealing with purely mathematical and deductive reasoning. Thus, a syllogism is a reasoning pattern involving and relating judgements in three different categories.

covered – assuming the knowledge elicitation is not deficient. It also has the advantage that where two techniques are used to reach the same conclusion then, if the results agree, the level of confidence in them is raised.

Data-centred approaches to software engineering begin with the data model while process-oriented approaches start with DFDs or activity diagrams. Some real-time approaches begin with finite state machines or STDs, but this is unusual for commercial systems developers. One problem with state transition diagrams is that, while they may be fine for systems with a small number of states – as with controllers – they are hopeless for systems with large numbers of, or even continuous, states. An object with n Boolean attributes may have 2^n states. Most commercial system objects have several, non-Boolean attributes. For this reason, it is necessary to focus on states that give rise to data changes significant to the business. This means that both the states and their related changes must be apprehended at the same time. The solution is to partition state space into chunks corresponding to significant predicates and viewpoints. For example, the anaesthetist's statechart for Person includes states {awake, asleep, dead}; the registrar's has {single, married, divorced, widowed, deceased}; the accountant's has {solvent, insolvent}. Each of these statecharts are simultaneously valid. But, of course, the partitioning can be regarded as subjective and care is needed.

Looking at early object-oriented analysis methods, certain things were noticeable. Some, such as Coad (Coad and Yourdon, 1990, 1991, 1991a) were simple but lacked support for describing system dynamics. Some such as OMT (Rumbaugh *et al.*, 1991) and Shlaer-Mellor were richer, but very complex to learn. Methods like OMT also offered little to help express business rules and constraints. Embley's OSA (Embley *et al.*, 1992) and Martin and Odell's (1992) synthesis of IE with Ptech were slightly simpler approaches. OSA allowed the analyst to write constraints on the diagrams as a sort of afterthought. None supported rules and you searched in vain for advice on how to combine the products of the three separate models into a coherent single model, though OMT did provide more help than others in this respect. In an attempt to address some of these weaknesses in these otherwise attractive methods I was led to the SOMA method. SOMA combined a notation for object-oriented analysis with knowledge-based systems style rules for describing constraints, business rules, global system control, database triggers and quantification over relationships (e.g. 'all children who like toys like each other'). It also addressed in this way issues of requirements engineering not addressed by other methods, as we shall see in Chapter 8. SOMA was also unique in supporting fuzzy generalization, which is important for requirements specification in some domains such as enterprise modelling and process control, though unfashionable in many software engineering circles

As the discipline has matured a purer object-oriented focus has meant that mature modern methods dispense with DFDs, constructing state models for individual objects. However, they also build models of interactions between a system and its users and external devices, usually in the form of use cases.

6.2.1 Responsibility-driven *versus* data-driven approaches

It is often said that data are more stable than functions and so data-centred approaches are to be preferred in most cases. However, one of the greatest dangers in adopting a method based too much on structured techniques is that of data-driven design. Two software engineers at Boeing (Sharble and Cohen, 1994) conducted an experiment with internal trainees with similar backgrounds. One group was taught the data-driven Shlaer/Mellor method of object-oriented analysis – a method consciously and deeply rooted in traditional entity-relationship modelling – while the other group was instructed in the Responsibility Driven Design techniques of Wirfs-Brock *et al.* (1990). The two groups were then asked to design a simplified control application for a brewery. The Shlaer-Mellor group produced a design wherein most of the classes represented static data stores while one class accessed these and encapsulated the control rules for most of the application: in much the same style as a main{} routine in C would do. The other group distributed the behaviour much more evenly across their classes. It was seen that this latter approach produced far more reusable classes: classes that could be unplugged from the application and used whole. It also demonstrated vividly that the method you use can influence the outcome profoundly. It is my firm conviction that data-driven methods are dangerous in the hands of the average developer and especially in the hands of someone educated or experienced in the relational tradition. Furthermore, I hold that the approach taken to requirements engineering can have a huge influence.

The study by Sharble and Cohen shows convincingly that data-driven methods *do* influence the thinking of designers and that they tend to produce un-reusable classes as a consequence. The usual effects are that:

- behaviour is concentrated in controller objects that resemble main routines; this makes systems much harder to maintain due to the amount of knowledge that these controllers store about other objects;
- other objects have few operations and are often equivalent to normalized database tables: not reflective therefore of sound object-oriented design.

In my commercial practice I insist upon or encourage responsibility-driven design and analysis, as we shall see in subsequent chapters. I will be concerned throughout this text to emphasize this in all we do, just as I shall stress adherence to the basic principles of object technology: encapsulation and inheritance. This is not the pedantic reaction of a purist but a stance of immense practical significance.

6.2.2 Translational *versus* elaborational approaches

Another important way in which we may classify object-oriented methods is as either translational or elaborational. Methods like Booch, OMT and RUP are evangelistically elaborational. They treat the passage from specification to implementation as a matter of creating an initial model and then adding more and more detail (elaborating) until eventually we press a button and the compiled code pops out.

Translational approaches, among which Shlaer-Mellor was the paradigm, regard the process as a sequence of separate models together with a procedure for linking them and translating from one to the next. Thus we can use the most appropriate modelling techniques and viewpoints at each stage of our thinking about the problem but still guarantee seamlessness and traceability – as will become apparent later in this chapter and in Chapter 7. Catalysis and SOMA fall *inter alia* into this camp and the next section will exemplify the approach.

6.3 Object-oriented analysis and design using UML

The Unified Modelling Language (UML) is probably the most widely known and used notation for object-oriented analysis and design. It is the result of the merger of several early contributions to object-oriented methods. In this section we use it to illustrate how to go about object-oriented analysis and design.

The first thing we need to know is how to represent objects. Figure 6.3 shows how classes and instances are represented.[2] Unfortunately, UML does not distinguish adequately between types and classes notationally; but we can add the stereotype «type» to the class icon to show the difference. Stereotypes are tags that can be added to objects to classify them in various ways. This useful idea was originally proposed by Wirfs-Brock and McKean (1996) but in the current version of UML (1.4) a class is allowed only one stereotype, which rather destroys their point. CASE tools then use the stereotype to render the object graphically, as we shall see later. I am convinced, with the majority of methodologists, that future versions of UML will permit multiple stereotypes and will assume it is so in this text. Users of current CASE tools can use free-text notes to do this. Notes are also illustrated in Figure 6.3. Notice that instance names are always underlined; otherwise the notation for an instance is exactly the same as that for a class (type).

A stereotype indicates a variation in the way the item should be interpreted, dealt with by tools, and presented. Standard stereotypes also include: «interface», «type» and «capsule». Stereotypes can be added to classes, associations, operations, use cases, packages, and so on. Actors are just objects, tagged with the «actor» stereotype. Most tools just use the stereotypes to display different icons; e.g. pin men. Stereotypes make the language extensible, adding extra meaning to the basic pieces of syntax, but to preserve the communicability of models please consult your friendly, local methodologist before inventing more.

In approaching object-oriented analysis we need to deal first with types and only during design is it appropriate to think of classes. Therefore, rather than use the stereotype, we interpret the class icon as a type unless otherwise noted.

---

[2] I have encapsulated information about association cardinalities, which – unfortunately – UML does not strictly allow for.

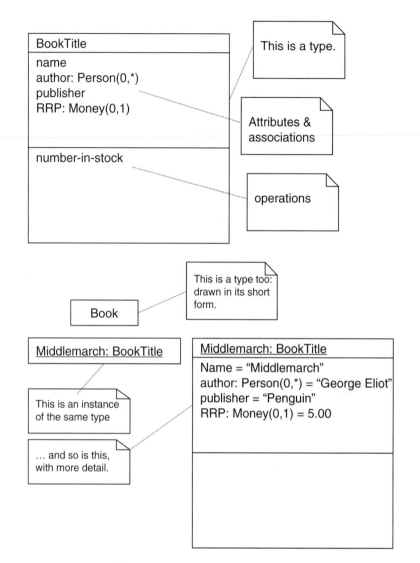

Figure 6.3 Types and their instances.

We have already met some UML notation in Chapter 1. If we compare Figure 6.3 with Figure 1.4(a) it can be seen that, in the absence of any difference of notation, I have adopted the convention that classes (which are collections of instances) are named in the plural, while types (which represent a single concept) are named in the singular. It should also be noted that rôles, such as the rôle of being an employee, are not the same as types or classes. The reason is that in object-oriented programming an instance belongs to its class forever; whereas a person can stop being an employee – on retirement say.

UML has no adequate distinction for rôles: although the short form shown in Figure 6.3 is the official usage, it is so useful for type diagrams as to make the restriction intolerable. We therefore usually model rôles as separate objects and indicate rôles with the stereotype «role» when the context so demands.

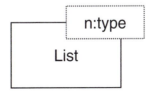

Figure 6.4 Generic types or templates.

Recall that we can distinguish between the features of a class and the features of its instances. Class methods and attributes refer to properties of and operations on entire collections. Operations that apply to instances, such as calculating a person's age from their date of birth, are called **instance operations**, and operations which apply to entire classes, such as calculating the average age of all employees, are **class operations**. Similarly there are **instance attributes** and **class attributes** though these are rarer.

The operations and attributes of an object are called its **features**. The features (and possibly the name) constitute the **signature** of the object. It is often useful to think of the features of an object as responsibilities. Attributes and associations are **responsibilities for knowing**. Operations are **responsibilities for doing**. Generic types (sometimes called templates) are shown as illustrated in Figure 6.4.

One of the great advantages of a conventional database management system is the separation of processes and data which gives a notion of data independence and benefits of flexibility and insulation from change, because the interface to shared data is stable. The data model is to be regarded as a model of the statics of the application. With object-orientation, processes and data are integrated. Does this mean that you have to abandon the benefits of data independence? Already in client-server relational databases we have seen a step in the same direction, with database triggers and integrity rules stored in the server with the data. With an object-oriented approach to data management it therefore seems reasonable to adopt the view that there are two kinds of object, which I call **domain objects** and **application objects**. Domain objects represent those aspects of the system that are relatively stable or generic (in supplying services to many applications). Application objects are those which can be expected to vary from installation to installation or from time to time quite rapidly. This approach resurrects the notion of data independence in an enhanced, object-oriented form. A conventional data model is a view of the domain objects, which latter also include constraints, rules and dynamics (state transitions, etc.). The goal is to make the interface to this part of the model as stable as possible.

The domain objects form the shared object model. Most interaction between components is via this model. We can go further and distinguish **interface objects** which are those whose sole *raison d'etre* is to enable communication, either with humans or with other systems and devices.

As an example of these distinctions in most business domains, Products and Transactions are unarguably domain objects, while DiscountCalculators might be a special application object. Classes like Sensors and InputValidators are likely to be interface objects.

These three categories can be regarded as stereotypes. Other stereotypes that are sometimes useful include controllers, co-ordinators, information holders and service providers. As Wirfs-Brock and McKean (1996) point out, such classifications are intentional oversimplifications to be refined during analysis and design.

ATTRIBUTE FACETS

The type icon shows lists of associations and operations. Associations are attributes that refer to other types. There are two ways of interpreting them: one can either think of them as shorthand for their corresponding *get* and *set* operations or as providing the vocabulary with which the type can be discussed. As shown by Wills (2001) the latter interpretation is the best one for component or system specification, and the associations can then provide the basis for part of the test harness. These viewpoints are both useful in different contexts as we shall see. However, when we come to requirements analysis in the next chapter it will be seen that a pointer viewpoint is often more valuable. Attributes are associations to more primitive types that are often left unspecified (such as String or Integer) and that we probably would not include on a structure diagram. What is 'primitive' is a rather subjective decision so that, technically, there is no distinction between attributes and associations.

UML allows classes to be tagged with extra information using the notation {tag=value}. The most useful tags include the following:

- description = descriptive text
- keyword = classification keyword; e.g. botanical, etc.
- object_classification = domain|application|interface
- stereotype = additional stereotype; e.g. deferred, rôle, etc.

Abstract classes are named in italics. In specification, when we are talking about types rather than classes, the notion of 'abstract' does not, of course, make sense.

UML supports the following annotations to, or **facets** of, associations:

- default (or initial) value (name:Type=expression)
- visibility prefix (+ = public, – = private, # = protected)

We would use notes or naming conventions to add additional facets of the following types:

- An attribute may have a list of allowed values (if it is of enumeration type) and a query preface (text used to preface any query on the attribute).

- An attribute may be declared as a state variable that represents one of a number of enumerated states that the object may occupy.
- Association types are qualified as either {set}, {bag}, {ordered set} or {list}.
- Attributes can be variable/fixed/common/unique. **Fixed** means that the value may not change during the lifetime of the object. Different instances may have different values and we need not know what these values are. **Variable** is the opposite of fixed and is the default. **Common** attributes require that all instances have the same value, again without necessarily knowing what it is. **Unique** attributes are the opposite of common ones; each instance has a different value. A well-known example is a primary key in a database table. The default is neither common nor unique. The notation is one of the following: {variable}, {fixed}, {common}, {unique}, {fixed,common}, {fixed,unique}, {variable,common}, {variable,unique}.[3]
- Security level may be specified.
- Ownership may be specified with a tagged value.
- Null values may be permitted or not. If not, the facet NON-NULL is set true. For associations this is shown by a minimal cardinality of 1; e.g. WorksFor: Dept (1,n).
- Valid range constraints may be specified; e.g. age > 16.
- $ before an attribute name indicates a class attribute. Its absence indicates an instance attribute. A class attribute is a property of a whole collection of the class's instances such as the maximum height of People. An instance attribute may have a different value for each instance such as the height of a person.
- × before an attribute name indicates that it cannot inherit its value.
- / before an attribute name indicates a derived (i.e. inherited) attribute.

Operations are the specifications of an object's methods. UML supports the following facets of operations:

- visibility (public = + , private = − , protected = #)
- protocol and return type (name(arg1:Type, ..., argN:Type):Type

These can also be used to specify the visibility of packages. We will see later that additional facets, such as pre-conditions, are essential.

6.3.1 Object structures

The next thing we may wish to do is illustrate how objects relate to each other graphically. We have already encountered some of the notation in Chapter 1. There are four principal ways in which objects interact. The most primitive of these is association, which indicates that a type is specified in terms of another type.

---

[3] This trichotomy is due to Dennis de Champeaux *et al.* (1993).

ASSOCIATION UML shows associations using the notation given in Figure 6.5. The rôlenames can be regarded as labels for the cardinality constraints or as attributes of the type furthest away from where they are written. For example, holder can be thought of as an attribute of **Account**, constrained to hold between 1 and 2 values of type **Customer**.

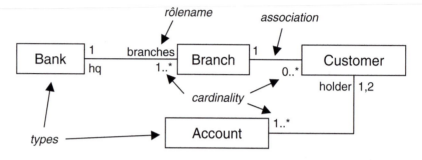

Figure 6.5 Associations in UML.

When an association has interesting properties in its own right it should be represented as a new type with the appropriate attributes and two new associations to the types it originally connected. For example, the association **married-to** between the types **Man** and **Woman** would be a plain vanilla association in an HR system but needs to be a type for a wedding registration system, with attributes including the people involved, the date of the marriage and so on. UML has a special notation for such 'association classes' but it is entirely redundant and so we will not use it (see Appendix C if you are interested).

As discussed in Section 5.2.1, association types should not be introduced merely to remove many-to-many relationships as one would do during relational database design. They should only be used where they can be given meaningful names. A counter-example would be the relationship between products and regulations already discussed (page 187).

Converting associations into types can also be used to distinguish between rôles and players: the types that play the rôles. Figure 6.6 shows a set of transformations or refinements of the same model to illustrate the point. Notice that the notion of having a job can be reified[4] into a type **Job** to allow the capture of work-related information. Converting this type back into an association allows us to be explicit about the rôles involved. This is rarely a good idea during specification but it is useful to know that it is possible, because at design time it may indicate how to design a class representing a plug-point, as we discuss in Chapter 9.

Graham *et al.* (1997a) showed that bi-directional associations of the kind depicted in Figures 6.5 and 6.6 violate encapsulation and thereby compromise

---

[4] I.e. made into a thing; from the Greek ρει or Latin *res*, meaning: thing.

reuse.[5] This kind of diagram is adequate for sketching out preliminary models and discovering the vocabulary of the domain but when documenting reusable components it is preferable to think of associations as one-directional pointers corresponding to the rôlenames in the figure. The reason for this will become even clearer when we discuss invariants.

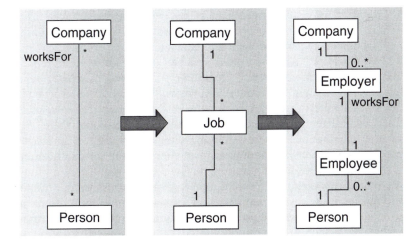

Figure 6.6 Distinguishing rôles and players.[6]

We already have the notion of the interface to an object containing an attribute and its facets. We can view associations as (generalized) attributes. In this sense an attribute contains zero or more values of a nominated type; an association stores values of a nominated user defined (or library) type. The only difference is that attributes point at 'primitive' types. What is primitive is up to the analyst and a key criterion for making this decision is whether the type (class) should appear on the class model diagrams.

Typical associations in an HR application might include ones that show that employees must work for exactly one department while departments may employ zero or more employees. These could be shown as follows.

worksIn: Dept(1,1) is an attribute of Employee.
employs: (Employee,0,n) is an attribute of Dept.

We regard attributes as split into two sorts: **pure attributes** and (attributes representing) **associations**. Technically, there is no difference between the two but the associations of pure attributes are not shown in association structure diagrams, mainly to avoid clutter. The default cardinality for a pure attribute is (0,1); if the

---

[5] The argument is summarized later in this subsection.

[6] This figure and several subsequent ones in this chapter and the next are reproduced courtesy of TriReme International Ltd.

attribute is non-null this should be shown as a facet.

This definition of associations is slightly different from that of methods and notations such as OMT, Shlaer-Mellor, Coad or UML. These view associations as external to objects and their metamodels require a new primitive to accommodate them. This shows up most clearly when bi-directional associations are used.

As we have seen, one of the two basic and characteristic features of object-orientation is the principle of encapsulation. This says that objects hide the implementation of their data structures and processing, and are used only via their interface. An object-oriented model uses object types to represent all concepts and divides these types (or their implementations as classes) into a public interface representing the type's responsibilities and an implementation that is hidden completely from all other parts of the system. The advantages of this are that it localizes maintenance of the classes and facilitates their reuse via calls to their interfaces alone. Modifications to classes are avoided by creating specialized subclasses that inherit basic responsibilities and can override (redefine) them and add new ones.

Bi-directional associations violate encapsulation. Stating that class A is associated with class B in some way or other is a statement of knowledge that concerns *both* classes. There are three obvious approaches to storing this knowledge:

- If the knowledge is separated from either class then we must return to a system of first- and second-class object types such as the one that plagued semantic data modelling. This means that, when we reuse either A or B, we have to have knowledge that is external to both of them in order to ensure that important coupling information is carried into the new system. Since this knowledge is not part of the classes it is quite conceivable that it could be lost, forgotten or overlooked by a hasty developer.
- Alternatively, we could place the knowledge inside one of the object types, A say. This will not work either, because now B will have lost track of its coupling with A and could not be reused successfully where this coupling was relevant.
- Finally, we could store the knowledge in both A and B. This last approach leads to the well-known problems of maintaining two copies of the same thing and cannot usually be tolerated.

Thus, separating objects from relationships violates encapsulation and compromises reuse. However, I will demonstrate later how the knowledge can indeed be split between the two types without loss of integrity, using invariants encapsulated in the objects.

Another way to violate encapsulation is to write remarks about associations, including constraints, on the type diagrams rather than encapsulating them with the interfaces. Constraints on the way objects are related can be written on UML diagrams near the associations that they refer to and connected to them by unadorned dotted lines. Clearly no class encapsulates them. For a particularly striking example of how foolish and unnecessary this is, consider the {or} constraint shown in Figure 6.7(a). This example was actually taken from the original UML documentation (www.rational.com). It shows that a bank account can be held by a person or an organization, but not by both.

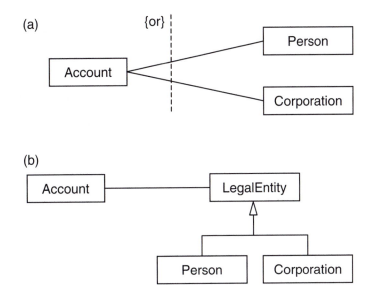

Figure 6.7 (a) A UML constraint violating encapsulation; **(b)** how appropriate use of polymorphism makes the constraint unnecessary.

The amazing thing is that any object-oriented designer should know perfectly well that, instead of this bad design, one should utilize inheritance polymorphism to represent the disjunction, as in Figure 6.7(b).[7] Here exactly the same information is conveyed and encapsulation is preserved. In addition we have forced the discovery of a very reusable class and – I would assert – an analysis pattern. Fowler (2000) calls half of this pattern EXTRACT SUPERCLASS.

INHERITANCE One special kind of association, and one that is characteristic of object-oriented models, is the generalization association, which is a class attribute whose value is the list of classes (or types) that the class inherits features from. Diagrams of these associations are called **inheritance structures**. Figure 6.8 illustrates some of these. Note that inheritance can be single or multiple as explained in Chapter 1. Also note that type inheritance can be distinguished from class inheritance because in type inheritance only the specification and no implementation is inherited. UML lacks

---

[7] We could also specialize Account to the same end.

specific notation for this but uses a dotted line with an arrowhead identical to those in Figure 6.8 to indicate interface inheritance (which it calls realization).

Associations can be inherited (or derived) and this is shown by placing a / mark on the association line at the rôlename end and/or before the attribute name. A good CASE tool would allow automatic suppression or display of derived associations.

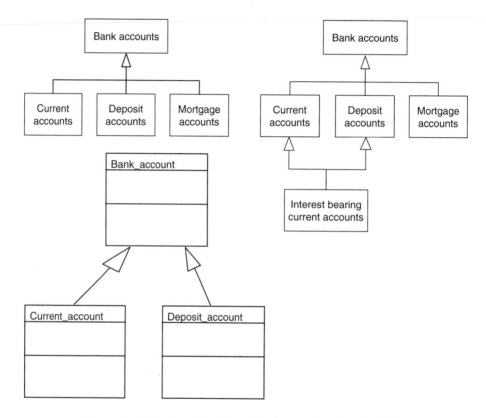

Figure 6.8 Single and multiple inheritance structures in UML.

Unfortunately, as shown by Wills (1991), it is not possible to make any general statement about the way cardinality constraints are inherited except that it depends on the entire interface of the subtype. This, of course, depends on how we interpret the diagrams: as a domain model or as part of a requirements description. Thus, we must make the weakest assumption: that inherited cardinalities are zero-to-many. Additional knowledge of the subtype and the domain allows us to strengthen this. For example, if all full-time employees work in exactly one department, we may wish to allow part-timers to work in several but, of course, they must work in at least one. We will be able to say more about this topic when we come to deal with invariants.

AGGREGATION AND COMPOSITION Another special kind of association is aggregation or composition. This occurs when there is a whole–part relationship between instances of a type. However, great care should be taken when using it unless you really understand what you are doing. It is somewhat dangerous for type modelling but will be essential when we examine use cases later.

An aggregation or composition indicates that a whole is made of (physically composed of) its parts. A good heuristic test for whether a relationship is a composition relationship is to ask: 'if the part moves, can one deduce that the whole moves with it in normal circumstances?'. For example, the relationship 'is the managing director of' between People and Companies is not a composition because if the MD goes on holiday to the Alps, the company does not. On the other hand, if his legs go the Alps then the MD probably goes too (unless he has seriously upset some unscrupulous business rivals).

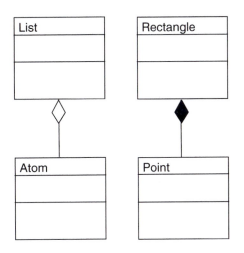

Figure 6.9 Aggregation and composition in UML.

Strictly in UML, aggregation and composition are represented by empty and filled diamonds respectively as shown in Figure 6.9 and represent programming language level concepts. In UML the empty diamond of aggregation designates that the whole maintains a *reference* to its part, so that the whole may not have created the part. This is equivalent to a C++ reference or pointer construction. The filled diamond signifies that the whole is responsible for creating its 'parts', which is equivalent to saying in C++ that when the whole class is allocated or declared the constructors of the part classes are called followed by the constructor for the whole (Texel and Williams, 1997). It is clear to me that this has little to do with the analysis of business objects; nor does the definition of composition in terms of ownership and lifetime constraints on instances (Rumbaugh *et al.*, 1999). We continue to use the terms composition and aggregation interchangeably for the common-sense notion of assembled components. The semantics of this notion were explored in detail by Odell (1994) whose argument may be summarized as follows.

Odell classifies composition relationships according to three decisions: whether they represent a structural relationship (configurational), whether the parts are of the same type as the whole (homeomeric) and whether the parts can be detached from the whole (invariant). This evidently factors APO into eight types. He then discusses six of them and names his different interpretations of composition as follows:

1. Component-integral (configurational, non-homeomeric and non-invariant).
2. Material (configurational, non-homeomeric and invariant).
3. Portion (configurational, homeomeric and non-invariant).
4. Place-area (configurational, homeomeric and invariant).
5. Member bunch (non-configurational, non-homeomeric and non-invariant).
6. Member-partnership (non-configurational, non-homeomeric and invariant).

We will only use configurational, invariant composition. All other types of so-called composition (such as the manages relationship alluded to above) are handled by either associations or attributes (which are merely a special case of associations). What difference these distinctions make to the programmer is arguable. I like the idea of aggregation as a form of refinement: the constituents are what you find if you look closer.

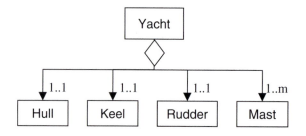

Figure 6.10 Composition structure for a yacht.

As with inheritance, composition is directional: it is improper for the part to know what whole it belongs to because this would compromise reuse. To emphasize this I have adorned the example of a composite yacht in Figure 6.10 with arrowheads. Each composition link can have a cardinality constraint at the part end as also shown. If a similar constraint were to be used at the whole end, not only would this compromise encapsulation, but we would have to introduce a distinction between type level and instance level composition (as indeed I did in previous editions of this text). I now think that a better way to handle this is to use Odell's notion of a 'power type' (Martin and Odell, 1998). A power type is just a type whose instances are subtypes of another type. Types may have more than one power type corresponding to separate subtype discriminators. For example, if we divide employees into male and female subtypes we could create (slightly redundantly in this case) a power type called GenderType; but if we classify them according to job type a different (and perhaps more useful) power type may be used. Returning to aggregation, if we regard a bicycle as being composed of a frame and some (two?) wheels then a particular wheel can belong to only one bike. However, the type of wheel that it is can be fitted to several types of bike. This leads to the need to distinguish type level from instance level aggregation unless we introduce a power type corresponding to the catalogue description of the wheel: its WheelType. This phenomenon is referred to as 'reflection'. The term is usually used when there is some facility to extend the model 'at run time'; the idea is that the analyst defines a model in which there is a type of types, which can be used at run time to add new types, but over which relationships are nevertheless asserted in the base specification language.

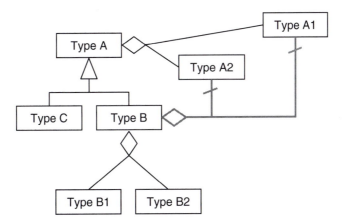

Figure 6.11 Derived composition dependencies.

Like other kinds of association, composition can be inherited and the same convention as for ordinary associations is used to show this: a / mark on the link. A subtype inherits the components of all its supertypes. Consider a type A with subtypes B and C. A also has components A1 and A2. Class B has components B1 and B2. The composition structure for Class B therefore includes two derived components as shown in Figure 6.11. The derived dependencies are shown in grey for greater clarity. I have not shown the derived dependencies for C. It is easy now to see how including all such derived links can quickly make diagrams unreadable, which is another reason why CASE tools should let them be toggled on and off.

Some authorities regard the notion of composition as undefinable and others definable only in terms of some specified set of operations defined on the whole. I recommend that composition is used sparingly in business object modelling but we will see that it is absolutely essential when modelling actions as objects, as we do in the next section and in Chapter 7.

UML also allows dependencies of arbitrary type between types and classes. These are shown by the labelled, dashed arrows. The label is a stereotype. The most usual and useful dependencies relate to interfaces and packages and we shall return to them later in those contexts.

Usage relationships signify that not only does a client know about the existence of a feature of a server but that it will actually send a message to exercise that feature at some point. Ordinary associations might never be exercised. The difference between an association and a usage dependency is akin to that between knowing the address of the editor of the *Financial Times* and being its Wall Street correspondent. This is not, as many of my critics have claimed, an implementation concept but a key part of the semantics of a model. Saying that two classes are associated does not imply that the structural link between them will ever be traversed. For example, there may be many relationships in a database that are there to support *ad hoc* queries that may never be made by any user. A usage link on the other hand states that there will be some interaction or collaboration. The existence of usage links removes the need for a separate notion for collaboration graphs as found in RDD (Wirfs-Brock *et al.*, 1990). One class 'uses' another if it is a client to the other class acting as a server. Any associations introduced may subsequently be replaced by more specific usage or (more rarely) composition relationships. This kind of relationship is also extremely important in requirements engineering and business process modelling, as we shall see in Chapter 7 when we come to modelling agents in businesses as objects. It is a concept missing from both OML and UML, although in UML one can use a dependency labelled «uses» to represent the idea. Henderson-Sellers (1998) argues for the inclusion of a uses relationship in OML.

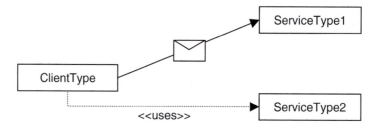

Figure 6.12 Usage associations.

Figure 6.12 shows an easily memorable icon to represent the stereotype «uses», and the more usual notation.

6.3.2 Using use cases to discover types

So far we have seen how to describe and draw pictures of objects but little has been said about how to go about discovering them. The most popular technique starts with a set of use cases that describe how a system interacts with its environment: typical interactions involving its users.

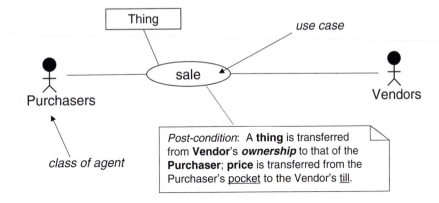

Figure 6.13 Use cases and the types they refer to.

Catalysis introduced the idea of actions, which generalize both use cases and operations. An **action** is any goal-oriented collaboration, activity, task, operation or job connecting agents in a business, system or project. When specifying systems, the most interesting actions are use cases. A **use case** is a goal-oriented collaboration between a system and an actor; where an **actor** is a user adopting a rôle. Such a 'user' can be a device or component as well as a person. An **agent** is anybody or anything adopting a rôle; as opposed to a user doing so. We regard agents and actors as objects, because they exhibit state and behaviour and have identity. If we know the initiator of a collaboration then we can think of a usage dependency as representative of the action. Consider the simple act of buying something illustrated in Figure 6.13. The ellipse represents an interaction between two agent instances which results in something changing ownership between them in return for money changing hands in the other direction. This is represented by an informal post-condition on the action written in the note illustrated. This post-condition only makes sense in terms of the objects it refers to: its **parameters**. In this case we have identified Thing as a type that must be included in our vocabulary and shown it on our initial drawing. Additionally, we have picked out some of the nouns in the post-condition. This is a very useful technique for inferring the type model from the use cases. We show candidate types in bold, with attributes underlined and potential associations italicized. We discuss this method of so-called textual analysis further in Section 6.5. It was popularized by Abbott (1983).

We can see from this example that an action always results in a change of state that can be expressed by a post-condition. Catalysis (D'Souza and Wills, 1999) introduced the idea of illustrating this change using **instance snapshots**. We draw instances of the candidate types and their associations at a particular point in time, before the occurrence of the action. Then the result of applying the use case is expressed by showing which associations are deleted and added to the diagram. In

Figure 6.14 the association between sock17 and the vendor is crossed out from the 'before' diagram (indicating deletion) and added to the 'after' diagram. Associations in after snapshots are shown by thick grey lines in this book. Note also that the values of the pocket and till attributes are crossed out and replaced with new values.

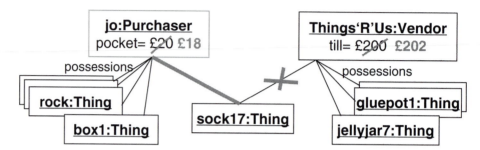

Figure 6.14 An instance snapshot.

Any snapshot must conform to the type diagram associated with the use case it illustrates. Snapshots are useful as an aid to clear thinking during analysis and design. They represent instances of use cases. Although simple ones may be included in formal documentation, I usually recommend against this. After drawing them, the type model can usually be updated. Note in particular that neither the action post-condition nor the snapshots say anything about the sequence of events; they only describe the outcome, regardless of the precise sequence of events leading to it. This is important when we come to the design of reusable components because two components (or two business units) may implement the use case quite differently. The interface to a reusable component should only specify the outcome and the vocabulary, not the sequence of implementation operations that leads to that outcome.

Every action, and *a fortiori* every use case, has a name, a goal, a list of participants (usually two in business analysis) and a list of parameters: the objects involved (actively or passively) that are different from one occurrence of the use case to another. The goal represents its specification: the result(s) it achieves, and/or a condition that it maintains. There may also be a pre-condition: a statement defining under what conditions the use case makes sense. Thus, when documenting an action the following form is recommended:

> <u>type</u> name (parameters)
> pre-condition
> post-condition

For example, referring to Figure 6.13, we might write:

> <u>use case</u> buy_thing (Purchaser, Vendor, Thing)
>   *pre*:   vendor owns the thing and purchaser can afford it
>   *post*:   vendor.possessions reduced by thing
>   and   purchaser.possessions increased by thing

```
and      vendor.till += thing.price
and      purchaser.pocket –= thing.price
```

We could even express this with full mathematical formality using UML's Object Constraint Language (OCL) as follows:

<u>use case</u> buy_thing (Purchaser, Vendor, Thing)
     pre: vendor.possessions -> includes thing
     And   purchaser.pocket >= thing.price
     post: vendor.possessions = vendor.possessions – thing
     and   purchaser.possessions = purchaser.possessions + thing
     and   vendor.till = vendor.till@pre + thing.price
     and   purchaser.pocket = purchaser.pocket@pre – thing.price

In the above, the expression @pre refers to the value held by the attribute in the before state and ->includes indicates set membership. The + sign is an abbreviation for –>union (ditto the – sign *mutatis mutandis*). Another convention used here is inherited from Fusion (Coleman *et al.*, 1994): if all the parameters have different types, their names are the same as the type names, but starting with lower case. The same convention is used for unlabelled associations. Using upper case means one is saying something about the type. Notice also that there is no attribute of **Thing** named price. The only purpose of the attributes is to provide a vocabulary for the action specifications.

    OCL specifications are not to everyone's taste and do not need to be used. But it is reassuring for those of us who work on high-integrity or safety-critical systems that such formality is possible. I will not use OCL very much in this text.

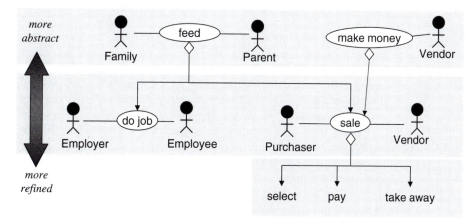

Figure 6.15 Composing and decomposing use cases.

    The static type model provides a vocabulary for expressing use cases. The use case model defines behaviour using the vocabulary from the static model. Snapshots illustrate use case occurrences and help clarify thinking about the type model.

Use cases (and other actions) are objects; so that they can be associated, classified and aggregated just like other objects. In our example of a sale, we can see that there can be various kinds of sale that specialize the concept. Note that the post-conditions are all strengthened in the sub-actions. Pre-conditions, if any, must be weakened. We will see later that this is a general rule for inherited pre- and post-conditions. It is also possible to abstract and refine use cases using aggregation as illustrated in Figure 6.15 and using inheritance as Figure 6.16 shows. Figure 6.16 gives an example specialization of sale; note that a specialized use case achieves all the goals of its parent(s).

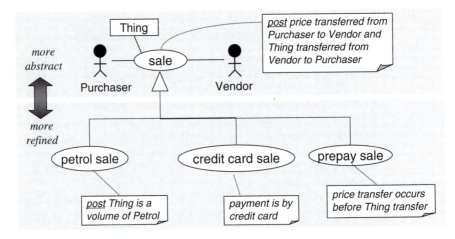

Figure 6.16 Generalizing and specializing use cases.

Figure 6.16 contains a deliberate *faux pas*, intended to illustrate a common error. It is quite wrong for the same inheritance arrow to be used to connect the completely incomparable notions of a petrol sale and a credit sale. We should show the two orthogonal hierarchies separately; each inheritance arrow corresponds to a **discriminator** such as 'fuel type' or 'payment method'. Always ask yourself 'what is the discriminator?' when drawing a specialization diagram of any sort.

The left-to-right ordering in aggregation diagrams like Figure 6.15 does not imply any temporal sequence; the use cases could happen in any sequence, be repeated or be concurrent. However, we can add such information by creating associations between actions as we will see in Chapter 7 where we will also discuss how to handle exceptions using «uses» dependencies. UML specifies two particular dependencies designated «include» (originally «uses») and «extend» (originally «extends»). However, since these are poorly and inconsistently defined and since «extend» violates encapsulation (Graham *et al.*, 1997a) I will not use them in this book. My experience is that their use sows confusion and, besides, the standard object semantics that we have laid down for static models enables us to do everything without introducing additional terminology. I will say more about this in Chapter 7.

The goals of use cases provide the basis for building a test harness very early on in analysis, because they relate directly to the purpose and function of a system. Again, more will be said on this in Chapter 8. This also facilitates eXtreme Programming (Beck, 2000).

Notice how the actors in the use case model correspond to types in the type model in our preliminary attempt. Also, if we regard the type model as providing the vocabulary for defining the use cases, we can see that this provides a link between two different kinds of UML diagram. It was a major innovation of Catalysis to show how the UML diagram types were related.

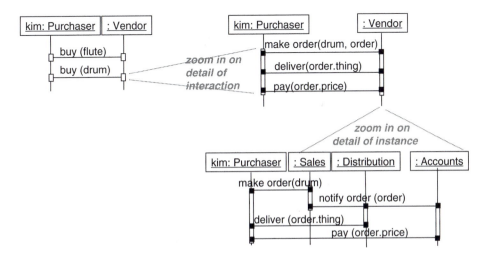

Figure 6.17 Sequence diagrams and refinement.

Just as snapshots help us visualize the type model, scenarios and sequence diagrams help with the visualization of use cases. Scenarios are stories about how the business works. They can be written out in prose and this is often a useful thing to do. They describe typical sequences that occur when a use case is realized and can include variations on the basic sequence. They can be illustrated with UML sequence or collaboration diagrams of the kind shown in Figure 6.18 or, better, with the Catalysis-style sequence chart of Figure 6.17. The distinctive feature of the latter is the action-instances, each of which may touch more than two objects, and need not be directed.

UML sequence diagrams only describe OO programming messages, each with a receiver and sender. In both cases the vertical lines represent the instances of the types indicated above them and the horizontal lines represent actions that involve the instances that they connect. Both dimensions can be expanded to refine the analysis and provide more detailed steps and a finer scale; each event can be expanded to more detailed sequences and each object to more detailed objects. In the figure we see that one can zoom in on the details of the buy(drum) use case to show details of the vendor's business process sequence. We can also zoom in on the vendor object to reveal details of his business organization as well. The trick is to choose the level and scale that you are working at: *essential* 'my pay was credited to my account yesterday, so I went to get some cash today'; *detail* 'to get money from your account, you insert your card into a cash machine, enter PIN, ...'; *grandiose* 'A good way of making money is to run a bank. Provide accounts with higher rates of interest in exchange for less accessibility. They should be able to get cash from the most accessible accounts at any time of day or night.' We will look further at the notion of essential use cases in Chapter 8.

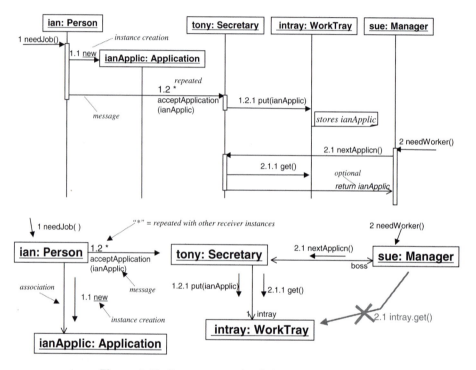

Figure 6.18 Sequence and collaboration diagrams.

Sequence charts for scenarios help to identify the different participants in the action and their interactions and to show the sequence of events. This helps with the conceptualization of the rôle of time and with understanding dependencies between instances. Sequence charts assist the designer in allocating instances among distributed system components and are often useful during testing. They also help with exploring interference between multiple use cases.

Notice that zooming is based on aggregation in the examples given above. Inheritance can also lead to refinements; so we could zoom from buy(drum) to buy(bodhran), which would involve the purchaser selecting a tipper and testing the goatskin for usefully melodious imperfections.

Refinement is one of the basic principles of Catalysis and aids traceability by linking specification level use cases and types to implementation interfaces and their vocabularies. Typically, the different levels of refinement will be contained in different implementation packages.

Sequence diagrams emphasize visualizing the allocation of responsibility: it is easy to shift tasks sideways. They are equivalent to collaboration diagrams which emphasize static relationships rather than temporal ones. Collaboration diagrams help you see what associations are being affected, and the dependencies between the objects (which, of course, you want to minimize). Sequence diagrams are good at illustrating the assignment of responsibilities but cannot express control flow variation well. Collaboration diagrams are better at showing associations and control flow. This helps us to think about better decoupling. Figure 6.18 shows a sequence diagram and its associated collaboration form. Arrows or lines joining the instances in the latter represent associations. Messages are indicated by the unattached arrows and their numbering indicates their calling sequence. Detailed as they look, collaboration diagrams still abstract from the precise details of implementation. In this case we see that the association between the manager and the work tray represents a poor design. S/he would be better to access these data through a secretarial service, which can be provided either by Tony or by an access function to a database. A change in the way the job-applications are stored would result in a change to both Secretary and Manager if they both access the Worktray. The moral is that we can reduce dependencies by assigning responsibilities properly; the collaborations help us understand how to assign responsibilities. Figure 6.18 also shows that collaboration diagrams can be used as snapshots.

6.3.3 Invariants and rulesets

In performing object-oriented analysis and building a model, a large number of lessons can be learnt from AI systems built using semantic nets and from semantic data modelling. Specifications that exhibit encapsulation of attributes and operations are all very well but do not necessarily contain the meaning intended by the analyst or the user. To reuse the specification of an object we should be able to read from it what it knows (attributes), what it does (operations), why it does it and how it is related to other objects' interfaces. It is my position that this semantic content is partly contained in the structures of association, classification, composition and usage and by the assertions, invariants and rulesets which describe the behaviour.

The fact is that all semantics limit reuse, although they make it safer. For example, inheritance does so; and so does anything that makes the *meaning* of an object more specific. In system specification, both aspects are equally important and the trade-off must be well understood and managed with care, depending on the goals of the analysts and their clients.

One must also be aware of the need to decide whether rules belong to individual operations or to the object as a whole. There is no principled reason why operations cannot be expressed in a rule-based language. However, the distinction to be made here is not between the form of expression but the content of the rules. Rules that relate several operations do not belong within those operations and rules which define dependencies between attributes also refer to the object as a whole. Conversely, rules that concern the encapsulated state of the object belong within one of its operations. The most important kind of 'whole object' rules are control rules which describe the behaviour of the object as it participates in structures that it belongs to: rules to control the handling of defaults, multiple inheritance, exceptions and general associations with other objects.

The introduction of encapsulated rulesets was a novel aspect of SOMA. It enhances object models by adding a set of rulesets to each object. Thus, while an object is normally thought to consist of Identifier, Attributes and Operations, a SOMA object consists of Identifier, Attributes, Operations and Rulesets. **Rulesets** are composed of an unordered set of assertions and rules of either 'if/then' or 'when/then' form. This modelling extension has a number of interesting consequences, the most remarkable of which is that these objects – which are local entities – can encapsulate the rules for global system behaviour; rather as DNA is supposed to encapsulate the morpheme. A further consequence is that objects with rulesets can be regarded as intelligent agents for expert systems developments.

It is widely agreed that it is quite insufficient to specify only the attributes and operations (the signature) of an object. To specify the object completely we must say how these are allowed to interact with each other and what rules and constraints must be obeyed by the object as a whole to maintain its integrity as such. Some languages, such as Eiffel, and some methods, such as BON, Catalysis or Syntropy, achieve a partial solution by using assertions. Assertions in such systems are of two kinds: assertions about the operations and assertions about the whole object. The former are typically pre- and post-conditions while the latter are called class invariants. SOMA and Catalysis add invariance conditions to the operational assertions and SOMA generalizes class invariants to rulesets – which can be chained together to infer new information. There are also assertion facets representing attribute constraints. Here are the definitions:

Attribute assertions
- **Range constraints** give limits on permissible values.
- **Enumeration constraints** list permissible values.
- **Type constraints** specify the class that values must belong to. Type constraints are always present and generalize the former two cases.

Operational assertions
- A **pre-condition** is a single logical statement that must be true before its operation may execute.
- A **post-condition** is a single logical statement that must be true after its operation has finished execution.

- An **invariance condition** is a single logical statement that must hold at all times when its operation is executing. This is only of importance for parallel processing systems (including business process models). Invariance conditions were first introduced as part of SOMA (Graham, 1991a). Catalysis (D'Souza and Wills, 1999) distinguishes two kinds of invariance conditions: guarantee and rely clauses.

- A **rely** clause states a pre-condition that must remain true throughout the execution of the operation it refers to. Should it be violated, the specification does not state what clients can expect as a result. The server is not responsible for maintaining the condition.

- A **guarantee** is a statement that the server must maintain as true throughout the execution of the operation.

The facets of an operation may include more than one assertion of any of these types. Assertions may be represented by state-transition diagrams as we shall see.

Object assertions and rulesets

- A **class invariant** is a single (possibly quantified) logical statement about any subset of the features of an object that must be true at all times (in Eiffel, which has direct support for invariants, this only applies to times when a method is not executing). Cardinality constraints on attributes are invariants. Invariants can also be called **rules**.

- A **ruleset** is an unordered set of class invariants (or **rules**) and assertions about attributes together with a defined inference régime that allows the rules to be chained together. **External rulesets** express second order information such as control strategy. **Internal rulesets** are (first order) sets of invariants. They may be written either in natural language, OCL or in an executable rule language.

- An **effect** is a post-condition that is conjoined with all other operation post-conditions of a type. An effect is usually of the form: (any change $f(x, x@\text{pre}) \Rightarrow$ condition). Effects can be expressed as rules. They are useful for the designer of a supertype who wants to impose restrictions on the operations that may be invented by subtype specifiers.

The normal assumption behind the above definitions is that the logic to be used is standard first order predicate calculus (FOPC). We make no such assumption although FOPC is the usual default logic.[8] Other logics that can be used include temporal, fuzzy, deontic, epistemic and non-monotonic logic. Each ruleset in a class determines its own logic locally, although it would be unusual to mix logics in the same class.

---

[8] In Catalysis the default is Logic of Partial Functions (Cheng and Jones, 1990) which has clear treatment of undefined values. Recommended reading for anyone who has applied logic to program specifications in real earnest.

We have already seen the distinction between a type and a class: a type has no implementation. We can now distinguish between types and interfaces. An **interface** is a list of the messages that can be sent to an object with their parameters and return types. Depending on the interpretation, this may include the get and set operations on attributes. This concept is sometimes referred to as the **signature** of a type. A type on the other hand is a full specification including all the assertions that may be made about the type and its instances and all rulesets.

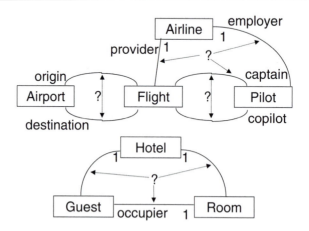

Figure 6.19 Cyclic associations suggest invariants.

An invariant, or constraint, is a single rule that is always obeyed by the object whose scope it lies in. It is expressed using the vocabulary provided by the type model. Example invariants for an airline management system might include: 'Every pilot must be the captain or co-pilot of up to one flight per day', 'The captain and co-pilot cannot be the same person' or 'Every flight must be flown by a captain who is qualified for this plane type'. Clearly, the invariant of a type can refer to the public interfaces of other types. Invariants can be expressed informally, as above, or using the high precision of OCL or other formal logic systems.

One possible source of invariants is the existence of cycles in type diagrams. In fact, as we shall see later, any bi-directional association usually requires a pair of invariants – precisely because the pair of rôlenames is a loop. In Figure 6.19 we can see that all the indicated loops may possibly imply the need for one or more invariants to be stated.

For example, in the upper diagram the pilot of a flight must work for the airline that provides the flight. The reader is encouraged to write invariants for the other cycle in Figure 6.19.

Rulesets generalize class invariants and permit objects to do several things:

- ■ Infer attribute values that are not stored explicitly.
- ■ Represent database triggers.

- Represent operations in a non-procedural fashion.
- Represent control régimes.

Rules specify second order information, such as dependencies between attributes; for example, a dependency between the age of an employee and her holiday entitlement. Global pre- and post-conditions that apply to all operations may be specified as rules. A typical business rule in a human resources application might include 'change holiday entitlement to six weeks when service exceeds five years' as a rule in the **Employee** type. With rulesets the notation can cope with analysis problems where an active database is envisaged as the target environment.

Rules and invariants are used to make an object's semantics explicit and visible. This helps with the description of information that would normally reside in a repository, such as business rules for the enterprise. It can also help with inter-operability at quite a low level. For example, if I have an object which computes cube roots, as a client of that object it is not enough to know its operations alone; I need to know that what is returned is a cube root and not a square root. In this simple case the solution is obvious because we can characterize the cube root uniquely with one simple rule: the response times itself twice is equal to the parameter sent. If this rule is part of the interface then all other systems and system components can see the meaning of the object from its interface alone, removing thus some of the complexities of repository technology by shifting it into the object model.

The rules which appear in the rule window may be classified into several, not necessarily exclusive, types, as follows.

- Business rules
- Exception handling rules
- Triggers
- Control rules

CONTROL RULES

The last application of rulesets is by far and away the most esoteric. Object-oriented methods must obviously deal with multiple class inheritance. This extension must include provision for annotating the handling of conflict arising when the same attribute or operation is inherited differently from two parent objects. Of course, types compose monotonically so this problem doesn't arise. This kind of discrimination can only be done with a class. One way to deal with it is to use rulesets to disambiguate multiple inheritance. One can then also define priority rules for defaults and demons. (A demon is a method that wakes up when needed; i.e. when a value changes, or is added or deleted.) That is, these rules can determine how to resolve the conflict that arises when an attribute inherits two different values or perhaps specify whether the default value should be applied before or after inheritance takes place or before or after a demon fires. They may also specify the relative priorities of inheritance and demons. As with attributes and operations, the interface of the object only displays the name of a ruleset. In the case of a backward chaining ruleset this might well include the name of the value being sought: its goal;

e.g. If Route: needed SEEK Route:

Control rules are encapsulated within objects, instead of being declared globally. They may also be inherited and overridden (although the rules for this may be slightly complicated in some cases – see (Wills, 1991)). The benefit of this is that local variations in control strategy are possible. Furthermore, the analyst may inspect the impact of the control structure on every object – using a browser perhaps – and does not have to annotate convoluted diagrams to describe the local effects of global control. Genuinely global rules can be contained in a top level object, called something like 'object', and will be inherited by all objects that do not override them. Alternatively, we can set up global rules in a special 'policy blackboard' object. Relevant classes register interest in Policies, which broadcasts rule and status changes to registrants as necessary. This uses, of course, a publish and subscribe pattern (see Chapter 7). Just as state transition diagrams may be used to describe the procedural semantics of operations, so decision trees may be found useful in describing complex sets of rules.

Control rules **concern** the operations and attributes of the object they belong to. They do not concern themselves. Thus, they cannot help with the determination of how to resolve a multiple inheritance conflict between rulesets or other control strategy problem related to rulesets. This would require a set of metarules to be encapsulated and these too would require a meta-language. This quickly leads to an infinite regress. Therefore multiple inheritance of rules does not permit conflict resolution. A dot notation is used to duplicate any rulesets with the same name. Thus, if an object inherits rulesets called POLICYA from two superclasses, X and Y, they are inherited separately as X.POLICYA and Y.POLICYA. The case of fuzzy rules is slightly different since fuzzy rules cannot contradict each other as explained in Appendix A. Therefore multiply inherited fuzzy rulesets with the same name may be merged. In both the crisp and fuzzy cases, however, the careful user of the method should decide every case on its merits, since the equivalent naming of the inherited rulesets could have been erroneous.

It is sometimes possible, in simple cases, to specify rules that must be obeyed by all control strategies for multiple inheritance. In the case where objects are identified with only abstract data types – i.e. constructed types representing relations, say, are not permitted – we have a clear set of three rules for inheritance:

1. There must be no cycles of the form: x is AKO y is AKO z is AKO x. This rule eliminates redundant objects.
2. The bottom of an AKO link must be a subtype, and the top must be a subtype or an abstract type (i.e. not a printable object; not an attribute).
3. It must be possible to name a subtype of two supertypes. This rule prevents absurd objects, such as the class of all people who are also toys.

These rules are commended as design checks.

RULE CHAINING

Rule-based systems are non-procedural. That is, the ordering of a set of rules does not affect their interpretation. Rules may be grouped into rulesets which concern the derivation of values for one object. In some environments, such as KEE, rules are each *bona fide* objects, but this approach begs the question of the relationship of a rule to another object. Most expert systems shells and environments encourage the developer to write the rules first and only later identify the objects used by the rules. This enforces a top-down approach and can be useful as a discipline but contradicts an object-oriented approach.

Regime = 'Backward';

Goal = bestProduct;

If client.status is 'Retired'
        and client.preference is not 'RiskAverse'
        then bestProduct is 'Annuity';

If client.status is 'Young'
        and client.preference is not 'RiskAverse'
        then bestProduct: is 'Endowment';

If client.preference is 'RiskAverse'
        then bestProduct is 'Bonds';

If Client.Children: > 0
        then client.preference is 'RiskAverse';

Figure 6.20 A ruleset.

Rules may be of several different types. For instance, we may have triggers, business rules and control rules. Business rules typically relate two or more attributes and triggers relate attributes to operations. For example:

Business rule: If Service_length > 5 then Holiday=25
Forward Trigger: When Salary + SalaryIncrement > 35000
                run AwardCompanyCar

The first of the two simple business rules above is interesting because we could evidently implement it in two completely different ways. We could place a pre-condition on **getHoliday** that always checks Service_length before returning the value. Alternatively, we could place a post-condition on **putService_length** that detects whether Holiday should be changed on every anniversary. Clearly, the former corresponds to lazy and the latter to eager evaluation. The important point here is that we should *not* be making design decisions of this nature during specification or analysis. Using a rule-based approach defers these decisions to a more appropriate point.

Quite complex rules can be expressed simply as rulesets. For example, an InsuranceSalesmen class might contain the rules for giving the best advice to a customer in the form shown in Figure 6.20. The rules fire when a value for BestProduct is needed. Note that these rules do not compromise the encapsulation of Client by setting the value of RiskAverse in that object. The salesman is merely making an assumption in the face of missing data or prompting the Client for that information. If the Client.preference attribute is already set to RiskAverse, these rules never fire. Note also the non-procedural character of this ruleset. The rule that fires first is written last. The ruleset executes under a backward chaining régime to seek a value for BestProduct. Thus, we can see that the language is non-procedural. That is, the ordering of a set of rules does not affect their interpretation.

UML AND RULES

UML's qualifiers may be expressed as rules. For example, consider the many-to-many association between DOS files and directories. The Filename qualifier reduces this to a many-to-one association as illustrated in Figure 6.21. In general, qualification only partitions the sets. This is because qualification is relative; there is a degree of qualification. To avoid confusion we use rules such as 'Every file in the ListOfFiles attribute must have a unique name', a rule encapsulated in Directory. If FileNames is an attribute this can be avoided by writing FileNames[set of names] as opposed to [bag of ...] or [list of ...].

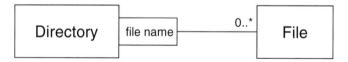

Figure 6.21 Qualified association.

In UML we can write invariants and rulesets in an (optional) fourth named compartment underneath the operations compartment of a type icon.

Rule-based extensions to object-oriented analysis help enrich the semantics of models of conventional commercial systems. This makes these models more readable and more reversible; more of the analysts' intentions are evident in the model. This provides a truly object-oriented approach to the specification of advanced database and knowledge-based systems.

As we have seen, control rules are not the only rules in an application. We have mentioned business rules already. In both cases, encapsulating these rules in objects makes sense and enhances reusability and extensibility. System-wide rules belong in the most general objects in the system; i.e. the top of the hierarchy (or hierarchies if there is no catch-all class as there is with Smalltalk's 'object'). They are propagated to other parts of the system via inheritance. All kinds of rule are stored in the rulesets of the optional fourth window of the object icon.

QUEST   Let us examine a simple but amusing example involving control rules for multiple inheritance and the default values of attributes. Suppose that we wish to construct an old-fashioned, text-based adventure game on the model of Colossal Cave, which I will call Quest. We usually have the following sorts of objects: locations, actors and things. The game has locations that may contain movable objects (we'll call them 'things' to avoid confusion) listed in their contents attribute or have mysterious properties described by operations. The attributes of locations also describe the various entries and exits and where they lead. There are players and the computer pretends to contain an anthropomorphic guide who will describe your current location and, if you ask it to eat the snake, say, will reply to the effect: 'I just lost my appetite'. These actors may be conveniently regarded as persons and fitted into a classification structure as shown in Figure 6.22. Note that the guide is not allowed to pick up objects (indicated by the ×) but inherits the ability to move from place to place. Players can issue commands such as 'take gem', 'go west' or 'hit troll with bucket'.

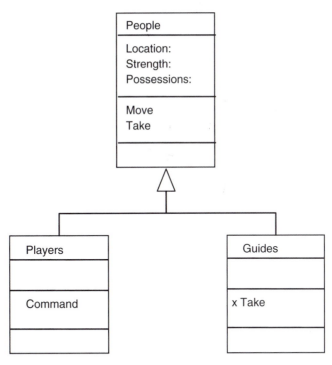

Figure 6.22 The actor classification structure of Quest.

Consider the Thing structure now. Things can be classified into treasure, which has a default value of 10 points, weapons, which do not, and utility items such as food, bags and the like. A provisional classification structure for Things is shown in Figure 6.23, where it can be seen that multiple inheritance has intruded; the jewelled sword is both treasure and a weapon. Treasure has positive value in points, and weapons have zero value. So what is the value of the jewelled sword, which could inherit from both weapon and treasure?

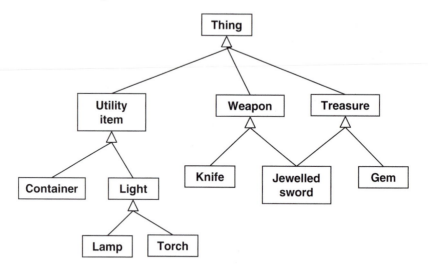

Figure 6.23 The classification structure of things.

There are several strategies for handling inheritance conflicts of this type. The system may report the conflict to the user and ask for a value, and this is the most common strategy. Unfortunately, stopping runs in a batch environment is usually more than merely annoying; it is costly. All other approaches require that the system is coded with some of the semantics of the application. Touretzky (1986) and others have suggested various 'shortest path' (or longest path) strategies based on the idea that the most direct inheritance represents the most specific knowledge. This can be useful but the assumption is not always justified and the strategy breaks down when the path lengths are equal. Other work by Touretzky (Horty *et al.*, 1990) suggests that conflict implies ignorance and means we should inherit the null value 'unknown'. The problem with this is that it reproduces all the logical problems that arise with null values in databases but in some applications it makes sense. It may also lead to run-time errors. If possible, the inheriting object can be given the answer in advance and told, by the default control rule, for example not to allow inherited wealth to override existing resources. Lastly, in the case of attributes rather than operations, the inherited values can sometimes be combined. One could, for example, take the average or weighted average of two numerical inherited values. Lenzerini *et al.* (1991) provide a survey of work in this general area of the interpretation of multiple inheritance lattices, now called 'terminological logic'.

Appendix A outlines a completely different scheme for combined value inheritance of this type. It also shows how to implement partial inheritance (inheriting something to a certain extent – a bit like inheriting your mother's singing voice) and even how to inherit partial properties (like being a bit rich) using notions from artificial intelligence and fuzzy set theory. But we still have not resolved the problem of the jewelled sword. A good practical suggestion in this case is to embody the rule 'If conflicts occur on the Value: attribute, combine values by taking their maximum' in the Thing class. The jewelled sword inherits this rule. This ensures that the sword gets its points and can still kill the troll.

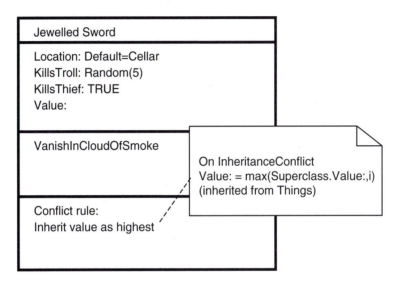

Figure 6.24 Including a conflict breaking rule.

Some researchers have applied this kind of rule-based idea to program browsers. These researchers believe that developers know much about their code that cannot be expressed formally which leads to time being wasted searching for implicit relationships. They suggest that the code should be related to a descriptive level that can be searched and manipulated. For example, the CogBrow research system supports operations such as: 'Find all the routines written last week by J. Smith and change every occurrence of GOTO 32767 to GOTO END:'. Similarly assertions and rules can be manipulated as if they were at the descriptive level. There have also been attempts to apply objects with rules to object-oriented network modelling (Bapat, 1994).

It may be enlightening to know that I was first motivated to add rules to the Coad/Yourdon method in 1989 when using it, not to describe a computer system, but to build a model of an organization. This kind of activity, known these days as enterprise modelling or business process re-engineering, brings to the fore the need to record business rules, often expressed at a high level or vaguely – just the sort of thing knowledge-based systems builders are used to.

SACIS

For a more concrete and realistic example, we will examine some objects in SACIS with their rules. The scenario involves a particular kind of event, a sale. A sale involves a customer, who may be an adult or a child, and a list of items, which may be of various types. There is a bar-code reader that reads and updates the stock system and a system whose task is to ensure that the sold items are suitable for the customer's purpose. The term suitable encompasses various 'fitness for purpose' criteria, one of which is safety. Let us assume that a particular customer is trying to buy a tube of glue. Note that there are a number of multiple inheritance structures involved; specifically, the one for glue shown in Figure 6.25.

Item
Drug
Office_equipment
Toy
Tube_of_glue

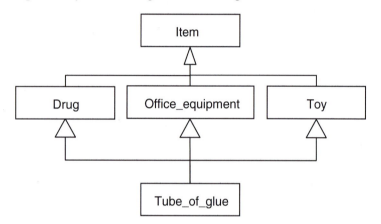

Figure 6.25 A multiple inheritance structure in SACIS.

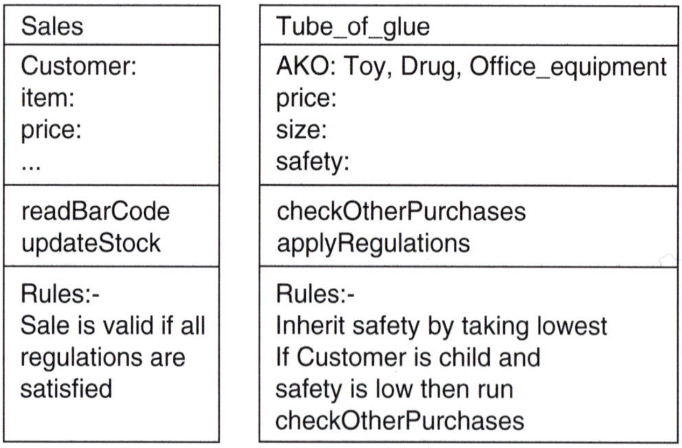

Sales
Customer:
item:
price:
...
readBarCode
updateStock
Rules:-
Sale is valid if all regulations are satisfied
Tube_of_glue
AKO: Toy, Drug, Office_equipment
price:
size:
safety:
checkOtherPurchases
applyRegulations
Rules:-
Inherit safety by taking lowest
If Customer is child and safety is low then run checkOtherPurchases

Figure 6.26 Some objects in the SACIS model.

The question is how to model the derivation of safety for this tube of glue.

Since glue inherits from office supplies and toy there should be no safety issue. However, the structures illustrated show that we have modelled the fact that glue can be abused as an intoxicating drug. Most shops now decline to sell glue to children for this reason; the structural modelling of this fact represents a business rule for such shops. However, it is also possible that there is a *bona fide* reason for a child purchasing glue, if perhaps a model has been purchased which must be glued. In such a case the system should either permit the sale or, more strictly perhaps, refuse to sell either the glue or the model (which is useless without the glue in any case).

To implement this, the system should flag the value of glue safety as low and scan the entire transaction to look for glue-related purchases. Figure 6.26 shows two of the objects that must be recorded during the analysis of this problem to convert the outline data model to object-oriented form.

6.3.4 Invariants and encapsulation

We have seen already that cyclic associations imply invariants and that bi-directional associations violate the principle of encapsulation and are therefore incompatible with object-orientation. The object-oriented principle of encapsulation implies that bi-directional associations must be abandoned in object-oriented modelling, in favour of either uni-directional pointers or conversion to *bona fide* classes.

In my formalism as we have seen, objects encapsulate rulesets, along with the usual attributes and methods. In this section we examine the notion of associations and their 'inverses' in some depth and point out some inconsistencies in current terminology within the database community that go back as far as Abrial's work. With the new foundation I then construct, I show how referential integrity rules can be embedded in classes rather than attached to external associations, as is the current normal practice. Finally, I argue that classes with rulesets are capable of modelling any semantic integrity constraint. This has, I believe, implications for the design of object-oriented CASE tools as well as for database design. Because of this argument it can be seen that to maintain the principle of encapsulation, objects *must* have rulesets; they are not an optional extra. I prove that the absence of bi-directional associations *requires* the presence of encapsulated rulesets in order to represent the integrity of relationships. The material is a little technical compared to the remainder of the text and the reader may skip to Section 6.3.5 at a first reading. However, I think the results are of great importance and lie at the roots of object modelling theory.

Most of the popular first-generation methods for object-oriented analysis (e.g. Coad and Yourdon, 1991; Rumbaugh *et al.,* 1991; Shlaer and Mellor, 1988) and several of the less widely used ones offered a construct that placed a link between object types depicting static connexions other than generalization and composition. This construct is generally called an association. Some authors use the term 'relationship' as its synonym; whilst yet others use 'relationship' as a higher level abstraction which groups together association, usage, aggregation, collection, various flavours of inheritance, etc. Such associations describe one aspect of the connectivity between object types. This approach is familiar to most developers who have used entity-relationship techniques and is semantically identical since these associations refer only to the data structures of the objects and not to their behaviour (except in those rare instances where associations are used to denote messaging; e.g. object-oriented SSADM (Robinson and Berrisford, 1994)).

A study of the literature of semantic data modelling reveals that there are two fundamental ways to connect data structures or entity types: constructors and pointers. Delobel *et al.* (1995) explain that in the first approach, emphasis is placed on building structures using constructors such as the tuple or the set. In the second, the stress is on linking types using attributes. In the 1980s the former approach was dominant, largely because of the popularity and widespread use of relational databases. In entity-relationship models there are two logical types: entity-relationships and relationship-relationships. Both are represented by sets of tuples and no links between them are stored; the run-time system of the DBMS must search for the linkages. Attempts to enrich the relational model led quickly to systems with more than two relationship types. This unsatisfactory situation soon led to suggestions to replace these arbitrary type systems with a single notion of classes reminiscent of object-oriented programming. (See Chapter 5 for a brief history of these developments.) The pointer-based approach is far more natural to an OO thinker but one suspects that the popularity of methods such as OMT was due largely to the fact that developers with a relational background found its approach familiar and anodyne. The danger here is that object-oriented principles will be ignored and highly relational models produced instead of truly object-oriented ones.

ASSOCIATIONS AS TYPES I think that associations should point in one direction only because to do otherwise would violate the principle of encapsulation. Several object-oriented methodologists have argued against my position, saying that you can always add link attributes to an association and create from it an association object type. However, this new object type must retain links to its progenitors. Therefore, if we accept this as a solution, these new relationships must in turn give rise to new association object types. At some point we must stop this process and will still have to represent the residual associations connecting our, now more numerous, set of classes. This is not to deny the utility of association object types. Some associations are so important that they are themselves concepts; i.e. object types. An often quoted example is the marriage relationship between people, discussed below.

Of course, in any particular case, one can find a natural place to stop this process. It is usual to create types out of associations only when the association has interesting properties in its own right. This still leaves us with associations between the newly constructed types and the types that were previously linked by the original associations. Thus, in *all* practical cases, we will have failed to convert *all* associations to types although we will typically have removed all the many-to-many associations through this process. It is worth noting that while relational databases forbid the use of many-to-many relationships, they are not precluded by modern object-oriented databases. Thus the habit of always removing them, common among traditionally educated database designers, is no longer necessarily a good one.

I will now begin to show how the problems alluded to above are overcome by abolishing bi-directional associations in favour of uni-directional associations or **mappings**, which can be thought of as pointers embedded in object types, coupled with rulesets to preserve referential and semantic integrity. This last point is crucial. Without encapsulating class invariants in objects there can be no way of storing referential integrity rules apart from as a part of some external and generally bi-directional association, and thus violating encapsulation.

A class may encapsulate public rulesets that concern the other public features of the class. They provide second order information about the class. For example, a single rule within a ruleset could represent a database trigger that causes a method to execute when an attribute changes value or it could represent necessary sequencing among methods. More unusually rules can represent the control régimes under which the class operates. For example, the rules could state whether default values should take precedence over multiple inheritance conflict resolution or vice versa. Rulesets for resolving multiple inheritance conflicts on numerical attributes can include mathematical formulae. For example, we could use such a formula to average the values of two conflicting, inherited attributes. Rulesets are unordered sets of production rules and are always subject to a defined inference régime. This means that classes can infer facts that are not stated explicitly.

Some existing object-oriented methods already regard associations as mappings. MOSES (Henderson-Sellers and Edwards, 1994) advocates uni-directional associations or mappings as does SOMA where they are simply called 'associations' or 'association attributes'. In the latter method, certain associations are designated 'pure attributes' when they point at primitive types. This is what permits some tools to generate uncluttered association diagrams automatically. In fact, undirected connexions ('associations') are often all that need to be presented on such diagrams but the underlying model, which describes completely what is likely to be implemented, must contain the richer uni-directional 'pointers'. Several other methodologists have noted that associations can be represented as mappings though they still work with associations directly and fail to explain how integrity is to be represented when mappings are used.

With uni-directional associations (mappings) we can still construct object types from them if needed. If aMan is married to aWoman, then both aMan and aWoman should know this. From the point of view of these two individuals this is often sufficient. However, to a registrar of births, deaths and marriages, the **Marriage** object type itself is important and has attributes like date, time, and place and may even exhibit behaviour, such as computing the correct substance to give as an anniversary gift. In which case it is indeed an object type. But it is NOT synonymous with the mapping of aMan to aWoman. Its nature is more substantive. Now the marriage object type must be responsible for knowing the identities of the partners involved and the partners must store uni-directional associations (mappings) to the marriage instance. This does not break encapsulation since Man then maps to Marriage and Woman maps to Marriage. It is not a (second class or even first class) *relationship type* but a true *object type*.

Odell (Martin and Odell, 1995) suggests that associations are really pairs of 'mappings' corresponding to the *rôles* of an association (Bachman, 1977). A mapping is a one-way connexion. It is part of the object (the client object) and therefore does not break encapsulation. An association *à la* UML, Coad, Rumbaugh or Shlaer/Mellor is external and does break encapsulation. We will examine Odell's argument and present a slightly firmer foundation in much the same spirit.

INTEGRITY CONSTRAINTS
The obvious problem with replacing bi-directional associations with mappings is that there is now no obvious container in which to store referential integrity constraints. I must therefore now show how this is accomplished using mappings. Fortunately, rulesets provide a neat solution.

In order to regard 'associations' as pairs of rôles or mappings we must be prepared to store the relationships, if there are any, between these pairs of mappings. An example where this is important arises when there are integrity rules. Take marriage again but forget the registration object. aMan is married to aWoman and aWoman is married to aMan. If aMan unmarries (divorces) aWoman it is necessary (in most countries at any rate) that aWoman unmarries aMan too. But aMan has no knowledge of what aWoman knows. Therefore aMan and aWoman must store rulesets that encapsulate this 'business rule' or at least trigger a call to some external rule base. The absence of rulesets in methods such as UML prevents them from this expedient — though they could hard code some methods to the same effect. Of course, such rulesets are not always necessary. For example, aMan and aWoman could remember each other's telephone number and aWoman could forget aMan's number with no effect on the adjoint relationship.

'INVERSES'
Basing himself on the terminology prevalent in work on databases and, especially, functional databases (Gray, 1984), Odell suggests that pairs of related mappings pointing in opposite directions are inverses (in the sense of set theory). This is actually incorrect but close enough to the truth to make it worthwhile reiterating his set-theoretic foundations more rigorously. I suspect that related pairs of uni-directional associations (or, more accurately, mappings as we will call them from now on) are adjoint functors in the sense of category theory, which means that they give rise to inverses in a comma category (McLarty, 1992). This idea will not be explored further herein as the assertion about adjoints does not affect my arguments, although I have assumed it to be true by using the term *adjoint* rather than *inverse* above.

In mathematics, a relation is a set of ordered n-tuples and a mapping is a single-valued relation. Consider two object types A and B. Forget that they are types and regard them simply as sets. Strictly speaking, a mapping takes elements of A to elements of B. However, such an interpretation does not capture the notion of association that we require, because it cannot represent one-to-many relationships such as the 'has children' association where A and B are both the set of all people. Odell, following a suggestion of Abrial and in conformity with the literature of functional data models, asserts that mappings are from the set to the power set and that an association consists of two 'inverse' mappings (Martin and Odell, 1995). This definition does not stand up to close scrutiny. To see this, consider the bi-directional publications association of Figure 6.27.

Figure 6.27 A bi-directional association.

This can be broken into two mappings:

$$f': \text{Papers} \longrightarrow \mathcal{P}(\text{People}) \qquad (f' = \text{writtenBy});$$

$$g': \text{People} \longrightarrow \mathcal{P}(\text{Papers}) \qquad (g' = \text{wrote}).$$

where $\mathcal{P}(A)$ represents the power set of A: the set of all subsets of A. Actually, we could work with power types but only the set theory is relevant to the present argument. These functions cannot even be composed, much less satisfy the definition of being inverse to each other:

$$f'.g'=1 \qquad (g' \text{ is a right inverse of } f')$$

$$g'.f'=1 \qquad (g' \text{ is a left inverse of } f')$$

The correct formulation is to say that the mappings should go between the power sets, so that:

$$f: \mathcal{P}(\text{Papers}) \longrightarrow \mathcal{P}(\text{People})$$

$$g: \mathcal{P}(\text{People}) \longrightarrow \mathcal{P}(\text{Papers})$$

These mappings are completely determined by their values at singleton subsets since, for all subset S and T, $f(S \cup T)=f(S) \cup f(T)$. In this sense, these mappings may always be reconstructed from mappings whose domain is the set rather than the power set by setting, for example, $f(\{p\}) = f'(p) \ \forall \ p$.

Observe that, for any A, $\mathcal{P}(A)$ is a complete lattice with the preorder relation defined by set inclusion: $\supseteq$ (read 'contains'). In fact, the power lattice is a category with these inclusions as arrows. This is the basis of my claim that the two mappings are adjoints rather than inverses.

Taking any two arbitrary mappings in opposite senses between a pair of power types is not sufficient for a true association. Intuitively there must be some relationship between the pair. This definition enables one to represent many-to-many relationships properly and to compose the two mappings as originally claimed. However, in general, we still do not have to have an inverse pair as claimed by Odell. What we must at least have, is that these mappings should be left and right **semi-inverses** (where the $=$ in the definition of inverse is replaced by $\supseteq$):

$$\text{Rule 1: } f.g(\{p\}) \supseteq \{p\}$$

($f.g(\{p\})$ is the set of all the people that wrote (or co-wrote) papers written by p; this contains $\{p\}$.)

$$\text{Rule 2: } g.f(\{q\}) \supseteq \{q\}$$

($g.f(\{q\})$ is the set of all papers written by people who wrote q; this contains $\{q\}$.)

Intuitively, these two rules represent the minimal referential integrity constraint on a pair of mappings for them to constitute an association. In fact, we *define* an **association** as a pair of opposed mappings on the power types such that rules 1 and 2 above are satisfied. An association need not be strong enough to enforce referential integrity and I will show in Section A.2.3 how these conditions must be strengthened to achieve this.

INTEGRITY RULES AND ENCAPSULATION

The above two conditions can be expressed by rulesets (or, more specifically, class invariants) encapsulated in the classes as follows.

Each object type corresponds to a set of classes that implement it. We choose one class as a representative. The mapping f is an instance attribute of the class **Papers** which can be written as writtenBy(People,1,n). This pointer to the **People** class indicates that a paper may be written by one to many people (authors). Then, in this example, g is an instance attribute of **People** which would normally be written as wrote(Papers,0,n).

Since the associations are attributes that form part of the interface, an instance q of the class **Papers** can determine the set of instances of **People** that wrote the paper. Call that set of identifiers AuthorsOf(q). For each member of AuthorsOf(q), **People** can check its **Wrote** attribute and return the set of papers written by this author. Call this set WrittenBy(AuthorsOf(q)). Rule 2, above, just states that q is a member of this set, for all q in **Papers**. The rule is encapsulated by **Papers**. Dually, Rule 1 is encapsulated by **People**. The reader should work through the dual processing steps.

Inserting the obvious cardinalities we could write the attributes and Rule 2 in a more familiar style:

- For all papers there must be someone, possibly many people, who wrote the paper.
- For all papers q, q is a member of the set of papers written by people who wrote q.

For those readers more familiar with Smalltalk-like programming languages than with databases, the above can be thought of as being implemented by message sends rather than mappings.

It should also be noted that, since *f* and *g* are in the public interfaces of their respective classes, there is no violation of encapsulation when the rules are encapsulated. The existence of a mapping implies that the class stores the identity of the associated class and this, of course, gives access to its interface. Encapsulation would be violated if a class referred to an instance of another class, because this would be an assumption about the instantiation of the other class. Therefore, it is assumed that reference to instances happens via the class extension (which is part of the public interface of the class).

Using this approach, no integrity information is lost and encapsulation is totally maintained. The approach to rules taken in other methods such as OMT (Blaha and Premerlani, 1998; Rumbaugh *et al.*, 1991), or Martin and Odell (1995) wherein rules are extraneous to objects does not have this advantage. Encapsulating rulesets not only makes classes more reusable but increases the effectiveness of rules since they are propagated readily via the classification structure (by inheritance). Rulesets have an inferencing capability that makes them more general and powerful than class invariants. However, in the example given, exactly the same effect could be achieved with class invariants as in the MOSES (Henderson-Sellers and Edwards, 1994) or BON (Waldén and Nerson, 1995) methods.

The suggestion above does not allow us to search for the association member that caused the integrity violation (as the rule is applied *a postiori*), although this is a necessity for any DBMS. To be able to provide a solution for this, the assumption that the other class can process its *g* function in the reverse direction (starting from the result) is not a violation of encapsulation. Starting from this, the first step would be to retrieve the set of authors of aPaper, wrote(aPaper), by sending a message to the People class. To ensure integrity it is then sufficient to compare the image of the returned set wrote(aPaper) under writtenBy with the Papers class's instance aPaper. This argument is made clearer in the next section.

RULES FOR REFERENTIAL INTEGRITY

Another way of looking at Rule 1 is to say that *q* is contained in the *union* of the individual sets of papers written by each author who wrote *q* (who are represented in the writtenBy association of the Papers class). These sets are found in the People class by checking the wrote association for each author who wrote paper *q*. This, in itself, is insufficient to ensure referential integrity.

For example, imagine the case when a paper *q* establishes that it is in writtenBy({Hugh}). Author Hugh would then have to establish that paper *q* is in the image of its wrote association. In case author Hugh could not establish this association for any reason, Rule 1 in the Papers class would compare the union of the sets of papers written by the Authors who wrote *q* as provided by the People class. If paper *q* had also been co-written by other authors, the resulting set would contain *q*, even though author Hugh's wrote association does not contain paper *q* and integrity would be violated. Thus, the rule given does not allow us to search for the association member that caused the integrity violation, although this is a necessity for any DBMS.

SEMANT INTEGRIT

6.3.5 State models

For objects with significant complex state it is useful to use UML state charts or state transition diagrams (STDs). These diagrams are used to capture the dynamics of individual objects and are related to the object model as effective specification of operations and their assertions. Statecharts represent possible sequences of state change from a particular point of view. Each transition is a realization of an action or use case. Depending on the domain. it is recommended that the technique is used sparingly during specification as I believe it will not always be of use for many objects that occur in MIS systems and that its prime benefits arise during physical design. On the other hand, the technique is a familiar, useful and possibly anodyne one for many workers in Telecommunications.

Another problem with over-zealous use of STDs is that they can be very complex very quickly. However, for some objects with complex life histories the technique is invaluable for capturing information about both the business and the system. A good example of an object where the technique is suitable is a loan application. However, the very act of representing this business process as a class is highly questionable in itself. It is often better to capture this kind of information in a use case model which then refers to classes such as loans. The individual circumstances will dictate the best approach. We will discuss the representation of business processes in Chapter 7.

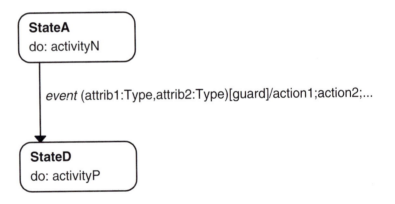

Figure 6.29 States and transitions.

An object's significant states are determined by key arrangements of its attribute values. These and the valid transitions between them are captured by a state transition diagram. Figure 6.29 illustrates the basic notation. States, which can be regarded as Boolean attributes of the type or values of a particular 'state attribute', are represented by rounded rectangles labelled with their names. Transitions are labelled arrows connecting states.

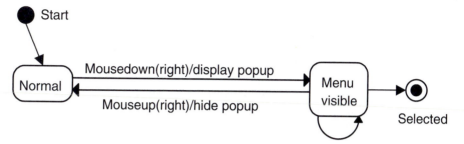

Figure 6.30 An example.

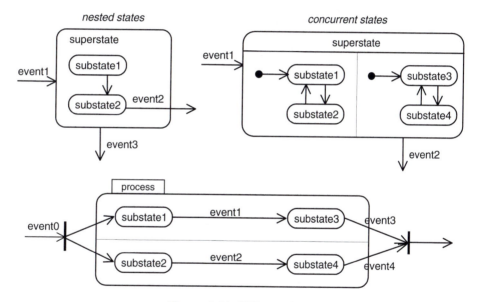

Figure 6.31 STD notation.

Events that cause transitions to occur are written next to the arrows. Events may have attributes. For example, thinking of a calculator object, the event of pressing a key may have the attribute key_number. This avoids the need to have a separate event for each key. Events may have guards or pre-conditions. A guard determines a logical condition that must be true before the transition can take place. An action is a function that is executed – effectively instantaneously – after the transition occurs. States may have activities. These are functions that begin execution as soon as the state is entered and continue executing until completion or until the state is left, whichever is the earlier. A guard may mandate that the state may not be left until an activity is completed.

Henderson-Sellers (private communication) points out that novices often misuse and overuse activities. They effectively use their STDs as DFDs in this way. The use of activities is therefore not encouraged.

Figure 6.30 gives a simple example showing part of the life history of a pop-up menu. Initial and final states are shown as filled circles and ringed filled circles respectively as shown in this example. Start and End (Selected here) are not states but represent the creation and destruction of instances, so that the attributes become undefined.

States may be nested and partitioned into concurrent states to make the structure neater. Figure 6.31 summarizes most of the rest of the notation. We have omitted some details such as start and end states to avoid clutter that would add little in the way of understanding the basic ideas.

Subtypes inherit the state models of their supertypes as illustrated in Figure 6.32, where the context is a simple graphical editor.

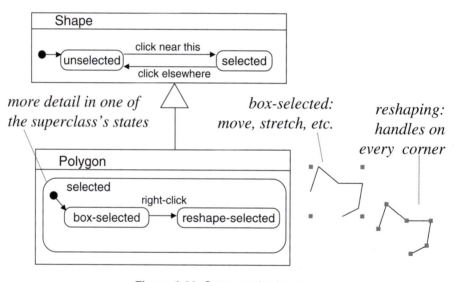

Figure 6.32 States and subtypes.

Sometimes it is useful to represent the states of a type as *bona fide* types; so that rather than considering people as employed or unemployed we could create types for employees and so on. These can be considered as rôles, as discussed earlier, or as **stative types**. The latter view is useful when the attributes and behaviour are very different.

State charts, along with sequence diagrams, are useful for exploring and documenting use case refinements and making explicit the way a particular business process is implemented.

STDs describe the local dynamics of each object in the system. We still need some techniques to describe global behaviour. However, the use of rulesets helps to encapsulate locally some aspects of global behaviour, as we have seen. Statecharts provide an additional way to visualize the problem and usually expose use cases that one has missed on the first pass. It is therefore important to cross-reference them against use cases. They make clear which action sequences are permissible.

6.3.6 Moving to component design

As we refine our specification into the design of a system and the set of components that constitute that system, we need to add more detail to any state, sequence and collaboration diagrams we have produced – focusing on the use cases at the system boundary. Typically, we will add timing constraints, guards, inter-object dependencies (such as «uses») and specify whether messages are sequential or asynchronous, and if the former, balking or subject to timeout.

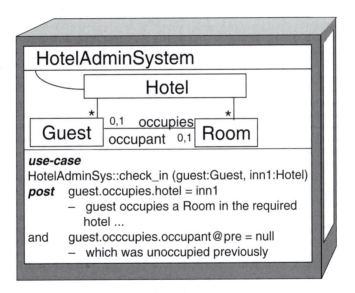

Figure 6.33 A Catalysis specification = type model + effects of use cases.

The types contained in the specification of Figure 6.33 represent a model rather than a mandate for the implementer. Any design is acceptable if it produces the behaviour implied by the use case specifications; the model supplies the vocabulary for expressing them. Only the use cases in the bottom section are required. Operations can be assigned to contained types but they are interpreted as 'factored' specifications. If we assign the operation reallocateRoom to Guest, this means that the system provides a facility with that name, one of whose parameters is Guest. It says nothing about how that facility is implemented.

RETRIEVALS The specification is like the label on the box the system comes in. It says how the system will behave: the responsibilities specified by the uses cases and their goals. It also declares the vocabulary that can be used to describe these responsibilities: the type model. However, it is not making any statements about the responsibilities of the individual types within the model other than their associations. Catalysis illustrates such specifications in the manner shown in Figure 6.33. A component module may have several such interfaces corresponding to different sets of use cases and actors. In the figure, the front label shows part of the interface concerned with a guest checking in. There may be other labels concerning, say, room service, room allocation or staff payment.

The specification doesn't really say what is inside the box. The objects on the label could be a mere illusion created by some façade. However, to describe the interface at all we usually need a conceptual model of the internal state, which makes it permissible to draw state and sequence diagrams.

Catalysis introduced the important idea, borrowed from formal specification languages, of **retrievals**. A retrieval is a function that determines the value of an abstract attribute from the actual implementation. It shows how the attributes map to the abstraction, providing that the two models are in conformance with each other; i.e. there is a mapping from the specification to the design with a justification for the design decisions taken. Thus, while models need not be real they must be retrievable. For an example, suppose that we have a specification of a queue that reads:

Queue
length: Integer
...
put (*post:* length = length@pre + 1 and ...) get (*post:* length = length@pre − 1 and ...)

Now suppose that we also have two array-based implementations. In one a variable len maintains the length and is incremented and decremented each time an element joins and leaves the queue as part of the put and get methods. The retrieval function is then (trivially): length = len. In the second implementation two pointers in and out are maintained which point at the elements of the array where a new element may be added and removed respectively. Now the retrieval function is: length = (out − in) mod n, where n is the rank of the array.

Writing retrievals in this way enables us to check post-conditions at run time in debug mode.

Mathematicians may be interested to know that, as functors, retrieval is adjoint to refinement. Refinement is a representation functor from the specification to its implementation while retrieval is 'forgetful'. This is interesting because it leads us to suspect that no method can be considered complete without *both* concepts; the reason being that adjointness theorems (often representation theorems) are central to every mathematical theory.

PACKAGES, MODULES AND WRAPPERS
We will also usually organize our classes into discrete packages. Any modelling language with ambitions to describe non-trivial systems or systems of great magnitude must adopt some sort of packaging strategy to reduce the complexity of its models. Many other methods have a fairly informal approach, so that the unit of packaging is only loosely defined by some heuristic such as: keep closely related classes in the same package.

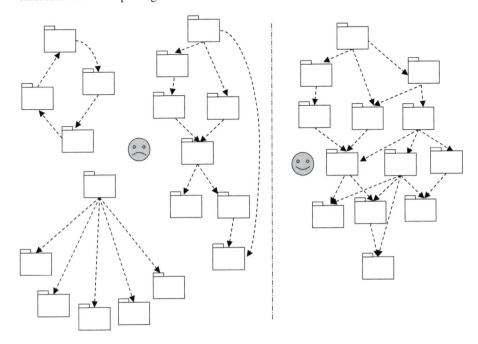

Figure 6.34 Dependency between packages.

Packages are groups of related classes, associations and use cases. This kind of packaging gives a way to organize large models, separate domains and enforce a cleaner architecture. A package can make use of items defined in other packages in which case there is a dependency; the package will not work on its own. Such usage dependencies between packages should preferably be non-circular to ensure that the model has a clear meaning and to allow anyone who imports one package not to have to import all the others. Figure 6.34 shows the UML notation for packages and indicates the goodness or badness of different architectures using it. Dependency relationships between packages can be drawn automatically by most tools and packages can usually be exported and imported between models. The most obvious correspondence between the UML package notation and the features of a language is the notion of a package in Java. Catalysis **model templates** are parametrized packages.

UML module or component diagrams use the 'Gradygrams' that we met in Chapter 1. Components can be assigned to 'nodes': physical computers. Nodes are displayed as cuboids like the one in Figure 6.33. Components with several interfaces show each one as a 'lollipop', but we will return to this when we discuss component-based development as an application of object-oriented design in Chapter 9. The one remaining UML notation, that for activity diagrams, will be dealt with in Chapter 7.

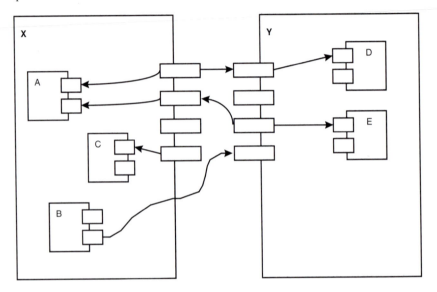

Figure 6.35 Wrappers and delegation.

It is sometimes useful to have a stronger notion of what constitutes a package. I feel the need for a more rigorously defined notion based on the idea that the packages encapsulate (i.e. hide) their contents. Originally this concept was called a layer in SOMA, but it is now clear that this word should be reserved for the idea of client-server or architectural layers connected via API ports, as found in the OSI seven-layer model or the layers of the ROOM method (Selic *et al.,* 1994). Therefore, we now call these encapsulating packaging units **wrappers**. Wrappers encapsulate their components. No new notation is needed for wrappers because a wrapper is merely a composite object and we can fall back on the standard UML composition notation. Since wrappers are components and component specifications are types we can use the UML type or component symbols for them. We may also, as we saw in the last chapter, overload the term wrapper to mean also an object encapsulating a conventional legacy system. This does no violence to our language because, after all, a plain vanilla object is nothing other than a simple conventional system consisting of functions and data.

Wrappers delegate some or all of the responsibilities in their interfaces to the operations of their components. These delegations are referred to as implemented-by links. They are as yet unsupported directly in UML but, pending this, one may readily annotate an operation with the syntax:

```
/* Implemented-by    Classname.operation_name */
```

This notion corresponds to the idea that wrapper operations delegate some or all of their responsibilities to the operations of their components. Notationally, layers might also be shown using a Gradygram notation as in Figure 6.35, which is sometimes preferable since it is easier to show implemented-by links in this way. Note that inbound messages cannot penetrate a wrapper but outbound ones can.

Wrappers encapsulate business functions and facilitate the use of existing components that are not necessarily object-oriented. A typical application is the application layer of a normal three-tier architecture.

A viable alternative to the informal notation we have used here is OML's **cluster** notation (Firesmith *et al.,* 1997), which we do not present here because it would take us too far from our main theme. One can also use UML's **package** notation. For an interesting comparison of the two notations in the context of wrappers see O'Callaghan (1997a).

TEMPLATES OR MODEL FRAMEWORKS Objects interact through contracts with other objects and these interactions define rôles for the objects. When an object plays several rôles its state is affected by all of them. For example, if someone is an employee and a parent then one rôle replenishes the bank account drained by the other. From this point of view the collaborations are just as much reusable chunks as are the objects themselves.

Collaborations have always been a key focus in object-oriented design. Distributing the responsibilities among objects is the key to successful decoupling. In fact most design patterns describe the relationships among a set of several objects, focusing on particular rôles; e.g. SUBJECT-OBSERVER (Gamma *et al.,* 1995). Catalysis introduced a way of modelling such patterns of collaboration with the idea of a model framework or template (Wills, 1996). 'Model framework' and 'model template' are synonyms and correspond to the UML 1.3 idea of a 'Collaboration' – not to be confused with the UML 'collaboration' (*cf.* Fowler, 1997, p.116).

A **model framework** is a related group of packages for the developer to build upon. It only makes sense when you can substitute fairly concrete things for its abstract concepts. Catalysis shows how to do this with the notion of substitutable placeholders. Typically, a framework represents a reusable pattern.

In Figure 6.36, we assume that we have completed first a model of the plumbing domain and later realized that we can abstract away from the detail of plumbing and consider the more general problem of resource allocation to conform to the same pattern. We therefore create a 'macro' version of the model. The terms that will vary from domain to domain are replaced with abstract placeholders. When the template is realized the placeholders are replaced by 'real' types according to the renaming rules written in the shaded box.

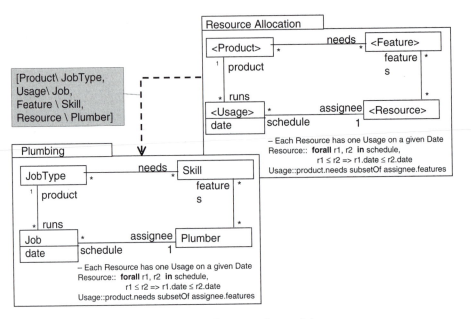

Figure 6.36 Framework templates.

A framework template, or template for short, is thus a package with placeholders written: <placeholderName>. This is not the same as inheritance, because the placeholders contain nothing that may be 'inherited' in the strict sense. However, anything that replaces them 'inherits' all the associations and their cardinalities – so that, in a way, this is a slightly stronger notion than inheritance. All types, associations and constraints are generated from the macro's instantiation.

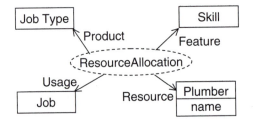

Figure 6.37 Framework pattern application.

We can use the UML collaboration symbol to iconize the concept. In Figure 6.37 the links to the types indicate the application of a template called ResourceAllocation. The attributes in the template are added to these types. The ellipse is not a use case but a UML collaboration **pattern**. Quoting the pattern adds macro-instantiated features to existing types.

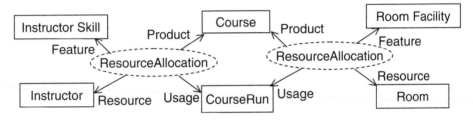

Figure 6.38 Multiple pattern application.

We can apply the pattern more than once in the same application. Figure 6.38 shows how it might be applied twice in the context of teaching administration. The resource placeholder maps to Instructor in one case and to Room in the other. In this example we need to amend the type model, not only by making explicit type substitutions but by disambiguating associations by renaming them, as shown in Figure 6.39. We also need to specialize any ambiguous invariants. Thus, the invariant displayed in Figure 6.36 becomes:

– Each Instructor has one CourseRun on a given Date
Instructor:: forall r1, r2 in schedule,
        r1 ? r2 => r1.date ? r2.date
CourseRun:: product.needsInstructorSkills
        subsetOf assigneeInstructor.features

for Instructor and has different terms for Room.

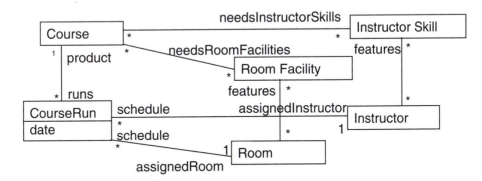

Figure 6.39 Unfolded type model for pattern application.

Frameworks may include use cases and their post-conditions as well as types and associations. These can be shown either graphically (as ellipses) or textually. This helps greatly with component design as we shall explore in Chapter 9. Even the simple Sale use case that we met early in this chapter can be viewed as a template as we can see in Figure 6.40. Figure 6.41 details the unfolding type and use case specification for this composite. Tools that support the framework idea will be able to complete partial models by applying the framework to classes.

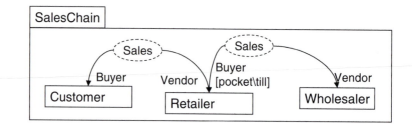

Figure 6.40 Instantiating generic models.

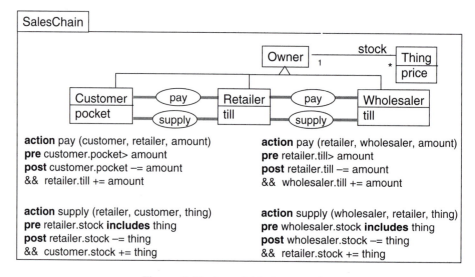

Figure 6.41 An unfolded composite.

6.3.8 The design process

Catalysis recommends the micro-process for system and component specification and design illustrated in Figure 6.42. One may begin either with actions or with objects, or perhaps both. In the former case one elicits the actions that the system partakes in, finding out also who (or what) the actors are. Writing post-conditions on the actions then teases out the vocabulary that the type model must clarify. Now the techniques of snapshot, sequence and state diagrams are used to clarify and refine the model, leading to new and additional actions. And so on round the loop, introducing more detail and eventually moving from a specification to a design and implementation.

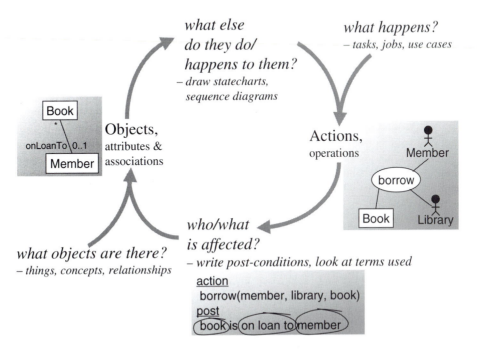

Figure 6.42 The Catalysis specification and design micro-process.

The important design principles that should be applied during the process are as follows.

- Assign responsibilities to objects evenly, trying to get objects of roughly similar size.
- Ensure that all associations are directional.
- Clarify invariants by using snapshots.
- Avoid circularity and high fanouts (as already shown in Figure 6.34).
- Make sure that dependencies are layered.
- Minimize coupling and visibility between objects.
- Apply patterns throughout the design process. (See Chapter 9.)
- Iterate until model is stable or deadline approaches.

6.3.9 Documenting models

One of the great dangers that comes for free when you buy an OO CASE tool is the temptation to produce huge class diagrams documenting every class in a system, along with masses of supplementary pictures. The tools make this easy to do. Such work products will be completely useless a few weeks after they are produced and probably not readable by anyone but the developer who produced them.

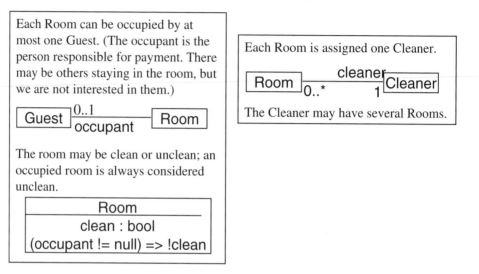

Figure 6.43 Documentation style.

Small diagrams are sometimes useful for illustrating narrative documentation, but remember: only developers speak UML. Don't expect users to be able to interpret them – at least not without help. The text must therefore explicate the information summarized in the diagram. Figure 6.43 illustrates the style of documentation that I favour. There will also be state and sequence diagrams where these illuminate the text.

A project glossary or dictionary is usually an important component of the documentation. It defines the types and all attributes, operations and invariants associated with them. It could also include coverage of business concepts that are relevant to the domain but which do not show up in the type model. Classes should be assigned keywords to help with finding them automatically. A good syntax for this is: topic = Biology; owner = Smith; etc.

Strictly speaking, all the diagrams are redundant because they could all be generated automatically from the type descriptions (Graham, 1998). However, illustration can be helpful to some readers and help with the precision of one's thinking.

6.3.10 Real-time extensions

Applets running in browsers and many real-time applications bring issues of concurrency to the fore. This kind of program can (or can appear to) do several things at once. A thread represents a concurrent sequence of steps and there may be many of these that can start, stop and signal to each other. A simple and familiar example is a GIF image being downloaded to a browser while the user continues to be able to click on hyperlinks. Threads are a key part of the Java object model. Buhr and Casselman (1996) describe Ray Buhr's important and powerful technique of **time threads.** Time threads (re-badged – I think rather opportunistically – in the cited book as 'use case maps') enable designers to visualize the way a system transfers control amongst its components. In this sense a thread is rather like the internalization of a use case. However, these authors routinely confuse use cases with scenarios and most examples that they give deal with using time threads to model scenarios rather than, more generically, use cases. A time thread map shows the components of a system (which could be machines or people) and one or more wiggly lines that pass through the components and which are annotated with (possibly shared) responsibilities. Components can be objects or pure processes. Time threads can branch and join. They can be synchronized according to a number of protocols. In fact, one can make an exhaustive list of the different patterns of inter-process coupling that can occur. Threads can access 'pools' of information and populate object 'slots' dynamically.

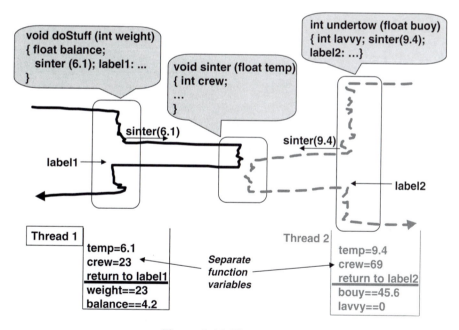

Figure 6.44 Time threads.

A number of commonly recurring design patterns can be presented using time thread diagrams. These vary from abstract and general patterns like PRODUCER/CONSUMER, through those specific to GUI design such as MVC to quite specific real-time ones such as dynamic buffering. The notation is fairly complex and I can't help feeling that I wouldn't use it on a system that didn't involve complex inter-process coupling of some sort. However, were one to take up network design or really low level tool-smithing, then learning the technique would pay dividends. For the run-of-the-mill MIS system though it is just too complex. Figure 6.44 shows how concurrent threads might look on a thread diagram.

The technique is a high level design technique that finds its apotheosis mid-way between use case analysis and object modelling. In fact, the time thread technique could be usefully added to most methods, especially where there is a need to model concurrency or real-time behaviour. Time threads could be usefully added to the task scripting techniques described in Chapter 7. The root task script associated with a message in the business process model gives rise to a time thread map that is less committed than the associated sequence or activity diagrams, because it enables the designer to defer commitment as to which classes own or share the necessary responsibilities.

The ROOM method for real-time object-oriented design (Selic *et al.*, 1994) introduced ports and the idea of representing their protocols as classes. It was the basis for the real-time UML notation. We will have more to say about these issues when we discuss component design in Chapter 7, where we also look at the idea of capsules.

⊟ 6.4 Identifying objects

Now, and only now that we have the intellectual tools necessary to describe and model objects, we can start to think about how to discover and invent them. We have seen that spotting the nouns and verbs in the post-conditions of use cases is a very useful technique for establishing the vocabulary of the domain and thereby the static type model. However, detailed discussion of how to go about identifying objects has been deferred until now, because we could not have described what we would have been looking for had we dealt with this earlier. The second reason for this is that object identification is recognized as a key, possibly the key, bottleneck in applying both object-oriented design and analysis. In this respect the topic deserves the attention of a separate section, in which I will try to show that the object identification bottleneck is as chimerical as the famous Feigenbaum knowledge acquisition bottleneck. Techniques exist to help apprehend objects, mostly those in use already in data modelling and knowledge engineering, and good analysts do not, in practice, stumble badly in this area.

TEXTUAL
ANALYSIS

Booch's original object-oriented design method began with a dataflow analysis which was then used to help identify objects by looking for both concrete and abstract objects in the problem space found from the bubbles and data stores in a data flow diagram (DFD). Next, methods are obtained from the process bubbles of the DFD. An alternative but complementary approach, first suggested by Abbott (1983), is to extract the objects and methods from a textual description of the problem. Objects correspond to nouns and methods to verbs. Verbs and nouns can be further subclassified. For example, there are proper and improper nouns, and verbs to do with doing, being and having. Doing verbs usually give rise to methods, being verbs to classification structures and having verbs to composition structures.[1] Transitive verbs generally correspond to methods, but intransitive ones may refer to exceptions or time-dependent events; in a phrase such as 'the shop closes', for example. This process is a helpful guide but may not be regarded as any sort of formal method. Intuition is still required to get hold of the best design. This technique can be automated as some of the tools developed to support HOOD and Saeki *et al.* (1989) showed.

For example, a SACIS requirements statement transcript might contain the following fragment:

> ... If a **customer** *enters* a **store** with the intention of *buying* a **toy** <u>for</u> a **child**, then **advice** must *be available* within a reasonable <u>time</u> concerning the <u>suitability</u> of the toy <u>for</u> the child. This will depend on the <u>**age range**</u> of the child and the **attributes** of the toy. If the toy is a **dangerous item**, then it is unsuitable. ...

I have emboldened some candidate classes (nouns) and italicized some candidate methods (transitive verbs). Possible attributes or associations are underlined. The process could be continued using the guidelines set out in Table 6.1, but it must be understood that this is **not** a formal technique in any sense of the word. The table is intended merely to provoke thought during analysis.

Most of the methods descended from Booch's work, including those based on UML, use some form of textual analysis of this sort.

HOOD, RDD and some other methods used Abbott textual analysis but otherwise there are no precise, normative techniques. Coad and Yourdon (1991) say that analysts should look for things or events remembered, devices, rôles, sites and organizational units. The Shlaer-Mellor method offers five categories: tangible entities, rôles, incidents, interactions and specifications. This is all very well, but rather fuzzy and certainly not complete. Coad *et al.* (1999) say that there are exactly five kinds of archetypal objects and gives standard features for each one. Each

---

[1] One point of caution here is that verbs include stative verbs (verbs that indicate that a state of affairs holds) which are compound constructions in English; 'to be present' is a stative verb whereas 'to increase' is not. This suggests perhaps that Chinese, where stative verbs are distinguished, is a good intermediate language for object-oriented design; and it's probably easier to learn than Ada.

archetype is associated with a colour – based on the colours of commercially available pads of paper stickers. His archetypes are objects representing:

- descriptions (blue);
- parties (e.g. people, organizations), places or things (green);
- rôles (yellow);
- moments in or intervals of time (pink); and
- interfaces and plug-points (see Chapter 9).

It is difficult to be completely convinced that the world is really so simple, but the idea is a useful one and emphasizes the recurrence of analysis patterns. We shall look at the latter in Chapter 9. This section provides several, quite precise, normative techniques for eliciting objects. They are founded in knowledge engineering, HCI[9] practice and philosophy.

Table 6.1 Guidelines for textual analysis.

Part of speech	Model component	Example from SACIS text
proper noun	instance	J. Smith
improper noun	class/type/rôle	toy
doing verb	operation	buy
being verb	classification	is an
having verb	composition	has an
stative verb	invariance-condition	are owned
modal verb	data semantics, pre-condition, post-condition or invariance-condition	must be
adjective	attribute value or class	unsuitable
adjectival phrase	association operation	the customer with children the customer who bought the kite
transitive verb	operation	enter
intransitive verb	exception or event	depend

6.4.1 Philosophy of knowledge and classification theory

To understand object identification approaches it is useful to pause and consider some of the insights that philosophers have had on the topic. The dominant philosophical view in Western scientific thinking has been, for a very long time, Empiricism. I believe that this clouds our view of what objects are in various subtle ways and must be overcome by the object-oriented analyst. For example, Empiricism holds that objects are merely bundles of properties. As pointed out in Chapter 1, an Empiricist would maintain that objects are out there just waiting to be perceived, and an extreme version holds that this is easy to do. A Phenomenologist

---

[9] Human-Computer Interaction

view, on the contrary, recognizes that perception is an active, iterative, creative process and that objects come both from our intentions and from the objectively existing world in an ever-repeating dialectical process. When we see a tree we bring our ideas about trees to bear before we make the perception. As the leading biologist J.Z. Young (1986) puts it, when we look 'we know already what we are going to see'. An even richer view suggests that real-world abstractions are a reflection of social relations and processes, as well as having an objective basis. We perceive the tree as mediator of our own human processes of production both of wooden artefacts and of ourselves – as when we enjoy the tree for its beauty. Ehn (1988) and Winograd and Flores (1986) explore these issues in relation to computer systems in general. Objects may be apprehended by an analyst familiar with an application in many different ways and choosing the 'best' representation is a fundamental contribution that human intelligence always makes to computer systems. Some objects correspond directly to real-world objects such as people or chairs, but others, such as stacks or quarks, correspond to invented abstractions. Abstractions sum up the relevant divisions of the domain. What is relevant may depend on the application, but this will compromise the reusability of the abstraction and so the designer should try to think of abstractions with as wide an applicability as possible. On the other hand, care should be taken not to compromise efficiency with over-general objects. The more high level our systems become, the more they are to be regarded as tools for enhancing communication between humans. The more the human aspect is emphasized, the more the subjective factor in object identification comes to the fore.

As I have suggested, most object-oriented analysis methods give little help on the process of identifying objects. It is a very reasonable approach to engage in the analysis of nouns, verbs and other parts of speech in an informal written description of the problem or a set of use case post-conditions. Rules of thumb here include: matching proper nouns to instances, and improper nouns to types or attributes; adjectival phrases qualifying nouns such as 'the employee who works in the salaries department' indicate relations or may indicate methods if they contain verbs as in 'the employee who got a rise'.

The Abbott technique is useful, but cannot succeed on its own. This semi-structured approach is only a guide and creative perception must be brought to bear by experienced analysts, as I have already emphasized. Using it involves difficult decisions. Analysts and designers can learn much from two key branches of Philosophy: Epistemology and Ontology. Epistemology is the theory of knowledge; what knowledge is, how it is possible and what can be known. Ontology is the science of Being; what is and how it comes about. These two sciences are intimately related because we are interested in true knowledge: knowledge of what really is. Both disciplines are concerned with the nature of objects, and are therefore directly relevant to the identification of objects in object-oriented analysis and design. This view is taken by Wand (1989), who proposed a formal model of objects based on Bunge's mathematical ontology. Unfortunately, this ontology is atomistic; it conceives things as reducible to irreducible components. Nevertheless, the principle of an ontologically based model, albeit not a formal model, is a sound one.

Fred Brooks (1986) notes the difference between essence and accidents in software engineering. The distinction is, in fact, a very old one going back to Aristotle and the mediaeval Scholastics. The idea of essence was attacked by modern philosophers from Descartes onwards, who saw objects as mere bundles of properties with no essence. This gave rise to severe difficulties because it fails to explain how we can recognize a chair with no properties in common with all the previous chairs we have experienced. A school of thought known as Phenomenology, represented by philosophers such as Hegel, Brentano, Husserl and Heidegger, arose *inter alia* from attempts to solve this kind of problem. Another classical problem, important for object-oriented analysis, is the problem of categories. Aristotle laid down a set of fixed pairs of categories through the application of which thought could proceed. These were concepts such as Universal/Individual, Necessary/Contingent, and so on. Kant gave a revised list but, as Hegel once remarked, didn't put himself to much trouble in the doing. The idealist Hegel showed that the categories were related and grew out of each other in thought. Finally, the materialist Marx showed that the categories of thought arose out of human social and historical practice:

> My dialectic method is not only different from the Hegelian, but is its direct opposite. To Hegel, the life-process of the human brain, i.e. the process of thinking, which, under the name of 'the Idea', he even transforms into an independent subject, is the demiurgos of the real world, and the real world is only the external, phenomenal form of 'the Idea'. With me, on the contrary, the ideal is nothing else than the material world reflected by the human mind, and translated into forms of thought. (Marx, 1961)

So, we inherit categories from our forebears, but also learn new ones from our practice in the world.

All phenomenologists and dialecticians, whether idealist or materialist, acknowledge that the perception or apprehension of objects is an active process. Objects are defined by the purpose of the thinking subject, although for a materialist they correspond to previously existing patterns of energy in the world – including of course patterns in the brain. A chair is a coherent object for the purposes of sitting (or perhaps for bar-room brawling) but not for the purposes of sub-atomic physics. You may be wondering by now what all this has got to do with object-oriented analysis. What does this analysis tell us about the identification of objects? The answer is that it directs attention to the user.

User-centred analysis requires that we ask about purpose when we partition the world into objects. It also tells us that common purpose is required for reusability, because objects designed for one user may not correspond to anything in the world of another. In fact reuse is only possible because society and production determine a common basis for perception. A clear understanding of Ontology helps to avoid the introduction of accidental, as opposed to essential, objects. Thus, Fred Brooks, in my opinion, either learned some Ontology or had it by instinct alone.

Some useful tips for identifying important, rather than arbitrary, objects can be gleaned from a study of philosophy, especially Hegelian philosophy and modern Phenomenology. Stern (1990) analyses Hegel's concept of the object in great detail. The main difference between this notion of objects and other notions is that objects are neither arbitrary 'bundles' of properties (the Empiricist or Kantian view), nor are they based on a mysterious essence, but are conceptual structures representing universal abstractions. The practical import of this view is that it allows us to distinguish between genuine high level abstractions such as Man and completely contingent ones such as Red Objects. Objects may be judged according to various, historically determined, categories. For example 'this rose is red' is a judgment in the category of quality. The important judgments for object-oriented analysis and their relevant uses are those shown in Table 6.2.

Table 6.2 Analysis of judgments.

Judgment	Example	Feature
Quality	this ball is red	attribute
Reflection	this herb is medicinal	relationship
Categorical	Fred is a man	generalization
Value	Fred should be kind	rules

The categorical judgment is the one that reveals genuine high level abstractions. We call such abstractions **essential**. Qualitative judgments only reveal contingent and accidental properties unlikely to be reusable, but nevertheless of semantic importance within the application. Beware, for example, of abstractions such as 'red roses' or 'dangerous toys'; they are qualitative and probably not reusable without internal restructuring. Objects revealed by qualitative judgments are called **accidental**. Accidental objects are mere bundles of arbitrary properties, such as 'expensive, prickly, red roses wrapped in foil'. Essential objects are universal, in the sense that they are (or belong to) classes which correspond to objects that already have been identified by human practice and are stable in time and space. What they are depends on human purposes; prior to trade money was not an object. Reflective judgments are useful for establishing usage relationships and methods; being medicinal connects herbs to the sicknesses that they cure. Value judgments may be outside the scope of a computer system, but can reveal semantic rules. For example, we could have, at a very high business analysis level, 'employees should be rewarded for loyalty' which at a lower level would translate to the rule: 'if five years' service then an extra three days' annual leave'.

Attributes are functions that take objects as values; that is, their ranges are classes. They may be distinguished into attributes whose values are abstract (or essential in the sense alluded to above) objects like employee, and those with printable, i.e. accidental, objects as values like redness. This observation has also been made in the context of semantic data models by Hull and King (1987).

For business and user-centred design, the ontological view dictates that objects should have a purpose. Operations too should have a goal. In several methods this is accomplished by specifying post-conditions. These conditions should be stated for each method (as in Eiffel) and for the object as a whole in the rules compartment of an object.

Lenat and Guha (1990) suggest that instances are things that something definite can be said about, but point out the danger of relying too much on the structure of natural language. They suggest that a concept should be abstracted as a class if:

■ several interesting things can be said about it as a whole;
■ it has properties shared by no other class;
■ there are statements that distinguish this class from some larger class it belongs to;
■ the boundaries of the concept are imprecise;
■ the number of 'siblings' (e.g. complementary classes whose union is the natural generalization of this one) is low.

They also emphasize the point I have made: that purpose is the chief determinant of what is to be a class or type.

A useful rule of thumb for distinguishing essential objects is that one should ask if more can be said about the object than can be obtained by listing its attributes and methods. It is cheating in the use of this rule to merely keep on adding more properties. Examples abound of this type of object. In a payroll system, an employee may have red hair, even though this is not an attribute, or be able to fly a plane, even though this is not a method. Nothing special can be said about the class 'employees who can fly' unless, of course, we are dealing with the payroll for an airline. What is essential is context sensitive.

Very long methods, objects with hundreds of attributes and/or hundreds of methods indicate that you are trying to model something that normal mortals couldn't apprehend in any conceivable perceptive act. This tells me, and I hope your project manager, that you haven't listened to the users.

It is not only the purposes of the immediate users that concern us, but the purposes of the user community at large and, indeed, of software engineers who will reuse your objects. Therefore, analysts should keep reuse in mind throughout the requirements elicitation process. Designing or analysing is not copying user and expert knowledge. As with perception, it is a creative act. A designer, analyst or knowledge engineer takes the purposes and perceptions of users and transforms them. S/he is not a *tabula rasa* – a blank sheet upon which knowledge is writ – as older texts on knowledge elicitation used to recommend, but a creative participant.

Johnson and Foote (1988) make a few suggestions for desiderata concerning when to create a new class rather than add a method to an existing class which seem to conform to the ontological insights of this section.

Epistemology has been studied by knowledge engineers involved in building expert systems. Many of the lessons learnt and the techniques they have discovered can be used in building conventional systems, and this is now routine in my work.

In particular, they can be applied to HCI design (Johnson, 1992) and within object-oriented analysis and design.

6.4.2 Task analysis

Several of the methods which have been developed by knowledge engineers trying to elicit knowledge from human beings with the aim of building expert systems can be used to obtain concepts in any domain. These concepts often map onto objects. This is not the place for an exegesis on methods of knowledge acquisition, but we should mention the usefulness of methods based on Kelly grids (or repertory grids), protocol analysis, task analysis and interviewing theory. The use of the techniques of Kelly grids for object identification is explained later in this section. Protocol analysis (Ericsson and Simon, 1984) is in some ways similar to the procedure outlined earlier of analysing parts of speech, and task analysis can reveal both objects and their methods. Task analysis is often used in UI design (Daniels, 1986; Johnson, 1992). We return to interview theory in Chapter 8.

Broadly, task analysis is a functional approach to knowledge elicitation which involves breaking down a problem into a hierarchy of tasks that must be performed. The objectives of task analysis in general can be outlined as the definition of:

- the objectives of the task;
- the procedures used;
- any actions and objects involved;
- time taken to accomplish the task;
- frequency of operations;
- occurrence of errors;
- involvement of subordinate and superordinate tasks.

The result is a task description which may be formalized in some way, such as by flowcharts, logic trees or even a formal grammar. The process does not, however, describe knowledge directly. That is, it does not attempt to capture the underlying knowledge structure but tries to represent how the task is performed and what is needed to achieve its aim. Any conceptual or procedural knowledge and any objects which are obtained are only elicited incidentally.

In task analysis the objective constraints on problem solving are exploited, usually prior to a later protocol analysis stage. The method consists in arriving at a classification of the factors involved in problem solving and the identification of the atomic 'tasks' involved. The categories that apply to an individual task might include:

- time taken;
- how often performed;
- procedures used;
- actions used;
- objects used;

- error rate;
- position in task hierarchy.

This implies that it is also necessary to identify the actions and types in a taxonomic manner. For example, if we were to embark on a study of poker playing we might start with the following crude structure:

Types: Card, Deck, Hand, Suit, Player, Table, Coin
Actions: Deal, Turn, See, Collect

One form of task analysis assumes that concepts are derivable from pairing actions with types; e.g. 'See player', 'Deal card'. Once the concepts can be identified it is necessary to identify plans or objectives (win game, make money) and strategies (bluff at random) and use this analysis to identify the knowledge required and used by matching object–action pairs to task descriptions occurring in task sequences. As mentioned before, this is important since objects are identified in relation to purposes.

As a means of breaking down the problem area into its constituent sub-problems, task analysis is useful in a similar way to data flow analysis or entity modelling. Although the method does incorporate the analysis of the objects associated with each task, it is lacking in graphical techniques for representation of these objects, and therefore remains mostly useful for functional elicitation.

The approach to cognitive task analysis recommended by Braune and Foshay (1983), based on human information processing theory, is less functional than the basic approach to task analysis as outlined above, concentrating on the analysis of concepts. The second stage of the three-step strategy is to define the relations between concepts by analysing examples, then to build on the resulting schema by analysing larger problem sets. The schema that results from the above analysis is a model of the knowledge structure of an expert, similar to that achieved by the concept sorting methods associated with Kelly grids, describing the 'chunking' of knowledge by the expert. This chunking is controlled by the idea of expectancy according to the theory of human information processing; i.e. the selection of the correct stimuli for solving the problem, and the knowledge of how to deal with these stimuli. As pointed out by Swaffield (1990), this approach is akin to the ideas of object modelling due to the concentration on the analysis of concepts and relations before further analysis of functions/tasks.

A task is a particular instance of a procedure that achieves a goal. There can be many tasks that achieve the same goal. Use cases are examples of tasks; they should always state their goal. We hope to be able to extract eventually a business object model from the tasks we have discovered.

The method of hierarchical task analysis can be better understood through the use of an example. Figure 6.45 is based on a project I once ran, concerned with the selection of input technology for a financial trader. The overall task to be described is that of recording a deal when the trader, in this case an equities trader, agrees to buy from or sell to some counterparty (the person at the other end of the transaction in 'dealerspeak').

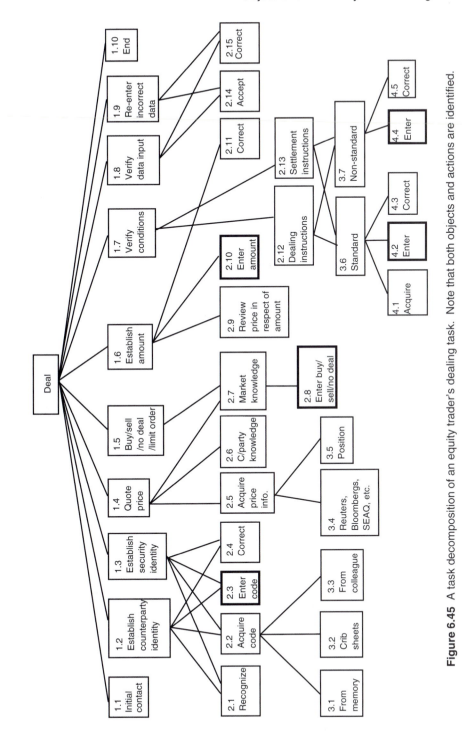

Figure 6.45 A task decomposition of an equity trader's dealing task. Note that both objects and actions are identified.

The diagram in Figure 6.45 is to be interpreted from the top level, which represents the overall task of striking a bargain and recording it, downwards and from the left-hand side. Note that the hierarchy is represented as a network at some points. This is only to avoid repetition of common subordinate operations and recursion.

We decompose the top level task into ten steps starting with the initial contact. This task is complex but does not impinge on the deal capture process and so is not expanded further. This, of course, refers to the receipt or initiation (usually by telephone) of a communication in which a dealing situation is identified. Once this complex activity is initiated the next step (possibly carried out in parallel) is to establish to whom the dealer is talking, and it is here that computer systems have a rôle to play. Thus, this task requires further decomposition. For example, 2.1 could refer to recognizing someone's voice or spotting their identity from the lights on a dealer board. Next, the counterparty identity must be validated as an authorized one by finding its code. This can be done either from the dealer's memory, from paper lists kept at hand, from a screen display or by calling out to a colleague who, in turn, may have all these resources available. Thus, there are recursive processes implicit in the diagrams but which have not been expanded. If the code is not obtained either the process can terminate (1.10) or a new code can be created. Having acquired the code it must be entered into the record keeping system, computerized or manual. This is the first point where there is significant interaction with the technology of deal capture, and the heavily drawn box indicates this interface. Further decomposition in terms of *inter alia* finger, arm and eye movements is not shown in the diagram precisely because it will now depend on the selected technology. The code must now be validated and if incorrect we either return to 2.1 or correct the entry (2.4) before re-entering stage 2.3. At this point we can return to level 1 and proceed to a similar process in order to identify the instrument being traded. Notice that this process revisits stages 2.1 through 2.4, which explains the tangle of descent paths in the diagram. The remainder of the diagram may now be interpreted in a similar fashion.

Note incidentally that 2.8 descends from 1.5 directly and that 1.8 refers to the verification of the entire transaction.

It will be seen that most of the tasks involve complex cognitive processes, especially perhaps 1.1, 1.4, and 1.5. However, the benefit of the task analysis is that it enables abstraction of those tasks where there is an interface with the deal capture technology from this background.

This rather detailed example is included here to give a feel for the practical problems in applying task decomposition. It should be clear, in particular, that there is value in using task analysis for designing systems and user interfaces, but we assert that other applications where it is necessary to conceptualize procedural knowledge can benefit from the approach. The example also shows the way in which task analysis can reveal the presence of objects, such as price information and settlement instructions, quite incidentally to its analysis of tasks. Thus in applications where the functions are more immediately apparent to consciousness than the objects and concepts, task analysis is a useful way of bootstrapping an object-oriented analysis. This is often true in tasks where there is a great deal of unarticulated, latent or compiled knowledge. Task scripts can be deepened into task analysis tree structures where this is helpful.

Task analysis will not help with the incorporation of the many psychological factors which are always present in deal capture or similar processes, and which are often quite immeasurable. Other incommensurables might include the effects of such environmental factors as ambient noise and heat, and the general level of distracting stimuli.

Readers familiar with Jackson System Development may notice a similarity between the task decomposition of Figure 6.45 and a JSD entity structure diagram. It could have been obtained from considering the time-ordered actions of the life history of a 'deal'. Any common sub-tree can be 'dismembered' (to use the JSD term) and regarded as either a separate group of actions or as a new object in its own right. It can then become the result of a JSD 'operation' or, in other words, a method. I am grateful to David Lee of GEC for pointing out this similarity to me. One striking thing about this observation is how it shows that different disciplines within IT keep reinventing the same wheel under different names.

In some ways it could be held that the use of a formal technique such as task analysis in the above example can add nothing that common sense could not have derived. However, its use in structuring the information derived from interviews is invaluable for the following reasons. Firstly, the decomposition of complex tasks into more primitive or unitary actions enables one to arrive at a better understanding of the interface between the tasks and the available implementation technology, as will be seen in the above analysis. This leads to a far better understanding of the possibilities for empirical measurement of the quality of the interface. The second factor is that the very process of constructing and critiquing the task hierarchy diagrams helps to uncover gaps in the analysis, and thus remove any contradictions.

Task analysis is primarily useful in method identification rather than for finding objects, although objects are elicited incidentally. We now turn to methods borrowed from knowledge engineering which address the object identification problem more directly.

Basden (1990 and 1990a) suggests, again in the context of knowledge acquisition for expert systems, a method which may be of considerable use in identifying objects and their attributes and methods. He offers the example of a knowledge engineer seeking for high level rules of thumb based on experience (heuristics). Suppose, in the domain of Gardening, that we have discovered that regular mowing produces good lawns. The knowledge engineer should not be satisfied with this because it does not show the boundaries of the intended system's competence – we do not want a system that gives confident advice in areas where it is incompetent. We need to go deeper into the understanding. Thus, the next question asked of the expert might be of the form: 'why?'. The answer might be: 'Because regular mowing reduces coarse grasses and encourages springy turf'.

What we have obtained here are two attributes of the object 'good turf' – whose parent in a hierarchy is 'turf', of course. Why does regular mowing lead to springy turf? Well, it helps to promote leaf branching. Now we are beginning to elicit methods as we approach causal knowledge. To help define the boundaries, Basden suggests asking 'what else' and 'what about ...' questions. In the example we have given the knowledge engineer should ask: 'what about drought conditions?' or 'what else gives good lawns?'. These questioning techniques are immensely useful for analysts using an object-oriented approach.

6.4.3 Kelly grids

One of the most useful knowledge engineering techniques for eliciting objects and their structure is that of Kelly, or repertory (repertoire), grids. These grids were introduced originally in the context of clinical psychiatry (Kelly, 1955). They are devices for helping analysts elicit 'personal constructs'; concepts which people use in dealing with and constructing their world. Constructs are pairs of opposites, such as slow/fast, and usually correspond to either classes or attribute values in object-oriented analysis. The second dimension of a grid is its 'elements' which correspond to objects. Elements are rated on a scale from 1 to 5, say, according to which pole of the construct they correspond to most closely. These values can then be used to 'focus' the grid; a mathematical procedure which clarifies relationships among elements and constructs. In particular, focusing ranks the elements in order of the clarity with which they are perceived, and the constructs in order of their importance as classifiers of elements. The details can be found in any decent book on knowledge acquisition; e.g. (Hart, 1989; Graham and Jones, 1988).

To illustrate the usefulness of Kelly grids, suppose we need to interview a user. The technique involves first identifying some 'elements' in the application. These might be real things or concepts, but should be organized into coherent sets. For example, the set {Porsche, Jaguar, Rolls Royce, Mini, Driver} has an obvious odd man out: Driver.

The use of the Kelly grid technique in its full form is not recommended. However, questioning techniques based on Kelly grids are immensely powerful in eliciting new classes and attributes and extending and refining classification structures. There are three principal techniques:

- asking for the opposites of all elements and concepts;
- laddering to extract generalizations;
- elicitation by triads to extract specializations.

Considering Figure 6.46, we might have discovered that SportyCars was a key class. Asking for the opposite produced not 'Unsporty' but 'Family' cars; not the logical opposite but a totally new class. Thus, asking for the opposite of a class can reveal new classes.

In laddering, users are asked to give names for higher level concepts: 'Can you think of a word that describes all the concepts {speed, luxury, economy}?' might produce a concept of 'value for money'. This technique is known as laddering, and elicits both composition and classification structures. It generally produces more general concepts. Asking for a term that sums up both Fast and Sporty we might discover the class of 'ego massaging' cars for example.

Elicitation by triads is not a reference to Chinese torture but to a technique whereby, given a coherent set of elements, the user is asked to take any three and specify a concept that applies to two of them but not to the third. For example, with {Porsche, Jaguar, Mini}, top speed might emerge as an important concept. Similarly, the triad {Mini, Jaguar, Trabant} might reveal the attribute CountryOfManufacture: or the classes BritishCar and GermanCar. As a variant of this technique, users may be asked to divide elements into two or more groups and then name the groups. This is known as card sorting.

All these techniques are first-rate ways of getting at the conceptual structure of the problem space, if used with care and sensitivity. Exhaustive listing of all triads, for example, can be extremely tedious and easily alienate users.

	ELEMENTS					
CONCEPT	Rolls Royce	Porsche	Jaguar	Mini	Trabant	OPPOSITE
Economical	5	4	4	2	2	Costly
Comfortable	1	4	2	4	5	Basic
Sporty	5	1	3	5	5	Family
Cheap	5	4	4	2	1	Expensive
Fast	3	1	2	4	5	Slow

Figure 6.46 A Kelly grid. Scores are between 1 and 5. The left-hand pole of the concept corresponds to a low score for the element and the right (its opposite) to a high one. The grid is not focused.

There are several computer systems which automate the construction and focusing of these grids, such as ETS (Boose, 1986) and its commercial descendant AQUINAS (Boose and Bradshaw, 1988). These systems convert the grids into sets of rules. It is curious that these automated tools throw so much of what is captured by the repertory grid analysis away. It is clear that laddering and sorting produce classification structures, for example. These are then disguised as production rules with a consequent loss of information. I predicted in the first edition of this book that tools would evolve which would capture such structural information directly. That this did begin to happen was illustrated by the work of Gaines and Shaw (Gaines and Shaw, 1992; Shaw and Gaines, 1992) but the work is not yet commercialized to the best of my knowledge. In the interim the technique must be used manually, and preferably informally, for object-oriented analysis.

Object templates have been used in knowledge acquisition for expert systems. Filling in the templates is a structured method for gathering semantic information which is of general applicability. The knowledge engineering approach emphasizes that classes should correspond to concepts held by users and experts. High level classes represent abstractions that may be reusable across several similar domains. The abstraction 'object' is universal in all domains, but 'account' is usable across most financial and accounting applications. Mortgage account is more specialized and therefore reusable across a narrow set of applications. The key skill for analysts seeking the benefit of reuse is to pitch the abstractions at the right level. Prototyping and interaction with users and domain experts all help to elicit knowledge about objects.

Thus, ontology and epistemology help us find objects and structures. They should also help us know how to recognize a good object when we meet one, either in a library or as a result of our own efforts. The third requisite tool for this purpose is, of course, common sense. A few common-sense guidelines for object identification are worth including at this point.

- Always remember that a good reusable object represents something universal and real. An object is a social animal; its methods may be used by other classes. If not, ask what its function is or delete it from the model.
- Although an object should not be so complex as to defy comprehension, it should encapsulate some reasonably complex behaviour to justify its existence.
- A method that doesn't make use of its current class's own attributes is probably encapsulated in the wrong object, since it does not need access to the private implementation.

Measuring the quality of an abstraction is very difficult. Guidelines can be taken from an analogy with the design of machinery. As with a machine, there should be a minimum number of interchangeable parts and the parts should be as general as possible. Suggested criteria, with their corresponding metrics, include several that we have already met in the context of object-oriented programming.

- Interfaces should be as small, simple and stable as possible.
- The object should be self-sufficient and complete; the slogan is: 'The object, the whole object and nothing but the object'. As a counter-example to this notion of complete objects, consider a class for objects whose names begin with the letters 'CH'. In other words, avoid accidental objects. Objects must not need to send lots of messages to do simple things: the topology of the usage structure should be simple.

Similar guidelines apply to methods. Methods too should be simple and generative. For example, the method 'add 1' generates a method 'add n' for all n. Look for such commonalities. They should be relevant; that is, methods must be applicable to the concept, neither more specific nor more general. Methods should depend on the encapsulated state of the containing object, as mentioned above. A very important principle of object-orientation is the principle of loose coupling or the

'Law of Demeter'[10] which states that 'the methods of a class should not depend in any way on the structure of any class, except the immediate (top level) structure of their own class. Furthermore, each method should send messages to objects belonging to a very limited set of classes only' (Sakkinen, 1988). This helps classes to be understood in isolation and therefore reused.

Recall that analysts should avoid objects arising solely from normalization or the removal of many-to-many relationships. The rule is: if it's not a real-world entity then it's not an object. For example, the many-to-many relationship between ORDERS and INVOICES may be removed by introducing a new class ORDER-LINE. This is fine, the lines are real things; they get printed on the invoice. On the contrary there seems to be no such natural object that would remove the many-to-many relationship between cars and the colours they may be painted.

The last point I wish to make is that analysts should not be expected to get it right first time. They never do. This is the mistake of the waterfall model, and we know all too well that the costs of maintaining incorrectly specified systems are high. Prototyping and task-centred design, if properly managed, allow the analyst to get it right; but third time round.

⊟ 6.5 CASE tools

There are several commercial CASE tools supporting UML or aspects of UML. Most of them are drawing editors that check the syntax of UML models and often generate code from the latter. Perhaps the best known is *Rose* from Rational Inc. *Rose* starts by default with two packages, one for use case diagrams and the other for class diagrams. But this isn't always the most sensible separation: you can put either kind of diagram into any package, and mix classes, use cases, and actors in a diagram as you judge appropriate. Use cases can be dragged onto class diagrams and *vice versa*. You can mix them in one diagram or not, as you prefer. Keywords, invariants and rulesets are not well supported and so one must use comments on for descriptions, rulesets, invariants and pre- and post-conditions.

In *Rose*, class diagrams and statecharts are always in separate diagrams. Also, *Rose* does not permit more than one statechart per class; if there are more, one must draw them all on one diagram.

One advantage, if such it is, of *Rose* is the fact that it integrates well with other Rational tools for configuration management, testing, requirements documentation and so on. There are also tools from third parties such as *RoseLink*, which enables C++ or Java application skeletons for the Versant OODBMS to be generated, converting associations into C++ or ODMG collections. The temptation with all such tools is to create huge diagrams. As I have argued, this is not a good idea; the ideal is a good narrative punctuated by small diagrams that help disambiguate and

---

[10] The Greek goddess of agriculture and therefore of cyclical rebirth.

illustrate the text. Tools, such as *Soda*, can be used to help embed diagrams in the narrative. It is a good idea to put any use case specifications in the main comment box – where they are more visible – and in attached notes, or both.

A more impressive tool of the same type is *Together*, which comes in C++ and Java variants. *TogetherJ*, for example, supports genuine round-trip engineering: as you draw a diagram the Java code appears in a separate window and, better still, the diagram changes as you edit the Java code. *Rose* does something similar, but not nearly as well.

Computer Associates' *Paradigm Plus* and its COOL suite of products also support UML diagram making. COOL Jex supports some of the Catalysis techniques. The component model underlying the COOL products is discussed by Cheesman and Daniels (2000).

Princeton Softtech's *Select*, Aionix's *Software through Pictures* (StP) and Popkin's *System Architect* are further examples of UML-compliant CASE tools. There are also UML tools that support specific methods such as Shlaer-Mellor rather than just the UML notation.

	Data (What)	Function (How)	Network (Where)	People (Who)	Time (When)	Motivation (Why)
Scope (Planner)	List of things	List of processes	List of locations	List of organizations	List of events	Strategy Goals, etc.
Business model (Owner)	ERD Semantic model	Process flow diagram	Logistics network	Organogram	Business schedule	Business plan
System model (Designer)	Logical data model	DFD Application architecture	Distributed system architecture	HCI architecture	Processing structure	Knowledge architecture
Technology model (Builder)	Data design	System design (Structure chart)	System architecture	HCI design	Control structure	Knowledge design
Detailed representation (Subcontractor)	Data definition	Program	Network architecture	Security, architecture	Interrupts etc.	Knowledge base

Figure 6.47 The Zachman framework with sample representations in each cell.

In additional to UML and structured methods support, *System Architect* has features that support business modelling using the Zachman framework (Zachman, 1987; Sowa and Zachman, 1992): a widely used classification scheme for descriptive or notational representations of enterprises. The framework allocates notations to the cells of a matrix as shown in Figure 6.47. The columns and rows are certainly a complete classification scheme – there are only those six question words. Notably, the rows are based on an analogy with building construction and represent the perspectives taken by different trades during the construction process. This can provide a useful guide, but it is difficult to see how the data/function split can be reconciled with object-orientation. In fact, as shown by Graham (1995), the framework collapses to many fewer cells when OO concepts are substituted for such representations as 'logical data model'.

No tool yet properly supports the Catalysis framework substitution described in Section 6.3.7, although *Platinum Plus* may do soon; others will probably follow and the technique is likely at some stage to appear in the UML standard. *TogetherJ* already does something fairly similar with its support for patterns.

What is lacking mostly on the CASE scene are good object-oriented business simulation tools; these would allow one to animate business process models. We also lack what one might designate 'anti-CASE' tools, which can generate most UML diagrams automatically. Ideally these types of tool should be integrated into a single package and have interfaces with popular conventional CASE tools and drawing packages.

My favourite everyday tools for drawing diagrams are the low-cost *Visio* and *PowerPoint* drawing tools. They intrude less on my thinking and allow me to innovate where necessary. UML templates for *Visio* are readily available.

6.6 Summary

This chapter gave a brief history of object-oriented analysis and design methods and distinguished between translational and elaborational approaches and between data- and responsibility-driven ones. I argued that translational, responsibility-driven methods were best.

The basics of object-oriented analysis and design were introduced using the UML notation and the Catalysis method was explained and recommended as best practice. Its concepts of refinement, reflection, retrieval and frameworks were explained. Considerable emphasis was placed on the rôle of invariants – and rulesets as introduced by SOMA.

We also dealt in detail with techniques for object identification, including several with their origins in knowledge elicitation for expert systems.

Finally a short review of current CASE tools was given.

6.7 Bibliographical notes

The treatment of object-oriented analysis and design in this chapter has been mostly based on a synthesis of the insights of Catalysis and SOMA and the UML standard. These insights, of course, are in themselves derivative of the work of many other methodologists. Much of this work is surveyed in Appendix B, whose bibliographical notes provide references to the original sources.

D'Souza and Wills (1999) defined Catalysis as a method for object-oriented and component-based development that made sense out of UML for the first time. The notion of rely and guarantee clauses comes from Cliff Jones' (1986) work on VDM.

SOMA (The Semantic Object Modelling Approach) arose out of attempts to combine object-oriented analysis with ideas from business process modelling and knowledge-based systems (Graham, 1991a, 1995, 1998). This book redefines SOMA as an extension of Catalysis, introducing rulesets and adding the requirements engineering techniques of Chapter 8 and the process innovations of Chapter 9. Most of the material in Section 6.3.4 is based on (Graham *et al.*, 1997a).

A good, concise, popular summary of UML is (Fowler, 1997) with (Booch *et al.*, 1999) and (Rumbaugh *et al.*, 1999) being the original definitive references. The most current definitive reference will be found at www.omg.org.

Lenzerini, Nardi and Simi (1991) survey the different interpretations of inheritance in knowledge engineering and object-oriented programming. They provide useful insights into the problems of multiple inheritance.

6.8 Exercises

1. How many methods or fragments of methods for OOA/D have been published?
   a) 12
   b) between 13 and 25
   c) 17
   d) between 26 and 44
   e) 44
   f) over 44

2. Which of the following OOA/D methods is associated with Jim Rumbaugh?
   a) CRC
   b) HOOD
   c) Ptech
   d) Objectory
   e) OMT

3. Define 'object' (one sentence). Name the four components of an object.

4. What is the difference between types, classes, instances and rôles?

5. What is a 'facet'? Give three completely different examples.

6. Why is analysis more important for OO systems?

7. Define (a) analysis, (b) logical design and (c) physical design. What is the difference between (a) analysis and logical design and (b) logical design and physical design?

8. Name 10 OO methods or notations. (Hint: Appendix B may be of use.)

9. Name the four principal structures of an object model.

10. Redraw the inheritance structure of Figure 6.16 with due attention to different discriminators.

11. What is the difference between a wrapper and a subsystem or package in most OOA methods?

12. Write invariants that might apply for all the cycles in Figure 6.19.

13. Name three things that rulesets can be used for.

14. Name six types of things that could be reused.

15. Define: (a) pre-condition; (b) post-condition; (c) assertion; (d) invariance condition; (e) class invariant; (f) guarantee; (g) rely clause.

16. Compare three OO methods known to you.

17. How do you decide whether something is to be modelled as an attribute or a class?

18. Bi-directional associations violate encapsulation. Why? How can this problem be easily overcome? Is this true in analysis as well as design? If not, why not?

19. Discuss the use of normalization in object-oriented and conventional modelling.

20. Discuss the use of functional decomposition in object-oriented and conventional modelling.

21. Write a small ruleset to describe the behaviour of a technical analyst (chartist) dealing in a single security.

22. When should state models be used and what for?

23. Give an example of a question that might elicit an abstract class from two more concrete classes. Give an example of a question that might elicit more concrete classes from a list of objects. Give an example of a question that might elicit a yet unmentioned concept.

24. Give some simple guidelines for textual analysis.

25. *'A type's existence is independent of the existence of its instances.'* Discuss, with reference to Plato.

26. Why is analysis important for OO programmers?

27. Does God throw exceptions?

28. Using the approach described in this chapter specify either:
    a) a simple public library lending administration system, where books can be borrowed, reserved and returned; or
    b) a simple drawing tool, where shapes can be drawn, moved, deleted and grouped.

7

Architecture, patterns and components
with Alan O'Callaghan and Alan Cameron Wills

A spider conducts operations that resemble those of a weaver, and a bee puts to shame many an architect in the construction of her cells. But what distinguishes the worst architect from the best of bees is this, that the architect raises his structure in imagination before he erects it in reality.

K. Marx (*Capital, Volume I*)

This chapter examines various issues that arise in modern object-oriented development. In particular, we examine the emerging discipline of software architecture and review current debates from the particular perspective of object-oriented designers who, arguably, have more choice open to them than most other software developers. In the context of that discussion we then look at the phenomenon of patterns, which are regarded as essential for good object-oriented design. Lastly we look at the application of object-oriented ideas to component-based development, which is the area where we expect to see the delivery of most of the benefits discussed in Chapter 2. As in Chapter 6, our treatment of component-based development follows the approach of Catalysis closely.

7.1 Software and system architecture

Software architecture is a hot topic in software development generally as well as within object-orientation. It has been palpably growing in importance, for reasons we discuss below, since at least 1992, with a clear separation in schools of thought surrounding its nature appearing more recently. However, the metaphor has a much longer genealogy than the modern debate is sometimes prepared to admit. The notion of software architecture has a pedigree at least as long as those of 'software engineering' and the 'software crisis'. These latter two terms are commonly accepted to have originated in the famous NATO conference of 1968 (Naur and Randall, 1969). Fred Brooks Jr. refers in a number of the influential articles in his Mythical Man-Month collection to architecture (Brooks, 1975), but credits Blaauw (1970) with the first use of the term five years previously. However, according to Ian Hugo, a delegate at that historic NATO conference, the idea of 'software architecture' and the rôle of 'software architects' were common currency in its deliberations (Hugo, personal communication with Alan O'Callaghan) – the analogy was, however, considered by the proceedings' editors too fanciful a notion to be reflected in the official minutes. It is symbolic indeed that the idea co-originates with that of the software crisis and that it was largely discarded in the intervening period, while the discipline of software engineering as it has been practised for more than three decades has manifestly failed to resolve the situation it was ushered in to redress. It is perhaps unsurprising then that the modern discussion of software architecture lies at the heart of a debate that is reassessing the very basis of the discipline(s) of software and system development. And in that debate, experience of both object-orientation and software patterns provides critical insights.

ARCHITECTURE AS GROSS STRUCTURE

There is as yet no clear and unambiguous definition of what software architecture is. What consensus does exist to date seems to revolve around issues of high level design and the gross structure of systems, including both their static and dynamic properties. Larry Bass and his colleagues (Bass *et al.*, 1998), for example, in a since oft-quoted definition, say that:

> The software architecture of a program or computing system is the structure or structures of the system, which comprise software components, the externally visible properties of those components and the relationships among them.

Mary Shaw and David Garlan in their influential short volume on software architecture go so far as to date its origins from the moment software systems were first broken into modules (Shaw and Garlan, 1996). At the same time they recognize that, historically, such architectures have been implicit. In attempting to render architecture more explicit and formal, they introduce the important notions of software *architectural style* and of *Architectural Description Languages* (ADLs).

They treat the architecture of a specific system as a collection of computational components together with a description of the interactions, or connectors, linking these components. An architectural style, according to Shaw and Garlan, defines a family of systems in terms of this structural organization. Clients, servers, filters, layers and databases are all given as possible examples of components, while example connectors are procedure calls, event broadcasts, database protocols and pipes. Table 7.1, which is adapted from their book, gives a list of common architectural styles.

Shaw and Garlan's position and that of others at Carnegie Mellon University (CMU) and at the Software Engineering Institute (SEI), which is home to such as Bass *et al.*, may be characterized as the view that architecture is equivalent to the high level structure of a system. The inclusion of OO in the table itself highlights an issue with an approach that reduces architecture to one of *components plus connectors*. Many of us believe that architecture is more than just boxes and lines, however much semantics is attached to them. To make sense it must include a notion of architectural vision: the unifying concept that we all recognize equally when we see an elegant software system or a Nash terrace or, more importantly, when we have to build one.

Table 7.1 Common architectural styles (after Shaw and Garlan).

Dataflow Systems	*Virtual Machines*
Batch sequential	Interpreters
Pipes and filters	Rule-based systems

Call-and-Return systems	*Data-centred systems (repositories)*
Main program and subroutine	Databases
OO systems	Hypertext systems
Hierarchical layers	Blackboards

Independent Components
Communicating processes
Event systems

Shaw and Garlan focus on the implementation technology and regard objects merely as instances of abstract data types. They note that an object is both responsible for preserving its representation and simultaneously hiding that representation from its clients. However, they seem to miss the significance of this; for, as Cook (1994) and O'Callaghan (1994) amongst others have pointed out, the fact that an object presents itself as abstract behaviour (through its operations), encapsulating both the implementation of its operations and the (localized) data they manipulate, isolates the programmer from the digital architecture of the underlying machine. As a consequence of this freedom from the constraints of Von Neumann architecture developers can use objects as building blocks to create any number of software architectures, especially ones which reflect the vocabulary of the problem space. Cook says that objects are in this sense 'architecture free'. This means, amongst other things, that objects can be used to build pipes-and-filter structures, layered architectures, blackboard systems and, arguably, any of the other styles listed by Shaw and Garlan.

The reduction of object-orientation to just one of a number of implementation styles further ignores Graham's (1998) identification of objects as a 'general knowledge acquisition mechanism'. This means that the use of objects in spaces other than the implementation space is ignored, and therefore their potential significance for software architecture grossly underemphasized. This seems to be an important gap in the current orthodoxy of software architecture thinking, since often it is precisely this 'modellability' of objects and the promise of systems that are consequently flexible to business change that makes them an attractive proposition. When Shaw and Garlan contrast what they call 'implicit invocation' architecture (i.e.

actor or blackboard systems where objects register interest in events) with object technology, they seem to be unwilling to admit that implicit invocation is readily modelled using object-oriented methods. Their view of object-orientation seems to be limited to the models of current object-oriented programming languages. Yet in the same work they use object-oriented design for their architectural design tool AESOP – implicitly admitting that OO can describe other styles. Worse still, they criticize OO for not being able to represent stylistic constraints. This narrow view of OO excludes object-oriented methods where objects with embedded rulesets can represent such things as semantic integrity constraints and the like.

On the other hand, Shaw and Garlan do present some sound arguments for the extension of the object-oriented metaphor. It is argued, for example, that ADLs imply a need for rôle modelling (and thus dynamic classification). Of course this does not mean that objects are the best choice for every requirement that can be imagined. Through the use of case studies such as Tektronix Inc.'s development of a reusable architecture for oscilloscopes, and another on mobile robotics, Shaw and Garlan effectively demonstrate that different topologies reflect different costs and benefits and therefore have different applicability. But they are somewhat unconvincing in arguing that components and connectors add up to architecture. For practising object technologists such a reductionist view of architecture is little help in helping them create software systems when they have so many different architectural possibilities open to them.

The other significant contribution made in the Shaw and Garlan book is to introduce ADLs. The authors point out that structural decomposition is traditionally expressed either through the modularization facilities of programming languages or through the special medium of Module Interconnexion Languages (MILs). These are criticized for being too low-level in their descriptions of interconnexions between different computational elements and because 'they fail to provide a clean separation of concerns between architectural-level issues and those related to the choices of algorithms and data structures' (page 148). Newer, component-based languages such as Occam II (Pountain, 1989) and Connection (Mak, 1992) or environments such as STEP (Rosene, 1995) which enforced specialized structural patterns of organization are criticized for their narrow scope. Instead six key requirements for a higher level kind of language, the ADL, are enumerated as follows.

1. *Composition.* It should be possible to describe a system as a composition of independent components and connectors.
2. *Abstraction.* It should be possible to describe the components and their interactions within software architecture in a way that clearly and explicitly prescribes their abstract rôles in a system.
3. *Reusability.* It should be possible to reuse components, connectors, and architectural patterns in different architectural descriptions, even if they were developed outside the context of the architectural system.
4. *Configuration.* Architectural descriptions should localize the description of system structure, independently of the elements being structured. They should also support dynamic reconfiguration.

5. *Heterogeneity*. It should be possible to combine multiple, heterogeneous architectural descriptions.
6. *Analysis*. It should be possible to perform rich and varied analyses of architectural descriptions.

Shaw and Garlan point out, quite correctly, that the typical box-and-line diagrams that often pass for 'architectural description' focus on components often to the virtual, and sometimes actual, exclusion of the connectors between them. They are therefore underspecified in a number of crucial contexts, notably third-party 'packaged' components, multi-language systems, legacy systems and, perhaps most critically of all, large-scale real-time embedded systems. Additionally the boxes, lines and the adjacency between boxes lack semantic consistency between diagrams and sometimes even within the same diagram and ignore the need to structure interface definitions. This points to a minimum of two levels of structure and abstraction that are typically missing: abstractions for connexions, and segmentation of interfaces. As it stands, such diagrams rely heavily on the knowledge and experience of the person in the architect's rôle, and this is held informally.

UniCon (short for 'Universal Connector language') is an example ADL developed at Carnegie Mellon University (Shaw *et al.*, 1995). It is characterized amongst other things by having an explicit connector construct which represents the rules by which components can be hooked up, and by having a defined abstraction function that allows an architectural description to be retrieved from low level constructs. A component has players – the entities visible and named in its interface; a connector has rôles – the named entities in its protocol – that have to be satisfied by players. UniCon supports the checking of associations between players and rôles, the checking of the types of components and connectors themselves, and the adherence of the components and connectors to architectural styles.

UniCon and other ADLs have undoubtedly added rigour and formality to the description and analysis of structure. This is of first-rate importance in certain classes of application, notably real-time systems. In this context, Selic *et al.* (1994) argue for the importance of an approach to architectural design in their real-time ROOM method and the ObjecTime tool that supports it. ObjecTime and Rational Software Inc. have been working together since 1997 to align their respective technologies and, following a period of strategic co-operation in which ObjecTime were Rational's exclusive supplier of modelling tools and automatic code generation technology for the real-time domain (and Rational had world-wide distribution rights for ObjecTime Developer), Rational Software announced the acquisition of ObjecTime in December 1999. As a result the architectural description concepts that originated in ROOM have now found their way into real-time extensions for UML (Rumbaugh and Selic, 1998). Arguably, UML with real-time extensions is the most widely used commercial-strength ADL. UML models the structure of a system by identifying the entities of interest and the relationships between them. In the category of real-time systems that form the domain described by ROOM (complex, event-driven and potentially distributed systems such as those that occur in telecommunications, aerospace and defence systems) two of UML's total of nine diagram types are the focus of the real-time extensions: class diagrams and collaboration diagrams. Class diagrams in UML capture relationships that are universal; that is, they apply to all possible instances in all possible contexts. Collaboration diagrams on the other hand capture relationships in just one particular context. Collaboration diagrams therefore are able to distinguish between different usages of different instances of the same class. This notion is captured in the concept of a *rôle*. Typically the complete specification of a complex real-time system in terms of its structure is obtained, using these extensions, through a combination of class diagrams and collaboration diagrams.

Three constructs are defined in order to use UML as an ADL for such systems:

- capsules (formerly known as *actors* in ROOM – and not to be confused with the concept of the same name used with use cases);
- ports;
- connectors (formerly known as *bindings* in ROOM).

A **capsule** is a complex, physical, possibly distributed architectural object that interacts with its environment through one or more signal-based boundary objects called ports. It completely contains all its ports and sub-capsules. That is, these cannot exist independently of their 'owning' capsule (unless the sub-capsule is a 'plug-in' capsule). This makes the capsule the central modelling element in real-time extended UML. A **port** is also a physical object, part of a capsule that implements a specific interface and plays a specific rôle in some collaboration between capsules. Being physical objects, ports are visible from the inside and from the outside of capsules. From the outside ports are distinguishable from each other only by their identity and the rôle that they play in their protocol. From the inside, however, ports can either be *relay* ports or *end* ports. Relay ports differ from end ports in their internal connexions. Relay ports are connected, through other ports, to sub-capsules and exist simply to pass on signals. End ports, in contrast, are connected to a capsule's state machine and are the ultimate sources and sinks of signals. Both capsules and ports are modelled with stereotyped class icons in UML, but an additional stereotype icon, a small black square (or, alternatively, a white one for a conjugated port in a binary protocol) is available. A *connector* is a physical communication channel that provides the transmission facilities for a particular, abstract, signal-based protocol. A connector can only interconnect ports that play complementary rôles in the protocol with which it is associated. Connectors are modelled with UML associations. Figure 7.1 shows the visual syntax of these constructs in UML extended for real-time. The approach forces capsules to communicate solely through their ports, permitting the decoupling of the capsules' internal representations from any knowledge about their surrounding environment, and enabling reuse.

The broader question arises, however, as to how much increased formality in and of itself will help in addressing the fundamental problems of software development. The roots of the research into architecture at Carnegie Mellon lie in Mary Shaw's pursuit of a definition of the Software Engineering discipline itself (e.g. Shaw, 1990). She opines that the maturity of an engineering discipline is marked by the emergence of a 'sufficient scientific basis' to enable a critical mass of science-trained professionals to apply their theory to both the analysis of problems and the synthesis of solutions. Further progress is observed when science becomes a forcing function. She presents, therefore, a model that contends that the emergence of a sound engineering discipline of software depends on the vigorous pursuit of applicable science and then the reduction of that science to a practice.

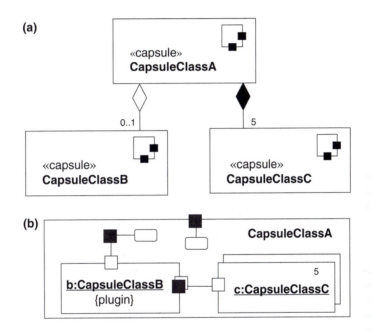

Figure 7.1 UML for Real-Time as an ADL (adapted from Rumbaugh and Selic, 1998): **(a)** a UML-RT class diagram; **(b)** one possible corresponding collaboration diagram.

This linear model of science preceding practice and reducing engineering to 'mere' problem-solving is, of course, the received wisdom of traditional Computer Science. But the problem is what is the 'applicable science'? There is a growing challenge to the old orthodoxy, which sees computing as essentially a specialized branch of mathematics. Borenstein (1991), for example, in his marvellously named book *Programming as if People Mattered* notes that the most interesting part of the process of building software is the human part, its design and its use: 'Inasmuch as human-oriented software engineering is the study of this process, it could be argued that it is more properly a branch of anthropology than of mathematical sciences. The study of software creation may, in fact, be grossly mis-classified in the academic world today, leading to a distorted overemphasis on formal models and a lack of basic work in collecting raw material that comes, most often, in anecdotal (or at least non-quantitative) form.' (p. 36)

Interestingly Borenstein upholds what Shaw and Garlan and indeed everyone else at CMU and the SEI appear to bemoan, the informality and unquantifiable characteristics of current software design practice. Bruce I. Blum, a former VP of Wolf Research and an erstwhile research scientist at Johns Hopkins University, has called for the redesign of the disciplines of Computer Science and Software Engineering on similar grounds to those advocated by Borenstein (Blum, 1996, 1998). In his work he has questioned the epistemology of the received orthodoxy on both the grounds of the philosophy of science and of practice. He points to a dialectical contradiction in the making of software that traditional Computer Science is blind to. He distinguishes between the 'program-in-the-computer' and the 'program-in-the-world'. The program in the computer is subject to the closed abstractions of mathematics and is, theoretically at least, verifiable against some specification. Indeed the core of interest in the 'program-in-the-computer' is the extent of the difficulty of its construction. But what is in the computer must also exist, on completion, as a 'program-in-the-world' where the one and only test is its usefulness. Its value depends upon its ability to transform the pre-existing situation into which it now inserts itself, both impacting upon and being impacted by that situation. As a result the 'program-in-the-computer' exists in a stable, well-known and formally representable environment, but the very same software as 'the program-in-the-world' is dynamic and incompletely understood. A key issue is this: formal approaches work primarily by a process of selection from an existing or theoretical universe of extant, well-defined formal abstractions. Selection is easier than creating from scratch and therefore all such gains are valuable, but a total solution using formal methods is possible only once *all possible* design solutions have been formalized. Hence, no doubt, the SEI's interest in collecting architectural styles. However, Blum's criticism suggests that such a task is not only an Herculean labour but that, because it too rests on a mythology – the received wisdom of Computer Science – it can never be completed.

PROBLEM FRAMES

A more profound approach is due to Jackson (1995). He defines a problem frame as a structure consisting of principal parts and a solution task. The principal parts correspond to what we have called agents, business objects, conversations, actions and use cases. The solution task is the work one has to do to meet some requirement concerning these parts or objects. He then abstracts from the objects to problem domains and the phenomena that are shared between them: in the sense of the elements that can be described in the languages of both domains. More importantly, each frame may have a set of rules that connect pairs of domains. We think that problem frames provide not only a requirements engineering technique but potentially also an architectural technique because they describe not a solution but a suitable approach to finding a solution. They also suggest the patterns that we deal with in the next section. The idea is focused more on the problems of the requirements analyst trying to understand a problem and select an approach than the object-oriented designer who has already selected the architectural style and implementation technology.

Typical problem frames include the following:

- CONNEXION: introduces a separate problem domain between the application and solution domains. Examples: a post office; CORBA.
- JSP: helps to describe a program in terms of its input and output streams. Example: a typical accounting or stock control system.
- SIMPLE CONTROL: describes the situation where known control rules are applied to a controllable phenomenon. Examples: embedded real-time controllers; vending machines.
- SIMPLE INFORMATION SYSTEMS: the real-world analogue of the JSP frame, the problem concerns users requesting and updating information about some domain. Example: database systems.
- WORKPIECES: describes the way operators' commands are linked to the manipulation of objects. Example: text editors.

Problem frames taken together represent a pattern language (see below) since realistic problems usually involve several frames. Jackson argues that identifying the frame is a precursor to selecting an appropriate method. He characterizes, by way of example, the use case approach as such a method and points to some of its limitations – as we shall in Chapter 8 – with the aim of showing that its use is restricted to problem frames where user I/O dominates. This is quite correct, but we feel that viewing object modelling as a form of knowledge representation frees us from this criticism. Although object technology undoubtedly has frame-dependent limitations, it can be specialized to deal with quite a variety of frames. The main reason for this is the semantic richness provided by rulesets and, for example, the inclusion of invariance conditions as well as pre- and post-conditions.

We would encourage readers to think about their own set of familiar problems and ask if there are other frames at this level of generality. Our contribution and experience are beginning to suggest that there is a frame that abstracts the common order processing or trading problem, one for modelling agents (called Assistant) and one for general simulation problems. Describing these frames in Jackson's language of domains and shared phenomena is left as an exercise for the interested reader.

Picking up similar themes from different roots, those of Syntropy (Cook and Daniels, 1994), O'Callaghan (2000a) has argued that object technology, to deliver its full benefits, needs to be used for modelling in two conceptually distinct spaces: the problem space, which is a conceptual model of the real-world situation, and the solution space where the software part of the solution is created. Object types capture observed behaviour of key abstractions in the problem space, but specify the behaviour of a to-be-designed solution in the implementation space. The programmer controls the latter, but can never do so in the former. Despite the 'seamlessness' of the use of the object as the basic metaphor in both spaces, the fundamental differences in the nature of the spaces themselves and therefore of the abstractions that are modelled within them, makes traceability a non-trivial issue. He posits the need for a Janus-like entity which sits between these two spaces, looking both ways at once. It is this he calls the software architecture. What is interesting is that while Borenstein, Blum and O'Callaghan, to which we might add the voices of Mitch Kapor (1991) and

Terry Winograd (1996), appear to be take an view orthogonal to the currently dominant view of software architecture, they actually have more in common with the historical roots of the notion of software architecture than does the SEI.

Fred Brooks Jr., in his article *Aristocracy, Democracy and System Design* (in Brooks, 1975), argued that the single most important consideration in system design is its conceptual integrity. This was for him the defining property of software or system architecture, and the chief charge of the architect. Brooks stated that it is far better to reflect a coherent set of design ideas, and if necessary omit feature or functionality in order to maintain that coherence, than it is to build a system that contains heterogeneous or uncoordinated concepts, however good they each may be independently. This raises the following issues.

- How is conceptual integrity to be achieved?
- Is it possible to maintain conceptual integrity without separation between a small, 'architectural' elite and a larger group of plebeian implementers for a system?
- How do you ensure the architects do not deliver unimplementable or over-costly implementations?
- How do you ensure that the architecture is reflected in the detailed design?

It was in answering these questions that Brooks made a conscious appeal to the metaphor of architecture in the built environment. He carefully distinguished between architecture and implementation. Echoing Blaauw he gave the simple example of a clock, whose architecture consists of its face, its hands and its winding knob. Having learned the architecture of a clock a child can tell the time whether using a wristwatch, a kitchen clock or a clock tower. The mechanism by which the time-telling function is delivered is a detail of implementation and realization, not architecture.

'By the architecture of a system', says Brooks, 'I mean the complete and detailed specification of the user interface'. For a computer this is the programming manual. For a compiler it is the language manual. For a control program it is the manuals for the language or languages used to invoke its functions. For the entire system it is the union of the manuals the user must consult to do his entire job'(p. 45).

While this definition seems inadequate today, it has at least the virtue of establishing that the architect is the client's agent, not the developers'. It strongly suggests that the conceptual integrity of the system, represented by the architecture, gains its shape from the perceived needs of the client and that the final test of what constitutes a 'good' architecture is its usefulness. In this important aspect there is a strong thread of continuity between the ideas of Brooks and Blum, although ironically Blum does not use the term 'software architecture', and a symmetrical discontinuity between Brooks and the SEI despite their claim to it. It is also worth noting that this view of the software architect as the client's agent is also a preoccupation of the recently founded World Wide Institute of Software Architects (WWISA, 2000).

Again following Blaauw, Brooks suggests that the overall creative effort involves three distinct phases: architecture, implementation and realization. For Brooks, architecture appears to end with the complete and final specification of the system; the design 'of module boundaries, table structures, pass or phase breakdowns, algorithms, and all kinds of tools' belongs to implementation. Brooks believed that all three phases could occur to some extent in parallel and that successful design requires an ongoing conversation between architects and implementers. Nevertheless the boundaries of the architects' input to the dialogue are confined to the external specification of the system. There is clearly some tension between this idea of the architect's rôle and Brooks' insistence on the need to maintain the conceptual integrity of the system. In modern systems at least, which involve issues of scale and distribution that did not exist in 1975, traceability of a construction back through its structure to its specification and to the need that spawned it is crucial in maintaining the integrity of the system.

ARCHITECT-URE AS DESIGN RATIONALE

There appears to be the need for a marriage between the idea of the architect as the client's agent championing the conceptual integrity of the system on the one hand, and ideas about the internal structures of the system on the other. Many modern theorists of software architecture draw inspiration from a seminal paper written by Dewayne Perry and Alexander Wolf (Perry and Wolf, 1992). They defined software architecture in terms of an equation:

Software Architecture = {Elements, Form, Rationale}

Barry Boehm has apparently qualified the last of these three terms to read 'Rationale/Constraints'. A powerfully influential interpretation of this idea, applied specifically to object-oriented development, has been offered by Phillipe Kruchten in his '4+1 View Model' of software architecture (Kruchten, 1995). This view underpins the Unified Process and is responsible, in large part, for the claims it makes to being 'architecture-centric'. Kruchten concedes that software architecture deals with abstraction, with composition and decomposition, and also with style and aesthetics. To deal with all these aspects, especially in the face of large and challenging systems developments, Kruchten proposes a generic model made up of five different views as follows.

- The *logical* view: an object model of the design.
- The *process* view: which models the concurrency and synchronization issues of the design.
- The *physical* view: a model of the mapping of software onto the hardware elements of the solution, including distribution issues.
- The *development* view: the static organization of the software in its development environment.
- A *scenarios*-based view: the usage scenarios from which the architecture is partially derived, and against which it is validated.

Kruchten applies the Perry and Wolf equation independently on each view. The set of elements in terms of components, containers and connectors is defined for each view, as are the forms and patterns which work in the particular context in which the architecture is to be applied. Similarly, the rationale and constraints for each view are also captured, connecting the architecture to the requirements. Each view is captured in the form of a blueprint in a notation appropriate to the view (in the original paper, which predated the UML, subsets of the Booch notation were used for each view), and may have an architectural style, à la Shaw and Garlan, to it.

Criticizing a rather linear, four-phase (sketching, organizing, specifying and optimising), twelve-step process for architecture proposed by Witt *et al.* (1994), Kruchten proposes an iterative, scenario-driven approach instead. Based on relative risk and criticality, a small number of scenarios are chosen for an iteration. Then a straw-man architecture is put in place. Scenarios are scripted to derive the major abstractions (classes, collaborations, processes, subsystems, etc.) and then decomposed into object–operation pairs. The architectural elements that have been discovered are laid out on to the four blueprints: logical, physical, process and development. The architecture is then implemented, tested, measured and analysed, possibly revealing flaws or opportunities for enhancement. Subsequent iterations can now begin. The documentation resulting from this process is in fact two sets of documents: a *Software Architecture Document* (the recommended template for which is shown in Figure 7.2) and a separate *Software Design Guidelines* which captures the most important design decisions that must be respected to maintain the conceptual integrity of the architecture. The essence of the process is this: the initial architectural prototype evolves to be the final system.

Astute readers will recognize in this approach the bones of the Unified Process (Jacobson *et al.*, 1999), itself a public domain subset of the proprietary Rational Unified Process, as well as a submission to the OMG's ongoing effort to define a standard, generic process for object-oriented development. In its modern, post-UML form Kruchten's '4+1' model has been retained but with some renaming. The logical, process views and development views remain, but the physical view is now called the Implementation View and/or the Component View (Grady Booch has recently used these names interchangeably in the same presentation) and the scenarios-based view is called the Use Case View, firmly tying the '4+1 Model' into the UML as well as the Unified Process. In a keynote speech to UML World, Booch has gone further and defined an architecture metamodel, depicted in Figure 7.3 (Booch, 1999). We will return to it later, but here we can note that the metamodel states that a *Software Architecture* is represented by a *Software Architecture Description* composed of *Architectural Views* (*Logical, Process, Implementation, Deployment* and *Use Case*) each depicted in an *Architectural Blueprint* and an *Architectural Style Guide*. It also shows a binary relationship between *Software Architecture* and *Requirements*. Allowing for a renaming of Kruchten's original *Software Design Guide* as *Architectural Style Guide*, the metamodel is entirely consistent with the '4+1 Model'.

There can be little doubt that the '4 +1' model and its successors have made a significant contribution to developing software architecture as a practical discipline. It does so in two particular ways when compared to the reductionist view of software architecture. Firstly, it extends the scope of architecture beyond mere structure. In Booch's UML World presentation already cited, one slide devoted to the domain of software architecture describes it not only in the traditional terms of the answers to the 'what?' and the 'how?' of system development, but also the 'why?' and the 'who?'.

Booch *et al.* (1999) offer a definition which, besides the usual structural stuff, adds 'Software architecture is not only concerned with structure and behaviour, but also with usage, functionality, performance, resilience, reuse, comprehensibility, economic and technology constraints and trade-offs, and aesthetic concerns' (p. 458). Secondly, it places software architecture on the critical path of software development by insisting that the first prototype be an architectural one. In *The Unified Software Development Process* (Jacobson *et al.*, 1999) this prototype is referred to as a 'small, skinny system'.

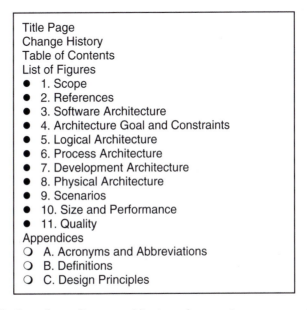

Figure 7.2 Outline of a software architecture document, as proposed by Kruchten (1995).

The '4+1 Model' and the Unified Process are designed to reveal the architecture as part of the software development process itself. In Kruchten's original paper he shows how the process works in domains as distinct as the Télic PABX architecture and Hughes Aircraft's Air Traffic Control System but it is less clear how it works when what is being created is an architecture for a domain, a family of systems or a product-line system all of which require leverage from a common architecture. After all, if every project is free to discover the architecture then there is an accentuated possibility, if not a clear probability, that each such 'architecture' will be different.

Jan Bosch has recently published a contribution to the problem of adopting and evolving a product-line approach based on the work of the RISE (Research in Software Engineering) group at the University of Karlskrona/Ronneby in Sweden and its collaborations with companies such as Securitas Alarm AB and Axis Communications (Bosch, 2000). Product-line approaches stand close to those of

Component-Based Development. The core of Bosch's approach involves first the development of what he calls a 'functionality-based architectural design' from the requirements specification. At the centre of this activity is the search for key problem-driven architectural abstractions which he calls 'archetypes'. Archetypes appear to be object types whose roots are in the problem space[1] but which, for product-line development, normally have to be generalized and abstracted further from the concrete phenomena that the analyst or architect first encounters. Bosch posits further that many archetypes are actually cross-domain in character.

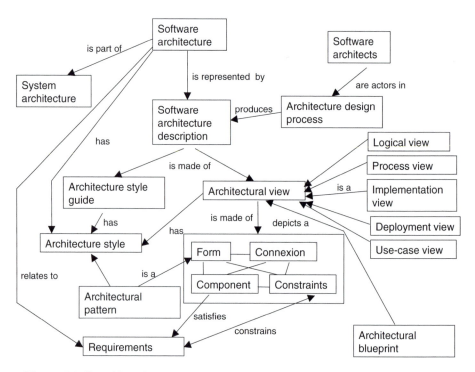

Figure 7.3 Booch's software architecture metamodel (adapted from Booch, 1999).

A small and stable set of archetypes is chosen from a wider candidate list, often merging initial candidates to produce higher level abstractions. The abstract relations between these archetypes are then identified and selected. The structure of the software architecture is then created by recursively decomposing the set of archetypes into well-defined components and establishing the relationship between them. A

---

[1] The notion appears to be close to the notion captured in the ARCHETYPE pattern in the ADAPTOR pattern language (O'Callaghan, 2000b) but distinct from that of Peter Coad who uses the term to describe one of four meta-level collaborations he believes to be endemic in object systems (Coad *et al.*, 1999).

system instantiation can then be described in order to validate the work done thus far. This requires the further decomposition of components into lower level components and the population of these components with instantiated archetypes. Since product-line architectures have to support a wide variety of systems with different specifications as well as different implementations, variability has to be addressed at this early point. Therefore, multiple such instantiations are produced to validate the match between the architecture and the requirements.

Architectural assessment involves another fairly novel idea: that of a *profile*. A profile is a set of scenarios, but they are not necessarily usage scenarios. That is to say, even if use cases are deployed in order to give traceability to functional requirements they will form only a subset of the overall number of scenarios described. Other scenarios, related to quality attributes (non-functional requirements), such as *hazard scenarios* (for safety-critical systems) or *change scenarios* for flexible maintenance, are also specified. The profiles allow for a more precise specification of quality attributes than is typical in most software development. Bosch reports that between four and eight categories of scenarios are typical. Scenarios are identified and specified for each category, and each one assigned a weighting. Weightings are, if necessary, normalized. Scenario-based assessment follows in two main steps: impact analysis, and quality attribute prediction. The impact of the running of each scenario in a profile is assessed and then a predictive value for a quality attribute measured. So, for example, the number of changed and new components resulting from a change scenario in a maintenance category estimated in impact analysis could lead to a cost of maintenance effort estimation when brought together with a change frequency figure, based, say, on historical data in the second (predictive) phase. Profiles and scenarios can be used in a variety of ways, including simulated assessments in which both an executable version of the system and implemented profiles can be used to dynamically verify the architecture.

In the course of these assessments it is normal for one or more quality requirements to fail to be satisfied by the architecture, normally as a result of conflicting forces acting upon the overall design – for example, performance constraints being violated because of the levels of indirection built into the architecture in order to meet changeability requirements. In these circumstances what Bosch calls 'architectural transformations' are required. Four categories of architectural transformation are identified and used in the following order, each next transformation having an expectancy of relatively decreasing impact:

- Impose architectural style (as per Shaw and Garlan, *op. cit.*);
- Impose architectural pattern (or mechanism) – by which Bosch means apply a rule locally to specify how the system will deal with one aspect of its overall functionality, e.g., concurrency or persistence[2];
- Apply design pattern (as per Gamma, 1995 – see below);

---

[2] This is clearly a different concept from that of (Buschmann *et al.*, 1996) discussed later in this chapter.

■ Convert quality requirements to functionality – e.g. extend functionality to deal with self-monitoring, or redundancy for fault tolerance.

The final step is to distribute quality requirements to identified components or subsystems in the overall architecture. We restrict ourselves here to the discussion in Bosch's book to software architecture. A second and substantial part deals with the actual development of product lines. To the interested reader we recommend the purchase of the volume itself.

There is actually a fair amount in common among the '4+1' view and the approach to product-line development software architectures used by the RISE research group. Both authors pay due attention to the full scope of software architecture and deal with conceptual integrity, rationale as well as structure.[3] Both attach non-functional requirements to components or subsystems originally identified by analysing functionality. Both, at a certain point in the process, recommend the application of architectural styles and then design patterns. We discuss issues involved therein below. The key difference is that Kruchten's approach is bottom-up, working from the abstractions discovered in a system requirements specification, while Bosch's approach is decidedly top-down, working from archetypal abstractions and then imposing them upon the development of a particular application or system.

7.2 Patterns, architecture and decoupled design

One of the most important recent ideas in software development is that of a design pattern. Design patterns are standard solutions to recurring problems, named to help people discuss them easily and to think about design. They have always been around in computing, so that terms such as 'linked list' or 'recursive descent' are readily understood by people in the field.

Software patterns have been described as reusable micro-architectures. Patterns are abstract, core solutions to problems that recur in different contexts but encounter the same 'forces' each time. The actual implementation of the solution varies with each application. Patterns are not, therefore, ready-made 'pluggable' solutions. They are most often represented in object-oriented development by commonly recurring arrangements of classes and the structural and dynamic connexions between them. Perhaps the best known and useful examples of patterns occur in application frameworks associated with graphical user interface building or other well-defined development problems. In fact, some of the motivation for the patterns movement came from the apprehension of already existing frameworks that led people to wonder how general the approach was. Nowadays it is more usual to deliver frameworks in the form of flexible class libraries for use by programmers in languages that support

---

[3] Although in a panel session on 'What is Software Architecture?' at TOOLS Europe 2000 on which sat two of the the co-authors of this chapter amongst others, Bosch put Kruchten firmly in the 'structuralist' camp of software architecture.

the class concept, often C++ and Java. Examples of frameworks range from class libraries that are delivered with programming environments through the NeXtStep Interface Builder to the many GUI and client-server development systems now on the market such as Delphi, Visual Studio, Visual Age or Visual Basic.

Patterns are most useful because they provide a language for designers to communicate in. Rather than having to explain a complex idea from scratch, the designer can just mention a pattern by name and everyone will know, at least roughly, what is meant. This is how designers in many other disciplines communicate their design ideas. In this sense they are an excellent vehicle for the collection and dissemination of the anecdotal and unquantifiable data that Borenstein (1991) argues need to be collected before we can see real advances in the processes of building software. As with software architecture there are two different views of patterns abroad, both of which have value. To examine these we will first look at the roots of the patterns concept which lie outside the domain of software development, in the domain of the built environment. Hardly surprising then that patterns are closely related to software architecture.

Patterns are associated with the radical architect of the built environment, Christopher Alexander. From the outset of his career Alexander has been driven by the view that the vast majority of building stock created since the end of World War II (which constitutes the great majority of all construction works created by human beings in the history of the species) has been dehumanizing, of poor quality and lacking all sense of beauty and human feeling. In his earliest publication Alexander presented a powerful critique of modern design (Alexander, 1964) contrasting the failures of the professional *self-conscious* process of design with what he called the *unselfconscious* process by which peasants' farmhouses, Eskimos' igloos and the huts of the Mousgoum tribesmen of the Cameroon amongst others create their living spaces. In the latter '…the pattern of building operation, the pattern of the building's maintenance, the constraints of the surrounding conditions, and also the pattern of daily life, are fused in the form' (p. 31) yet there is no concept of 'design' or 'architecture', let alone separate designers and architects. Each man builds his own house.

Alexander argues that the unselfconscious process has a homeostatic (i.e. self-organizing) structure that produces well-fitting forms even in the face of change, but in the self-conscious process this homeostatic structure has been broken down, making poorly-fitting forms almost inevitable.[4] Although, by definition, there are no

---

[4] Mature biological systems are homeostatic. Consider how a tree, for example a mighty oak in a wood, is formed. The shape of an individual tree appears well adapted to its environment. The height of the tree is a factor of its competition with neighbouring trees. If used as a windbreak on the edges of farms, it will typically be bent in the direction of the prevailing wind patterns. The number of branches it has depends on the number of leaves it produces to accommodate local sunshine and rainfall conditions, etc. If alone on a hilltop, the pattern of growth is normally symmetrical, but if constrained in any way, the tree reflects the constraints in its own growth pattern. The tree's adaptiveness is of course a function of its genetic code. More recently Alexander has talked of his own approach as being a 'genetic' approach and the

explicitly articulated rules for building in the unselfconscious process, there is usually a great weight of unspoken, unwritten, implicit rules that are, nevertheless, rigidly maintained by culture and tradition. These traditions provide a bedrock of stability, but more than that, a viscosity or resistance to all but the most urgent changes – usually when a form 'fails' in some way. When such changes are required the very simplicity of life itself, and the immediacy of the feedback (since the builder and homeowner are one and the same) mean that the necessary adaptation can itself be made immediately, as a 'one-off'. Thus the unselfconscious process is characterized by fast reactions to single 'failures' combined with resistance to all other changes. This allows the process to make a series of minor, incremental adjustments instead of spasmodic global ones. Changes have local impact only, and over a long period of time, the system adjusts 'subsystem by subsystem'. Since the minor changes happen at a faster rate of change than does the culture, equilibrium is constantly and dynamically re-established after each disturbance.

In the self-conscious process tradition is weakened or becomes non-existent. The feedback loop is lengthened by the distance between the 'user' and the builder. Immediate reaction to failure is not possible because materials are not close to hand. Failures for all these reasons accumulate and require far more drastic action because they have to be dealt with in combination. All the factors that drive the construction process to equilibrium have disappeared in the self-conscious process. Equilibrium, if reached at all, is unsustainable, not least because the rate at which culture changes outpaces the rate at which adaptations can be made.

Alexander does not seek a return to primitive forms, but rather a new approach to a modern dilemma: self-conscious designers, and indeed the notion of design itself, have arisen as a result of the increased complexity of requirements and sophistication of materials. They now have control over the process to a degree that the unselfconscious craftsman never had. But the more control they get, the greater the cognitive burden and the greater the effort they spend in trying to deal with it, the more obscure becomes the causal structure of the problem which needs to be expressed for a well-fitting solution to be created. Increasingly, the very individuality of the designer is turning into its opposite: instead of being a solution, it is the main obstacle to a solution to the problem of restoring equilibrium between form and context.

In his 1964 work, Alexander produced a semi-algorithmic, mechanistic 'programme' based on functional decomposition (supported by a mathematical description in an appendix) to address the issues he identified. He has long since abandoned that prescription. It is the rather more informal drawings he used in the worked example that seem to have a more lasting significance. These became the basis, it seems, for the patterns in his later work.

Alexandrian 'theory' is currently expressed in an 11-volume-strong literary project that does not include his 1964 work. Eight of these volumes have been published so far (though, at best, three of them, referred to as the patterns trilogy, *The Timeless Way of Building*, *A Pattern Language* and *The Oregon Experiment*, are

---

job of patterns is to instil this genetic code into structures.

familiar to parts of the software patterns movement).[5] The ninth volume in the series, *The Nature of Order*, is eagerly awaited as it promises to provide the fullest exposition yet of the underlying theory. A common theme of all the books is the rejection of abstract categories of architectural or design principles as being entirely arbitrary. Also rejected is the idea that it is even possible to successfully design 'very abstract forms at the big level' (Alexander, 1996, p.8). For Alexander architecture attains its highest expression, not at the level of gross structure, but actually in its finest detail, what he calls 'fine structure'. That is to say, the macroscopic clarity of design comes from a consistency; a geometric unity holds true at all levels of scale. It is not possible for a single mind to envision this recursive structure at all levels in advance of building it. It is in this context that his patterns for the built environment must be understood.

Alexander *et al.* (1977) present an archetypal pattern language for construction. The language is an interconnected network of 253 patterns that encapsulate design best practice at a variety of levels of scale, from the siting of alcoves to the construction of towns and cities. The language is designed to be used collaboratively by all the stakeholders in a development, not just developers. This is premised, in part at least, by the idea that the real experts in buildings are those that live and work in them rather than those that have formally studied architecture or structural engineering. The patterns are applied sequentially to the construction itself. Each state change caused by the application of a pattern creates a new context to which the next pattern can be applied. The overall development is an emergent property of the application of the pattern language. The language therefore has a generative character: it generates solutions piece-meal from the successive addressing of each individual problem that each of the patterns addresses separately.

WAIST-HIGH SHELF (number 201 in the language) is an example pattern. It proposes the building of waist-high shelves around main rooms to hold the 'traffic' of objects that are handled most so that they are always immediately at hand. Clearly the specific form, depth, position and so on of these shelves will differ from house to house and workplace to workplace. The implementation of the pattern creates, therefore, a very specific context in which other patterns such as THICKENING THE OUTER WALL (number 211) can be used since Alexander suggests the shelves be built into the very structure of the building where appropriate, and THINGS FROM YOUR LIFE (number 253) to populate the shelves.

The pattern which more than any other is the physical and procedural embodiment of Alexander's approach to design, however, is pattern number 208, GRADUAL STIFFENING:

The fundamental philosophy behind the use of pattern languages is that buildings

---

[5] These three books along with *The Linz Café*, *The Production of Houses, A New Theory of Urban Design, A Foreshadowing of 21st Century Art* and *The Mary Rose Museum* are published by Oxford University Press. In preparation are *The Nature of Order, Sketches of a New Architecture* and *Battle: The Story of an Historic Clash Between World System A and World System B.*

should be uniquely adapted to individual needs and sites; and that the plans of buildings should be rather loose and fluid, in order to accommodate these subtleties....

Recognize that you are not assembling a building from components like an erector set, but that you are instead weaving a structure which starts out globally complete, but flimsy; then gradually making it stiffer but still rather flimsy; and only finally making it completely stiff and strong. (Alexander et al., 1977, pp. 963–9.)

In the description of this pattern Alexander invites the reader to visualize a 50-year-old master carpenter at work. He keeps working, apparently without stopping, until he eventually produces a quality product. The smoothness of his labour comes from the fact that he is making small, sequential, incremental steps such that he can always eliminate a mistake or correct an imperfection with the next step. He compares this with the novice who with a 'panic-stricken attention to detail' tries to work out everything in advance, fearful of making an unrecoverable error. Alexander's point is that most modern architecture has the character of the novice's work, not the master craftsman's. Successful construction processes, producing well-fitting forms, come from the postponement of detail design decisions until the building process itself so that the details are fitted into the overall, evolving structure.

Alexander's ideas seem to have been first introduced into the object-oriented community by Kent Beck and Ward Cunningham. In a 1993 article in *Smalltalk Report* Beck claimed to have been using patterns for six years already, but the software patterns movement seems to have been kicked off by a workshop on the production of a software architect's handbook organized by Bruce Anderson for OOPSLA'91. Here met for the first time Erich Gamma, Richard Helm, Ralph Johnson and John Vlissides – a group destined to gain notoriety as the Gang of Four (GoF). Gamma was already near to completion of his PhD thesis on 'design patterns' in the ET++ framework (Gamma, 1992). He had already been joined by Helm in the production of an independent catalogue. By the time of a follow-up meeting at OOPSLA in 1992, first Vlissides and then Johnson had joined the effort and, sometime in 1993, the group agreed to write a book that has been a best-seller ever since its publication in 1995. In fact, outside the patterns movement itself, many in the software development industry identify software patterns completely and totally with the GoF book.

However, the 1991 OOPSLA workshop was only the first in a series of meetings that culminated first in the formation of the non-profit Hillside Group[6] (apparently so-called because they went off to a hillside one weekend to try out Alexander's building patterns) and then the first Pattern Languages of Programming (PLoP) conference in 1994. PLoP conferences, organized and funded by the Hillside Group, take place annually in America, Germany and Australia and collections of the patterns that are

---

[6] The founding members were Ken Auer, Kent Beck, Grady Booch, Jim Coplien, Ward Cunningham, Hal Hildebrand and Ralph Johnson. The initial sponsors were Rational and the Object Management Group.

produced are published in a series by Addison-Wesley – four volumes to date. In addition the Hillside Group maintains a web site and numerous pattern mailing lists (Hillside Group, 2000). These communication channels form the backbone of a large and growing community that is rightly called the patterns movement.

A characteristic of the way patterns are developed for publication in the patterns movement is the so-called pattern writers' workshop. This is a form of peer-review which is loosely related to design reviews that are typical in software development processes, but more strongly related to poetry circles which are decidedly atypical. The special rules of the pattern writers' workshop (which are the *modus operandi* of the PLoP conferences) have been shown to be powerful in producing software patterns, written in easily accessible, regular forms known as **pattern templates**, at an appropriate level of abstraction. Rising (1998) reports on their effectiveness in producing a patterns' culture in the telecommunications company AGCS; and they are *de rigeur* in parts of IBM, Siemens and AT&T, all of which are known to have produced their own in-house software patterns, as well as publishing them in the public domain.

While the GoF book has won deserved recognition for raising the profile of patterns, for many it has been a double-edged sword. The GoF patterns form a catalogue of standalone patterns all at a similar level of abstraction. Such a catalogue can never have the generative quality that Alexander's pattern language claims for itself and, to be fair, the Gang of Four freely admit that this was not the aim of their work.

The GoF book includes 23 useful design patterns, including the following particularly interesting and useful ones:

- FAÇADE. Useful for implementing object wrappers: combines multiple interfaces into one.
- ADAPTER. Also useful for wrappers: converts interfaces into ones understandable by clients.
- PROXY. Mainly used to support distribution: creates a local surrogate for a remote object to enable access to it.
- OBSERVER. This helps an object to notify registrants that its state has changed and helps with the implementation of blackboard systems.
- VISITOR and STATE. These two patterns help to implement dynamic classification.
- COMPOSITE. Allows clients to treat parts and wholes uniformly.
- BRIDGE. Helps with decoupling interfaces from their implementations.

Some cynics claim that some of the GoF patterns are really only useful for fixing deficiencies in the C++ language. Examples of these might arguably include DECORATOR and ITERATOR. However, this very suggestion raises the issue of language-dependent vs. language-independent patterns. Buschmann *et al.* (1996) (also known as the Party of Five or PoV) from Siemens in Germany suggest a system of patterns that can be divided into architectural patterns, design patterns and language idioms. They present examples of the first two categories. Architectural patterns include: PIPES AND FILTERS, BLACKBOARD systems, and the MODEL VIEW

CONTROLLER (MVC) pattern for user interface development. Typical PoV design patterns are called:

- FORWARDER RECEIVER;
- WHOLE PART; and
- PROXY.

The reader is advised by the PoV to refer to all the GoF patterns as well. The PoV book can therefore be regarded as an expansion of the original catalogue, not merely through the addition of extra patterns, but by addressing different levels of abstraction too. The WHOLE-PART pattern is exactly the implementation of the composition structures that form part of basic object modelling semantics. In that sense it appears to be a trivial pattern. However, since most languages do not support the construct, it can be useful to see the standard way to implement it. It is a rare example of an analysis pattern that maps directly to an idiom in several languages: a multi-language idiom. The best known source of idiomatic (i.e. language-specific) patterns is Jim Coplien's book on advanced C++ which predates the GoF book by some three years (Coplien, 1992). C++ 'patterns' (the book does not use the term) that Coplien presents include:

- HANDLE CLASS, used to encapsulate classes that bear application intelligence;
- REFERENCE COUNTER, managing a reference count to shared representation;
- ENVELOPE-LETTER permits 'type migration' of classes;
- EXEMPLAR enables the creation of prototypes in the absence of delegation;
- AMBASSADOR provides distribution transparency.

Whilst experienced object-oriented programmers will feel immediately familiar with many of these patterns, almost everyone will recognize the ideas behind caches and recursive composites. These too can be regarded as design and/or analysis patterns. CACHE should be used when complex computations make it better to store the results rather than recalculate often; or when the cost of bringing data across a network makes it more efficient to store them locally. Clearly this is a pattern having much to do with performance optimization. It is also worth noting that patterns may use each other; this pattern may make use of the OBSERVER pattern (see below) when it is necessary to know that the results need to be recalculated or the data refreshed. This can be done eagerly or lazily, depending on the relative read and update profiles.

Although it is often good practice – unless dealing with derived dependencies – to document structures such as inheritance and aggregation separately, as we saw in Chapter 6, documenting patterns often requires that they are expressed in terms of more than one structure. Recursive, extensible structures such as binary trees and lists are a good example: a list is recursively composed of an atomic head and a tail which is itself a list, and a program is made up of primitive statements and blocks that are themselves made of blocks and statements. We can use a Catalysis framework template to document a general case as in Figure 7.4, in which one might substitute Block for <Node>, Program for <Branch> and Statement for <Leaf>.

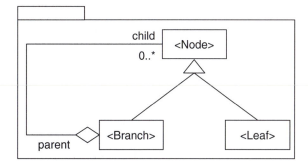

Figure 7.4 Recursive composites.

We process recursive structures by recursive descent and need to specify – in the template – whether looping is prevented by including constraints. In OCL such a constraint can be written[7]:

context Node::ancestors = parent + parent.ancestors AND
context Node:: not(ancestors includes self)

The list and the block patterns can be regarded as whole objects or wrappers and the pattern merely describes their internal structure.

The above examples indicate that a standard pattern layout may be beneficial, and many proponents adopt a standard based on Alexander's work: the so-called Alexandrian form. This divides pattern descriptions into prose sections with suitable pictorial illustrations as follows – although the actual headings vary from author to author.

- Pattern name and description.
- Context (Problem) – situations where the patterns may be useful and the problem that the pattern solves.
- Forces – the contradictory forces at work that the designer must balance.
- Solution – the principles underlying the pattern and how to apply it (including examples of its realization, consequences and benefits).
- Also Known As/Related patterns – other names for (almost) the same thing and patterns that this one uses or might occur with.
- Known uses.

Kent Beck has produced a book of 92 Smalltalk idioms (Beck, 1997) and there have been a number of language-specific 'versions' of the GoF book, notably for Smalltalk (Alpert *et al.*, 1998) and Java (Grand, 1998; Cooper, 2000). Although many of the PoV architectural patterns exist also among the SEI's 'styles', it is crucial to note their different purposes. Both are abstracted from software development best practice, but by the SEI in order to collect and formalize (and presumably later

---

[7] Strictly speaking, addition is not defined over sets in OCL. The plus sign is an abbreviation introduced in Catalysis, with the advantage of symmetry. The correct OCL form is: Set1 -> union(Set2).

automate) them, by the PoV in order to further generalize that practice.

The overwhelming majority of software patterns produced to date have been design patterns at various levels of abstraction but Fowler (1997) introduces the idea of analysis patterns as opposed to design patterns. Fowler's patterns are reusable fragments of object-oriented specification models made generic enough to be applicable across a number of specific application domains. They therefore have something of the flavour of the GoF pattern catalogue (described in that book's subtitle as 'elements of reusable object-oriented software') but are even further removed from Alexander's generative concepts. Examples of Fowler's patterns include:

- PARTY: how to store the name and address of someone or something you deal with.
- ORGANIZATION STRUCTURE: how to represent divisional structure.
- POSTING RULES: how to represent basic bookkeeping rules.
- QUOTE: dealing with the different ways in which financial instrument prices are represented.

There are many more, some specialized into domains such as Health or Accounting.

The problem with these patterns is that even the simplest ones – like ACCOUNTABILITY – are really quite hard to understand compared to the difficulty of the underlying problem that they solve. One of us had three goes at reading the text before really understanding what was going on. At the end of this process he found that he knew the proposed solution already but would never have expressed it in the same terms.

Maiden *et al.* (1998) propose a pattern language for socio-technical system design to inform requirements validation thereof, based on the CREWS-SAVRE prototype discussed in Chapter 8. They specify three patterns as follows:

- MACHINE-FUNCTION: this represents a rule connecting the presence of a user action (a task script in our language) to a system requirement to support that action (an operation of a business object that implements the task). We feel that it is stretching language somewhat to call this rule a pattern.
- COLLECT-FIRST-OBJECTIVE-LAST: this pattern tells us to force the user to complete the prime transaction after the subsidiary ones; e.g. ATMs should make you take the card before the cash. (For a discussion of the psychological phenomenon of *completion* in user interface design, see Chapter 9.)
- INSECURE-SECURE-TRANSACTION: this suggests that systems should monitor their security state and take appropriate action if the system becomes insecure.

The value of these patterns may be doubted because, like Fowler's analysis patterns, they seem to state the obvious; and they fail to address the sort of task or system usage patterns represented by our task association sets or use case refinement. Also, it could be argued that they are nothing but design principles; just as *completion* provides a well-known design principle in HCI. On the other hand, their operationalization in the CREWS-SAVRE system indicates that they may have a specialized practical value in this and certain other contexts.

OTHER PATTERN TYPES

There has also been interest in developing patterns for organizational development (Coplien, 1995; O'Callaghan, 1997, 1997a, 1998). Coplien applies the idea of patterns to the software development process itself and observes several noteworthy regularities. These observations arose out of a research project sponsored by AT&T investigating the value of QA process standards such as ISO9001 and the SEI's Capability Maturity Model. Working from a base concept that real processes were characterized by their communication pathways, Coplien, together with Brad Cain and Neil Harrison, analysed more than 50 projects by medium-size, high productivity software development organizations, including the Borland team charged with developing the Quattro Pro spreadsheet product. The technique they used was to adapt CRC cards and to get, in a workshop situation, representatives of the development organization under focus to enumerate rôles (as opposed to job descriptions), identify and categorize the strength of the relationships between those rôles (as either Weak, Medium and Strong) and then to rôle-play the development process in order to validate their judgements. The information was then input into a Smalltalk-based system called Pasteur that produces a variety of different sociometric diagrams and measures. From these, Coplien *et al.* were able to identify the commonly recurring key characteristics of the most productive organizations and develop a 42-strong pattern language to aid the design of development organizations. Included in the language are patterns such as these:

- CONWAY'S LAW states that architecture always follows organization or *vice versa*;
- ARCHITECT ALSO IMPLEMENTS requires that the architect stands close to the development process;
- DEVELOPER CONTROLS PROCESS requires that the developers own and drive the development process, as opposed to having one imposed on them;
- MERCENARY ANALYST enables the 'off-line' reverse engineering and production of project documentation;
- FIREWALL describes how to insulate developers from the 'white noise' of the software development industry;
- GATEKEEPER describes how to get useful information in a timely manner to software developers.

A typical application of such organizational patterns is the combined use of GATEKEEPER and FIREWALL in, say, a situation where a pilot project is assessing new technology. The software development industry excels at rumour-mongering, a situation fuelled by the practice of vendors who make vapourware announcements long in advance of any commercial-strength implementations. Over-attention to the whispers on the industry grapevine, let alone authoritative-looking statements in the trade press, can seriously undermine a pilot project. Developers lose confidence in Java, say, because of its reputation for poor performance or a claimed lack of available tools. Yet, at the same time, some news is important: for example, the publication of Platform 2 for Java. A solution is to build official firewalls and then create a gatekeeper rôle where a nominated individual, or perhaps a virtual centre such as an Object Centre, is responsible for filtering and forwarding the useful and usable information as opposed to unsubstantiated scare stories, junk mail and even the attention of vendors' sales forces.

More interesting than the individual patterns themselves, however, is the underlying approach of Coplien's language which is much closer to the spirit of Alexander's work than anything to be found in the GoF or PoV books, for example. First, since its very scope is intercommunication between people, it is human-centred. Second, it is explicitly generative in its aim. Coplien argues that while software developers do not inhabit code in the way that people inhabit houses and offices, as professionals they are expert users of professional processes and organizations. Therefore, just as Alexander's language is designed to involve all the stakeholders of building projects (and, above all, the expertise of the users of the buildings) so process designers have to base themselves on the expertise of the victims of formal processes – the developers themselves. Coplien's attempt to create an avowedly Alexandrian pattern language seems to push the focus of his patterns away from descriptions of fragments of structure (as is typical in the GoF patterns) much more towards descriptions of the work that has to be done. In going beyond mere structure Coplien's patterns have much more of a feel of genuine architecture about them than do many other pattern types available.

In fact, it is clear that from common roots there are two polarized views of patterns abroad today. One view focuses on patterns as generic structural descriptions. They have been described, in UML books especially, as 'parameterized collaborations'. The suggestion is that you can take, say, the structural descriptions of the rôles that different classes can play in a pattern and then, simply by changing the class names and providing detailed algorithmic implementations, plug them into a software development. Patterns thus become reduced to abstract descriptions of potentially pluggable components. A problem with this simplistic view occurs when a single class is required to play many rôles simultaneously in different patterns. Erich Gamma has recently re-implemented the HotDraw framework, for example, in Java. One class, Figure, appears to collaborate in fourteen different overlapping patterns – it is difficult to see how the design could have been successful if each of these patterns had been instantiated as a separate component. More importantly, this view has nothing to say about how software projects should be put together, only what (fragments of) it might look like structurally. The other view regards them simply as design decisions (taken in a particular context, in response to a problem recognized as a recurring one). This view inevitably tends toward the development of patterns as elements in a generative pattern language.

Support for this comes from the work of Alan O'Callaghan and his colleagues in the Object Engineering and Migration group and Software Technology Research Laboratory at De Montfort University. O'Callaghan is the lead author of the ADAPTOR pattern language for migrating legacy systems to object and component-based structures. ADAPTOR was based initially on five projects, starting in 1993, in separate business areas and stands for Architecture-Driven And Patterns-based Techniques for Object Re-engineering. It currently encapsulates experiences of eight major industrial projects in four different sectors: telecommunications, the retail industry, defence and oil exploration. O'Callaghan argues that migrating to object technology is more than mere reverse engineering, because reverse engineering is usually (a) formal and (b) focused purely on the functional nature of the legacy systems in question and (c) assumes a self-similar architecture to the original one. The most crucial information, about the original design rationales, has already been lost irretrievably. It cannot be retrieved from the code because the code never contained that information (unless, of course, it was written in an unusually expressive way). The best that traditional archaeological approaches to reverse engineering can achieve is to recreate the old system in an object-oriented 'style' which, more often than not, delivers none of the required benefits.

The approach, pioneered by Graham (1995) and O'Callaghan, was to develop object models of the required 'new' system and the legacy system and, by focusing on the maintainers and developers (including their organizational structure) rather than the code or design documentation, determine only subsequently what software assets might already exist that could be redeployed. O'Callaghan's group turned to patterns in the search for some way of documenting and communicating the common practices that were successful in each new project (legacy systems present especially wicked problems and are, overall, always unique unto themselves). At first, public domain, standalone design patterns were used but quickly his team were forced to mine their own. Then problems of code ownership (i.e. responsibility for part of a system being re-engineered belonging to someone other than the immediate client), caused by the fact that migrations typically involve radical changes at the level of the gross structure of a system, required that organizational and process problems be addressed also through patterns. Finally, observations that the most powerful patterns in different domains were interconnected suggested the possibility of a generative pattern language.

ADAPTOR was announced in 1998 as a 'candidate, open, generative pattern language'. It is a candidate language for two reasons: first, despite the overwhelming success of the projects from which it is drawn ADAPTOR is not comprehensive enough in its coverage or recursed to a sufficient level of detail to be, as yet, truly generative. Secondly, O'Callaghan has different level of confidence in the different patterns with only those having gone through the patterns workshops of the patterns movement being regarded as fully mature. Patterns yet to prove themselves in this way are regarded as candidate patterns. ADAPTOR is open in a number of senses too. First, like any true language, both the language itself and the elements that comprise it are evolvable. Many of the most mature patterns, such as GET THE MODEL FROM THE PEOPLE, which was first presented in 1996 at a TelePlop workshop, have gone through numbers of iterations of change. Secondly, following Alexander *et al.* (1977), O'Callaghan insists that patterns are open abstractions themselves. Since no true pattern provides a complete solution and every time it is applied it delivers different results (because of different specific contexts to which it is applied), it resists the kind of formalization that closed abstractions such as rules can be subject to. Finally, and uniquely amongst published software pattern languages, ADAPTOR is open because it makes explicit use of other public-domain pattern languages and catalogues, such as Coplien's generative development-process language already cited, or the GoF and PoV catalogues.

Patterns in ADAPTOR include the following.

- GET THE MODEL FROM THE PEOPLE requires utilization of the maintainers of a legacy system as sources of business information.
- PAY ATTENTION TO THE FOLKLORE treats the development/maintenance communities as domain experts, even if they don't do so themselves.
- BUFFER THE SYSTEM WITH SCENARIOS gets the main business analysts, marketers, futurologists, etc. to rôle-play alternative business contexts to the one they bet on in their requirements specifications.
- SHAMROCK divides a system under development into three loosely coupled 'leaves' – each of which could contain many class categories or packages; the leaves are the conceptual domain (the problem space objects), the infrastructure domain (persistence, concurrency, etc.) and the interaction domain (GUIs, inter-system protocols, etc.).
- TIME-ORDERED COUPLING clusters classes according to common change rates to accommodate flexibility to change.
- KEEPER OF THE FLAME sets up a rôle whereby the detailed design decisions can be assured to be in continuity with the architecture – changes to the gross structure are permitted if deemed necessary and appropriate.
- ARCHETYPE creates object types to represent the key abstractions discovered in the problem space.
- SEMANTIC WRAPPER creates wrappers for legacy code that present behavioural interfaces of identifiable abstractions to the rest of the system.

Something of the open and generative character aspired to by ADAPTOR can be gained from looking at the typical application of patterns to the early phases of a legacy system migration project. Underpinning ADAPTOR is the model-driven approach described earlier. O'Callaghan's problem space models comprise object types and the relationships between them, which capture the behaviour of key abstractions of the context of the system as well as the system itself. ARCHETYPE is therefore one of the first patterns used, along with GET THE MODEL FROM THE PEOPLE and PAY ATTENTION TO THE FOLKLORE. At an early stage strategic 'what-if' scenarios are run against this model using BUFFER THE SYSTEM WITH SCENARIOS. SHAMROCK is applied in order to decouple the concept domain object types from the purely system resources needed to deliver them at run time. The concept domain 'leaf' can then be factored into packages using TIME-ORDERED COUPLING to keep types with similar change rates (discovered through the scenario-buffering) together. Coplien's CONWAY'S LAW is now utilized to design a development organization that is aligned with the evolving structure of the system. CODE OWNERSHIP (another Coplien pattern) makes sure that every package has someone assigned to it with responsibility for it. An ADAPTOR pattern called TRACKABLE COMPONENT ensures that these 'code owners' are responsible for publishing the interfaces of their packages that others need to develop to, so that they can evolve in a controlled way. The GoF pattern FAÇADE is deployed to create a scaffolding for the detailed structure of the system. It is at this point that decisions can be made as to which pieces of functionality require new code and which can make use of legacy code. The scaffolding ensures that these decisions, and their implementation consequences, can be dealt with at a rate completely under the control and at the discretion of the development team without fear of runaway ripple effects. For the latter, SEMANTIC WRAPPERs are used to interface the old legacy stuff to the new object-oriented bits.

Even with this cursory example we can see how the language addresses all of the important issues of architecture (client's needs, conceptual integrity, structure, process and organization, etc.) as well as getting quickly to the heart of the issues of legacy migration. O'Callaghan reports that, when outlining this approach at a public tutorial, one member of the audience objected that the model-driven approach was not re-engineering at all but just 'forward engineering with the reuse of some legacy code'. In reply, O'Callaghan agreed and stated that that was just the point. On further consideration, he decided that many of ADAPTOR's patterns were not specific to legacy migration at all. As a result ADAPTOR is currently being regarded as a subset of a more general language on architectural praxis for software development in a project codenamed the Janus project (O'Callaghan, 2000b).

The debate about the nature of software patterns ('parametrized collaborations' *versus* 'design decisions'; pattern catalogues *versus* pattern languages) itself both reflects, and affects, the debates about software architecture discussed in the previous section. That relationship has been sharply exposed by Coplien's guest editorship of *IEEE Software* magazine in the Autumn of 1999. The issue was a special feature on software architecture in which Coplien published, amongst others, Alexander's keynote talk to the OOPSLA conference in San Jose, California in 1996 (Alexander, 1999). In his editorial, re-evaluating the architectural metaphor, Coplien identified two fundamental approaches to software development: the 'blueprint' or 'masterplan' approach *versus* that of 'piecemeal growth' (Coplien, 1999). Coplien suggests that the immature discipline of software architecture is suffering from 'formal envy' and has borrowed inappropriate lessons from both the worlds of hardware engineering and the built environment. Symptoms of its crisis are the separation of the deliverables of architecture from the artefacts delivered to the customer and the reification of architecture as a separate process in a waterfall approach to software development. Following the architect of the built environment Ludwig Miles van der Rohe, Coplien proclaims, as does Alexander as we have seen, that 'God lives in the details' and that clarity at the macro level can only be judged by whether it incorporates the fine details successfully. He further asserts: 'The object experience highlights what had been important all along: architecture is not so much about software, but about the people who write the software' (p. 41).

The main point about coupling and cohesion is that it permits people to work socially to produce a piece of software and both recognize and value their own particular contribution. Coplien points to CRC cards and their use in object-oriented development as the classic example of software design's anthropomorphic nature. From this perspective, software patterns were the next wave in the advance of a software architectural practice of this kind. As Coplien quite rightly points out, the patterns movement has always celebrated the otherwise lowly programmer as the major source of architectural knowledge in software development. Beyond that it recognizes the deep character of the relationship between code's structure and the communication pathways between the people developing and maintaining it. In doing so, Coplien argues, patterns have taken software development beyond the naïve practice of the early days of objects, which fell short of its promise because it was still constrained by a purely modular view of software programs, inherited from the previous culture. Further advance requires liberation from the weight of 'the historic illusions of formalism and planning' (p. 42).

Richard Gabriel, who is currently a member of the Hillside Group, a master software practitioner as well as a practising poet,[8] suggests that there are two reasons why all successful software development is in reality piecemeal growth. First, there is the cognitive complexity of dealing not only with current, but possible future, causes of change which make it impossible to completely visualize a constructible software program in advance to the necessary level of detail with any accuracy (Gabriel, 1996). Second, there is the fact that pre-planning alienates all but the planners. Coplien, Gabriel and the entire patterns movement are dedicated to developing practices that combat this social alienation. In doing so they impart a profound social and moral obligation to the notion of software architecture. In the face of these stark realities the only alternative to piecemeal growth is the one once offered by David Parnas: fake the blueprints by reverse engineering them once the code is complete.

7.2.1 Design patterns for decoupling

To get the true benefits of polymorphism – or 'pluggability' – in a program, it is important to declare variables and parameters not with explicit classes, but via an interface (abstract class in C++, interface in Java, deferred class in Eiffel). Looking at the metaphor of a café used in Figure 7.5, our initial model has **Food** used by both **Kitchen** and **Cash Register**. But these clients need different behaviour from **Food**, so we separate their requirements into different interfaces: **Edible** for the kitchen's requirements of food, and **Saleable** for the till's. By doing this, we have made the design more flexible – and the business too: because now we can consider edible things that are not saleable (ingredients such as flour), and saleable things that are not edible – we could start selling newspapers in our café. Our original **Food** class happens to implement both interfaces. Some good programmers insist that we should always use interfaces to declare variables and parameters. Simple multiple inheritance of rôle-types can be considered a pattern for composing collaborations. (In untyped languages such as Smalltalk, the difference appears only in our design

---

[8] The rules of the pattern writers' workshops, which are the way of working of the PLoP conferences, are attributed to Gabriel.

model, and does not appear in the program.)

Using interfaces is the basic pattern for reducing dependencies between classes. A class represents an implementation; an interface represents the specification of what a particular client requires. So declaring an interface pares the client's dependency on others down to the minimum: anything will do that meets the specification represented by the interface.

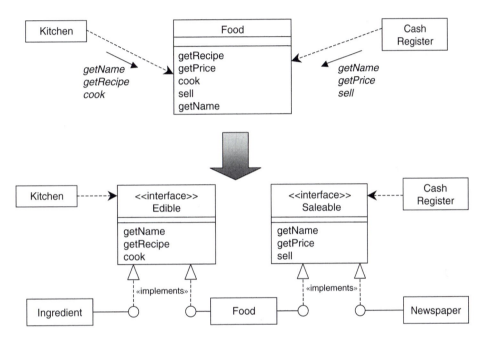

Figure 7.5 Interface decoupling.

DECOUPLING WITH FACTORY   When we add a new class to a program, we want to alter code at as few places as possible. Therefore, one should minimize the number of points where classes are explicitly mentioned. As we have discussed, some of these points are in variable and parameter declarations: use interface names there instead. The other variation points are where new instances are created. An explicit choice of class has to be made somewhere (using **new Classname**, or in some languages, by cloning an existing object).

FACTORY patterns are used to reduce this kind of dependency. We concentrate all creations into a **factory**. The factory's responsibility is to know what classes there are, and which one should be chosen in a particular case. The factory might be a method, or an object (or possibly one rôle of an object that has associated responsibilities). As a simple example, in a graphical editor, the user might create new shapes by typing 'c' for a new circle, 'r' for a new rectangle and so on. Somewhere we must map from keystrokes to classes, perhaps using a switch statement or in a table. We do that in the shape factory, which will typically have a method called something like make ShapeFor(char keystroke). Then, if we change the design to permit a new kind of shape, we would add the new class as a subclass of Shapes and alter the factory. More typically, there will be a menu that initializes from a table of icons and names of shape types.

Normally one would have a separate factory for each variable feature of the design: one factory for creating shapes and a separate one for creating pointing-device handlers.

A separate factory class can have subclasses. Different subclasses can provide different responses as to which classes should be created. For example, suppose we permit the user of a drawing editor to change mode between creating plain shapes and creating decorated ones. We add new classes like FancyTriangles to accompany the plain ones but, instead of providing new keystrokes for creating them explicitly, we provide a mode switch – whose effect is to alter this pointer in the Editor:

ShapeFactory shapeFactory;

Normally, this points to an instance of PlainShapeFactory, which implements ShapeFactory. When given the keystroke 'c' or the appropriate file segment, this factory creates a normal circle. But we can reassign the pointer to an instance of FancyShapeFactory, which, given the same input, creates a FancyCircle. Gamma *et al.* (1995) call classes like ShapeFactory ABSTRACT FACTORIES. It declares all the factory messages like makeShapeFor(keystroke), but its subclasses create different versions.

DECOUPLING WITH DELEGATION Programmers new to object-oriented design can get over-enthusiastic about inheritance. A naïve analysis of a hotel system might conclude that there are several kinds of hotel, which allocate rooms to guests in different ways; and a naïve designer might therefore create a corresponding set of subclasses of Hotel in the program code, overriding the room-allocation method in the different subclasses:

```
class Hotel {...
    public void checkInGuest(...)
    ...
    abstract protected Room allocateRoom (...);
    ...}
class LeastUsedRoomAllocatingHotel extends Hotel
{   protected Room allocateRoom (...)
    {      // allocate least recently used room
    ...}
}
class EvenlySpacedRoomAllocatingHotel extends Hotel
{   protected Room allocateRoom (...)
    { // allocate room furthest from other occupied
```

This is not a very satisfactory tactic: it cannot be repeated for other variations in requirements, for example if there are several ways of paying the staff. Overriding methods is one of the shortest blind alleys in the history of object-oriented programming. In practice, it is useful only within the context of a few particular patterns (usually those concerned with providing default behaviour). Instead, the trick is to move each separate behavioural variation into a separate object. We define a new interface for room allocation, for staff payment, and so on; and then define various concrete implementations for them. For example, we might write:

```
class Hotel {
    Allocator allocator; ...
    public void checkInGuest (...)
    {... allocator.doAllocation(...);..}
...}
interface Allocator{
    Room doAllocation (...); // returns a free room
...}
class LeastUsedAllocator implements Allocator
{  Room doAllocation (...) {...code ...}}
class EvenSpaceAllocator implements Allocator
{  Room doAllocation (...) {...code ...}}
```

This pattern of moving behaviour into another object is called DELEGATION. It has some variants, described differently depending on your purpose. One benefit of delegation is that it's possible to change the room allocator (for example) at run time, by 'plugging in' a new **Allocator** implementation to the allocator variable. Where the objective is to do this frequently, the pattern is called STATE.

Another application of DELEGATION is called POLICY: this separates business-dependent routines from the core code; so that it is easy to change them. Room allocation is an example. Another style of POLICY checks, after each operation on an object, that certain business-defined constraints are matched, raising an exception and cancelling the operation if not. For example, the manager of a hotel in a very repressed region of the world might wish to ensure that young people of opposite genders are never assigned rooms next to each other; the rule would need to be checked whenever any room-assigning operation is done.

DECOUPLING WITH EVENT, OBSERVER AND MVC Interfaces decouple a class from explicit knowledge of how other objects are implemented; but in general there is still some knowledge of what the other object does. For example, the **RoomAllocator** interface includes **allocateRoom(guest)** – it is clear what the **Hotel** expects from any **RoomAllocator** implementation. But sometimes it is appropriate to take decoupling a stage further, so that the sender of a message does not even know what the message will do. For example, the hotel object could send a message to interested parties whenever a room is assigned or becomes free. We could invent various classes to do something with that information: a counter that tells us the current occupancy of a room, a reservations system, an object that directs the cleaning staff, and so on.

These messages are called **events**. An event conveys information; unlike the normal idea of an operation, the sender has no particular expectations about what it will do; that is up to the receiver. The sender of an event is designed to be able to send it to other parties that register their interest; but it does not have to know anything about their design. Events are a very common example of decoupling.

To be able to send events, an object has to provide an operation whereby a client can register its interest; and it has to be able to keep a list of interested parties. Whenever the relevant event occurs, it should send a standard notification message to each party on the list.

An extension of the EVENT pattern is OBSERVER. Here the sender and listener are called Subject and Observer, and an event is sent whenever a change occurs in the sender's state. By this means, the observers are kept up to date with changes in the subject. New observers may be added easily as subtypes as shown in Figure 7.6.

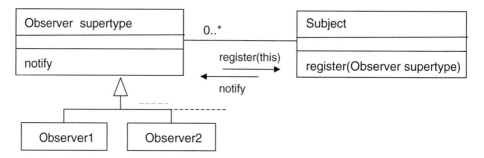

Figure 7.6 OBSERVER.

A very common application of OBSERVER is in user interfaces: the display on the screen is kept up to date with changes in the underlying business objects. Two great benefits of this usage are:

1. the user interface can easily be changed without affecting the business logic;
2. several views of a business object can be in existence at a time – perhaps different classes of view.

For example, a machine design can be displayed both as an engineering drawing and as a bill of materials; any changes made via one view are immediately reflected in the other. Users of word processors and operating systems are also familiar with changes made in one place – perhaps to a file name – appearing in another. It is only very old technology in which a view needs to be prompted manually to reflect changes made elsewhere. Another common use of OBSERVER is in blackboard systems.

The OBSERVER pattern has its origin in the MODEL-VIEW-CONTROLLER (MVC) pattern (or 'paradigm' as it is often mistakenly called), first seen in the work of Trygve Reenskaug on Smalltalk in the 1970s, and now visible in the Java AWT and Swing libraries. The MVC metaphor also influenced several object-oriented and object-based visual programming languages such as Delphi and Visual Basic.

An MVC **model** is an object in the business part of the program logic: not to be confused with our other use of the term 'modelling'. A **view** is an observer whose job it is to display the current state of the model on the screen, or whatever output device is in use: keeping up to date with any changes that occur. In other words, it translates from the internal representation of the model to the human-readable representation on the screen. **Controller** objects do the opposite: they take human actions, keystrokes and mouse movements, and translate them into operations that the model object can understand. Note, in Figure 7.7, that OBSERVER sets up two-way visibility between model and controller as well as model and view. Controllers are not visible to views, although part of a view may sometimes be used as a controller: cells in a spreadsheet are an example.

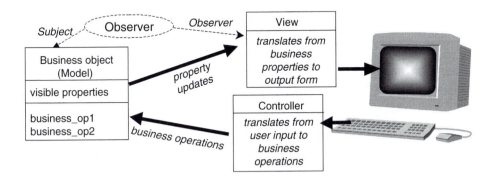

Figure 7.7 MODEL-VIEW-CONTROLLER instantiates OBSERVER.

Views are often nested, since they represent complex model objects, which form whole–part hierarchies with others. Each class of controller is usually used with a particular class of views, since the interpretation of the user's gestures and typing is usually dependent on what view the mouse is pointing at.

DECOUPLING WITH ADAPTER   In MVC, View and Controller are each specializations of the ADAPTER pattern (not to be confused with the ADAPTOR pattern language). An **adapter** is an object that connects two classes that were designed in ignorance of each other, translating events issued by one into operations on the other. The View translates from the property change events of the Model object to the graphical operations of the windowing system concerned. A Controller translates from the input events of the user's gestures and typing to the operations of the Model.

An adapter knows about both of the objects it is translating between; the benefit that it confers is that neither of them needs to know about the other, as we can see from the package dependency diagram in Figure 7.8.

Any collection of functions can be thought of as an adapter in a general sense; but the term is usually used in the context of event; that is, where the sender of a message does not know what is going to be done with it.

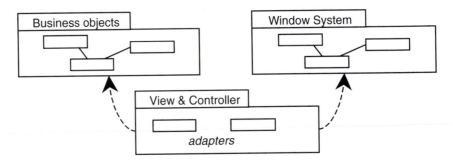

Figure 7.8 Adapters decouple the objects they connect.

Adapters appear in a variety of other contexts beside user interfaces, and also on a grander scale: they can connect components running in separate execution spaces. Adapters are useful as 'glue' wherever two or more pre-existing or independently designed pieces of software are to be made to work together.

DECOUPLING WITH PORTS AND CONNECTORS Adapters generally translate between two specific types – for example, from the keystrokes and mouse clicks of the GUI to the business operations of a business object. This means, of course, that one has to design a new adapter whenever one wants to connect members of a different pair of classes. Frequently, that is appropriate: different business objects need different user interfaces. But it is an attractive option to be able to reconfigure a collection of components without designing a new set of adapters every time.

To illustrate an example of a reconfigurable system, Figure 7.9 shows the plugs that connect a simple electronic system together, using the real-time UML instance/port or **capsule** notation. Ports are linked by **connectors**. A connector is not necessarily implemented as a chunk of software in its own right: it is often just a protocol agreed between port designers. We try to minimize the number of connector types in a kit, so as to maximize the chances of any pair of ports being connected. In our example, two types of connector are visible, which we can call **event connectors** and **property connectors** – which transmit, respectively, plain events and observed attributes. You can think of the components as physical machines or the software that represents them *a piacere*. The button pressed interface always exports the same voltage (or signal) when it is pressed. The start and stop interfaces interpret this signal differently according to the motor's state machine. The point about this component kit is that careful design of the interface protocols and plug-points allows it to be used for a completely (well, not quite completely!) different purpose as shown in Figure 7.10. The members of this kit of parts can be rewired to make many different end products, rather like a construction toy. The secret of this reconfigurability is that each component incorporates its own adapter, which translates to a common 'language' understood by many of the other components. Such built-in adapters are called **ports**; they are represented by the small boxes in the figure.

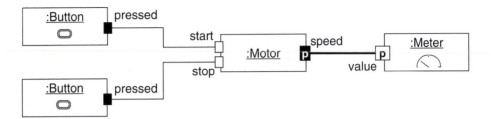

Figure 7.9 Component ports and event and property connectors.

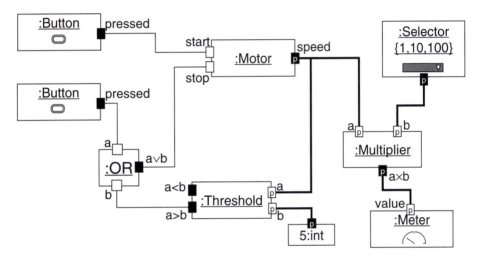

Figure 7.10 Creating different products from the same components.

The connector is such a useful abstraction that it deserves a notation in its own right: we have used the UML-RT notation here (with some artistic licence to highlight our two types of connector). The objects in this notation are stereotyped «capsule». The small black squares in this example are output ports and the white ones input ports. A 'p' indicates a continuous 'property' port: these transmit values as often as necessary to keep the receiving end up to date with the sender – in other words, an observer. Unmarked ports transmit discrete events. Property connectors are shown by bolder lines than event connectors.

Once we have understood what the ports represent, we can get on and design useful products from kits of components, without bothering about all the details of registering interest, notification messages, and so on.

Ports can contain quite complex protocols. Each component must be well-specified enough to be usable without having to look inside it. So let's consider one way a port might work, as shown in Figure 7.11. An output port provides messages that allow another object to register interest in the event it carries; when the relevant event occurs (for example, when the user touches a button component) the port sends a standard 'notify' message to all registered parties. An input port implements the LISTENER interface for these notify messages; when it receives one, it sends a suitable message into the body of its component. For example, the 'start' port of the **Motor** component, when it receives a standard notify( ) message, will pass start ( ) to the principal object representing the motor.

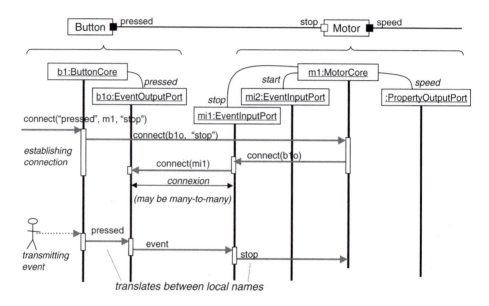

Figure 7.11 Connectors abstract protocols.

Property output ports in this scheme transmit events whenever the named attribute in the sender object changes – in other words, they implement the OBSERVER pattern. Property input ports update the named attribute in the receiver object. Thus the meter's value keeps up to date with the motor's speed, while they are connected.

A component **kit** is a collection of components with a coherent interconnexion architecture, built to work together; it is characterized by the definitions of its connectors – the protocols to which the ports conform. A **component kit architecture** defines how plugs and sockets work and what kinds there are. Of course, these definitions have to be standardized before the components themselves are written. Common object types (int, Aeroplane, etc.) should be understood by all kit members. The kit architecture is the base upon which component libraries are built. Applications may then be assembled from the components in the library – but without the kit architecture, the whole edifice of CBD collapses. There are usually many architectures that will work for any scheme of connectors: the Java Beans specification provides a slightly different (and better performing) set of protocols to the ones we have described here.

Designing the architecture involves design decisions. A port should be realized as an object in its own right. The port connectors abstract away from the details of the port's protocol, but this must be specified eventually. For example, the sequence diagram in Figure 7.11 shows just one way in which the button–motor interface can be implemented. The property coupling port could be similarly implemented, but with regular update of new values.

Although we have illustrated the principle of the connector with small components, the same idea applies to large ones, in which the connector protocols are more complex and carry complex transactions. The current concern with Enterprise Application Integration can be seen as the effort to replace a multiplicity of point-to-point protocols with a smaller number of uniform connectors.

When specifying ports, or capsules, specify the types of parameters passed, the interaction protocol and the language in which the protocol is expressed. The interaction protocol could be any of:

- Ada rendezvous;
- asynchronous call;
- broadcast;
- buffered message;
- call handover;

- complex transaction;
- continuous dataflow;
- FTP;
- function call;
- HTTP, and so on.

The interaction language could be:

- ASCII, etc.;
- CORBA message or event;
- DLL/COM call;
- HTML;
- Java RMI;
- Java serialized;

- plain procedure call;
- RS232;
- TCP/IP;
- UNIX pipe;
- XML;
- zipped.

7.3 Designing components

Writing in *Byte* John Udell tells us that 'Objects are dead!' and will be replaced by components. But he wrote this in May 1994, whereas objects didn't really hit the mainstream of information technology until around 1996/7. In fact, most CBD offerings that were around in 1994 didn't survive for very long after that: think of OpenDoc, OpenStep, Hyperdesk, etc. Probably the only significant survivor was the humble VBX. Currently, there are several understandings of what the term 'component' means. Some commentators just use it to mean any module. Others mean a deliverable object or framework: a unit of deployment. Still others mean a binary that can create instances (of multiple classes). Writers on object-oriented analysis tend to mean a set of interfaces with *offers* and *requires* constraints. The *requires* constraints are often called **outbound interfaces**. Daniels (2000) questions this and shows that while these aspects of a component must be defined, they do not form part of the component's contract. Szyperski (1998) defines a component as 'a binary unit of independent production, acquisition and deployment' and later 'A unit of composition with contractually specified interfaces and explicit context dependencies only'. We prefer: a unit of executable deployment that plays a part in a composition.

In many ways, VB is still the paradigm for component-based development. Components were needed initially because OOPLs were restricted to one address space. Objects compiled by different compilers (even in the same language) could not communicate with each other. Thus arose distribution technologies such as RPCs, DCOM, CORBA, and so on. In every case interfaces were defined separately from implementation, making OOP only one option for the actual coding of the objects.

In the late 1990s ERP vendors that surfed on the crest of the year 2000 and Euro conversion issues did well because their customers needed quick, all-embracing solutions. When that period ended their market was threatened by a return to more flexible systems that were better tailored to companies' requirements. One vendor was even quoted as saying that a large customer should change its processes to fit the package because the way they worked was not 'industry standard'. This arrogance would no longer be tolerable after 2000 and the vendors were seen to rush headlong to 'componentize' their offerings; i.e. introduce greater customizability into them.

A lot of the talk about components being different from (better than) objects was based on a flawed idea of what a business object was in the first place. Many developers assumed that the concept of an object was coextensive with the semantics of a C++ class or instance. Others based their understanding on the semantics of Smalltalk objects or Eiffel classes or instances. Even those who used UML classes or instances failed to supply enough semantic richness to the concept: typically ignoring the presence of rules and invariants and not thinking of packages as wrappers (see Chapter 6). Furthermore, an object will only work if all its required services (servers) are present. This was the standpoint of methods such as SOMA from as early as 1993. SOMA (Graham, 1995) always allowed message-server pairs as part of class specifications. These are equivalent to what Microsoft COM terminology calls outbound interfaces.

From one point of view, outbound interfaces violate encapsulation, because the component depends on collaborators that may change and so affect it. For example, the client of an order management service should not have to know that this component depends on a product management one; an alternative implementation might bundle everything up into one object. For this reason John Daniels (2000) argues that collaborations do not form part of an object's contract in the normal sense. He distinguishes usage contracts from implementation contracts. The latter do include dependencies, as they must to be of use to the application assembler. That more research is needed in this area is revealed by one of Daniels' own examples. Consider a financial trading system that collaborates with a real-time price feed. The user of the system should not care, on the above argument, whether the feed is provided by a well-known and reputable firm, such as Reuters, or by Price, Floggett & Runne Inc. But of course the user cares deeply about the reliability of the information and would differentiate sharply between these two suppliers. This example suggests that we should always capture the **effects** of collaborations as invariants or rulesets in the usage contracts, if not the collaborators themselves. The rules in this case would amount to a statement about the reputability of the information provider.

Current component-based development offerings include CORBA/OMA, Java Beans/EJB, COM/DCOM/ActiveX/COM+, TI Composer and the more academically based Component Pascal/Oberon. What these approaches all have in common is an emphasis on composition/forwarding, compound documents, transfer protocols (e.g. JAR files), event connectors (single or multi-cast), metadata and some persistence mechanism. Differentiators between the approaches include their approaches to interface versioning, memory management, adherence to standards (binary/binding/etc.), language dependence and platform support.

From a supplier's point of view components are usually larger than classes and may be implemented in multiple languages. They can include their own metadata and be assembled without programming (!). They need to specify what they require to run. These statements could almost be a specification for COM+ or CORBA. Such component systems are not invulnerable to criticism. The size of a component is often inversely proportional to its match to any given requirement. Also, components may have to be tested late; an extreme case being things that cannot be tested until the users downloads them (although applets are not really components in the sense we mean here). There is a tension between architectural standards and requirements, which can limit the options for business process change. Finally there is the problem of shared understanding between developers and users that we will discuss in Chapter 8. Szyperski discusses at length the different decision criteria used by each of infrastructure vendors and component vendors. He says nothing about the consequences for users. Can we deduce that users don't care about how components are developed? They certainly care about how they are assembled into applications.

Object modelling is about not separating processes from data. It is about encapsulation: separating interfaces from implementation. It is about polymorphism: inheritance and pluggability. It is about design by contract: constraints and rules. OO principles must be consistently applied to object-oriented programming, object-oriented analysis, business process modelling, distributed object design and components. However, there is a difference between conceptual models and programming models. In conceptual modelling both components and classes have identity. Therefore components are objects. Inheritance is as fundamental as encapsulation for the conceptual modeller. In programming models on the other hand components and classes do not have identity (class methods are handled by instances of factory classes). Thus components are not objects, class inheritance (or delegation) is dangerous and pluggability is the thing. So is there a rôle for inheritance? CBD plays down 'implementation inheritance' but not interface inheritance, but at the conceptual level this distinction makes no sense anyway.

When it comes to linking requirements models to analysis models, we can either 'dumb down' to a model that looks like the programming model (as most UML-based methods tend to do) or introduce a translation process between the models (e.g. the SOMA to Catalysis transformation suggested in Chapter 8). The trade-off concerns the degree to which users and developers can share a common understanding.

7.3.1 Components for flexibility

Component-based development is concerned with building extensible families of software products from new or existing kits of components. The latter may range in scale from individual classes to entire (wrapped) legacy systems or commercial packages. Doing this has hitherto proved an elusive goal for software developers. The trick is to realize that we need to define the interface protocols of objects in such a way that they can be plugged together in different ways. The number of interfaces needs to be small compared to the number of components. To improve flexibility these interfaces should permit negotiation in the same way as with facsimile machines or clipboard interfaces in Microsoft's OLE and the like.

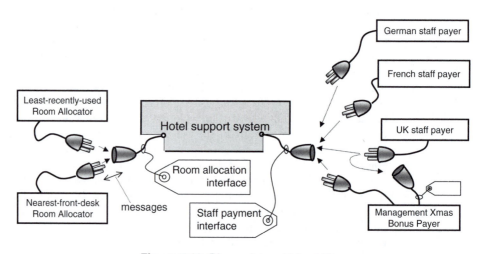

Figure 7.12 Plug-points add flexibility.

An example may suffice to explain the point. Consider an hotel support system that is originally written for a small chain of Scottish hotels. The original is a great success and pays for itself quickly. But the price of success is rapid expansion and the company now acquires several more hotels in England, Wales, France and Germany. In Scotland rooms are always allocated to new arrivals on the basis of the empty room nearest the reception desk – to save visitors wearing out their shoes walking long distances. But the spendthrift and gloomy English want peace and quiet more than these savings; so that rooms are allocated alternately, to leave empty rooms separating occupied ones when the hotel is not full. The Germans allocate rooms with French widows first. The different states involved also have different rules about wage payments. The system is amended piecemeal and soon there are several versions to maintain: one with nearest desk allocation and French payment rules, another with least-recently-used room allocation and UK staff payment laws and an *ad hoc* patch for management christmas bonuses in Ireland and the Netherlands, and so on. A maintenance disaster of some proportion!

A considerable improvement on arbitrary modification is shown in Figure 7.12. There is a basic framework, which does everything that is common between the requirements of all the hotels. Each separate variable requirement has been moved into a plug-in component: for example, there are different room-allocators; and different staff payment components. This arrangement makes it much easier to maintain and manage variants of the system. We separate the rôles of the framework-designer and the designers of the plug-in components – who are not allowed to change the framework.

This makes it very clear that **the most suitable basis for choosing components is that they should correspond to variable requirements**. This is a key rule which people sometimes forget, while still claiming to be doing component-based development.

One problem is that it is not always easy to foresee what requirements will be variable in the future. The best advice we can give here is as follows.

- Follow the principle of separation of concerns within the main framework, so that it is reasonably easy to refactor.
- Don't cater for generalizations that you don't know you are going to need: the work will likely be wasted. Observe the eXtreme Programming maxim: 'You ain't gonna need it!'.
- Where you do need to refactor the framework to introduce new plug-points, make one change at a time, and re-test after each change.

7.3.2 Large-scale connectors

In the previous section, we introduced the idea of connectors, using a Bean-scale example to illustrate the principle; the connectors transmitted simple events and property-values. But we can also use the same idea where the components are large applications running their own databases and interoperating over the internet. Recall that the big advantage of connectors over point-to-point interfaces was that we try to design a small number of protocols common to the whole network of components, so that they can easily be rearranged. In our small examples, that meant that we could pull components out of a bag and make many end-products; for large systems, it means that you can more easily rearrange the components as the business changes. This is a common problem being faced by many large and not-so-large companies.

For example, our hotel system might have a web server in Amsterdam, a central reservations system in Edinburgh, a credit card gateway in New Zealand, and local room allocation systems in each hotel world-wide. We would like to define a common connector, a common 'language' in which they all talk to one another, so that future reconfigurations need not involve writing many new adapters. Typical events in our hotels connector protocol will be customers arriving and leaving, paying bills; properties will include availability of rooms. The component kit architecture for such a network will have to specify:

- low level technology – whether it will use COM or CORBA, TCP/IP, etc.;
- a basic model of the business – what types of object are communicated between the components, customers, reservations, bills, etc.
- the syntax of the language in which the model will be transmitted – XML is often the solution;
- business transactions – e.g. how a reservation is agreed between the reservations system and a local hotel;
- business rules – is a customer allowed to have rooms in different hotels at the same time?

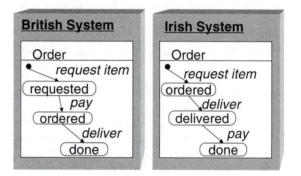

Figure 7.13 Incompatible business processes.

This point about business rules is sometimes forgotten at the modelling stage. But it is very important: if one component of the system thinks a customer can have two rooms whereas another thinks each customer just has one, there will be confusion when they try to interoperate. And it is not just a question of static invariants: the sequences in which things should happen matters too. For example, imagine a company that comprises two divisions in different states as a result of a merger. In Great Britain the business demands payment before delivery is made, whilst in Eire payment is demanded after delivery is made. The different business régimes can be illustrated by the two state transition models in Figure 7.13. Problems will arise if these systems pass orders to each other to fulfil, because when a British customer orders a widget from the Dublin branch, they pass the request to the British system in the ordered state. That system assumes payment has been made and delivers – so that lucky John Bull never pays a penny. Obversely, poor Paddy Riley, who orders from the London branch, is asked to pay twice.

7.3.3 Mapping the business model to the implementation

Catalysis provides specific techniques for component design. Actions are refined into collaborations and collaborations into ports. Retrievals (see Chapter 6) are used to reconcile components with the specification model. Consider the situation illustrated in Figure 7.14. Here there are two coarse-grained components for accounting and dispatch, but they are based on different business models. Any system that integrates them must be based on a type model that resolves the name conflicts in the base components. For example, our model must define customer in such a way that the subsidiary customer and payer concepts are represented. We must also include invariants to synchronize operations.

Interfaces cannot be fully described in programming languages; the context in which they are used (pragmatics) is relevant. Often the only reason people accept lists of operations as specifications is because their names suggest the expected behaviour. We must say what components do as well as what they are; i.e. include type models, invariants, rulesets and protocols. The first three were covered in Chapter 6, now let us now see how we can describe the protocols rigorously.

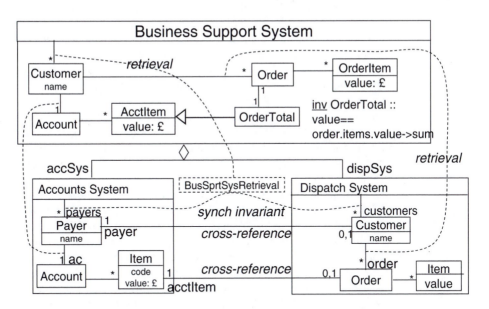

Figure 7.14 Retrieving a model from components.

Just as connectors must be encapsulated in objects, they can also be specialized and generalized. Templates, or frameworks, (see Chapter 6) are used to define connector classes. We define and specify each class and its interfaces. Next the connector classes are defined. Then message protocols for each class of connector can be defined using sequence and/or state diagrams. We must always ensure that a business model, common to all components, is clearly defined using a type model rich enough to define all parameters of the connector protocols. Points of potential variation should be handled using plug-points. Business rules should be encapsulated by the interfaces.

Components will be used in contexts unknown to their designer(s) and so need far better 'packaging' than simple, fine-grain classes in class libraries. They should be stored and delivered with full documentation, covering the full specification and all the interfaces and ports and their protocols. It is mandatory that components should be supplied therefore with their test harnesses. Good component architectures require that components should be able to answer queries about their connexions at run time: complaining rather than collapsing under abuse by other software.

7.3.4 Business components and libraries

There seem to be three competing conceptions of a business object in use. Perhaps the oldest is due to Oliver Sims (1994) who meant something representable by an icon that means something sensible to users. Ian Graham's conception of a business object developed independently at around the same time. He meant any *specification object* that is mentioned in business process and task descriptions. The third conception emerges from discussion within the OMG. Their Business Object Modelling interest group promulgated the idea of a business object as a commonly used **software** component that occurs in the domain terminology. We have problems with this last definition insofar as it restricts business objects to the territory of commercial software vendors and excludes our ambitions of being able to model businesses, tasks and agents and of keeping our reusable objects totally machine and language independent. The OMG conception of a business object in its current form excludes intelligent agents from being business objects because IDL objects cannot easily express semantics equivalent to rulesets. We expect, however, that this will change at some point in the future.

Components occur at all scales from GUI frameworks – like the Java AWT, VBXs and OCXs – through program parts – such as Java Beans – up to entire applications crossing the language barrier delivered as UNIX pipes or COM and OLE components – such as Excel. As we leave the boundary of a single computer and enter distributed space-time we encounter components packaged by CORBA, DCOM and Java RMT. There are several companies now claiming to offer libraries of business objects in vertical markets. These mostly consist of code libraries, an early, well-known one being the Infinity model for financial instruments. We have already mentioned the componentized ERP packages that are emerging at the time of writing these words. IBM's San Francisco was an early attempt to provide a whole library of business level components and design patterns (Monday *et al.*, 2000; Carey *et al.*, 2000). The Infinity offering uses a proprietary, but relational, data model known as Montage as the sub-structure upon which its C++ object model is built. This leads to performance problems, especially when complex derivative instruments are involved, because the database has to do many small joins to compose these complex composite objects. There is also a degree of incompleteness, with several instruments not being included in the model; users are expected to complete the model themselves. However, the product has been successfully used by several banks and is well suited to the smaller such institutions or to those not specializing in high volume derivatives markets. Infinity does not sell its abstract object model; it only offers the code. Some other offerings, that do represent themselves as abstract object models of financial instruments, are usually, in our experience, little more than re-badged data models.

Continuing with Finance as a typical domain for business object modelling, let us pause to consider what types of thing are suitable for modelling as business objects or not. The class of financial instruments seems to be a good candidate because every instrument has a clear, stable and unambiguous definition. However, there are well over 300 classes in even the crudest model of financial instruments. This means that building a stable classification structure is extremely difficult, even allowing for the use of interface decoupling. Furthermore, many financial products are composites. This leads to two completely different ways in which instruments can be modelled. The simplistic way is to build a broad, deep classification structure, noting the composition structures of each instrument as it arises. We have built such models and found them useful, if unwieldy. This is the approach taken by Infinity. A possibly more elegant approach exploits a theorem of financial engineering that says that every instrument is a composite of fundamental commodities and options on them. This means that instead of relying solely on classification structure we can also exploit composition. At least one important and successful risk management system at the Chase Manhattan Bank uses this approach. However, these general classification problems are still very tricky and should not be tackled by the inexperienced modeller. Smaller classification structures, however, are good candidates for inclusion in your first library of reusable specifications.

Corporate actions are a very good example of ideal candidates for business objects. There are (arguably) exactly 42^9 of them and they can easily be classified. Figure 7.15 shows a fragment of this classification structure. It can be seen immediately that even this structure is reasonably complex. Imagine what a structure with 350 classes would look like!

On the face of it, pricing algorithms appear not to be good candidates because they are pure function and, of course, proper objects must have data too. Reasoning in this way, the product should know how to price itself. However, in Finance there are many, many ways to price the same product, all of the algorithms being subject to evolution as new discoveries are made in financial engineering. It is therefore crazy to pack all these algorithms into Products. Here is a definite case where algorithms should be objects; these of course are nothing more nor less than function libraries resurrected in object-oriented form. And why ever not!

---

[9] Possibly answering a question posed by Douglas Adams.

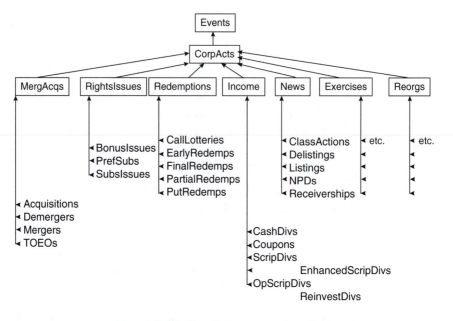

Figure 7.15 Classifying corporate actions.

Events, such as trades, payments, cash flows, etc., are more problematical. Trades go through complex life cycles that could perhaps be represented by state machines. We are thinking of states such as: quoted, agreed, affirmed, confirmed, matched, settled, etc. The difficulty here is that different instruments have very different life cycles: foreign exchange settles quite differently from equities. The question is whether we should attempt to design a business object **Trades** that covers all eventualities or have different ones for the different kinds of instrument. Our instinct as object designers tells us that a single **Trades** class should refer to a complex instrument hierarchy with each instrument responsible for knowing its peculiar life cycle. However, we have already mentioned that the instrument hierarchy is extremely complex, so that making it more so may be considered unattractive. In practice, this is a difficult decision that will be taken according to the circumstances and judgment of different organizations.

But what of our customers, regulators, and so on? These are the worst candidates for business objects that we can think of because there is no such thing as a customer. Look at your own company's computer systems. The likelihood is that every system has a different definition of what a customer is. This is not because all past generations of developer were brain dead. It is because each department relates **differently** to its customers. Looked at one way, customerhood is a *rôle* adopted by a legal entity. Equivalently we can say that customerdom is a *relation* between your organization and another. Thus your business object library should have what Martin Fowler would call a **Parties** class and a series of relations representing concepts like account customers, overseas customers, etc.

Business processes are often advanced as candidates for modelling as business objects. This is, we feel, both right and wrong. Having actual software objects to represent a process is only apposite for the simplest processes and can lead to horribly rigid workflow systems in our experience. However, the approach presented in the next chapter does use objects (agents, conversations and actions) to model business processes, albeit indirectly. This gives more flexibility and expressive power. Beware therefore of people selling 'business process objects'.

There seem to be several current conceptions of what a business object model is. We regard one as a model of the domain concepts expressed in terms of objects. Of course, it is not (in this sense) a model of the business and its processes. Neither is it a pure system model (until refined by logical design). Some commercial offerings labelled 'vertical business object model' are little more than re-badged data/process models, replete with false assumptions about business processes taken from the small number of other organizations that were used to finance the original development. Creating a business object model of your own may be thus a better solution. It will provide a tailor-made resource and gives you more control. Such a strategy permits you to optimize performance if necessary, for example by choosing appropriate database technology. Your approach can take advantage of new technology as these innovations come along. However, it can be very expensive.

Business objects have been hyped. If you are considering buying a commercial business object model, then ask yourself if the model fits your business or if you will have to adapt to its foibles. Beware particularly of data models in disguise as object models. These are common. Beware too of models extracted from coded implementations, especially when the implementation is in some non-object-oriented language such as PowerBuilder or Visual Basic. Ask the supplier to give you the history of the product with this consideration in mind. Ask too, if the model is implemented, how the database is implemented and designed: is performance going to be adequate for the type and scale of application you have? Use binaries only when you trust them. Buy or build the right middleware; and be prepared to pay for it. An architecture based on sound middleware decisions is the only basis for profitable gains from reuse.

The emphasis of CBD is on deployment architecture and packaging, and new design methods such as Catalysis are clearly indicated; but component-based *analysis* is something of an oxymoron. What is needed is a mapping from sound BPM/OOA techniques to component-based design, which derives use cases and actions from process models. Catalysis 'refinement' techniques then ensure traceability down on through the modelling to implementation.

It is still unclear whether there really is a mature component market. We have OCXs, we have Java Beans, we have San Francisco even; but undoubtedly the range and types of component on offer will grow. As this happens we will increasingly distinguish component building from application assembly, both requiring new development process models. We will also need to make methodological changes.

In our new methods inheritance must treated differently at the conceptual and component levels. It remains a fundamental concept for conceptual modelling and knowledge representation, and is readily understood by users. However, inheritance is not the ideal way to build flexibility into components, as we have seen; plug-points based on the patterns we have presented give far greater flexibility. We are, of course, endangering seamlessness slightly, but the price is well worth paying. In the same way, the principle of substitutability is crucial for the design of flexible components, but it is often counter-intuitive during conceptual modelling.

CBD is often contrasted with object-oriented development, as though they were quite different. One reason for this is that some (bad) object-oriented programming practice concentrated on very small objects at the expense of enterprise level ones and completely ignored collaborations (outbound interfaces) and interface semantics (rules, etc.). Emphasis was on weak object models based on languages rather than the sort of semantically rich conceptual models that OOA methods like SOMA always advocated. In this sense CBD merely tells us where some of us got OO wrong.

We may also conclude that successful CBD will require a heightened focus on architecture and patterns together with the semantically rich object modelling techniques mandated by methods such as Catalysis and SOMA. An organization adopting CBD should always discuss architecture and reuse up front. It must also **manage** the reuse process, as we discuss in Chapter 9. The main methodological changes are at the level of design, architecture and implementation.

Remember that models are powerful representations of knowledge, not just computer stuff! Object models can be used to represent many things: any kind of object knowledge, that is. The semantics of the modelling language you use must therefore be powerful enough to express this knowledge, which means that it should include class invariants (ideally rulesets), usage links and other features necessary to model business processes. This is because it is never enough just to model the computer system. A good model should include users' conversations, contracts, goals and tasks. Take control over the specification yourself rather than relying entirely on external suppliers.

Remember also that greenfield sites are the exception; most components will be used within a context of existing systems and these must be modelled as design level components. In many cases there will be a strong need for a repository of existing and buyable components and previous specifications (processes, objects, etc.). There should be a relatively fixed architectural framework.

⊟ 7.4 Summary

This chapter surveyed the emerging fields of software architecture, patterns and component design. We argued that architecture was more than just structure and must include vision or rationale. We also argued for its importance.

Several design, analysis, architectural and organizational patterns were introduced and we touched on the idea of pattern languages and related concepts like problem frames.

Building on this base, we made extensive use of patterns and concepts from Catalysis, such as retrievals, to show how to design robust, flexible component-based systems. Our emphasis was on techniques for decoupling components. Finally we looked at some issues surrounding the emergence of a market for components.

⊟ 7.5 Bibliographical notes

Shaw and Garlan (1996), Bass *et al.* (1998) and Bosch (2000) all discuss software architecture from a broadly structural perspective. Alan O'Callaghan's series of articles in *Application Development Advisor* [sic] provide a different view closer to the one expressed in this chapter.

Design patterns were introduced by Gamma *et al.* (1995). Buschmann *et al.* (1996) cover these together with architectural patterns. Pree (1995) is another early contribution in this area and introduced the idea of metapatterns. Fowler (1996) discusses analysis patterns, the idea of which was earlier suggested by Coad (1992). The annual proceedings of the PLoP conferences (Coplien and Schmidt, 1995; Vlissides *et al.*, 1996) are full of interesting exegesis and new patterns including the earliest work on organizational patterns (Coplien, 1995). Beck (1997) is an excellent exposition of how to use patterns in the context of Smalltalk, well worth reading by those not interested in that language. Coplien (1992) describes C++ idioms. Mowbray and Malveau (1997) discuss patterns for CORBA implementations. Much current work on patterns has been inspired by the work of Christopher Alexander and his colleagues (1964, 1977, 1979) in the built environment. Lea (1994) gives a concise summary of Alexander's ideas. Richard Gabriel (1996) also provides much insight into the relevance of Alexander's ideas.

Madsen *et al.* (1993) discuss a different conception of a pattern in the context of the BETA 'pattern oriented' language. This makes patterns a generalization of classes but it is still unclear what this conception has to do with the patterns we have described in this chapter.

Jackson (2001) describes problem frames as patterns for requirements or, more precisely, analysing software development problems rather than solutions, extending the treament in his earlier work (1995).

Gardner *et al.* (1998) discuss their idea of cognitive patterns based on the task templates of the Common KADS knowledge engineering method. The idea is that common problem solving strategies, such as diagnosis, planning and product selection, can be classified as patterns that show how each kind of inference proceeds.

Brown *et al.* (1998) discuss **anti-patterns**: common solutions to frequently occurring problems that **don't** work – and provide suggested solutions. The idea has much in common with the 'software ailments' of Capers Jones (1994).

OORAM (Reenskaug *et al.*, 1996) was an influential method, tool and language in which collaborations and their composition were the central design mechanisms; it is discussed briefly in Appendix B.

D'Souza and Wills (1999) describe the Catalysis method for component-based development. Wills (2001) is a more recent and (we hope) readable introduction. Cheesman and Daniels (2000) describe a simple process for specifying software components and component-based systems, using UML notations and drawing on ideas from Catalysis. Substantial parts of Sections 7.2 and 7.3 are based on a TriReme technical white paper written by Alan Wills.

7.6 Exercises

1. Compare two architectural styles from the following list: layers, blackboard, pipes and filters, CORBA, peer-to-peer, client-server.

2. Define what you understand by software architecture. Why is architecture not merely high level structure?

3. Define the terms: pattern, design pattern, analysis pattern, organizational pattern architectural pattern. Give examples of each.

4. Distinguish between a patterns catalogue and a pattern language, giving examples.

5. Write a pattern in Alexandrian form showing how to decouple the various shapes that could be drawn in a drawing editor from the core editor. In doing this, consider the problems of how to 'smooth' and 'unsmooth' polygons and increase or decrease the number of their vertices in a sensible way.

6. Write patterns to deal with the following situations:
   a) the need to inform all users of e-mail of a change to their e-mail addresses, when some may be on holiday;
   b) users in a workshops continually disagree with each other;
   c) management resist object technology because they consider it too risky.

7. Discuss the pros and cons of inheritance *versus* delegation.

8. Discuss the differences between Catalysis and another OO method known to you with respect to component-based development.

9. What is a retrieval? Give an example.

10. **Mini project**
    Produce a framework template for school timetable preparation: allocating suitable classrooms, qualified teachers, ten subjects and five one-hour time-slots per weekday. Include all invariants; e.g. Chemistry needs a classroom with sinks and there must be at least five hours of Maths and English per week. Are there

any rules that are hard to express in OCL? Why is this? Apply the same framework to factory production scheduling.

8

Requirements engineering

There are many reasons why novelists write, but they all have one thing in common – a need to create an alternative world.

John Fowles (Newspaper article)

Most approaches to object-oriented analysis and design ignore the issues of requirements engineering and knowledge elicitation completely. UML, which we studied in Chapters 6 and 7, assumes that use cases and word-processor-based traceability tools are sufficient for this purpose. We will see in this chapter that there are deep theoretical and practical reasons why such an approach cannot be sanctioned. We shall also see how this can interfere with the process of business re-engineering and the creation of genuinely alternative futures for the organization. I will then describe a mature approach to object-oriented business process modelling and requirements engineering, SOMA, that maps seamlessly onto advanced analysis methods such as Catalysis and which may also be used with standard UML techniques and tools. En route, we can also look at a few research issues in this rapidly developing field.

8.1 Approaches to requirements engineering

Pohl (1993) defines requirements engineering as 'the systematic process of developing requirements through an iterative co-operative process of analysing the problem, documenting the resulting observations in a variety of representation formats, and checking the accuracy of the understanding gained'. This definition, while it leaves some questions unanswered, is a good starting point because it suggests that there is more to requirements engineering than just writing a functional specification. By contrast, the IEEE (Dorfman and Thayer, 1990) define a requirement as one of the following.

1. A condition or capacity needed by a user to solve a problem or achieve an objective.
2. A condition or capability that must be met or possessed by a system or system component to satisfy a contract, standard, specification or other formally imposed documents.
3. A documented representation of a condition or capability as in 1 or 2.

This leaves out the issue of context completely and emphasizes the presence of a requirements document but is notable for the inclusion of the idea of a contract.

Macaulay (1996) suggests that the Pohl definition raises a number of important questions, including whether one can be systematic in the face of vaguely understood requirements, how one can know whether the requirements are complete in the context of iteration, how to define co-operation among agents, what representation formalisms can be used and, finally, how can a genuine shared understanding be reached. The approach laid out in this book offers answers to all of these questions but specifically in the context of object-oriented development.

FORMAL OR INFORMAL?

We distinguish two aspects of requirements engineering: requirements elicitation and requirements analysis. Requirements elicitation is the process whereby a development agency discovers what is needed and why. It is a branch of the discipline of knowledge elicitation and will use many techniques developed within that discipline. Requirements analysis, on the other hand, is the process of understanding the requirements that have been or are being elicited. This is where the requirements engineer will ask questions about the completeness and consistency of the knowledge discovered. This distinction is represented by the division of most work on requirements engineering into two fairly distinct camps. One group focuses on knowledge elicitation techniques and is represented by work that uses *inter alia* ethnomethodology, human factors theories, soft systems methods and ergonomics. A second group emphasizes formal methods of systems analysis. Examples range from traditional systems analysis approaches such as JSD (Jackson, 1983) to overtly mathematical formal methods such as VDM and Z. In the context of object-oriented development there have been several attempts to extend object-oriented analysis with formal theories.

One of the problems with formal specification is that it can actually ignore the true requirement just as easily as an informal document-oriented approach. An example will suffice to illustrate this. An infamous case occurred in the case of aircraft design. A requirement was stated that an aeroplane's reverse thrusters should not cut in until the aircraft was in contact with the runway. The designers reasoned that one could only be sure that the plane had touched down when its wheels began to spin forwards, which would be the case when in contact with a runway or similar. Therefore they arranged the system such that the thrusters would fire automatically when the wheels so span. This worked very well ... until the first time the plane had to land on a runway covered with water and aquaplaned! The plane overshot the runway. So, even if the system can be proved to meet its specification – and there is no principled reason why this could not have been done in our aircraft example – then there is still no guarantee that the specification meets the true requirement. This is especially the case when there are conflicting requirements. In the example just given the conflict was between the need to eliminate human error and the need to land safely in all conditions.

Formal methods emphasize proving the correctness of the code against the specification. This is achieved by writing the specification in a language based on some variant of formal logic. Mathematical proofs of correctness may then be constructed. There are two major problems with this. First, the proofs require great mathematical skill and for large systems can be quite intractable. On the other hand the effort may be worthwhile for safety-critical systems or systems upon which mission-critical systems depend. One of the largest projects of this kind involved the specification of the CICS transaction monitor. The second defect is, in my opinion, far more damning. The problem is that using logic as a specification language is tantamount to programming in logic. All the formal proofs can do is to show the equivalence of the two programs; they say nothing at all about whether the specification meets the users' requirements. The approach presented in this chapter addresses precisely this problem, as we shall see.

Examples of object-oriented approaches to formal specification include Object Z (Carrington *et al.,* 1990; Duke *et al.,* 1991) and Paul Swatman's work on the FOOM modelling language based upon it (Swatman and Swatman, 1992). In this work the formal language is used to express contracts in the form of logical assertions. Catalysis (D'Souza and Wills, 1999) is another method that emphasizes formality but without the extensive use of mathematical notation. Syntropy (Cook and Daniels, 1994) uses state-transition diagrams to achieve similar ends. What all these approaches have in common is that they are chiefly concerned with analysing requirements that are already known and understood and with specifying systems. These methods on their own say little about the knowledge elicitation process.

A similar comment can be made about the approach of Wieringa (1996) who provides extensive guidance on how to analyse requirements using functional decomposition, entity-relationship models and JSD, and emphasizing the production of written requirements specifications. The approach is basically an extension of Information Engineering or SSADM and, as such, would not suit either an object-oriented or evolutionary approach to development.

Jackson (1995) emphasizes the use of problem frames in requirements understanding and analysis. His approach is fundamentally that of an analyst but he pays far more attention to the human issues than is traditional in requirements analysis. He stresses formality but without using the kind of alienating symbolism found in the formal methods tradition. Most importantly of all, Jackson points out that the generality of a method is in inverse proportion to its applicability. To this end he proposes the building of a library of problem frames to cover commonly encountered problem types and appropriate methods to go with them. We discussed problem frames already in Chapter 7 in the context of patterns.

ETHICS   In contrast to formal and semi-formal techniques, approaches such as ETHICS (Mumford, 1986) stress participation and the harmonization of the social and the technical aspects of systems. ETHICS (Effective Technical and Human Implementation of Computer-based Systems) advocates twelve main steps:

1. Specify the work mission.
2. Describe current activities and needs.
3. Consider and measure job satisfaction.
4. Decide on changes needed.
5. Set objectives for job satisfaction, efficiency and effectiveness.
6. Consider the organizational options.
7. Reorganize.
8. Select computer solutions.
9. Train the staff.
10. Redesign jobs.
11. Implement.
12. Evaluate.

ETHICS thus is strongly echoed by more recent work on business process re-engineering and workflow analysis, though it is less associated with rigid and bureaucratic workflow systems of the sort commonly implemented in Lotus Notes and the like. I feel that all the above twelve issues must be addressed during requirements engineering and systems analysis, though not necessarily in that order. Implicitly ETHICS encourages the empowerment of teams and the use of formal inspections to facilitate self-correction of defects. The major problem with ETHICS is that it provides no guidance on how to go about modelling itself, which is the critical success factor for step 8. Nor does it integrate ideas from business process re-engineering, rapid application development or object technology into its approach. Thus, while not ignoring the advances of ETHICS, we must go well beyond it.

SOCIALLY CENTRED TECHNIQUES   Ethnography and ethnomethodological techniques, deriving from Anthropology, have been applied to requirements engineering in order to recognize that task analysis based on studies of individuals is flawed if it fails to recognize that all business activity takes place in a social context. The behaviour of groups is studied over some time and conclusions about requirements drawn. Suchman (1987) provides an excellent case study: applying the method to the design of photocopying machinery. We adopt an approach in this chapter which focuses on networks of social commitments but does not require extensive observational studies; though these are by no means ruled out.

Participatory design is a general label for approaches that emphasize user involvement throughout the specification and design process. Leading proponents include Ehn (Ehn *et al.*, 1990; Ehn and Kyng, 1991). Requirements are not fixed at some arbitrary point as in conventional structured approaches. This view is consistent with the evolutionary process model described in Chapter 9. Also important to the advocates of participatory design is that systems should not be used to downgrade and de-skill users' work. Webster (1996) provides some pretty horrifying counter-examples in the context of the degradation of work when looked at from a gender-specific viewpoint – and that includes the degradation (or elimination) of the work of both sexes. I believe that all relevant social factors should be taken into account when designing systems (including perhaps, age, culture, gender and physical ability) and that designers have a social responsibility at least to *predict* the effects of their technology.

Research into human–computer interaction (HCI) has led to approaches based on user-centred and task-centred design. These can utilize direct user involvement, observational studies or even questionnaires and surveys. Eason (1989) is a leading exponent of user-centred design whose approach has much in common with ETHICS although he gives more emphasis to socio-technical design and cost–benefit analysis. The task-centred approach descends from the educational technology movement of the 1950s and 60s. User task analysis is a key influence on the approach presented in this chapter, but we combine these ideas with those of use cases, semiotics (part of ethnomethodology) and script theory from artificial intelligence. SOMA advocates the use of a number of other techniques, such as Kelly grids, derived from knowledge engineering. Chapter 6 has already presented several such techniques.

Contextual enquiry (Beyer and Holtzblatt, 1997) is a set of tools and techniques whose basic tenet is that business processes are best apprehended in the context of the workplace. It has its origins in work done at DEC in the early 1990s. Modelling techniques include flow models, task scenarios, artefacts used, culture and the physical environment. It does not emphasize user interface design and is most suitable for automating existing manual processes rather than for re-engineering.

Usage-centred design (Constantine and Lockwood, 1999) builds on many of the above ideas and emphasizes user interface design, task analysis, user rôles and the use of 'essential' use cases (see Section 8.6). It has much in common with the SOMA approach presented herein.

Quality function deployment or the so-called 'house of quality' has been put forward as a way of discovering users' requirements based on correlating them pairwise with product features. I believe that the techniques described in this book make this kind of approach superfluous.

The CREWS approach to requirements engineering (Maiden *et al.,* 1997) emphasizes techniques based on scenarios for checking that specifications are consistent and – more especially – complete. This important work is discussed further in Section 8.10.

An approach to the analysis of workflow systems developed by Winograd and Flores (1986) has much to recommend it and is integrated into our approach. It emphasizes the network of commitments that exists between the agents in a business and their sequenced conversations. However, the approach has been criticized for leading to over-rigid work practices in the implementations that it arrives at. I believe that this can be overcome by delving deeper than the workflow aspects of the conversations and analysing the stakeholders' tasks as well. We will return at length to the subject of Flores nets, as they are known, in Section 8.5.

ORCA

ORCA (Object-Oriented Requirements Capture and Analysis) (MacLean *et al.*, 1994) represents one of the few attempts to make requirements engineering for object-oriented development in any way rigorous. It advocates the use of soft systems style 'rich pictures' as a starting point and then, like Catalysis, SOMA and Syntropy, makes a clear distinction between models of the world and models of intended systems. ORCA's approach relies on the differentiation of *purposive* and *behavioural* entities and provides two distinct notations to represent each aspect of its models. Purposive entities are things not directly observable, such as countries, and correspond to our agents, which will be discussed in Section 8.5. Behavioural entities correspond to UML classes. MacLean *et al.* (1994) point out that the two may coincide, as in the case of organizational structures. Here the correspondence is with the agent classes of SOMA, which internalize (or 'cartoon') real-world agents inside the computer system. Clearly, ORCA has some points in common with SOMA, not least in addressing requirements engineering at all – unlike most other object-oriented methods. However, there are differences, among which is ORCA's inability to provide a formal link between its two modelling languages and its reliance on a good deal of modelling techniques derived from entity-relationship approaches; e.g. bi-directional associations and even SSADM-style exclusion arcs are permitted in ORCA.

ORCA emphasizes business process re-engineering and the environment in which systems are embedded. In this sense it is innovative and powerful. However, its use of object modelling techniques is somewhat pedestrian. Workshops and rapid development are not stressed, but business objectives are discussed as part of the knowledge discovery process.

ORCA's world model consists of objects that represent purposive entities and the contracts that exist between them, expressed in terms of services with pre- and post-conditions and constraints (class invariants). These classes may also embed non-functional requirements (to the credit of the method). From this model a behavioural model (basically a conventional object model) is intuited and then described using a mixture of extended entity-relationship diagrams and diagrams that are essentially an extension of UML sequence diagrams, though with clearer semantics and less related to the program code. A key contribution of ORCA is the provision of formal syntax for both its modelling languages. This enables the models to be checked more easily for consistency and errors and is the main basis for ORCA's claim to be rigorous. ORCA cannot, however, and despite this rigour, prove that its system model meets the requirements as stated in the world model. We will see later in this chapter that it is the ability to do precisely this that lays the foundation for the claim that SOMA is rigorous – though SOMA has no formal syntax defined currently.

SOFT SYSTEMS

Soft systems research (Checkland, 1981; Checkland and Scholes, 1991) is concerned with apprehending an entire, situated problem in the context of an organization and the purposes of the whole problem solving activity. Emphasis is on elicitation of behaviour and problem dynamics from multiple perspectives. The foundation of soft systems work was in general systems theory and Cybernetics. The same traditions are at the root of approaches to business process re-engineering such as that of Senge

(1990). The approach usually begins by drawing a so-called rich picture of the problem situation. Such a picture is not unlike a freehand, annotated SOMA business process model.

It is possible to make a number of specific remarks concerning the relationship between Checkland's soft systems method (SSM) and SOMA as there are evident similarities. Checkland's famous mnemonic, CATWOE – standing for: Customers, Actors, Transformation processes, Weltanschauung, Owners and Environment – is used within SSM as a guide to what the components of a system model should cover. These items have a direct correspondence with SOMA concepts as shown in Table 8.1. Furthermore, Checkland's concept of a root definition for the system problem corresponds to our mission statement in a direct manner.

Table 8.1 Concepts in Soft Systems Method and SOMA.

SSM	*SOMA*
Customers = victims or beneficiaries of T	External agents = Stakeholders, users, sponsors, regulators, external systems, etc.
Actors = those who would do T	Actors, internal agents
Transformation process (T) = conversion of input to output	The system
Weltanschauung = Worldview that gives meaning to T in context	Goals, objectives, measures, assumptions, exclusions, etc.
Owners = those who could stop T	Sponsors
Environmental constraints = elements outside the system over which we have no influence	External objects, timers, assumptions, etc.

In SOMA, as a modelling approach, we are not concerned with the fine distinction Checkland and Scholes (1991) make between the system as a model of the world and the world as a system. It is not relevant here precisely because we are modelling. Also, I agree with these authors on the importance of the active rôle of the subject in cognition but disagree that there is no objective basis to cognitive acts.

The world is a system in some objective sense but 'system' is also a subjective idea imposed on it. However, in SOMA we do have a 'world model' in the form of the business process and task models and a 'system model' in the shape of a Catalysis specification model. This text is not the place to explore these important philosophical ideas further. In practice there is no problem in using SOMA as a method for modelling soft systems, and its fuzzy extensions (see Appendix A) may be apposite.

The SSM requirements engineering process is also remarkably similar to SOMA.

In the former there are seven stages which have been annotated with their SOMA equivalents in Table 8.2.

Table 8.2 SSM stages and SOMA techniques.

SSM	*SOMA*
Find out about problem situation	Mission grid, Objectives, Business Process Model
Express the situation (rich picture)	Business Process Model
Select viewpoint and produce root definitions	Mission grid, Objectives
Build conceptual models of what the system must do for each root definition	Business Process Model, Task Object Model
Compare the conceptual model with the world	Task Object Model, Business Object Model, Walkthrough traces
Identify feasible and desirable changes	Objectives, Workshop discussions

This section has provided only a brief and fairly cursory review of approaches to requirements engineering (RE), since my main purpose is to present my own approach. Many of the techniques for requirements engineering described only briefly in this section have been incorporated into SOMA and I acknowledge my debt to them. My approach emphasizes the need to prove that system specifications actually do service the requirements as represented. Mathematical formalism is possible within SOMA but I choose not to go down that route in this book – and indeed in the vast majority of practical problems that I face from day to day.

▤ 8.2 Requirements engineering *versus* system specification

The commonest misconception in computing is that understanding a client's requirements is the same as specifying a system that will meet those requirements. On such a premise one can then blithely state that use case analysis is the only requirements modelling technique needed. Jackson (1998) pours scorn on this idea, arguing that use cases are useful for specifying systems but that they cannot describe requirements fully. Use cases connect actors, which represent **users** adopting rôles, to systems. Requirements, on the other hand, may be those of people and organizations that never get anywhere near the system boundary.

In Figure 8.1 we see part of Jackson's argument illustrated pictorially. A requirements document must be written in a language whose designations concern things in the world in which the system is embedded (including of course that system). Specifications need only describe the interfaces of the system and therefore depend on different designations. The specification S describes the interface of phenomena shared between the world and the system; use cases may be used to express these. The requirements model R is a description over these and other phenomena in the world. R depends on both the specification *and* the world. He also states that 'the customer is usually interested in effects that are felt some distance from the machine'.

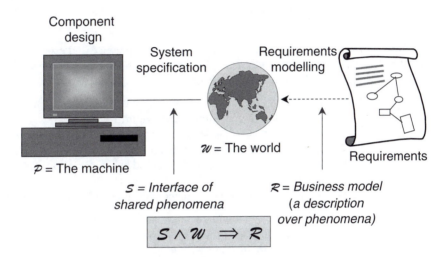

Figure 8.1 Specification models are not requirements models.

Ignoring the non-user interactions can lead to us missing important re-engineering opportunities. I worked on a rule-based order processing and auto-pricing system, whose aim was to take orders from customers electronically and price them automatically using various, often complex, pricing engines via the corporate ORB. The problem was that some orders were too complex or too large to admit of automatic handling. These had to be looked at by a salesman who would of course have an interface with the 'system'. So far, so good: a rule engine would screen 'illegal' or 'handle manually' orders. The salesman would then apply his various spreadsheet and other routines to such orders. But a further problem existed; some orders were so complicated as to be beyond the skills of the salesman, who did not have expertise in financial mathematics. For these orders, the salesman had to go across the office and talk to a specialist trader. She did have the requisite PhD in Financial Engineering. Because we were using SOMA we also modelled this non-use-case conversation and, as a result, when our domain expert looked at the simulation we had built, she realized immediately that if we gave the trader a screen we could radically improve the workflow, and thereby customer service. Even this relatively minor excursion away from the system boundary thus had a big cash import. In many, more complex cases, the importance of going beyond the boundary will be greater still.

My interpretation of Jackson's argument is that we need a specific technique for modelling business processes distinct from, but compatible with, use case models of specifications. The alternative is to fall back on a veritable 'Russian doll' of nested models described in terms of 'business use cases' (Jacobson *et al.*, 1995): an approach that is not only clumsy but fails to address the above arguments. Thus, we need to know the answers to the following two questions before we can proceed.

- What is a model?
- What is a business process?

THE NATURE OF MODELS Modelling is central to software engineering practice and especially to object-oriented development. A **model** is a representation of some thing or system of things with all or some of the following properties.

- It is always *different* from the thing or system being modelled (the *original*) in scale, implementation or behaviour.
- It has the shape or appearance of the original (an iconic model).
- It can be manipulated or exercised in such a way that its behaviour or properties can be used to predict the behaviour or properties of the original (a simulation model).
- There is always some correspondence between the model and the original.

Examples of models abound throughout daily life: mock-ups of aircraft in wind tunnels; architectural scale models; models of network traffic using compressed air in tubes or electrical circuits; software models of gas combustion in engines. Of course *all* software is a model of something, just as all mathematical equations are (analytic) models.

Jackson (1995) relates models to descriptions by saying that modelling a domain involves making designations of the primitives of the domain and then using these to build a description of the properties, relationships and behaviour that are true of that domain. For example, if we take the domain of sending birthday cards to one's friends, we might make designations:

p is a friend;
d is a date (day and month);
$B(p,d)$ says that *p* was born on *d*.

Then we can make descriptions like: For all *p*, there is exactly one *B*. Jackson suggests that modelling is all about ensuring that the descriptions apply equally well to the model and to the original domain. In the context of computer models this might mean that the instances of a class or the records of a database are made to correspond uniquely to domain instances of our friends. Most usefully, Jackson presents this concept as the M configuration shown in Figure 8.2.

The Domain and the Machine are different; in the domain friends do not reside in disk sectors. There are many things in the domain that are not in our model, such as our friends' legs or pimples. There are also things that go on in computers that we are not concerned with in a model, such as time sharing. The model comprises the features shared between the domain and the machine.

This understanding of what a model is can be applied to the problem of object modelling. We must understand clearly that a so-called Business Object Model is both a model of the domain and a potentially implementable machine model. But we must begin with a model of the domain to understand and validate the requirements.

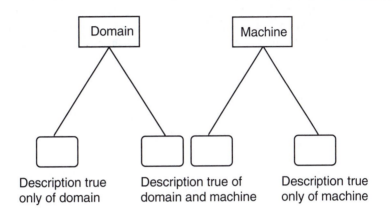

Figure 8.2 M is for 'model' (after Jackson, 1995).

It is my thesis that object modelling is a very general method for knowledge representation. There is little that cannot be modelled with objects – provided, of course, that we do not restrict ourselves to the semantics of some particular object-oriented programming language. We can model both the domain and the machine using objects. This is not to say that the world consists of our model objects, but it is to say that we can almost always model the domain as if it was made of objects. A good example is provided by Cook and Daniels (1994), who also make a strong distinction between *essential* (i.e. domain) and *specification* models. They argue that the world is not made of objects, citing by way of example the fact that the sun does not wake the birds up each morning by sending each one a message. However, if we want a correspondence between our domain and specification models, it is quite permissible to model the sunrise event as recorded on a 'blackboard' object in which each instance of the class Birds has registered interest. That is not what happens physically but it is a good model insofar as object semantics do not include a broadcast metaphor. There are of course many exceptions where object modelling is inappropriate, but the sheer discipline of trying to model with objects is beneficial in terms of scientific parsimony and ordered thought. For example, I doubt whether the solution of a differential equation is best modelled with objects. Here another idea promoted by Jackson (1995) may be useful. He argues that one can recognize analysis patterns (which he calls problem frames) that recur and which imply suitable modelling methods. This classification-based approach provides references for solving future problems of the same or similar types. One example is the 'simple IS frame', which indicates that a JSP approach is suitable. The arguments in this case are convincing, but generally I find that object modelling gives more chance of success than any other general approach and that JSP can be accommodated as a technique within an object-oriented approach. Kristen (1995), for one, does this within his KISS method. Jackson's problem frames can be criticized for being *post facto* rationalizations of only a few well-known situations, so that they do not help much with the discovery of solutions to new problems. Nor does Jackson provide a concrete process for applying the approach. However, this can be said of any pattern-oriented approach and the power of such approaches is widely recognized.

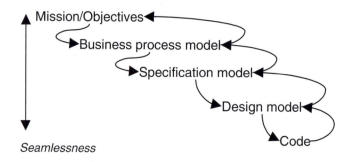

Figure 8.3 Traceable models.

Jackson's M metaphor provides us with an understanding of the correspondence between two worlds – the domain and the machine in the example above. However, if we are to apply object modelling to a realistic business problem it turns out that this is often too simplistic a view. In practice we must build a linked series of models more reminiscent of a tasty *mmmmm* than single M. De Champeaux (1997) offers some more support for this view. He distinguishes between two approaches to object modelling that he characterizes as constructivist (neat) and impressionist (scruffy). Scruffies do not emphasize the precise semantics of object modelling. They opine 'the design fleshes out the analysis' without being precise about what this means. Precision is only introduced in the implementation models when the semantics of a programming language has to be faced. The neats are different. They want to 'exploit the analysis computational model' and observe that analysis models are 'nearly executable'. Examples of approaches close to the spirit of the neats include those of Cook and Daniels, D'Souza and Wills (1999) and of de Champeaux himself. This, of course, is closely related to the elaborational *versus* translational debate discussed in Chapter 6. We will model the business mission and objectives, the interactions among the agents involved in the business, the tasks that they perform and the business objects that they use and refer to before implementing a system. Each of these models is transformed into the next, as we shall see. At each model transformation we validate the consistency of the models as suggested by Figure 8.3. Doing so guarantees that the resultant system meets its stakeholders' objectives. As we will see, some of these models are object models and some are not.

BPR   Business process re-engineering (BPR) became a fashionable topic during the first half of the 1990s and received much attention. It was locally, but not universally, successful, and did help several businesses reorganize their operations and change their relationship to information technology radically and irreversibly. Typically this has been also associated with a move to evolutionary development and sometimes with the adoption of object technology and e-commerce.

Business process re-engineering is the radical rethinking and redesign of an entire business, its processes, organizational structure, management, jobs and value system. Its aim is dramatic performance improvement. It is accomplished by first identifying the key processes needed to do business and then breaking through organizational and functional divisions that could impede these processes. Processes are viewed from new angles and new organizational structures invented to support them. With increased global competition and the threat of new internet rivals, many businesses feel compelled to consider BPR.

BPR must be driven by business requirements and backed fully by senior management, with regular and open feedback to staff. IT is usually an enabler of BPR, because the legacy must be removed or wrapped before changes become feasible. Also, IT staff often have a cross-functional perspective that eludes many line managers.

BPR redefines jobs by making corporate information accessible to all and giving those in direct contact with the task the power to make decisions. Unfortunately, it is largely an art rather than a science because the analyst has to leap intuitively to what is sometimes called 'the great idea'. The examples quoted in the literature all have such a great idea; e.g. (Hammer, 1990 and Davenport and Short, 1990). Ford was able to reduce the size of its Accounts Payable headcount from 500 to 125 by paying for goods on receipt rather than matching invoices and orders. This was enabled by a computer system, but the great idea was generated from the observation that Mazda had an equivalent department with only five people in it. Mutual Benefit Life similarly reduced its underwriting turnaround from 24 to 4 hours by making a 'case manager', equipped with expert systems technology, responsible for the whole process. Here it seems the great idea arose directly from the technological potential of expert systems combined with the propensity to think outside current organizational constraints. I think the main lesson to be learnt from these and many other case studies is that a more systematic approach is necessary. Re-engineers need representational and simulation tools so that they can perform 'what-if' analyses on a model of the existing or projected business process; tools that do for the re-engineer what spreadsheets have done for management accountants. Object technology offers a solution here because business processes can be modelled as arrangements of communicating objects with state, responsibilities and, importantly, knowledge of business policies and rules. Another lesson is that sometimes only IT makes BPR possible. A story is told about the managing director of an insurance company who was at his desk at 7pm when the telephone rang. Since he had access to the company's workflow model via a terminal he was able to call up the customer's records and deal with her problem there and then.

IT helps eliminate unnecessary flows and makes managers into clerks as much as it makes clerks into decision makers (a better word might be executives). This questions the classical conceptions of the division of labour of Adam Smith and Frederick Taylor in a fundamental way. In fact, the arguments of the modern management science gurus are faintly reminiscent of the argument used by Lenin in his *State and Revolution* (Lenin, 1964)[1], where it is argued that in a genuinely free and productive society the division of labour would wither away. His slogan was 'the administration of things – not the management of people'. This sounds very much like Tom Peters' (1992) exhortations to empower the workforce and eliminate chains of permission to act. However, the evident result of juxtaposing these disparate political views is to ask whether current politico-economic structures will either tolerate or support such radical restructuring of the way work is done. Peters evidently believes it will, but it is unproven and unlikely that the beneficial effects of empowerment will continue to apply when spread from a handful of advanced companies to all the world's enterprises unless there are concomitant social changes. Another, more immediate, social issue that arises with workflow systems is the fact that managers can monitor employees' work with them. This could lead to resentment against snooping. Gary Marx (1992) argues that if managers think such monitoring is useful, they should submit to it themselves.

The BPR literature emphasizes that businesses organized around functional models are rigid and inflexible due to excessive functional specialization. No one in this circle has suggested that object models are better but it is widely agreed that the unit of analysis should be the business process. The rôle of objects is to provide direct support for modelling processes as flows of communication between actors. I would assert that any natural language description of a business process translates naturally to an object model – at least when rules can be represented. A rule-based, object-oriented description may be animated to provide business process simulations that may be used for scenario modelling to help find the 'great idea'.

The quality and BPR movements have both emphasized process over functional specialization. An orientation towards process, it is said, helps to produce:

- increases in efficiency and effectiveness;
- cost reductions;
- greater process flexibility and therefore adaptability;
- greater job satisfaction; and
- higher quality products.

It has become commonplace to appoint a 'process engineer' to oversee the delivery of these benefits. The lessons of BPR can be applied to the process of software engineering itself and, with object-oriented developments in mind, the rôle of the process engineer will be largely adopted by the domain modeller.

---

[1] Lenin was undoubtedly familiar with Taylor's ideas, as evinced by his jocular slogan: 'Electrification + Taylorism = Socialism'.

BPR projects fail for many reasons:

- refusal to dispose of IT assets, existing management structures and business practices;
- over-reliance on package software (such as ERP systems) to solve all problems at a stroke;
- lack of clear strategy and resistance from 'robber barons' in management positions;
- failure to flatten management structures radically;
- resistance to multi-skilling and multi-tasking among staff and management;
- excessive focus on cost-cutting;
- lack of patience – the budget is cut before tangible results emerge;
- lack of understanding of customers.

Along with the failures, there have been many widely-reported successes at companies such as Baxter Healthcare, IBM, British Telecom, Lucas, Nabisco and Xerox. The National & Provincial Building Society re-engineered itself between 1990 and 1995 and in the last year could report a 45% increase in both profit and revenue without any significant cut in its cost base.

Many current IT practices tend to lock organizations into their existing methods of working. This is chiefly because changes to computer systems take too long. The move to rapid development is thus very important for IT within a business that is adopting BPR. OT supports this move by providing programming environments that are very flexible, based on the polymorphic characteristics of the languages and dynamic binding. Prototypes can be built quickly and evolved easily. Reuse libraries make rapid development even faster, where they exist. Finally, object-oriented methods should pay close attention to the flexibility of the life-cycle model.

Of course, business process re-engineering cannot be accomplished without business process modelling and the object metaphor is ideally suited to modelling businesses. Also, evolutionary development is nearly always an opportunity to re-engineer some aspect of the business. This chapter shows how an object-oriented approach to system modelling can be integrated with business process modelling and requirements engineering techniques. We will see how to apply the object modelling language developed in Chapter 6 to modelling businesses and to modelling users' tasks. I show how starting with an object model of the business leads seamlessly to an object model of agents' tasks that is clearly related to the objectives and mission of that business. This, in turn, leads to a UML use case model. Finally I show how a more conventional object model can be extracted from these earlier models and validated against both them and the business's objectives. Furthermore, I demonstrate that this use case model can be linked seamlessly to an executable specification of the computer support system that we may want to build.

8.2.1 Collaborative work, workflow automation and groupware

While labour in manufacture has seen massive increases in its productivity in the last 50 years, the productivity of office workers has stagnated despite increased usage of computers (Brynjolfsson, 1993; Roach, 1991). According to the Association for Image and Information Management and other researchers, between 94% and 95% of office information still resided on paper – pre-web anyway – and 15% to 30% of office workers' time was spent in locating it.

This section illustrates how IT can enable BPR and deals with some technology for amplifying the productivity of office workers. It is variously known as computer supported co-operative work (CSCW), workflow automation, groupware and collaborative work support. It involves various technologies from document image management, scanners, CD storage, multimedia display, broadband networks, full-content database retrieval, and specialized technologies based on insights from linguistics, AI, biology, anthropology and other social sciences. There are also strong links to the ideas of business process re-engineering (BPR).

Workflow software automates existing, repetitive, multi-actor processes while **groupware** supports *ad hoc* forms of co-operation and co-ordination. Some software products support both approaches. The split reflects a dichotomy within the business process re-engineering community, which either emphasizes the automation and streamlining of existing processes and the enforcement of 'best practice' or the entire obliteration of unnecessary work. Successful introduction of groupware correlates with flat organizational structures where the norm is people working in teams to solve problems rather than individuals reporting upwards in order to have their decisions authorized. Often workflow and groupware systems are delivered via an intranet.

To see where a business can benefit most from groupware it is often effective to construct an application grid of the type shown in Figure 8.4. In this figure we compare the level of social interaction required to carry out the task with the management level at which the task usually occurs. The cells of the grid contain some typical applications and it can be seen that groupware may be suitable for a range of applications across all management levels at the high interactivity level. More surprising is that medium interactivity applications tend to be concentrated at the operational level, again emphasizing collaboration and the empowerment of line workers. Furthermore, workflow applications, emphasizing control, are more appropriate at the low interactivity end of the scale. Where organizational change is expected it would seem prudent to adopt systems flexible enough to cover both control and collaboration applications.

Tools for workflow automation fall into three main classes. They are either document image management (DIM) systems such as Filenet with its integral Workflo language, office automation systems or specific groupware products. Such systems are highly effective in large bureaucracies such as local government departments where paper flow and rule adherence are considered to be important factors in public accountability. The amount of paper storage and concomitant costs can also be dramatically reduced in these contexts. Products like Lotus Notes and the various internet-based systems enable incoming documents to be scanned, stored and distributed by e-mail. This helps to avoid massive waste where many photocopies are circulated to people with no interest in the information while genuinely interested parties are omitted from the circulation. Many products offer two modes: one for developers and one for users. The developer mode usually utilizes some kind of high level scripting language. Some products, such as Beyond Mail, attempt to apply rules to the mail routing problem to support workflow applications. It is possible, for example, to store and send a standard reply to mail from nominated individuals – useful for junking junk mail I would hazard. The approach need not be restricted to a local LAN. Many e-mail products support the X400 and X500 protocols.

Interaction level	Management level		
	Operational	Middle	Top
Low	Database access	Reporting	Executive information systems
Medium	E-mail, Resource sharing	Scheduling meetings	Decision support systems, Expert systems, Warehouses
High	Informal discussions, Meetings, Panics	Decision support systems, Expert systems, Warehouses	Group decision support

Figure 8.4 Application grid for groupware and workflow systems.

HCI design concentrates on the detailed performance of specific tasks. This is fine for analysing the use of a computer system by an individual at a workstation but less so in workflow environments where many users have to co-operate. HCI draws heavily on work in cognitive psychology and this means that the results of HCI can be extended to CSCW. Work on this at Xerox' research centre in Cambridge, England has emphasized the use of contributions from the other social sciences such as anthropology, ethnomethodology and social psychology. Ethnomethodology, as we saw in Section 8.1, is concerned with the relationships between people, groups, work patterns and technology. It has considerable application to studying the organizational impact of IT. Group work emphasizes the social aspects of work and thought and CSCW has emphasized this further. In fact, Diaper (1993) has claimed that CSCW is little more than HCI for groups. Ethnomethodologists may film people at work in groups and record physical movement, gestures, eye focus, posture and their relationship to conversation. Conversation analysis provides notations for recording such things and the results can be surprising. For example, it turns out that sound cues are very important, and when a door is heard closing at the end of a conversation via a multimedia system, this augments user satisfaction because it helps them achieve closure. Subtle hand positioning and movement can provide cues for the counterparty to begin speaking. People in video conferences are less sensitive to small but significant movements in peripheral vision than in face-to-face conversations. Some users learn to exaggerate their gestures for this reason. However useful in the video context, this can make people look very silly when viewed from across the office. I have also heard it reported that users of an early video-conferencing system in a large corporation gave up using it when they realized that the unreality of the experience led to tarnished images within the organization. An extreme case was a senior manager who had a tendency to pick his nose throughout video meetings. He did not do this in real meetings. Obviously I cannot name the company.

It is often useful in designing workflow and groupware systems to analyze use cases and, more generally, agent interactions. Each interaction script is associated with a set of objects, which will often be documents or database records. A script analysis leads directly to an object-oriented description and this model may be used to critique the current workflow in order to obliterate some work. A process view is integral to many object-oriented analysis and design methods, notably methods such as Ptech which was actually named as a contraction of Process technology long before it became fashionable to describe the method as object-oriented (*cf.* Appendix B).

It would be a mistake to assume that the benefits of collaborative computing arrive without costs being incurred. Beyond the costs of the new software there are training and change management costs. I would assert that this style of working requires that every member of staff has a workstation of their own. Where this is not already the case, it must be paid for. On the other hand there are some latent benefits too. Instant access to information can speed up time-to-market considerably. For example, a first-rate groupware system can reduce the number of meetings required to reach a critical decision, since no one has to go off to collect missing information and reconvene the meeting later.

8.3 De-scoping large problems – the mission grid

Returning to the main stream of our exposition of method, the aim is to construct an object model of a business. For a small business this is straightforward but, unfortunately, building an object model of a corporation as large as AT&T, British Petroleum, Chase Manhattan or IBM is likely to produce a model of such complexity as to be virtually meaningless. Like earlier attempts to produce corporate data models, the exercise is likely to take so long that it would be out of date years before it was complete. Approaches based on Soft Systems' rich pictures or ORCA rôle models will not help a great deal with problems of this sort of scale. What then can be done to de-scope such a large problem to a scale where object modelling is apposite and effective? To answer this question, I propose a technique which I designate the MISSION GRID.

In analysing any commercial enterprise, the first question we must ask is: 'who are the customers and other stakeholders in this business?'. Typical stakeholders might include – in addition to the ever-present customers – suppliers, regulatory bodies, trade associations, information providers and competitors. Once these are identified, we can define external goals that are shared with the customers and others. These are variously called shared goals or customer value propositions (CVPs) in the literature (e.g. Jacobson *et al.*, 1995). These statements sum up a state of affairs that both the customer and the enterprise would like to achieve on a regular basis, such as delivering a high quality product at a reasonable price while remaining profitable. This suits the customer who wants such a product but wants to buy from a reliable supplier who is going to stay in business and continue to improve the product. The mission grid technique mandates that we write these goals along one axis of a grid or spreadsheet. The external goals are insufficient to characterize the goals of a business; we must also define internal goals. Internal goals are those that the organization holds to for it own, private reasons and could be to do with cultural or ethical principles or more mundane issues such as keeping the managing director out of gaol. The latter consideration leads, for example, to the need to file proper accounts and tax returns. To clarify the separation, these goals are written against separate columns from the external goals on our spreadsheet, typically at the opposite edge of the page as in the example shown in Figure 8.5. The orientation of the grid is irrelevant. In this case the logical rôles are written along the top, the customer value propositions on the left and the internal goals on the right.

The next step in completing the grid is creative and challenging; it involves establishing what processes must be carried out in order to contribute to or accomplish the goals, internal and external. These processes must then be rearranged around yet to be identified 'logical rôles'. A logical rôle is a sort of abstract job description that unifies a coherent set of processes that could be accomplished using one basic set of skills, such as those likely to be within the capabilities of a single human agent or department. Assigning the processes to the rôles is quite a difficult thing to do well and the process is bound to be iterative and to involve a lot of interaction with domain experts and users within the business. In Figure 8.5 the rôles are the columns.

Often, two mission grids are developed: the first representing the existing situation and the second a vision of a re-engineered business. Ideally the AFTER grid is developed without reference to the BEFORE grid. One may also prepare separate grids for different geographical divisions of the organization.

The mission grid has been found to be an excellent tool for communicating with business leaders about the nature of the business and its strategy in the large. These experts should always be asked to justify the CVPs and challenge every process: Is it necessary? Do we really want to be in that business? Will that goal be sustainable in forecast market conditions?

Certain rows or columns of the grid, or particular groups of cells (processes), may be candidates for outsourcing. The key desiderata in this respect are:

- Is the process a customer facing process?
- Is the process differentiating?

	Butcher	Master butcher	Cleaner	Accountant	
Make/offer product	Prepare product	Visit markets			
	Cutting	Define cuts	Clean workspace		
Inform public of products	Offer advice	Train butchers			
		Advertise & promote			
				VAT Analysis	**Produce VAT return**
	Take cash		Keep hands clean	Accounting	**Produce accounts**

Figure 8.5 A fragment of a mission grid for a butcher's shop.

The phrase **customer facing** signifies that the process involves direct contact with the customer. It is usually unwise to outsource such processes to third parties. The many companies that outsourced their help desks in recent years are beginning to realize their error in relation to this principle. **Differentiating** activities are those that your company does that actually characterize it in the eyes of its customers. For example, if you saw a hoarding advertising an organization that 'guarantees to take a percentage of your income every year while providing no direct service in return', then you could be pretty sure that the ad. referred to the Revenue. This statement differentiates that organization from all others. It is a capital error to outsource customer facing, differentiating processes. Processes that are neither customer facing nor differentiating are usually the most appropriate for outsourcing. Thus, the mission grid is a powerful tool for discussing business process re-engineering with the business. It is also the starting point for the implementation of the systems that must underpin such an enterprise and for object-oriented business modelling.

The processes in each cell of the grid can be thought of as mission statements for each process-oriented 'business area'. Each of these is likely to be: (a) small enough to make the construction of an object model of the business area feasible; and (in many cases) (b) suitable for enhancement with a fairly well-focused computer support system. Sometimes the business area corresponds to a small group of closely related cells.

⊟ 8.4 Discovering business objectives and priorities

Having focused down to a particular process-oriented business area and defined its mission, we are now in a position to define the specific objectives of this process. Ideally, a joint requirements workshop will be the forum for this activity. In a workshop, the facilitator will ask other participants to call out and discuss objectives. These are written on a flip chart or other visible medium (e.g. text can be projected from the computer with which the requirements analyst or scribe records the session). Experience has taught that there are usually about 13 objectives, either due to the fact that people run out of ideas after that much discussion, that 13 objectives comfortably fills two flip chart pages or, as a more remote possibility, reflecting some obscure law of nature yet to be articulated by rational Man.

The SOMA philosophy is that no activity should be allowed to produce a deliverable without it being tested. This principle is applied to the objectives by seeking a measure for each objective. For example, if our business is running an hotel and an objective is to provide a high quality service then the measure might be a star rating system as provided by many tourist boards or motoring organizations. Of course, there are cases where a precise measure is elusive. Discussing the measures is an important tool for clarifying, elucidating and completing the objectives shared and understood by the group. The discussion of measures helps a group think more clearly about the objectives and often leads to the discovery of additional ones or the modification of those already captured. Setting aside plenty of time for the discussion of the measures is seldom a waste of time.

The minimum requirement is that it must be possible to prioritize all the objectives. A formal preference grid can be elicited by asking that each pair of objectives be ranked against each other. In workshops, this is too time consuming and a quicker, more subjective technique is needed. One way to come quickly to the priorities is to allow participants to place votes against each objective. We usually permit each person a number of votes corresponding to about 66% of the number of objectives; e.g. 9 votes for 13 objectives. A good way to perform the voting is to give each eligible participant a number of small, sticky, coloured paper disks, of the sort that are sold in strips by most stationers. Then the rules of voting are explained: 'You may place all your stickers on one objective or distribute them across several, evenly or unevenly according to the importance you place on the objectives. You need not use all your votes; but you are not allowed to give – or sell – unused votes to other participants.' Then everyone must come up to the flip charts all at once. No hanging back to see what others do is permitted. This helps inject a dynamic atmosphere into the proceedings and stops people waiting to see what the boss does before voting.

Sometimes two rounds of voting should be done, under different interpretations, and the results added to reach a final priority score for each objective. Of course, two colours are then needed for the sticky disks. An example of two possible interpretations that can be combined is:

1.   Vote from your point of view as an individual user.
2.   Vote from a corporate viewpoint.

Another pair might be:

1.   Vote from the supplier's viewpoint.
2.   Vote from the customer's viewpoint.

The results often generate further useful discussion. Also one should allow for re-prioritization at this point, if surprising results have emerged. This is often due to overlap between objectives that is highlighted by the priorities given.

An objective that cannot be measured and/or prioritized must be rejected or, at least, consigned to a slightly modified mission statement. The priorities are a key tool for project management since they determine what must be implemented first from the point of view of the business sponsor. Technical dependencies must also be allowed for, of course. Often a discussion around these issues elicits new objectives, clarifies existing ones or leads to their recombination or even placement in the overall mission statement. Issues that cannot be resolved are recorded with the names of the people responsible for resolving them. Specific assumptions and exclusions should also be recorded.

We now have one mission grid for the whole organization, consisting of multiple processes, each expressed by a mission statement. Each mission statement is linked to several measurable and prioritized business objectives. We can now begin to construct a model of the business area and its processes.

8.5 Agents, conversations and business processes

Once the objectives are clearly stated with defined measures and priorities we can construct our first object model: an object model of the business area that we are dealing with. To do this we must understand what a business (process) actually is. Most vendors of business process modelling tools and techniques find it very difficult to answer the question: 'what is a business process?'. Typically, they might answer that a business is a set of processes connected by data flows, with timings for each process and (possibly) allocations of process responsibility to functional units. In other words, data flow diagrams enhanced with timings or perhaps UML activity diagrams are all that is needed. Neither approach is object-oriented (cf. Kleppe and Warmer, 2000). Typical of product offerings of this kind, in the general area of process modelling and workflow management, are Beyond Inc's BeyondMail, Computron's Epic/Workflow, DEC's TeamRoute, HP's WaveFlow, IBM's Folder Application Facility, ICL's ProcessWise, NCR's ProcessIT, Plexus' Imageflow, Recognition Equipment's ImageFlow and the eponymous Filenet and Staffware. Many of these tools rely on object technology even though they fail to have an object-oriented view on what a process is. For example, ProcessWise claims that object-oriented techniques are used to let it build business process simulations and to develop the computer systems needed to support business process re-engineering. ICL's approach involves finding measurable improvement objectives and using ProcessWise WorkBench to build the simulations to be measured against these objectives. ProcessWise Integrator then helps to develop the workflow management system. This approach is remarkably similar in some respects to the approach of SOMA to modelling both enterprises and systems but still has a data flow emphasis. It also illustrates the intimate connexion between groupware products and business process re-engineering. What all these approaches have in common is that they lack an adequate *theory* of what a business process is.

Unlike many approaches to business process re-engineering and requirements engineering, SOMA offers a very definite, theoretically based, perspective on the question of what a business process is, which I now present. The theory is rooted in the science of Semiotics, and the work of Winograd and Flores (1986) on workflow systems. Rather than taking use cases as a starting point, we extract them from a process model.

As I have said, a key part of the SOMA approach to system development is the use of joint user and developer workshops for requirements capture and analysis. The technique, of course, pre-dates object technology and I used it long before there were any methods for object-oriented analysis available. Running such workshops, I have found that data-centred or static modelling approaches to object modelling are not a good place to start with users. Obtaining an entity model or business object model takes quite a long time if attempted at the start of a workshop. Worse still, the developers in the group tend to dominate the procedure since they have more experience of modelling in this way. Quite often this leads to a neglect of behaviour and processes in favour of a static model. Many people with similar experience have observed that users respond better to a process-oriented approach. However, if we want to extract an object-oriented model from the activity, constructing data flow diagrams is really worse than useless and likely to: (a) be ignored by real object-oriented programmers; or (b) lead to a horrid functional decomposition that poorer programmers can use as an excuse to write functionally oriented code – or 'flat C++' as I once saw it euphemistically described (Cox, 1994). My experience has shown that all these problems can be overcome by basing the requirements model on business processes using a modelling technique that is strictly object-oriented and is a generalization of both the data flow, use case analysis and the soft and human-centric approaches discussed in Section 8.1. As a side effect of the approach, it turns out that if an entity model view is required for a conventional implementation, it can be extracted from the object model and agreed with users literally in a matter of moments.

8.5.1 Business process models

Both requirements engineering and business process re-engineering must start with a model of the communications and contracts among the participants in the business and the other stakeholders, customers, suppliers and so on. We should have already identified these 'external agents' as part of our mission grid construction. If not, doing so is a first step.

Consider some business or enterprise. It could be an entire small company, a division or department of a larger one or even a sole trader. A **business process** (or business area) is a network of communicating agents. Flores (1997) refers to this as a network of *commitments*. An **agent** is any entity in the world that can communicate; so it could represent a customer, regulator, employee, organizational unit, computer system or even a mechanical device of a certain type, such as a clock. Agents are autonomous and flexible. They respond to appropriate stimuli and they can be proactive and exhibit a social aspect; i.e. communicate. Typically agents exhibit some level of intelligence; human agents certainly so but mechanical agents insofar as they can initiate and respond to communication. This now begs the question of what it means for two agents to communicate.

Agents can be **internal** to the business we are examining or **external** to it. This has nothing to do with whether they are system users; i.e. actors. Agents – like actors – are to be thought of as adopting a rôle.

This 'business' must communicate with the outside world to exist at all and, if it does so, it must use some convention of signs and signals thereto. We can call these signals between agents **semiotic acts**. They are *carried* by some material substratum. They involve a number of semiotic levels from data flows up to implicit social relationships[2]. For example, the substrate may consist of filled-in forms in a paper-based office environment and the social context might be that one assumes that no practical jokes are to be played. If the substratum is verbal (or written) natural language then we can speak instead of **speech acts** or **conversations**. These are the speech acts of Austin (1962) and Searle (1969). Flores (1997) argues that business conversations have a constant recurrent structure based on only five primitive speech acts: assert, assess, declare, offer/promise and request.

Semiotic acts (or conversations as I shall call them from here on) can be represented by messages, which are directed from the initiator (source) of the communication to its recipient (target). By *abus de langage* we can identify semiotic acts, or conversations, with their representation as messages although strictly they are different; the same semiotic act may be represented by many different messages.[3] This defines equivalence classes of messages and we can think of our actual message as a generic representative of its class; many contracts may express the same relationship so we choose one to represent its equivalence class.

A typical conversation is represented in Figure 8.6 where a typical external customer agent places an order with some business. This message includes the

[2] Semiotics is the comparative study of sign systems and has been important in such diverse fields as mathematical logic, natural language processing, anthropology and literary criticism. It holds that signs can be analysed at at least three levels: those of syntax, semantics and pragmatics. There can be as many as five levels, up to and including the level defined by the social relations of production.

[3] For a trivial example consider that the same conversation may be represented by a message in English, Chinese, German or Urdu.

definition of the reply: {order accepted|out of stock|etc.}. We have, quite legitimately I think, used the UML use case symbol to represent the conversation, but overloaded the UML actor symbol to represent agents in Figure 8.6(a). If a distinction between actors (who are users) and other agents (who are not) is required, symbols like those of Figure 8.6(b) can be used.

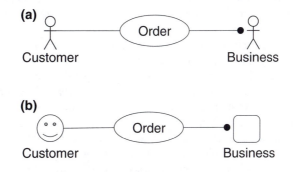

Figure 8.6 A conversation.

A message implies that data flow, so that this approach generalizes data flow modelling. However, it also enriches it considerably. For one thing, data flow in both directions along message links (via the request and hand-over stages discussed below). This is why we have chosen to terminate message links at the recipient end with a filled circle rather than an arrowhead. The line segment is directed from the *initiator* of the communication, not from the origin of the data.

We now begin to see that agents can be modelled as objects that pass messages to each other. Clearly agents can also be classified into different types as well. Therefore it seems well justified to refer to our business process model as an Agent Object Model (AOM). The question we face now is how to go about analysing the messages. So far as I am aware, apart from the ORCA approach which overlaps my approach somewhat, there are only three candidate techniques:

1. Jackson System Development (JSD) (Jackson, 1983) can be used or some object-oriented variant of it such as KISS (Kristen, 1995). In my view this type of approach is far too close to system design to work well at the requirements elicitation stage, except for a very limited range of problem types.
2. Use cases (Jacobson *et al.,* 1992) are probably the most widely used alternative and constitute the recommended technique within UML. However, as we have seen, they are limited when not dealing with system specification.
3. It therefore seems that an approach based on semiotics such as the one proposed here is all that is both available and realistic.

A semiotic or speech act is characterized at the semantic and pragmatic levels by a (possibly implicit) contract that both parties understand. The pragmatics of this contract represent a social relation, just as a message represents a semiotic act.

We think of a business process as a network of related conversations between agents, represented by messages. It is inconceivable in most businesses that the message initiator does not wish to change the state of the world in some way as a result of the communication. This desired state of the world is the **goal** of the conversation and every conversation (or message) has a goal or post-condition, even if it is often unstated: the contract representing the conditions of satisfaction of the conversation.

A goal is achieved by the performance of a **task**. The innovation here is twofold. Firstly, there is the realization that the tasks we perform can often be reduced to a few stereotypes: typical tasks that act as pattern matching templates against which real tasks can be evaluated and from which real tasks (or use cases) can be generated. This overcomes a possible objection that there could be an explosion in the number of use cases, as I have often found. My experience indicates that there is no such explosion of tasks. For example, in a simple foreign exchange deal capture model there are only eleven tasks of which eight are atomic (defined below and illustrated in Figure 8.14). Second comes the appreciation that tasks can be modelled as objects within a *bona fide* object model in the task domain, as we shall see in the next section.

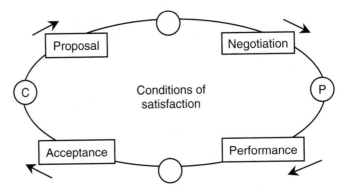

Figure 8.7 A Flores conversation for action.

In business, only serious, goal-oriented conversations are relevant and therefore we can argue that each conversation has a sixfold structure as follows:

1. A **triggering event**: a world event that triggers the interaction.
2. A **goal**: a world state desired by the initiator of the conversation.
3. An **offer** or **request**, which contains the data necessary for the recipient to evaluate the offer or request.
4. A **negotiation**, whereby the recipient determines whether the goals are shared and the conditions of acceptance, leading to either a **contract** being agreed or the offer rejected. The contract formalizes the goal and provides formal conditions for knowing when the goal has been achieved satisfactorily.

5. A **task** that must be performed by the recipient of a request to achieve the goal and satisfy the contract. This is what is normally thought of as a use case when one of the agents is an actor.

6. A **handover** of the product of the task and any associated data, which checks that the conditions of satisfaction of the goals have been met.

This structure accords generally with that of a *conversation for action* in the terminology of Winograd and Flores (Flores, 1997; Winograd and Flores, 1986), although I have added the notion of a triggering event. Note also that there is a symmetry of offers and requests, so that we can replace every offer with an equivalent request by swapping the initiator with the recipient. In SOMA one always deals with messages in this **request canonical form**. Flores presents the theory, as shown in Figure 8.7, in terms of a customer (our initiator) and a performer (our recipient) who executes the primitive speech acts – shown in italics in what follows. The customer *assesses* her concerns and *asserts* a request to the performer (dually the performer makes an offer). A process of negotiation then ensues, aimed at defining a contract that can be *promised* by the performer and accepted by the customer. This, and other stages in the conversation, may involve recursion whereby subsidiary conversations are engaged in. At the end of negotiation the contract defines the conditions of customer satisfaction, and then some task must be executed to fulfil their promise. Finally, the results of this work are *declared* complete and handed over to the customer who should *declare* satisfaction.

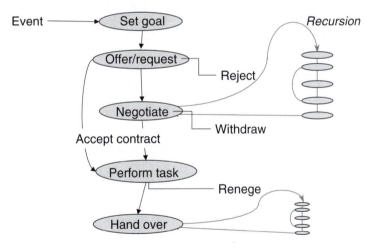

Figure 8.8 The structure of a conversation in SOMA.

Figure 8.8 shows the structure of a SOMA conversation and illustrates that recursion can occur in each segment of the conversation and that either party may withdraw at each stage.

Consider the concrete example of buying a house. An initiator might say 'would you like to buy my house?' and the recipient would need to know, and would negotiate on, the price. This negotiation could well involve (recursively) subsidiary conversations between the recipient and a mortgage provider and a building surveyor. If everything is agreed then a contract will be agreed and signed (literally in this case). Now there is work to do; in England it is called conveyancing. The work involves searching local government records and land registry documents along with many other – all fairly straightforward – tasks. So this is the place where we might rely on a standard task script, as exemplified for example by the words (or flowcharts) in a book on conveyancing. Finally, when this task completes satisfactorily we can hand over the keys and the contract is said to be *completed*.

A BPR EXAMPLE Of course, in business process re-engineering, we are eager to capture not just the messages that cross the business boundary, such as order placement, but to model the communications among our customers, suppliers, competitors, etc. This provides the opportunity to offer new services to these players, perhaps taking over their internal operations – for a fee of course.

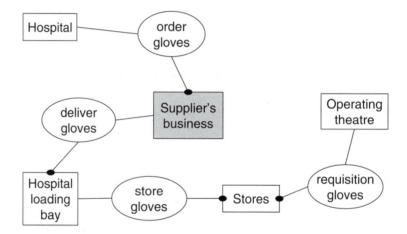

Figure 8.9 Re-engineering delivery logistics: before.

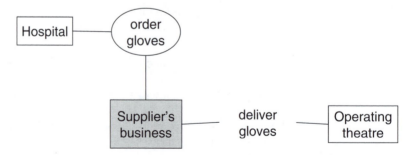

Figure 8.10 Re-engineering delivery logistics: after.

Figures 8.9 and 8.10 show how this might be applied in the simple case of delivering medical supplies, based on what happened at Baxter Healthcare (Short and Venkatramen, 1992). Originally, Baxter took an order from the hospital's procurement department and delivered to its loading bay. Then the hospital was responsible for storing the goods and delivering them to the appropriate operating theatre (Figure 8.9). After re-engineering, goods such as surgical gloves are delivered direct by the supplier to the operating theatre where they are required (Figure 8.10). Of course, the message labelled OrderGloves has been modified. This gives an advantage over other suppliers in terms of service, reduces the hospital's inventory and logistics costs and means that a higher price can be charged by the supplier while remaining competitive. It also makes the hospital more dependent on the supplier.

MATCHING MODELS   Having analysed the business process in terms of conversations, we now focus on the task performance segment of the conversation: the use case if actors are involved. Before doing so let us remind ourselves of the model sequence. We started with a mission grid leading to several processes. Each process has several objectives. Also, there is now a network of conversations (messages). We should now ask two critically important questions:

- Does every message support the achievement of *at least one* objective?
- Is *every* objective supported by at least one message?

If the answer to either question is 'no', then the model must be amended. Either we have missed some conversations or we are modelling conversations that do not contribute to the achievement of any stated business objective. Of course, it is possible that we have missed an important objective and, in that case, the users should be consulted to see if the statement of objectives needs to be modified. If not, we have a clear re-engineering opportunity: just stop doing the work that supports no objective.

8.5.2 Activity diagrams and business process modelling

UML provides only one notation for business process modelling: the activity diagram. Activity diagrams are said to be a special case of state charts, which implies that they must describe the state of some thing – or object. However, the way they are used, as Martin and Odell (1998) point out, makes them look dangerously like data flow diagrams; albeit with some characteristics of flow charts added. Their origins are in Ptech and Martin/Odell event schemata. The states are usually 'process states'. Figure 8.11 shows an activity diagram in the domain of order processing. You will see that it is entirely unclear which object(s) the process states are states of – unless order processing is itself an object of some sort. We can improve the situation somewhat by adding swimlanes, as we have done in this figure.

In the figure, process states are rounded rectangles and arrows represent, possibly conditional, threads of control flow. The diamonds are decision branches, as in a flowchart. The thick horizontal bars represent forks and joins of control. It is distinctly better to annotate these with pre- and post-conditions, as we have done with the 'order prepared' fork. I have shown two swimlanes with grey outlines and names.

The problem is that, without swimlanes, the processes are entirely 'disembodied' and the notation is not object-oriented at all. By 'disembodied' I mean that the processes are not encapsulated within any business object. The advantage of this is that no assumptions about the allocation of responsibilities have been made, so that attention is not focused on any particular implementation of the business process. However, this is only apparently so; the diagram is a state chart, so the states must be states of something – we just haven't said what explicitly. Using swimlanes makes our assumption more clear. But even here there are problems. Remarkably, Rumbaugh *et al.* (1999) state that, as an organizational unit for activity diagrams, the swimlane 'has no inherent semantics': it can mean whatever you like! Most people seem to use them to represent functional units within the organization; so we are straight back to a set of assumptions about business process implementation.

Our agent conversation diagrams offer a convenient alternative to activity diagrams which makes all implementation assumptions very explicit and, more importantly, in a way more readily understandable by users; the activity notation is quite hard to remember, understand and explain. Of course, there may be occasions when activity diagrams are helpful, but I have found few occasions when this is so.

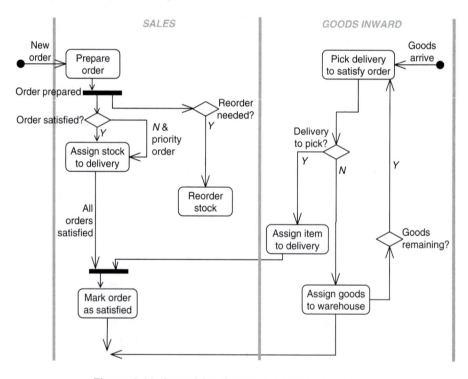

Figure 8.11 An activity diagram for order processing.

Martin and Odell (1998) give the following criteria for deciding whether or not to use this kind of state-based representation. Consider using activity charts if:

- an object has complex, significant state (use state charts);
- there is complex interaction between a few objects which trigger state changes in each other – as often found in real-time control systems;
- object behaviour is event driven and single threaded and objects have only one state variable (note that business processes are notoriously multi-threaded);
- the user culture supports their use – as in the telecomms sector.

Avoid them if:

- there are several threads (as in a typical business process);
- there is complex interaction between large numbers of objects;
- objects have several significant state variables.

Odell's arguments seem to support mine, although I know he does use the notation for process modelling.

I find that the 'embodied' approach of agent and use case modelling is easier to understand for most non-technical people. Also, provided that the 'make before and after models' discipline is enforced, the approach is very productive in a re-engineering context, with implementation assumptions seldom appearing. Another reason that I avoid this notation is that it is very hard to discuss what causes transitions between states or how these occur.

Activity diagrams are reminiscent of what O&M experts in the 1960s used to call procedure flow charts. One useful application of them is to document system (or system simulation) executions, as we discuss later in this chapter. Sequence diagrams can be used for the same purpose, but activity charts may be better if we want to show control or decision branching, or both. It is very much a pragmatic decision as to which notation is best in each case one meets.

8.6 From conversations to tasks and use cases

Task modelling is a powerful, generic variant of use case modelling. It enables us to drill down into the agent model and model users' task performance in a very concise and thoroughly object-oriented manner. Our focus now moves chiefly to the task segment of the conversations. We now show that we can represent tasks as *bona fide* objects. Because of this we need no new notation and can rely entirely on the techniques presented in Chapter 6. This is in contradistinction to UML, which introduces a whole new set of notation to represent use case dependencies; principally «include» and «extend». We are in the happier position of being able to stick to the known representations for objects and the basic four structural links of UML:

classification, composition, usage and association.[4] The model is a model of a different subject matter but the modelling concepts are identical in structural terms. Remember that we are using the precepts of the object metaphor to model task actions, and so use cases are treated as objects. Classification and composition relationships allow us to group similar objects together into networks. Thus with tasks too!

Decomposing tasks into components is another important feature of the process, for two reasons. Disaggregating tasks into components uncovers tasks which can feature as components in more than one high level task; this supports reuse by containment. In addition, the count of 'atomic' tasks within a model, referred to as the *task point* count, provides an important metric on the system's scope and complexity. This metric and other metrics are discussed in Chapter 9.

The operations of task objects are methods that invoke exception handling tasks. Exception tasks, or 'side-scripts', represent unusual tasks which are executed in specific circumstances. We often find that exception tasks are reusable in the context of a variety of high level tasks. As with other associations between tasks, there may be some level of iteration: there can be exceptions to exceptions. For example, we usually interrupt our normal work by taking a break in the summer. But if unexpected circumstances, such as a death in the family, should sadly arise, we might well suspend our holiday activities and rush off home.

Although we model tasks as objects, a task can also be viewed as an aspect of the behaviour of an agent. It parallels the idea of an operation of a type.

SCRIPT THEORY

Tasks can be described in several ways but it is most useful to describe a task using a **task script**. A task script represents a *stereotypical* task. It is a textual description of such a task (ideally a single sentence) with lists of nominated supertasks, component tasks and tasks that describe exceptions (side-scripts). This provides a notion of generalized exception handling that does not seem to be natural to users of the use case approach, where an exception (extends) path is often specific to the use case. Jacobson *et al.* (1992) define a use case as 'a behaviourally related sequence of transactions *in a dialogue with the system*' and 'a sequence of transactions *in a system* whose task is to yield a result of measurable value' (Jacobson *et al.,* 1995). My added emphasis indicates a slight conflict between these two definitions. I will take the view, shared by most users of the technique, that a task describes a dialogue in the world and not in the system and that use cases are restricted to describing the system interface. Task scripts are part of a model of the world but differ in that they are not restricted to the interface. What is more important, task scripts describe *stereotyped* behaviour in the world.

As an example, consider a task script that describes the task of going to a restaurant. The idea is that one *always* does the same thing when visiting a restaurant. One *always*:

---

[4] Dan Rawsthorne of Dimensions Inc. (private communication) also has a theory of use cases (with goals) that uses standard UML notation to connect them. His semantics coincide with a subset of mine. Cockburn (1997) also argues for adding goals to use cases.

1. Enters the restaurant
2. Attracts the attention of a waiter
3. Takes one's seat
4. Reads the menu
5. Chooses a meal
6. Eats it
7. Pays
8. Leaves

This is certainly a good stereotype of the situations normally met with – at least in a US restaurant. However, no visit to any restaurant follows this script exactly. One may, for example:

1. Enter the restaurant
2. Attract the attention of a waiter
3. Go to take one's seat
4. Slip on a banana skin ...

The script is broken and must be repaired before our culinary cravings can be assuaged. This is accomplished by permitting what we will call side-scripts, which deal with stereotypical exceptions. **Side-scripts** are scripts for well-known situations that may be invoked when an exception occurs in another script; we have the mental model of a script 'sending a message' to a side-script to ask for its help. In this particular case the side-script might proceed:

1. Get up
2. Brush oneself down
3. Look around to see who is laughing
4. Abuse them verbally or punch them
5. Return to the interrupted task

The point to note here is that the banana skin script does not just work in the context of the restaurant script. It will work anywhere: in the street, on the factory floor or in the office (if there are no carpets). In practice, scripts can become complicated and have to allow for many exceptions; e.g. what happens when the bill arrives and you find you have lost your wallet? However, the script describes a well-known and stereotypical situation: one that has been encountered many times before. To process such exceptions, task objects are able to send messages to each other. It turns out that task scripts can also be classified and (de)composed. For example the scripts for paying one's electricity, gas and water bills can be generalized into a 'pay bill' task script. In other words, they can be regarded as objects within an object model. This Task Object Model is not the Business Object Model (BOM) that we will derive eventually. The Task Object Model is a model of the world and the Business Object Model is a model of a potentially implementable system.

The idea of task scripts has its theoretical roots in the AI script theory of Schank and Abelson (1977) and in the hierarchical task analysis popular in HCI work. Also, task scripts can be regarded as generic use cases. Use cases may be one sentence or an essay whereas atomic task scripts should consist of a single sentence. This means that measurement of process models based on task scripts is much easier than with use cases. Parenthetically, we should note that a side-script has exactly the same semantics as what Schank and Abelson called a 'subscript'. The renaming is necessary to avoid confusion with notions of specialization where the prefix 'sub' is commonly used.

So, tasks can be modelled as *bona fide* objects, where the attributes are the task script and various performance-related items and the operations are exceptions to the script to be handled by other tasks. The most common approach to analysing a task that arises from a conversation is to decompose the task into components and to keep doing this until the tasks are atomic. The scripts can be written using a task action grammar if desired, which we call SVDPI form because all sentences can be arranged into the form: Subject–Verb–Direct object(s)–Preposition–Indirect object(s).

It is always possible to keep on decomposing tasks *ad infinitum*, merely by adding more detail or descending to a lower level of Physics. We stop when words that are not in the vocabulary of the normal user would be introduced at the next stage of the decomposition. For example, in order capture the script 'the clerk moves the mouse to the Quantity field and enters ...' is not atomic because the word mouse is not part of the ontology of ordering. We should have stopped at 'the clerk enters the quantity ...'. In other words an **atomic** script is arrived at by decomposing task objects until:

1. the task script is a single sentence – ideally in SVDPI format;
2. further decomposition would introduce terms that are not in the domain ontology.

TASKS AND USE CASES

Use cases were introduced as a technique for object-oriented requirements capture by Jacobson *et al.* (1992) and have been almost universally recognized as a brilliant and useful idea by the object-oriented methods community. Most methodologists have integrated use cases into their methods. Use cases offered possibly the first technique within object-oriented development that did not assume that a written requirements specification existed at the start of object-oriented analysis.

Task scripts were first introduced within the SOMA method and have three main intellectual ancestors: Jacobson's use cases, hierarchical task analysis as found in the HCI literature and the scripts found in the conceptual dependency theory of Schank and Abelson (1977). Rubin and Goldberg (1992) use the term SCRIPT in their work on OBA and one suspects that this usage is derived in a similar way, though this was not stated explicitly; nor were their conclusions the same as mine.

At first sight, the use case approach appears to have a more functional flavour than the object-oriented practitioner would be comfortable with. Blaha and Premerlani (1998), leading thinkers behind OMT, go so far as to include a treatment of use cases within the dataflow-based Functional Model of OMT. This has led critics to claim that use cases are not really object-oriented at all. However, when use cases emerged it was clear that object-oriented analysis and design methods lacked an approach to system requirements specification. Furthermore, most of these methods were entirely data-driven and this led to difficulties in communicating with users who were more comfortable with functionally oriented descriptions than with data-centred ones. So, while use cases and the Objectory method within which they were situated were rather 'functional' there was at least a small step forward beyond the methods that assumed the pre-existence of the requirements statement. The challenge was to integrate this advance and its functional viewpoint within a genuinely object-oriented, responsibility-driven approach, rather than cobbling it together with a data-driven one.

Far more seriously, the lack of a precise and universally accepted definition has led to a proliferation of approaches all calling themselves 'use case' based. It seems that every company has their own version of the theory. At a goldfish bowl session at Object Technology 96, held in Oxford, England, participants were asked if they used use cases. Of the 14 who said they did, each was asked to give a definition of a use case. The result was 14 different definitions; even though three of the respondents worked for the same company (in different divisions). Cockburn (1997) has obtained similar results in the USA. At a workshop on use cases at OOPSLA'97 the present author asked the other participants if they would deduce that this meant that a precisely defined notion of use cases (such as task scripts) should use a different name to make the issues clearer. The consensus that emerged from the discussion was, yes, we should really rename the idea but, no, the industry had bought the idea of use cases and so we had to live with the label – however ill defined. I disagree with this pessimism and continue to talk about task scripts, while recognizing our deep debt to Jacobson. Precision matters in Science and Engineering.

My experience with use cases dates back to about 1991, when I attempted to use them to capture the requirements for part of a banking application: deal capture. I quickly discovered that this relatively simple application was generating hundreds of use cases; far too many to be manageable! With task scripts there were eleven: an order of magnitude improvement! This defect is potentially very serious, though in some domains (designing equipment such as vending machines or switch gear for example) it may not happen. In MIS domains I have often found that there are hundreds or even thousands of use cases precisely because there are many exceptional paths through a business process. The exceptions are not 'errors' as they would be in a computer program; they are important – often business-critical – variants on the use case. Nor are they concrete scenarios, because they themselves are implemented in a multiplicity of concrete executable scenarios corresponding to actual use. From a practical point of view there was no longer any doubt which technique we would use in future, but the theoretical question of why this explosion in number took place remained. We now understand that there are several reasons that lead to this problem of multiplying too rapidly.[5]

First of all we want to be able to treat use cases as *bona fide* objects so that we can reuse them, as we did routinely in Chapter 6. This turns out to be problematical because of the granularity of the typical use case, the fact that a use case can span

---

[5] This violation of Ockham's razor first emerged from several users' comments during a Birds-Of-a-Feather session at Object Expo Europe in 1993. It is confirmed by anecdotal evidence from several projects known to me and the observations of other practitioners.

several linked but independent tasks and because of the poor exception handling semantics in the theory.

Severe problems arise if we try to treat pure UML use cases as objects: a treatment that Jacobson hints at in several places. One structural link between use cases, the «extends» arrow, points in the wrong direction from the point of view of encapsulation. Therefore we are not able to treat use cases as *bona fide* objects. Therefore they are not really reusable. If we agree that use cases are pure objects, we do not need to invent «includes» and «extends» links but can use existing and properly defined object-oriented linkage concepts such as composition and usage to cover the same semantics and, additionally, we get the notions of inheritance and task associations for free. Usage links give us a much better way of handling exceptions than is available with standard use cases, which suffer from the poor semantics of «extends».

INCLUDES AND EXTENDS

One use case 'uses' or 'includes' another if the latter is 'part of its own description' (Jacobson *et al.,* 1995). Thus, the Objectory 'uses' relationship (ako UML «includes») certainly corresponds to task decomposition using the aggregation relationship in UML. The difference here is one of interpretation. Objectory does not emphasize the discovery of use case components of this kind by top-down decomposition.

A use case 'extends' another if it may be 'inserted into' the latter (Jacobson *et al.,* 1992). Thus, «extends» would correspond to 'is a side-script of', though the arrows are drawn in the opposite sense in the latter to preserve encapsulation; an extension of a task should not know that it is part of something bigger.

To use an example from Jacobson *et al.* (1992), consider the design of a vending machine, which accepts used containers for recycling. Returning item is the use case that describes a customer inserting a used container into the machine. The Item is stuck use case extends Returning item and describes what happens when the container jams in the chute. However, it does so in a foreseeable course of events, whereas the restaurant script only uses the BananaSkin script (discussed above) in the most exceptional circumstances, which may not be foreseen. One of the consequences of this in terms of implementation is that EnterRestaurant may have to perform a search for an appropriate script such as BananaSkin rather than store a reference to it statically. Once again, for reasons of encapsulation and the promotion of reuse, it is important that side-scripts do not know which scripts they 'extend', which is why it is important to model this relationship as a message-send to the side-script, possibly involving a search.

The reader may be tempted to confuse our side-script notion with UML's 'includes' or 'extends' relations. A careful reading of both the works of Jacobson cited and the UML reference material reveals that this is not exactly the case, though there is a considerable overlap. Our intention is to use a very pure concept of object modelling to model tasks. In this way the developer has to learn only one set of terminology and concepts to model both tasks and business objects.

ATOMICITY   As project managers we would like to believe that the number of use cases in a requirements analysis gives some indication of the business benefit or the final system or even of the amount of effort involved in building it. This would help with product pricing and project estimation. However, use cases are notoriously hard to measure, since a use case can be any length.

The lack of a notion of *atomicity* means that no metrics can be reasonably defined for use case models – unless we change their definition as many companies have indeed done: numbering the sentences of a use case, for example. The task script notion includes a notion of atomicity that permits developers to measure task complexity by simply counting the single-sentence atomic scripts.

ASSOCIATION SETS OF TASKS   A use case covers a sequence of several possibly interchangeable tasks. For example, consider a system that automatically prices orders and provides automatic quotations or diverts them, under certain criteria, to a salesman for manual pricing or quotation. It would be normal to have four use cases at the highest level of abstraction: autoprice quote, autoprice order, manual order and manual quote. This is not a parsimonious approach because the process of applying diversion rules that decide whether to re-route orders or quotes to the sales desk may be different for quotes and orders while the notification process is the same (or *vice versa*). For this reason it is better to have independent task scripts for the different components of the use case. These can then be assembled to model complete business processes. This promotes greater reusability of task objects.

The upshot of this is that, while in most cases task scripts are merely generic or essential use cases, it may be the case that a conventional use case corresponds to a sequence or network of tasks linked by an association set; i.e. in a, possibly concurrent, activity or sequence diagram. Task association sets are explained in Section 8.11.

RESTRICTION TO INTERFACE   While they have been utilized successfully on many projects, use cases have been criticized for dealing only with the external, interface aspects of systems. This refers of course to all interfaces and not just the human–computer interface.

The defect, if such it is, is deliberate. The intention was to focus designers' attention on what the system did for its users, rather than how it did it. While this is a laudable aim, and is quite the correct approach to take when building a telecommunications switch or a process controller, in many MIS applications – especially those replacing paper flow systems – the development team, consisting of users and developers, has expectations about how the system (not necessarily the computer system but the business system) will operate internally. These expectations are often the basis of insights into business processes and opportunities for re-engineering them. Thus, a variant on use cases that permits internal modelling can be desirable in such circumstances.

This is the inverse of the earlier criticism that says that use case analysis does not extend *outside* the system boundary; here the problem is that it does not look *inside*. We are not suggesting that encapsulation be violated, of course.

CONTROLLER OBJECTS

These problems with use cases are not the end of our critique of OOSE and, by implication, Objectory and UML. OOSE recommends that its use cases should be linked to three kinds of implementation object: entity objects [*sic*], interface objects and controller objects. The introduction of controller objects later in the analysis process can seriously violate the principle of encapsulation, leading to severe maintenance problems downstream. This is because controllers often act as main routines (especially when a data-driven approach is adopted) and have to know a great deal about the other objects that they control. Thus, when one of these objects changes, the controller may have to be modified. This style of implementation, where the controller objects access several entity objects (i.e. datastores), was shown to be inferior to a responsibility-driven design in the study of Sharble and Cohen (1994) discussed in Section 6.2.1. A far better approach is the use of rule-based agents as discussed in Chapters 6 and 10.

USE CASES AND SCENARIOS

There has been some further confusion over the exact meaning of the term SCENARIO among users of Jacobson's Objectory and OOSE methods and, therefore, of UML. The problems referred to above are mostly compounded by confusion over whether a use case is the same as a scenario. At OOPSLA 1994 a panel was posed the question of the relationship between scenarios and use cases. Jacobson and Booch agreed that a scenario was 'an instance of a use case' but the point was not elaborated further. The distinction is far better understood as that between abstract and concrete notions than between classes and instances. Use cases and scenarios are *both* instance level concepts. One difference is that scenarios also include sequencing information.

The use case approach asks developers to begin by discovering behaviourally related sequences of transactions in a dialogue with a system whose task is to yield a result of measurable value to actors who use the system. These descriptions are then mined for concepts and actions that will be implemented as classes and methods in a future system. Several other approaches recommend the study of scenarios of system use. In most cases a scenario is more detailed and specific than a use case and may mention individuals by name. Thus, 'The user enters the number' is a use case whereas 'John enters his wife's number' is a scenario – at least that is the understanding that will suffice for the purposes of this book.

ESSENTIAL OR GENERIC USE CASES

Another reason for the tendency to find too many use cases is the lack of any notion of essentiality or genericity.

There appears to be an overlap between the notion of task scripts and Constantine's *essential* use cases. However, the motivation is different and the embedding of the theory of task scripts within the approach to business process modelling described in this chapter justifies its separate presentation.

Essential use cases abstract away from the detail of a use case in a different dimension from task scripts. As an example, the use case that deals with extracting cash from an ATM (Automatic Teller Machine) refers to inserting a card, entering a PIN and so on. The corresponding essential use case merely refers to withdrawing cash. This corresponds to what I have referred to as the *atomicity* of tasks. The atomic level depends on the purpose of the description and excludes terms foreign to the domain at that level of purpose. Constantine (1995) defines an essential use case as:

> an abstract use case describing the common structure of use cases representing a single intent or purpose of users in some rôle (Jacobson's 'actors', simplified and generalized to represent the essential core of something such users want or need to accomplish independent of implementation in a specific user interface or interface technology. An essential use case is expressed in user application domain terms and assumes idealized technology or is technology independent.

In other words, an essential use case is a structured narrative, expressed in a language that users can understand. It is a simplified, abstract, technology-free and implementation-independent description of a user's task, embodying the goal underlying an interaction. These definitions combine what I have called 'generification' and 'atomicity'. I think it is better to separate these concerns. As I show in the next section, a task script represents a generic use case. Thus, I would suggest that a task script that is atomic – or contains (has parts) nothing more specific than atomic tasks – should be called an essential task script. It then appears that an essential task script is the same as what Constantine calls an essential use case. Eliciting essential use cases is a key part of Constantine's Usage-Centred Design method (Constantine and Lockwood, 1999): a method that has much to recommend it and which overlaps – in spirit at least – with the ideas presented in this chapter.

Now we are in a position to define the differences and relationships between the concepts of task actions, use cases and scenarios. To overcome the lack of essentiality referred to above, what is required is a generification[6] of the idea of use cases that prevents this explosion in their number. Task actions are just such a generic concept that, additionally, allows developers to model the internals of the business process and its implementation.

As remarked earlier, a scenario is often seen as an instance of a use case: it describes an actual occurrence of the use case. Intuitively, too, a use case could be thought of as an instance of a linked set of task actions: it describes a typical path through the business model. Unfortunately, this terminology does not bear closer scrutiny because a scenario is an instance of the class of scenarios and the class of *all* scenarios will not correspond to a sensible use case. The idea, however, is sound and can be rephrased by saying that task actions *generify* use cases in the sense that a set of task scripts is a generic use case or an equivalence class of use cases. They do not *generalize* use cases; they make them generic. Similarly, a use case is a generic scenario.

We may now view a **use case** as an equivalence class of scenarios. Task actions *generify* use cases in the sense that a task action is a **generic** or **essential** use case

---

[6] The OED describes this word as more precise than GENERALIZATION: 'the abstraction which carries up species into genera'. It is used here in the sense of 'making a generic representative'.

segment. Similarly, a use case is a generic scenario instance. A use case is equivalent to the set of scenarios that can implement it and a task action sequence is equivalent to the set of use cases that can implement it. The equivalence relations are easily defined informally but may often be fuzzy relations in the sense of Zadeh (1971). For example, the relation could equate all scenarios where some individual enters the phone number of some other individual, or all 'eating out' use cases. For an example of the fuzzy case, we could instantiate the EnterRestaurant script with the use case for entering a fast food establishment although, so far as I can see, most of the latter bear a very fuzzy relationship to any normal concept of a restaurant. In fact, we know that the term restaurant is misapplied *precisely* because of our sense of dissonance when we try to apply the term RESTAURANT to a McDonald's outlet: the script doesn't fit.

The three levels of abstraction correspond (informally) to the three traditional levels of information systems modelling: data, information and knowledge. The levels are nothing to do with the difference between abstract and concrete use cases as Jacobson has suggested.[7] That distinction only tells us how we classify or generalize scenarios and use cases. We can do the same thing with task scripts and define an abstract task as one having no instances. What is needed is not generalization but generification.

As we saw earlier, the advantage of moving to the essential level is principally that we abstract away from specific exceptions that tend to increase the total number of use cases to an unacceptable extent

As if all these criticisms were not enough, there is even a problem with the phrase USE CASE itself being, I suspect, a literal translation of a Swedish construction. It makes for very unwieldy and unprosodic expressions in English, such as 'using uses links between the use cases we use is used to show ...'.

What can be done to fix all these problems? What is needed is an approach with a sound, theoretical basis and a precise definition. We need a notion of *genericity* and a notion of *atomicity* for use cases or their equivalent. Use cases have no clear link to a business process model and are offered as such a model in their own right, which I feel does not make good sense. Finally, we need an approach that is properly object-oriented in supporting encapsulation and inheritance. The task modelling approach of SOMA fulfils all these criteria.

I suspect that the different ways of thinking about the problems of requirements engineering partly reflect differences in the domains within which Objectory and SOMA grew up, and especially differences among the typical users that are encountered in these domains. Telecommunication engineers are usually quite happy with detailed specification and will be comfortable with, for example, state machine notations. Bankers do not often respond well to such approaches. A further practical consequence is a vast reduction in the sheer size of the model. Booch, who has accumulated experience of the technique, remarked that: 'Most systems are characterized by 10 [high level] use cases, an order of magnitude more primary use cases and an[other] order of magnitude more secondary use cases' (Grotehen, 1995).

---

[7] Private communication.

The chief reason for this explosion seems to be the lack of generic exception handling and the nature of the «includes» and «extends» notions as discussed above.

☐ 8.7 From the Task Object Model to the Business Object Model

In this section I explain how a UML specification, or Business Object Model, can be elicited from a reading of the task scripts together with a good helping of creativity and design acumen.

Recall that external agents differ from internal agents in two senses: internal agents work within our business; and we know more about the tasks they are carrying out. External agents may conceal tasks we have no knowledge of, which will affect us because they lead to events that trigger messages or **triggering events**. In the case of messages initiated by actors or agents internal to the business, we usually know the causes of these events, because they are the direct result of task execution. When the initiator is an external agent we nearly always lack this knowledge and the triggering event appears as a given. **Actors** are users of a system (adopting a rôle) and thus could be either internal or external agents but are normally internal. Therefore, we may routinely confuse internal agents with actors in practice and use the UML pin-man icon. Messages always have triggering events, though for internal agents and system agents we will usually know the task that has led to the event.

CARTOONING AGENTS In the normal style of object-oriented development, agents – such as customers and clerks – are usually represented in the Business Object Model by rather unintelligent objects with few or no operations but typically several attributes. It is important not to confuse these internal representations, which cannot do anything except store static data, with their real-world counterparts that do exhibit, often complex, behaviour. Such internal representations of agents external to the system are nearly always persistent objects. The more usual object-oriented approach models intelligent customers and clerks as mere dumb data structures and the orders – which are dumb pieces of paper in the real world – as intelligent objects responsible for several operations, such as the validation of customer credit limits or checking stock levels. There is a powerful alternative to this, which is to internalize part of the intelligence of the entities in the world as *intelligent agents* in the system.

In Figure 8.12 an internal agent (the clerk actor) receives the customer's order and enters it into a business support system. The order is triggered by some unknown condition within the customer. Of course, this business support system is likely to be the computer system that we are trying to construct, but it could just as well be a card index or similar. Our task as analysts is to find the business objects. We evidently have a clerk, a customer, a product and, of course, an order. Is the credit limit an attribute of customer or is it the responsibility of a credit manager agent? In banking systems it is often the latter because credit lines are handled by specialized systems; usually legacy systems. But now we come to the really fascinating question from the agent-oriented perspective: How intelligent is the order itself? Do the credit validation rules belong to the **Orders** class?

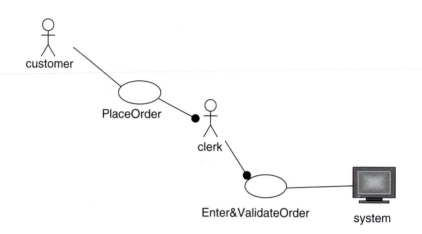

Figure 8.12 Order entry conversations.

The knee-jerk reaction of the typical object-oriented designer is to place the rule and a good deal of the behaviour in **Orders**. But does this make sense to a typical user? I do not think so. In the world, customers and clerks are intelligent and exhibit behaviour. The order is a very dead, behaviour-free piece of paper. But our systems push all the behaviour into the order and strip it away from customers and clerks who are usually represented in database tables which store details like name, address and login codes. The most these objects do is to calculate things like current debt, usually by collaborating with other classes such as **Orders**. In one way this is sensible; real customers can place orders with us, but we certainly do not want the system representation of customer to be able to do this. Business would become too easy – except that we probably either would not be paid or would be charged with fraud. However, in the case of the clerk it is less clear that this strategy is the right one.

The agent perspective allows us instead to visualize an agent in the system called **Clerk's Assistant**. This agent can take responsibility for all the order validation and confirmation behaviour that is needed and let us strip it away from **Orders**. This has three significant advantages:

1. If we are in a distributed system we can allow the assistant agent to be mobile with the attendant benefits of reducing network traffic and improving overall control structure.
2. Stripping the order of its behaviour may reduce the impedance mismatch between our new systems and legacy databases where orders are still stored, without behaviour usually.
3. The 'cognitive dissonance' between the system and the world is reduced. This means that discussions between users and developers are easier because

they share a common model of the application. Smart clerks in the office are modelled as smart creatures in the computer (or partially so, because real intelligent computers don't and can't exist). Electronic orders are just as dumb as their paper counterparts.

Whether this approach is correct will depend entirely on the application and its circumstances. However, knowing that it is possible gives developers an extra tool of their trade. Next time you model a system consider the choice at least.

It is a coincidence that, while the insertion of rulesets into objects in SOMA was not motivated by agent technology at all, this addition to object modelling seems to be pretty well all that is needed to model intelligent, possibly mobile agents. The original motivation was actually provided by a business process re-engineering project as long ago as 1989. Now it should be possible to see why precisely the same extension to object-oriented analysis needed to model business processes is needed to model system agents. The underlying metaphor is the same. We will return to the topic of agent-based systems in Chapter 10.

We can use internalized (or **cartooned**) agents to model the responsibilities of the sales clerk. The agent stereotype can be thought of as internalizing within the system the real agents in the business world. With agents representing more of the business logic, the order is modelled as a data structure that will probably correspond far more closely to the representation that may exist in the legacy order database.

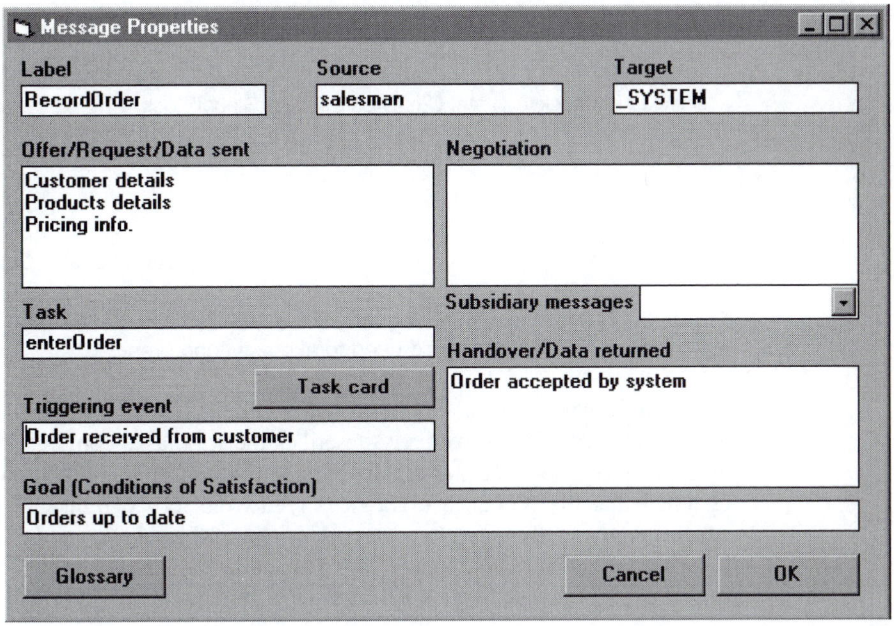

Figure 8.13 Suggested conversation dialogue box.

Nevertheless, for the purposes of the present exposition we will stay with the more usual approach of putting the intelligence into the order class. Let us examine the Enter&ValidateOrder message in more detail. The detailed description of this message can be based on the sixfold structure of a message or conversation described earlier in this chapter. If automated support in envisaged the dialogue might look something like that shown in Figure 8.13.

The whole decomposition may then be displayed in graphical form as shown in Figure 8.14. Tasks have complexity and take time. This is usually only recorded for atomic tasks since it can often be inferred for the composite tasks; the time taken is assumed to be the sum of the times for the components at the next level and so on. This of course can be overridden. Complexities are also additive unless otherwise stated.

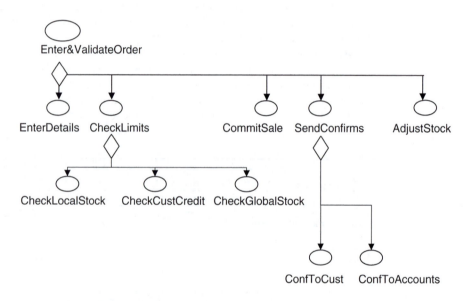

Figure 8.14 Decomposition diagram for the task action 'enter deal'. Task associations or rulesets can be used to express concurrency.

Task associations can be used to allow the sequencing and co-ordination of tasks to be described. This effectively describes the way tasks combine to form complete business processes. However, in the situations most commonly found, it will be assumed that the sequence of tasks is read from left to right and that there is no concurrency. If the situation is more complex then the expressive power of task associations and rulesets together is sufficient to ensure than any level of complexity can be described. See Section 8.11 for more details.

Class Name	Abstract/~~Concrete~~*
Product	~~Domain~~/Application/~~Interface~~*

Description/Keywords

A product has a code, a name, a description, and a price

Superclasses/Interfaces: *Commodity*

Component classes:

Attributes and associations

Product Name

Product Description

Product Price

Product ID

Stock level

Operations	'Collaborator-message sent' pairs
SetProductCode	*(Product - Create Product)*
Establishes the product code and other details in the system database	
ProductMargin	

Rulesets/Invariants

ProductPricingPolicy

* Delete as applicable

Figure 8.15 A SOMA class card.

There is also some complexity in the way that inheritance and composition structures interact, which again is rarely met in practice but which must be allowed for. The rules for handling this interaction were described in Section 6.3.1 in relation to derived dependencies for business objects. Task objects are handled in exactly the same way.

Once the analysis of the process models, business processes and messages is completed, we end up with a set of decomposed tasks. It is assumed that the decomposition continues to 'atomic' level where an atomic task is one that cannot be further decomposed without introducing terms foreign to the domain. Each atomic task is represented by a sentence – in a standard Subject/Verb/DirectObjects/ Preposition/IndirectObjects (SVDPI) form where possible. The sentences in the task model are now analysed (preferably, I find, by users during workshops) to discover the true business objects that will be the basis of the system model. The technique is basically a textual analysis where nouns indicate candidate objects and verbs candidate operations. Unfortunately this process is not seamless, violating one of the key benefits claimed for object-oriented methods; it is irreducibly creative. The next section explains how the seam can be mended. The classes so discovered can be recorded using the class cards shown in Figure 8.15 for use in 'CRC'-style walkthroughs or rôle-play simulations. This micro-process creates the Business Object Model (BOM) that will be the basis of later system design.

The walkthroughs produce a set of UML sequence or activity diagrams that effectively describe the way business objects execute operations that support each of the business tasks. This provides a test that the two object models are consistent and complete and usually leads to the model being 'debugged'. These walkthroughs can be recorded by drawing the sequence or activity diagrams by hand or using a conventional CASE tool. These form the basis for system test scripts later in the project.

8.8 Seamlessness

It is important to realize that – normally – in passing from a business process model to a system model we are crossing the Rubicon, as it were. There is no way back. Should we change our model of the system, as a result of a coding improvement say, then we cannot detect the impact of the change on the business model or objectives. In SOMA each task tree corresponds to a *plan* for a business process. The root nodes of our task trees are containers for the atomic tasks that constitute the detail of the plans. What we must do is create a set of classes in the system model (BOM) that can help a user execute this plan. Now, such an implementation must start somewhere. Therefore, each 'root' task corresponds to **exactly one** system operation (and therefore *a fortiori*) to exactly one class. This operation initiates the system process that implements the plan. The identity of this class and operation are recorded as part of the task properties and this enables us in principle to produce a complete set of event traces, *validating* that the system can implement all business processes specified. Thus, our task-oriented approach offers possibilities for seamlessness in the transition from the business to the system model that seem to be unavailable in use-case-oriented approaches. It also has implications for testing, as the event traces can be regarded as test scripts.

I have introduced the reader to SOMA's twin object models: the Task Object Model (TOM) and the Business Object Model (BOM) and suggested that they could be linked using CRC-style walkthroughs with users and developers. I now want to show how this linkage can be automated to provide a truly seamless link between a system and its requirements. This link means that if the system changes we can explore the impact on the business objectives and processes. It also offers the possibility of a new notion of provable correctness: proving that the specification meets the requirements.

SOMA uses a uniform object modelling technique to model several things. The process life cycle, for example, is modelled as a network of activity objects and contracts between them. The Agent Object Model is a model of the business process(es). The Task Object Model is a model of the tasks performed by users (and other agents) as part of their business processes. The Business Object Model is a model of the business objects that constitute a computer system specification. In that sense we could call the TOM part a model of the world or *world model*. The BOM could be called a *system object model*. Sometimes there is a more refined system model, built later on, called the Implementation Object Model. Alternatively, one can produce an executable specification using code generation facilities.

While conventional methods offer different modelling techniques for almost every life-cycle activity, object-oriented methods introduce no such seams between analysis and logical design. There may be a 'seam' between logical and physical design when language-dependent features are introduced, but using a language such as Eiffel effectively eliminates this seam too. Thus object-oriented development is claimed to be seamless. However, leaping from the requirements model to the system model, there remains more than a seam: a veritable abyss which, once leapt over, cannot be easily re-traversed. There is a neat solution to this problem of the World/System seam which I will attempt to explain using a simple example.

AN EXAMPLE In the SOMA approach to object-oriented requirements capture for a business area, the first thing we do is establish the project mission and then drill down to a number of specific, measurable, prioritized objectives as previously described. Next, we build a business process or context model showing: external agents (the stakeholders in our business area), internal agents and support agents (systems). Messages representing conversations between these agents are then introduced. Figure 8.16 shows how this might be applied to a system designed to capture foreign exchange trades. In this figure, the external agent c/party[8] sends a message to an internal agent (dealer)

---

[8] A bank's trading customer is often referred to as its counterparty.

inviting him to strike a foreign exchange bargain. The dealer then must negotiate the terms, validate the trade and enter it into the system. This is represented by the message enter deal.

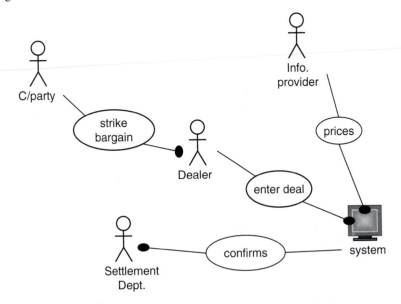

Figure 8.16 Business process model for trade capture.

We must find a goal for each such message and its associated task. This is called the root task because it is at the root of a composition tree structure. The tree for enter deal is shown in Figure 8.17. We analyse and decompose the tasks for each goal in this way, ending at the atomic tasks, which are the leaf nodes of this tree. Next we write task scripts for the atomic tasks.

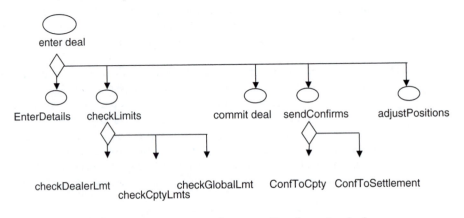

Figure 8.17 Use case decomposition for enter deal.

Figure 8.18 shows the atomic script for the task EnterDetails. It is easy to see from this script that a number of classes are mentioned; e.g. Instruments, Counterparties and (implicitly) Deals. Also there are some obvious attributes, such as Buy/Sell. Finally the operation enter is mentioned. After a preliminary analysis of this and all the other scripts and a walk through the system design, we realize that the task enter deal at the root of the tree corresponds to a responsibility of the business object class Deals: captureDeal in this case.

We record this as the ImplementedBy operation of the root task object enter deal with the value: 'captureDeal', an operation of the Deals class. This makes a permanent link between the process plan represented by the root task and the software that will help the user execute this plan. Because of this link we can, in principle, easily animate the specification.

The dealer enters the following data:
counterparty, instrument, amount, rate, buy or sell,
special settlement conditions

Figure 8.18 Atomic task script for EnterDetails.

LINKING
TASKS TO
CLASSES

Another way of looking at the seamless nature of the specification process that we have described by way of this example is illustrated schematically in Figure 8.19. This shows the mission statement of a project fanning out to its various objectives. Each objective relates to a number of communication acts (conversations) in the model. Each conversation has exactly one goal and exactly one root task. The root tasks correspond to one or more atomic tasks. So far, all these links are totally traceable; at least in principle. For that reason, it is easy to arrive at the TOM in an iterative fashion.

Now we take the leap from the world to the system. We identify the business objects partly based on the nouns discovered in the scripts. We define classification, composition and association structures. For each class we find responsibilities and rules, partly based on the verbs found in the scripts. This is a creative process that cannot be automated. We have lost traceability; we have crossed the Rubicon.

However, we can at least validate the mutual consistency of the two models using a group of users and developers. They walk through with class cards (rôle-playing the classes) to prove that all tasks are correctly supported and that there are no processing or storage absurdities. The automatic linking of the two models described above amounts to finding a means to record and replay this dynamic scenario interaction.

How did we make the leap from world model to the system model seamless? The trick is to notice that the task trees constitute 'plans' for interaction during task performance and, thus, for system execution. Each root task corresponds to *exactly one* system operation: in the class that initiates the plan. Making this link means that we can generate event traces automatically. Now we have a seamless link from mission down to the code – *and back!* Because we can refine the business object model and generate working code, we can trace changes to the code back to their effects on the task models and even the mission. Activity diagrams or sequence diagrams can be used to represent the way the object model supports the use case model.

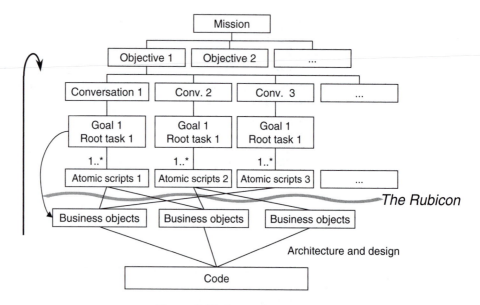

Figure 8.19 A seamless process.

We saw earlier that there was an attribute of a task called **implemented by** which allows the class implementation of a task to be described. Of course, since the two domains are not in any sense a one-to-one mapping, this implemented by link simply acts as the gateway from one domain to another and allows us to specify the operation of the implementation class that begins the system's support for the task. When first documenting a task, these data will not be known. Only after the Business Object Model has been constructed can we return to the task descriptions and fill in these data. This closing of the loop is of great importance to the overall process. It is the means by which task simulations can be set up for execution and validation of the model.

The implications of this approach to software engineering for quality and testing are, I hope, obvious:

1. The event traces constitute acceptance test scripts for later verification of the system built.
2. The involvement of users in the creation of these traces (during the walkthrough) proves that the Business Object Model supports the Task Object Model accurately and completely.

The second point is that we have a technique for 'proving' the correctness of system specifications against the requirements model. Normally, the notion of correctness is only applied to proving that the implementation meets its specification. This suggests an approach that glues the two technologies together.

Strictly speaking, the technique that we have described *validates* the Business Object Model rather than *proves* that it is correct in the mathematical sense. But this is in accordance with our desire to build shared understanding between users and developers. The slogan is: 'Don't prove that it works; convince me'. Validation against task scripts and, ultimately, scenarios approaches proof in the limiting case, when we can be sure that we have exercised every scenario. Therefore we now turn to current research into how to ensure that this is the case, or at least maximize the completeness of the set of scenarios.

The arrangement of use cases shown in Figures 8.14 and 8.17 is actually a common one and suggests what is now widely referred to as a *pattern*, although it is a pattern related to business processes rather than to design or systems analysis, where most currently known patterns have been discovered.

8.9 The syllogism pattern for use case generation

Diversion

Another completely different kind of pattern – this time a pattern for knowledge elicitation – is suggested by the way SOMA workshops are conducted. In such workshops, users walk through the dynamics of the system they have defined, rôle-playing the class cards that represent the Business Object Model to ensure that every use case can be executed by the combined class cards working together in parallel. The walkthrough tests that the Business Object Model actually supports all the users' tasks. It is instructive to analyse exactly what goes on during such a simulation from the point of view of the pattern given in Figure 8.20. The event trace that the walkthrough produces represents a use case but this use case is generated from the task script and the process is initiated by the workshop facilitator giving a very concrete scenario. For example, for the order capture task, the facilitator might – in acting the rôle of the order clerk – say: 'Elvis, my pal down at ZapMart has just phoned in a order asking for 200 chocolate-covered widgets for delivery next Tuesday'.

The movement here is from the individual to the particular via the general: start with the (individual) scenario and then use the (universal) task script to generate a corresponding (particular) use case. This is a particular case of a syllogism, although the reader should be aware that we are using the term in the very general sense used by Hegel in his *Science of Logic* (Miller, 1969) rather than in the common manner that refers only to Aristotle's syllogism of deduction: Gaius is a man, all men are mortal, therefore Gaius is mortal. Hegel's syllogisms dealt with the various relationships between categories, notably between Particular, Individual and

Universal. The deductive syllogism can be represented by the triplet: I-P-U.[9] In the syllogism pattern of Figure 8.20 we are dealing with the same I-P-U triplet but using it to generate the particular (use case – event trace) out of the universal (task script) together with the individual (scenario). Clearly, this is not the same as ordinary deductive logic but it is a syllogism in this Hegelian sense and it is, from a more practical viewpoint, a formula for a certain process of knowledge elicitation or requirements capture. Nor should this pattern be thought of as or confused with a 'design pattern' in the sense of Gamma *et al.* (1995); it is more akin to a pattern of thought that recurs in many analysis contexts but one that may have little relation to program design. Thus, I make no attempt to present it in the so-called Alexandrian[10] form.

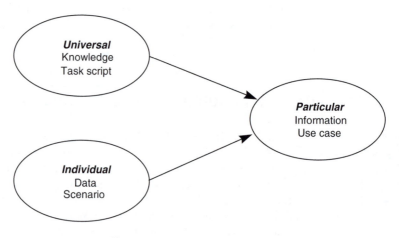

Figure 8.20 The syllogism pattern.

While this pattern might seem rather abstruse, it is actually of tremendous practical value in guiding requirements elicitation. Furthermore, it hints at the relationship between sequence diagrams, use case diagrams and activity diagrams, with the latter arising from a synthesis of the first two.

---

[9] Hegel describes this syllogism as follows: 'Individuality unites with universality through particularity'. The first term is a statement of a subsistent universal, the second relates an individual (instance) to a particular (class) leading to the proposition in the third term.

[10] As discussed in Chapter 7, the architect Christopher Alexander was responsible for inspiring among software engineers a standard way of presenting patterns (Alexander *et al.*, 1977).

⊟ 8.10 Ensuring the completeness of scenarios

Diversion

Requirements engineering can be divided into requirements elicitation and requirements analysis. The former finds out what people want and need, expressing it as an agent communication and task model, and the latter builds a model that can execute to support the needs defined in the earlier models. We have now seen that this process can be made seamless in the sense that we can prove that the Business Object Model will actually support the task in the Task Object Model and *a fortiori* the business objectives and the conversations of the Agent Object Model. This is a step forward from proving that the implementation model meets its specification, which is the territory of traditional formal methods and 'proofs of correctness'. What is not, however, guaranteed is that the requirements expressed in the agent and task models are in any sense complete with respect to human frailties.

Recently there has been some interest in this question in Academe and results are just beginning to emerge from research. One of the most interesting developments is the SAVRE system (Scenarios for Acquisition and Validation in Requirements Engineering), developed as part of the European Union funded CREWS (Co-operative Requirements Engineering With Scenarios) project. The CREWS-SAVRE project (Maiden *et al.*, 1997) sets out to achieve systematic scenario use and generate useful scenarios, taking into account problem-specific patterns of normative behaviour and the insights of human error theory (Reason, 1990), cognitive science and software engineering. As Pohl *et al.* (1997) have pointed out, current methods and tools such as Objectory provide little support or guidance in this area. The CREWS project aims to make scenario generation and walkthrough more systematic, useful and cost-effective.

The SAVRE tool generates scenarios to acquire and validate user requirements in a semi-automatic fashion based on parameters set by its user. A wizard then supports a systematic walkthrough of the generated scenarios, ensuring that all paths are explored and all requirements are validated. In the course of this, the tool suggests generic requirements statements that the user can add to the specification. Each scenario consists of hypothetical situations in the target environment, acting as a sort of test script. CREWS has developed theories of standard and alternate courses based on normative behaviour specific to certain problem classes and non-normative events and states for general situations (*cf.* Maiden and Sutcliffe, 1994). The user can either retrieve reusable use cases (task scripts) or choose NATURE object system models (normative behaviour for pre-defined problem domains) from which to generate them. NATURE (Maiden and Sutcliffe, 1994) is a set of object models for specific domains developed as part of another ESPRIT project. The current tool has about 250 types of problem in its database. Task scripts are viewed as having one initial event and at least one each of the following: end events, agents, sub-actions and objects. The states of the object may change as a result of the task execution. The tasks are linked using pre-conditions on the actions defined in the object model. The wizard now guides the user through scenario generation based on the following five selection types of alternative courses:

- Agent Interaction Patterns.
- Generic Exceptions (e.g. actions that start but never end).
- Permutation Exceptions (e.g. combining two events that occur concurrently).
- Permutation Options (e.g. temporal links between events and actions).
- Problem Exceptions (e.g. HCI handshake failure).

For example, in a command and control system the normal course script might be presented as 'crew reads mobilization instruction'. The system then asks a series of questions such as: 'What happens if the event does not occur?' or 'What happens if this event occurs twice?' The user must then add a note to the specification.

Ensuring that scenario sets are complete is important if we want to argue, as in the last section, that SOMA proves the correctness of the object model against the requirements as expressed in the agent and task models. The ability to check the requirements model exhaustively in this way may be critical for certain applications. Furthermore, the classification of problem exception classes and the work on the temporal logic of task sequencing will be of lasting value. However, keeping the requirements document as a piece of text rather than in the form of task objects is a limitation.

8.11 Task association sets and sequence diagrams

When faced with a number of users' tasks, or use cases, it is intuitively clear that there must be relationships among them. For instance, a library loan cannot be recorded until an access record for the book concerned has been located in the library database. We can conclude from this that the task of setting up a record for a book *enables* the task of issuing the book on loan. We cannot lend a book before buying a copy of it, so that the purchasing task *precedes* the lending task. A delinquent lender who fails to return overdue books will normally be placed on a suspended list. In this case, suspending the lender *disables* lending to that person. A librarian may be talking with a researcher while recording a loan for someone else at the same time: the give advice task *parallels* the lend book task.

These kinds of relationship are modelled in SOMA using task associations and task association sets. A **task association** is a named, directed relationship between two tasks. Possible task association types include: Succeeds, Precedes, Enables, Disables and Parallels.

As we have seen, tasks are operations of agent objects, and so a task association written *Assoc01(AgentX.A,AgentB.Y)* might represent a message transmitted from AgentX in the course of executing its task A to AgentY invoking the execution of task B. The agents can be internal, external or system agents. A **task association set** is a named collection of task associations. It represents a time-ordered, possibly parallel collection of tasks, and is an object in its own right. It is a directed graph whose nodes are tasks and whose arcs are task associations. It represents a related, coherent set of tasks that support a business goal. A task association set is equivalent to one or more sequence diagrams. Such sequence diagrams may involve branching and concurrency. A simple linear association set will have only one realization as a sequence diagram, whereas branching association sets have a unique sequence diagram for every path through the network represented by the association set. Therefore a UML sequence diagram, which cannot show these aspects of a model, represents a strict subset of an association set, not expressing the complete situation.

As we saw in Chapter 6, refinement of sequence diagrams is a powerful technique for analysis and comprehension. Task associations, like use cases or any other objects, can be linked by any of the four object structures, notably that of composition. Large task association sets can be disaggregated into components, and so a hierarchical set of views of tasks can be generated. For example, an association set called 'Process Order' could contain the tasks concerned with validating the external system that issued the order, checking to see whether the order violated any legal or compliance constraints, deciding whether the order should be priced manually or automatically and so on.

Other processes represented as task association sets can be reusable in many contexts within an organization – a good example being transaction capture which is structurally identical whether pencils or zlotys are being purchased, even though the subject matter is quite different: stationery *versus* foreign exchange. Task reuse of this kind can simplify the diagrammatic representation of large-scale processes enormously. The capability for drilling down through different diagrammatic levels is also supported, as we shall see.

The reader should note carefully the difference between an association set of tasks and a task decomposition: all component tasks in a task composition structure are carried out by the same agent; tasks within a task association set will be carried out co-operatively by a set of agents. In this sense, therefore, a task association set corresponds more closely to a joint action in the sense of Catalysis (D'Souza and Wills, 1999) than does a unitary task.

Recall from Section 8.5.1 that a conversation between agents has a recursive sixfold structure. We can use sequence diagrams based on task association sets to represent the recursion in conversations illustrated previously in Figure 8.8. To illustrate the general idea of this, consider the simple process of buying a cup of coffee. Conversations, like all use cases, can be realized in sequence diagrams. A sequence diagram representing such a conversation is shown in Figure 8.21. The task association set behind this diagram covers the four stages of *request, negotiate, perform* and *handover*. A 'thirst' event causes the customer to initiate the process by asking for the price of a cup of coffee (the *request* or *preparation* stage of the transaction). The seller proposes a price, which the customer ponders (*negotiation*) and accepts in this case. If the price is tolerable, the vendor makes and delivers the coffee (*task execution* or *performance*). If the coffee is hot and strong enough, the customer takes and pays for it (*handover*).

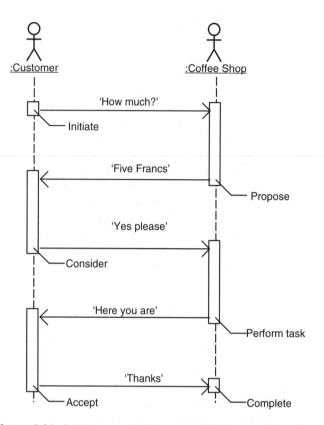

Figure 8.21 A sequence diagram representing a conversation.

One of the strengths of this way of grounding sequence diagrams in a model of task associations is that the various failure branches that could occur can be added, and we could, in principle, auto-generate sequence diagrams covering all the possibilities for discussion by the development team and the users.

The process could fail at the proposal stage, perhaps because the shop is about to close or has run out of the basic ingredients of coffee making. The negotiation could collapse because the customer thinks the price is too high. Failure at the perform stage could occur because the espresso machine breaks down. At the acceptance stage the customer might abort the process because the coffee is too weak (no reference to Java is intended here). We could add task associations at each of these failure points.

One important aspect of the approach of Flores, which has influenced SOMA's treatment of conversations, is the idea of *nesting* conversations. Any stage of a conversation may involve recurrence to a further level. Catalysis refinements represent a similar insight. The association set approach uses nested association sets to reduce and manage model complexity.

The approach taken by Flores is exemplified quite differently in the tool produced by his company Action Technologies Inc. (ATI). Their Action Technologies Workbench enables modellers to draw conversations, using a notation based on that shown in Figure 8.7, and generate workflow applications in products such as Lotus Notes. As a result of this approach the work of Winograd and Flores has been criticized in the requirements engineering literature as leading to rigid, inflexible régimes disliked by users who have to follow the workflow system's laid down rules. I feel that this does not detract from the basic theory though and anyway, our purpose is not to build workflow models but to provide a starting point for object-oriented analysis.

SEQUENCE DIAGRAMS AND UML

UML sequence diagrams describe phenomena that occur in a specified sequence, but nothing in the semantics of UML sequence diagrams shows causality. It is important to understand the implications of this. The arrows on a UML sequence diagram represent the steps in a sequential process – and nothing more than that. The following sequence of events:

1. The sun rises.
2. The birds begin to sing.
3. The rush hour traffic grinds to a halt.

can of course be easily represented in UML by a sequence diagram. Common sense dictates that the first and second phenomena are causally linked. (In a certain sense, the sun sends an electromagnetic message to the birds, which causes them to sing.) The causal links between the first two steps and the third are less clear. Of course, singing birds do nothing to alter traffic conditions. The sun rising has equally little direct effect. Although most of us have electric light nowadays, we nevertheless tend to go to work during daylight, and in this sense the rising of the sun will presage a traffic jam. However, to explain this synchronicity, we would have to expand our model to include some representation of people, land use, traffic patterns and transport modes. This is both a strength and a weakness of the UML version of sequence diagrams. Hidden and essentially irrelevant stages in linked sets of actions can be eliminated, thus simplifying the diagrams. On the other hand, viewing an incomplete diagram that takes advantage of this simplification can lead to erroneous assumptions about causality between the arrows of the diagram. This becomes especially significant when an analyst hands over a specification to a developer. Eventually, a program must be written, and it must be complete and without discontinuities in its control flow. Without clear guidance, the developer may just make assumptions about the sequence of control. To deny this is to ignore the time and budget pressures that exist in real organizations. Gaps in design turn up not as discontinuities in program control flow, but as *ad hoc* conceptual leaps. These can materialize as bugs, which are fixed only at great cost – particularly since this kind of error cannot be traced back to the specification. This is one manifestation of a well-known process model relationship: time saved during analysis leads to extra costs in maintenance.

AN EXAMPLE In the training material supplied with the UML version of Rational *Rose* we find the advice that sequence diagrams can be used early on in the analysis of requirements. An example is given concerning simple order processing, whereby one constructs a sequence diagram based on the idea that a customer asks a clerk to place an order. Naturally, the customer and the clerk appear on the sequence diagram. The clerk needs to know the stock availability and the price, so he looks these up on a price list and a stock record. Here the temptations of the devil begin and we can posit instances called stock_record and price_list_item. *Rose* adds to the temptation by making it easy to convert these instances into classes: **StockRecords** and **PriceList**. Now, to any seasoned object designer this is patently the wrong thing to do. It would be obvious to such a person that the Products class should know (or be able to obtain) the stock and price for any of its instances, or indeed the averages of these numbers. Creating the sequence diagram before the basic class model is therefore very dangerous for any but the most experienced object designer.

Thus, the *Rose* approach can lead to an absurdly bad design from the viewpoint of object-orientation. I recommend a completely different approach whereby the Business Object Model is built from the Task Object Model and the designers are encouraged to see that the Products class should have features corresponding to product price and stock level long before any sequence diagrams are drawn. The latter should be used to document and validate complex business processes only after the first-cut object model has been built.

Another problem with UML sequence diagrams is that they are interpreted as instances of system classes, the operations of which send messages to each other represented by horizontal arrows. Catalysis views these arrows as representing use cases, which is a slightly better interpretation. The vertical boxes on such charts, similar to the ones of Figure 8.21, therefore represent operations. In my approach the instances are thought of as real-world agents and the boxes represent their tasks. The horizontal arrows represent task associations such as *precedes*. I think this is a better approach in the context of requirements engineering because, rather than think of the unwinding of the operation stack frame, we situate our model firmly in the world of the user. This leads to a more fruitful dialogue between users and developers during requirements analysis and an improved chance of a shared understanding of the problem at hand. The Catalysis interpretation can then be resurrected during specification, where it is appropriate.

8.11.1 Conjunctive, disjunctive and nested association sets

As we have seen, task association sets can include parallel paths. As an example, consider this time the process of making a cup of *instant* coffee. The process involves filling a kettle with water and putting it on to boil. While the kettle is heating, the cups and (optionally) milk and sugar are located. Next the coffee granules must be dissolved using the hot water, after the kettle has boiled. These tasks and their relationships imply a task association set, which can show the parallelism between the two main activities. It is hard to show this information on UML sequence diagrams.

Concurrent branches can, of course, be represented one at a time on separate sequence diagrams.

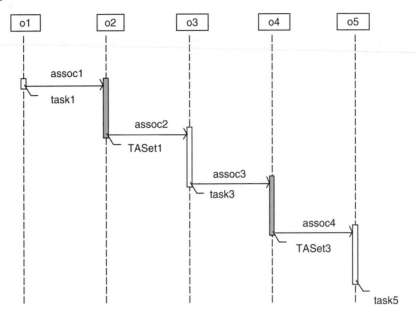

Figure 8.22 Nested task association sets.

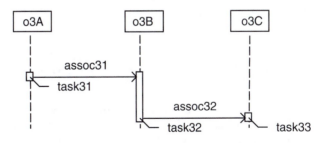

Figure 8.23 A component task association set.

On occasion, task association sets and their realizations as sequence diagrams may become rather large. In such a case, using the Catalysis refinement idea, we can decompose an association set into smaller sets to help us apprehend the structure more clearly. Thus we can substitute a single composite task for an entire association set, thereby imposing a nested structure. In Figure 8.22, the association *assoc1* links the task *task1* to a complete association set *TASet1*. The association can be thought of as precedes for the purposes of the example. Similarly *assoc2* and *assoc3* both link task3 to entire association sets. Expanding either of these association sets (by clicking their icons) will reveal a diagram of the whole nested association set. This is depicted in Figure 8.23 for the case of the association set *assoc3*.

COMPOSING ASSOCIATION SETS Association sets are themselves *bona fide* objects, and as such can be linked by all four structural relationships between objects, including composition. In the example just given, *TASet1* and *TASet3* are nested in (i.e. are components of) an association set called *Main*. The composition structure for *Main* is shown in Figure 8.24. This shows the components *TASet1* and *TASet3* and that *TASet1* has a component *TASet2*.

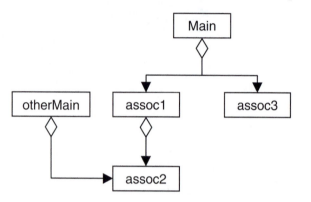

Figure 8.24 Association set composition structure.

Expanding *TASet2* shows us that *TASe2* is in turn a component of another association set called *otherMain*. Note that the idea of specification reuse is, once more, central to the approach.

8.12 Executable specifications and simulation

A central idea of SOMA and some other methods such as ROOM (Selic *et al.*, 1994) is that of being able, with suitable tool support, to *execute specifications*. People can experience considerable difficulty in understanding the dynamic behaviour of a system when provided only with static representations of it. With this in mind, good support tools should provide for the definition of operations in a high level scripting language which allows the class and agent collaborations to be viewed dynamically. Such a language could be a subset of Java with a few additional keywords. This would allow each relevant task identified in the earlier phases of business process modelling and analysis to be tested against the system as designed, automating some of what we do with walkthroughs in workshops – though *not* replacing them. It also tests the classes and operations that have been agreed upon during the requirements engineering process. An operation is then defined by its script, which serves as a precise definition of the operation's specification and as a method implementing that operation, thus enabling validation of the specification as we saw in Section 8.8. The language is thus characterizable as a *scripting* rather than *programming* language. It should remove from the designer the responsibility of grappling with the syntax of complex language.

Recall that a message in the business process model represents a conversation and that a task script defines the work performance aspect implied by the contract implicit in the conversation. When a task is to be supported during a simulation run, as a result of an event occurring in the Agent Object Model, we move sequentially from the Agent Object Model to the Task Object Model and then to the Business Object Model. It is important to understand the meaning of these transitions clearly. The AOM and the TOM are in the world of the users and their business processes: part of what Cook and Daniels (1994) call the **essential** model. These models are concerned with the activities that must be carried out if the proposed system is to be of use to a business. The BOM lies in the systems world: Cook and Daniels' **specification** model. It specifies the classes that must be created if the system is to be made operational; or at least one possible design of such classes – there may be many alternative decompositions that could be imposed at design time due to architectural and other considerations. The purpose of an animation and simulation, however, is to confirm that the BOM classes actually do support the user tasks which our analysis has determined must be supported for a valid business process.

We can validate a particular class design by linking these three models together by a simulation of the class model's support for the tasks of agents. An agent in the business process modelling knows about triggering events for the conversations it engages in, together with their associated tasks and 'implemented-by' operations.

Messages always have exactly one root task but may have several component tasks. Furthermore, the same task may be (re)used by several conversations; or rather by one of the agents involved in them to be precise. Task objects and classes (i.e. business objects in the BOM) do not correspond to each other in a one-to-one fashion: the mapping can be more complex. However, it is equally important to remember that there is only one initiating class supporting each root task, as we have already seen in Section 8.8. Although several classes may collaborate to achieve the apotheosis of a particular task, it is also true that there is only *one* class which is the instigator of the Business Object Model's support for this task. Execution always begins with the execution of a unique operation. This initiation point is recorded in the task. It is the link to the class domain from the task domain: the **implemented by** class and operation.

Once the principal parts of the business process have been modelled correctly, we could use sequence diagrams to create regression tests which can be re-executed at appropriate points in the development to ensure that modifications to the business object model have not corrupted our understanding of the problem or diverged too far from our mission. The resultant sequence diagram can be used to confirm the class design and for regression testing purposes.

8.12.1 Discrete event and time-based simulation

Simulation was at the very root of object technology from the early days of object-oriented programming and the Simula language. Simula came out of work on discrete event simulation and operational research dating back to 1949, with the motivating problem being the design of nuclear reactors. The differential equations involved in such problems were too hard for even numerical solution, so alternative techniques had to be developed from first principles. A successful technique is to simulate a world which moves (transforms its state) in discrete steps corresponding to time intervals. With such simulations, which can be run and re-run on a computer, the effects of different parameters can be observed rather than calculated. This is analogous to the use of spreadsheets for 'what if' analysis. However, the languages available in the 1960s were not particularly suited for simulation. Whereas the abstractions of conventional languages like FORTRAN attempted to describe processes in the computer, Simula, with its abstractions, essayed to describe real-world processes.

The seminal simulation problem involved objects which were neutrons and absorbent rods in a nuclear reactor. A more readily understandable example is the simulation of traffic passing through a complex intersection which involves random arrival rates, saturation flow rates, traffic light settings and queuing. The vehicles are generated and tracked through the system as it passes through discrete time steps, rather like time-lapse photography, and the behaviour can be observed, at each time step, in terms of queue lengths, delay times, junction locking and similar features. It is also possible to observe global phenomena such as stability or convergence to a stable state. A simulation of a system, once constructed, can be tested under different assumptions on such variables as volume, signal linking or cycle times.

The sort of simulation discussed so far in this section is based on events triggering messages between agents, which in turn imply the execution of tasks that cause operations of business objects to be invoked, but not with respect to any particular flow of elapsed time. Discrete event simulation is traditionally held to involve the simulation of discrete time steps. It is also possible to base simulations on the passing of simulated time.

The properties of a task object should include any constraints placed on the performance of a system; such as:

- the mean time to execute the task;
- the maximum (and minimum) time to execute the task;
- the variance and standard deviation of the execution time;
- the probability distribution that times are to be sampled from – normal, lognormal, Poisson, uniform, exponential, gamma, etc.;
- the number of queues and queue servers available; and
- the time units used.

This specification includes probability distributions representing the way events arrive at event queues. If the model is of things arriving in a queue at random then the Poisson distribution is normally chosen. A very familiar example of a Poisson process is given by vehicles arriving at a set of traffic signals. If the model is of the time taken to perform some manual task, such as completing a tax return, the normal distribution is more appropriate.

Note that the task performance specification includes the number of queues and queue servers. An airline check-in area, for example, often has a number of desks (servers) and a separate queue for each. Post offices on the other hand have multiple servers but only one queue. This arrangement was adopted as a result of one of the very earliest Operational Research projects in the 1950s.

Discrete event, or time-based, simulation enables designers to observe the apparent development of a system in time, but where time is modelled rather unrealistically as a sequence discrete evenly spaced points.

MULTIPLE THREADS
In real businesses there will usually be multiple independent paths (or threads) of execution for at least some important business processes. This increases the complexity that modellers must deal with when it occurs. The threads may also need to be synchronized at various points, making life more complicated still.

Simulation tools should provide support for modelling multiple parallel threads. Inter-process synchronization could be provided by a semaphore model or similar, in which concurrent executing processes can be spawned from any operation of any class. All operations specified inside the scope of a thread are fired ostensibly at once and in parallel. Of course, a simulation will actually be carried out on a normal sequential (i.e. Single Instruction stream, Single Data stream or SISD) machine in most cases. This means that the processes are not really processed in parallel; it only appears to be so. We also need a variable that will respond to other process instances that request notification of state changes, using perhaps the OBSERVER pattern discussed in Chapter 7. Such messages can originate from any operation of any class that has the appropriate directives included in its operation scripts. Semaphores should be able to be set and cleared.

It must be possible to suspend process execution. The period during which a process is suspended can be set either as a fixed or calculated time period. Alternatively, the process can be suspended until one or more semaphores are set.

Event and time-based simulation can be combined. One of the primary motivations behind the provision of time-based simulation facilities is to create a background against which discrete event simulations of interactions among classes can be studied. This could be accomplished by overlaying an event sequence on top of a time-based simulation.

8.13 Organizing and running requirements workshops

Several times in this chapter there have been references to the use of joint user/developer workshops. Here we pause to look in detail at how these workshops, an important component of the SOMA process, should be organized and managed.

There is a number of different ways of structuring workshop sessions, so this chapter is not so much a prescriptive tutorial on how precisely to execute workshop events, but rather a set of guidelines, based on my experience of running workshops over the past two decades.

The focus of the chapter is on the organization and management issues involved in setting up and executing a successful workshop. Details on the stages that a workshop passes through are (in this context) implicit in the SOMA method, as described earlier. The macro development process within which the micro workshop process occurs is dealt with in Chapter 9.

Historically, system requirements were captured from users during a series of interviews. Systems analysts would interview individual users, or sometimes small groups of users, on an aspect of the required system. The results of these interviews would be collected into a systems analysis report, which would then be circulated for comments. Based on the comments received, a revision would be issued for further comments, and so on. Such reports were usually very large and often quite unreadable. It is difficult to believe that anyone ever both read and understood them all. One suspects that they were often signed in default of a full understanding, rather than provoke a fruitless confrontation.

There are several problems that arise from this approach:

- Each user being interviewed is inclined to focus on the system seen from their own perspective. This is natural and proper but the absence of comments from other users involved in using the system being proposed means that trade-offs in function and ease of use by the various members of the user group are not made visible until after the report has been circulated – and then only if it was read and understood thoroughly.

- The approach is inclined to inculcate into people an 'us and them' attitude for the users and the developers, and sometimes between different groups of users. The users ask for features and state requirements. The developers go away and produce something. That which is produced never exactly matches the users', perhaps not properly articulated, original requirements. Blame and finger-pointing inevitably follow.

- Setting up a complete interview round, recognizing that each user has a busy diary of their own, can be a lengthy process. Two or three months may be spent on the initial round of interviews, particularly if users are geographically dispersed. A second round of interviews for elaboration or clarification is often necessary. All this increases the elapsed time of the overall project, and in a shifting environment this in its own right causes problems with the delivered system. The requirements the users claimed at the beginning of the process will inevitably change as the business circumstances change. The longer the development process, the greater the guarantee that the delivered system will fail to match the requirements current on the delivery date – a phenomenon commonly characterized as: requirements drift.

In contrast, workshops offer the following advantages:

- They reduce the elapsed time needed to establish the requirements.
- They ensure that all participants have heard at first hand the contributions of other users, which eases the problem of arriving at compromises where these are necessary.
- Developers gain a first-hand appreciation of the real goals of the users implicit in their requests, as opposed to a mediated set of requirement statements.
- They develop a shared ownership of the project between and among the developers and users.
- The monetary and other costs of the requirements elicitation and refinement process can often (but not always) be reduced.
- The tempo of a rapid development process is established. Introducing these ideas into an organization where users have experienced the all too familiar pattern of projects being delivered late, over budget and under specification can be met with a not unjustified degree of scepticism. Visibility of a documented requirements specification produced by co-operative effort in a matter of a few days can go far to overcome this response.

8.13.1 Rôles adopted during a workshop

The participants in a workshop are the sponsor, users, domain experts, the facilitator, the requirements engineer, the project manager and the team members. In addition, observers may attend the workshops (which provide excellent opportunities for training) where they may have contributions to make in specific but limited areas of expertise.

The **requirements engineer** (sometimes also called the **scribe**) is an experienced systems analyst – who must understand SOMA and object modelling – who documents the requirements during workshops. I dislike the term 'scribe' because the word tends to diminish the importance of the rôle, the contribution being made and indeed the very high levels of skill required to carry out the task effectively. For a large workshop, it can be useful to have two individuals allocated to the rôle, to assist each other and spread the burden of typing.

The **sponsor** is a senior executive responsible for the business area under review. Her rôle is to approve the cost and results of the workshop, resolve issues that cannot be resolved during the event itself and ensure that the appropriate participants are selected and committed to the project. The sponsor should attend the scoping session but does not need to attend the detail sessions.

The core team is made up of developers and between two and twenty key business users who are experts in the business area being analysed. Their rôle is to provide the business requirements, as elicited by the facilitator, and to verify that requirements are correctly documented.

The **facilitator** is almost the key determinant of the success of a workshop. S/he is an experienced business analyst who:

- conducts the scoping and detail sessions;

- ensures the requirements are captured in a complete and consistent way;
- ensures the right level of detail is achieved for input into the next project activity.

8.13.2 Who should attend workshops

Not everyone affected by a proposed new system can always be present at requirements capture workshops. A good and oft-quoted example is dealers in financial trading rooms who are reluctant to leave their investment positions unattended. Furthermore, such events would be too large and unwieldy to be managed comfortably. Therefore, some users act as delegates for their immediate colleagues, managers and subordinates. In the example given, dealer management often stand in for actual dealers. The selection of the right delegates for the task is a key determinant of the success of the event and the participants must at least include representatives of both the users of the proposed system and the development team.

USERS The presence of key users is both more important and potentially more difficult to organize than one might think. Surely the identity of the correct participants from the user side is obvious and unarguable. Not necessarily! There are several factors to weigh:

- Seniority: more senior people may have a better grasp of the wider business issues being addressed in the workshop (or maybe just think they do) but the devil is always in the details, and operational level staff are more likely to be familiar with the detailed intricacies of operations, which will be the things that will break a proposed system if they are not taken into account. So we need people from different levels of seniority – but then we need to be aware that some people will not like to be seen to contradict their boss in public. This is where the facilitator's job of setting ground rules and ensuring fair play becomes important.
- Every stakeholder present *must* have delegated signatory authority to commit to the findings of the workshop. There is an escape path in the shape of the open issues which we will discuss later; but it is not acceptable for someone to say at the end of the session when the sign-off sheet is going round that they do not have the authority to sign it. Apart from causing delay, this vitiates the purpose of a workshop in gaining consensus; it makes the deliverables the subject of editing by people who were not present. Ensuring that this signatory authority is in place is a key job of the sponsor.
- The number of people present: the complexity of the interactions will rise exponentially with the number of participants, so life is easier the smaller the number – and the workshop is cheaper to run. Everyone affected by the proposed system should be represented; but, in the limit, this could mean half the company. What must be avoided is the situation of somebody feeling later that they were improperly overlooked. When the delivered system has a flaw, you do not want to be told that that some stakeholder or user was

never consulted in the first place.

The above list indicates that before setting up the workshop, the sponsor, project manager and facilitator should have a prior meeting, generally led by the facilitator, to establish the participant list. They should examine all the options in terms of inclusions and exclusions, probe the emerging list for weaknesses and seek to rectify them and document the reasons for the final invitation list. It can be useful to develop a matrix of candidates, enumerating all the people who could conceivably attend, and then compare possible combinations of candidates from the grid in terms of the impact on the workshop's success. Start with the company's organization chart, and collapse the relevant components into a matrix where the rows are the organizational units, the columns represent approximate seniority levels within the organization, and the cells contain names of logical job descriptions and possible candidates. Note especially that this document is *not* a formal deliverable, because the logical rôles may be the subject of discussion and change during the workshop.

	Strategic management	*Tactical management*	*Operational management and clerical staff*
Sales	Sales Director National Sales Manager	Account managers Regional managers	Sales staff Clerical and telesales staff
Marketing	Marketing Director	Product managers	Marketing assistants
Production	Distribution Director	Production engineers	Warehouse supervisors Machinists

Figure 8.25 Workshop participation grid.

As an example, consider a system to support a new process for product presentation, sales, order taking, and manufacturing. This would affect *inter alia* the Sales, Marketing and Production divisions. A possible workshop participation grid is shown in Figure 8.25. One should ensure that the grid reflects the actual organizational structure, then fill in the names of the candidates for participation. Considering the options, one representative for each group may make the workshop too large. Beware of the dangers of arguing that a manager can always speak for the troops as well – because he used to be one. This may be true, but it is difficult for people to represent their own needs sincerely as well as those of someone else. The inevitable exceptions that do occur, as with the dealers alluded to above, should be handled with extra care and sensitivity. Otherwise, if any rôle is not to be represented at the workshop, then there is an assumption this rôle will not be affected by the new system – and this should be documented. Some sensitive issues can arise if this is a business process re-engineering project: some rôles may disappear altogether, and asking possible victims of reorganization to contribute enthusiastically to planning the wake may be regarded as unproductive, or in bad taste at the very least. The aim is to produce a participant invitation list along with a supporting document justifying the rôles represented and not represented, and the reasoning behind the choices made.

Users should attend the entire workshop. This is often easier said than done. Freeing people from important work, even for a few days, can have a significant business impact and cost implications. It is also sometimes the case that people will not wish to appear in any way 'dispensable'. Having people attending for a couple of hours, disappearing for a while, then coming back can be very harmful to the progress and ultimate value of a workshop. The sponsor and project manager must work hard with departmental managers to ensure that a block of time is made available to run the event as a block and not as a set of piecemeal sessions with a floating population of participants.

DEVELOPERS   Where at all possible, the complete development team should attend the workshop(s). An absolutely central idea SOMA is that of a *joint* development team, made up of users and technical people. The challenge is to avoid the development of an 'us and them' attitude: where the user group states its requirements, the developer group goes away and produces something with little contact with or reference to the users. Only later do the users have the opportunity to tell them where they went wrong, when it is often too late to avoid project deadline pressure freezing the mistakes into the end product. The reason for having the whole development team present at the workshops is to help gain *shared* ownership of the system requirements: to understand more fully the content of the formal documents they may be dealing with later in the project. Importantly, all developers should feel involved in all parts of the project. Of course, someone may be on the team because of specialist skills, say in network design and management, because it is known that this will be a key component of the delivered system; but that person should not have the feeling that their contribution is just at the level of their own narrow specialism – they should be regarded as significant contributors to the system as a whole.

8.13.3 Selecting a location

Having decided to run a workshop rather than conduct interviews, a major choice faced by the organizer of a requirements engineering workshop is whether to hold the session on or off the site where the users normally work. There are arguments for and against both strategies as summarized in Table 8.3.

The most usual off-site location is an hotel. Choose one that is not near to the normal workplace, preferable in an idyllic country setting that offers comfort and suitable recreational facilities. Alternatively, if a software house is building the system and has a suitable location, that may suffice if there is no chance that the developers will be interrupted by their company; and if the users can be so persuaded.

Table 8.3 Comparison of on-site and off-site workshop location strategies.

	On-site	Off-site
For	It is easier to persuade users and domain experts to attend	A change of environment often relaxes the participants, especially if they normally work in a stressful environment
	On-site space is usually less costly	There is less opportunity for the users and domain experts to be called away for meetings, fire-fights, 'urgent' jobs, etc.
	Travelling costs may be lower	Catering facilities are usually better
		You have more control over the allocation of rooms and facilities
Against	There may be constant interruptions and users may be called back to their work often. This is really the most important and common reason for workshops failing apart from poor facilitation	Accommodation costs are usually higher
	Users are less likely to be able to take their minds off their normal duties	There may be significant extra travelling costs

8.13.4 Workshop logistics

Ideally, arrange to have a main room, as discussed below, and a break-out room which can be quite small, containing only a table, chairs and a flip chart. More than one break-out room may be needed if the workshop is a large one. The break-out room may be useful if a sub-group needs to split off to resolve some important but not necessarily mainstream point. Coffee and refreshments can be served in the break-out room, but in any case should be served outside the main room, even if this is in the corridor outside. This ensures that a break really is a break, giving people a chance to stretch their legs, cool down if things are getting warm, or just refocus in a different environment for a few minutes. Even more importantly, the arrival of coffee is de-coupled from the session in progress; this sounds like a minor point, but so often you find when facilitating that the group are just reaching towards some important consensus or insight when a hardworking hotel employee comes clanking in with the tea-trolley and fractures the flow and concentration just at the wrong moment.

The layout of the room or rooms in which the sessions are conducted is important. Figure 8.26 shows a typical but not necessarily ideal layout. For example, in many circumstances it is an extremely bad idea to allow coffee to be served in the main room as this can distract from the proceedings. On the other hand if there is no other room available then in-room coffee is better than no coffee. The main table is U-shaped to support the walkthrough sessions when bean bags are thrown about and the facilitator needs quick and easy access. All the participants can have eye contact too. This is important. A horseshoe table like this is easily the best layout; a boardroom-style table is second best, but not as good because the facilitator must then either stay at the head of the table at all times, or lose contact with participants by walking behind them as s/he moves around. Separate tables should not be used. Groups from the same department sitting at a separate table may easily get a subconscious feeling that this is their turf, which they will defend against all comers – reaching a wider group consensus becomes more difficult.

Figure 8.26 Facilitator's-eye view of a typical room layout.

The other table in the figure should really be several tables to support the printer and other items. At least two flip charts are needed and a whiteboard is useful too, especially one that can produce hard copies of what is drawn or written on it. Get plenty of marker pens, check they all work before you start, and make sure they are erasable or water-soluble before you write all over the whiteboard. Figure 8.26 shows an ordinary whiteboard and flip-chart pages 'blu-tacked' to the wall at the rear. Some hotels don't permit fixing paper to their walls like this: avoid them.

On the right we can see the requirements engineer with the computer, which is equipped with any CASE or other tools needed, and probably a standard suite of office automation software such as MS Office. This machine is connected to a fast laser printer and to an LCD palette set atop of the overhead projector that projects on the screen to the right.

Not shown are all the little items needed but catalogued in the checklists below. Nor do we see the video or audio recording equipment that it is advisable to use sometimes.

Whatever tools you use, some artefacts will need to be distributed during the workshop. Therefore, make sure that the hotel can provide adequate photocopying facilities. At break times, the current state of the project document should be printed and photocopied, so that after the break participants sit down with the absolute current state of the workshop in front of them. You need to check that the hotel understands this time schedule. Often, the management may quite sincerely say they offer photocopying, when in practice this means you can hand a couple of sheets in at the desk and get a single copy in an hour or so when someone gets round to it. Make sure the management is clear that you may need 20 copies of a 30-page document prepared on demand in a 20-minute period (and you are prepared for one of the team actually to do the copying). And if they can't service the requirement, use somewhere else.

Get set up and tested in good time, and preferably the night before. This is particularly true if you are using hired equipment. Check everything; has the computer got the printer driver for the printer? Does the printer have adequate paper and toner? Do you have a splitter cable for the projector so the scribe can see the terminal as well as project on the screen?

There will also need to be the rooms allocated for break-out sessions and syndicate work. These sessions are used to resolve specialized issues and especially to allow the users to work on the first cut at class descriptions (class cards). I find that keeping the development staff away from the early stages of this process of discovery is beneficial in terms of getting a good, business-oriented model. The developers should look over the resultant model later to apply solid object-oriented design principles. Another useful approach is to split the users into two teams and then merge the resultant class cards in the plenary session. This can appear to take longer, but often reveals important conflicts and alternative approaches. Also, small groups usually get results faster than large ones. The layout for these secondary rooms can be much simpler: just a large table, chairs, one flip chart and stationery such as blank acetates.

8.13.5 Workshop organizer's and facilitator's checklists

The checklists on the next three pages are intended to help the organizer of workshops and the facilitator. They are to be treated as reminder lists and not adhered to slavishly. Look at each item and think: 'Do we need (to do) that?'. These checklists have been used by the organizers of many projects and may be considered tested; but I would be interested to hear readers' views on whether anything useful could be added.

The first two checklists cover the suggested order of business for scoping and detail workshops respectively. The third list is perhaps the most useful; it is a list of useful or essential items to procure before the workshop starts.

Checklist 8.1: Running scoping sessions

Introduction to approach (optional)
Mission statement
Objectives
Measures
Voting on priorities
Discussion of priorities
External process model
      External agents and conversations
Internal process model
      Agents and actors
      Conversations
      Triggers and goals
      Key tasks
Exclusions
Assumptions
Outstanding Issues – who will resolve?
Implementation priorities
Reuse candidates?
Next steps
Obtain sign-off

Checklist 8.2: Running detailed analysis sessions

Introduction to approach (if needed)
Scoping session output (if any)
   Mission, objectives, measures and priorities
   Business process model
Process modelling
   For each conversation analyse
   Goal – Offer/Request – Negotiation – Root task – Handover
   Triggers for agents
   Top level (root) tasks for each message
Examine business process re-engineering opportunities
   Is there one or more conversation(s) supporting each objective?
   Is there at least one objective underlying each conversation?
Decompose task scripts into sub-scripts to atomic level
Exceptions: side-scripts
Syndicate work
   Textual analysis to find candidate classes
   Class cards
   Structures (classification, composition, association and usage)
   Card sorts or repertory grids to refine structures
   Assign attributes to classes
   Assign operations to classes
   Assign rules to classes
   State models if necessary
Consolidate syndicates' work
Confirm associations (by drawing 'entity' model) – optional; ten minutes
   maximum
Rôle play – record sequence diagrams for each root task
Review library classes
Discuss implementation priorities
Reuse candidates
Have open issues from scoping been resolved?
Operational aspects dealt with?
Legal aspects dealt with?
Security policy dealt with?
Disaster recovery dealt with?
Sign off document

Checklist 8.3: Organizer's logistics checklist

Book the hotel/rooms
Number of participants
  Room big enough?
  Enough syndicate rooms?
Specify room layout(s)
Catering arrangements
  Meal/drinks schedules?
  Meals/drinks/special diets?
  Coffee taken outside the main room
Photocopying arrangements
Inform the participants, facilitator(s), analysts
  Have they confirmed availability?
  Travel arrangements – flights booked?
  Facilitator briefed?
Book computer equipment and install and test software
  Computer, printer, drivers, display screen, palette or projector
  Software installed and tested?
      MS Office, Visio or similar
      Other CASE?
      Existing repository classes and class cards
      Sufficient disk space?
      Appropriate printer driver installed?
Video/audio equipment ordered, installed and tested
Flip charts, pens, overhead, blank foils, video/audio, blank tapes,
  paper for printer and participants, pencils, glow pens, Post-It® notes,
  BLU-TACK®, Sellotape®, coloured stickers, etc.
Spare bulbs, batteries, etc.
Is there a (copy generating) whiteboard?
Prepare foils, handouts
  Handouts duplicated?
Collect and take documents from earlier sessions
Collect class and task descriptions from earlier workshops
Prepare agenda
Create sign-off document

8.13.6 Facilitation skills

Effective facilitators require a rare combination of talents. They must be knowledgeable in the method and techniques – UML, Catalysis and SOMA in this case – and about the business, at least to the extent of being comfortable with the terminology and familiar with the main ideas. Presentation and communication skills are key. They must be assertive but know when to keep in the background and just listen. They have to be able to encourage diffident participants and give them confidence while knowing how to deal with troublesome personalities, often very senior ones, without upsetting or belittling them. Setting up and agreeing ground rules for the workshop (discussed below) is a very helpful technique.

A sense of humour helps put people at ease and the facilitator should not be afraid of quips and even risqué remarks, as long as this does not get out of hand. The key skill is that of being able to pull out the essence of an argument and see its principal contradictory elements quickly. My approach is always to look for two opposites in analysing anything and then explore the dialectic and mediations between them. With practice this can be done very quickly. Probably, the only way to learn to be an accomplished facilitator is by apprenticeship. Perhaps some people are just born and grown as natural facilitators. I have never had formal training in facilitation; I learnt through practice, theory and imitation. Perhaps a study of group dynamics would be a useful background; it is certainly very important.

Importantly, the facilitator must be neutral with respect to groups of participants, and moreover be *seen to be* neutral. There must be no perceived bias towards any user group, and no perception that the facilitator 'represents' in any sense the development group. This is important because occasionally the facilitator will be a member of the development organization. Life's experience will often have left users with a feeling that they are going to get what the developers want to deliver, rather than what they asked for.

Voting is an important way of reaching consensus but should be handled carefully. A vote may not indicate the truth, merely the current conjuncture of opinion. The results of voting should be presented as such: softly and as a guide only. The facilitator is responsible for obtaining the sponsor's and other users' sign-off. This too requires a combination of tact and determination. We present the group with a form offering a single choice between 'I agree that this model is a good representation of the requirements' and 'I *strongly* disagree ...'; nothing in between will do.

The facilitator is responsible for maintaining the time-box discipline within the workshop and should have approximate time targets for each step on the agenda. S/he should also have a clear mental model of what will happen and where delays are likely. The facilitator must be aware of the tasks of the requirements engineer and clarify issues or slow the pace for him when necessary. A good rapport between these two is essential and telepathy would be a distinct advantage – although subtle hand signals and nods usually suffice.

Potential indicators of a poor facilitator include any tendency to be a bully or autocrat, timidity, lack of confidence when presenting, fixed ideas, inability to sit back and listen, any tendency to sycophancy in the face of senior management, lack of awareness of general and specific business issues and general lack of authority or charisma. Curiously, you cannot discover these faults reliably without watching the person actually do the job. Interviews and – especially – psychometric tests are of little use.

8.13.7 Who should record the session

As I have remarked above, the word 'scribe', frequently used in the literature, demeans both the importance and the difficulty of the task of correctly recording the proceedings. This is why I prefer the term REQUIREMENTS ENGINEER. There are two basic prerequisites: absolute familiarity with the selected documentation tool and its underlying method, if it has one; and fluency and accuracy in typing (not necessarily touch typing though). But there is much more. The engineer must be able to turn shorthand notes thrown up on the board or flip chart by the facilitator into grammatical connected text; but without recording every jot and tittle of conversations that, while they may lead to important conclusions, may also contain much that is irrelevant. On the other hand, if there is any doubt about relevancy, it is better to record it than not. The text can be amended later.

It is sometimes useful to record the proceedings of a workshop using audio tape or even video. In this section I want to present, very briefly, a few guidelines and rules of thumb on the use of such technology.

Having a taped record is mainly useful for the scribes and analysts who may have failed to understand or record some nuance of the argument or detail of a required feature. This applies to completing the workshop report and refining the analysis into a more detailed specification or systems analysis report. I have found that the difference between audio and video recording is of little significance when using the tapes for this purpose. I therefore feel that the additional cost of video can really only be justified if the physical actions of users are being studied in some way. Of course the organizers of the workshop may wish to impress the users with all their high-tech equipment, but that is another issue.

My experience, and indeed common sense, tells us that there is hardly ever any point in having tapes transcribed into typescript. No one ever reads such documents and the process is time-consuming and expensive. The exception to this rule is when the users have described a complex knowledge-based task and a protocol analysis is to be applied.

Whether using audio or video, the facilitator must always ask the group's permission to record the proceedings and offer to turn the tape off at anyone's request, perhaps if a particularly sensitive issue is being discussed. The group should be assured that the tapes will be confidential to the project team and that they will be destroyed after use or, if required, returned to the lead user for destruction. Identifying a LEAD USER, whom the other participants usually defer to, at the outset of the event is a key way of managing disagreements. This is one of many patterns for running workshops. We will also meet TEN-MINUTE RULE.

8.13.8 Running a workshop

A SOMA workshop can last from one to five days. A workshop taking longer than a week should be broken down into separate workshops. Apart from the difficulty of taking people away from their normal jobs for so long, if the workshop will last longer it means that there is too much to do in the time for the technique to work properly. Half-day workshops do not usually work well for detailed sessions but can be used to define scope and partition the job among subsequent detailed workshops.

Deciding on how much time should be allocated for a particular workshop is still something of a black art. After all, we are asking how much time will a group of people, who have perhaps never worked together before in this way, take to agree on an unquantifiable number of points. But we are obliged to come up with some sort of estimate, in order to allocate people for the requisite time. Taking three days as a norm we might allocate half-a-day to a day scoping and two to two and a half days on the detail; the more people involved, the longer it will take. If the scoping indicates that there will not be enough time to cover everything in detail, it is important to cover all the issues discovered at a reasonably high level, and then schedule further workshops for the detail, rather than to exhaust the detail on some areas and not cover others at all.

The facilitator should have a mental model of the temporal structure of the workshop and the issues that must be covered. The checklists provided in Section 8.13.5 provide a useful *aide mémoire*. Usually I find it best not to publish this in too much detail in advance. Certainly publish and review the *sequence* of the agenda – but refrain from a blatant announcement of specific times. It is easier to estimate the time requirements for the entire workshop than for each session. Often, extra time spent on one issue will ease the discussion and reduce the time taken on a subsequent one. Furthermore, the iterative nature of developing consistency at each level means that no stage is necessarily complete until all stages have been covered. But if there exists a piece of paper saying something like:

9:30 Mission Statement
10:00 Objectives
11:00 Business Process
12.30 ... etc.

then people will feel uncomfortable if the workshop is straying too far from the (rather arbitrary) timings that were assigned at the outset, and they may wonder if things are growing successfully to a point. Sometimes, for example, the sponsor may already have thought through the mission statement in some detail, and be able to state it to everyone's satisfaction in a couple of minutes. On other occasions, the real mission may only become clear after analysing an initially diffuse set of more detailed issues. So, as facilitator, give yourself enough leeway in timings so that no one can question whether the workshop appears to be running early or late. An exception to this must be made when there is a need to schedule slots for specialists such as legal or security experts to participate.

Take a full one-hour break for lunch. Plan for this and keep to the schedule – it is a courtesy to the participants to let them know that they can rely on a break say between 12:30 and 13:30 to make phone calls and deal with other commitments. Schedule coffee and tea breaks mid-morning and mid-afternoon but, for these, do not guarantee the precise time; come to a suitable break-point and then stop for 20 minutes. Remember also the need for regular comfort breaks – especially when there are smokers present.

The facilitator can make her own job easier, and the workshop experience more satisfactory for everyone involved, by laying down some ground rules right at the start – and inviting participants to specify their own rules, add them to the list and then agree to follow those very rules. If things get a little emotional later on, it can help to defuse the situation by referring to the abstract rules, rather than heightening tension further by the facilitator becoming involved on a personal level. If it is a clearly stated and established rule that only one person is to speak at a time, without interruption, then when two people start having a highly vocal argument, pointing out that the rule has been violated is a more emollient intervention than telling people to shut up. The ten-minute rule is possibly the most useful rule in this respect. Having said all this, the facilitator must have the *gravitas* to take charge in a positive way, if that is what it takes. Here are some rules that have proved useful:

- One speaker at a time and no private, parallel conversations.
- No hogging the floor; ten minutes is the maximum and the facilitator can instruct offenders to stop after that time.
- Politeness dictates that interrupting other speakers is not on.
- Personal reflections are to be avoided strenuously.
- Job titles and grades are left outside the room; the participants are here to work together.
- Mobile phones are switched off. Pick up messages during breaks.
- Everyone gets a chance to speak on any point of discussion. That's the facilitator's responsibility. This can be quite a tricky issue for the facilitator. In a big workshop, one cannot ask everyone in the room every time a topic arises. In such a case, one should encourage people to raise their hands or make some signal that they have something to say – but be sure to be alert enough to notice and include them. Otherwise the more vociferous individuals will dominate while the more taciturn will rarely get a chance to comment.

An important technique for closing down redundant discussion and ensuring wider participation is to explain at the beginning of the workshop that there will be a TEN-MINUTE RULE. This means that, at the facilitator's discretion or on the request of other participants, any topic that has been discussed for too long is placed on the open issues list for later resolution by fewer people. The ten-minute rule can be applied to defuse group dynamics conflicts. If consensus on a topic is not emerging after ten minutes, the facilitator, or anyone else, can point this out and have the topic shelved.

The issue should be noted as open for subsequent resolution. This requires judgment and discipline on the facilitator's part. After all, looked at from one viewpoint, the whole event relates to one topic. When does one topic segue into another? This is why it is so important to keep the current focus clear in everyone's mind – keeping a keyword on the whiteboard until this area has been exhausted helps here.

Enforce the rules fairly, consistently and thoroughly. Being seen to be prepared to enforce the rules early on, perhaps on a minor issue, can serve as an object lesson and in itself reduces the need to enforce the rules later.

KEEPING MOMENTUM

As with ordinary interviewing, there is a difficult path to tread between the pastures of rambling but productive discussion and the quagmire of the unfocused talking shop. It can be useful to write the current topic of discussion on the whiteboard, to refer to when someone is wandering off track. Use a flipchart to note down topics that are raised but are divergent from the current issue on the whiteboard. This allows you to abort some branch of discussion without being negative towards the person raising it. An interesting point can be returned to later.

Make a point of telling people the *time* that the meeting will be reconvened after breaks. It is useful to have a clock in the room. It helps to get the meeting restarted on time after such interruptions. If you announce a ten-minute break people will tend to extend their off-line activities to the next round half hour. At least a few minutes will be lost at every break. If you can point at the clock and say that the much-needed ten-minute leg stretch will bring us up to 11:20 (a nice round number even though it's actually 11:06 now) then people will tend to return and be ready at the appointed time.

If people appear to be losing concentration, do not be afraid to take short (five to ten minute) breaks at unscheduled times – other than the planned refreshment points.

ENDING THE WORKSHOP

After several days' hard work, the time comes for everyone to return to their normal jobs and various locations. It is central to the philosophy of SOMA that workshops are used to build shared understanding between the user and development groups. The construction of object models has a key rôle to play in this, but the way in which the facilitator closes the workshop is also critical.

It is vital that before concluding the proceedings, a sign-off sheet is circulated to all the participants and their signature obtained. They can either sign as being in agreement that the project should proceed based on the high-level object model developed, or as being in **strong** disagreement with the final report produced. No intermediate position can be countenanced. Strong disagreement, it should be explained, is tantamount to signing the 'project delay form'. Remembering that the workshop report is a document covering the results agreed during the workshop, there is usually no legitimate reason why anyone should be in disagreement. This is particularly true if the facilitator and requirements engineer have ensured that the developing document has been re-circulated and reviewed at various key break-points during the event, so that people have had a chance to review it as it develops and raise any divergent issues at the time.

The open issues section of the report offers an escape valve for divergent opinions, so that people in violent disagreement over some aspect can still agree to sign the document as agreeing with the fact that the open issue has been recorded and awaits resolution. When an open issue is recorded, it is important to record who is responsible for resolving it and by when.

It is important that everyone goes away with the warm fuzzies. Nobody should be left with the feeling that the event has been a waste of their time. At close, review the progress made, summarize the findings and talk about the next stages and the next key milestones that can be expected.

8.13.9 Using interviewing techniques in a workshop context

Many techniques that can be used in normal interviews can be readily extended for use in workshops once they are well understood. This subsection discusses just a few of the techniques that I have found particularly useful.

It is usual to divide interviews into structured and focused interviews. Typically, structured interviews are at a high level of generality and take place earlier in the discovery process. A structured interview aims to grasp an overview of the topic which is broad but shallow. It will result in elicitation of the key objects and concepts of the domain but not go into detail. In a workshop this corresponds to running a scoping session, where the same techniques can be used.

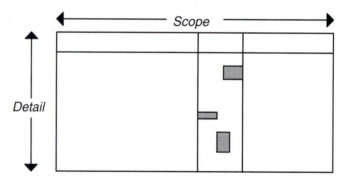

Figure 8.27 Narrow and deep *versus* broad and shallow approaches to interviews and prototyping.

Focused interviews or detailed workshops go into the detail of one area and are typically narrow and deep. During the elicitation process it is essential to search for reusable elements – the grey rectangles in Figure 8.27. Analysts should select the area that gives either 80% of the benefit or 80% of the predicted complexity or reuse potential as the first area to explore – preferably both. This corresponds, ideally, to about 20% of the scope of the system. This broad and shallow followed by narrow and deep scenario corresponds closely to the approach that should be followed during prototyping.

Structured interviews follow a plan that should be prepared in advance and state the objectives of the interview. At the start of the session, participants should agree an agenda. Then, for each agenda topic, interviewers or workshop facilitators ask questions, put out **probes**, review the results at each stage and move to the next topic. Finally, one must review the overall results and compare them with the plan, asking whether the objectives have been achieved. If not, the exercise can be repeated. It is essential that questions are open rather than closed. Open questions do not permit an answer such as 'Yes' or 'No' that closes further discussion or elaboration. Probes are merely particularly useful types of open question. Table 8.4 sets out some probe types with examples. Probes use all six question words alluded to by Kipling as follows.

> *I keep six honest serving men*
> *(They taught me all I knew);*
> *Their names are* What *and* Why *and* When
> *And* How *and* Where *and* Who.

Table 8.4 Types of probe.

Probe type	Example
Definitional	What is a ...?
Additive	Go on ...
Reflective	What you're saying is ...
Mode change	How would your colleagues view that?
	Can you give a more concrete example?
Directive	Why is that?
	How?
	Could you be more specific?

Focused interviews are less easy to describe in abstract. Their form depends more on the domain in question. However, techniques such as teachback, repertory grids and task analysis are commonly the ones used. Teachback involves interviewers presenting their understanding to the users formally and receiving corrections thereby. The other techniques are described below.

A good interviewer or facilitator plans and prepares sessions and sets clear objectives. However, adaptability is the key skill and one must be prepared to adapt or even abandon a plan that is not working. Some domain knowledge is prerequisite to facilitate open discussion, as is a good understanding of object-oriented technology itself, especially object modelling.

⊟ 8.14 Summary

This chapter presented the workshop-based, SOMA requirements engineering micro-process in some detail. We also reviewed other approaches to requirements engineering and showed that it needed different techniques to system specification. So while use-case-driven methods were usual for the latter, a business-driven conversation analysis worked better for the former. In support of this we reviewed the theory of business process modelling and re-engineering.

The mission grid was introduced for scaling very large business models and we saw how to elicit business objectives and their priorities.

I pointed out several other problems with the use case approach and introduced task actions and scripts for them. Use cases are not abandoned but they cease to be either the starting point for requirements capture or the units of business process reuse.

We saw how the SOMA approach supported traceability and discussed the idea of executable specification. Finally, we learnt how to organize and run requirements engineering workshops.

Practical experience has borne out the advantages of the approach on over 100 projects undertaken since 1993. This experience confirms that the method of requirements engineering based on task script elicitation within a business process model and described in this book is intensely practical. I conclude that it is of wide applicability and should be used as a precursor to the use of UML-based specification and design methods such as Catalysis. I recommend it to practitioners for their further evaluation.

⊟ 8.15 Bibliographical notes

The theory of business process modelling presented in this chapter is largely original, although I have been motivated by the work of many others; notably Jacobson, Flores and Winograd. Some of the material in this chapter was first presented in a series of articles in the SIGS journal *Object Expert*. Graham (1998) also covered much the same ground.

The field of CSCW is surveyed in Greenberg (1991) and Wilson (1990). Diaper (1993) is a collection of papers on the state of the art. Khoshafian *et al.* (1992) is a manifesto about building office automation systems using a combination of techniques from relational databases, object-oriented databases, expert systems, CSCW, graphical user interfaces, multimedia storage systems, network technology and full-content information retrieval. They are effectively proposing a product to meet the needs of office automation and, presumably, are building such a thing for sale. However, the book is a useful survey of the underlying technology covering a broad range of topics not usually brought together.

Although SOMA always allowed for associations between tasks, Peter Jones first elaborated the theory of task association sets and their equivalence with sequence diagrams. He also developed many of the ideas concerning time- and event-based simulation presented in the digression of Section 8.12.1.

Martin and Odell (1998) provide a far better explanation of activity diagrams and their use than any of the core references on UML such as the OMG web site or Rumbaugh *et al.* (1999). Tony Simons found 30 more things that could go wrong in object modelling with UML (Simons and Graham, 1999).

Leffingwell and Widrig (2000) survey the field of requirements engineering with an emphasis on traceability using their *Requisite Pro* tool and on use cases and RUP.

For a very readable overview of requirements capture in group sessions, evidently based on a lot of practical experience, see Gause and Weinberg (1989). Macaulay (1996) lists several approaches to the management of group sessions and gives checklists and guidance for each approach.

8.16 Exercises

1. Why are use cases useful for specifying systems? Why are they not suitable for requirements analysis?

2. Define the following terms: agent, actor, conversation, message, action, use case, script.

3. Discuss the differences between any two approaches to requirements engineering.

4. Draw a sequence and activity diagram for a visit to your local supermarket.

5. What is the first thing a facilitator does in a workshop? What is the last?

6. Name ten of the key tasks of a workshop – in order.

7. Discuss the use of voting in workshops.

8. Discuss the difference between task scripts, actions and use cases.

9. What is a (a) side-script (b) component script (c) subscript?

10. What is the grammatical structure of an atomic task? Define atomic. How else can scripts be specified?

11. Discuss the validation of requirements models.
    a) How is the Business Object Model tested?

b) How are objectives tested?

c) How is the Task Object Model tested?

12. How is a Task Object Model transformed into a Business Object Model? How is a Business Object Model transformed into an Implementation Object Model?

13. Discuss the use of activity diagrams for business process modelling. What are the boundaries to their successful use?

14. Complete the following well-known phrases and sayings:

a) Better _____ faster!

b) I keep six honest serving men,
They taught me all I knew.
Their names are _____ and _____ and _____
And _____ and _____ and _____.

15. Sketch a class card in detail.

16. What techniques can be used to restrict or extend discussion in a workshop?

17. What is a probe? Give two examples and name the type of probe.

18. **Mini-project**

A dealer has already found an opportunity to deal in the FX market with a certain counterparty. The dealer is obliged to execute the deal only within given counterparty limits and within her personal position limits. They must complete the deal once they have agreed it verbally. If these conditions are satisfied then:
The dealer strikes a bargain with the counterparty at agreed terms and rates;
A confirmation must be sent to the counterparty;
The Settlements Department must be notified of the deal so that they can arrange payment. Settlements also provide standing settlement instructions and notify the Accounts Department of the deal;
Accounts post on the deal date and on its value date;
The dealer's position and the counterparty's limit availability must be adjusted to reflect the new position.

Based on the above scenario, draw a business process model for the above situation, including agents and conversations and the tasks associated with them. Write a task script for one of the tasks. Sketch a Business Object Model using any elements that seem appropriate. Try to find the key objects and their four structural relationships: classification, usage, composition and association. Make up some class cards. If you are part of a group try to walk through and debug your model. Use the walkthrough to produce sequence charts and/or activity diagrams.

9

Process and project management

I tell you, the only safeguard of order and discipline in the modern world is a standardized worker with interchangeable parts. That would solve the entire problem of management.

Jean Giraudoux (*The Madwoman of Chaillot*)

It is often thought that software engineering process models aim to automate and thereby de-skill the development process. Unfortunately, this has led to over-bureaucratic methods that, at best, produce reams of documentation that are never looked at by either developers or their clients. Such 'shelfware' is mainly used to soothe a too-nervous management that has little understanding of the development process itself. It is also often claimed, with some justification, that a good developer needs no process. On the other hand it is clear that real projects are not entirely staffed by top-rank developers (or top-rank managers for that matter) and that if a process is to improve then it must be written down.

My view therefore lies somewhere between the possible extremes. I think that a defined, repeatable, measurable process is highly desirable but that it should not be large or bureaucratic. Nor should it attempt to demean the rôle of the human beings involved in development or set at nought the importance of their creativity.

This chapter surveys the current state of thought on object-oriented development processes, project management and measurement. We will pay particular attention to rapid application development and make some recommendations as to the minimal process that should be adopted. It has a truly object-oriented process model – an instantiation of the OPEN process framework (Graham *et al.*, 1997b; Henderson-Sellers *et al.*, 1998) that is compatible with DSDM, RUP and XP. It extends RUP by offering more definite guidelines for process management and, while we use use cases extensively, is business process rather than use case driven; i.e. it is *contract driven*.

⊟ 9.1 Why follow a process?

Repeated biennial surveys by the Standish Group since 1995 have shown that nearly two-thirds of US software development projects fail, either through cancellation, overrunning their budgets or delivering software that is never put into production. It is not incredible to extrapolate these – frankly scandalous – figures to other parts of the world. What is harder to believe is that our industry, and the people in it, can tolerate such a situation. We should be too ashamed of ourselves ever to bid for work again. The Standish surveys also looked into the reasons why people involved in the sample projects thought such projects fail so often. The reasons given – in descending order of importance – were:

- lack of user involvement
- no clear statement of requirements
- no project ownership
- no clear vision and objectives
- lack of planning

With a move to object technology some things are unchanged: good software engineering and project management practices remain critical; sound knowledge of the business is still as important as development skills and there is still need to understand the legacy. Infrastructure issues, the need for documentation, testing and sound configuration management practices all remain. This is good, in the sense that it allows developers and management to build on what they already know. However, some things do change as a result of the new approach. Project managers now must understand incremental delivery along with new languages, frameworks and components (Java, C++, Beans, San Francisco, CORBA, EJBs, COM, etc.). As I have repeatedly stressed, object-oriented design methods do not separate processes from data, so that is different too. Recall that over 16% of our costs are due to changes in data structures; the new approach must address these costs at least. Lastly, object-oriented methods permit far more seamless modelling and traceability.

As we will see shortly, conventional processes are often far too bureaucratic and prone to 'paper bloat'. In an evolutionary and iterative culture we need a much more lightweight process. In our consultancy practice at TriReme we try to document the complete development process for any client in fewer than 100 pages. Specifically, companies moving to object technology need a better process: lightweight but still rigorous. But solid requirements capture remains a key issue; so they need a new approach to requirements, as suggested in the previous chapter. They also need a new object-oriented analysis and design mind-set. The slogans for such organizations should be these.

- Only produce documents that will really be used (rather than produced to placate line management).
- Keep it short (100 pages or fewer – modulo statutory *diktat*).

- Make sure activities are properly sequenced.
- Start with a clear understanding of the requirements; but let them evolve.
- Better systems faster!

A defined software engineering process is needed because organizations do not just want isolated islands of success, they want their successes to be repeatable. This then creates the possibility of process improvement and provides a basis for measurement and estimation. The latter, in turn, offer the hope of improvements in product quality. In other words, organizations want to improve their process maturity. This does not imply adherence to the much-vaunted SEI Capability Maturity Model illustrated in Figure 9.1 (Humphrey, 1989) but it does recognize that such models represent an extremely good idea in principle. Jones (1994) regards the CMM levels as arbitrary, and it is certainly difficult to see how something that is not defined can be repeatable; how would you know what had been repeated?

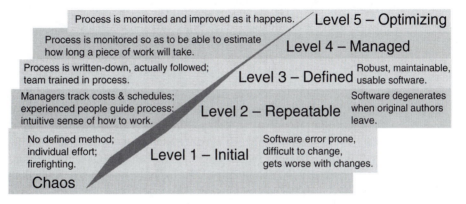

Figure 9.1 The SEI Capability Maturity Model.

9.2 What must an object-oriented method do?

For a system to be successful it must satisfy the requirements of three kinds of stakeholder: project sponsors, system users and system support personnel. It is unlikely that the requirements of these three groups will coincide exactly. In particular, if a system is to make the transition from a concept and plan to an industrial-strength application supporting the business then the requirements of group one – the project sponsors – must be completely satisfied. Once the system is live this group of people will judge the system based on the evidence they receive from group two – the users. The users' view of the system will be more favourable if the system is easy to use, performs to business needs and the support they receive is prompt and effective. However, before the system is live the project sponsors have little evidence with which to judge the future success of the project.

Specifically, all they have available to them is the track record of the development team and the arguments put forward in favour of the system in the preliminary documentation.

Development organizations migrating to object technology need to recruit and hold on to the best developers, and produce both systems and documentation of the highest quality, usability and clarity. Their methods need to reflect existing practice – that is, what is actually done successfully now – rather than impose bureaucratic methods that few developers will understand the need for. Such methods are only beneficial in the presence of unskilled developers.

Computers provide solutions to problems specified by industry and commerce. In theory, a new development should be a new solution to an unsolved problem. In practice the solution may already exist but not have been adequately communicated to interested parties. In either event, there will be uncertainty present in the analysis and design of a new system. Effective analysis and design will rapidly reduce this uncertainty to manageable proportions. Use must be made of existing and established technologies and systems in order to manage this uncertainty successfully. Specifically, use must be made of stable platforms as a foundation for development at the outset, as well as throughout the life cycle of a project. Booch (1994) quotes Gall on this subject:

> A complex system that works is invariably found to have evolved
> from a simple system that worked ... A complex system designed
> from scratch never works and cannot be patched up to make it work.
> You have to start over, beginning with a working simple system.

We should build evolutionary systems in an incremental fashion, not offer 'big-bang' solutions. Such an approach not only follows the guidelines alluded to by Booch and Gall but also allows the users and sponsors to comment on the intermediate products and have a greater input into the design of a system throughout its development.

Sponsors should be made aware of the management of uncertainty and the evolutionary approach to building systems. Statements of such aims should be made in project proposals and systems analysis reports. In addition, specific statements of what will constitute a deliverable after each evolutionary cycle should be made. This should tie in with close user and sponsor involvement during the requirements, systems design and construction activities. While this is certainly already standard practice within some successful systems in existence, it should be adopted as a conscious policy by all organizations.

The difficulty in implementing such a policy is that the level of user or sponsor involvement will vary according to the product being developed. Many GUI designs lend themselves readily to user/sponsor involvement and comment. In addition, the tools available to support the development of these GUIs enable rapid implementation of cosmetic changes in response to user requests. However, it may be more difficult to generate the same level of user enthusiasm for complex transaction processing and computation with no graphical representation of the processes.

Nevertheless, closer user involvement throughout the development of a project should be formally encouraged. Closer user involvement raises the profile of the development organization, gives greater visibility of developers to the user and sponsor communities and enables more open and effective communication between the development organization and these communities. This will enable users to articulate their needs more clearly and developers to understand them more precisely. This will result in the development organization delivering systems that the business *needs,* not what the business wants nor what the developers think it should have.

A good system development method must enforce a reasonable level of discipline on developers without hampering their productivity by unnecessary bureaucracy and endless deliverables that do not contribute to the product. Neither should it assume that it has all the answers, because there will be situations and types of system that have not been foreseen. A method should contribute to the business goal of continuous process improvement. This means that some means of measuring the output and efficiency of the process must be mandated, so that it is possible to discover the existence and the amount of any improvement. Productivity is enhanced when the imperatives of the method correspond to the steps that an ideal developer would take in the real world, under pressure, without the benefit of the method. Deliverables should be natural, essential and be actually used by someone for some valuable purpose. Many methods mandate deliverables that may only be used under certain circumstances or that are really only there to cover managers against potential criticism. Methods adopted by governments are often the worst offenders in this respect because it is too often the case that *being seen* to do the job properly is more important than doing the job properly for both civil servants and politicians.

A method should contribute to meeting real business needs by helping to ensure that quality is maintained and enhanced, requirements are captured accurately and fully, needs are not swamped by wants, deadlines are met and developers are productive. It should encourage the creation of flexible systems that can evolve with the business at minimal cost. It must help to control and shorten time-to-market in the sense that users should not have to wait for years for the system that they have specified while the inexorable changes in requirements march on.

The method proposed in this chapter shortens time-to-market through the use of an evolutionary development approach based on time-boxes, so that important layers of the system can be delivered in a maximum period of six months. Less important modules can be delivered and incorporated later. This approach recognizes that it is unrealistic to expect all of a huge, complex system to be built in the twinkling of an eye and that some systems just will not decompose in this way. I would not, for example, wish to travel on an aeroplane whose in-flight systems had been only 80% delivered. However, it is my observation that the majority of commercial systems will yield to this approach. In fact, a senior software engineer at Boeing once told me that jumbo jets were indeed built using exactly these evolutionary methods; they (fortunately) restrict the partial deliveries to the test bed. They don't fly them like that!

An object-oriented method should enhance productivity through direct support for and encouragement of a reuse culture and the use of appropriate and powerful development tools. Of course, the cost of the development and the tools must be offset against the benefits derived in the end-product. Taking the view popularized by Booch (1991, 1994), that object-oriented development is mainly justified by allowing us to manage complexity better, this whole argument amounts to building more valuable, bigger, trickier systems faster. The quality of the systems must be maintained too and this means that product as well as process and accounting metrics should be collected. The best of methods is of no use if developers find its imperatives onerous; they will inevitably devise ways of avoiding them. A good object-oriented development method should be small, simple, usable – and used.

An object-oriented process should support seamlessness by using OO modelling from wall to wall. This will in itself improve traceability, although model linking techniques must be made explicit – as discussed in Chapter 8.

A sound OO process will support lower times to market, provided that project management and component design disciplines are obeyed and reuse is managed properly.

A complete OO process should cover and include:

- requirements and business process modelling
  – workshops, animation, validation and BPR;
- a lightweight, customizable process framework;
- project management
  – an activity model, techniques, metrics, configuration, testing, etc.
  – reuse management;
- component architecture;
- system specification
  – use cases/actions, Catalysis process patterns, UML, architecture, etc.;
- component design and decomposition;
- testing through the life cycle;
- QA, commissioning and configuration management; and
- process patterns.

The term PROCESS PATTERN refers to any process of software or system development and maintenance. Such patterns are encountered often, easily recognized and readily nameable. Process patterns are of the form:

Whenever your goal is A
and your current situation is B
then try doing C
 (but be aware of prerequisite P, risk R,
 side-effect S, time-scale T, etc.)

The idea is to capture the wisdom of software strategy and tactics in digestible chunks. One of the problems with prescriptive software methodologies is that they tend to assume a fixed starting point – for example, they may assume that the developer is designing a product from scratch. In practice, this is a rare situation; a believable programming process should cater for many different starting points. We try to distil our process experience into a set of discrete patterns. Each is in the 'production rule' form given above: trigger ⇒ action. The actions often set sub-goals, for which other patterns can be found, so that patterns can be chained together to produce higher level ones.

To use process patterns, you find all the ones that apply to your current goals and situation; these form the basis of your plan. There may be several that describe different aspects of the plan; for example, ones about building the team, estimating time-scales, as well as the main outline of the plan. Because they are informally expressed, you need to apply your intelligence to choose and fit them together. It is not a mechanical process. But by choosing a pattern (or perhaps combining several), you start on the development of a custom process. Each pattern will yield some sub-goals, which you can then hope to find some other patterns to match. Choosing and applying these, you put more detail into your plan. Process patterns work best within an overall process framework into which they can be plugged.

The process described in this chapter has its origins *inter alia* in MOSES, SOMA, DSDM and Catalysis. It is a fully object-oriented process in the senses that:

- it is aimed at projects that model the world with objects;
- any new code produced will be OO code (except perhaps for wrapper code);
- the process itself is described as a set of communicating objects;
- its metrics are OO metrics;
- it is evolutionary and iterative.

For maximal flexibility, it includes both the high level metaprocess described in this chapter and componentized process patterns, including those for the requirements and design micro-processes presented in earlier chapters.

From the point of view of rapid application development, our process may be regarded as an object-oriented variant of DSDM – whose principles it adheres to strictly. Equally, from the systems builders' viewpoint, it can be seen as an extension of RUP; although we offer more flexibility and process life-cycle guidance than does RUP.

Unlike DSDM and RUP, the process is in the public domain. It is much more lightweight while retaining process rigour; to paraphrase Einstein it is 'as simple as possible but no simpler'. Many ideas from extreme programming (XP) are built-in; for example, we encourage the use of techniques such as pair-programming and the use of short, rapid cycles.

9.3 Classic life-cycle models

This section provides a critical review of software engineering life-cycle models that pre-date object technology.

9.3.1 Waterfall, V and X models

There have been several suggestions as to how IT projects should proceed based on analogies with other industrial or natural processes and structures. The oldest and best known is the waterfall model which is often justified as being equivalent to the process model of the construction industry. The earliest documentation of the idea is (Royce, 1970). The idea is that only after a complete set of requirements has been defined can analysis begin. After analysis is complete, and only then, logical design may commence and so on. Iterations are sometimes permitted but should be avoided since the cost of iteration is high and increases as the backward move crosses more phases of the life cycle, as indicated by Figure 9.2.

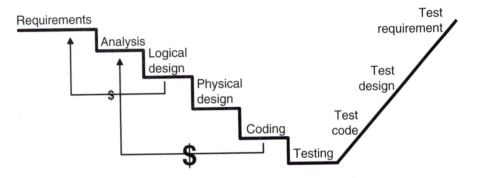

Figure 9.2 The waterfall model with iteration and its extension into the V model. The greater the number of stages reworked, the greater the cost. Testing happens far too late.

Closely related to waterfall models are the so-called 'V' models. These relate testing sub-stages to the earlier waterfall stages; unit testing tests the code, integration and stress testing tests the design and, finally, acceptance testing and post-implementation reviews test the analysis and requirements. The later a test failure occurs, the more costly the fix.

It has been argued that the waterfall model was never put forward by software engineers as a prescription for system building but that it was designed by suppliers to control delivery and payment schedules. Once an external contractor had produced the analysis report it could be paid for the work. Naturally, buyers often felt that once they had paid for something it ought to work, so that redoing the analysis was resisted unless the supplier would do so at no charge; something that they were – equally naturally – reluctant to do. This led to contractors inventing rigorous methods to maximize the completeness of each phased deliverable, even unto the time-honoured practice of stating that if the customer didn't explicitly state it then it won't be done – even if it was evidently needed. These methods consisted mainly of heuristics and manual instructions or checklists. Current pressures indicate a widely agreed need for more flexible approaches that permit prototyping and rapid development in a highly iterative manner.

Hodgson (1991) proposed an extension of the basic V model that takes account of reuse, called the X model. It is illustrated in Figure 9.3 with a few terminological changes for greater clarity. The model emphasizes the way that components and frameworks move in and out of the repository using an analogy between accounting and computing. This model is certainly an improvement over the traditional V model and does throw light on the reuse issue. However, I consider such models inadequate for modern object-oriented development because they fail to provide for early testing, prototyping and iterative development.

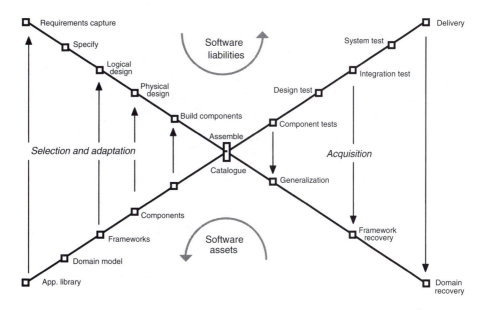

Figure 9.3 Hodgson's X model.

9.3.2 Spiral models

Barry Boehm of TRW is credited with the first formalization of an iterative process model. His key idea was that software development should be risk and product driven. A modernized representation of his spiral model is given in Figure 9.4. This is interpreted as follows. Development begins with a survey and review of the existing situation in the business with due regard to existing systems. The situation must be monitored and measured so that an analysis of the risk of proceeding with any change can be made. If the positive risks outweigh the negative ones sufficiently, the next stage is to plan what is to be done. Doing it implies that a mini-waterfall process takes place. This could represent the complete development, a prototype, a pilot or an incremental deliverable component of the final system. Next, the situation should be reviewed to establish if further development is required and, if so, plan the next step. This process can be repeated indefinitely or a number of times fixed in advance. Clearly, it is more general than the waterfall model. Some critics have argued that it is really a linear process with repetition rather than a genuinely iterative one (Henderson-Sellers and Edwards, 1994). Indeed, it can be viewed as little more than a wrapped-up waterfall but the emphasis on risk and producing usable products at every stage makes it quite different. Boehm (1981) points out that the model is inappropriate for putting work out to contract with external suppliers. The main contribution of the spiral model is its emphasis on risk analysis.

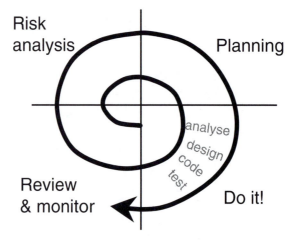

Figure 9.4 A modern version of the Boehm spiral model.

9.3.3 The fountain model and MOSES

Brian Henderson-Sellers and Julian Edwards were the originators of a life-cycle model that uses an analogy with fountains rather than waterfalls. In this model the spiral model is implicit and it emphasizes that phases overlap, that layers and subsystems emerge at various points in development and that the development of individual components is uneven. It permits a division between domain and application objects and is designed to encourage reuse. The deliverables pass up the middle of the fountain, building on the existing reuse pool at the base and falling back into it as completed. The simile includes the idea of intermediate catchment basins. New components rise up through testing and program use into maintenance and further development. Both new and existing components may pass through a generalization and re-evaluation phase before falling back into the reuse pool.

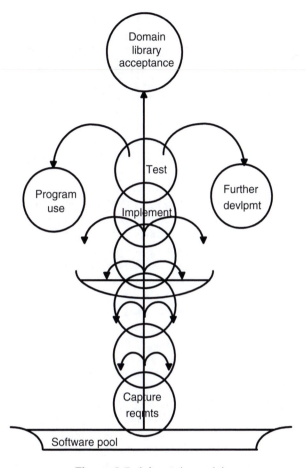

Figure 9.5 A fountain model.

There are three routes through the fountain model corresponding to the situations where: (a) all classes are new and pass through all life-cycle phases; (b) some reuse is possible so that classes are modified, messaged and subclassed rather than designed and built; and (c) systems are merely assembled from existing classes based on a thorough domain analysis. The first scenario corresponds to the organization that is naïve in object-oriented methods and the last to one which is unlikely to be achieved even in dynamic user organizations in the foreseeable future. The fountain model is a useful metaphor but contains insufficient detail to guide the development process on its own. In the sequel we will incorporate its ideas into a more prescriptive but flexible approach.

MOSES defined the activities appropriate to the process phases using a table similar to Table 9.1.

Table 9.1 Simplified MOSES phases and activities.

Phase	Activities
Planning	Estimation, scheduling, objective setting, resource commissioning, risk analysis
Investigation	Requirements capture, information gathering, problem understanding, scoping
Specification	Analysis, high level logical design
Implementation	Low level physical design, coding, testing
Review	Quality audit, project plan assessment, metrics assessment, tests against task scripts

The planning phase is a reprise of the business planning stage with a shorter-term focus. Investigation involves collecting existing textual sources, previous models and existing reusable class descriptions, running interviews or workshops and establishing scope and constraints. This process continues into the specification stage where again joint workshops are used and analysis performed. A system analysis report is produced from the first iteration. Later iterations may involve designs that take account of computer constraints. Implementation converts the object model representing the logical design to a physical design that is usually language specific and moves on to code production. The design model must include decisions on database storage, conversion of classification structures into inheritance networks, use of public/private/protected/friend, etc., implementing composition structures, concurrent inter-object communication and architectural considerations. Unit and integration tests are performed here too. Review involves further testing against use cases and both product and process quality assessment.

We do not follow this model exactly because the investigation process takes place both within and outside of the time-boxes. Workshops gather requirements that apply to all the iterations within at least one time-box; but each user review within the time-box is capturing additional requirements – at least in principle. If we admit that planning is primarily objective setting and scheduling then it is also clear that objective setting takes place during workshops and is only modified during the build. Review too is split between the time-box (use-case-based testing) and the evaluation stage (which corresponds to MOSES' Review). The next section defines the time-box approach in detail.

9.3.4 Fractals, conches and pinballs

Other variants on the spiral and suggestions intended to support prototyping and/or RAD abound. McGregor and Sykes (1992) describe a fractal model due to Forte and based on the observation that development is self-similar at various levels of granularity: class, layer, system, etc. Henderson-Sellers and Edwards (1994) criticize this approach on the grounds that fractals are infinitely recursive and deterministic because, they claim, development is not. However, I find the analogy useful and would expect to see use made of it in future methods. The issue of determinism is always contentious; *viz.* arguments about hidden variables in quantum physics and open and closed system arguments in cybernetics. The Catalysis micro-process for specification and component design is highly fractal.

There are several variants on the spiral model in the literature such as the 'conch' model, which is really only a different, and more detailed, diagrammatic representation of the spiral and, in fact, Boehm's original representation had such a shape. My own experience with this kind of model soon showed that, while the metaphor was of some use, it did not give real guidance on what to do. Something better would have to be developed. The remainder of this chapter describes the result of my efforts to arrive at a truly object-oriented process life-cycle model. This approach has by now been used for a large number of commercial projects and adopted in various customized forms by several large organizations.

There are even models based on the idea that a project is like a pinball table, with deliverable bouncing among activities that redirect and re-energize them. This isn't so crazy as it sounds, but I dread the appearance of software engineering rock operas based on the idea.

9.4 Workshops, time-boxes and evolutionary development

Rapid Application Development or RAD, as a development approach, began to be popular in the late 1980s but its origins remain obscure. The Joint Application Development (JAD) workshop technique used at IBM was certainly an influential component. Rapid prototyping had been used for years and also penetrated the RAD approach. James Martin is sometimes accused of first coining the phrase but the earliest formal declaration seems to be the Ripp (Rapid Iterative Production Prototyping) method developed at El du Pont de Nemours and sold later under the catchy slogan: 'Your system in 128 days – or your money back'. Ripp was followed by many proprietary imitations and soon every consultancy had its own version and name. What they all had in common is the use of workshops and time-boxes. A 'time-box' sets a rigid limit to prototype iterations to ensure management control over prototyping. A small team is mandatory and the tested prototype is both end-point and deliverable. RAD methods vary in the extent to which users participate in the prototyping process and the kind of tools used. Some, as with Ripp, insist on the use of 4GLs and repositories. Others emphasize CASE tools and code generation. I want to emphasize building a bridge between the understanding of users and developers and integrating their effort.

RAD is highly beneficial, whether object-oriented tools are in use or otherwise, and there is a growing amount of empirical evidence for this. Scott Gordon and Bieman (1993) report that ease of use and correct requirements capture are unarguably improved, based on a study of 34 projects. There is some evidence that maintainability is improved but only when throwaway prototypes are not allowed to evolve into the final product. These authors found no support for 'the common notion that rapid prototyping cannot be used for developing large systems' and recommend that an object-oriented approach is used within a disciplined framework such as that used in Hekmatpour (1987) and the one present in this chapter. When workshops are used, costs are often lower than those implied by multiple interviews with users and much time is usually saved. They give structure to the requirements capture and analysis activity but are dynamic, interactive and co-operative. They involve users and often cut across organizational boundaries. Workshops help to identify and prioritize needs and resolve contentious issues. User ownership of the end-product is promoted from the beginning and the analysis process gets a healthy kick-start. Decisions and compromises are agreed and recorded during workshops and the first workshop is the first opportunity to begin managing both users' expectations and their attitudes to change.

The time-box technique offers the following benefits. It imposes management control over ripple effects and uncontrolled iteration. Control is achieved by setting a rigid elapsed time limit on the prototyping cycle and using a small project team. Furthermore, it has a usable system as both the end-point of the process and its deliverable. There is no distinction between production, evolution and maintenance as with conventional approaches, which usually ignore maintenance costs during project justification.

Time-boxes tackle the following management issues:

- Wants *versus* needs – by forcing requirements to be prioritized by negotiation between users and developers. Users and the project team are forced to concentrate on the real needs of the business.
- Creeping functionality – in the traditional life cycle the long delay between specification and delivery can lead to users requesting extra features. The use of a time limit reduces this tendency.
- Project team motivation – the developers can see a tangible result of their efforts emerging.
- The involvement of users at every stage reduces implementation shock.

The approach reduces time-to-market, not by a magic trick that makes hard things easy but by delivering an important usable subset of the entire system in no more than a few months.

It is absolutely critical to maintain credibility; build on success and manage expectations during the process. This is achieved by several means. Users should be warned that a quickly developed prototype may conceal much complexity. A working system will take time in proportion to the complexity of the tasks it assists with. Equally, users should be stimulated by many small, incremental deliveries. With my approach, they agree prioritized objectives and developers should show that corners that are cut to keep within time limits are low priority corners. Developers can thus afford to accept reasonable changes to requirements, provided that existing, low priority requirements can be eliminated by mutual agreement based on the priorities. This expectation management is a key task for the project manager. If it is neglected the project will usually fail.

This technique prevents paralysis by analysis, errors due to delay, spurious requirements and implementation shock. It usually motivates teams better than the waterfall approach.

One possible criticism of evolutionary and iterative rapid development is that its benefits may derive largely from the Hawthorne effect observed on many O&M studies, whereby merely paying more attention to users and developers makes them more productive regardless of the techniques used. It can also be argued that highly trained and motivated users and developers are the cause of the success, since many RAD-aware companies are also innovators with skilled staffs. I cannot disprove either of these assertions but remain confident of the utility of RAD nevertheless.

The process offers a synthesis of JAD, RAD and OT. In one company I worked for, both RAD and object-oriented programming had been introduced simultaneously but separately, with considerable and beneficial effects on productivity in each case. Workshops gave many of the benefits mentioned above but, unfortunately, they were run using structured techniques and typically produced normalized entity models and huge functional decompositions. The developers were prone to saying 'nice pictures', filing them somewhere and then going off to find a user who could help them prototype something. The contract-driven life-cycle model was created, in part, to help this company reconcile RAD with OOP.

9.4.1 Principles of dynamic system development

The Dynamic Systems Development Method (DSDM) is a 'framework of controls for rapid application development' (Stapleton, 1997). Unlike OPEN, RUP or SOMA, there are no prescribed techniques. DSDM has a rudimentary and high level process model that can be tailored for individual organizations' requirements. It was developed as a potentially standard approach by a consortium of 17 UK user organizations in 1994 that now has over 1,000 members world-wide. It eschews affiliation to any particular style of development and Version 2 removed any reference to object technology for this reason. This was perhaps fortunate because the few remarks that the Version 1 manual made about object-orientation (OO) were largely wrong. On the other hand the view taken by the DSDM Consortium – that OO is a mere technique – is arguable from my point of view, which characterizes OO as a general method of knowledge representation. DSDM has nine fundamental principles, all of which the process described below adheres to totally. They are:

1. Active user involvement is imperative.
2. Teams are empowered to make decisions.
3. The focus is on the frequent delivery of products.
4. Fitness for business purpose is the essential criterion for acceptance of deliverables.
5. Iterative development and incremental delivery are necessary to converge on an accurate business solution.

6. All changes during development are reversible.
7. Requirements are defined at a high level.
8. Testing is integrated throughout the life cycle.
9. A collaborative and co-operative approach between all stakeholders is essential.

These principles enable an organization to determine whether a particular project is suitable for the approach. For example, if you know perfectly well that under no circumstances will a representative sample of users be available, then forget it. Of course, under many circumstances it may be permissible to make do with representatives of users, rather than the users themselves. Although this is not ideal, it is usually better than returning to the old, rigid, ineffective way of doing things.

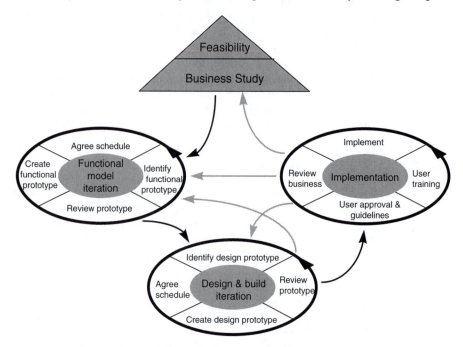

Figure 9.6 The DSDM development process model (after Stapleton, 1997).

Figure 9.6 illustrates the DSDM development process model. The approach starts with feasibility and business studies, which are followed by three iterative and overlapping phases: essentially based on the spiral model.

DSDM is not entirely suitable for object-oriented development because it cannot perforce assume the kind of flexibility that an object-oriented approach gives. Nor does it support any notion of contract-driven or responsibility-driven design or development. It is necessary to modify the life cycle to take full advantage of object technology. DSDM has no model of reuse management. Nor does it have a formal notion of a 'programme' decomposing into smaller 'projects' as do, for example, both OPEN and SOMA. Furthermore, DSDM fails to distinguish adequately between process and product life cycles. These issues are discussed in Section 9.6, where we will see that DSDM phases can be reconciled with the object-oriented contract-driven life-cycle model discussed later.

What DSDM does give is a framework that can be informed with the concrete political and organizational characteristics of a project. The commitment to time-boxing (principle 3) means that milestones are equated with deliverables, making the approach very product oriented. Testing is performed throughout the life cycle, rather than as an end-stage activity, and this leads to far higher quality and far fewer implementation surprises. Very importantly, the products and documentation mandated by DSDM are as minimal as possible, while still ensuring adequate quality and progress towards delivery and maintenance. Unfortunately, if an object-oriented approach is not adopted there can be no guarantee that the resultant system will be easy to maintain in the face of further evolution of the requirements – as was explained in Chapter 1.

We have already noted that DSDM is product oriented. However, I think we should be stricter in enforcing the frequent delivery of operational components than DSDM. The latter has to compromise slightly because the products of conventional development are typically coarser grained than those of object-oriented development. Thus, in DSDM a data model might be the end-product of a time-box. In an object-oriented RAD method we can argue that all the object models produced are, at least potentially, executable – as we shall see later. In either method, this product focus is far more flexible than a task-oriented approach whereby low level tasks are assigned to individual team members. With the latter regimen it is much harder for a team to modify tasks to meet a deadline and it is here that principle 2 (empowerment) finds its apotheosis.

Principle 9 not only implies that team members should include both users and development staff, it mandates certain organizational principles too. As Stapleton (1997) points out:

> Some organizations put up artificial barriers between different parts of the IT department. *It is useless* for the application development staff to put a system together quickly, if the operational staff do not view its take-on as important and delay it because of their own conflicting set of priorities. (*emphasis added*)

Thus, an organization that maintains traditional mainframe-oriented user acceptance testing (UAT) and roll-out practices or one that has maintenance and engineering teams that report to a different line management from that of the developers will find RAD far more difficult to implement and far less beneficial.

DSDM, like OOSE (Jacobson *et al.*, 1992), restricts attention to the system interface. This is perfectly valid for simple MIS systems or for the specification of machinery such as vending machines or telecommunications switches, but it is far from adequate for more complex systems as we saw in Chapter 8. SOMA's requirements engineering techniques allow the analysis to 'penetrate' the user interface in order to build a shared understanding of how the system will actually work. Recognizing this limitation perhaps, DSDM is not advanced as suitable for applications with any computational complexity. That this need not apply, at least, to an object-oriented RAD method is evinced by my experience in the financial services industry where there are often complex calculations behind option pricing or the generation of yield curves or volatility surfaces and where SOMA has proved successful.

DSDM recommends an approach to prototyping that parallels our approach to knowledge discovery in general. We proceed with a broad and shallow analysis (prototype) covering all the key features of the target system in outline. This is followed by an in-depth analysis (prototype) of one area of the problem. Here there are three possibilities:

1. tackle the easiest area first to boost developers' confidence;
2. tackle the area that solves 80% of the business need first; or
3. tackle the area with the greatest technical challenge first.

The first approach is seldom the right one, because there can be some nasty shocks awaiting the team downstream and because it is not a good way to impress users with the team's skills. A combination of the other two approaches is ideal. With an object-oriented approach to the analysis, far more emphasis must be placed on the search for potentially reusable components as each successive functional area is attacked. The focus too is on the essential requirements early on, rather than those features that the users (or developers) would like the system to have ideally.

One useful contribution from DSDM (suggested first by Dai Clegg of Oracle, I understand) parallels the prioritization of objectives in SOMA workshops. DSDM classifies requirements into: Must have, Should have, Could have and Want to have (but not in this release). This categorization is referred to by the contraction: MoSCoW.

DSDM recommends the use of specialist human – computer interaction consultants. I disagree fundamentally with the separation of the user interface design from the design of the system as a whole. It is not possible to design a good interface to a system with an inappropriate architecture. My solution is to ensure that sufficient developers are skilled in user interface design.

Finally DSDM introduces a fourfold categorization of prototypes as follows:

- business prototypes (or demonstrators);
- capability/design prototypes;
- performance and capacity prototypes;
- usability prototypes.

This reflects the separation of functional and design iterations in the DSDM life cycle (Figure 9.7) and is incompatible with a more seamless object-oriented approach such as the one described in this book. We instead distinguish only research, throwaway and evolutionary prototypes. This also reflects my view that it is quite wrong to separate functional and non-functional requirements.

⊟ 9.5 Process and product life-cycle models

Most writing on software engineering process, as we have discussed it, has focused on how to find the best one. The assumption is that there is only one. The MOSES work included the discovery that there are actually two life cycles. This observation arose from work on software measurement, where it was always clear that there were two kinds of metric; product metrics measured what was produced and process metrics measured how production was accomplished. Analogously, we can see that there are two life cycles in software development. The product life cycle describes the way products are delivered to their purchasers. I have already argued that the waterfall model was a model of this contractual process. The simplest such model of product development says that we first make a business case for some development – i.e. get a budget – then build the thing and install it into use. The process of production, however, need not follow a waterfall at all, and could be a complex network of parallel activities. This dichotomy is illustrated in Figure 9.7. We are familiar with such complex, concurrent process in Manufacture and software need not be different.

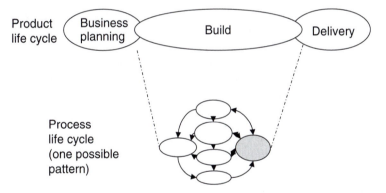

Figure 9.7 The relationship between the product and process life cycles.

This new perspective throws some light on arguments about software development processes. It enables us to reconcile waterfall and iterative approaches rather than having to choose between them. It also explains why replacing waterfalls with spirals looks defective: spirals appear to be wrapped-up waterfalls. The solution is to see that the process life cycle is separate and that it must be concurrent – except in the simplest of cases. It describes the activities we engage in to make the product and how they are related to one another. It is about manufacture rather than delivery; it is about work rather than payment for work.

This view also allows us to envisage the conception of software maintenance in a quite new way. Traditionally, software maintenance is seen as a percentage of the build cost: a tax on the use of software. It is seldom budgeted for explicitly.

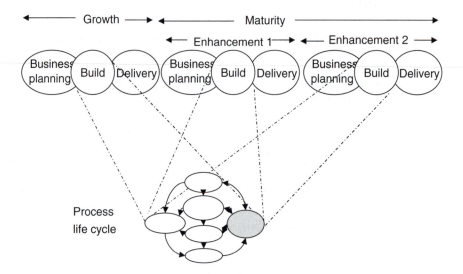

Figure 9.8 Growth and maturity epochs of the product life cycle and the embedding of the process life cycle within each build stage.

Figure 9.8 illustrates the idea that we could abolish the whole idea of maintenance if every new enhancement were to be seen as a new project. The initial product life cycle is labelled as the growth epoch of the software and subsequent enhancements are seem as replacement products in the maturity epoch, each subject to their own product life cycle – but each using the same process and needing independent budget justification. This is extremely resonant with the ideas of extreme programming and refactoring, albeit on a coarser scale.

9.5.1 OO life-cycle models

There are several published processes claiming to support object-oriented development. Coad *et al*. (1999) describe an evolutionary process that they call feature-driven development (FDD). FDD emphasizes the frequent delivery of tangible, working results. It has many similarities to OPEN, with which consortium Coad was for a while involved. A feature is a small block of functionality of some value to clients. A feature must be produced every two weeks or less. Planning and process templates are part of the method. FDD is an advance over classic life cycles but does not depart radically from the spiral model. It largely ignores the fact that early deliverables may be in the form of something that is not code, such as a requirements statement.

Beck (2000) describes the principle of eXtreme Programming (XP): a method that goes even further than FDD in its emphasis on the frequent delivery of tangible, working results. XP is test-driven and defines simplicity as 'just enough code to make all the tests work'. Unit tests are written by developers and functional tests by users. It also uses the output from its short cycles to refactor code. Examples of refactoring include creating a superclass to abstract common features, creating new plug-points, splitting classes or methods into two, and renaming components to be more descriptive. Doing this frequently relies on the presence of automated testing tools, of course.

One of the most important and useful techniques advocated (though not invented) by XP is pair programming. The idea is that no one person ever writes code alone. One person sits and codes while another watches, thinks and comments. The two then swap around. Furthermore, the pairs are not permanent and anyone may (and will) alter someone else's code. This sounds as though it should halve productivity but, curiously, all the studies that have been done indicate that productivity doubles – or better. Beck called the approach extreme because it attempts to take commonplace good ideas and apply them aggressively. For example, as he puts it:

- If code reviews are good, review code all the time (pair programming).
- If short iterations are good, make them *really* short (hours not months).
- If testing is good, then everyone tests all the time.
- If simplicity is good, then build the simplest thing that could work.

It is an implicit principle of XP that one should listen to the business all the time (refactoring). However, some particularly extreme advocates of XP take this to mean that there is no need to establish the requirements before coding: 'all that matters is the code!' These people take the view that if you get it wrong you can change the code easily, so why bother. I think this is wrong for two reasons. First, misunderstood requirements may not bite until the development team has moved on to other projects. Secondly, I don't believe Beck when he tells me that programmers with 'ordinary skills' can make it work. Take the example of a very widely reported success story for XP – at Chrysler. In this case there were very considerably talented people on the team (including Beck himself). Furthermore, the project followed on from an earlier, failed project and many of the team from that project were used. It is inconceivable to me that these very experienced people did not have a good grasp of what the requirements were before the project started. I think that XP is an excellent way of building systems and that all its techniques are useful. However, I think it must be accompanied (not necessarily preceded) by sound requirements engineering techniques. Also, it is not suitable for companies trying to migrate and re-skill staff with a non-OO background; they already have enough to learn if we are to avoid the mistakes of the early adopters of C++, for example.

If one of the most fundamental principles of object technology is encapsulation then can we not deduce that undisciplined hacking can after all be permitted within our organized approach? The argument is that since an object is defined by its specification and contract alone the implementation can change without impact on other systems components. Therefore, we do not care exactly how an object gets implemented as long as it meets the specification and goes fast. This is where the talented hacker comes in. S/he can write really clever, efficient code; and who cares if it looks like spaghetti, contains no comments and is unmaintainable. We won't maintain it; we'll subclass from it if we need refinements. If not, we'll throw it away and hire another hacker to re-implement. Thus, the rôle of the undisciplined genius – the hacker – is restored to its rightful place in software engineering.

There are some organizations where this argument could actually be applied and I would not dismiss the argument completely. However, the major flaw is that it is not always possible to create variants by subclassing alone. More usually an abstract superclass must be created by generalizing the code. This involves examining the code and understanding it. For any large organization this means that some standards must be applied because developers will have to understand, at some point, someone else's code. XP seems to combine the best of both worlds in this respect.

This point aside, there is another way in which our method supports what would usually be regarded as hacking as a structured activity. Within development it is supposed that analysis, design and coding all go on, but no order is imposed. This means that it is perfectly permissible to do the design *after* writing the code. This assumes that the requirements capture activities are complete but not that the requirements are complete. In that sense, analysis too can follow coding as we go through successive prototype iterations. The testing and evaluation of the time-box products ensure that this practice is valid. As long as the tests are passed, we need not care how the products were arrived at. The time-box itself controls any tendency to creeping functionality. Thus, we have imposed perfect management controls on a totally unstructured creative process. Our 'hackers' can work in the way they find most productive while not endangering the quality or maintainability of the product.

HP's *Team Fusion* method includes a proprietary, but lightweight and tailorable, process that emphasizes early architectural design. It is risk-driven and also stresses frequent delivery. Like XP the idea is to do 'just enough'. It was one of the first methods to include the idea of a process pattern. Otherwise it is based on a rather ordinary spiral model. CA's *Process Engineer* tool is built around a tailorable process that has much in common with both *Team Fusion* and the process described in Section 9.6, although it does not handle parallel tasks well. It includes many Catalysis techniques and has a strong component focus. The *Perspective* process (Allen and Frost, 1998) also offers management guidance on component-based development but is light on actual design techniques.

9.5.1 Objectory and the Rational Unified Process

Objectory had a life-cycle model based on use cases as long ago as 1988. When Jacobson joined Rational Inc. in 1995, that company began to sell it and, following the adoption of UML by the OMG, it was renamed as the Rational Unified Process (RUP). Whether because of its apparent association with UML or perhaps because of aggressive marketing, it has become the most widely quoted example of an OO development process. Kruchten (1999) describes RUP in outline and Jacobson *et al.*

(1999) describe part of it – which they designate the Unified Software Development Process (USDP) – in detail. Royce (1998) gives a project management perspective on some aspects of RUP. Although there are many contradictions between what is said in these three books, we will view the ideas contained therein as a unified set and refer to them all as RUP in this necessarily terse review.

Table 9.2 RUP terminology.

RUP	*Normal term*	*Definition* [emphasis added throughout]
Activity	Task	A unit of work for a person in a rôle that creates a deliverable artefact.
Activity step	Subtask	Part of an activity (task).
Artefact	Deliverable	Things produced by people carrying out tasks. RUP defines deliverables as artefacts of use to a customer.
Iteration	Iteration	A planned *sequence* of activities resulting in a tested release (or milestone).
Phase	Phase/Stage	A period of time between major milestones.
Worker	Rôle	The responsibilities of a development agent described as a set of activities.
Workflow	Activity	A *sequence* of activities that produces a result of measurable value *to an actor.* Identified (in USDP) with a UML activity diagram.

RUP defines activities, artefacts (deliverables), workers (project rôles), 'phases' and 'workflows' for projects. The terminology is strange: for example, most project managers would call RUP workflows *activities*. In fact there is an ISO standard to this effect. The definitions are given in Table 9.2.

Notice that everything (though iterative) is sequential; there is no provision for parallelism and synchronization in the model. The relationship between phases and workflows is described Figure 9.9, which also indicates a product life-cycle waterfall with four stages: inception, elaboration, construction and transition. These are each achieved by sequential iterations, so that the process model is basically a conventional spiral.

The basic sequence of an RUP project goes something like this.

- Get the team together.
- Decide what system will be built (there is apparently no other option than to build a system).
- Build a use case model and UI prototype.
- Use the UML process extensions to build an analysis object model.
- Segue into the more conventional UML stuff to do the design – class, state, sequence diagrams and the like.
- Think hard about architecture while you assign the designed classes to modules and packages.
- Test against the use case model. RUP provides some excellent guidance on testing.

■ Transition to live system and do the post mortem.

RUP permits a limited amount of organization-specific tailoring. An RUP development case is the result of changing the workers, activities and so on that are included in the process. However, changing the sequencing is more problematical and describing concurrent processes would require a major extension.

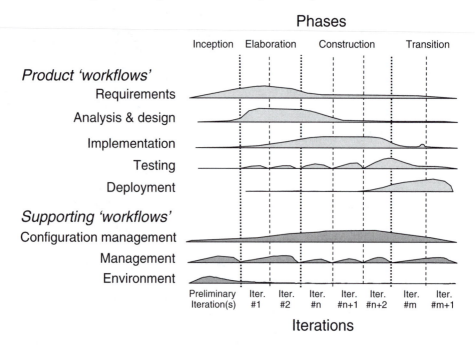

Figure 9.9 Workflows and phases in RUP.

RUP also includes guidance on the use of techniques and tutorials on the use of Rational's tools that support these techniques. In the USDP version considerable emphasis is placed on the use of the UML process extensions in the analysis workflow. Here, instead of drawing UML class diagrams, a preliminary model using the symbols for interface, entity and controller objects is used. I have already alluded to the dangers inherent in this approach in several places.

RUP has several positive features compared to older approaches. It uses UML throughout and includes several specifically OO techniques. Most important among these is its use of use cases to drive specification and testing. It is thoroughly iterative and incremental and, for an existing user of Rational's tools, it is well integrated with them.

RUP is said to be architecture driven. This too is a positive feature, though it must be said that it takes the restricted view of architecture as mere structure that we criticized in Chapter 7. RUP is also use case driven. Again this good providing that one is only concerned with system specification; RUP has nothing to say about business requirements or business process modelling – except that use cases are enough. We saw in Chapter 8 how wrong this view is.

One advantage of RUP is also a disadvantage: being tied to the tools of one supplier makes many organizations feel uneasy and makes it harder to take advantage of tool innovations as they arise. I have already said that RUP must be extended to deal with requirements engineering. However, we have shown clearly how to do this with the micro-process of Chapter 8. There is also nothing in RUP about GUI design. Once again it is easy to extend, as I show later. It has nothing profound to say about CBD but the Catalysis techniques and micro-process explained in Chapters 6 and 7 can readily be added on. Metrics are not specified in RUP, though they are expected to be collected. Here too extension is possible as we show in Section 9.7. Perhaps the worst feature of RUP, as a modern process, is its sheer size: well over 1,700 pages. I don't call that lightweight. We show from here how it is possible to extend and generalize RUP with a genuinely lightweight and flexible process.

9.5.2 The OPEN Process Framework

Starting from around 1995, the OPEN Consortium grew into an informal group of about 30 methodologists, with no common commercial affiliation, that wanted to see greater method integration but felt strongly that methods should include a process, should be in the public domain, should not be tied to particular tools and should focus strongly on scientific integrity as well as pragmatic issues. The founding members of OPEN were Brian Henderson-Sellers and myself who began to integrate the MOSES and SOMA process models. The result, the OPEN process, was published by Graham *et al.* (1997b). We were soon joined by Don Firesmith who started work on an integrated notation (OML) with the aim of a more pure object-oriented character than the OMT-influenced UML and one that would be easier to learn and remember (Firesmith *et al.*, 1997). This notation, though it started from some simple ideas, became very complex and (perhaps partly because of this) was largely ignored following the adoption of UML by the OMG.

The OPEN process consisted of an adaptable framework based on an object model of the product and process life cycles, with the product life cycle being a waterfall and the process life cycle a network – as described above. In the next section we will look at an instantiation of this framework. The consortium went on to publish a further book describing the ways in which various software engineering techniques related to the activities and tasks of the process (Henderson-Sellers *et al.*, 1998). In my opinion there can be no definitive relationship between all the techniques in our armoury, but the work stands as an interesting example of how a particular organization might set about constructing such a matrix – which would be a valid exercise. The principal innovation of this work was the development of a matrix showing how techniques related to process tasks and activities. For example, the Gantt chart technique could be recommended for the project planning activity.

Furthermore, techniques could be given a deontic match, such as Recommended or Mandatory, to the tasks they were associated with. This too will be explained the next section. OPEN was designed to be fully customizable, as we shall also see.

⊟ 9.6 A contract-driven process model

The remarkable thing about most of the seminal object-oriented analysis and design methods is that their life-cycle models remained thoroughly procedural. Some were nothing more than 'structured' methods with objects added to the entity model. OMT had a rudimentary micro-process for analysis and design. MOSES was the first method to publish a full life cycle, although Objectory had a proprietary one. MOSES retained a slightly procedural flavour because it still had phases, although these could be may be executed in any order. Other methods had no life-cycle model at all and the remainder had very weak ones; e.g. Booch (1994). Successful object-oriented rapid development requires the total abolition of the notion of development 'phases'.

The contract-driven life-cycle model of OPEN (Graham *et al.*, 1997b) defined projects as networks of activities that have dependencies but no explicit sequence. It distinguishes two life cycles: a waterfall-like product life cycle and a network-like process life cycle. In OPEN, an activity produces a result which must be a *tested* result. In particular, we test objectives by measuring them and requirements object models by walkthroughs, as in Chapter 8. Use case scripts are captured very early on and are used as test scripts. This helps address the debugging problem in a tool-independent fashion and places the emphasis on quality first. This tested time-box (or 'right on time') philosophy means that it is quite permissible and safe to write the code before the design is done – or *vice versa* if that's how you like to work – very much in the spirit of XP. Both business objects and task scripts are accumulated in a repository for reuse in subsequent workshops and projects. It is not so much that OO enhances RAD with additional benefits or *vice versa*; it is more that modern IT requires the benefits of both techniques applied in such a way as to be consistent with one another. A major benefit of the combined approach is that it makes it possible to move to specification level, rather than code level, reuse.

This section describes my approach to systems development for software projects. It presents the development of any computer-based system as a set of activities with a subsection devoted to each one. The tasks outlined in it are viewed as current best practice for systems development and project management. The process has been used successfully at organizations such as Swiss Bank Corporation, Chase Manhattan Bank and several of TriReme's clients, always with some tailoring. This chapter only covers the process model. The associated object-oriented analysis and design techniques have been largely covered already.

One difference in emphasis between conventional and object-oriented development is that object-oriented development blurs the distinction between analysis and logical design but splits logical and physical design. In our approach there is only one major, deliverable document that passes through three phases: Workshop Report, Analysis Report and Design Report. In each activity chapters are added and some existing chapters modified. User Acceptance Testing (UAT) is much more distributed throughout the project activities rather than concentrated at the end. The User Review activity is of particular importance in this respect. This, however, does not remove the need for a sound UAT environment. Change management is subject to the same disciplines as usual. We offer specific guidance on user interface design.

DEFINITIONS A **project** is defined as any work that is expected to take more than five staff days. The optimum size of a project is between one and twelve man-months' effort, with two to four people in the project team, and a duration of up to six months (but see next paragraph but one). Work that takes less than five days is called a Request For Service (RFS), and is prioritized by management. A Change Request (CR) will usually be raised for work of up to one man-week, or some other specified period.

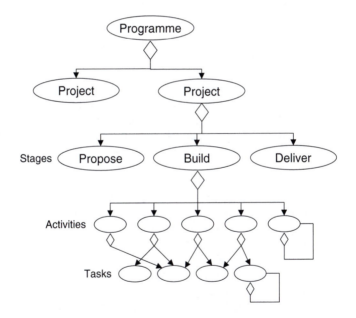

Figure 9.10 Programmes, projects, stages, activities and tasks.

A **programme** is a collection of projects designed to satisfy a major corporate objective. Programmes must be decomposed into projects before the approach described in this document can be applied. Such decomposition may itself constitute a project. This recursive composition structure is shown in Figure 9.10.

In order to maximize efficiency, provide predictable testing workloads and deliveries to users and focus development teams on achieving delivery dates, development projects are 'time-boxed'. A time-boxed project will ideally take from 30 to 180 days elapsed and will occupy two to six staff members. Where a project cannot be limited to this amount of effort because its requirements are too complex, the work will be split into sections that will conform to the above standard. Where the scope of a project is limited, so that the required effort is too little, then a number of requirements will be bundled together to create an effective project. Note that, in this case, all requirements should be related and assigned a priority by the user(s) and other stakeholders. Production failures take precedence over both project work and work done on service requests.

The procedures outlined in this book are only relevant for projects that are expected to take between four and 36 man-months of effort; smaller projects should use an abbreviated form of the life cycle. This is described in Section 9.6.16.

THE CONTRACT-DRIVEN MODEL

In this approach, there is not a linear arrangement of 'workflows' or 'phases' but there are activities, both bounded and unbounded. Bounded activities are time-boxes, limited by predetermined periods of elapsed time. Some unbounded activities are continuous but must still pay attention to cost control by setting and meeting objectives. Others are embedded within bounded activities and the project manager is required to balance their time and resource consumption within the overall bounded activity. Some, small, bounded activities correspond to the iterations of RUP.

The product life-cycle model was inspired by that of MOSES. There are three stages: Propose, Build and Implement. The most complex of these is Build. The process life cycle overlaps all three, but is mainly concerned with the Build.

Activities produce deliverables. We regard activities as objects whose interfaces consist of tasks. Developers and users adopting rôles are responsible for carrying out tasks and producing deliverables. They do these using **techniques** such as 'draw sequence diagrams', 'code in Java' or 'use case modelling'. Techniques are not covered in this chapter but are assumed known. Each dependency between activities is a guarded message so that all message sends are 'guarded' by the defined tests. Each guard is a ruleset or assertion: often a pre- or post-condition. Each rule is implemented by a test. Mandated deliverables are set out as post-conditions on the activities as a whole, as detailed in subsequent subsections. Activities are the building blocks of projects and correspond to the workflows and phases of RUP, but we can go further than just drawing activity diagrams to represent them. Specifying the guards amounts to constructing a network of the relationships between activities that can be highly parallel. Review and testing are carried out within every activity.

The principles that are applied are:

1. Quality first: everything is tested as it is created, removing some of the need for post-implementation reviews, so that these may be deferred with the agreement of IT and the client.
2. Continuous improvement: based on reuse of software and specifications and on measurement of the products and processes.

3. Minimum time-to-market: through the use of the time-boxed RAD approach.
4. Flexibility and robustness: through a total commitment to object and component technology throughout the life cycle.

HIGH LEVEL STRUCTURE OF A PROJECT

The high level object model of a project in the contract-driven model is illustrated in Figure 9.11 in which the core intra-project activities are represented in white and extra-project activities in grey. Note that this life-cycle model is a *bona fide* object model, where the objects are activities whose 'methods' are tasks.

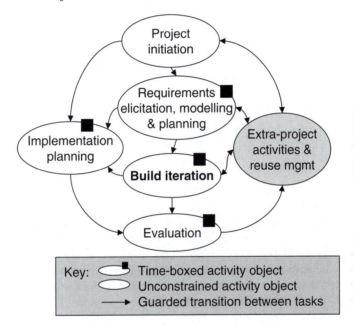

Figure 9.11 The contract-driven life cycle.

Each ellipse in the diagram represents an activity object; they are actions or use cases. Boxes on these actions' outlines mean that they are bounded by elapsed time. Every activity has completion criteria so that its output is tested. Each activity has prerequisites that must be met before any or some of its tasks may commence and/or finish. Activities can also be viewed as objects that send guarded (i.e. tested) messages to each other in the form of deliverables. The guards are assertions or, equivalently, pre- and post-conditions on the activities or tasks. An activity is comprised of **tasks** that correspond to the operations of the activity objects. Some assertions are pre- and post-conditions on individual tasks. Tasks use techniques to produce work products.

Project initiation, or inception, involves getting approval for the project, using whatever means are necessary: be it cost–benefit analysis or plying the MD with gin! The post-condition is a signed project initiation form specifying a budget. Once this unbounded activity is complete we can start the requirements, elaboration and project planning workflows and the implementation planning activities in parallel, as well as trigger various activities outside the project itself. Once we have elaborated the requirements, usually as a business object model, we can start the iterative build activity. Implementation planning may continue in parallel. It involves all those boring little things that have to get done to complete the project successfully: make sure the developers have desks; order the kit; etc. Finally we evaluate the results and decide whether to deliver the product into use or not.

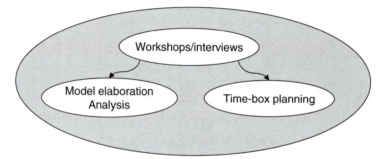

Figure 9.12 Pre-build activities.

AFORE YE GO ... Looking inside the requirements use case, as shown in Figure 9.12, we see that it begins with a knowledge elicitation activity: requirements workshops or interviews. Of course we will assume the workshops are used. The end of a workshop triggers tasks in the model elaboration, analysis activity. Notice how this clarifies the relationship between the RUP ideas of the elaboration phase and analysis workflow. Other workshops may continue in parallel. We also see that project planning tasks to decide the iterations are triggered.

BUILD ITERATIONS The build involves short-cycle iterations as indicated by the message loop in Figure 9.13. Notice that no ordering of analysis, design, coding, testing or documentation is implied. In a contract-driven project all that matters is that the goals of the activity are achieved: there must be good design documentation; the code must be tested; etc. Some people like to code before they design. Others base the design on pre-written documentation. It does not matter what order you do things in. I think people should be allowed to work the way they work best, rather than be forced to follow some conventional wisdom. Users review the results frequently and this may lead to modified requirements. Negotiation on such changes is controlled by the prioritized objectives established during requirements engineering. When time runs out or the product is deemed satisfactory, the team must consolidate the product with the results of earlier or parallel time-boxes and check that standards have been adhered to, documentation produced, code tested and so on. They may also flag interest in potentially reusable components and pass this to the domain library team. They are not mandated to make their code reusable. XP fits well into this scenario.

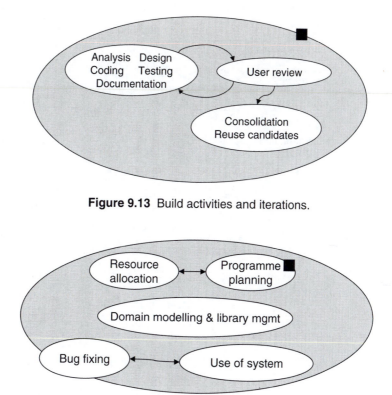

Figure 9.13 Build activities and iterations.

Figure 9.14 Extra-project (programme) activities.

PROGRAMME ACTIVITIES
The project interacts with activities outside the project itself. We have already seen the developers passing potential reuse candidates to the library team. Undoubtedly they will have reused corporate assets maintained by this team as well. Clearly, programme and project managers must interact with each other and company-wide resources allocation is interdependent with project resources. When the system goes into use some of the team will be allocated to hand-holding and bug fixing, working alongside the early users and sorting out teething troubles. Others take a sabbatical with the reuse team, making their potentially reusable component really so. This is discussed further in Section 9.7.

THE FULL LIFE CYCLE
All possible message interactions between all the activities are shown in Figure 9.15. The diagram looks complicated at first sight but if its activities are set up as HTML hot spots then it actually provides a very user-friendly interface to a process document. It is also included here for completeness.

This process model is one where evolutionary prototyping and rapid development are the rule rather than the exception. Throwaway prototypes may also be produced during the Project Initiation, Requirements or Analysis activities.

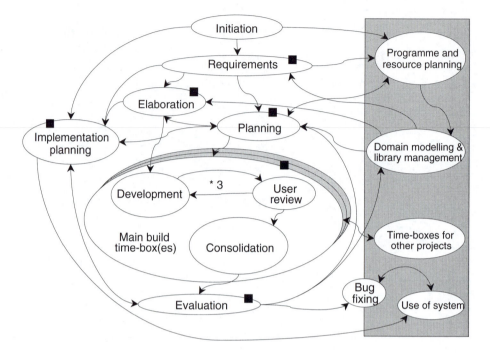

Figure 9.15 The full contract-driven process object model.

The IT organization is subject to its overall strategy. Management controls financial allocations to projects at a high level and its decisions enter the project planning activity box and initiate workshops aimed at establishing the scope of the application and the goals of the users of each of its features. These are followed by intensive requirements workshops which deliver business process models, task scripts and an outline business object model and then by a more thorough and critical elaboration which refines that model and produces a complete Analysis Report (AR). Output from the requirements workshops and subsequent analysis goes into the development planning and domain modelling activities for two reasons. First the planners must be made aware of the resource requirements that the preliminary scoping implies. Second, the trustees of the domain model need to examine the Business Object Model to see if there are any existing class descriptions in their repository that match. Conversely the developers are drawing upon project resources from the departmental planners and harvesting reusable specifications and code from the domain team.

Every activity's completion is a milestone and results in output and deliverables. Output is that which is inevitable but not delivered to anybody beyond the producers. Deliverables are seen by others and are classified as optional, recommended and mandatory, indicting the level of duty attached to them. **MANDATORY** deliverables must be delivered in all circumstances. **RECOMMENDED** deliverables may be omitted provided that their omission can be justified. **OPTIONAL** deliverables may be omitted at the discretion of the project manager. Completion criteria always include tests of the products of the activity. Tasks and activities are thus marked as M, R or O. This structure may be applied recursively to substages, subtasks and subactivities. We have not made use of the two other deontic[1] levels available within the OPEN specification: **DISCOURAGED** and **FORBIDDEN**.

This method emphasizes that system development and business process re-engineering are the same thing. Every requirements workshop will explore the possibilities for radical process innovation and not be bound by the existing functional organization of the company or its departments. Our object modelling approach begins with the description of business processes and the tasks that underlie the conversations represented in this model. Large process models are represented using a Mission Grid.

TIME LIMITS   Elapsed-time limits are imposed on all rapid development activities apart from project initiation, project planning and domain modelling. Requirements capture and elaboration should take no more than four weeks. A one-week minimum may be expected. The time-box planning activity will normally last for between one and four weeks as well. Each time-box may last for between one and five months and a three-month period is to be considered normal. Evaluation should never take more than two weeks and a half day is the target. These limits are subject to an overall maximum of six months' elapsed time from the end of the workshops to implementation. The shortest time-box I have ever seen was eleven and a half hours.

The sign-off of the products of the workshops and especially the AR fixes both the project plan and the elapsed time limits on the project. Requirements may evolve but only within the limits agreed at this time. Failure on the part of users to attend workshops, User Reviews, or sign off requirements will result in the cancellation of the project. This may only be avoided if a delay agreement is signed.

PRESENTING THE METHOD   Each ellipse in Figure 9.15 corresponds to an activity. Each of the activities in the contract-driven model are described in a document section with the following invariable structure.

> Activity title
> Activity description and justification
> Prerequisites
> Tasks (with level of duty)
> Deliverables and post-conditions (including completion criteria and time limits)

This process description presented in this chapter refers to many techniques that are documented elsewhere. Appendices to an organization's tailored process manual should include references to its IT strategy, particular standards for relational

---

[1] Deontics is the science (or logic) of obligation or duty.

database development, the IT security and network security policies, and so on. Where the project involves a graphical user interface an appropriate style guide should be adhered to. Where coding and API standards have been developed for the language or environment in use, they should also be followed.

Section 9.7 provides a sample instantiation of the contract-driven process life cycle described here. The reader whose primary interest is not in process may wish to skip this long section or glance through it fairly quickly, at least at a first reading.

9.7 Details of a contract-driven process

This section shows just one way the process could be instantiated but leaves out some detail. In practice a real manual for the method will include various appendices providing checklists, optional activities, related documents, site-specific issues, a discussion of rôles within projects and the like. Subsections 9.7.1 to 9.7.12 cover the core system development activities. Subsections 9.7.13 to 9.7.16 describe the supporting tasks of project management, quality and security that cut across the core activities, along with exceptions that apply to such things as small projects. Throughout these subsections we refer to the generic development organization by the initials IT and to the generic stakeholders by Users. The last subsection enumerates project rôles and responsibilities.

9.7.1 Project Initiation stage and activity

This subsection presents the Project Proposal stage and the initiation activity that comprises it. This stage is mandatory. It corresponds to the RUP inception phase.

The development process starts with business planning. A request from part of the business or even external legislation can initiate the process. The product is a project proposal which should be short and to the point. It should contain a statement of the project mission and cost and other constraints.

A project will be started on receipt of an approved and signed project page from a user department. It is the responsibility of the user department to sign the project page, which must contain the following items:

- A problem definition stated in terms of business processes and its commercial impact
- The names of a sponsor, domain experts and key users
- The broad scope of the project and its critical success factors
- A justification in terms approved by the organization
- Completion criteria and main deliverables

It may also include cost–benefit, feasibility, risk and critical success factor statements. It may be accompanied by a proof-of-concept prototype. A standard Project Initiation Form should be used if desired. Submission by e-mail is usually preferred. Once the proposal has been prepared and presented to the appropriate committee(s) for its priority to be set, it will be placed in a project book and the development can proceed.

A proposal, once agreed and approved, leads to the running of a requirements workshop – with interviews as a second choice. There is no definite assumption at this stage that the solution will be computerized and the workshop is free to explore the possibilities of business process re-engineering.

PRE-REQUISITES

There are no pre-conditions for this activity.

TASKS

	IT	Users	M/R/O
Problem definition in business terms	Assist	Y	M
Identification of scope – specific inclusions/exclusions of deficiencies or processes	Assist	Y	M
Justification for further investigation	Assist	Y	M
Identify sponsor willing to take responsibility for the project, and be accountable for its success or failure	Assist	Y	M
Specification of completion criteria	Assist	Y	M
Estimate (at a high level) the size of the project in man-days and task points where possible	Y		R
Estimate the cost of the next activity of the project and the costs of the complete project, including future running costs	Y		M
Identify resources/rôles for workshop	Y	Y	R
Identify training requirements for workshop personnel and initiate training as necessary	Y		R
Review existing systems to find existing components for possible reuse, especially existing models	Y		R
Schedule workshop dates and obtain commitments from participants	Y	Y	R
Schedule participants part-time for specific sessions	Y	Y	O
Obtain approval to proceed and sign-off from sponsors and management	Y	Y	M
Initiate workshop	Y		R
Initiate preliminary development, implementation and time-box planning. Liaise with Production.	Y		R

DELIVERABLES AND POST-CONDITIONS

The major deliverable is the **Project Proposal**, a document generated jointly by users and IT. This document can be as little as a page in length in which case it is known as the **Project Initiation Page**. For larger projects, a second document called the **Project Quality Plan** will be used to record progress through the various project stages, in terms of both expected and achieved dates, and responsibilities. Management will then allocate a priority to the project.

The Project Proposal document has the following recommended form.

1. Project name.
2. Business requirement and problem definition.
3. Scope.
4. Justification, with the payback. Where cost saving is the justification, use NPV to evaluate cash flows.
5. Executive sponsor, project sponsor and dependencies (people whose activities may affect the success of the project).
6. Assumptions and exclusions.
7. External constraints.
8. Completion criteria.
9. Projected cost of proceeding, including projected future running costs (including hardware and software maintenance).
10. Training plan for workshop personnel.
11. Where applicable, the estimated size of the system in task points and/or function points.
12. For large projects, a quality plan.
13. Glossary of terms.

The Project Proposal should be complete but need not be longer than a page. It must contain evidence of approval by sponsors and steering committees. The justification should be reasonable and in the format approved by the appropriate senior management. All mandatory and recommended tasks (as listed above) must be complete; or there must be a justification for any recommended tasks not included. There should also be a project quality plan form for large projects and this should be approved by senior management. The layout is given in Appendix A2.

This is an unbounded activity with no elapsed time limits.

9.7.2 Requirements activity

Requirements elicitation can proceed using joint user–developer workshops or more traditional interviews, depending on the circumstances. I recommend workshops strongly whenever they are possible. I assume here that workshops will be used.

The SOMA workshop is a process pattern designed to improve the quality and efficiency of systems analysis within the project life cycle. A team of systems and business experts attend workshop sessions to define the business area's requirements. A model of the business process, users' tasks and a model of the business objects and their relationships are produced. This will be followed by an elaboration of the business object model using rigorous object-oriented analysis. Where appropriate, package evaluation is performed during Elaboration with a list of appropriate packages determined at the end of this activity. Extensive user involvement is required. Workshops are highly beneficial and there is a growing amount of empirical evidence for this.

While the time-box activity uses prototypes as an evolutionary technique to move the build forward through successive iterations, any prototype built during a workshop will almost certainly have to be thrown away. This implies that expectations must be managed accordingly.

SCOPING

Scoping workshops, or sessions within workshops, define the project mission or charter and define the boundaries of the problem, issues that must be resolved, objectives, priorities and user goals. It should also begin a review of business processes. Scoping will also involve splitting up large programmes into projects.

The product is a scoping document that should contain the project mission statement, objectives, measures and priorities. It should identify external objects and the main rôles in which users will interact with the system and each other, the events that trigger these interactions and the information exchanged. For each interaction its post-condition should be stated. Assumptions, exclusions and outstanding issues are documented.

We first deal with the workshop that elicits the scope of the project. It is followed by one or more workshops to elicit the detail. These are dealt with below although they may follow on from a scoping session directly. Alternatively, the scoping and detail activities can be combined.

The objectives of this activity are as follows:

- To establish a high level understanding of existing and proposed business processes, the context in which they operate, the actors involved, events that occur, messages sent and their post-conditions
- To establish the mission, boundaries and objectives of the project
- To set clear targets, priorities and acceptance criteria for a new system
- To review financial and business justification and identify other benefits
- To complete the activity in a short time-scale via the use of intensive workshop sessions

PRE-REQUISITES

Project initiation, as specified in Subsection 9.7.1, should be complete and suitably approved. All tools should be available; e.g. word processor, drawing package.

TASKS

	IT	Users	M/R/O
Arrange accommodation and facilities	Y		M
Confirm availability	Y	Y	M
Collect relevant documents	Y	Assist	M
Collect reusable object specifications from repository and other projects	Y		R
Prepare agenda	Y	Assist	R
Hold scoping session or workshop	Y	Y	R
Explain approach to participants, including responsibilities of sponsors and users	Y		O
Establish and agree mission, objectives, measures and priorities	Y	Y	M
Record assumptions and exclusions	Y	Y	M

Identify open issues and responsibility for solving them	Y	Y	M
Produce business process model	Y	Y	M
Identify all significant conversations	Y	Y	M
Establish the post-condition of each interaction	Y	Y	M
Agree implementation priorities	Y	Y	M
Sign-off agreements and models	Y	Y	M
Produce and publish Scope Document	Y		M
Review and approve Scope Document	Y	Y	M
Initiate detailed workshop	Y	Y	M

DELIVERABLES AND POST-CONDITIONS The activity is complete when the **scoping workshop report** is produced and the user sign-off has been obtained. Objectives are tested by trying to apply measures and by voting. The mission and objectives are tested against consensus. The report should contain the following:

1. Table of contents
2. Management summary (R)
3. Introduction and project overview (O)
4. Project name and mission (M)
5. List of participants and date of workshop (M)
6. Objectives, measures and priorities (M)
7. Assumptions and exclusions (M)
8. Open issues and responsibilities for closing them (R)
9. A business process model containing external and internal agents and the messages that are passed between them (M)
10. Design notes and business process definitions, including security and controls, disaster recovery, business transactions with volumes and frequencies, expected response times, major interfaces to other systems, object ownership (R)
11. User sign-off (M)

Review the scoping document to ensure it provides a clear statement of:

- the scope of the project;
- the project's objectives;
- reuse considerations, in code, data- and business-models;
- the model of the proposed business process and its actors and interactions;
- the post-conditions of each interaction.

A scoping workshop will normally last one day or less.

DETAIL WORKSHOPS Detail workshops follow scoping and refine the business process model into a Task Object Model by identifying the tasks necessary to accomplish each goal or post-condition identified in the former. These are decomposed, classified and related to exceptions. A textual analysis of the task scripts leads to the construction of a Business Object Model that comprises the business objects and their relationships with further detail as appropriate.

The objectives of this activity are:

- To produce a detailed statement of system requirements
- To produce a set of task action scripts (use cases)
- To identify opportunities for process innovation
- To produce a Business Object Model (BOM) (UML class diagram(s))
- To test the BOM against the use cases
- To make further recommendations on the resources and equipment required
- To revise development and implementation plans

The workshop will include a review of compliance, legal and security issues.

PRE-REQUISITES Scoping activity (if applicable) is complete and scoping signed off by sponsor and other participants.

TASKS

	IT	Users	M/R/O
Arrange accommodation and facilities	Y		M
Confirm availability	Y	Y	M
Collect relevant documents	Y	Assist	M
Collect reusable object specifications from repository and other projects	Y		M
Prepare agenda	Y	Assist	R
Explain approach to participants, including responsibilities of sponsors and users	Y		O
Confirm results of scoping session	Y	Y	M
Confirm project mission and objectives	Y	Y	M
Confirm assumptions and exclusions	Y	Y	M
Confirm unresolved open issues and responsibility for solving them	Y	Y	M
Confirm business process model	Y	Y	M
For each conversation, produce a task script	Y	Y	M
Use the process model as the basis for identifying and modelling potential process improvements	Y	Y	R
Decompose to atomic tasks (use cases)	Y	Y	M
Carry out textual analysis of scripts to produce class cards	Y	Y	M
Add repository classes to model produced	Y	Y	R
Add structures to model	Y	Y	M
Identify components and wrappers	Y	Y	O
Walk through all significant task scripts to produce sequence diagrams	Y	Y	M
Produce conversation/objectives matrix	Y	Y	O
Agree implementation priorities	Y	Y	M
Sign-off agreements and models	Y	Y	M
Produce and publish Requirements Definition	Y		M
Obtain approval for Requirements Definition	Y	Y	M

Produce metrics and send to Domain Modelling	Y	R
Initiate elaboration	Y	R
Initiate or inform Time-Box Planning	Y	R

Models from the workshop should be printed off, reviewed and signed off (daily if possible) by all participants.

DELIVERABLES AND POST-CONDITIONS

A **Workshop Report** with the following contents:

1. Table of contents
2. Introduction and project overview (O)
3. Management summary (R)
4. Project name and mission (M)
5. List of participants and date of workshop (M)
6. Objectives, measures and priorities (M)
7. Assumptions and exclusions (M)
8. Open issues and responsibilities for closing them (R)
9. A business process model containing external and internal actors and the messages that are passed between them (M)
   For each conversation, a task script together with a decomposition of the script into atomic component task scripts (M)
10. A Business Object Model comprising
    Completed class cards (M), UML class diagrams (R), state models (O)
11. A set of sequence diagrams documenting walkthroughs (M)
12. Planned reuse of previous workshop output, including business models, definitions and designs, including a list of objects to be reused from earlier projects (R)
13. Design notes and business process definitions, including security and controls, disaster recovery, business transactions with volumes and frequencies, expected response times, major interfaces to other systems, object ownership (R)
14. Next steps and recommendations (including process improvements) (R)
15. Glossary of business terms and other business information (R)
16. User sign-off (M)

All mandatory and recommended tasks (as listed above) must be complete; or there must be a justification for any recommended tasks not included.

The main tests applied are the walkthroughs carried out by rôle-playing which test the Business Object Model principally but also the Task Object Model. Objectives are tested by trying to apply measures and by establishing priorities using such techniques as placing a number of preference markers against objectives. These are counted to establish the implementation priorities attached to the objectives.

It must be checked that the company's security policy has been followed with respect to data ownership and classification. Each object in the Business Object

Conduct inspection	Y Y	R
Sign-off Analysis Report	Y Y	M
Pass result to Time-Box Planning and System Security	Y	M

If the analysis determines that a package solution is appropriate then the following package evaluation tasks should be carried out.

	IT	Users	M/R/O
Identify evaluation criteria	Y	Y	M
Produce Invitation to Tender (ITT)	Y	Y	M
Identify short-list of packages	Y	Y	M
Send ITT to package vendors			R
Perform detailed evaluation of short-listed packages	Y	Y	M
Review auditability			M

DELIVERABLES AND POST-CONDITIONS The main deliverable of this activity is the **Analysis Report (AR)**, which extends and refines the workshop report. Its purpose is to model and specify the proposed system in detail and work out its costs and benefits, to enable a decision to be taken as to whether to continue to the next activity. The report is originated by the project team. Its complete contents are not given here. It should, however, contain:

- an up-to-date version of everything covered in the workshop report;
- a review of the impact of systems-based risk;
- a complete UML model of the proposed system, including state models as necessary;
- a complete set of task scripts with pre- and post-conditions and as many sequence diagrams as practicable;
- a preliminary list of components to be reused and candidates for further reuse;
- a review of the impact of change on production systems;
- a development plan, including a projected end date;
- an estimate of the metrics of the system, including non-development costs.

All mandatory and recommended tasks (as listed above) must be complete; or there must be a justification for any recommended tasks not included.

The formal time limits are from one day to two weeks. There are overall limits on the workshop and Analysis activities combined of between one day and four weeks elapsed. A one-week minimum may be expected for the combined activities. Time used in this activity is to be deducted from the overall maximum of six months to implementation.

9.7.4 Time-box planning activity

The time-box plan outlines the activities and resources required to build an agreed part of the system by a fixed date. Time-box planning also involves estimating and resource and infrastructure procurement.

The plan takes account of the overall project plan and should be sent to those responsible for the overall plan.

Where parallel time-boxes are planned or there is substantial interaction with the results of parallel projects, extra time should be allowed for cross-time-box co-ordination. This is discussed in detail in Subsection 9.10.

PRE-REQUISITES The project initiation should be complete at the start of this activity. Requirements capture activities and the AR (except for the time-box plan) should be completed before this activity can reach completion.

TASKS

	IT	Client	M/R/O
Review the requirements discovered in the workshops and review the AR	Y		O
Review domain model and existing systems and identify existing components for possible reuse, especially existing models	Y		R
Ensure participant training programme planned	Y	Y	R
Apply source code control tools to existing system if proposed solution is a change to an existing system	Y		M
Revise development plans (to 30% accuracy)	Y		R
Identify impact of proposed change on hardware, including batch and on-line response times	Y		M
Set the time-box objectives and publish them	Y		M
Set the number of planned prototype iterations	Y		R
Establish development team. Confirm the lead user, project manager, developers and the sponsor	Y	Y	M
Establish the evaluation team – sponsor, project manager, user representatives, facilitator, demonstrator/reader, auditor, operations representative, reuse librarian, legal expert, etc.	Y	Y	M
Complete Training Requirements Report	Y	Assist	M
Send plan to development manager and inform Change Management of deadlines and requirements	Y		M
Initiate Build	Y		M

DELIVERABLES AND POST-CONDITIONS Time-box planning produces a **time-box plan**, including a Gantt chart, and an estimate in task or function points, and of staff days with resource requirements and delivery dates. A **participant training requirements report** is produced to ensure rôles, systems training and business training needs of Systems and Business participants are clearly understood and planned. Emphasis is placed on requirements and testing. The project manager is responsible for creating both reports. The contents of the training requirements report will include:

1. Project rôles and names (R)
2. Training requirements (R)
3. Training schedule (high level plan) (R)
4. Training costs (R)

The training requirements report identifies the broad skills required to undertake the project, then the skill set of the individuals allocated to it, to identify the mismatch. Ensure that:

- staff members are named;
- training requirements are identified and scheduled;
- business and technical needs are covered;
- inspections are included in the plan.

All mandatory and recommended tasks (as listed above) must be complete; or there must be a justification for any recommended tasks not included.

Approvals may be required from the development manager and sponsor.

The formal time limits are from one day to four weeks. A one-week minimum may be expected. Time used in this activity is to be deducted from the overall maximum of six months to implementation.

9.7.5 Development within a time-box: The Build activity

This activity consists of a number of nested and iterated subsidiary activities as follows.

Build	
– Analysis	See Subsection 9.7.3 and Figure 9.15
– Design	See Subsection 9.7.6 and Figure 9.15
– Programming	See Subsection 9.7.7 and Figure 9.15
– Testing	See Subsection 9.7.8 and Figure 9.15
User Review	See Subsection 9.7.9 and Figure 9.15
Consolidation	See Subsection 9.7.10 and Figure 9.15
Reuse potential evaluation	See Subsection 9.7.11 and Figure 9.15
Documentation	See Subsection 9.7.12 and Figure 9.15

A waterfall or 'V' process model was once used for applications with heavy transaction processing requirements to be implemented in conventional languages on centralized architectures. This approach is not appropriate for development of OO systems. Development of applications of this type is better approached with an iterative approach. The objective is to provide the user with a system that is correct and easy to use, and to achieve this in as short a time as possible. We accomplish this by:

- extensive reuse of existing components where they exist;
- applying an interface style that is consistent with other applications;
- being supportive of user goals and tasks based on business processes rather than narrowly defined functional responsibilities;
- eliminating a large number of steps in the full 'V' model process whilst still providing a disciplined framework within which to work;
- supplying management control by testing the products of every activity and imposing an elapsed time limit;
- imposing management control over ripple effects and uncontrolled iteration – this activity has a usable system as both the end-point of the process and its deliverable;
- not requiring a distinction between production, evolution and maintenance as with conventional approaches, which usually ignore maintenance costs during project justification.

The time-box approach reduces time-to-market, not by a magic trick that makes hard things easy but by delivering an important usable subset of the entire system in no more than six months. This subsection summarizes this approach.

A computer system development project is divided into time-boxes to allow effective cost control to ensure, as far as possible, delivery of predicted benefits within time and cost limits. At the end of each time-box, a number of walkthroughs, reviews and tests are performed to validate the product against earlier documentation, especially the Project Proposal. This evaluation allows both defect analysis and configuration control to take place at each stage, and provides data to allow a decision to halt the project to be taken if necessary. The time-box is followed by a formal evaluation as described in Subsection 9.7.11.

The developers immediately produce a first-cut prototype system and may incidentally sketch out a design in the process. This is reviewed with users and typically is a broad and shallow prototype. User reaction is taken back to a second iteration and a deeper, narrower prototype produced. Here it is likely – but still not compulsory – that a design document will be produced. In many cases the code can be produced straight from the class cards in the AR. When this is done any design changes should result in new or revised class cards being prepared. This may affect the domain model and should be flagged for review at the evaluation stage. Iterations – each with a strong user involvement – should be limited to about three but the actual number is determined partly by the absolute time limit on the time-box; a maximum of six months. Adequate time must be left for tasks such as consolidation with the products of other time-boxes, database integration, documentation and the identification of candidate classes for reuse. Note that the developers are not responsible for creating reusable classes, only for identifying their potential, and that the latter is subject to review by the evaluation team. Design documentation before release is at the discretion of the time-box project manager and is not a compulsory deliverable unless otherwise specified at the outset. The important thing is that the end-product satisfies the interface specification and that design documentation exists – not the order in which the deliverables are produced.

The analysis notation of UML gives the required level of documentation and will be poured back into the library for use in other workshops.

It is absolutely critical to maintain credibility, build on success and manage expectations during the process. This is achieved by constant user involvement and candour on the part of developers. Other guidelines to be aware of may be summarized as follows.

- Define the time-box and project objectives clearly and objectively.
- Remain within the scope of the project where possible.
- Architecture is important; attend to it.
- Consider performance as early as possible.
- Use high level tools and packages wherever possible.
- Manage the user review process so as not to raise expectations too high or reduce them too much.
- Impose an informal change control discipline on the user reviews.
- Include conversion time in estimates where a revolutionary approach is used.
- Never keep a prototype that was intended to be discarded.

During the time-box an Implementation Object Model (including reused, interface and data management objects) is produced or refined where necessary. The only mandatory deliverables, however, are the working code, a 'candidates for reuse' report and user and technical documentation. Whether the technical documentation includes a full Implementation Object Model (IOM) is at the discretion of the project managers involved. As a guide, one should be produced for more complex systems. In case implementation from the Business Object Model is feasible even these are not necessary. The crucial thing is that all design decisions are traceable back to the Business Object Model, either via the IOM or directly. The time-box evaluation report must make traceability visible in the prototypes and/or their documentation.

Time-boxes include testing activities and should deliver test results against both task scripts and a technical test plan of the normal kind; i.e. tests that answer the questions: Does an enhancement leave previous things that worked working? Does the system work well under stress and high volume I/O? Also deliverable from this stage are the source code and the executable system. Project managers are responsible for ensuring that all elements of security policy have been attended to and this document includes a checklist and appropriate references to this end.

PRE-REQUISITES Once planning is complete, the resources are available and the equipment and environment are commissioned, the time-box may be entered. A workshop should have been held and the AR produced.

TASKS

	IT	Users	M/R/O
Review the objectives and the AR	Y	Y	R
Convert analysis to design and document design decisions. Modify the class cards if necessary but only produce detail design documentation for complex systems	Y		M
Review existing systems and identify existing components for possible reuse	Y		M
Prototyping (system build) 2–5 iterations. Construct broad and shallow followed by deep and possibly narrow prototypes. Basics first, rare exceptions later.	Y		M
User review for each prototype iteration	Y	Y	M
Identify candidate classes for future reuse	Y		M
Attend to security, GUI, network, coding and other standards compliance	Y		M
Documentation	Y		M
Consolidation of results of other time-boxes and the class library	Y		R
Inspection	Y	Y	R
Document defect analysis	Y		R
Test against requirements definition task scripts and a standard technical test plan	Y		M
Produce User Manual		Y	R
Produce Conversion Plan	Y		R
Initiate Evaluation	Y		M

DELIVERABLES AND POST-CONDITIONS

Each of the time-boxes results in deliverables in the form of one or more of the following:

- a system and its documentation;
- documentation on any divergences from strategy; e.g. systems architecture; standard components;
- a specification/report, including defect analysis and other metrics;
- a service;
- a set of candidate classes for reuse ('candidates for reuse' report).

The system is complete when all the task scripts in the AR can be exercised successfully and all systems tests are passed satisfactorily. The activity is complete when the system, its documentation and the reuse candidate list are all complete. The system will be integrated with all necessary components to be deliverable. The following five subsections give detailed completion criteria for the sub-activities of the time-box.

All mandatory and recommended tasks (as listed above) must be complete; or there must be a justification for any recommended tasks not included.

Each time-box may last between one and six months subject to an overall limit that the time from the end of the workshop activity to implementation is under six months. The ideal time-box lasts three to four months.

9.7.6 Design activity

The purpose of this activity is to establish that the documentation describes the system in sufficient detail for it to be supported by persons not involved in its creation. It also states how the application fulfils the requirements specified in the AR.

The Design activity follows completion of the Analysis Elaboration activity, normally within a time-box. During this activity computer system design is carried out to produce a computer solution in terms of program, database, interface and file specifications. Design may precede or follow programming. However, this assumes the architecture is defined in advance. Both specification and design will follow the Catalysis micro-process that we discussed in Chapter 6.

Standards must be followed where appropriate. UML is the standard notation for design.

Only limited user participation will be required in this activity, although the user should take part in the review/test process at its completion.

Objectives:

- To produce a technical design which meets the business objectives as simply as possible while taking account of performance, security and control requirements and system-based risks, quality, flexibility, ease of reuse and reuse
- To specify technical details of how the system will operate in terms of programs, files and database usage
- To produce the necessary documentation for subsequent program maintenance and operational running
- To finalize the physical formats of input and output for all types of systems. Include the conversation structure of interactive transactions for on-line systems as appropriate
- To estimate the likely utilization of hardware and software resources, identifying likely requirements for change
- To revise the development and implementation plans

PRE-REQUISITES	Completion of AR and Analysis, confirmation of it within the current time-box iteration.
TASKS	The detailed tasks depend on the method selected, the time-box iteration reached and the type of project but may include:

	IT	Users	M/R/O
Convert analysis model by assigning responsibilities and adding interface objects	Y		R

Identify system components, interfaces and define architecture	Y	M
Confirm compliance with architecture and standard component libraries	Y	R
Develop detailed physical design and Implementation Object Model	Y	R
Revise development and implementation plans, including hardware changes and impact on batch and on-line timings	Y	R
Identify sources of existing data and method of conversion	Y	R
Data modelling and database design, object/relational mapping design	Y	R
Develop program test plan and data	Y	R
Produce system test plan	Y	R
Produce acceptance test plan	Y	Y	R
Complete documentation and seek approval	Y	R
Collect or generate metrics	Y	M
Perform inspection or informal walkthrough	Y	R
Document and package objects developed	Y	M

DELIVERABLES AND POST-CONDITIONS The major deliverables are the Design Report, Unit Test Plan, System Test Plan and the Acceptance Test Plan. The **Design Report** (DR) is a stage of the project document. It modifies and extends the AR stage. Standard templates for these documents are advisable.

The purpose of the **Unit Test Plan**, written by the project leader, is to summarize the class test design and the resources required. Its contents should include:

1. Testing method/approach, including use of automated testing tools (R)
2. Source of test data (O)
3. Test run (O)
4. Purpose (O)
5. Test cycles (O)
6. Test conditions (R)
7. Files used (R)
8. Data checked, together with exclusions and reasons (R)

The **System (Integration) Test Plan** summarizes the method to be used in system testing. It is kept as program documentation and considers the internal architecture of the system. It should test that program invocation is as defined in the design, and that individual data fields correspond to the design. Control flags should also be verified to the design. The author is the project leader. Contents include:

1. Testing method/approach/tools (M)
2. Regression testing plan (R)
3. Systems integration plan (R)

4. Performance testing plan (overnight and on-line) (R)
5. Completion criteria (M)
6. Files and objects used (R)
7. Objects checked (M)

The purpose of the **Acceptance Test Plan** is to specify a plan that will control the user acceptance test activity. It describes the method to be used during acceptance testing. It is kept as application documentation and should verify that the system works as defined in the Project Proposal, workshop and systems analysis reports and that all use cases can be executed as described. Contents include:

1. Testing method/approach/tools (M)
2. Satisfactory completion criteria (M)
3. Source of test data (R)
4. Test plan and timetable (R)
5. Test cycles (R)
6. Test conditions (R)
7. Identification of user responsible for approval (M)

A design review confirms that the documentation is adequate for maintenance. Test the System Design to ensure that the designed system meets the business and technical needs, the system is secure but not over-complex, the project as designed is still justified in terms of costs and benefits and all functions have been addressed in the design, including hardware/operating software requirements.

All mandatory and recommended tasks (as listed above) must be complete; or there must be a justification for any recommended tasks not included.

Review the test plans and reports to ensure completeness,

TECHNIQUES   Catalysis refinement and retrieval definition. Design patterns. Informal walkthrough, or inspection for larger systems.

9.7.7 Programming activity

This activity converts the model as designed into a working system or fragment of a system. The first prototype will generally be broad and shallow, covering the whole scope. Subsequent prototypes will extend earlier ones and treat all or part of the system in depth. Narrow and deep prototypes will be used to identify reusable components for subsequent iterations.

During this activity individual programs are coded and tested. These programs are then linked and their interfaces tested. Users will have little input to programming and the associated testing processes, but they will be required to specify the acceptance test plan, construct test cases and review the results.

IT will be required to provide an environment that is as close as possible to the production environment. Acceptance testing is designed for the users to determine that the system works as originally specified, and satisfies the business requirement, using actual terms and procedures.

Objectives:

- To code and test each program object
- To ensure that objects and layers link together
- To ensure that the system performs as specified, and meets the business requirement
- To establish that any conversion programs are working as specified in the conversion plan, and are in a position to be implemented
- To verify that the system works within machine operating requirements
- To establish that the completed system is in a position to be released to users for acceptance testing

Use of testing aids is mandatory during this activity where it is possible.

The objective of this activity is to design, code and test each object or layer individually (program test) before testing the system as a whole (system test).

No formal approvals are required.

The project leader is responsible for ensuring that the project quality plan is complied with.

PRE-REQUISITES

The time-box has started and the project infrastructure is in place. User reviews have been planned. The analysis and design activities have been carried out within the time-box.

TASKS

	IT	Users	M/R/O
Select the section of the model to be coded	Y		R
Code objects	Y		M
Write test harness and unit test the coded objects	Y		M
Incorporate library classes and record design decisions			R
Create system test environment	Y		M
Review against coding standards	Y		M
Review against interface standards	Y		M
Create acceptance test environment	Y		R
Produce user documentation	Y		R
Stress test	Y		R
Note potentially reusable objects	Y		M
Collect metrics	Y		M
Initiate User Review			

DELIVERABLES AND POST-CONDITIONS

The major deliverables from this activity are any code or prototypes produced, user documentation and technical documentation, including metrics. Each object produced should be delivered with its test harness.

All mandatory and recommended tasks (as listed above) must be complete; or there must be a justification for any recommended tasks not included.

Confirm that product and documentation conform to standards and that test harnesses are delivered.

9.7.8 Testing activity

This activity involves both developers and users and is embedded in all activities, especially Programming and User Review. During Design the test plans have been refined. The tested prototype is demonstrated to the users and if possible exercised by them. The developers must carry out unit and integration (system) tests on the software modules (objects and components) they produce and ensure that all sequence diagrams can be reproduced. Use cases are the basis for system testing. Where appropriate, mass usage stress tests must be performed after Consolidation, ideally using automatic testing software.

Wherever possible, programmers should perform white-box tests on their own code but *not* be permitted to black-box test their own products. For large or high risk projects, formal testing by an outside test team is Recommended.

PRE-REQUISITES Coded prototype produced and all programming criteria satisfied. Users available.

TASKS

	IT	Users	M/R/O
Obtain test plans	Y	Y	M
Obtain testing tools	Y		R
Design usability tests	Y		R
Perform system testing on prototype, including external interfaces	Y		M
Test against relevant use cases and sequence diagrams	Y		M
Produce program and system test report	Y		M
Refer results to QA department	Y		M

DELIVERABLES AND POST-CONDITIONS The main deliverables are test reports for each object produced and the system as a whole (integration and acceptance). The **Object and System Test Report** confirms that the objects, as coded, work as described in the workshop documentation, the design document, and the Project Proposal, for handover to users for acceptance testing. Its originator is the project leader. Contents include:

1. Introduction
2. Conclusion – confirmation that the system works as defined in Project Proposal, workshop and design documentation
3. Areas of acceptable divergence from specifications
4. Error log and actions

All mandatory and recommended tasks (as listed above) must be complete; or there must be a justification for any recommended tasks not included.

Confirm that the test results are adequate, that product and documentation conform to standards and that metrics are within acceptable ranges.

Confirm that all relevant sequence diagrams can be handled correctly and that the usability checks are satisfactory. Confirm that all tests are successful. Tests are tested by tester signature.

9.7.9 User review and UAT activity

This activity involves both developers and users. The tested prototype is demonstrated to the users and if possible exercised by them.

The user(s) on the project team perform acceptance testing during this activity, removing the need for a major acceptance test when the system goes live. However, a UAT environment is still necessary in most cases. Note that if an application in UAT publishes data to a live environment then a private segment should be created to hold these data.

The final iteration through this activity is to be regarded as formal User Acceptance Testing and will need to be run in the UAT environment.

PRE-REQUISITES   Coded prototype produced and all programming and testing criteria satisfied. Users available.

TASKS

	IT	Users	M/R/O
Demonstrate prototype to user	Y	Y	M
User exercises prototype following sequence diagrams and acceptance test plan	Y	Y	M
User exercises prototype not following sequence diagrams (elbow test)	Y	Y	R
Identify potential reuse	Y	Some	M
Iterate through all users affected	Y	Y	R
Report results of reviews	Y		M
Agree and sign off necessary changes	Y	Y	M
Agree next iteration through Programming or application complete	Y	Y	M
Produce Review Report		Y	R
Ensure production standards followed	Y		M
Initiate Consolidation	Y		R

DELIVERABLES AND POST-CONDITIONS   The only deliverable is the **Review Report**, including agreements and sign-off. It should be very brief, ideally less than a page. This report should confirm that the system, as coded, works as described in the Project Proposal and the analysis documentation to the users' satisfaction, in a pseudo-production environment; and that the user manual satisfactorily describes procedures to be followed on and after implementation. Areas of acceptable divergence from specification are also recorded. The project team may all contribute to this report.

All mandatory and recommended tasks (as listed above) must be complete; or there must be a justification for any recommended tasks not included.

Confirm that all relevant sequence diagrams can be handled correctly and that the usability checks are satisfactory. Confirm relevant standards have been followed.

9.7.10 Consolidation, co-ordination, reuse and documentation

This activity takes place after a number of iterations through Analysis, Design, Programming and User Review. It consolidates the products of this time-box with those of earlier time-boxes or other projects and systems. It confirms the candidate classes identified as potentially reusable and consolidates user and technical documentation. The remarks of this subsection are also relevant to the Time-Box Planning activity where extra time must be planned for projects with parallel time-boxes.

The process model described in Figure 9.15 makes the assumption that time-boxes can be run in parallel. Clearly, this implies a means of dealing with the extra complexities of distributed, concurrent development. We have to co-ordinate across projects and time-boxes. The problem is to ensure that integration of time-box products is adequately planned for and that time-box synchronization is accomplished. The model we adopt is shown in Figure 9.16.

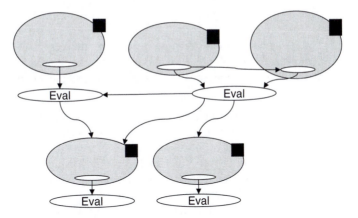

Figure 9.16 Co-ordinating concurrent development.

The diagram shows how the consolidation activity within each time-box integrates the results of other efforts to produce a product which is then subjected to evaluation. In some cases the time-boxes communicate directly and informally, in others only after evaluation. If the products of the two final time-boxes interact there will be a combined evaluation. Cautious project managers will double their estimates when this kind of parallelism occurs and, if at all possible, avoid it.

The outstanding co-ordination questions that we must discuss concern co-ordinating products from the repository, managing updates to the repository and releasing updates to the repository. We will discuss the specific issues raised by reuse in Section 9.7.

PRE-REQUISITES Results of prototype iterations signed off for consolidation and delivery by users on time-box team.

TASKS

	IT	Users	M/R/O
Identify components to be assembled	Y		M
Perform all programming tasks on the complete system	Y		R
Confirm reuse candidates	Y		M
Produce user and technical documentation	Y		M
Review user documentation with users on team	Y	Y	M
Confirm technical documentation	Y		R
Estimate application impact on comms systems	Y		M
Liaise with network team to determine requirements	Y		R
Consider impact of actual system on batch and on-line response times	Y		M
Notify client	Y		M
Perform inspection	Y	Y	R
Conduct defect analysis	Y		R
Complete metrics	Y		M

DELIVERABLES AND POST-CONDITIONS The complete system is now ready for delivery. The system will be fully demonstrable at this point. It should be checked that all use cases can be exercised and all reports produced without error. The technical documentation set will ensure that:

- all objects and design decisions are documented;
- interfaces to other systems are described;
- any modifications to the AR have been documented;
- a design report is included, preferably using a CASE tool;
- links between code objects and design objects and design objects and specification objects are described;
- there is a conversion/cut-over report where appropriate;
- a test report exists;
- infrastructure implications and required actions are documented.

The development team shall deliver the following to the production department:

- All source code and necessary compilers/linkers;
- Complete installation instructions;
- Running instructions.

Every user task should be described in the user documentation set. That document may also include sample screens and reports with a commentary on how they are used. There will be on-screen help for key user tasks and system features.

Originated by the project team, an **implementation and conversion plan** outlines the steps to be followed cutting over to the new system. This should include specific details of tasks required of the technical infrastructure team. The plan should define the business processes that will be changed as a result of the implementation; i.e. the boundaries of the change should be defined. Special consideration should be given to testing where a phased conversion is planned. Contents:

1. Summary
2. Approach
3. Contingency, back-out and disaster recovery plans
4. Completion criteria
5. Preparatory work required
6. Cost of conversion
7. Timetable and plan
8. Change boundaries
9. Resources required

Where there is an existing system, this plan indicates:

- satisfactory conversion criteria;
- the method to be used;
- work that is required to existing system prior to conversion;
- the layout of any reports required specifically for conversion.

All mandatory and recommended tasks (as listed above) must be complete; or there must be a justification for any recommended tasks not included. Check that:

- system runs in target environment;
- test results are accepted by users;
- product and documentation complete and conform to standards;
- metrics within acceptable ranges (to detect collection errors);
- all relevant use cases can be handled correctly;
- usability checks satisfactory;
- time-box team user sign-off completed;
- documentation complete and conforms to standards;
- conversion plan satisfactory.

9.7.11 Evaluation and reuse evaluation activity

Evaluation for each time-box produces an evaluation report including reuse recommendations, reuse candidates approved, a quality report and an outline implementation plan. The report should confirm the results of the tests against task scripts and consolidate all metrics from this and earlier time-boxes.

Evaluations will be included as part of the project method, reviewing progress at the end of each time-box. The objectives of an evaluation are:

- To authorize the project to continue, or not
- To authorize delivery of the product of a time-box, or not
- To identity potentially reusable components produced within the time-box
- To identify candidate classes produced by other projects or time-boxes for incorporation into the system being constructed in subsequent time-boxes
- To review stage tolerances, security issues and provide data for QA
- To act as a collection point for project metrics
- To review progress on both the current activity and the whole project against plan
- To review and approve any exception plans
- To review the plan for the next stage
- To identify the effect of current and potential problems, and plan remedial actions if necessary

Efficiency will be enhanced by the reuse of software. Hitherto designers have been responsible for packaging code so that it can be reused as many times as possible in subsequent projects. The problem with this is that well-constructed, reusable classes take time and care to produce and this presents a contradiction to the philosophy of rapid development within a time-box. Developers will be required to consider code reuse specifically for each project but only insofar as they identify reuse potential. The end-stage assessments have the task of confirming candidate classes for reuse. These should be passed to a specialist class constructer for refinement, testing and reissue to projects. Class constructers will be evaluated on the number of times their classes are reused, number of defects in them reported and productivity improvements resulting from reuse.

As part of the evaluation process, defect analysis will take place at the end of each time-box. The volume of defects identified will be compared to industry standards and past performance in order to track improvements in productivity and accuracy in specifying and coding systems. Software metrics will be used to measure changes in trends in productivity and quality levels. For object-oriented projects the number of atomic tasks supported will be taken as the equivalent of traditional logical business transactions. Usability metrics should also be collected where possible; e.g. time to complete a task, time to forget, etc. Comparisons of reliability (mean-time-to-fail), cost and programming efficiency (task points per man-month development time) will be made, amongst others. Reuse metrics will also be collected where appropriate, including number of classes reused and number of candidate reusable classes created. Metrics for each project must be completed before the project goes live, and must be maintained at each stage of the life cycle.

The evaluation activity is most important. Here it is decided whether the time-box deliverables are adequate and whether implementation should proceed or the work needs to be redone or even abandoned as infeasible. The evaluation team must involve the sponsor and personnel who are not on the time-box team. Reference should be made during evaluation to the quality plan which should have stated what elements of the method would be used and what deliverables mandated. There should be reference back to existing architectures, networks, operations and hardware. Suitably knowledgeable people should be co-opted if necessary.

The inspection technique may be used where appropriate and coding standards reviewed. The team will need to be assured that the testing was adequate by reference to both the task scripts and normal system test plans.

Senior management and QA will be present for major projects and are required to sign off the evaluation in that case.

PRE-REQUISITES This activity takes place after the end of a time-box. The evaluation team should have been assigned during Time-Box Planning.

TASKS

	IT	Users	M/R/O
Confirm candidates for reuse library identified by the developers and suggest new ones	Y	Y	R
Check that tests are adequate	Y		M
Check that performance is adequate	Y	Y	M
Check that appropriate standards have been followed	Y		R
A usability check should have been carried out	Y	Y	R
Check that the architecture is maintainable	Y		R
Review issues of security, recovery, etc.	Y		M
Review User Manual	Y		R
Review Conversion Plan	Y	Y	R
Review acceptance test plan	Y		M
Decide between redo, release or abort	Y	Y	M
Confirm deadlines	Y	Y	M
Confirm technical solution	Y		R
Initiate implementation	Y	Y	M

DELIVERABLES AND POST-CONDITIONS The deliverables are:

1. Minutes of the review.
2. A decision as to whether to release, repeat or abort the time-box. Note that **the evaluation team have no authority to delay implementation to correct defects**. This will be done as part of normal 'bug fixing' or as part of a subsequent project time-box. They may only recommend redo or abort should the project be completely undeliverable. Otherwise, their suggestions will form the basis of a new Project Proposal, CR or RFS.

All mandatory and recommended tasks (as listed above) must be complete; or there must be a justification for any recommended tasks not included. The completion criteria for earlier activities should have been met.

All parties must agree that the review is complete or decide by simple majority in case of dispute. In the latter case senior management and the project sponsor must approve. IT senior management must attend reviews for all major projects.

Review the time-box products to ensure that:

- the program documentation is complete and that the Program Test Plan has been executed correctly;
- completion criteria have been achieved for both unit and program testing and that the programs are now ready for acceptance testing;
- the programs are maintainable;
- operation of the system has been successfully demonstrated;
- the techniques used and the documentation conform to standards;
- all required metrics information is complete;
- reuse candidates acceptable;
- the justification from the Project Proposal remains valid;
- there are no decisions or items pending;
- security policy adhered to;
- Data Protection Act and other relevant legislation adhered to.

This activity should never take more than two weeks and should typically last half a day.

9.7.12 Implementation planning activity

The objective of the Implementation Planning stage is to ensure that all necessary activities are completed prior to the system starting live operation. This activity involves three component activities: implementation planning, training and installation.

If the time-box products are released the implementation activity can begin. Implementation issues include the following.

- Training.
- Education.
- Change management (through the sponsor).
- H/W and S/W resources.
- Environment/locations.
- Support.

The planning for the implementation planning activity begins in the workshop activity. Implementation planning is concerned with ensuring that all necessary activities are complete prior to going live and satisfactory cut-over to the new system. The approval requirements should also be stated in the Project Proposal.

The objectives are:

- To ensure that the production environment has been set up
- To provide for, and ensure, complete and accurate file conversion and take-on
- To convert to the new system
- To provide support and assistance at and beyond changeover to the new system
- To obtain formal acceptance of successful system implementation

■ To ensure Change Management group informed of impact of proposed changes

PRE-REQUISITES Sign-off from evaluation stage is required before this activity can complete, although much planning may have been completed earlier. Project initiation must be complete and there is input from workshops, Rapid Analysis and the main build time-boxes.

TASKS

Task	IT	Users	M/R/O
Complete implementation plan	Y		M
Notify engineering and production support groups of technology requirements	Y		M
Plan back-out facilities	Y		R
Define, commission, test and QA hardware and bought-in software	Y		R
Create installation instructions and setup kit	Y		M
Complete training plan	Y	Y	R
Train users	Y	Y	R
Data take-on	Y	Y	R
Prepare beta test plan	Y		O
Complete beta tests with selected users	Y	Y	O
Complete usability tests	Y	Y	R
Review beta test report	Y	Y	R
Create change management record of change, report to Change Management group	Y		M
Establish that approval given for implementation	Y		M
Define security profiles	Y		R
Ensure users and project team trained in new system	Y	Y	R
Establish that metrics are complete for project	Y		M
Establish operational environment	Y		M
Perform take-on and conversion	Y		M
Test conversion		Y	M
Approve conversion		Y	M
Support users of new system	Y		M
Install system	Y		M
Monitor fault reports	Y	Y	M

DELIVERABLES AND POST-CONDITIONS Deliverables and documentation include:

■ user acceptance of conversion, a formal document from the user accepting the new system;

■ implementation pack.

All mandatory and recommended tasks (as listed above) must be complete; or there must be a justification for any recommended tasks not included.

Review the implementation of the system and ensure that:

- the system has been accepted by both the users and IT;
- the appropriate hardware/software has been installed;
- the network has been installed (if required);
- production libraries have been set up;
- all special stationery has been approved and obtained;
- all required system documentation is available and conforms to standards.

Approvals may be required from the Project Sponsor, Development Manager and IT Management.

This activity is constrained by the overall six-month limit but should take less than two weeks.

9.7.13 Development planning and resource planning activities

This is the first extra-project, supporting activity to be discussed. Project planning comprises two types of activity, the detailed planning of an individual time-box, which is dealt with separately in Section 9.7.4, and the planning of a whole project composed of several time-boxes. This latter activity cannot be separated from the need to balance the resource requirements as a whole. Where there is only one time-box these activities are combined. This subsection considers the development planning activity as one that starts from both global and site considerations and apportions work to various time-boxes given the discoveries and imperatives of the earlier activities: project initiation, workshops, analysis and other time-boxes and their plans. In parallel with this activity the identification of potentially reusable classes from the repository is conducted. This latter is discussed in Section 9.7.14. As shown in Figure 9.15, this activity crosses the boundary between the project and the organization as a whole.

There are plans and estimates at various levels. At the highest level there should be a plan covering the entire scope established and perhaps recording the predicted tasks concerned with linking to other systems and the timing implications of dependencies on undelivered components in other systems. Within this plan there will be an overall iteration plan. Then there is a plan for each time-box. The extent to which these plans are formal deliverables is questionable. They should exist but may be recorded in minutes of meetings or as common agreements among teams. In that sense they may not be 'delivered' to anyone but the originators.

Development planning involves two separate but related planning activities: planning the project itself and working out the implications of this project on other projects in the company and resolving issues of interaction. The second issue is closely related to domain modelling and is considered with that topic in the next section. The development manager must also engage in resource planning. This involves establishing the availability of manpower, hardware, software, and other resources along with the appropriate budgetary approvals. This section concentrates on the planning of the application. The project and development managers must plan checkpoints for integration with other projects, infrastructural services, etc.

Project planning starts when the Project Proposal has been signed off by the user sponsor and the manager responsible or when scheduled by a steering committee. Metrics should be updated at every phase of the project. A cut-over plan will also be prepared for use by the implementation planning activity.

The project manager is responsible for ensuring that initial user training is performed, because it has a direct impact on the success of the implementation. S/he will be in the best position to determine who actually does the training, which may well be one of the full-time users seconded to the project team, or the supplier if it is a package solution. The project manager should decide.

However, users also have an interest in ensuring that training is done, so they are not absolved of all responsibility. Users also have responsibility for ensuring that their requirement is defined in terms of content and attendance. They are also required to release the staff at the appropriate time. This should be **before** implementation. Post-implementation training is the responsibility of the user group.

The development manager is responsible for liaison between the project and other parts of the organization: users, other projects, steering committees and so on.

The objectives of this activity are:

- To identify and allocate resources to the project in balance with other projects
- To plan user training as necessary
- To plan the sequencing and slicing of time-boxes
- To identify checkpoints with other projects and potential for reuse
- To plan the cut-over to the new system

PRE-REQUISITES The Project Proposal Page is completed and approved.

TASKS

	IT	Users	M/R/O
Submit project to next Steering Committee meeting	Y	Y	M
Allocate priority to project	Steering Committee		M
then according to the given priority:			
Allocate resources (IT and User)	Y	Y	M
Define a high level plan	Y		M
Decide on time-box decomposition, concurrency and sequencing (with reference to project team and management)	Y		M
Define training requirements and gain approval for cost from project sponsor	Y	Y	M
Schedule and implement training plan	Y	Y	R
Complete Quality Plan, where appropriate	Y		M

| Plan checkpoints for integration with other projects/infrastructural services etc. | Y | M |

In the initial stages of a project, estimating tools should be used to determine size in terms of both elapsed days and task points where possible.

Projects will be set up on an appropriate planning tool so that management can review the progress of all projects in each group's portfolio. Time will be recorded against each project and, where there are specific project hardware and software budgets, costs are to be recorded as the budgets are drawn down.

One person in each project team will be designated as the person responsible for change control who will be the project manager by default. Changes include correction of errors and alterations to specification. The effect of changes will be reflected in the revised plan, which will be reviewed and approved by the project steering committee.

DELIVERABLES AND POST-CONDITIONS The key deliverables from this activity are a steering committee proposal and a quality plan. The **steering committee proposal** is written by the project manager and provides sufficient information to prioritize the project and allocate funds. Its contents include:

1. Project title
2. Project reference
3. Brief project description and benefits
4. Estimated costs to 50% accuracy
5. Estimated task points
6. Project leader
7. Sponsor + cost centre(s) to be charged
8. Justification reference
9. Drop down rate
10. High level project plan. This enumerates, sequences and sizes the time-boxes and indicates any parallel running.
11. Budget
12. Resource requirements should include training requirements

The **quality plan** helps to identify the major milestones in the project, how quality is assured, methods used (e.g. review methods) plus how changes are to be controlled. The quality plan should list CSFs and the criteria by which the project will be judged. Contents:

1. CSFs (R)
2. Major milestones (M)
3. Inspection methods (R)
4. Metrics to be collected (R)
5. Change control method (M)

The quality plan will be reviewed by senior management for all major projects. It is laid out to show key deliverables, review methods, dates promised and delivered for each project activity. Those responsible sign for each activity's completion. Typical review methods include inspections, sponsor signature and walkthroughs.

Development planning is a continuous, unbounded activity with no specific time limits.

9.7.14 Domain modelling and repository administration activity

This subsection refers to repository administration. The subsection presupposes that the library team will administer this function and provide core staff.

Domain modelling is the continuous activity of defining and refining the objects that represent the business regardless of the particularities of applications. It is closely related to the issue of repository management.

It is beneficial to divide analysis into various layers. In particular, we separate domain analysis from application analysis. These are parallel activities. Domain modelling covers those objects and structures that concern all of the business and not those areas that are peculiar to an application. The boundary is fuzzy but the principle is clear. Domain objects are potentially reusable and, as such, deserve greater care in analysis, design and implementation. They should be improved by experienced developers but these people need to be freed from the concerns of project deadlines while they are re-engineering and improving domain classes. Candidate classes for reuse are checked out of the applications, improved and checked in to the repository for subsequent use by projects.

The domain model is a Business Object Model (BOM) consisting of domain objects, application frameworks, task scripts and so on. It is owned by the whole business and has the same general character as a conventional entity-based enterprise model. It is unlikely that it will work well without some sort of computerized repository. That repository should be capable of storing, without loss of detail, business process models, message tables, task scripts, class descriptions and structures. It should compute metrics automatically and provide both keyword and hierarchical browsing facilities.

Information from the domain model and rapid analysis provide input, along with company-wide project planning imperatives, to the time-box planning activity. This activity involves deciding if the project can be divided up into different segments that can be implemented independently or almost independently. The layers identified during analysis are the obvious basis for this fragmentation. In some cases, the time-boxes will have to be run sequentially and in a certain order due to dependencies. In others, it will be possible to run parallel time-boxes if resources permit or delivery dates so imply. Otherwise, the aim is to build the layer with the highest priority first – and the priorities have been established at the first workshop if all has gone well.

		Programme team	Project team
PRE-REQUISITES	None.		

TASKS

Task	Programme team	Project team
Respond to requests for information from project teams	Y	
Check in candidate classes for inspection	Y	
Inspect candidate classes and structures	Y	
Examine repository for similar or identical classes	Y	Y
Inform project manager that registered candidate has synonyms	Y	
Report incomplete project models to project manager	Y	
Rework class definitions and add to repository	Y	
Build and document links to code level classes	Y	Y
Publish changes in domain model to all projects	Y	
Attend project meetings to advise on reuse of repository classes	Y	
Maintain register of applications, specification objects, design objects, code objects and their linkages	Y	Y

DELIVERABLES AND POST-CONDITIONS

Every class defined in a workshop or time-box and approved as a reuse candidate at the evaluation stage shall be examined for potential addition to the repository. A report on the result will be transmitted to the originating project leader. The repository itself documents the inclusion of classes and the links between applications, specifications, design objects and code objects. Additions can be reported in a monthly newsletter or by e-mail.

The linkages will be recorded in the following form, as a textual annotation to each object and application.

Application	• List of specification objects in the AR
	• List of design objects
	• List of code objects used
Specification object	• List of equivalent objects in the design
	• List of applications that use the specification
Design object	• List of code objects that implement the design
	• List of related specification objects
Code object	• List of design objects implemented by the code object
	• Applications that use this object

The task is never complete and there are no time limits.

9.7.15 Bug fixing activity

This activity allows for the inevitable defects that occur in any newly delivered software. It involves rapid response to bug reports from users by the remnants of the project team allocated this responsibility.

When a project is delivered a fragment of the project team is assigned responsibility for correcting any remaining defects. When the situation stabilizes this resource can be released and the system passes into use fully.

PRE-REQUISITES The system has been delivered and responsibility for customer service allocated during Implementation Planning.

TASKS

	Project team	Users
Use the system and fill in bug report forms, CRs or RFSs		Y
Correct faults and perform regression tests	Y	
Deliver new versions	Y	
Update status reports	Y	Y
Report defect metrics	Y	Y
Document fixes and inform Change Management	Y	

DELIVERABLES AND POST-CONDITIONS Fault reports include the fault description, time reported, status and responsibility. When they are closed the time closed is added.

This activity ceases when the system ceases to reveal faults. Normally, this activity would cease within at most two months. A greater level of faults should generate a new Project Proposal.

9.7.16 General project management tasks and issues

A diagrammatic representation of the process life cycle relating its different activities was given as Figure 9.15. The associated project and development management tasks are covered together in this subsection as well as under the individual activities.

PROJECT INITIATION A project manager initially supports the user department in production of the Project Proposal. Then, when agreement to proceed with a project is given, it is scheduled into the current operating plan by a development manager.

Normally, once a quarter, a project manager is appointed to the project. That person needs to liaise with the development manager who must (with the project manager's help) perform the following tasks.

Initiate the project

- Review the Project Proposal, ensuring that it conforms to standard.
- Obtain sign-off for the proposal, including estimated cost of proceeding.

Submit Proposal to Steering Committee(s)

- Distribute proposal to members of relevant Steering Committee(s).
- Ensure proposal is reviewed by committee, which attaches a priority to it.
- Obtain approval to proceed to workshop, to be confirmed in the minutes of the meeting.

Plan first workshops and likely subsequent development

- Create high level plan.
- Initiate the requirements process.
- Obtain commitment from user for dedicated resource for the project.
- Estimate costs for the development, together with outline project plan. Use an estimating model to verify the estimated costs.

RISK ANALYSIS

Impact and risk analysis should be performed before starting any significant activity. For each system ask:

- what can go wrong?
- what would be the cost?
- what is the probability of occurrence?
- what preventative measures are possible?
- what would they cost?
- what is the cost of not doing the project?

Find measures for each risk and consider simulation.

ACTIVITY INITIATION

There are certain activities within a project activity that are associated only with the start of that activity.

• Approvals	Verify approval previously given to proceed to this activity and prerequisites met.
• Review Development Plan	The latest version of the project plan is reviewed and any changes are published and authorized.
• Assign Activities	Ensure that project members are aware of the objectives of the activity, and the time frames.
• Manage Project Change Control	The procedures to be adopted for agreeing changes in the project will have been documented in the Quality Plan.

ACTIVITY EXECUTION

The majority of tasks defined in the project plan will be completed during these sections of the project life cycle.

All project leaders/managers should submit **regular progress reports** to their steering committees, at least monthly but possibly verbally. Specifically, the project status report should be updated at the end of each activity. The project leader should update monthly reports of planned progress against actual and forecast, and other performance metrics. Project managers must comply with all established reporting requirements.

The project manager should ensure that the procedures for **change management and version control** are followed to:

- ensure requirements changes follow change control procedures (separately defined);
- evaluate the impact of each change on the project.

Milestone reviews should be held throughout the project. Material divergence from planned time frames should be reported to the Development Manager and the Sponsor.

Use **Inspections** and other tests to review the output from every activity to identify defects. Inspections will be performed on all major documents/systems, produced from the systems development process. These include the AR, systems design, code, and the various test plans. Inspections will take place as part of a process to instil a quality culture within IT, and will provide support to the end-stage assessments performed at the end of each project activity. Each document should be inspected before the sponsor's approval or sign-off; inspections will not be performed after sign-off.

Inspection is a formal peer review of a document. It is intended to identify defects, but not to provide solutions. The inspection team comprises the following:

- the moderator – an independent person, specifically trained in the role, who ensures that practical arrangements are made for the inspection, and that all participants are prepared and involved;
- the reader – to present the report being investigated;
- the person responsible for the document;
- the person responsible for input to the document;
- the person responsible for using the product of the document under inspection.

Participants should have been trained in Inspection techniques. The inspection meeting will take no more than two hours, but participants should have made themselves aware of the systems and products involved beforehand, as well as having read the document to be inspected. Defects will be identified in the meeting, however.

The output of the inspection process is a defect list; these are reworked by the person responsible for the document with the moderator following up to ensure completion. There would usually be one inspection meeting per document. A second inspection may be required if the moderator deems this necessary. The moderator is also responsible for maintaining control sheets for inspections held to be used in the collation of Inspection Metrics, i.e. analyses of defects found during the inspection process.

End-Stage Assessments require that the project sponsor ensure that the evaluation follows each time-box activity in the project. This is a formal process of approval for the project to proceed to the next activity (or not, as the case may be).

For large projects, senior management will be involved in these. The project plan and quality plan should be made available. A nominated scribe should record the project name, stage being assessed and date of the meeting. The following points should be covered:

- Status of deliverables against plan
- Cross-reference to previous system life-cycle activities
- Total man-months actual against plan
- Quality assurance undertaken
- Review exception plan, if any (see below)
- Named person responsible for change control. Changes since last baseline? MM changes due to date
- Risks and dependencies, one-page review
- Review tolerance for next stage
- Named senior user
- User deliverables

A project has been completed when it has concluded its implementation planning activity and delivered, or when it has been terminated. The project completion activities will act as a trigger to change the status of the project in the various tracking systems.

- Close the project documentation.
- Complete the Project Completion Form.

QUALITY PLANNING

Quality is assured by adherence to the procedures laid down in this document whereby every product is tested and accepted as it is produced. Company-specific procedures, or those required by regulators, may need to be added.

SECURITY

The process mandates adherence to appropriate disaster recovery, security and network security policies.

<u>Check</u>	<u>Activity where relevant</u>
for the object model:	
Every object has an owner	Workshop, Analysis, Testing, Evaluation
Every attribute/method has a security level (default is owner only)	Workshop, Analysis, Testing, Evaluation
Every object, attribute and method has a security sensitivity level	Workshop, Analysis, Testing, Evaluation
for the system:	
Are passwords enforced at system or network level? If system then:	Testing,
Should system be physically isolated (e.g. mergers and acquisitions)?	Design, Programming, Testing, Evaluation

Has database security policy been followed?	Design, Programming, Testing Evaluation
Has network security policy been followed?	Design, Programming, Testing Evaluation
What is the frequency that passwords are changed?	Design, Programming, Testing Evaluation
There are no passwords embedded in code/files.	Design, Programming, Testing Evaluation
Who deactivates old passwords?	Implementation Planning
Are there audit trails of access violations?	Design, Programming, Testing Evaluation

Generally:

Which office is responsible for the security of this system?	Implementation Planning
Has a separate test environment been created?	Implementation Planning
Inform Systems Security of system release/implementation	Implementation Planning

Here is a useful checklist for project management.

1. Create and obtain sign-off for Project Proposal.
2. Obtain approvals.
3. Identify team.
4. Organize and run requirements workshop.
5. Obtain sign-off for Workshop Report.
6. Complete AR and process innovation.
7. Obtain sign-off for AR.
8. Plan time-box, training and organize evaluation team.
9. Initiate Implementation Planning, plan delivery, liaise with Production staff and commission infrastructure.
10. Build and test systems.
11. Produce DR.
12. Ensure all deliverables created and correct.
13. Complete evaluation activity.
14. Obtain sign-off for systems.
15. Install systems.

SMALL PROJECTS

There are some differences between the full cycle and the shortened cycle appropriate for small projects. A small project is defined as one taking less than three man-months' total effort, irrespective of the number of people involved in the project team, and one that is not making use of the process. The following documentation is required, irrespective of the size of the project:

■   Project Initiation Form (M)

- Abbreviated Systems Analysis (including conversion details) and Systems Design sections of Project Report (M)
- User documentation or help (R)
- Program and System Test Plan and Report (R)
- Acceptance Test Plan and Report (M)
- Implementation Document (R)

The following documents are not required for small projects.

- Participants Training Requirements
- Scoping Documents
- Requirements Document
- Conversion Plan – include details in Analysis Report

A small project should follow the same steps as any other, apart from the stages within the workshop activity. A formal workshop activity would not normally be undertaken, although most of the products of this stage are required and would be produced as a result of discussions with users or interviews.

POST-IMPLEMENT-ATION REVIEWS

Post-implementation reviews (PIRs) should be held after a system has been live for three months. They may be skipped with the documented agreement of both IT and the client when both sides feel there are no problems and there is little to be learnt. Their purpose is to examine the production process with a view to improving it in future and this can be of immense value to the organization. They may also be used to institute formal usability testing.

If either side requests a PIR it becomes mandatory on both sides. A PIR should be requested whenever feasible.

The review is a specific activity providing a picture of the current position, and reviewing the history of the project to see what lessons may be learnt and what changes may be required to either the System or the Development process. This is an opportunity for the success of the project to be assessed in terms of the operation of the system and the development process used to produce it.

A review of the system normally takes place approximately one month after implementation when the system has 'bedded in'. The review of the development process occurs immediately after the implementation. The system review should include an appraisal of its impact on other systems, batch times and network traffic where applicable.

The review report will be presented to the appropriate steering committee on its completion.

The objectives of a post-implementation review are:

- To review the performance of the system against targets
- To determine whether the system met the business requirements
- To review actual costs and benefits compared with original estimates
- To review operational procedures
- To review development techniques and procedures

- To review and measure usability
- To identify strengths and weaknesses, and decide whether or not an in-depth review of any area is necessary
- To assess and categorize requested changes
- To recommend any necessary changes

A PIR is documented by a **system review report** and **project assessment forms**, both produced by the project leader, to review the operation of the live system and identify any further action needed; it also reviews the project development process and assesses if and how it could be improved. Project assessment forms are used to record and review metric-related data on each completed project and provide data for project audits. Contents for the system review report are as follows.

1. Management summary
2. Findings
3. Conclusions and recommendations
4. An appendix containing
   Terms of reference for post-implementation review
   Draft terms of reference for further work
   Current cost–benefit analysis
   Justification check
   Metrics review

With suitable user involvement, a PIR should:

- confirm scope and objectives;
- review operational system;
- review system development;
- review project costs and metrics;
- complete metrics preparation;
- complete defect analysis;
- complete project assessment forms;
- produce documentation;
- prepare final project review statement;
- present results to the steering committee.

SUPPORTING DOCUMENTS AND TOOLS

Documents relating to and supporting the process are likely to include:

- IT strategy
- IT security regulations
- Network security policy
- Database design guidelines
- Application architecture and component standards
- Quality and metrics guidelines

Any published list of corporate approved tools should include *inter alia* the following.

- Project management and control tools, such as MS Project.
- Documentation and Office Automation Tools, such as MS Office, Visio, etc.
- Workshop and analysis tools such as Visio or a CASE tool.
- Design tools, including CASE.
- Source code control and change management tools.
- Estimating and metrics tools.
- Risk evaluation tools.
- Languages, components and libraries.

9.7.17 Project rôles and responsibilities

This subsection covers the responsibility to a project of each rôle in which people interact with the project, with the exception of the workshop rôles explained in Chapter 8.

GROUP RÔLES Each project is associated with a **steering committee**. Management is responsible for authorizing the start of each project after a Project Proposal has been produced, then for monitoring progress against previously agreed milestones up to project completion. Steering Committees work within the budgetary constraints determined by management.

Senior management are responsible for ensuring that IT provides the overall service required by the business, and that the service is consistent with the defined objectives for quality, cost and timeliness. New projects are prioritized by the business area concerned and approved by the Board for being placed on the central project list.

PROJECT RÔLES The **Project Sponsor** is the individual user who is responsible for the project, has authority to approve initial and continued expenditure on it within the agreed budget constraints and authority to approve implementation of any changes to production systems. The Project Sponsor is charged with the full cost of the project and is thus of key importance. S/he should be kept informed of all significant milestones and involved in review points, especially the evaluation stages. The sponsor will sign off each workshop, AR, time-box and change of plan.

Responsibility for day-to-day management of a project is given to a **project or 'development' manager** from either IT or a user department. This project manager advises his/her **Manager**; the Manager and the Project Sponsor both in turn report on the project to the appropriate Project Steering Committee. Project managers are responsible for day-to-day liaison with users and for product quality.

Steering committees only review projects by exception; they exist to take policy decisions and distribute resources in IT on user request. They authorize divergence from previously agreed timetables, and should meet no more than monthly locally or once per quarter regionally, when priorities can be reassessed.

The evaluation activity report will be presented to the appropriate steering committee as part of the project closing procedure.

Project managers are responsible for the technical and commercial success of the project, and for maintaining quality standards through the development. Both may occasionally act as **time-box managers.**

Specific responsibilities of project managers include:

- ensuring all work carried out is covered by defined tasks as contained in the plans for the project;
- reviewing the proposals with specific reference to exposure to system-related risk;
- ensuring all methods used by the individual are appropriate and are consistent with the project's overall objectives for quality, cost and time-scale;
- checking the quality of their own work before indicating its completion;
- ensuring that all necessary communication channels with other groups have been established;
- identifying and resolving issues and problems which influence the quality, time-scale or cost of the project as a whole;
- promoting the profile of total quality within the system development process;
- considering the implications of the new system on the production environment;
- managing changes requested by users;
- reporting status to IT management;
- diagnosing and resolving problems.

DEVELOPER RÔLES

The **developer** plays, of course, a key rôle in the process. The developer's skill set may/must include Java, O/S skills, client management, finance, pragmatism, GUI design, project management, database techniques and object-oriented analysis/design. In the method proposed here the developer is not responsible for making classes reusable but only for spotting opportunities for reuse. Evidence shows that practice helps developers do this earlier in the process. There are not analysts, designers, coders, etc. There are just developers. This implies that horizontal stratification is the order of the day rather than vertical structuring. Standard career grades are obsolete. This does not imply that there is no division of labour or that special skills are not exploited. It does imply a flat organizational structure and a flexible approach.

Domain analysts need broad business knowledge and the skills and dispositions of the systems programmer; an impossible combination it seems. Our current thinking is that the job should rotate until suitable staff are discovered by trial and error. Domain analysis is a long-term investment that will pay off when workshops begin to use its products. At the outset there may be only small visible benefits.

USER RÔLES Best practice in system development places emphasis on iterative development, hence the degree of user involvement should be high. In order for the process to be successful, users must also supply a number of devoted resources, ones that are aware of the business requirements relating to the development.

Users are responsible for approving progress at major project milestones, in that the project sponsor has to sign off documentation at the end of each activity. Users have to perform the acceptance test activity, having previously written the acceptance test plan. They are responsible for generating test data for this activity.

Users agree to the project being migrated to the production environment, and decide whether the cut-over has been successful. This is done within a mutually agreed time frame, with variances approved by the project steering committee.

More details are given in individual sections relating to project activities.

The user is no less important than the developer. Users, ideally, need computer awareness, management skills, enthusiasm and commitment. However, we recognize that only unskilled users are not busy and that project involvement will not always be full-time. It must, however, be a committed and planned involvement.

A **lead user** should be appointed early in the project to resolve disputes. This person will be one respected by other users and need not always be the most heavily involved in terms of time spent.

The project manager may well be a developer as well. He should possess all key project management skills and be responsible for steering committee and sponsor liaison.

The **project leader** is usually the project manager of the systems area under analysis. His/her role is to plan and co-ordinate the Rapid Analysis and Rapid Transition sessions and liaise between the business customers and the facilitator/analyst.

OTHER RÔLES **Evaluators** need reuse awareness and both technical and business skills. Some evaluators must not have been part of the project team and can benefit from training in inspection techniques.

The **change controller** has the key rôle of ensuring the continuing integrity of systems as they are upgraded. Other key rôles include the **support team** and representatives from the **system security** and **legal** functional areas.

⊟ 9.8 Reuse management

Making objects of sufficient quality to be genuinely reusable, with good, stable well-defined interfaces, is not possible within the constraints imposed by rapid, time-box-constrained development. I advocate the establishment of a separate reuse team to do this. However, commercial experience of such separated teams has been generally poor. The reason for this is that they quickly become isolated from the businesses and development teams that they serve and ossify into ivory towers with concerns of their own and less and less knowledge of what is really needed. To overcome this Graham (1995) advanced the idea of the 'hairies and conscripts' model for reuse management.

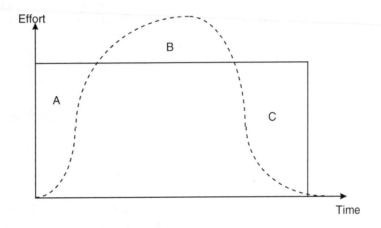

Figure 9.17 Project resource profiles.

Figure 9.17 shows two alternative resource profiles for a software project. The dotted line shows the true resource loading during the lifetime of the project but the solid line shows how the typical project manager allocates resources: grabbing all he expects to need at the outset and holding on to them until the end of the time-box. This dichotomy has a number of interesting effects. First, the under-utilization indicated by the area marked A may be used for learning and generally getting up to speed. The area marked B indicates a period of hard work, long hours and often heightened angst. But the under-utilization labelled C is not the ideal way to relax and recuperate; it is usually a boring time and is always wasteful. Developers deserve a genuine break after the high intensity work and stress that characterizes time-box-based development. Adopting the view that a change is as good as a rest, we can advocate that the developers so under-utilized can take one of two routes. They can be assigned to hand-holding and fixing the inevitable post-implementation bugs: the Bug Fixing activity. Or, they can be 'conscripted' to a sabbatical with the reuse or library team for a period.

Special skill is required to spot potential components, generalize and create a coherent component library; so we need reuse specialists. This reuse team must be populated by permanent staff too: people dedicated to software excellence who are responsible for the architecture of the library and knowing its contents inside out. Unfortunately perhaps, such skills are not always to be found in the same individuals as the customer facing skills that application developers need so crucially.

Graham originally characterized the library staff as 'hairies' by analogy with the IBM systems programmers of the 1960s, who were often bearded, besandalled and replete with anorak and train spotters' manual – but *very* good at their job. The resultant 'hairies and conscripts' model of reuse management is then a model of knowledge interchange designed to prevent the reuse initiative becoming a separate ivory tower. Developers (the conscripts) take the business knowledge that they have acquired on their projects into the library domain along with the new classes that they will help make more reusable. During their sojourn in the library they learn reuse and architectural skills from the librarians and, what is more important, learn what is in the other parts of the library. When they return to their next project they then act as reuse ambassadors and mentors to other team members. This **knowledge circulation** model is illustrated by Figure 9.18.

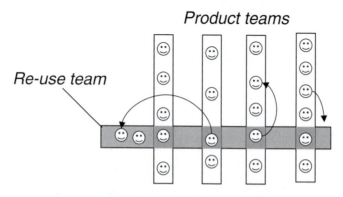

Figure 9.18 The knowledge circulation model of reuse management.

In the context of CBD reuse becomes even more critical. We must distinguish between the rapid assembly of products for users and the creation of the component kits from which families of products are built. The components in a kit are likely to be used many times and a higher degree of ceremony in the design process is required in their definition and creation; perhaps even formal specification should be used. This is probably a responsibility of the library team. Experience with the use of the kit will generate new requirements and fixes to the kit and its architecture. Products within a defined family can be put together far more quickly and a lower ceremony process is needed. Users will feed their reactions back to the application developers and would like rapid response to their changing requirements. These two feedback loops are shown on the right-hand side of Figure 9.19. On the left we see slower, broader feedback processes going on. Market analysts will be trying to understand and anticipate users' needs and wants. They set strategy for the next generation of component kits. Architects intervene, in creating the new architecture and establishing a baseline for the kits as they evolve.

Products are quickly-created specialized solutions. As far as possible we want to build them from the reusable assets in the library. New assets should be created by generalizing from designs of known products and feedback from users, not from bright ideas about what might be useful. The reuse team enhances the component kit based on what is learnt, but must avoid galloping generalization: 'we might need a …, and it could also do …'. They protect and cultivate these assets and devote resources to maintaining their 'design capital'. Application builders select and specialize components from the kit and the users certify the end-product's quality and fitness for purpose. Their observations can then be fed back to the kit builders.

Architects and strategists plan the evolution of the library, which must be separately resourced from products to avoid panic fixes that could destabilize the architecture.

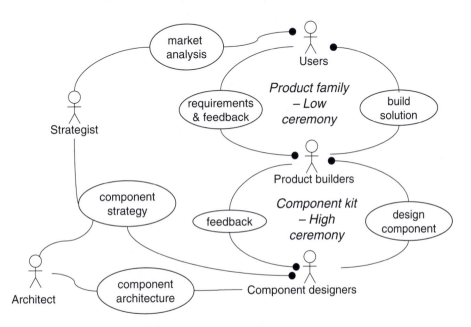

Figure 9.19 Reuse feedback loops.

REUSE LIBRARY MODELS

The outstanding specific issues raised by reuse that we must discuss concern co-ordinating products from the repository, and managing and releasing updates to the repository. Henderson-Sellers and Pant (1993) describe four different models of reuse co-ordination. In their **end of life cycle** model the generalization activity is carried out after projects complete. My observation has been that there is a severe danger that this activity is omitted due to the demands of new projects for the newly released personnel who are the ones expected to carry out the generalization. Even if these resources are made available, as Henderson-Sellers and Pant point out, it is unlikely that the customer will be altruistic enough to fund the apparent extension to his project after he has taken delivery of a satisfactory end-product. The obvious alternative is to make developers responsible for creating reusable classes during the project. Menzies *et al.* (1992) call this the G-C1 model. I refer to it as the **constant-**

creation model. The arguments for this approach are strong. The costs can be attributed to the customer during development. Furthermore, good developers have a tendency to produce reusable code 'as a silk worm produces silk'; as a by-product of what they are doing anyway. However, in practice this increases costs and increases time-to-market and is often the victim of time pressures within projects. Obviously, nothing should be done to discourage the production of high quality, reusable classes during projects but it cannot be enforced in practice. When this régime is in place we tend to observe a lot of source code copying and improvement rather than subclassing. To overcome problems with both these approaches Henderson-Sellers and Pant suggest two models, appropriate for small to average and very large companies respectively: the **two-library** model and the **alternative cost-centre** model.

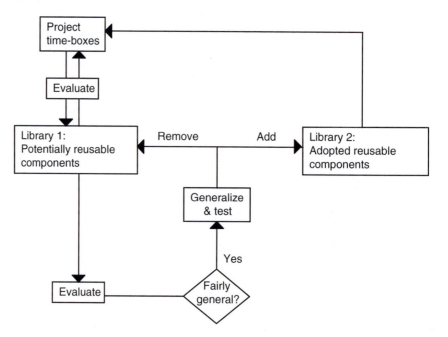

Figure 9.20 A two-library model.

My version of the two-library model is illustrated schematically in Figure 9.20. Here there is a library of potentially reusable classes identified during projects and another of fully generalized and adopted classes maintained by the domain team. How an object's potential for reuse can be determined is almost impossible to legislate for. Business knowledge and development skills combine to determine the result in concrete circumstances. Developers will typically ask if the concept is important to the business, likely to be used in other systems, fundamental to technical components of applications and so on. Attentive readers will have already noticed that we have adopted a two-library approach.

The only additional effort specific to the project in this approach is the recognition of potentially reusable classes and the extra cost is almost zero. As we have seen, early on in projects, from workshops to prototyping in the time-box, library components are scanned. If the classes identified in this way happen to reside in Library 1 then an additional generalization cost is incurred by the project, but this is entirely as it should be and the costs can be happily borne by the sponsor. The two-library model directly addresses the danger of over-generalization alluded to earlier.

The alternative cost-centre model involves creating and funding a separate cost-centre centrally. It is not funded by projects and initially runs at a loss, costs being recovered by selling classes to projects long-term. This model is only thought to be appropriate for very large organizations. My process is compatible with this approach too, as long as the hairies and conscripts technique is firmly applied.

9.9 Metrics and process improvement

Accurate estimation of the resource and elapsed time requirements for delivery of a defined project is clearly a matter of the highest importance in effective management of the IT function. The drive is to move accurate estimation of the resources demanded by a project further back up the life cycle of the project. If we want to understand and improve the way we develop software we must measure ourselves and our products. In other words, we must collect both product and process metrics. Conventional measures of software products include lines of source code, function points, defects found in testing and so on. Measures (the proper word for metrics) of the process include time taken.

9.9.1 Metrics

Historically, the SLOC (Source Lines Of Code) approach has been widely used; but the volume of code is only known when the work has been completed; and prior to that, the estimate is based largely on experience of similar projects. Attention more recently has been focused on the *function point analysis* approach, which at least moves us back up to the point where a detailed functional specification has been developed. The problems here largely reside in the definition of what exactly constitutes a function point: experience shows that given a definition, competent analysts may come up with widely differing estimates of the function point content. In addition, there is a problem in applying function point analysis in a pure object-oriented development environment, in that there are no functions in such a system that are separate from data structures and arguably therefore no function points in the accepted sense.

This section focuses attention on task point analysis – estimating on the basis of the business task points in a requirements definition: the number of atomic tasks that the users are helped to do by the system. This has many benefits. For one thing, the estimation is carried out at the requirements capture stage of the life cycle – early enough to assist in project justification and estimation. Also, business task points at the requirements definition stage do not presuppose any particular delivery vehicle or strategy. Before defining the SOMA metrics suite, including task points, we review the state of the art in the field of object-oriented metrics.

The MOSES method (Henderson-Sellers and Edwards, 1994) collects metrics as part of its quality evaluation activity to permit code testing and reuse assessment. MOSES distinguishes three kinds of metric: internal (intra-) class metrics, inter-class external (i.e. interface) metrics and system metrics. Intra-class metrics are concerned with size and complexity, inter-class metrics with coupling and cohesion. Other metrics are concerned with cognitive complexity: how hard it is for programmers to understand. MOSES is one of the most complete methods published in respect of metrics yet it remains consciously tentative in its prescriptions. Its intra-object metrics are size, average operations per class and average method size (in SLOCs). Size is defined as

$$W_A*A + W_M*M$$

where A is the number of attributes and M is the number of operations or methods. W_A and W_M are empirically determined weights. W_A is expected to be close in value to 1 and W_M in the range 5–20. Complexity is measured by a variant of McCabe's cyclomatic complexity (McCabe, 1976).

The inter-object metrics are average system fan-out, depth of inheritance and the 'reuse ratio' of the number of superclasses to the total number of classes. Average system fan-out does not distinguish between the different structural relationships that objects may enter into. MOSES also permits the collection of the metrics suggested by Chidamber and Kemerer discussed below.

THE MIT METRICS

Two workers at MIT, Chidamber and Kemerer (1991), developed a suite of six collectable metrics as follows.

Weighted methods per class (WMC) is the sum of the static complexities of the methods of a class. If the complexities are taken to be unity this reduces to a simple count of methods. They do not state how the complexity is to be determined and presumably it could be a subjective estimate or a formal measure like cyclomatic complexity. This is an intra-object metric.

Depth of inheritance tree (DIT), an inter-object metric that should more properly be called depth of inheritance network, is the maximal length of a chain of specializations or the distance from the root of the tree when viewed as a class rather than system metric.

Number of children (NOC) is the fan-in in the classification structure: the number of subclasses. Of course this is a global system metric since classes do not know their children. It is not made clear whether this metric allows for dynamic classification schemes where NOC can change at run time.

Coupling between objects (CBO) is a count of the non-classification structure couplings. It fails to make a distinction between association, composition and usage – effectively treating them all as messaging. This is an inter-object metric.

Response for a class (RFC) is a measure of the structural coupling of the class and the most novel of the six. It counts the number of methods available to the class either directly within it or via one message to another class and could be regarded as closely related to the fan-out of the usage structure. According to Chidamber and Kemerer, RFC should be minimized although this militates against subcontracting.

Lack of cohesion in methods (LCOM) is also innovative. It measures the non-overlapping of sets of instance variables used by the methods of a class. An alternative, operational definition is: the percentage of methods that do not access an attribute, averaged over all attributes. The lowest, and most desirable, value of LCOM occurs when all the methods use all the instance variables and the highest when no instance variable is used by more than one method. This measures structural cohesion but not logical or semantic cohesion and there may be no correlation between the two. High LCOM may be an indicator of the need to split up a class but this should never be done automatically or without due reference to semantic cohesion.

These metrics have been quite widely adopted. For example, the McCabe Tools software product collects five out of six of them, adds more and provides an additional degree of structuring. That is, the McCabe Tool divides its 13 object-oriented metrics into four categories: quality, encapsulation, inheritance and polymorphism. The encapsulation metrics are LCOM together with measures of the features of the class that are public and protected (Pctpub) and the number of accesses to these features (Pubdata). Inheritance measures are the number of root classes (Rootcnt), fan-in, NOC and class level DIT. Polymorphism is measured by WMC, RFC and the percentage of calls not made to overloaded modules (Pctcall). Quality is measured using the maximum cyclomatic and essential complexity of a class's methods and the number of classes that depend on descendants.

The six MIT metrics are also said to be founded on a sound theoretical basis in measurement theory and mathematics. The basis used is Wand's version of Bunge's mathematical ontology (Wand, 1989). Here, the work is less than convincing because this ontology itself suffers from some grave philosophical defects. It is atomistic: it conceives things as reducible to irreducible components. Further, it can probably not stand up to the Phenomenologist critique that an object's identity is independent of its properties (i.e. they could all change), although Whitmire (1997) overcomes this objection by stating that if we perceive two objects as identical, then we have not identified all the important properties; i.e. have not discovered the identities. Whether the demolition of the base affects the correctness of the superstructure is arguable. Having arrived at the proposed metrics by an incorrect route need not necessarily mean that they are flawed.

As remarked above, in some systems NOC may vary at run time due to dynamic classification. I would suggest that max, min, mean and mode values for NOC should be collected in such circumstances.

Coupling depends on interaction. One is tempted to suspect that the type of interaction matters. My solution is to collect separate metrics for all the structures of an object model: classification, composition, usage and association. This view can be applied to fan-out and fan-in and to RFC.

Cohesion based on LCOM is purely structural cohesion. It is logical or conceptual cohesion that matters most from the point of view of reuse. I am also concerned that only instance variables are referred to in these metrics. Class attributes should not be excluded from the definition since they contribute to complexity and cohesion.

Henderson-Sellers *et al.* (1996) found that there were some inconsistencies and errors in the MIT metrics. They reference various versions of the paper by Chidamber and Kemerer (1991, 1993, 1994) which offer radically differing definitions of the CBO and LCOM metrics. This paper remarks that although Chidamber and Kemerer evaluated their suite against the axioms proposed by Weyuker (1988), the latter are known to be inconsistent and have dubious validity. It is shown that the 1991 version of LCOM always gives zero – whatever the input – and that the later version does not discriminate between classes that intuitively have radically different structural cohesion. Furthermore, LCOM seems to increase with cohesion where it should decrease. The other metrics are subjected to a detailed critique as well but that need not concern us directly here. The 1996 paper's main contribution from our perspective is a new definition for LCOM that overcomes all these problems.

Consider a class with m methods $\{M_i\}$ and a attributes $\{A_j\}$. Let $a(M_i)$ represent the number of attributes that M_i accesses. Also, let $m(A_j)$ be the number of methods that access A_j. Define:

$$LCOM^* = \frac{\left(\dfrac{1}{a}\displaystyle\sum_{j=1}^{a} m(A_j)\right) - m}{1 - m}$$

This definition provides a metric that decreases as cohesion increases, gives values in the unit interval and gives values that discriminate classes of intuitively different cohesion (for details see Henderson-Sellers, 1996). This is an improvement over the McCabe version described in the preceding section, which does not give values in the unit interval and therefore makes comparison harder. It turns out that it is possible to construct classes for which LCOM* takes values outside the unit interval. However, if one examines these examples it soon becomes apparent that they have been very badly designed from an OO standpoint. I therefore suggest that the magnitude of a negative value of LCOM* is a measure of the class's degree of 'non-object-orientation'.

The MIT suite was an important and seminal contribution and the flaws that Henderson-Sellers *et al.* point out can easily be corrected as I will show.

CONNASCENCE An intriguing possibility is to attempt to unite coupling and cohesion as is done in Page-Jones' *connascence* metric (Page-Jones, 1992). This generalizes Constantine's classic notion that good design minimizes coupling and maximizes cohesion by defining connascence[2] and three kinds of encapsulation. Level 0 encapsulation represents the idea that a line of code encapsulates a certain abstraction. Level 1 is the encapsulation of procedures into modules and level 2 is the encapsulation provided in object-oriented programming. Two elements of a system are connascent if they share the same history and future or, more exactly, if changes to one may necessitate changes to the other. Good design should eliminate unnecessary connascence and minimize connascence across encapsulation boundaries and maximize it within them. For level 0 and level 1 encapsulation this reduces to the principle of coupling and cohesion. In general, inheritance compromises reuse. The connascence principle tells us that inheritance should be restricted to visible features or that there should be two separate hierarchies for inheriting the implementation and the interface. It would also discourage the use of friends in C++. Page-Jones classifies several kinds of connascence as name, type, value, position, algorithm, meaning and polymorphism. Polymorphism connascence is particularly interesting for object-oriented design and is closely related to the problems of non-monotonic logic. For example, if FLY is an operation of BIRDS and PENGUINS is a subclass of BIRDS then FLY may sometimes fail and sometimes succeed. This causes maintenance problems should the system be changed. Rules, as in SOMA, may be used to avoid this problem, as may the fuzzification of objects and inheritance. It is not yet clear how connascence could be measured in practice.

Another attempt to unify coupling and cohesion can be found in Cox and Novobilski (1991) where a hardware analogy is used to show how objects at different levels can coexist inside an application.

In SOMA, attribute values can be fuzzy sets and inheritance links can have a certainty factor attached. It is unclear whether this fuzziness of attribute values or classification increases or reduces complexity according to the metrics discussed so far. Intuitively one would expect fuzziness to reduce complexity since it does so in other areas of application; e.g. a fuzzy process controller needs fewer rules than a numerical one. The same question arises for multiple inheritance. It is likely that the use of multiple inheritance will reduce WMC but increase some of the inter-object metrics.

Another open question is whether cohesion metrics can be made to deal with the fact that a whole may be greater (more cohesive) than the sum of its parts.

Metrics are often related to reward structures. Those used to measure domain class developers may not be appropriate to application developers and vice versa.

---

[2] Literally, connascence means being 'born together'.

Lorenz and Kidd (1994) seek to draw on their experience of managing object-oriented projects and recommend a list of metrics suitable for such projects together with useful heuristics for their use. Some of the metrics are obvious (such as number of methods per class) and some are novel (such as the number of support classes per key class and the number of scenario scripts). Support classes are those that support the solution without being essential to modelling the business. I would call them 'implementation classes'. Examples include Stacks, Windows, Buttons and so on. The scenario scripts used seem to suffer from the same weakness as use cases since there is no attempt to emphasize their 'stereotypical' character, nor are they reduced to 'atomic' components. SOMA shows how this decomposition gives an important new metric analogous to the function point as we will see below.

The advice given is soundly based in experience. However, fundamentally this is just an arbitrary list of metrics with no theoretical cohesion and no compelling arguments for either including or excluding a particular metric. Little account is taken of other work done in this area (notably that of Henderson-Sellers and his students in Australia) and the book castigates the only work referenced (Chidamber and Kemerer, 1991) for being 'grounded in theory'. For me, this is adding insult to injury: a sound approach to metrics must be grounded in both theory **and** practice. Such a grounding would perhaps reduce the unmanageably long list of metrics given by Lorenz and soften the arbitrary character of some of these metrics. On the other hand Lorenz gives valuable heuristics and advice on thresholds which are not to be found elsewhere in the literature.

De Champeaux (1997) presents three sets of metrics for analysis, design and implementation, each linked to a fairly informal micro-process model. His idea of analysis is very different from my idea of requirements engineering; he sees it as a matter of rewriting an existing requirement document. He also emphasizes the central rôle of state-transition diagrams much more than I do. On the other hand, he also makes use of use cases and insists on defining a domain ontology or vocabulary in ways analogous to those of SOMA. The analysis process is defined by stating how the existence of each deliverable or artefact contributes to the production of other artefacts; notably, in the case of analysis, of class diagrams and sequence diagrams. The metrics for analysis are mostly based on counting such things as vocabulary items, use cases and classes appearing on the various diagrams. These are used to predict the effort associated with the production of analysis artefacts. The danger here, of course, is the creation of a 'deliverables fixation' of the type associated with structured methods; the focus should be on the end-product rather than intermediate deliverables. But in bureaucratic organizations the approach would be popular. All of Chidamber's metrics except LCOM are included in de Champeaux's suite.

De Champeaux makes the absolutely crucial point that analysis objects should be viewed as independent, parallel processors with their own threads of control, whereas design must eliminate this implicit parallelism because implementation objects usually share a single thread per process. De Champeaux pays a lot of attention to eliminating high 'arity' associations. In SOMA we do not need this machinery because of our insistence on uni-directional mappings in place of bi-directional associations. The design process focuses on creating an executable model, mainly from the state transition diagrams. This is then organized into clusters for each distributed process, which are then serialized and optimized. Design metrics focus on quality and effort estimation. Finally, the implementation metrics introduced are all based on C++. However, both the design and implementation metrics are essentially extensions of the metrics introduced for analysis. The product metrics introduced have much in common with the SOMA business object metrics suite discussed in the next section.

In another interesting book on object-oriented metrics, Scott Whitmire (1997) also ties the issue of metrics to the development process. Whitmire's approach is undoubtedly the most theoretically based approach among those discussed so far. Most creditable is his attempt to provide a firm foundation for both his metrics and object modelling in general. He does this using category theory, a branch of applied algebra dealing with abstract mathematical structures, and measurement theory. Briefly, he views a class as a category whose *objects* are attribute domains and state spaces defined on them, and whose *arrows* are the set theoretic projections from the Cartesian product of these domains together with functions representing state transitions. In other words a class is a *diagram* of arrows. These categories then become the objects in a category of categories representing the designed class model. The arrows are functors and represent associations, including inheritance, aggregation and usage relationships. For non-trivial classes these diagrams become extremely complicated and therefore the resultant method is probably too complicated for the average development organization, but it does mark an important step forward in our understanding of both metrics and the foundations of object modelling. One minor problem with Whitmire's approach is that it is not clear that, in this model, classes can be objects; which would mean that the theory would have to be so extended to be compatible with SOMA. Multiple inheritance also is not catered for. Some category theorists might find the categories rather pathological because arrows that represent associations (except inheritance) do not compose. This is quite unlike the categories found in most of mathematics and suggests that a different formulation may be possible. Whitmire provides a recipe for developing metrics rather than merely suggesting things to measure in the manner of the other approaches discussed in this chapter. This again makes his approach rather complex for normal organizations. What is very different is that he proposes a way to measure the goodness of a design. Formal properties are stated for all the metrics developed and considerable attention is paid to getting the measurement scales right.

THE SOMA METRICS

The suite of metrics proposed within SOMA represents an attempt to synthesize and add to the MOSES, MIT and Lorenz work described above. It should also be noted that MOSES and SOMA converge on a single suite of metrics in the OPEN framework.

Measures such as WMC are not quite sufficient to capture the complexity of a SOMA object since the former does not allow for complexity due to rulesets. Our metric allows for this but does not measure the effect of assertions where they are used. This is open to discussion since clearly some assertions stand for rules and should be counted. On the other hand this is more difficult to automate and one could argue that attribute constraints should be counted too. I propose that the following metrics should be collected. In every case, collection can be made automatic by appropriate software at the requirements, specification and code levels.

For the Business Object Model the metrics are:

BM1) The weighted complexity WC_C of each class C, defined as:

$$WC_C = W_A * A + W_M * L_M * M + W_R * N_R * R$$

where
- A = number of attributes and associations
- M = number of operations/methods
- R = number of rulesets
- N_R = number of rules per ruleset * average number of antecedent clauses per rule
- L_M is the proportional excess of SLOCs per method over an agreed, language-dependent standard (this definition ensures that the equation is dimensionally correct)
- W_A, W_M and W_R are empirically discovered weights.

BM2) The fan-outs and fan-ins for all four structures together with their averages.

BM3) The structure depths for the two acyclic structures: Dclass and Dcomp. This generalizes DIT.

BM4) The numbers of abstract and concrete classes.

BM5) The numbers of interface, domain and application objects incorporated into a project.

It should be noted that there is enough information collected here to reconstruct all the MIT metrics except LCOM.

For the action model the metrics are:

AM1) The weighted complexity WC_T of each task T, defined as:
$$WC_T = W_I * I + W_A * A + W_E * E + W_R * N_R * R$$

where
- I = number of objects (in the grammatical sense) per task. Usually this corresponds to the number of noun phrases
- A = number of associated tasks (if any)
- E = number of exceptions or side-scripts
- R = number of rulesets
- N_R = number of rules per ruleset * average number of antecedent clauses per rule
- W_I, W_A, W_E and W_R are empirically discovered weights, which may be zero

if empirical study shows that a factor such as *E* has no effect.

AM2) The fan-outs and fan-ins for all four structures in the use case model together with their averages; e.g. number of exceptions (side-scripts) per task (usage fan-out).

AM3) The structure depths for the two acyclic structures: Dsub and Dcomp.

AM4) The numbers of abstract and concrete tasks.

AM5) The numbers of interface, domain and application tasks incorporated into a project.

AM6) The numbers of external agents, messages and internal agents in the Agent Object Model.

AM7) The number of atomic tasks; i.e. those with no component tasks: the leaf nodes of the task tree.

This last metric, called the number of **task points**, is the most important and most novel SOMA metric. It offers a potential replacement for function points as a measure of overall complexity with the added benefit of automated collection. Furthermore, it can be collected earlier in the life cycle; i.e. at requirements capture.

SLOC measures are poor estimating tools because they are highly language, environment and programmer dependent and estimation is most needed before any language decisions have been made. Function point counts, which address these points, suffer because of the labour-intensive process required to collect them and their poor mapping onto object-oriented systems, event-driven systems, real-time systems, computationally intensive systems, GUIs and the like. What is required is a code-independent measure that can be collected at the requirements capture stage and onwards and which correlates well with the business benefits to be delivered. Fortunately, the SOMA Task Object Model suggests just such a measure and this measure has the additional benefit of being able to be counted automatically. The measure is the number of task points.

Task points represent atomic tasks that the system will help the user carry out. This includes autonomous tasks carried out within the system *en route* to the accomplishment of externally visible tasks. A task is **atomic** with respect to a problem if further decomposition would introduce terms inappropriate to the domain. For example, the register deal task might be decomposed into sub-tasks such as send confirmations, check positions and so on. We could go on decomposing until a level is reached where further decomposition would introduce sentences such as press key with finger. The nouns are no longer in the trading domain, though they may well be in the domain of user interface design. This is a clear rule, though it relies on the fuzzy evaluation of whether a term is a term of a domain or not. In practice, it is nearly always obvious when to stop decomposing. The atomic tasks are the leaf nodes (terminals) of the task tree (network) and the count can be automated by counting the tasks with no component tasks.

It is assumed that each task is expressed in a Subject, Verb, Direct Object,

Preposition, Indirect Object (SVDPI) sentence. The approach also assumes some skill and consistency on the part of developers in identifying when atomic task level is reached. It is recommended that one person, the class librarian is ideal, examine all task models with this in mind; at least at the beginning. Eventually, the cultural norm should be established and consistent.

Task points have two major significant advantages over function points: they can be collected automatically and earlier in the life cycle. Furthermore, they are a metric specifically and deliberately developed as part of an object-oriented approach to system building.

ESTIMATING MODELS   Estimation is a key task in software development. Most traditional estimation methods rely on either experience, using comparison with similar projects, or metrics which depend on first estimating the number of lines of code to be produced. Neither method is appropriate for the estimation of object-oriented systems. The heuristic methods will not work, simply because there is not yet enough experience of this kind of project in the world, and some people claim they lead to bias even in conventional projects. Secondly, the measure of lines of source code also relies on experience and is impossible to use except for a language, such as COBOL, in which many applications have been written within the same industry or organization. The obvious unit of estimation for object-oriented programming, or design for that matter, is the object. A concrete technique with appropriate metrics for object-oriented estimation was proposed by Laranjeira (1990). The only conventional estimation technique likely to be at all useful is Function Points Analysis (Albrecht and Gaffney, 1983). This method may give a rough first estimate if used with care and judgement.

It is proposed that effort estimation will be based on the same model as almost every other estimating technique; i.e.

$$E = a + pT^k$$

where E is effort in staff hours, T is the task point count, p is the inverse of productivity in task points per staff hour (to be determined empirically) and k and a are constants; a may be thought of as start-up and constant overhead costs. Productivity will itself be a function of the level of reuse and may depend of the ratio of domain to application objects in the BOM and on the complexity of the BOM based on weighted class complexity, fan measures and so on. Much empirical work remains to be done in this area.

9.9.2 Process improvement

Collecting metrics is central to process improvement, simply because you cannot know that you have improved upon your process objectively unless you have a measure of the goodness of both process and product. Process improvements that produce inferior products are all too common, as discussed by Morgan (1997). You must therefore measure defects, time to failure, satisfaction ratings and other product metrics, in addition to the SOMA metrics defined above. You need to measure, in addition, productivity: time spent on a project, time taken, resources used, etc. Soft factors should also be included in the metrics programme: educational background of developers, working environment and even personality traits. Then you can begin to see if there are ways to improve, and measure the amount of improvement. Visible success is a great way to motivate developers and gain credibility with business sponsors.

It is currently fashionable to cast process improvement programmes within a so-called 'process maturity model' such as the one promulgated by Humphrey (1989) and the Software Engineering Institute: the SEI Capability Maturity Model. The latter is given false credibility because parts of the US government will not buy from an organization not accredited as 'mature' at some level against this model. It divides organizations into five arbitrary categories labelled: Initial, Repeatable, Defined, Managed and Optimizing. These are in increasing order of brownie points. The absurdity of the labels is evident: how an undefined process can be repeatable beats me! But there is worse to come. It turns out that the cost of reaching the highest level is quite astronomical – and you have to pay a fee to be accredited as such. As far as I know only one organization in the world is at that level. Capers Jones (1994) puts it nicely: 'The kind of uncertainty in mapping the complexities of the real world into the constraints of the artificial taxonomy tends to create "priesthoods" of consulting specialists who assist in dealing with arcane topics.' For these reasons, I am rather against immature and arbitrary process maturity models.

⊟ 9.10 User interface design

The process includes an approach to user interface design. We outline its principles in this section.

THE HISTORY OF THE USER INTERFACE
User interfaces originated with the very first computers in the form of cathode ray tube displays showing base 32 arithmetic for output and plug boards for input. Programming was thus like rewiring the hardware and interpreting the magic symbols that came out. The early machines also made a noise so that experienced operators could guess what sort of thing they were doing and detect abnormalities such as endless loops (a constant whirring sound). Later Hollerith punched cards were used for input and batch line-printers for output. This represented a significant advance in user friendliness – until you dropped a large box of punched cards. The main problem with this approach occurred when the programmer missed a comma from a line of code and discovered that the program would not compile – only after a day or so – because of this simple slip. Paper tape was not so subject to being dropped but tore easily. Long turn-round times began to be addressed when conversational remote job entry (CRJE) was introduced, whereby the programmer could submit jobs via a golf-ball teletype machine attached to a remote computer via

a modem. As television technology became cheaper to manufacture these terminals were gradually replaced with screen terminals which emulated CRJE devices, but quietly. For this reason, these character display terminals were known as 'glass teletypes'. In the 1970s these displays began to be used by users who were not programmers and command line interfaces gave way to simple menu systems and tab-and-fill data entry screens. Meanwhile, Doug Englebart had invented the mouse but no one had yet exploited its potential.

The first well-known commercial application of the mouse came out of the work at Xerox PARC on the Star interface and later emerged in the form of the Apple Lisa and Macintosh. Rodents[3] made it possible to conceive of an entirely different style of user interaction with the display based on the metaphor of pointing and choosing rather than instructing and describing actions. The Xerox/Apple style was emulated by many others and eventually standardized into the systems we are now familiar with, such as MS Windows and X-Windows. There have been attempts to go beyond a Windows-style interface, some based on virtual reality techniques, but little consensus on the next standard is yet evident.

WHY GUI? Graphical user interfaces (GUIs) are popular because it is widely believed that they are easy to use, enhance user and developer productivity and lead to a greater degree of comfort and less stress. A GUI in and of itself is not the secret of productivity; it is a well-crafted GUI that is required. Interface usage also depends on the type of task being undertaken, as we shall see later. For me, greater benefits derive from the consistency of the interface. In Windows, for example, no matter what application is running, the File menu is always at the top left-hand corner of the screen and Help is always the rightmost pull-down menu. Even if you have no mouse, in MS Windows, Alt-F-X *always* closes the application. The exploratory style means that users can explore the structure of the application without commitment to actions. This is often achieved by 'greying out' inapplicable menu entries in the current mode; e.g. you cannot *cut* unless you have selected something, but you can see that cut and paste is supported in the system. An *undo* facility also promotes exploration since it is possible to try an action and then recover from it if the effects are undesirable. A further benefit is the use of a metaphor, the so-called desktop metaphor, to help users transfer knowledge from manual tasks to using the computer. I will discuss such transfer effects in more detail below.

The uses to which GUIs can be put are manifold. They can be used to hide multi-language implementations: systems connected by loosely coupling systems written in different products. A very common use of GUIs is to protect users from the interaction style of old mainframe systems or the complexities of networks. All these usages can be viewed as examples of object wrappers, when the GUI is built using an object-oriented language.

---

[3] We have to call them that because foot-operated mice which run along the floor have been developed and these and the large mice used for specialist graphics work are sometimes known as **rats**.

The apparent, main benefits of graphical user interfaces are consistency, ease of use, learnability and the ease with which multiple applications can be combined. However, there are drawbacks, including extra software, hardware, operational and support costs and more complex software development. The fact that the size of the memory required for an entry level PC has more than quadrupled in two years and the hard disk size gone up by almost an order of magnitude is a tribute to the hardware hunger of GUIs. On the other hand, the cash price of such a machine has not changed appreciably in the same period. Whatever one thinks about this there is no doubt that most organizations will install and standardize around GUIs. These companies will inevitably be using object-oriented tools and will need corresponding software engineering methods. All these extra costs will be paid for by better, more usable, more flexible applications and the consequent business benefits.

9.10.1 Designing the HCI

Design for human – computer interaction (HCI) is like other design problems and the same principles apply. Designed artefacts should be fit for their purpose. They should be natural in behaviour and conform to users' expectations. There should be no unpleasant surprises except where these are introduced deliberately as alarms. Use of the artefact should give feedback on progress of the task being undertaken. They should fit the mental and manual abilities of users. A very common example of bad interface design outside the context of computers concerns door handles. Recently I was walking through an office building with a colleague and, meeting a closed door, I grasped its handle and pushed. Nothing happened because the door only opened toward me. My colleague laughed and remarked that his old headmaster would have shouted: 'Stupid boy! Can't you see that the handle is there to be pulled?'. I had to explain that I had worked for over two years in a building that had handles on both sides of all the doors and that I had often strained myself by pulling doors that should be pushed. In the end I had become totally disoriented in my relationships with all doors. I still find the stupidity of builders or architects that design in this way quite exasperating. Further, someone paid them for the work; more stupid yet! I know of at least two systems that include the helpful advice: Press Enter to Exit. And, as I have to explain patiently to Mac users, to close down Windows you click on **Start**: obviously! As long as users continue to buy them, designers will continue to deliver such daft interfaces.

Similar examples of inane design abound. My feeling is that a good design is one that supports a conversational style of interaction. Barfield (1993) compares a computer with a human servant and pillories bad interface designers by asking how we would respond if such a servant replied to simple requests with sentences like 'Error code 42 Sir!'. Worse, he argues, if it behaves like the servant who, when asked to put a fiction writer's new manuscript in the filing cabinet, returns with the comment: 'Sorry Sir, the filing cabinet was full so I burnt the manuscript.' Something like that happened to me recently.

Criticizing other people's design is far easier than designing something well yourself. This long section attempts to set out a series of guidelines for good UI design, including good practice in the analysis required to design well. A key technique is task analysis, which is widely used by successful designers. We have already met it in Chapter 8. The key observation here is that user-centred design and, especially, the task-centred design favoured by most UI theorists are important for creating usable, useful, correct systems – even where the interface element is not the primary consideration. First, we look at the hardware issues.

SELECTING THE HARDWARE

Hardware for the user interface may be conveniently divided into hardware for input, output or both. There are many kinds of input device available, including plug boards, punched cards, paper tape, keyboards (QWERTY and otherwise), mice, tracker balls, light pens, pressure pens, joysticks, data gloves, graphics tablets, touch screens and microphones. There are several types of touch screen, including scanning infra-red, surface acoustic wave, capacitative overlay, conductive or resistive membrane types. This is not the place to discuss these in detail but continuous capacitative touch screens are probably agreed to be best for most kinds of application. In the common imagination, *voice input* must be the ideal form of input for the majority of tasks. There is no learning time because we mostly know a natural language already. It leaves our hands and eyes free and imposes a very low cognitive load due to the commonplace character of speech. On the other hand there are many disadvantages. Speech can be noisy and distracting to others in the work environment and voice input itself needs silence since ambient noise can interfere with the interpretation. Complex software is needed and in practice there is a trade-off between the training time required and a limited vocabulary. Correct interpretation can be affected by illness, alcohol, the weather and so on.

Though voice input is attractive for many applications, especially those where the user's hands are not free, there are problems with the recognition of continuous speech. To see why this is so consider the sentence: IT'S VERY HARD TO WRECK A NICE BEACH. Now try saying it out loud a few times, rapidly.[4] There are now continuous speech recognition systems but their vocabulary is very limited. The topic remains essentially in the research domain. Most speech input systems make fairly precise impositions on what can be said and how or require time-consuming training to recognize one user's voice patterns.

As well as devices for input, there are several options for the output devices including screens, printers and loudspeakers. Networks are both input and output devices. Only input devices, such as screens, raise serious HCI issues, not mostly concerned with physical ergonomics.

Virtual reality, which immerses the user in a simulated world and provides feedback through multiple senses as well as multiple media, offers perhaps the greatest challenge of all to user interface designers. Fortunately, all interactions in such a world can be described as interactions with objects satisfying contracts.

---

[4] If there was someone within earshot while you were doing this, they are probably agreeing with you by now that is indeed very hard to recognize speech.

However, it is not yet clear what the new psychological factors associated with immersion are. Many of the basic UI principles may need amendment and much care will be needed since there are many medical and social dangers.

Studies have shown that there is no 'best' input or output device. What is most appropriate and usable depends not only on the application but on the precise task or set of tasks being carried out. One unpublished study, carried out by Logica, concluded that foreign exchange traders would benefit from a keyboard but that a bond trader might do better using a graphics tablet for input. Given changes in both the task and the technology, whether these results apply today is unclear.

STYLES OF INTERACTION

There are many different ways of interacting with a computer system. These include menus, forms, command languages, natural language and graphical user interfaces. As with input and output devices, the best style of interaction depends mainly on the task being undertaken. There is no generic best style.

Menus have the advantage that they can be learned quickly. They generally require fewer keystrokes than other styles and can use dialogue management tools. Menus help to give structure to the dialogue and make it far easier for the designer to manage errors. However, there are several disadvantages too. The menu tree may be deep and difficult to remember and navigate. This may slow frequent users down significantly. Menus consume screen space, are inflexible and impose a need for a rapid display rate. The most significant factor with menu interfaces is the need for the task analysis to be complete.

Forms-based interfaces are mainly suitable for data entry and tend to make it easier. Users of such interfaces require modest training but they are not very good for casual users. They too consume screen space and tend to be inflexible. On the plus side, form generators can readily be used to cut down development times compared to coding everything at the 3GL level.

Modal dialogue boxes, where the dialogue is constrained strictly to the questions and values in the current box, represent a sort of combination of the forms- and menus-based approaches.

Command languages have the advantage of infinite flexibility and are usually tailorable with macros or a programming language. However, they are notoriously hard to learn, hard to remember and easy to make errors with.

The oldest command languages are natural languages and it has often been remarked that the computer should speak the user's language and interact in English or some other natural language. This would mean that the users had no new commands to learn but there are several very serious disadvantages. Natural languages are expressive but verbose and ambiguous. In work situations, even without computers, a more formal or structured subset of language is often used. Consider, for example, the use of 'roger' in military communications or technical jargon in most trades. Natural language conversations are invariably based on implicit, shared understanding and the fact that when this breaks down clarification is often needed – and this will slow dialogues unbearably. This and the context sensitivity of language means that artificial intelligence techniques are required.

Unfortunately these techniques are not very advanced yet and some of us believe that a speaking computer would be a thinking computer and that that is either impossible or so far beyond the scope of rational human engineering as to be absurd (Graham, 1994c). Natural language front-ends to databases have been written and exist as commercial products, but these do not attempt to solve the general language understanding problem; preferring rather to permit natural enquiries in a restricted context, based on a shared model of the data dictionary and its structure.

9.10.2 Fundamentals of cognitive psychology

In order to design a good user interface it is necessary to know a little about the way the human mind and body works. In particular it is useful to know how memory storage and retrieval works, how the eye responds to colours, what positions lead to fatigue and so on. The bodily aspects of human–computer interaction are often referred to as Ergonomics, though strictly this subject encompasses the mental aspects as well.

According to current theories of cognitive psychology, **long-term memory** (LTM) stores knowledge and data. To be used these memories must be activated and this takes time. They are normally stored in an inactivated state though not necessarily in a separate location from those immediately accessible in what used to be called short-term memory. **Working** or **activated memory** is limited and transitory. Items in working memory can be accessed directly and quickly. The activation of the linkages to these memories decays over time. Miller (1956) discovered that activated memory could hold a maximum of between five and nine items or *chunks* before filling up in some sense. These limits depend on the meaning of the material and an expert's chunk can represent far more knowledge than that of a novice. It is a crude mistake to interpret this as meaning, for example, that there should never be more than 7±2 items presented on a screen. For example, when a novice sees a display of a chess board s/he sees 32 pieces. A grand master, however, may see only five high level game patterns which s/he has chunked through long practice. Further, the units are stored in classification, composition and other structures which assist recall. **Rehearsal** of cues helps storage in LTM and retrieval, through reinforcing commonly used activation paths in the brain's neural network. Another way of activating these paths more quickly is **priming** where recalling one item helps to activate another semantically related one. Priming helps activate concepts in working memory (WM). When a user moves from one system's interface to that of another there are **transfer effects** due to both rehearsal and priming. These transfer effects can be both positive (beneficial) and negative (harmful) from the point of view of usability. The more that user interface designers are aware of memory characteristics the better they can do their job.

Other memory effects that may be significant include **interference**, which occurs when priming may activate the wrong things or at least activate memories that interfere with what should be recalled. This is an example of a negative transfer effect. Positive transfer effects can exploit the ability of users to classify their knowledge and this helps with the consistency and coherence of an interface. Generally speaking, positive effects will occur when the designer copies the structure of existing and well-known tasks. The success of the desktop metaphor can be regarded as evidence for this proposition, as can the popularity of tricks such as 3D button controls that appear to depress as they are clicked. A classic of negative effects was the use of the F3 key for the help function in WordPerfect when most packages use F1. When a WordPerfect user presses F1 the wrong things are primed and when trying to recall what key gives help there is no such support. An example of the exploitation of positive transfer effects is the support for Lotus syntax in Excel.

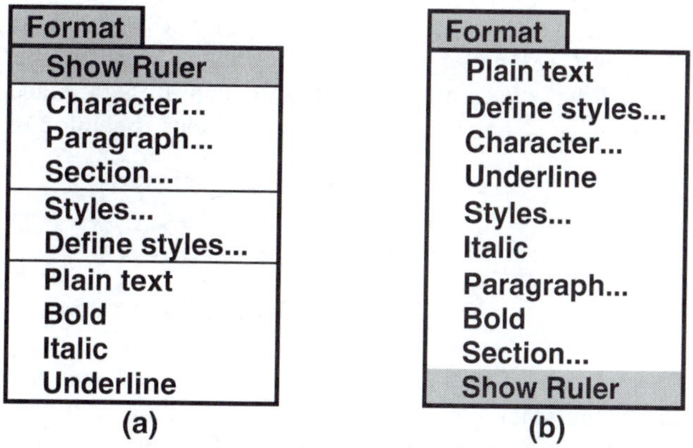

Format		Format
Show Ruler		**Plain text**
Character...		**Define styles...**
Paragraph...		**Character...**
Section...		**Underline**
Styles...		**Styles...**
Define styles...		**Italic**
Plain text		**Paragraph...**
Bold		**Bold**
Italic		**Section...**
Underline		**Show Ruler**
(a)		**(b)**

Figure 9.21 **(a)** Structured menu; **(b)** unstructured menu.

Structure and organization help priming. This can be seen readily by examining Figure 9.21. In 9.21(a) related items are adjacent and the lines emphasize this. In 9.21(b) there is no such organization and the menu is confusing to read and difficult to remember.

Face		Face
Courier		Courier
Helvetica		Helvetica
Script		*Script*
Symbol		Συμβολ
Times		Times

Figure 9.22 Priming the memory of typefaces.

Priming effects occur between semantically related words. For example, saying CAT primes DOG; showing *ITALIC* may prime **bold**. Another example of the beneficial exploitation of priming effects in a user interface occurs when the actual appearance of an item is used to reinforce the memory of what selecting that item may imply, often using a visual cue or an icon. Figure 9.22 illustrates this with an example of two different menu designs for the typeface selection within a word processor. The rightmost menu clearly helps the user remember what typefaces like Courier and Times Roman look like. However, this can go too far. A user unfamiliar with the Greek alphabet might well be very confused by the Hellenic appearance of the Symbol face. Priming is a context-sensitive effect and this should be understood by designers. For example, CAT could prime X-RAY rather than DOG in the context of medical diagnosis.

This example raises a general point about the use of symbols, icons and mnemonics. Icons are culturally dependent and their use depends on background knowledge that may not be shared by all users. For example, consider the symbol shown in Figure 9.23 for a moment. You either know what it means immediately or, I suggest, will never guess. Here is a clue. Most European or American readers over 35 will have used a device with this icon in its interface. The answer will be given later in the chapter. It is usually a good idea to reinforce icons with words.

Figure 9.23 An icon.

There are several guidelines that can be deduced from a knowledge of how users act when reading displays. Research has shown that the first items read from a list tend to be stored more readily in LTM. This is known as the **primacy effect**. The last items in a list tend to be stored in WM; the **recency effect**. One corollary of this is the need for interfaces to be standardized across applications and stable in time. Standard interfaces also exploit the classification structures of memory.

Standard user interfaces are important because of the memory limitations of users. The chief advantage for me of a GUI is that most applications work in the same way and I can utilize positive transfer when closing a window or calling for help because the positions of the features are standard. In my opinion, this is more important than ease of use itself.

Another important principle of user interface design that derives from an understanding of psychology is exploiting **closure**. We are all familiar with the 'I came in here for something but can't remember what' syndrome. It occurs because of the human tendency to be satisfied with tasks once we have achieved closure in one respect; we tend to omit to complete ancillary tasks. This is why most bank ATMs make you take your card before taking the money. The alternative sequence is likely to cause errors because once you have the cash (closure of main task) you are likely to depart, forgetting the card and receipt. Unfortunately for the street sweepers the same principle is rarely applied to the receipt as well. One of the CREWS patterns discussed in Chapter 7 is based on closure.

Cognitive dissonance occurs when a false consciousness is created to explain a bad design. Users create explanations for doing stupid things. If you do something often enough and have worked hard to learn how to do it, you will often invent reasons for continuing to do so. In this way bad designs become right by usage and bugs become features. Having invested the learning time you can make yourself an indispensable resource as the source of knowledge about the product. Now you can be the expert to whom others refer, even though a better designed product would eliminate the need for any expertise. I have observed this often with impenetrable mainframe operating systems, otiose programming languages such as RPG and write-only macro languages such as that of Lotus 123 and its ilk. Perhaps the QWERTY keyboard could be regarded as a particularly well-known example of this phenomenon.

Given this very high level knowledge of psychological principles, we can now establish some practical principles and guidelines for HCI design.

9.10.3 Principles for HCI design

Human computer interaction (HCI) involves computers, users, tasks, and requirements. For a time, user-centred design was emphasized. However, it is now widely realized that the user is not a stable given, because users adopt varying rôles in interacting with a computer system. The stable feature is often the task being performed for the rôle. Therefore, this section and this whole book focus on task-centred design. HCI uses principles from computer science, psychology, sociology, anthropology, engineering, aesthetics and many other areas. This book emphasizes insights from psychology, software engineering and knowledge engineering but attempts to take account of all other influences. The main insight from knowledge engineering is that the user interface includes the user's knowledge of the system and the system's model of the user. A personal insight that has greatly influenced this presentation is that most user interfaces are dreadful.

It is crucial that the interface designer, like the software engineer, does not stop at analysing and automating existing manual practices. Computers can change the tasks they were designed to assist with and this is often their largest contribution. Word processing has largely changed the nature of work in many offices and the impact of the web continues the trend.

HCI design involves the following issues.

- Functionality: How does the interface help users carry out tasks and how does it impede them? Does the interface itself make something possible or impossible?
- Aesthetics.
- Acceptability.
- Structure.
- Reliability.
- Efficiency.
- Maintainability.
- Extensibility.

- Cost.
- Usability, covering: Learnability; Memorability; Productivity; Propensity to make errors; Support for tasks (task analysis); Safety; Range of users; and Suitability for different locations and conditions.

Object-oriented programming contributes to maintainability, extensibility and some aspects of usability. Prototyping is widely seen as essential for the production of usable interfaces. Some authorities recommend the use of specialist graphic or industrial designers as part of the development team and some go further, suggesting the complete separation of the UI development within the life cycle. I think that this is a mistake and that sound practices of software engineering and object-oriented methods should integrate the specialist skills of interface designers into those of software developers in general. There is a danger here that my remarks will be interpreted to mean that developers can just design the interface from the use cases; which is in fact what RUP recommends. Of course, the use cases do **define** the permissible interactions, but we must also **design** each interaction. To do this requires the developer to become an expert UI designer. Because GUIs are so important, I believe that most developers should acquire such skills as the norm; if you can't then you'll have to hire a specialist.

It is remarkable that the most liked features of a given GUI are often the aesthetic ones. One of the most popular innovations in windows systems, for example, was the 3D push button that appears to depress when clicked or held clicked. It apparently contributes nothing, but is loved by users to the extent of being a prerequisite for all such systems nowadays.

General HCI principles are rare, though some have been suggested. IBM's (1991) CUA gave a set of remarkably clear and complete guidelines that are compatible with an object-oriented approach. It incorporated task analysis, user surveys, site visits and usability testing within the approach and constructs three models representing user, designer and programmer views on the interface and underlying system. CUA emphasized reducing user memory load, consistency and placing the user in command of the interface. In particular, in support of the last principle, it recommends not blaming users for errors, parsimonious use of modes with pre-emption to control them, immediate feedback, undo, accommodating users with different skill levels, providing helpful messages, customizability and transparency of the interface. Memory loads are reduced by using meaningful class interfaces to control interaction and using concrete instances and examples wherever possible. The CUA approach to consistency exploits the principles of aesthetics, continuity and priming via clear standards and visual metaphors. OO processes such as FDD, RUP and Perspective are deficient in this area.

GUEPs   Thimbleby (1990) introduces the concept of Generative User-Engineering Principles (GUEPs) – for both designers and users. Typical GUEPs he identifies include the following.

- Recognize and exploit closure.

- WYSIWYG = What You See Is What You Get!
- Fix the documentation and then make the program conform to it.
- The designer should be able to explain the interface concisely and completely.
- The designer must ensure that the user can construct an appropriate internal, mental model of the system

He also introduces a number of formal or algebraic GUEPs as follows.

- *Idempotence* $[T = T^2]$. Some operations should have no effect when reiterated. For example, when the escape key returns to the main menu hitting it twice should have no further effect. When deleting files, one should not be able to re-press the delete key to delete the next file without some other interaction intervening. The cut, copy and paste actions should also be idempotent. Idempotence is particularly important when the type-ahead buffer is active since unintentional actions might otherwise be performed when the machine cannot keep pace with typing.
- *Distributivity* $[A*(B+C) = A*B+A*C]$. This GUEP says that distributing operations over their arguments can enhance usability and convenience by reducing input. For example: 'delete file1; delete file2' should be equivalent to 'delete file1, file2'. In MS Windows Explorer, *delete file* distributes over *select file*, so that you can select a whole bunch of files and delete them at one stroke.
- *Commutativity* $[A*B = B*A]$. This says that the order of operations should not be important unless order is significant. For example, cursor movement (except at the screen boundaries) with the right and left arrow keys successively should leave the cursor position unchanged. This principle tends against the common modern innovation of permitting mouse wrap-around where the mouse appears on the opposite side of the screen when moved past the boundary.
- *Substitutivity* means putting an expression in place of a constant, as can be done in most programming languages or spreadsheets.
- *Associativity* $[A*(B*C) = (A*B)*C]$. This principle is equivalent to that of modelessness.

Modes in a user interface are defined as 'variable information in the computer system affecting the meaning of what the user sees and does'. In a **modal** system the user is required to know what mode the system is in because the same action may have quite different effects in different modes.

It is commonly agreed that modes should be avoided but that they are sometimes necessary. For example, having *user* and *novice* modes is widely agreed to be almost a principle in its own right. Certainly the system should inform the user of the current mode and it is good practice to attract attention to the change by a change of colour in the mode indicator, a status bar or some such device. Examples of modes in an interface include: pressing the ON button on a typical calculator, where the mode is either *on* or *off* and the effect is different in each case; a 'Cannot save file – disk not formatted' message reveals a mode; as does 'Overwrite existing file?'. Dialogue boxes are usually modal in that the behaviour of other visible options is suspended while they appear; the behaviour of part of the screen has thus changed. The notion of modes is closely related to that of polymorphism; polymorphic interfaces are precisely modal. However, what is useful in a language is not necessarily good in an interface.

It is very helpful to provide users with information about the context within which their actions will be interpreted. This includes information on state dependencies and modes and should explain the current task with its pre-conditions, post-conditions and side effects. Modes should only be used where it is absolutely necessary to restrict the user's freedom of interaction. Temporal modes can be used to enforce a certain sequence of operations but this implies burdening the user with a heavy load on memory. This should never be done useless out-of-sequence actions are catastrophic. The commonest example of this is the excessive use of cascaded modal dialogue boxes where a simple data entry form would do better. Spatial modes are common when several things are possible but only one can be done at a time. Highlighting icons and changing the mouse pointer are good ways to draw attention to spatial modes. Other contextual information can be given in a status bar, such as the state of the irritatingly-close-to-the-main-keyboard 'insert' key on most PCs.

It is generally wise to include *undo* and *redo* facilities to encourage exploratory learning and protect users from catastrophic errors. However, *undo* and modelessness can be incompatible as Thimbleby (1990) demonstrates, though the argument is too intricate to summarize here. It is largely because undoing multiple actions may change the state of the system in other ways. Modern interfaces often respond 'can't undo' when they encounter this situation.

Thimbleby gives the following GUEPs for modes, breaking them down into GUEPs for pre-emptive, inertial, input and output modes along with a general principle of **equal opportunity**.

- *Pre-emptive modes.* You should be able to do anything anywhere (e.g. there should be no Y/N questions or immovable dialogue boxes).
- *Inertial modes.* The layout of successive screens should change as little as possible. When you go back everything should be as you left it. The most [recently|likely|frequently] used menu selection should be highlighted.
- *Input modes.* The system should be sufficiently consistent to use with the display switched off (e.g. q or Alt-F-X for quit).
- *Output modes.* WYSIWYG.
- *Equal opportunity.* Output can become input and vice versa (e.g. aperture or shutter priority cameras).

A well-known example of equal opportunity is Query By Example (QBE), a widely used query method for relational and pseudo-relational databases. QBE offers the user a blank form such as the one in Figure 9.24. The user may then type fixed values for **Dept** and **Salary** and QBE will return all records which match the pattern. This is not dissimilar in principle from what occurs with Prolog queries which are resolved by pattern matching too. The **equal** opportunity arises because the user may choose **any** value to fix and is not constrained to a fixed, pre-designed dialogue, such as:

```
Enter Dept: Sales
Enter Salary: >10,000
<list of matching records>
```

Cut and paste facilities usually give equal opportunity, or at least should do.

Name	Dept	Salary
?	Sales	>10,000

Figure 9.24 Query By Example in database enquiry systems.

Thimbleby gives the example of a calculator of the sort illustrated in Figure 9.25(a). Simple calculators are not equal opportunity because the result and the operands are not interchangeable. For example, I can put in '13 * 4 =' and will (with luck and a good battery) get '52'; but I cannot put in '? * 4 = 52' and expect the unknown to be computed as '13'. Incidentally, these devices also have poor feedback in the interface. If you want to check that 0 * 0 = 0, you may equally well believe that the device is not working as that the algebra is vindicated.

Figure 9.25(b) illustrates an improved design based on this GUEP; set the symbols for the two button displays and put in any two numbers, and the third will display a consistent result. We could further improve the design by not using 0 as the default display.

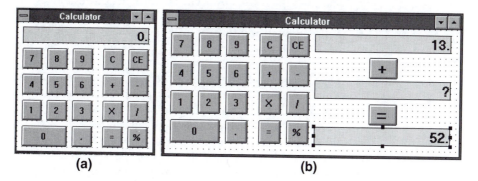

(a)   **(b)**

Figure 9.25 (a) Simple calculator; **(b)** equal opportunity calculator.

Other design principles that we advocate are the following.

- **WYSIWYG.** I have mentioned this term already without explaining it. It stands for What You See Is What You Get and implies the principle that all forms of output should be the same; e.g. the layout, fount and size of characters that appear on a screen will be exactly what a printer produces.

- **WYSIWYCU** stand for What You See Is What You Can Use. If there is an object on the screen you should be able do something to it or with it and what that something is should be as natural and obvious as possible. Future computer systems may, I hope, generalize this to: WYKAIWYCU (What You Know About Is What You Can Use). I know about cut and paste. Why can't I use it in a typical modal dialogue box?

- The principle of **commensurate effort** states that it should be as hard to delete something as to create it; as hard to undo as to do. Steve Jobs' slogan 'Simple things should be simple, difficult things should be possible' is a rephrasing of this principle.

- The interface should provide a **sense of progress**. Feedback is needed for this because effects can be thus related to causes and allows the user to see if the results of each step are contributing to the overall task. Slow tasks or network delays should be made visible in this way, so that the user can tell if the system has really crashed or is just plain slow. Changing the mouse pointer to an hour glass is a helpful and often used technique but one can still wonder whether the system has hung. Providing an estimate of the anticipated time in the form of a gauge is useful in such contexts.

- **Non-pre-emption**. This is a good principle because it restricts the flexibility of the interface and the range of tasks to which it can be applied. On the other hand, there is sometimes a real need for pre-emption to prevent catastrophic, inadvertent errors. The user might erase several pages by accident, delete or overwrite files unintentionally, forget to save some important work, lock the keyboard or system inadvertently or fill memory and abort the session by accident. Such dangerous moves are candidates for pre-emptive prompts.

- **Self-demonstrability**. Consider context-sensitive help, tutorials and – best of all – a completely intuitive interface based on transfer effects from a suitable metaphor.

- **Options should be settable by the user**. For example, the Microsoft Mouse driver offers options for wrapping the pointer round to the opposite screen edge and snapping its position to the latest OK button to appear in a dialogue box. Both these options are useful but to the experienced user just lead to 'mouse creep' as the physical position is constantly at variance with his expectations. Fortunately they can be switched off.

- **Avoid frequent channel switching**. Frequent switching of input between keyboard and mouse is evidently undesirable. Distracting messages from other screen areas than the one where attention is directed should be avoided, as should moving the focus of attention around too much.

So much for principles, now for some practical advice on user interface design.

9.10.4 Guidelines for user interface design

In the context of a user interface, both the user and the system must fulfil their responsibilities toward each other based on the known use cases. The responsibilities of the user include knowing what tasks can be attempted, being able to perform the procedures needed to accomplish these tasks, understanding and interpreting messages (including their interpretation under different modes) and being able to use the appropriate I/O devices. The responsibilities of the system include those of helping the user to carry out the tasks specified during design, responding correctly to commands, pre-empting destructive input, meeting performance constraints and sometimes explaining itself to the user. These responsibilities are task oriented rather than user oriented because the same user may have quite different responsibilities when adopting a different rôle when a different set of tasks is implied. For example, the same user might approach the systems as a manager enquiring on performance or as a data entry clerk adding new financial assumptions.

Designers should remember that there are considerable variations among users. Icons – images – are culturally dependent as demonstrated by the icon in Figure 9.23. For those who have still not guessed the meaning of this icon, it represents the choke of an automobile. Recognizing it as such depends either entirely on memory or on the knowledge that a carburettor contains within it a 'butterfly': a device consisting of a flat metal plate that pivots about an axial pin to allow more or less air into the combustion process. Once you know this, the meaning is obvious. If you don't have this fundamental engineering knowledge, you have to remember the meaning. Furthermore, users vary widely in their visual ability and will react accordingly. In addition to this natural variation in ability there may also be very great variation due to handicaps such as colour blindness, fingers missing, fatigue, illiteracy, memory disorders, deafness and so on.

The **power law of practice** says that practice has a log-linear effect on skill or that practice makes perfect. The more opportunity the users have to explore the interface the better they will become at using it. This implies that both regular use and an exploratory style will help. It also tells us that systems that will be used by infrequent users need more attention to the user interface.

Users come to the system with different backgrounds and knowledge levels. Psychology tells us that during skill acquisition knowledge is first stored as **declarative knowledge**, often in the form of rules and objects to which those rules apply, and can be directly recalled as such. Practice helps people store associations between items and form chunks based on these associations; this is **associative knowledge**. More practice compiles the rules into **procedural knowledge** by which stage it is often inaccessible to consciousness; as with the knowledge of how to ride a bicycle or read a sentence. On this basis designers should design for the knowledge level of the users they anticipate using the systems and preferably provide both novice and expert modes.

Here are some commonly used heuristics for user interface modelling which add to the above principles.

- Use strong, natural metaphors and analogies.
- Keep it simple (KISS).
- Model the domain objects directly.
- Use semantic structures (classification, composition, usage, association).
- Minimize semantic primitives.
- Capture rules.
- Remember that documentation, training and the user's knowledge are all part of the user interface.

Note the similarity with the guidelines for constructing object-oriented models to be found in earlier chapters.

DIALOGUE DESIGN

Dialogue design is a problem for all user interfaces, graphical or otherwise. Much work outside computer science may be drawn upon. Relevant fields include discourse analysis and semiotics. Speech act theory (Austen, 1962; Searle, 1969) is particularly relevant to groupware systems (Winograd and Flores, 1986) and has influenced SOMA's approach to requirements modelling as discussed in Chapter 8. Suchman (1987) applies anthropological and ethnomethodological principles to the design of photocopiers. Johnson (1992) describes a number of research attempts to formalize interaction using command language grammars and task action languages. Neither approach is yet proven to yield significant improvements in practice. Perhaps the most important observation that can be made in this context is that dialogues depend on shared understanding and knowledge of a common domain. This has long been known to designers of computerized natural language systems where it would be a wonderful achievement to get a computer to understand the sentence 'time flies like an arrow' because of the use of simile but how much harder it is to expect the same machine to respond intelligently, and soon after the last remark, to the observation that 'fruit flies like a banana'. We already made use of the idea of a **task-action grammar** when we expressed use cases and other tasks as **SVDPI** sentences of the form:

Subject – Verb – Direct.Objects – [Preposition – Indirect.Objects]

Typically, the verb will be a transitive verb. The subject corresponds to either an agent or to some active component or system.

Dialogues are used for several reasons: to give commands, to refine a common goal and plan tasks to achieve it, to convey information, data or knowledge, to pass the time. Most system dialogues are concerned with commands and conveying information and data. Commands imply a commitment on the part of the recipient to carry out the task mentioned. All interactions initiated by the user should therefore give an observable result, either confirming that the task is complete and giving any resultant information or reporting an exception. This goes beyond the goal of the use case. In other words, well-designed systems are *helpful*. They should also be *forgiving* of user errors.

Expert systems often include explanation facilities though the latter are more costly to write than is often supposed. Sometimes therefore a dialogue consists of an explanation that modifies the user's model of the system. If the user has a good model of a system, s/he will find it easier to use. Good feedback as well as explanation help the user to develop and refine a model. If the system has a model of the user it will be able to respond more appropriately. Examples of the latter occur frequently in intelligent computer-aided learning where the system asks easier questions of novices based on their test scores, or in systems that have a *novice* and *expert* mode switch of some sort.

Here are some heuristics for dialogue design.

- Minimize input movements.
- Maximize input bandwidth/channels.
- Use words and language carefully.
- The interface should look good.
- Be consistent (keys, positioning, etc.).
- Keep the system modeless or provide a high level of context-sensitive feedback.
- A natural response time is desirable.
- Process continuity should be sought.
- Ease of use should be paramount.
- Make your system customizable.
- Make it non-pre-emptive.
- Follow standards.

Good dialogue design requires consistency, informative feedback and simple error handling. Frequent users should be able to take shortcuts. The system should exploit and indicate the phenomenon of closure. *Undo/redo* facilities are often useful but can be problematic in cases where some actions cannot be consistently undone or redone. Dialogues should be user driven and not modal, when possible. The designer should attempt to reduce the load placed on the working memory of the user – exploiting priming, transfer effects, closure and other devices. Some designers stress that the use of words and language itself can be important. It is reported, for example, that some female users are disturbed by words like *abort*. Table 9.3 illustrates this point.

Table 9.3 Use of language in error messages.

Error message	Evaluation
ABORT: error 451	Bad
I'm tremendously sorry but I have discovered that a file you want to use is already open (error number 451).	Better but verbose
Error number 451. File already open. This error normally occurs when you forgot to close the file at the end of a previous subroutine.	Better but tedious
Error number 451: File already open. Explain?<Y/N>:	Good-ish
Left as an exercise to the reader!	PERFECT

Error messages should be consistent, friendly and constructive, informative, precise and use the users' terminology. Multiple levels of message are often helpful. Hypertext *help* systems are a simple way to meet most of these requirements.

Command languages should exhibit uniform abbreviation rules, be consistent and follow standards. Counter-examples from DOS include multiple ways of abbreviating directory commands (CHDIR, CD, DIR, etc.). Also, in different operating systems from the same manufacturer it used to be common to find several words being used for the same purpose; e.g. CATALOG/DIRECTORY or HELP/ASSIST/AID.

GAINING ATTENTION AND USING COLOUR

There are many tricks that designers employ for getting a user's attention to focus on a particular screen location, datum or message. Galitz (1981) reports that the guidelines provided in Table 9.4 have proved effective. Colour is useful for gaining attention but one should be aware that the eye is not colour sensitive at the periphery. It can help in emphasizing the logical organization of a screen, facilitating subtle discrimination and improving aesthetics. Use it parsimoniously. Beware of monochrome ports; i.e. people running an application on a black and white screen that was developed on a colour one and finding that certain contrasts obscure a function. This is more of a problem with printers than screens nowadays. Beware of poor contrast combinations. Allow users to change the colour scheme and above all be consistent. Another reason for avoiding thoughtless use of colour is the very large number of people, especially men, who have some degree of colour blindness.

Table 9.4 Gaining attention.

Intensity	up to 2 levels
Point size	up to 4
Founts	up to 3
Blinking	2–4 Hz
Colour	up to 5
Sound	soft tones except for emergencies
Symbols	bullets, arrows, boxes, lines

Other guidelines for using colour effectively were identified by MacDonald (1993) and, adding some deriving from my own experience, may be stated as follows.

- Use colour parsimoniously. Use no more than twelve colours and only five for critical tasks.
- Use colour to increase information flow. Colours should relate semantically connected items. Colour changes should nearly always be used to indicate mode changes to attract attention to them.
- Take advantage of colour associations such as red/danger but beware of cultural variations (white is the colour of mourning in China). Use industry-standard associations where possible; e.g. the colour coding of

electrical wiring, or red and yellow for healthy tissue in medical applications.

- Allow for human limitations. The eye is usually more sensitive to yellow and green than red or blue. The latter are therefore poor for displaying detail or small text. The luminance ratio between foreground and background should be 10:1. Embolden dark characters on light backgrounds. Use desaturated colours for backgrounds to avoid fatigue. Avoid bright colours at the display extremities to avoid flicker effects. Grey is usually best for this. Use complementary colours to avoid problems for colour-blind users.
- Consider the task being performed. Typeface design matters for textual presentation. Realism matters for pictures.
- Treat colour as part of the whole interface. Let the user change the colour scheme. Be consistent. Use colour as you use menu design – as a simplifier of tasks.
- Think about how the user will cope with motion, especially when using a mouse. When I upgraded my processor once I found that drag-and-drop, a feature I made much use of, had become unusable – simply because the screen scrolled too quickly for me to control the drop point. Mouse movement and screen refreshment or scrolling should accelerate in proportion to the time the button is depressed to overcome such problems.

It is often effective to prototype in monochrome and introduce colours later. Further, one should not clutter display. The same technique, sound or colour should indicate related items. Response times should normally be under one second. Messages should indicate significant variations. Pace-induced stress should be avoided. Novices should be allowed more time.

USABILITY TESTS AND METRICS

Evaluation of the user interface is very important. HCI reviews and expert walkthroughs are usually enormously useful. Other valuable evaluation techniques include questionnaires, observational studies and test script reports. Useful GUI metrics include the time it takes to learn an operation or to use a whole system, the time it takes to carry out a particular task, the average user's error rate, satisfaction indices and the skill retention over time. These metrics imply that a budget for experimentation and data collection be created. Also, it should be noted that the existing system should be measured with respect to these metrics during requirements capture if the metrics are to be of use in assessing benefits.

For mass market products it is often worth investing in full-scale usability workshops wherein trial users are recorded, observed and measured carrying out common operations. This is usually too expensive for custom developments but would be worthwhile for systems going into very wide use or where paybacks are very high and sensitive to usability. Observational studies of any kind imply the need for usability metrics to be agreed. One can measure learnability by comparing task execution times before and after extended use. Usability testing is easier if it is supported by specific software support tools although this is most beneficial for mature products where comparisons with earlier versions are possible. Usability testing also uses task analysis as a key technique.

Usability tests should examine users' rôles, skill levels, frequency of use and the possible social, cultural and organizational variations. Use case analysis emphasizes the centrality of user rôles; that is, neither the users nor their rôles but the combination of a user adopting a rôle: an actor. This notion combines the skill level and organizational rôle in a single, finer-grained concept. Usability studies may further distinguish computer and application skill levels and most approaches to HCI use a simple knowledge-level model such as:

1. Beginner (no knowledge);
2. Learner (knowledge incomplete, encoded as rules);
3. Competent (knowledge complete, compiled and not accessible to consciousness);
4. Expert (knowledge subject to critique and refinement).

Usability testing requires careful experimental design and statistical analysis. It is therefore expensive. At the simplest level it must identify the categories of the most frequent users, such as: frequent, competent with computers, domain learners, English-speaking or well-educated. The tests should take account of transfer effects between different environments and this may, for example, lead to the need for a user interface that looks the same on different platforms. An additional difficulty with testing GUIs arises from their graphical nature. Whereas a command line interface can be tested by producing a test harness that compares textual output across trials, often GUI tests have to compare bitmaps of output. This is complicated by the need to ignore irrelevant variations, such as the final position of the mouse pointer, which makes careful design of the tests very important. For all this, big savings can result from thorough usability engineering.

TASK ANALYSIS

One of the most important techniques available to the interface designer is task analysis. We have used it extensively in earlier chapters. Early versions of task analysis were developed independently, and somewhat differently, in the USA and Britain during the 1950s. In both places, the motivation and background was mainly training needs analysis to help overcome a chronic post-war labour and skills shortage. The British concentrated on the hierarchical decomposition of tasks and on taxonomies of human skills, while the Americans focused on issues such as psychometric testing. Substantive tasks were decomposed into their requisite psychological abilities, viewed as perceptual, motor and problem solving skills. The model of human cognition was fairly primitive at this time and not able to analyse complex tasks such as programming.

A **task** is an activity or set of actions undertaken by an agent assuming a rôle to change a system's state to some goal state. Goals may have subgoals and be achieved by executing procedures (sets of actions). It is a matter of some skill to set goals at the appropriate level; neither too abstract nor too specific. Tasks involve objects, actions and taxonomies (classification structures). Sometimes the goals are clear. In other cases the goal is not known at the start or may change during the task, as new factors emerge. UI designers should consider people, rôles, organizations and technology in their approach. A goal is a desired state and a task is the means of reaching it. For example, my goal might be to stop feelings of hunger. The corresponding task is to eat. This may involve setting subgoals (or implied tasks) such as finding food, chewing, etc.

There are two kinds of task: **internal tasks** are the tasks that the user must carry out to use the system (having knowledge, depressing certain keys in sequence, etc.); **external tasks** are those tasks that the user must perform using the system to support them (interpreting reports, writing documents, etc.). Internal tasks enable external tasks.

Just as there are two kinds of task, there are two approaches to design. We can attempt merely to support each of the external tasks; i.e. focus solely on the use cases. This approach does not challenge the underlying business processes or attempt to change them and Barfield (1993) suggests that it amounts to building 'intelligent notebooks'. The alternative is to attempt to build a model underneath the task level, including some understanding of what is being done and why. If the existing task can be modelled then the model can be criticized and optimized. As we have seen, this may lead to suggestions as to how to improve business processes. Building internal task models is tantamount to building a knowledge model in cases where the task is not merely a sequence of simple external tasks. The skills of the knowledge engineer are then useful. When the task normally involves group interaction, as with CASE or group work, then some internal task knowledge may become externalized. Typically these kinds of system are the hardest to model and Barfield points out forcibly, and correctly in my view, how this is evinced by most CASE tools, which usually enforce too many trivial tasks and sometimes miss out the important ones.

To be useful for system builders, task knowledge should be central, typical and representative. **Centrality** means that the task is critical to achieving the goal. If most users mention it, it is likely to be central. **Representativeness** holds when the mental model corresponds closely to the domain model that experts would hold. **Typicality** occurs when the task knowledge is typical of most users.

There are three fundamental activities (which may be regarded loosely as steps) involved in task analysis. These activities are: to define the objectives of the system, perform task knowledge elicitation and finally carry out a knowledge analysis – looking for the knowledge and skills involved in task performance. Again there is a strong link here to the domain of expert systems and the skills of the knowledge engineer. Typically, knowledge engineers carry a tool bag of more or less formal knowledge elicitation techniques which includes such approaches as task analysis itself, topic analysis, Kelly grids and card sorts, rating scales and frequency counts, skill profiles and taxonomies of human performance. Some of these techniques were described in Chapter 6 when we dealt with the object identification techniques. Other techniques include reading about the domain, introspection, examining sample output, observation (both direct and indirect), structured and focused interviews, protocol analysis (both concurrent and retrospective), brainstorming, questionnaires and having the analyst perform the task after instruction from the user or expert (also called teachback). Direct observation involves the physical presence of the observer whereas indirect observation could utilize video recordings. Both are time consuming and may be intrusive. Concurrent protocols require the expert to give a running commentary on the task being performed while retrospective ones are reports on task performance given afterwards.

Especially in the context of web site design it is crucial to respect the users' time; they may not wish to wait while all your fancy graphics download before being able to search or navigate the site. This will even more so when users access the site via dial-up lines.

USER INTERFACES AND OBJECT SYSTEMS

In Chapter 7 we met the MODEL VIEW CONTROLLER (MVC) pattern, which is key in UI design. Almost any system's interface may be interpreted in this way. The way a word processor stores text is not the way it is displayed. A simulation model may give the user access to some variables but block others, if changing them would violate the integrity of the model, say. Most GUI environments use an event handler to capture mouse and keyboard actions. This can be modelled as the controller that sends messages to the methods of the application. When designing interfaces, use this pattern to enforce a separation of concerns between the views of objects and their underlying state representations. This not only improves the interface but promotes greater architectural flexibility.

RESEARCH ISSUES

Johnson (1992) describes research into command language grammar (CLG) and other, as yet unproven, formal approaches to task analysis. CLG (Moran, 1981) offers a top-down, input/output model of interaction. CLG describes the interface as composed of three components at two levels of abstraction. The conceptual component has a task and a semantic level, so that task hierarchies are constructed and then objects and procedures to accomplish each task are expressed in a Lisp-style language. The communication component has syntactic (the command language) and interaction (physical actions) levels. Finally, the physical component has spatial and device levels. The approach is largely unproven.

Reisner's (1981) Task Action Language uses BNF-style grammar rules to describe user interfaces formally, and therefore provide a basis for measurement and comparison. This approach is promising but also unproven as yet. Johnson's (1992) Task Action Grammar extends Reisner's approach by incorporating insights from cognitive psychology and ideas about user modelling. It develops a rule-based model of the user's competence.

Programmable User Models (Young et al., 1989) treat the user as just another processor or object in the system. They draw the designer's attention to usability and cognitive aspects of a design and are intended to help with measuring usability. The approach has much in common with object-oriented user interface design.

One of the oldest formal approaches to UI design is GOMS (Goals, Operators, Methods and Selection rules) and cognitive complexity theory (Card et al., 1983).

The approach is task and rule based and predicts training time. It is based on a rather outmoded theory of human cognition that says there are three cognitive subsystems: perceptual, motor and cognitive. A model is built and decomposed to the level of these primitive skills. We first identify a goal or task sequence (a method) leading to each high level user goal. Each task is accomplished by a sequence of perceptual, motor or cognitive operators such as: see icon, move finger, recall password. Selection rules tell us when particular methods are appropriate. For example, we could find a book in a library by sequential search or by using an index. The trouble with these types of approach is that they are complex, time consuming and often need a trained psychologist. GOMS task descriptions can be extremely verbose too. Furthermore, GOMS assumes that a prototype exists to be measured so that the approach cannot be used in the early phases of requirements capture. In fact, most of the approaches discussed in this section are mainly useful for evaluative studies rather than original elicitation of the user interface. GOMS was seminal in the development of much of the theory of task analysis but is weakened by a crude, rule-based conception of cognition. Johnson (1992) presents a synthesis of ideas from task analysis and expert systems called Knowledge Analysis of Tasks that emphasizes not only the tasks but the user's knowledge of them. This is a promising area of research that deserves to be explored further. The approach we have adopted is much simpler and depends on expressing tasks as simple sentences concerning actions on objects with indirect objects.

GUI STANDARDS

The various style guides from Apple, IBM, Microsoft, NeXT, OSF and Sun all adopt a broadly object-oriented approach to user interface design. Therefore, given a sufficiently correct and expressive object model, these guides may be used to select standard components to represent the objects in the model. This is especially easy when there is an interface object library available. Standards for Java, for example, are largely encapsulated in the Swing libraries. Microsoft (1995) contains detailed guidelines on user interface design when the context is MS Windows. Apple, Sun and the Open Systems Foundation have all published style guides defining a standard for the Mac (Apple, 1987), Open Look (Sun, 1989) and Motif (OSF, 1990) respectively, with the Apple document being generally regarded as the paradigm for all the others mentioned so far. Most of these standards give a lot of detail, including positioning standards for controls (e.g. the Cancel button should be 3mm below the OK button or to its right), standard control types and layouts (such as those shown in Figure 3.9), standards for menus and naming conventions.

There are certain things that all the style guides have in common, despite terminological variations. All permit the display of one or more windows that can be divided into panes or child windows and used to provide views of different parts of an object, file or document. One may have either modal or modeless dialogue boxes to give additional information or contextual clues. The windows contain objects to be acted upon and there is a menu bar detailing the actions permissible. The style guides agree on issues such as the use of single words for menu items. Most require a status bar at the bottom of the screen and 'grey out' unreachable menu options.

They all support push buttons, radio buttons, check boxes, text fields, scroll bars, gauges and some kind of hierarchical menu display. Only some have spin buttons, list boxes, combo boxes, hierarchical scrolling lists, scrolling menus and so on, but there is usually an equivalent way to implement such features. Sometimes it is more profitable to look at a really first-rate implementation than to read the style guide.

International standards exist in this area too. ISO 9126 covers UI evaluation processes and ISO 9241 deals with ergonomic and safety requirements for displays. The latter is to be extended to deal with how to specify usability. There is also a European Community directive on health and safety that refers to software usability.

One word of caution about these interface standards is in order. These documents contain standards on issues like control positioning, colour and so on – but they mostly contain only guidelines on design. It is a capital mistake not to be willing to vary your design away from the standard when you can justify the deviation as an improvement that is at least roughly compatible with the guidance.

9.11 Testing

We have already said a great deal about testing when describing the process in Section 9.7. We also observed that the guidelines of Jacobson *et al.* (1992) were among the most useful published and that testing should be use case driven. Only a few other remarks need to be made here.

Testing object-oriented systems involves, as with conventional ones, verification and validation. Verification means ensuring that the code meets the specification and validation checks that the result actually meets current requirements. Testing often takes place in the reverse of the order in which the system is produced. Thus, unit tests of modules or classes occur first and whole system tests last with integration tests of whole layers between. After delivery, regression tests check that functions supported by the original release are still supported by subsequent fixes. Usually a test harness is built to automate regression tests. Test servers prior to client objects, because defects in servers may be propagated to their clients.

Jacobson *et al.* (1992) point out that polymorphism makes it harder to count the number of paths through a code module which in turn makes it harder to be sure that test coverage is complete; every sequence of mouse clicks is a potential path. The solution is to use the use cases to represent potential paths through the system. If possible, paths should be grouped into equivalence classes that can be tested as if one path. Another problem is that an inherited method may not work in the context of the subclass even though it worked properly in the superclass, meaning that the entire structure should be integration tested top-down. This can happen when the subclass has different values for attributes that the method uses and if multiple inheritance conflicts or overriding have modified the methods in some way. Perry and Kaiser (1990) discuss object-oriented unit testing further.

With an object-oriented language, testing should have been carried out during coding as each class is completed, preferably by a separate team. This includes integration: testing either each layer or the whole system with the new classes added. Thus the testing is largely completed by the testing stage, which must only look for unexpected effects of the systems working as a whole.

It is highly advisable to build a test harness: a suite of applications and user dialogues which are known to work as expected along with test runs. Do this at least as soon as prototypes are released to users. User feedback can be used to design the harness. It will pay for itself very quickly indeed, unless your programmers always write error-free code.

Follow all the usual, good, conventional testing practices (see for example (Myers, 1979)). State diagrams and decision tables remain useful. The main difference with object-oriented testing is that unit testing begins far earlier in the life cycle.

Since object-orientation emphasizes the interfaces rather than the implementation of objects, it might be expected that black-box testing techniques, where only the specification is used to construct tests, would suffice. This has been found to be empirically false in studies carried out at Hewlett-Packard (Fiedler, 1989), where white-box testing, which examines the implementation, was shown to increase the number of defects detected significantly. This implies that class designers and implementers must be intimately involved in the testing at the white-box stage as independent testers may be unfamiliar with the way low level functions work. The life-cycle model of this chapter implies that the sequence:

1. code,
2. white-box test,
3. incorporate library classes,
4. black-box test,
5. document,
6. train,
7. user test

should be the norm.

⊟ 9.12 Summary

This chapter surveyed the current state of the art in object-oriented process. It also described a concrete approach to running OO projects. The key points to remember are as follows.

- ■ Process is an essential part of a true object-oriented method.
- ■ Conventional waterfall processes are inappropriate for the iterative, incremental style of development made possible by object technology.

- Spiral models, such as DSDM and RUP, are needed to describe the **product life cycle**. But it is an error to fail to see that the product and process life-cycle models are **different**.
- In addition to describing product life cycles in outline, I presented in detail a full **process life-cycle** model framework and showed one instantiation of it. A process framework of this type must allow for the synchronization of parallel activities. We achieved this by building an object model of the activities and tasks of a project. The message passing metaphor was used to discuss the synchronization: using pre- and post-conditions. We also adhered to ISO standard terminology for project management.
- A **programme** is made of projects. A **project** consists of activity objects, whose operations are **tasks**. Tasks in one activity can trigger (or disable) tasks in other activities if their post-conditions are satisfied. Any process life-cycle model can be described in this way. Tasks have levels of duty (deontic) associated with them (M/R/O/F/D). Tasks also have deontically specified links to appropriate techniques. For example, the justify task of the project initiation activity could have the technique cost–benefit study marked as Recommended.
- We looked at various techniques for tailoring the framework: re-linking the activities; changing the guards; re-setting the deontic levels; etc. The use of **process patterns** to help tailor the process was also discussed.
- Catalysis was recommended as the pattern (or micro-process) for component and system specification and design. It was shown how the process was compatible with the DSDM and RUP product life cycles and how ideas from XP could be incorporated.
- The process includes thorough approaches to reuse management, testing, metrics and user interface design. The latter is based on principles from cognitive psychology and design theory.

We also covered the measurement of object-oriented software and projects. Task points were introduced as a potential alternative to function points. After a detailed consideration of the principles and practice of user interface design, we concluded by summarizing the key points about testing OO software.

9.13 Bibliographical notes

The idea of process patterns was introduced independently by D'Souza and Wills (1999) and Ambler (1998, 1999). The clearest exposition of RUP is by Kruchten (1999) but (Jacobson *et al.*, 1999) adds more detail. Royce (1998) adds a very considerable amount of information on RUP project management and issues like estimation. The three books are not always consistent. DSDM is clearly described by Stapleton (1997) and XP by Beck (2000). Other books on XP include (Beck and

Fowler, 2000) and (Jeffries *et al.*, 2000). The origins of this process life-cycle model described in this chapter lie in SOMA (Graham, 1995) and OPEN (Graham *et al.*, 1997b). Henderson-Sellers and Unhelkar (2000) show how OPEN (and by implication the process described in this chapter) can be realized in a software tool, in their case CA's Process Continuum.

Gilb and Graham (1993) explain their well-tried method of carrying out software and document inspections. The book includes several useful templates.

Henderson-Sellers (1996) gives a good discussion of the state of the art in object-oriented metrics.

Schneiderman (1987) has been a standard text on user interface design for a long time. Laurel (1990) discusses the art of user interface design in general and in relation to several emerging technologies. She collects several papers on the design aspects of systems using advanced UI technology, including virtual reality. Laurel's most interesting work is concerned with applying the principles of Greek drama to interface design. I am still waiting for my first experience of catharsis when using a computer but still consider this work as very important. Suchman (1987) applies anthropological and ethnomethodological principles to user interface design. Her book is highly recommended. Johnson (1992) deals with task analysis and especially the knowledge analysis of tasks. Thimbleby (1990) is one of the more thoughtful contributions to the subject of user interfaces and many of the principles presented in this chapter are derived from his work. Norman (1988) is essential background reading for user interface designers. Barfield (1993) is an intelligent contribution to the literature on HCI. Its humorous style only adds to the important messages it carries about good design and the need for humanity and intelligence on the part of designers. Read together with the books by Thimbleby, Johnson and Schneiderman it forms the basis of an excellent introduction to the subject. Other useful books include those by Cato (2000), Van Harmelen (2000) and Tognazzini (1992), one of the originators of the Apple Mac interface. Lee (1993) gives a reasonably complete and well-structured approach to GUI design based on object-oriented principles. The emphasis is on task analysis and interface design principles. Lee describes how to perform usability studies and bases his method of task analysis on the traditional 'Goals, Operators, Methods and Selection rules' model. He simplifies this model by expressing tasks as simple Subject/Predicate sentences and explains the approach well using a running personnel administration example. Especially clear guidelines on the use of user interface metaphors such as the desktop metaphor are provided and the architectural design of GUIs is covered briefly. Browne (1994) offers an approach located squarely in the structured tradition of SSADM and separated from the development of the non-interface components. It does, however, contain some useful insights. Another UI design process offering useful ideas, and similar in its basis to the principles covered in this chapter, is GUIDE (Redmond-Pyle and Moore, 1995). Baecker and Buxton (1987) provide a comprehensive collection of source papers on early user interface design theory, including many that pre-date the arrival of graphical interfaces. If you are embarking on an HCI project it may be useful to read the appropriate manuals and style guides for the system that you will use. The Apple (1987) *Human Interface Guidelines* is a classic reference. The NeXT style guide (1992) may be inspiring. Microsoft developers will need (Microsoft, 1992).

The seminal work on software testing by Myers (1979) is still relevant.

⊟ 9.14 Exercises

1. Why would a company wish to standardize on a development process? What disadvantages might they see?

2. Enumerate the benefits of time-boxes.

3. Give examples of product and process metrics. How might they be related?

4. Define the term ESTIMATION MODEL. Give an example of one.

5. Define Lack of Cohesion in Methods (LCOM). Take some actual designs and plot a graph of LCOM. What are its mathematical properties? Are they what one would expect?

6. Define fan-out and fan-in.

7. Define the terms:
   a) task point
   b) atomic use case
   c) essential use case
   d) function point

8. Define the three Task Object Model metrics and four Business Object Model metrics.

9. Describe the main tasks of two of the following activities:
   a) Time-box planning
   b) The build time-box
   c) Evaluation
   d) Implementation planning

10. 4. How long does it take to go from the end of a requirements workshop to implementation?

11. What is the difference between education and training? Which is the most important?

12. Sketch the waterfall, spiral, RUP and contract-driven life-cycle models.

13. Name eight project rôles. Describe two of them in detail.

14. Complete the phrase: Users should be _____ but not too _____.

15. What is the difference between a workflow in RUP and an activity and a task in ISO standard project management terminology?

16. Devise a menu similar to that of Figure 9.22 that supports priming without using Greek characters.

17. Discuss the use of icons in graphical user interfaces, including their advantages and possible misuse.

18. Should a mouse move the pointer further when the user's hand moves faster? If not, why not?

19. List seven principles that should guide user interface design; in each case discuss why it is important and give an example where not applying it leads to a bad experience for the user.

10

Applications

These things are beyond all use,
and I do fear them.

W. Shakespeare (*Julius Caesar*)

This chapter surveys some past and future applications of object-oriented programming and methods and points out some actual and potential limitations. Almost anything that can be done with conventional computing can be done equally well with object-oriented techniques. We have already covered many applications of object technology in the bulk of this text, but here we review some that are particularly characteristic, including some that there has been resistance to adopting so far. We then revisit some of the predictions for the future made in earlier editions of this text and review their accuracy with the benefit of hindsight, indulging *en passant* in some reiterated and some new speculations.

10.1 Web applications

Without doubt, the application that forced practically every organization in the world to adopt object technology was the world wide web and its attendant: e-commerce. It has been said that technologies, like animals, are subject to natural selection; when a new variation arises it only survives if the conditions are right for it. OT languished as an 'advanced' technology until the new business model of e-commerce forced businesses, rather than just IT departments, to consider using things like Java and application servers – often based on an OODBMS. If AI had found such a killer application, its history might have been very different. E-commerce depends on many interconnected technologies: networking, the internet, databases, middleware and object-oriented methods. It also implies that companies must re-engineer. Thus, BPR and these other technologies seem to have evolved and just sat there waiting for e-commerce to make their use into a survival trait.

The internet started in 1969 as ARPANET: the DoD's Cold War response to the perceived threat of nuclear communications disruption. It survived because its military and academic users found features like e-mail and FTP incredibly useful. It was based on packet switching rather than circuit switching, so that messages contain their own routing information and can thus be diverted along the most appropriate routes in the event of node or network failures. The similar system developed at that time at INRIA in France proved less resilient – probably because of its smaller user base. Nevertheless, it was Europe that spawned the web when Tim Berners-Lee and others at the particle research centre CERN developed the idea of a hypertext-based browser in 1990. The HTTP protocol supported graphics on top of the text-based internet protocols – TCP/IP, SMTP, etc. – and led to the creation of the world wide web.

Before the web and HTML there were several hypertext systems, such as Apple's Hypercard, running on stand-alone computers. The term hypertext refers to an idea first advanced by Doug Englebart – the inventor of the mouse – as early as 1963 (Englebart, 1963; Englebart and English, 1968), and to a number of computer systems embodying this idea. Even earlier, Roosevelt's wartime science adviser, Vannevar Bush (1945), had suggested similar ideas. The term itself came into use much later in the work of Ted Nelson (1980, 1981) when machines had become powerful enough for a reasonably fast implementation. Nelson's XANADU interactive reference, writing and conferencing system is still available, under UNIX. Hypertext systems are directed to two main aims, better navigation of complex information retrieval systems and improved user interfaces. The idea behind XANADU was more far-reaching still. Nelson's vision was of a huge, publicly accessible repository of data, connected to international networks, which could respond to requests for information from relatively untutored users in any medium; text, graphics, film or sound. It was the web that finally realized this vision. The charitable Gutenberg Project exists to make available on the web, in editable form, all the world's literature that is out of copyright. It is still far from complete – as I discovered when trying to double check a quotation used in this book – but is a massively useful resource.

Typically, a hypertext system may be viewed as a network of text fragments linked together by a complex network of pointers. A hypertext document is not read sequentially, like a novel, but according to content, like an encyclopaedia. One reads the text, spots a relevant or interesting term or concept and then is able to go directly to the text explaining the term, usually by pointing at – or clicking a mouse over – the phrase or icon concerned. Such a system will support multiple media, including text, graphics, music or video. Thus the more general term 'hypermedia' is to be preferred to 'hypertext'.

Hypermedia fragments are referred to as 'nodes' or 'pages' and the pointers as 'links'. Nodes can be given a 'type' if required, to indicate the subject matter or the form of the page; text or graphics say. Nodes may be combined into composite nodes for increased modularity. Links are of two types: 'from' links and 'to' links. The unique 'from' link at a node refers to the node last visited, and a set of 'to' links record the nodes currently available for the next step in the journey through the information world. A link between nodes is normally created by the developer, who highlights an item and records what it points at. Some systems create links dynamically or automatically. An example of this might relate to the production of a document contents list or index. From these features it is readily inferred that object-orientation had a strong influence on the design of such systems, and object-oriented programming languages are often the bases for their development. It is worth noting in passing that the artificial intelligence notion of semantic networks also had an influence.

Simple browsing systems are aimed primarily at the reader rather than the writer. They provide easy access to large volumes of information where ease of learning and usability are important, such as on-line policy and procedure manuals, help systems or maintenance handbooks. Many of today's web sites are simple 'brochures' describing some organization, product or person. More sophisticated ones are linked to databases giving access to shared information. These are also easier to maintain dynamically. In-house **intranets** make corporate data available to a firm's staff – enabling business process re-engineering thereby – without the security risks of the open internet. Many sites use Java applets, Active X controls or CGI scripts to include animation and forms, to allow users to send as well as read information – or just to prettify the site. Corporate **extranets** allow companies to interact with customers in a secure manner, giving external access to its intranet to authenticated sites. Sites such as amazon.com are paradigms of business-to-customer (B2C) e-commerce. Here the difficulty of predicting how many customers will access the site means that load balancing and caching using application servers, often based on object-oriented databases and middleware, are critical. Business-to-business (B2B) commerce provides opportunities for both supply chain integration and electronic ordering and payment, but without the high cost and inflexibility of traditional EDI. Companies can even auction their future production to the highest bidder.

True, world-wide businesses based on the web have yet to emerge, although Citibank has announced plans to do business with 16% of the world's population by 2012. Reuters' CORBA-based e-trading system already accounts for 15% of trading on the NASDAQ stock exchange.

Hypertext systems, which allow the attachment of procedures to their links, raise naturally the question as to whether some knowledge processing could be done at this point in order to simulate 'intelligent' traversal of the information network. Here XML has come to the rescue; but it depends also on the use of object-oriented middleware. New entrants to e-commerce can easily become experts in object technology and use it, but existing companies need to incorporate their legacy. It is here that CBD takes on a critical importance and a clearly defined application architecture is a prerequisite of success. The techniques of Chapter 7 are central to such endeavours. Another lesson of e-commerce is that poorly designed user interfaces can be tolerated no longer. As I write, the news is about sportswear supplier boo.com having to close. One contributing factor was that not all potential customers were able to access their site easily. In other words, Boo failed to understand the use cases for customers on dial-up lines and who did not have the very latest browser technology. The guidelines in Chapter 9 and the methods of Chapters 6 to 8 are intended to address this issue.

10.2 Other commercial applications

Throughout the last decade of the 20th century applications of object-oriented programming gained ground rapidly. Apart from e-commerce, the most active industry sectors were Finance, Telecomms, Manufacturing and the computing industry itself. As with all new technologies, object-oriented programming was met with a certain amount of scepticism from the established practitioners of the IT industry. To overcome this resistance, it was necessary for successful applications to become visible. Early flagship projects showed that very large object-oriented systems could be built, the biggest having around 900,000 lines of code and 3,500 classes, but this did not convince everybody.

10.2.1 Graphical user interfaces

The reason that the most popular application of object-oriented programming up to about 1990 was user interface design was partly the pervasive influence of Smalltalk, which emphasized the user interface and office automation applications from the early days of the Dynabook, and partly because of the complexity of the typical graphical user interface (GUI). The approach was pioneered at Xerox not only in Smalltalk but in InterLisp, their proprietary dialect of Lisp. The influence of this early work on the later development of the Apple Lisa and Macintosh user interfaces is well-known. This iconic style of user interface is almost totally pervasive now.

GUIs are tremendously expensive to develop. If over 200 man-years of effort were required for the development of the Apple Lisa, of which most went on software development, and a considerable amount of that was concerned with the interface, it is inconceivable that Apple could move on to the Macintosh and then the Macintosh II without reusing some of the Clascal code used for the Lisa. As the pace of hardware development accelerates, suppliers cannot afford a new 200 man-year development every few years. This applies not only to the developers of the computing environment but to its users as well. Most current GUIs just could not have been written without the use of object-oriented techniques. Furthermore, applications programming in such environments becomes almost impossible without libraries of reusable and extensible graphical objects. Under early versions of Microsoft Windows a simple 'hallo world' program took about 83 lines of C code, excluding the reuse of the Windows API code, and often had to be edited, compiled and linked outside the Windows environment. The API in such systems is huge, and the event-driven style of user interaction makes programming doubly difficult. The object-oriented programmer need not fight so hard with the API if new types of windows, scroll bars, radio buttons and so on can be defined as instances of existing classes that understand how to respond to events (messages) and whose methods can be inherited. The object-oriented style, or some style that supports reuse and extension, is really essential for productive programming in such environments. Maintenance is also eased by the use of object-oriented programming. Thus, there was a profound need for object-oriented solutions to the problems of the construction, maintenance and use of GUIs. With a good class library to hand, object-oriented programming can speed up applications development in a system such as Windows by up to 75%. Visual Basic, from the start, contained built-in UI objects that have changeable attributes and empty methods which correspond to interface events. For example, a command button object has a method called Click that can contain the code to be executed when the mouse is left-clicked over the button area. Additional objects of this type can be written in C or purchased from third parties. Visual Basic is an example of how the object-oriented style can be usefully embedded in a conventional language as an application framework. There is now a host of properly object-oriented application frameworks for GUI development, based usually on Java or C++.

Object-oriented programming is not only used by GUI developers and application programmers, but may be used by users to facilitate their tailoring of applications to some particular purpose. With the first generation of object-oriented interfaces, such as the Macintosh I, neither the user nor the application programmer had access to the icons as objects. With later systems, such as the NeXt machine and the HyperCard system, programmers had limited access and could make extensions to the interface. The trend is towards giving users this level of access.

Typical early applications of object-oriented programming to user interface development include UIMS – a complex user interface management system designed for electronic design applications written in C++ (Raghavan, 1990), and GLAD – a visual database interface written in Actor (Wu, 1990). Apple Computer developed a user-extensible visualization system, DoubleVision, which helps scientists produce flexible colour plots of two-dimensional data (Mock, 1990).

10.2.2 Simulation

Simulation of complex systems has been an application of object-oriented programming since the earliest days of Simula. Traffic systems, nuclear reactors, integrated office systems, financial systems and manufacturing processes have all been successfully subjected to the approach.

Nierstratz and Tsichritzis (1989) discuss the essential characteristics of an object-oriented office systems simulator. Sim City is an educational game which simulates city planning situations and allows players to explore the consequences of various budgeting, pricing, traffic control and environmental decisions.

10.2.3 Geographic information systems

Geographic information systems (GIS) are essentially computer systems that replace or automate aspects of analogue, paper-based cartography and record keeping. They typically comprise subsystems for:

1. data capture from existing maps, remote sensors, satellite images and so on;
2. data storage and retrieval of spatial data in a form which supports fast retrieval for analysis and rapid updates;
3. database management systems for handling information about the attributes of spatial defined features;
4. reporting and map display.

At a more detailed level, a typical GIS product will support the overlaid presentation of several line maps on a background map and the fast retrieval of information about the adjacency and proximity of polygons such as those representing postal sectors or counties. Also, it is often necessary to store attribute data for polygons, nodes and links and support quick panning, zooming and plotting. GIS can store information on demographics which could be useful for marketing purposes or on routing for the optimization of travelling costs. Most GIS store two kinds of data: mapping data and data concerning the attributes of the objects to be mapped. The performance of relational systems is poor on mapping data because of their inability to store complex, structured objects and their need to do joins to reconstruct them. For this reason the mapping data are usually stored in a proprietary file system. The attribute data are often stored in a relational database and also often shared with other applications. In many applications a change to mapping data must be reflected in changes to the attributes and vice versa. This close coupling has been a significant task for product developers. Relational systems that support BLOBS can be used but they cannot interpret the data.

The history of GIS has been compared to that of civil aviation (Peuquet and Marble, 1990). For the latter, it is claimed that there have been only three significant events: the Wright brothers' first flight, the first civil airliner – the DC3 – and the Boeing 707. The simile is constructed by noting that the first successful geographic information system, CGIS – the Canadian Geographic Information System, succeeded in being used where most others failed to get off the ground at all due to either poor design or bad software engineering practices. This occurred in the days when computing was almost exclusively a matter of batch processing mainframes taking punched cards as input and was a remarkable achievement in itself. The development of interactive computing in the seventies made it possible for a revolution in geographic information systems to take place, and the equivalent of the DC3 was ARC/INFO. Its authors took an existing pseudo-relational database (INFO) to hold attribute data and added a proprietary topologically structured database (ARC) to hold the map data. The analogue of the 707 is yet to appear, and we may safely assume that this will happen in the near future for two major reasons:

1. the huge amount of money being invested in this technology at present, which all market surveys predict will increase;
2. the new possibility of constructing both the attribute and map databases in an efficient but unified database management system using object-oriented technology. In particular, modern object-oriented databases combine the efficiency of the network, pointer-based approach with the flexibility of the relational as we saw in Chapter 5.

We may expect to see a new generation of GIS products emerge that will be based on a single object-oriented database that will provide an effective standard for data exchange among different GIS. In this way the current generation of products will become outdated in two major respects; lack of a data storage standard and reliance on inflexible topological storage schemes.

Current GIS rely heavily on CAD and database technology and usually operate on non-standard, proprietary file management systems. To see the reason for this it is necessary to understand that there is a fundamental reason why topological data may not be retrieved efficiently from a relational database. Cartographic data may be represented in a number of different ways: as analogue (paper), raster (bit maps) or vector images. Vector images are particularly suited to the storage of network data and this may be done with one of two basic data models: 'spaghetti' models and topological models. Spaghetti models give very efficient retrieval but are badly adapted for analysis. Modern products almost always adopt a topological model. Such a model stores not only the locations of points and lines but information about adjacency and intersection. This is accomplished by storing pointers linking the topological entities – points, lines and polygons – and sometimes by encoding the co-ordinate pairs locationally so that they are stored in a proximity ordered manner. A typical technique is the Peano ordering which stores points as numbers constructed by interlacing the bits from the binary representation of the longitude and latitude of the points. This makes zooming and nearness calculation very fast since points can be stored sorted in order of proximity. The problem with relational databases is that such systems need to store data in normalized tables, and these tables need not correspond to anything physical like a line or polygon. Such objects must be reconstructed at run time by joining several tables. Unfortunately a join operation is about the slowest thing a relational database can be asked to do. Network databases can be up 100 times more efficient for this kind of application. On the other hand, network databases are horribly inflexible and difficult to manage in the face of schema evolution. For this reason data concerning the attributes of map features, such as the capacity of a road, are best stored in a relational database because it is these data that are the most vulnerable to changes in the schema. The map data, however, are not so vulnerable and may be stored in a purpose-built network database. This is the way nearly all products since ARC/INFO have been constructed. Object-oriented databases offer the possibility of storing all the data in one database for the first time. Pacific Bell implemented a pilot system for network maintenance using an early version of ObjectStore (see Chapter 5). More recent geographic information systems, such as Smallworld, have opted for an object-oriented approach to storing mapping data. The authors of Smallworld chose to create their own persistent version of Smalltalk and object-oriented database because no commercial OODBs existed at the time they started. Vendors starting now have a much better choice.

Most PC products use the AutoCAD DXF standard to store maps. These range from full AutoCAD implementations such as Addmaps to Geo/SQL, which latter uses Oracle to store attributes and its image database. AutoCAD is used for display only and provides the user interface.

10.2.4 Concurrent systems and parallel hardware

Concurrency refers to processes which happen at the same time. If these processes happen outside the computer then we need ways for even conventional Von Neumann machines to cope with simultaneous, multiple demands on their processing power. Multi-user operating systems and locking strategies in databases are two solutions to this kind of concurrency problem. Another kind of concurrency arises when we can have two or more processes executing simultaneously inside the computer. This is parallel computation. We will deal with non-parallel concurrency first.

Models of concurrent computation usually involve a notion of message passing, although these are real messages as opposed to the metaphorical message passing of object-orientation. However, the analogy is so strong that it is difficult to resist the temptation of seeing object-oriented programming as the natural solution to problems of concurrency. Furthermore, as Tomlinson and Scheevel (1989) have pointed out, alternative shared memory models of concurrency do not lend themselves as well to parallel or distributed implementations as do encapsulated models. Object-oriented approaches support the clustering of objects that communicate frequently, and this too helps to support concurrent applications.

Concurrent object-oriented systems have to specify whether objects are synchronous or asynchronous with respect to their various methods. That is, whether the object or actor may continue processing after it has sent or received a message. The usual terminology refers to blocking sends, blocking receives, non-blocking sends, etc. The notion of message passing combines information transfer into a single construct, whereas the usual shared memory model of concurrency does not and involves the use of complicated semaphores. Furthermore, objects, which encapsulate both data and methods, are a very natural unit of distribution in distributed implementations.

There have been a number of suggestions for concurrent object-oriented programming languages and similar ideas very closely related to objects such as actor systems. Just as everything is an object in Smalltalk, everything is an actor in actor systems. Actors have unique permanent identity and current behaviour which may change over time and which determines how the actor will respond to the next message it receives. The behaviour is composed of attributes, called *acquaintances*, and methods, called its *script*. Acquaintances determine the other actors with which the actor may communicate. An actor with no acquaintances is a candidate for garbage collection. On receipt of a message the current behaviour may replace itself. If it does not have a method to handle the message, the actor may *delegate* to a *proxy*, which is an actor nominated among its acquaintances. This notion is similar to that of a superclass, but the methods are not inherited; that is, no code is copied, all that takes place is message passing. Unlike object-oriented programming, there is a well-defined semantics for actor systems, but actor languages are very low level and difficult to use.

In addition to actor languages, such as Act 3, there are also concurrent versions of pure object-oriented languages, such as ConcurrentSmalltalk (Yokote and Tokoro, 1987), and hybrids such as Orient84/K, which combines the Smalltalk and Prolog styles (Ishikawa and Tokoro, 1987). Eiffel has a rudimentary but useful concurrency facility and Java supports the idea of threads, as discussed in Chapter 3.

Object-oriented concurrent programming remains a field for researchers, but its future importance is assured by two incontrovertible facts. Namely, that distributed architectures involve concurrency if effective use of resources is to be made, and that no other programming style offers a clear and conceptually economical model for this kind of complex, co-operating concurrent system.

Parallel computation has nothing to do with the number of processors in a machine. A multi-processor can run several programs in parallel, a single one can simulate several processors (using time slicing) but a multi-processor mainframe usually is only able to process one application program instruction at a time, the other processors being devoted to specialized operations such as I/O.

There are several different kinds of parallel computer system. The basic division is between shared memory designs which use a coarse-grained decomposition of processes that each share the same data space, and distributed memory designs. Distributed memory systems distribute the data storage across several processors and usually implement a more fine-grained decomposition of processes. Distributed memory designs can be of two basic types: either all processors run the same program, as with connection machines and vector processors, or different processors can run different programs, as with database machines, transputer surfaces or hypercube architectures. Neural networks are examples of parallel machines in which all the processors are identical at a low level but which give the appearance of several processes running at a higher level of granularity.

Processors in distributed memory systems communicate by sending messages. The object-oriented metaphor therefore maps directly onto the problem of describing the topology of a process running on such a machine. Object-oriented programming languages and design techniques are therefore likely to become standard for such machines.

Since Simula, objects have been a way of implementing both data structures and processes where concurrency is involved. Distributed architectures involving networks and remote procedure calls emphasize the need to describe these systems.

Once again the object-oriented metaphor applies directly and is likely to become standard in applications of this kind.

Parallel computing is still an intriguing research problem. Many issues have yet to be resolved, before the technology matures and receives wide commercial application. It is a key technology and will mature in close connexion with object-orientation.

STRAND

One option for high level parallel programming languages is exemplified by Strand and Parlog (Foster and Taylor, 1990), which are logic programming languages in the tradition of Prolog. Prolog is based on the idea of expressing all program statements declaratively in the form of Horn clause logic, and then applying automatic inference algorithms at execution time, usually a form of backward chaining. This process is thought of as either pattern matching or theorem proving. A Horn clause is a special kind of logical implication rule with only one term in its consequent clause. For example, the rule 'If A and B then C' is in Horn clause form, whereas 'If A and B then C and D' is not. In the Edinburgh Prolog notation, the former would be expressed in the form 'C :- A, B'. Guarded Horn Clauses are an extension of logic programming used in parallel theorem provers, such as Parlog or Strand, which support parallel execution of all the descents of the proof tree. A guarded Horn clause has the following form.

$$H :- G_1, G_2, \dots, G_m \mid B_1, B_2, \dots, B_n$$

where H is the 'head', | is the 'commit' operator, $B_1, B_2, \dots, B_n$ is the 'body' of the clause and $G_1, G_2, \dots, G_m$ is the 'guard'. The guard specifies the pre-condition under which a process may execute. This style of programming combines formal specification with parallel execution.

One of the attractive features of Strand is the fact that it is portable from sequential to parallel machines. It has been found that the approach exemplified by Strand is more successful than object-oriented programming in certain application areas, such as telephony (Foster and Taylor, 1990). On the other hand, there seems to be no more natural way to model communicating processors than with the object-oriented metaphor. We saw in Chapter 3 that there are research initiatives aimed at amalgamating functional, logic and object-oriented programming. It is to be expected that the first applications of any successes from this research will be applied to programming parallel computers.

In object-oriented analysis, where every object has its own thread of control, we are always to think of our systems as parallel systems. The lack of concurrency support in object-oriented programming languages means that there is still a small 'impedance mismatch' between analysis and implementation. The concurrency and threading facilities in languages like Eiffel and Java do little to address this issue, and I still believe that more developments are both possible and needed.

10.2.5 Other applications

Currently, most user organizations are developing the client-end components of mainstream systems using object-oriented technology, and more and more base their entire development strategy on objects and CBD. The trouble is that object-oriented programming can be applied to almost anything. We have already discussed several applications in early chapters.

Application areas which have been widely reported include environments for visual programming, CASE tools, Computer Integrated Manufacturing (CIM) systems, electronic publishing systems, computer-assisted learning systems and quite a few CAD/CAM systems, where issues related to object-oriented databases are paramount.

Applications to the problems faced by software developers, in DP itself, have been fairly common. One such application is a branch path analyser for C programs (Pinson and Wiener, 1990). This program, written in Smalltalk, identifies branch paths; that is, blocks of code whose execution may be conditional on the value of one or more parameters. It also maintains statistics on which paths were used during test runs. Significantly, the system was re-implemented in C++ and Objective-C for greater efficiency.

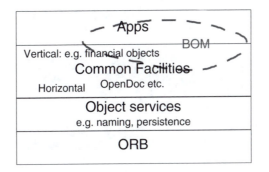

Figure 10.1 An object-technology-inspired architecture.

Much of the recent work on software design patterns can be lifted to the level of architecture, giving rise to architectural patterns such as blackboard and pipe-and-filter patterns. In parallel with this trend many modern software development organizations are planning their systems strategy around an ORB-enabled, service-based architecture. In such an approach the aim is to enhance opportunities for component reuse and increase system interoperability. Figure 10.1 sketches such an architecture. Notice that the ORB acts as a general bus, carrying service requests to various servers at different levels of abstraction. At the lower levels the organization hopes to buy nearly everything: naming services, databases, etc. At the top this organization will write most of its business-specific applications. The middle layers are more problematical; while it may be desirable to buy ready-made business objects, the fact is that there are few on the market and, anyway, the firm may not always reflect the way others do business. The best hope is that third parties will be able to supply horizontal components of use in all business sectors, such as GUI frameworks or database access tools. The vertical components will be far harder to agree upon. Thus we see the provenance of business objects (whether specifications or code) crossing the buy/make boundary. Notice the area labelled 'BOM' – denoted by the dashed ellipse – which designates that the organization's business object model overlaps both the common facilities and custom-built applications areas. This signifies the extreme unlikelihood of external suppliers being able to offer genuinely useful vertical business object libraries in generic domains such as finance, telecommunications or manufacturing. Such libraries will appear, but they will only contain a fragment of the classes needed.

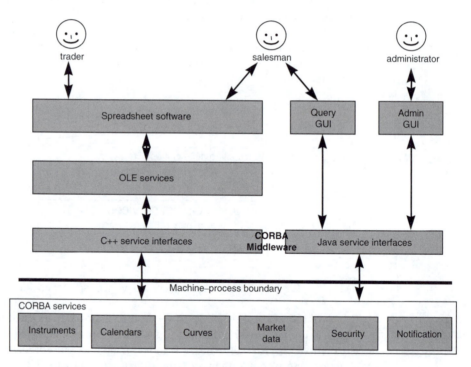

Figure 10.2 Applying the architecture to trading.

An alternative, more specific instantiation of this architecture is shown in Figure 10.2. In this set-up, common financial services such as curve generators (used for pricing) and calendars (that determine when markets are open) are represented as CORBA services. This is usually a C++ program with an IDL wrapper. Users rarely access these services directly or even uniformly. Traders pricing trades and sales staff bidding for business may access these services from Excel spreadsheets or custom-built applications. Other users may access the same services from a Web browser.

Object request brokers are at the centre of most early adopters' strategies for object-oriented systems. Many of these companies are also moving closer to agent-based technology. It makes sense to ask if object request brokers can be useful in this. Common sense and wishful thinking dictate that CORBA products ought to provide an infrastructure for agent-based systems, including, especially, a standard agent communication language. Currently, this is very far from the case, primarily due to the semantic limitations of IDL, which has no conception of rulesets or even invariants. However, many ORB vendors that we have spoken to would like to add this kind of functionality to their products and, if enough do so, we may well see some standardization of their efforts in the future. For now, each organization that wants to implement agent-based systems must write its own agent communication language. Doing this on top of CORBA still makes a great deal of sense. As we saw in Chapter 4, XML is commonly used on top of message-oriented middleware and/or an ORB.

The most flexible architectures are loose federations of components, with subsystems corresponding to business processes. The paths between them match the communication paths in the business itself. This gives three advantages over conventional, centralized database architectures:

- System crashes may affect only one department instead of an entire company.
- Each subsystem can be made to work in harmony with its local users' methods of working. It is easier to make local changes and negotiation with a centralized IT function can be eliminated in many cases.
- When the business is reorganized the system can be reorganized too.

Object-oriented methods can be used for organizational modelling or simulation as discussed in Chapter 8. This enables strategy studies to be conducted by simulation, so that alternative scenarios may be tested and compared.

10.3 Expert systems, AI and intelligent agents

One area where object-orientation has been influential for a long time is artificial intelligence (AI) and its commercial offspring, expert systems. AI, strictly speaking, is about using computational models to help understand the workings of the human brain. Expert systems (or knowledge-based systems) technology, on the other hand, is about using some of the lessons learnt from AI to solve practical problems. In particular, an expert system does not set out to model general problem solving capability but to simulate the behaviour of an 'expert' in some narrow discipline. One of the earliest systems, the well-known MYCIN system (Buchanan and

Shortliffe, 1984), simulated the diagnostic abilities of a physician in the area of infectious diseases of the blood.

For many years the language of choice for AI research was the functional language Lisp. It turns out that Lisp can be easily extended to deal with objects and messages – in fact Lisp is one of the easiest languages to extend for *any* purpose. For this reason AI researchers were among the first to exploit the benefits of object-oriented programming. In doing so they largely reinvented the subject – it has to be said also that OOP workers got many of their ideas from AI – and still use a slightly different terminology. In particular, AI people talk about 'frames'. Frames (Minsky, 1981, 1985) were invented to represent stereotypes of objects, concepts or situations, but implementations of frames look almost indistinguishable from the objects of object-oriented programming, especially in terms of their inheritance features. To understand frames we must understand the basic architecture of expert systems.

Expert systems are defined not only by what they do but how they do it. In a typical modern expert system the 'expertise' or 'knowledge' is stored separately from the reasoning strategy, often in the form of simple if/then rules. These rules can be readily changed, which means that expert systems are easier to maintain than some other kinds of computer system. This is important when it is realized that the majority of software cost these days goes toward the maintenance of existing systems rather than the construction of new ones. Furthermore, this architecture permits the systems to explain their reasoning to users, which can be important if humans are to act confidently on the basis of a computer's advice in critical or sensitive areas.

Expert systems attempt to represent domain knowledge within a computer system. Rules are good at representing causal knowledge, but there are many other types of knowledge: process knowledge, object knowledge, intuitive knowledge, etc. Representing knowledge about the shape and properties of a motor car's distributor cap, for example, would be unspeakably tedious, if not quite impossible, using if/then statements. A much better way, as we know, is to represent the object as a series of attributes and methods; as objects and classes of objects. In the world of AI such objects are sometimes called units, or scripts for procedural abstractions, but usually **frames**. Expert systems with rules and frames have the same expressive power as logic programming languages but are far easier to use, due largely to their ability to deal with higher order constructs and inheritance structures.

Frames, from the beginning, have been closely connected with notions of inheritance, as explained in Chapter 3. A frame is a structure with an extensible set of 'slots' which contain the attributes of a concept or object. A slot may have various **facets** such as a value, constraints, a default value and attached procedures. Thus, methods are viewed not so much as an interface, but as means to fill the value facet or to initiate action in the system. Some slots have the special purpose of determining inheritance. For example, the employee frame may have an AKO slot containing its superclasses: classes from which it may inherit. This slot too may have facets, representing inheritance from different perspectives. For example, from the dominant perspective of a payroll system, an employee is a kind of taxpayer, but from the point of view of zoological classification an employee might be usefully regarded as a mammal. What this suggests is the superposition of multiple non-interacting inheritance hierarchies for different purposes. In AI, frames (objects) inherit values, in object-oriented programming objects normally only inherit the ability to have a value. Frames contain pointers to attached procedures and these too are inheritable, though the attached procedures are not properly encapsulated and may be accessed independently of the frame. Also in AI, multiple inheritance is the norm rather than the exception.

Another characteristic of expert systems is their ability to work with vague or judgemental statements. This is required by systems which need to represent the sort of knowledge used by human experts such as 'invest in companies whose stocks are greatly undervalued' where the term 'greatly' has no precise meaning but is still perfectly understandable. There are several technologies available for this uncertainty management. One that is popular in Japan but less so in the West is fuzzy logic. Other methods abound and include probability theory, various belief theories and numerous *ad hoc* and descriptive methods. For an introduction to uncertainty and fuzzy logic in knowledge-based systems see (Graham and Jones, 1988). Appendix A describes a fuzzy extension to object-oriented analysis.

Summarizing, an expert system consists of a 'knowledge base', containing the objects and rules corresponding to specialist knowledge of the application, an 'inference engine', which is a program that applies the knowledge in the knowledge base to the data presented to the system, and some means of managing uncertainty. If the system is emptied of its application-specific knowledge and given the means for developers to insert easily some other knowledge base it is called an 'expert system shell'. Such shells are highly productive development environments for builders of expert systems.

Expert systems are now helping companies across the world in such diverse areas as insurance underwriting, financial trading, bank loan authorization, the control of complex plant such as cement kilns and blast furnaces, the diagnosis of faults in vibrating machinery, database optimization, the selection and combination of chemical coatings, the configuration of computers and telecommunications machinery, fraud detection for both banks and phone companies, planning and scheduling, chemical product formulation, laying out the Yellow Pages, the diagnosis of faults in an inter-bank payments system, and many others. Another key area of application is in data processing itself, with packages available for project estimation and methods support (as part of CASE tools). The 'hype' about expert systems which characterized most of the 1980s was supplanted in the 1990s by a burgeoning number of real applications, most of which are embedded in apparently conventional ones.

A number of expert systems 'shells', which are programming environments containing built-in inference and uncertainty handling methods and some means of adding knowledge, contain object-oriented features. The systems discussed in Chapter 3, such as Aion, ART, Kappa and Nexpert Object, are all expert systems development environments with more or less of the features of object-orientation. Their suppliers are now prone to repositioning them as 'object-oriented development environments' with varying degrees of justification and often can deliver them in the form of libraries of Java or C++ components; e.g. Nexpert. Usually, their strength lies in their inheritance features rather than their abstraction facilities. This makes them suitable for applications with complex process semantics or business rules – as opposed to data semantics. It thus carves out a set of niche applications that are usually, although by no means always, expert systems. Such applications are characterized not by being knowledge intensive (although they may be that as well) but by involving inheritance structures where the behaviour of the conflict resolution strategies reflects something important about the application.

AARDVARK In the case of SACIS, for example, we envisage a definite requirement for matching customer characteristics to product features. Aardvark's policy is to sell only toys that are safe. This is not as simple as it seems at first. A product that is safe for an adult (e.g. a sword-swallowing kit) might not be safe for a ten-year-old. A toy safe for a ten-year-old (e.g. a bag of marbles) should be considered decidedly risky in the hands of an infant with a natural penchant for swallowing things. What is required, within SACIS, is an expert systems component capable of matching product to client on the basis of rules and the properties of complex structures of product and customer types. Without attempting to describe the whole application, let us observe the inheritance structures involved.

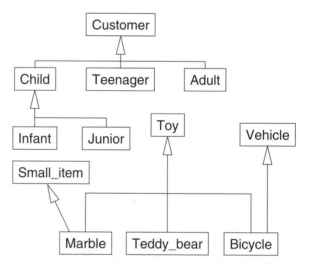

Figure 10.3 Fragments of inheritance structures in SACIS.

Customers are classified in advance as Child, Teenager and Adult, rather than merely encapsulating age. Child admits a further classification as Infant and Junior. Defaults and constraints on age, or date of birth, are encapsulated within the structures. Toys may be similarly classified according to their functional properties. Note that Marble inherits multiply from both Toy and SmallItem. Small items are those with overall dimension under, say, 30mm. This means that Marble inherits an additional property of being small and additional methods concerned with the manipulation of small objects within the stock system; they are stored in bins. Now we may encapsulate the rule 'if toy is small then safe is false' within the Infant object, without having an impact on other objects and eliminating much redundant code.

10.3.1 Blackboards and actor systems

We have already met blackboard architectures in Chapter 7. In complex systems, and especially in real-time systems, there may be many sources of knowledge and many plans and procedures. Typical application areas are fighter battle systems and financial trading rooms.

Blackboard systems have been applied in a military context where, for example, a fighter pilot has to process a vast amount of incoming data in order to select from a limited range of actions. The model is one of several independent knowledge-based systems monitoring the input and advising the pilot when something interesting occurs; e.g. when a real target or threat is identified among many dummy targets or threats. The financial trader is in a similar position, being the recipient of a vast amount of data from several information feeds; all of them in need of analysis to determine (a) if anything interesting has occurred requiring further analysis, and (b) what the appropriate action should be.

A blackboard system is so called because it imitates a group of highly specialized experts sitting around a blackboard in order to solve a problem. As new information arrives it is written up on the blackboard where all the experts can look. When an expert sees that s/he can contribute a new fact based on specialist knowledge, s/he raises a hand. This might be to confirm or refute an hypothesis already on the board or to add a new one. The new evidence will now be available to the other experts who may in turn be prompted to contribute to the discussion. The chairman of the group monitors the experts and selects their contributions in order, according to an agenda visible on the board. Common storage is the blackboard, and the agenda is under the control of a specialized inference program. In the trading context, our experts might be represented by a technical analysis expert system, a fundamental analysis system, an option strategy adviser, and so on. If, for example, new price information arrives from the wire, the chartist might detect a possible reversal but need to await confirmation before a sell signal is issued. However, the fundamental analyst only needed this small piece of confirmatory evidence to suggest a flagging in the security's fortunes. The combined evidence may be enough to generate a valid signal and thus, incidentally, beat all the pure chartists to the winning post. Perhaps also this action of selling the security will attract the attention of the option strategist who now sees a need to modify positions in order to maintain a risk-free hedge or to avoid an otherwise unexpected exercise in now unfavourable market conditions.

Actor and object-oriented systems allow objects to send and receive messages that have definite destination objects when sent. The blackboard model requires that we think of the blackboard as 'broadcasting' its contents; the messages are posted to a common data area. An object-oriented model of a system does not permit such a metaphor but there is a simple remedy. Sometimes the blackboard is partitioned into pigeonholes. We ask every agent (or other object) to register interest in the contents of particular pigeonholes. When the contents of a pigeonhole change, the agent is sent a message either with the new data or merely a 'has changed' flag. If the latter, the agent must decide whether to send a retrieval message to the blackboard object. The agent may notify the blackboard of any significant changes in its state: its 'opinions'. The architecture of the blackboard is shown in Figure 10.4. This notion is now widely recognized as an example of an architectural pattern. Here we merely point out the importance of this architecture for systems where intelligent agents need to co-operate in achieving shared goals or during collaborative problem solving.

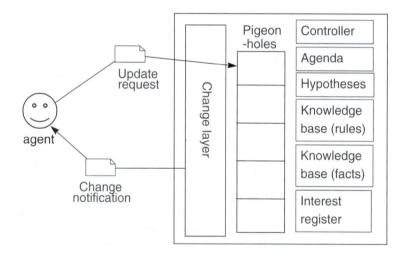

Figure 10.4 Blackboard architecture.

Usually, messages must be dealt with according to the order in which they arrive and the state of the receiving object at that time; thus all such systems tend to look like real-time systems and benefit greatly from parallel hardware architectures. Having said this, one of the earliest blackboard system was Hearsay-II which was addressed to the problem of speech understanding, which is only implicitly a real-time problem. Most applications since then have been in military real-time communication, command and control systems, so that little has been published openly. However, blackboard systems have been used in plant process control and complex currency dealing decision support systems, nearly always using some object technology.

BLOBS   Blackboard systems run into problems in continuous reasoning because of the accumulation of information in the common data area and the global accessibility of that data. Actor systems, on the other hand, need to know in advance which objects will need to communicate. For these reasons there have been attempts to combine the formalisms in some systems. One programming environment, BLOBS, was developed along these lines by Cambridge Consultants Ltd. and applied to such problems as ship positioning control. BLOBS supports an object-oriented programming style, so that instead of passing data to a program for manipulation messages are sent to objects. Objects are synchronized with a real-time clock and an 'agenda' object may be set up to schedule processing. An object (unsurprisingly in BLOBS) is called a 'blob'. Here is an example of a blob:

```
static blob Biggles
        private vars x,y,dx,dy
        on_message fly_north with s=speed do
                o --> dy; s --> dx;
                send 'biggles flies north to base';
        enddo
        ...
        on_message tick with t=time interval do
                x+t*dx --> x;
                y+t*dy --> y;
        enddo
        on_message where_are_you with s=sender do
                send 'biggles is at', x=x,y=y, to (s);
        enddo
endblob
```

A typical way to implement a blackboard system is to set up a family of frames representing a community of co-operating experts. Each frame has a slot containing a 'trigger' and one indicating priority of execution of the procedures attached to the frame. Some frames will fire their procedures on the trigger value denoting the start of processing and these are, *ceteris paribus*,[1] executed in order of priority. The priorities may be subject to dynamic alteration as earlier procedures write facts on the blackboard. Demons may be used to detect critical changes to the blackboard's data and amend the appropriate frames. Other frames are triggered directly by certain values in the database.

Object-oriented programming is a programming style rather than a control or knowledge representation strategy. It is designed to promote modularity and reusability of code as well as facilitating better representation in the user interface. However, in looking at systems like Xerox's LOOPS which combines object-

---

[1] Other things being equal

oriented programming with InterLisp, high quality graphics and a number of facilities for encoding knowledge-based systems, it is difficult sometimes not to end up confusing the two. If a generic object can inherit from multiple parents it is sometimes called a **flavour**. If all the attributes and methods associated with an object, flavour or blob can be filled in, then there is a case to be made for saying that we **understand** the object. The property attachment and procedural inheritance features lead us to a notion of meaning being inherent in an object-oriented description. Object-oriented control and meta-control strategies clearly have an interesting future. Much depends on sorting out the terminological mess wherein there is no clear distinction between objects, frames, semantic nets and so on.

10.3.2 Neural networks and parallel computing

Hardware design itself has already fallen under the influence of the object-oriented philosophy. It is claimed that the AS/400 machine is object-oriented in precisely the sense that the hardware and operating system was designed using object-oriented techniques. The operating systems of the NeXT and Rekursiv machines were also object-oriented. With the emergence of various models of parallel computation and the hardware based on them, object-orientation is a very natural way to model message passing between hardware units. Also, the Rekursiv offers direct hardware support for message passing, dynamic binding and so on. Parallelism comes in various levels of granularity; from simple four-processor transputer surfaces on PC cards up to massively parallel machines such as Fahlman's Connection Machine. The most massively parallel device in the known universe is the human brain. Neural networks are a kind of massively parallel machine loosely based on the structure of the brain. I will use them to illustrate how the object-oriented metaphor maps onto the implementation, or indeed simulation, of parallel architectures. First we must understand what a neural network is.

The study of neural nets is at least as old as the computer itself and can be traced back to the work of McCulloch and Pitts in the 1940s. As with AI, when commercial data processing came to dominate the use of the world's computer power, research in this area retired to the university. Nevertheless, it remained an active and promising area. Ross Ashby's influential books *Design for a Brain* (1956) and *Introduction to Cybernetics* (1960) show that the same set of ideas which we discuss below was being vigorously pursued by the Cyberneticians in the fifties. Neuro-scientists also expressed much interest, as well as posing many interesting problems for verification by means of neural models.

Probably the most significant early practical application of the idea came with Rosenblatt's PERCEPTRON and this device gives us an opportunity to explain the basic ideas behind neural computing.

Essentially, the idea is to design a computational device which, in place of the monolithic single processor of the Von Neumann machine, has many very simple processors rather like the neurons in the animal brain. These distributed processors or neurons have to work together in order to achieve anything but the most trivial computational tasks. To do this, organic neurons seem to send messages through an immense tangle of interconnexions, and a neural network system taking this as inspiration proposes that its processors too are connected in as complex a way as is needed. The PERCEPTRON is a simple example based on a model of the visual cortex, designed to be able to 'learn to see' coherent physical objects presented to it (in 2D) via a TV camera or similar. To see that this is in fact a very difficult problem, consider how hard it is to recognize a familiar object from a photograph taken from an unusual angle or close position. Some frame of reference is required. In the case of the PERCEPTRON and similar devices this is achieved by the introduction of a teacher who can tell the system when it has and has not recognized the object correctly.

The original PERCEPTRON is a relatively simple device compared to modern neural nets. (Technically, it is a one-layer network – see below.) Modern networks have been shown to be at least as powerful as digital computers (Turing machines). Nevertheless, important theorems can be proved about the PERCEPTRON's ability to learn to recognize patterns.

Conventional computers usually consist of a single, monolithic central processor together with various peripheral devices. Information is processed sequentially in accordance with a stored program of arbitrary complexity. This model of information processing differs radically from the structure of the human brain which, so far as we know, consists of millions (roughly 10^{11} it is believed) of very simple processors called neurons connected together by an even larger number of synaptic connexions to other neurons. To compensate for the simplicity of the neurons as computers and the slow rates of information transfer across synapses, the brain carries out its processing in a massively parallel fashion. These discoveries of neuroscience inspire attempts to construct computing machinery that mimics this parallel distributed kind of information processing. Implementations of this idea are thus often called neural networks.

The connexions in a neural network permit the units (neurons) to send very simple excitatory or inhibitory messages. Since an individual unit may receive many (in the brain, many thousand) signals it is necessary to propose that a 'weight' is given to each input and used to derive the total effect on the unit.

In detail a neural network consists of:

- a set of n units, which are simple computers capable of computing the 'activation' of the unit as a function of the input signals and weights and an output function of the activation;
- a rank n vector representing the current activation of each unit;
- an $n \times n$ matrix representing the connectivity and the weight distribution in the network; note that a weight of zero is equivalent to 'no connexion';
- a learning rule by which weights are modified in the light of experience.

This is a slightly simplified account but the interested reader may refer for more detail to the classic text by the PDP research group (Rummelhart and McClelland, 1986).

Figure 10.5 illustrates a simplified fragment of a neural network. Looking at a single unit j we take some function of the weights w_{ij} and the output values o_i of all the incoming connexions to arrive at the net input net_j. The simplest way to do this is to take the weighted sum of the input to j. Next we compute the new activation a_j of j as some function of the old activation and net_j. Usually this function will be a simple sigmoid function of net_j, as shown in Figure 10.6(a) which ignores the old value of a_j, but this will depend heavily on the properties required of the target application. The final step is to calculate the output which will be propagated to the units connected to j, which is often done by a simple threshold model as illustrated in Figure 10.6(b). That is, the net input has to reach a certain level before the neuron will 'fire'.

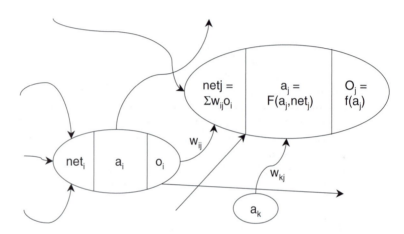

Figure 10.5 The structure of a neural network (after Rummelhart and McClelland).

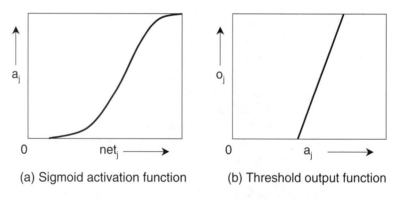

(a) Sigmoid activation function   (b) Threshold output function

Figure 10.6 Typical activation and threshold functions.

The learning algorithm models the ability of the brain to construct useful groupings of neurons which act as symbol recognition units or feature detectors. There are many ways in which this can be done, the oldest being the Hebbian learning algorithm which I shall describe in outline.

The Hebb rule strengthens the weight on the link between two units if both are active in proportion to the product of the activation of the second unit and the output from the first. Thus:

$$w_{ij} = ko_i a_j$$

A more complicated version of this rule allows for a 'teaching input' which is the activation resulting from a successful pattern match and is compared with the actual activation; so that

$$w_{ij} = k(t_i - o_i)a_j$$

This is one of many possible similar learning rules and is known as the Delta or Widrow-Hoff rule. Another popular idea is to regard learning as a process of minimizing the 'energy' or generalized cost of the network which is defined as a function of the weights and activations summed across all the connexions. The weights are altered by relaxation towards the local minimum and additional steps are taken to ensure that the global minimum is found with very high probability. These techniques are closely related to the genetic algorithms (Goldberg, 1989) found in machine learning systems on conventional hardware.

The details of which learning rules are best at what tasks need not detain us. This is in fact a topic of continuing research, but enough is known about some algorithms to show that real systems can be built with them.

It is convenient to divide the units of a neural net into hidden (or internal) input and output units. The input and output units are the only ones visible to the user and the hidden units are usually organized (at least conceptually) into layers. The idea here is that units at level $n+1$ represent the activation of abstract features represented by the activation of groups of units at level n. For example, we may want our network to be able to recognize printed words. The input units may take letters from an Optical Character Reader. Suppose there is only one output unit which fires if and only if the input sequence is a word. It is necessary to postulate hidden units that act as valid sequence detectors. The first layer is devoted to recognizing the letters. This, of course, is a simplification, and we should really include a layer of feature detectors for the components of the letters. If the input matches a letter unit then that unit is excited and all other letter units are inhibited. The letter detectors are connected to units in the next layer which will represent words. If all or some of the letters in a word are active then the word will become active. How these units evolve is either a matter for the learning algorithm (and the teacher) or the designer may hard-wire the appropriate excitatory links. A typical such scheme is shown as Figure 10.7.

Neural networks are good at pattern completion as well as pattern recognition. For example, in some of the early research work, it was found that some neural nets could learn to recognize partly obscured words, as shown in Figure 10.8(a). They could even learn to guess at non-words as indicated in Figure 10.8(b), possibly by having learnt some 'looks like a word' rules. Another important feature of these networks is that, as with the brain, if a few processors are damaged they can still continue to function, even if only to a limited capacity. This property is known as graceful degradation. Monolithic computer systems degrade most ungracefully when they go down.

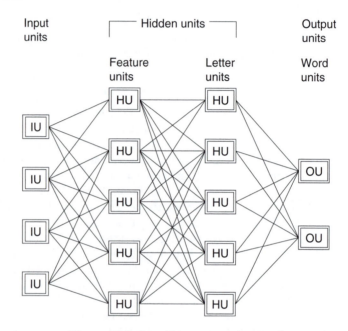

Figure 10.7 A multi-layer neural network.

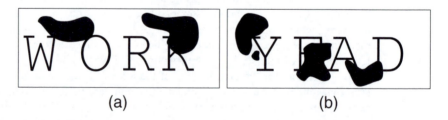

(a)   (b)

Figure 10.8 (a) A word recognition problem; **(b)** a similar non-word problem.

The main observation to be made here is that neurons are evidently objects with encapsulated behaviour and which communicate by passing messages. What better than an object-oriented programming language to simulate such a system? Blum (1992) provides the basics of an object-oriented framework for neural systems and gives source code for a C++ class library containing several learning algorithms. The second observation is that, although short-term memory resides in the units as activation, long-term memory resides in the weightings; in the system as a whole. This, I think, leads to some interesting conclusions about the global properties of object-oriented systems where the message passing topology may be viewed as containing unencapsulated control information. This observation influenced the treatment of methods in Chapter 6.

10.3.3 Intelligent agents

Increasing complexity of business problems is starting to generate market demand for 'smart' software systems that co-operate with end users by being able to reason about the tasks they perform: intelligent agents. Some problems are harder to solve with other technologies; e.g. searching the internet. Agent technology also provides an effective metaphor for domain analysis, systems design and implementation. It facilitates reuse at the knowledge level.

We need to understand how to model intelligent agents for two quite distinct reasons. First, to see how business processes can be modelled using objects that represent agents – as in Chapter 7 – and, second, to understand how object-oriented models can be used to describe the agent-based computer systems that are becoming increasingly important.

Adding rules to the interfaces of objects has the useful side effect of enabling us to model intelligent agents and multi-agent systems without any special purpose agent-based modelling machinery. Agents are autonomous, flexible software objects that can respond to changes in their environment or context, engage in 'social' acts via a common agent communication language and be proactive in the manner of the Intellisense agents in MS Office, for example.

One of the major reasons that corporations are adopting object technology is the move to distributed architectures, but even n-tier architectures are often beset with severe network bandwidth problems. Using mobile agents can reduce the amount of network traffic. The mobility of agents means that, when it is more efficient, we can send the program across the network rather than a request to retrieve unfiltered data. Smart agents can be used to personalize systems for individual needs and skills, which has the effect of reducing the cognitive and learning burden on these users. Agents that can learn, adapt and exchange goals and data can be used to speed up information searches, especially across networks or the internet.

Another area where agent computing is becoming influential, at least as a modelling metaphor, is in business process modelling and re-engineering. The focus in most work on BPR is on process and this is as it should be. However, as Taylor (1995) has pointed out, an exclusive obsession with process can be dangerous because business depends on the management of resources and the structure of the organization as well as on effective processes. Thus, any approach to business process modelling needs to be able to model all three aspects: resources, organization and processes. It turns out that the agent metaphor when combined with an object-oriented perspective on systems analysis provides an effective solution to this modelling problem. Furthermore, modelling a user's responsibilities with an intelligent agent can often reduce the cognitive dissonance between the user's mental model of a system and its actual structure.

WHAT IS AN AGENT?

Agent technology has its roots in the study of distributed artificial intelligence (DAI), although the popularity of the approach has had to wait for more mundane applications in mobile computing, mail filtering and network search.

Agents have been used to monitor stock markets and trade shares automatically, to find and buy cheap flights and to collect data on a user's use of a computer. They have evident uses in e-commerce where there are purchasing agents that can find the best price for a product, such as a book, across multiple web sites. An agent system handles malfunctions aboard the space shuttle. The White House uses e-mail agents to filter thousands of requests for information. MIT has built agents to schedule meetings. Researchers from the fields of robotics, entertainment, knowledge-based systems, human–computer interaction, databases, distributed systems, communications networks, cognitive science, psychology and virtual reality have all shown a keen interest. Sample applications of agent technology to date include data filtering and analysis, process monitoring and alarm generation, business process and workflow control, data/document retrieval and storage management, personal digital assistants, computer supported co-operative working, simulation modelling and gaming.

Agents in current systems perform information filtering, task automation, pattern recognition and completion, user modelling, decision making, information retrieval, resource optimization based on negotiation (e.g. in air traffic control), routing, simulation and planning.

Other current applications include:

- user interface agents (such as Microsoft's Office Assistant);
- battlefield command and control;
- process monitoring (of networks and of business processes).

Along with the plethora of new applications there is a great deal of very confusing terminology facing anyone attempting to understand the technology of intelligent agent computing. We read many conflicting and overlapping terms such as Intelligent Agents, Knowbots, Softbots, Taskbots, Personal assistants and Wizards. Also, we may often encounter writings on network agents which are not true agents in the sense of most of the above terms. Furthermore, there are several competing definitions of an intelligent agent in the literature. Russell and Norvig (1995) characterize an agent as 'anything that can be viewed as perceiving its environment through sensors and acting upon that environment through effectors. A rational agent is one that does the right thing'. A report from Ovum (Guilfoyle and Warner, 1994) tightens this slightly: 'An agent is a self-contained software element responsible for executing part of a programmatic process, usually in a distributed environment. An intelligent agent makes use of non-procedural process information

– knowledge – defined in and accessed from a knowledge base, by means of inference mechanisms.' But a more compelling definition comes from Genesereth and Ketchpel (Riecken, 1994): 'An entity is a software agent if and only if it communicates correctly with its peers by exchanging messages in an *agent communication language*.' This is a most important point if agents from different manufacturers are to meet and co-operate. Kendall *et al.* (1997) say that agents are objects 'that proactively carry out autonomous behaviour and co-operate with each other through negotiation', which further supports this view.

Agent communication languages (ACLs) perform a very similar rôle to object request brokers and may be implemented on top of them. ACLs are necessary so that agents can be regarded as distributed objects that need not know of each other's existence when created. There are two kinds of ACL, procedural ones such as General Magic's Telescript, and declarative languages such as the European Space Agency's KQML/KIF.

One might add that an agent is an entity that can sense, make decisions, act, communicate with other entities, relocate, maintain beliefs and learn. Not all agents will have all these features but we should at least allow for them. One way to do this is to classify agents according to the level of features they exhibit. We will consider four levels in order of increasing complexity and power:

- Basic software 'agents';
- Reactive intelligent agents;
- Deliberative intelligent agents;
- Hybrid intelligent agents.

It is common to apply the description AGENT to quite ordinary code modules that perform pre-defined tasks. This is an especially common usage in relation to macros attached to spreadsheets or database system triggers and stored procedures. Such 'agents' are usually standalone and have no learning capability, no adaptability, no social behaviour and a lack of explicit control. The term is also applied to simple mail agents or web macros written in PERL (Practical Extraction and Report Language) or Tcl (Tool command language) (Ousterhout, 1994). The PC automation scripts to be found in HP's NewWave environment were an even simpler example.

Reactive intelligent agents represent the simplest category of agent where the term is properly applied. These are data-driven programs; meaning that they react to stimuli and are not goal oriented. They perform pre-defined tasks but may perform symbolic reasoning, often being rule based. They are sometimes able to communicate with other agents. They may have learning capability and emergent intelligence. At a macro level they may sometimes exhibit explicit control but there is no explicit micro-level control. They cannot reason about organization. Homogeneous groupings of such agents are common. Examples of reactive intelligent agents include monitor/alert agents encoded as a set of knowledge-sources or rules with a global control strategy.

Deliberative intelligent agents are mainly goal-driven programs. They can have the ability to set and follow new goals. They typically use symbolic representation and reasoning; typically using a production rule approach. They typically maintain a model of their beliefs about their environment and goal seeking status. They may be mobile and able to communicate and exchange data (or even goals) with other agents that they encounter. Deliberative agents may have learning capability. They can reason about organization and are able to perform complex reasoning. Their intelligence is programmed at the micro level at which there is explicit control. Heterogeneous grouping of these agents is possible. Data retrieval agents that will fetch and filter data from a database or the internet are typical examples of this kind of agent.

According to some authorities (Kendall *et al.,* 1997) this is the weakest permissible use of the term AGENT. **Weak agents** on this view are autonomous, mobile, reactive to events, able to influence their environments and able to interact with other agents. **Strong agents** have the additional properties of storing beliefs, goals and plans of action, learning and veracity; although there is some dispute over the meaning of the latter property.

Hybrid intelligent agents are a combination of deliberative and reactive agents. Such agents can be mobile and may try actively and dynamically to co-operate with other agents. If they can also learn, they are **strong hybrid intelligent agents**. Such agents usually contain (or may access) a knowledge base of rules and assertions (beliefs) and a plan library. An interpreter enables the agent to select a plan according to its current goals and state. When an event occurs a plan is selected (instantiated) to represent the agent's current intention.

PITFALLS Although the potential benefits are enormous, there are still many open issues in intelligent agent technology. The theories of agents are still largely incomplete. There has been a complete absence of methodological guidelines hitherto. There is still a limited choice of development tools as discussed above. The underlying technology is potentially very complex. Finally, we have yet to accumulate large amounts of experience and expertise based on real-life, large-scale applications.

Agent design remains something of a black art because there are no published guidelines on how to select appropriate agent architectures for different classes of problem solving. A designer must also struggle to answer the questions of how an agent acquires its knowledge and how that knowledge should be represented. One must decide how a complex task should be decomposed and allocated to different agents. The question of the 'agent communication language' must be addressed too: how should heterogeneous agents co-operate and communicate with each other? Finally, there are new problems of a legal and ethical nature, such as whether an intelligent agent can ever be trusted. People might think that their jobs are threatened and this too could be a barrier to acceptance.

We have seen that there is a plethora of agent definitions and approaches – many of which seem dubious. The current trend towards endowing computers with more intelligence is expected to grow, but may be slowed down by a shortage of skilled resources. Further proliferation of agent-based software into mobile and WAN-based computing is likely to be the most visible symptom in the short term. Many challenges remain, both theoretical and practical. We can expect to see increasing use of OO methods and tools to model and deliver agent-based systems. It is clear that there will be increasing utilization of distributed object-oriented technologies such as CORBA with no use of agents. On the other hand, intelligent agents show great promise as an enabling technology to help realize large-scale OO developments. The emergence of standard agent-based architectures and ACLs may lead to a market in tradable agents.

AGENT ARCHITEC- TURE Intelligent agents are intelligent in the sense that they embody some kind of expertise or the ability to learn. This expertise may be encoded as production rules, in which case the agent must be equipped with an inference engine to process them. Learning algorithms are usually, of course, procedural in nature and may be based on decision branching (e.g. ID3), neural nets or genetic algorithms. Agents need to communicate with users and with each other. As I have mentioned, the best way to do this is via a standard agent communication language. Unfortunately, such a universal standard is not yet agreed so that designers are often forced to create one or work within a proprietary environment.

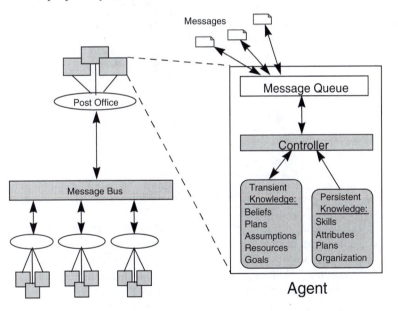

Figure 10.9 A typical architecture for an agent.

We can generalize about the basic architecture that most agent systems share. Figure 10.9 shows a typical architecture. Each agent has a controller that stores or can access its inference engine and problem solving strategy. The agent encapsulates two kinds of knowledge in its knowledge base: persistent and transient. The persistent knowledge often takes the form of attributes and methods that represent its skills in an object-oriented implementation, but the methods may be coded non-procedurally; Prolog is a common implementation language. The agent may also store knowledge about the rôles that it plays in the overall agent organization and about its plans. Plans, which are fixed, are to be distinguished from those that vary during execution, the latter being part of the agent's transient knowledge base along with its current assumptions, beliefs, acquaintances and short-term goals. Agents communicate via a message queue and deliver messages to 'post offices' on the network which deliver to other agents, systems or users. The reader will note the resonance of this communication architecture with that of object request brokers, and the latter can be used to implement agent-oriented systems. Actual agent-based systems vary considerably but share this basic approach in outline at least.

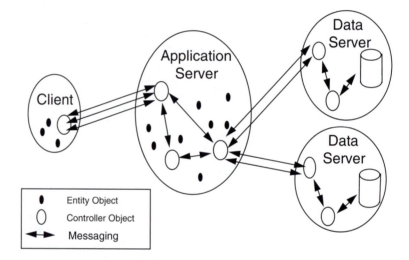

Figure 10.10 Three-tier client-server: RPC approach.

One of the chief problems with current client-server systems is the amount of network traffic generated. Even on high speed LANs this can lead to unpredictable performance levels: which is worse than predictably slow performance for most people. Many companies have tried to address the problem by moving away from their first generation two-tier systems, with all the additional problems of stored procedure calls, to three-tier systems based on the use of remote procedure calls (RPCs). In a three-tier system much of the processing logic is moved to an intermediate 'application server' that is accessed by clients needing an application's services, often nowadays via an ORB. The calls to the database are now mostly pure SQL data retrieval. The architecture of a typical such system is shown in Figure 10.10. Note how busy the network may become. This is largely because applications retrieve tables that contain many data irrelevant to the user's purpose. Note also the need to use controller objects. These dangerous beasties are objects that can control multiple execution threads and, because of this, may need access to the implementations of several other objects or have to maintain complex knowledge about them at the very least. There is thus a danger that this violation of encapsulation could throw away all the maintenance advantages of object-orientation.

Agents come to the rescue. With agents it is possible to send a program across the network rather than an RPC or SQL statement. As illustrated in Figure 10.11, this mobile (or missionary) agent takes over the responsibilities of the controller objects, and can do so without the heinous violation of encapsulation (because agents can be represented as *bona fide* objects). Since the agents can contain logic they can filter the data they retrieve and return to the client with a packet of relevant data only. In this way data traffic is reduced for a whole class of applications where searches are based on complex criteria. This blurs the distinction between client and server, bringing agent systems closer to peer-to-peer architectures. Therefore, decisions about the location of code can be made later in a project, thus reducing design risk.

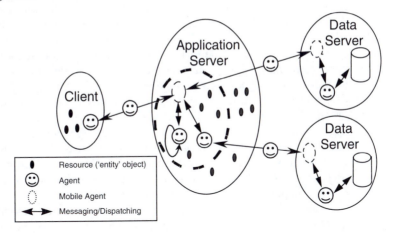

Figure 10.11 Three-tier client-server using agents.

The agent model is a model of distributed problem solving. There are several approaches to the co-ordination of distributed co-operating agents. These include centralized control, contracting models (as found in object-oriented approach or for example in Smith's Contract Net), hierarchical control via organizational units, multi-agent planning systems and negotiation models. These are not discussed further here, but one type of strategy is especially important for systems involving multiple, co-operating agents that each apply specialized knowledge to help solve a common problem. A common architecture for such applications is the 'implicit invocation' or blackboard architecture.

We now turn to a discussion of the relationship between agents and objects and show how suitably extended object-oriented methods can be used to model agents. This leads naturally to a discussion of how to use the agent metaphor to model business processes.

Developers designing agent systems need a modelling technique and it is natural to want to use the metaphors of object technology because agents, like objects, obviously encapsulate both state and behaviour. Certainly, object-oriented languages, such as Java, CLOS, and so on, can be used to build agent-based systems but most object-oriented methods find it *very* hard indeed to represent intelligent agents that encapsulate reasoning capability. Indeed most agent-based implementations use a mixture of procedural and non-procedural languages, such as C with Prolog. The difficulty with modelling is that most of these methods do not allow for objects to encapsulate second order information about themselves: how attributes and operations are related to each other. Methods that support class invariants, such as BON (Waldén and Nerson, 1995), go some way to solve the problem but still find it difficult to represent the inferencing capability of intelligent agents. BON invariants must be converted into procedural code in Eiffel, losing the non-procedural character of production rules in the process. Such methods fail to realize the need to chain rules together and perform inference (search) across them. The only method, to my knowledge, that encapsulates rulesets within objects is SOMA.

Any attempt to cobble together a method for agent-based systems from the first generation OO methods is therefore doomed to failure. I have encountered several attempts to use a goulash of techniques from OMT, Objectory, RDD and so on. All of them had problems. Comparing the agent metaphor with the terminology used by OO modellers we might note that agents need to monitor events in databases and trigger operations when they change, heterogeneous agents need ontologies to co-operate, intelligent agents contain rules and can reason and some intelligent agents need to reason in the presence of uncertainty. Object-oriented methods usually have no support for these ideas. Also, agents manage their own threads of control. There is scant support for this (except in Actor systems).

Other difficulties include modelling agent co-ordination, task allocation, knowledge sharing and interacting goals where agents might need to reason about the beliefs or co-ordination strategies of other agents. Notice that several requirements for modelling agent systems are entirely unsupported or only receive support in non-standard approaches that use delegation and active objects, as with methods that have tools to model actor systems. Where there is some support, we must ask: Is the support adequate for agents and does it conform to object-oriented principles? We might, for example, note that Jacobson's 'controller objects' are introduced to manage threads of control that pass through several other objects. Implementers are frequently tempted to allow controllers to violate the encapsulation of the controlled objects. Encapsulation must be preserved when we design agents to take on this control function. This is easier in the approach advocated here because agents only communicate with the interfaces of other objects and other agents (using an agent communication language preferably). This militates against the danger of very severe maintenance problems when 'control' objects violate encapsulation.

FUNCTIONAL UNIT (FUN) is a term introduced by Farhoodi (1994) to capture the idea of a composite agent: a set of agents organized into a group of co-operating agents within a defined organizational structure and encapsulated by a single interface. The interface intercepts all messages and delegates them to appropriate staff agents. This concept is called a WRAPPER in SOMA when applied to vanilla-flavoured objects. A more specialized use of FUNs in agent modelling involves modelling the rôles that an agent can adopt. Functional context can change expectations about an agent's behaviour and reduce communication thereby. Individual agents perform tasks that may be represented as operations in their interfaces. These tasks can be abstracted away from the class the agent belongs to and stored within rôles. Rôles are like classes except that their instances can migrate to other rôles (dynamic classification). In effect, agents are responsible for the tasks stored by a rôle. Also, the agent can be designated as a component of a FUN that stores rôles and can provide substitutes when the agent fails.

As it turns out, most of the problems referred to above are overcome by SOMA, even though its innovations were not designed for this purpose but to extend object modelling to business process modelling problems. I will try to explain this rather remarkable coincidence.

It should be apparent that rulesets, thus defined, are all that is necessary to make objects into agents. Forward chaining (data-driven) rulesets enable reactive agents and backward chaining (goal-driven) régimes support deliberative agents. Because each object can contain more than one ruleset and each ruleset may have a specified régime, hybrid agents can also be described. Note that learning abilities would not normally be represented as rulesets but, more likely, by operations – or a mixture of the two.

Repositories of business objects become, effectively, the domain ontology. This object-oriented ontology extends the concept of a data dictionary, not only by including behaviour in the form of operations but by encapsulating business rules in an explicit form.

Intelligent agents may have to operate in the presence of uncertainty and uncertainty comes in many guises: probability, possibility and many more. Modelling systems that restrict the logic in which rules or class invariants are expressed to standard predicate logic or first order predicate calculus (FOPC) are too restrictive. SOMA allows the designer to pick the logic used for reasoning: FOPC, temporal logic, fuzzy logic, deontic logic (the logic of obligation or duty), etc. Just as a ruleset has an inference régime, it has a logic. In fact the régime and the logic are intimately related. For example, standard fuzzy logic implies (usually) a one-shot forward chaining strategy that treats the rules as if they all fire in parallel. In SOMA support for fuzzy reasoning is particularly strong: fuzzy objects with fuzzy-valued attributes are possible and partial (fuzzy) inheritance is clearly defined.

Objects with rulesets support the modelling and design of intelligent agents and systems but agents are also the key to modelling business processes and reducing the cognitive dissonance between models of the world and system designs.

Up to now I have been writing about the technology of intelligent agents and the way object-oriented analysis methods can model agent-based systems. The assumption has been that someone who wants to develop a computer system using mobile intelligent agents can use SOMA to model the requirements before and during system development. So, our subject matter has been lifting the agent metaphor up from the code level to the more abstract analysis level, freeing the model of language and architectural dependencies in the process. Now I want to stand the approach on its head and ask: Can the agent metaphor be applied to describing systems in the world instead of systems inside a machine? SOMA places emphasis on intelligent agents in two areas:

- ■ as an implementation technique;
- ■ in the business process model.

It is to the latter topic that we now turn our attention.

An agent object model, which is a business process model, provides a framework in which activities may occur. It initially provides a description of the players involved in the activities and their interacting commitments (conversations). These players are agents, as discussed in Chapter 8. It provides a high level view of the ambit of the system being designed. What the agent model explicitly does not do is to introduce any concept of *sequence*. The further level of detail regarding sequence of activity is developed using sequence diagrams or task association sets.

As I have said, external agents are 'black boxes' outside our control and organization. Internal agents work within the context and have motives known to us. Either may adopt rôles as direct system users and become actors thereby. However, it is unusual for an external agent to adopt a user rôle. If this does happen the external agent is an actor. Internal, external agents and actors communicate with each other by passing messages. A message is emitted as a result of an event.

In conclusion we can state first that a rule-enhanced object-oriented method such as SOMA is highly suitable for modelling projected agent-based systems and that less semantically rich methods are likely to fail or introduce unnecessary complexity. Secondly, using the agent metaphor at the beginning of requirements engineering or business process re-engineering provides a theoretically sound way of deducing user requirements and their relationship to business objectives. We can reify these requirements as task objects with far more confidence that we have discovered them correctly than we would have with a more arbitrary and non-object-oriented technique such as use cases.

⊟ 10.4 Back to the future

In the previous editions of this book I made a number of predictions about what was then an evidently emerging technology. Now that object-oriented methods are more stable and accepted, it is possible to evaluate how accurate some of these predictions were.

LANGUAGE TRENDS I predicted that most 3GLs would acquire object-oriented features in the manner that C, Lisp, COBOL and Pascal already had. I went slightly further and predicted that these extensions would become standard and the provision of object-oriented features would be delivered willy-nilly with the core compiler and become part of the international language standards. Even COBOL would not be able to resist this trend. C has in fact been surprisingly resilient in the face of pressure to introduce classes into its definition. And Object COBOL seems to have failed to impress IT management. The requirement here is not to write new reusable code but to reuse the millions of lines of existing COBOL code and extend or replace it gradually. EAI is now the major route to this goal, rather than language extension superseding most re-engineering efforts, perhaps because of something I did point out: the poor quality of much COBOL code. Object-oriented programming languages have by now penetrated even the most Luddite DP organizations.

Paradoxically, I claimed, it was difficult to see the respectability of an Object COBOL being widely conferred on Ada, and this seems to have been justified by the decline in interest in that language. As predicted, C++ remained the language of choice for developments where the performance or single-user limitations of Smalltalk could not be tolerated. Of course I did not know in 1994 that Java would largely replace Smalltalk and Eiffel for many mainstream applications, with IDEs standing in for the prototyping facilities of Smalltalk. Where declarative semantics was important I said CLOS would be the language of choice. It seems that there are so few such applications that have caught the public eye that this too was a vain forecast. Embedded AI does exist but CLOS is not often heard of outside academic circles.

Open research issues in object-oriented programming languages included, and still include, the convergence of the functional and object-oriented styles, the relationships between object-oriented programming, logic programming and formal methods, efficiency, the development of type theories for object-oriented programming languages and the possibility of mixed language environments facilitated by small interfaces between languages regarded as encapsulated objects. The latter has been only partially addressed by the middleware developments discussed in Chapter 4. The introduction of the agent mechanism in Eiffel confirms the trend towards the convergence of functional and object-oriented programming. There are still a number of open questions about object-oriented databases, including those concerned with schema evolution, locking strategies, distributed access and query languages. I said that relational databases would continue to acquire object-oriented features and within ten years it will be hard to tell the difference. Performance issues aside, this has already largely happened – four years early – as we saw in Chapter 5.

As hardware costs came down, I said, the trend to garbage collection and dynamic binding would be reinforced. Java has vindicated this statement, but I now predict that Java is a long way from being the last word in object-oriented programming languages and we may well see completely new ones incorporating the lessons of both Eiffel and CBD. I probably over-emphasized the rôle of parallel hardware in all this but at least multi-processing is now commonplace.

4GLs have continued, as predicted, to acquire object-oriented features but have become less important – temporarily I expect – in mainstream development. However, my view that expert systems software would merge into that of 4GLs has so far been unfulfilled. The ideas from expert systems in object-oriented analysis that we have discussed in this book have yet to be influential in language design. In fact, the decline in interest in Eiffel is a step backwards in a way. I still have confidence that the future will be somewhat different. On the other hand, my prediction that evolutionary development would soon become the norm in commercial software engineering has been almost fully vindicated.

I argued that repository technology was very similar to that of object-oriented databases and that we could confidently expect CASE repositories to be uniformly object-oriented within a few years. The emergence of object-relational databases has made this forecast both true and false. Object-oriented databases have not replaced relational ones for small systems and for systems involving complex data types, except in a few key areas – so I was wrong again. I also said: 'existing RDBMSs will remain the environments of choice for mainstream commercial projects, but will include object-oriented features increasingly'; this happened.

OBJECTS, AI AND UNCERTAINTY I commented on the split in terminology between the artificial intelligence, database and object-oriented communities. Objects for the latter, entities in the middle and frames for the former have so few dissimilarities that I predicted a complete convergence of the concepts, offering SOMA objects with rulesets as one view of what the converged concept could be like. The principal points of convergence were to be as follows.

- AI frame systems must have a clearer notion of the way frames encapsulate methods and offer more in the way of information hiding.
- Frames must support the multiple inheritance of explicitly encapsulated methods as well as attribute values.
- Objects must encapsulate declarative semantics and control rules.
- Objects must be able to encapsulate the methods of their attribute's domains in the form of demons which fire if needed to establish an attribute value or when the attribute is updated.
- Object-oriented systems must permit the multiple inheritance of attribute values as well as methods.

■ Object-oriented systems should incorporate means of modelling and managing uncertainty.

We still have some way to go before this happens. Commercial interest has been focused elsewhere for the time being, but I remain convinced of the need in the long term. Fuzzy objects too have found only limited application in areas such as GIS, and much of what I wrote – and repeat below – about uncertainty management stands unchanged to this day.

Very little attention has ever been paid in the object-oriented literature to problems of handling uncertainty. However, it has long been recognized that managing uncertainty is a key problem in decision making and process control problems. Decision makers want answers quickly; their accuracy is not the key issue. Also, several approximately correct solutions may be acceptable and the input data may be irreducibly uncertain or too expensive to collect with absolute precision. Furthermore, it is known that probability theory is not able to represent every kind of uncertainty. Bellman and Zadeh (1970) put it like this:

> Much of the decision-making in the real world takes place in an environment in which the goals, the constraints and the consequences of possible actions are not known precisely. To deal quantitatively with imprecision, we usually employ the concepts and techniques of probability theory and, more particularly, the tools provided by decision theory, control theory and information theory. In so doing, we are tacitly accepting the premise that imprecision – whatever its nature – can be equated with randomness. This, in our view, is a questionable assumption.
>
> Specifically, our contention is that there is a need for differentiation between *randomness* and *fuzziness*, with the latter being a major source of imprecision in many decision processes. By fuzziness, we mean a type of imprecision which is associated with *fuzzy sets*, that is, classes in which there is no sharp transition from membership to nonmembership. For example, the class of *green objects* is a fuzzy set. So are the classes of objects characterized by such commonly used adjectives as large, small, substantial, significant, important, serious, simple, accurate, approximate, etc. Actually, in sharp contrast to the notion of a class or a set in mathematics, most of the classes in the real world do not have crisp boundaries which separate those objects which belong to a class from those which do not. In this connection, it is important to note that, in discourse between humans, fuzzy statements such as 'John is *several* inches taller than Jim', 'x is *much larger* than y', 'Corporation X has a *bright future*', 'the stock market has suffered a *sharp decline*', convey information despite the imprecision of the meaning of the italicized words. In fact, it may be argued that the main distinction between human intelligence and machine intelligence lies in the ability of humans – an ability which present-day computers do not possess – to manipulate fuzzy concepts and respond to fuzzy instructions.

Most uncertainty management techniques originate from work in operational research and expert systems. The methods which have been used, or suggested seriously, fall into two broad classes: those offering quantitative numerical representations of degrees of certainty in some way, and those which attempt to model uncertainty in a purely descriptive or qualitative way.

Numerical methods include fuzzy set theory, described in outline in Appendix A, certainty factors and Bayesian probability theory. The certainty factor model of the medical diagnosis expert system MYCIN, and its descendants, assigns to each proposition a certainty between -5 and $+5$ and incorporates a calculus, arithmetically similar to that of standard fuzzy set theory, for propagating those factors through long chains of reasoning. Rules themselves may also be hedged with certainty factors and the calculus takes this into account. A generalization of this approach, and one with a more elaborate mathematical justification is the Dempster-Shafer theory of evidence. Another system, the one used in the PROSPECTOR expert system, is based on Bayesian probability theory. Here the certainties are interpreted as subjective probabilities and propagated in accordance with Bayes Rule. Chapter 2 of (Graham and Jones, 1988) covers these methods in an introductory manner.

There is thus a need to be able to represent uncertain statements in object-oriented programming languages. At present, all the functionality to do this must be hand-crafted as no object-oriented programming language has the appropriate constructs built in. Expert systems shells are usually little better, offering usually no means, or at best one or two, of representing uncertain information.

One of the only commercial product offerings in this area which offers fuzzy-set-based uncertainty management is ES/KERNEL, which is an object-oriented expert system shell marketed in Japan by Hitachi. It has been used for a number of applications. ES/KERNEL offers the usual facilities of a shell but has a number of novel features. It supports knowledge representation by rules and objects with a noticeably object-oriented style, it has an excellent graphical user and programmer interface – using Japanese characters – and it is particularly notable here for incorporating a fuzzy inference capability as an extension to the basic product. Its fuzzy facilities are extremely well implemented. I will describe these very briefly.

Membership functions (of fuzzy sets) are defined by choosing from a set of seven graphically displayed templates which can then be modified by the user who changes two, or sometimes more, parameters. These parameters may be changed dynamically during reasoning. The fuzzy part of ES/KERNEL is derived from a successful fuzzy expert control system for the Sendai subway system mentioned below. This practical application is the basis for confidence in the generality of the seven shapes, but also probably restricts the range of applicability of the system in its present form. The fuzzy rule syntax is typified as follows (in a financial application):

> IF *Official rate is high* and *average stock price is high*
> THEN *buy less pounds*
> IF *Official rate is low* and *average stock price is low*
> THEN *buy more pounds*

I have italicized the phases corresponding to membership functions. The fuzzy inference engine is essentially an add-on to the basic ES/KERNEL offering. Communication between the fuzzy rule base and the core system is accomplished by message passing between rules or procedures (methods) and the fuzzy system invocation frames. Its background and reasoning methods make it particularly suitable for applications involving real-time control and prediction.

One of the most impressive applications of fuzzy expert systems is the automatic train operations system developed by Hitachi for the Sendai municipal subway system. The significant feature here is that Sendai's commuters are prepared to entrust their safety to a piece of mathematics that is often denigrated. The benefits they receive are principally a smoother ride and lower fares as the controller also optimizes fuel consumption and other aspects of the total systems performance. The key to the success of fuzzy control as opposed to numerical control is the elicitation of rules from skilled operators. These rules are, perforce, expressed in vague terms: 'if the speed is *far below* the limit then the power notch is selected'. Also the performance indices such as safety and riding comfort are readily expressed as membership functions. The standard methods of fuzzy sets can then be used to combine elastic constraints and produce control output via the compositional rule of inference and defuzzification methods.

The experiences in the use of fuzzy methods gained by Hitachi engineers on this project led them to be incorporated in the ES/KERNEL product. One of the largest building and civil engineering companies in Japan used ES/KERNEL's fuzzy set facilities in building a system to support bridge design decisions. A major Japanese bank also planned, at one point, to use the technology to construct a sophisticated system for financial chart analysis, with the long-term aim of distributing it for routine use. The application of fuzzy sets in expert system shells was surveyed in (Graham, 1991b, 1991c). Object/IQ is a Romanized version of ES/KERNEL but the fuzzy capability has been removed. XShell from Expersoft of San Diego is a set of object-oriented development tools that supports fuzzy systems for process control applications.

Real-world problems, especially decision-making problems, usually involve the management of uncertainty. For this reason object-oriented methods need a notion of fuzzy objects and therefore of inheritance under uncertainty and of uncertainty in the expression of business rules. A fuzzy object could be a fuzzy set, appearing as the value of some attribute, or it could be an object with several fuzzy attributes. At present, uncertainty management in object-oriented methods is an unsolved problem. In inheritance systems, we have the problem of modelling partial inheritance of both crisp and fuzzy properties. For example, we might quantify the extent to which a paper clip is A Kind Of mental puzzle. The problem is especially complex when multiple inheritance is involved. Here, the problem is how to combine the inherited fuzzy properties. The theory needs to be worked out and agreed. Appendix A is a small contribution to this programme.

DISTRIBUTED AND CLIENT-SERVER SYSTEMS

I hazarded that the trend towards open distributed systems would both require and support object-orientation. Require, because client-server architectures, distributed processing and complex UIs will need the modelling expressiveness and programming productivity delivered by the object-oriented style. Support, because user demands for robust, adaptable, friendly systems will flow from early successes with object-oriented systems. Without reusability, extensibility and semantic richness, true open and distributed systems cannot be delivered at a low enough cost. Practically every trend discussed in this book has been in vindication of this view: language APIs, middleware, CBD, EAI, Catalysis, etc. I also predicted that middleware concepts and the OMG would play an important rôle in this area, as they indeed have, as we saw in Chapter 4.

CONCURRENT SYSTEMS

This is an area where relatively little – though not zero – progress has been made since the last edition of this book, and research activity remains fairly intense.

FORMAL METHODS

Formal methods address the problems of vagueness in specifications and of matching the semantics of specifications to those of source code. While the latter aim is purely laudable, there can be two views on vagueness; either it should be factored out by more formality or it is an essential component of the very act of description. For example, every user knows what an *adequate* response time is, but formal methods require that it should be expressed as so many seconds (or as a function returning so many seconds) to remove all vagueness. More seriously, a requirement for 'a friendly user interface' must be formally stated. I cannot think of a reasonable way to formalize friendliness, and incline to the opinion that vagueness is an essential feature of specification and should itself be captured in the formalism. This view is exemplified in the treatment of inheritance semantics in Appendix A, but is not a fashionable one.

Alan Turing suggested using formal logic to program computers as early as 1948. The idea was taken up by Dijkstra and Hoare in the late 1960s, who showed that the semantics of a programming language could be formally characterized and that specifications could be expressed in a formal language. Formal proof systems enable mathematicians to take a specification, expressed in a formal language based on logic or set theory, and a piece of source code and prove that the code meets the specification. A more sophisticated approach, adopted by methods like Z and VDM, involves starting with a formal specification and then refining it through step-by-step mathematical transformations into a program. The difficulty with this approach is that it takes a great deal of mathematical skill and a great deal of time to produce these proofs of correctness, often skill at the level of a PhD in mathematics.

VDM, IBM's Vienna Development Method, now has a BSI standardization committee and a standard for Z is also projected. Other formal specification methods/languages include OBJ and STC's *me too*. Logic programming languages may also be used to produce executable specifications directly. The problem with this approach is twofold. First, FOPC may not be expressive enough to capture the specification, if vagueness is involved for example. Second, and more seriously, programming in logic is still programming and this approach merely shifts the position of the programming effort forward in the life cycle. Formal logic is not itself entirely 'design free'; for the very act of stating a problem in logic involves a commitment to certain positions about what can be validly expressed. This is why there are several different logics. Another problem is the need to retrain programmers in formal logic, which is a subtle and difficult subject to master. The most sophisticated approach of all is based on AI and proof theory. The philosophy here is that a program is identical to a proof of a theorem which represents the specification. Automatic theorem provers take the specification and search for a proof. If the search terminates, the stored result is executable code. The most successful proof-theoretic methods are based on non-standard logics, such as the Martin-Löf intuitionistic type theory (Martin-Löf, 1975, 1982). At present, and for the foreseeable future, this approach only works on trivially small problems.

Because of the time- and skill-intensive nature of formal methods they are usually only considered worthwhile in safety-critical domains. However, the ideas evolved in formal methods can be adopted informally with considerable practical benefit in commercial systems, especially when combined with object-oriented methods.

Formal specification maps onto object-oriented design through the notion of a contract between client and server objects. This contract is expressible as rules, invariants and pre- and post-conditions as described in previous chapters. No formal theory is required to make immediate use of this good idea.

Wills (1991) used formal methods to overcome the problems associated with using large object libraries. The basic idea was that programmers need to know what the objects in a library do, so why not attach a formal specification to them so that one can prove theorems about them and even form composite objects constructed from them? The work depends on the notions of pre- and post-conditions and effectively extended Smalltalk with notions from VDM and Larch (Guttag *et al.*, 1985). This added to Smalltalk features which were provided as standard in Eiffel. Many of ideas emerged in a mature form in Catalysis, which we have covered.

THE DEATH OF THE MAINFRAME   Reports of the demise of the mainframe have been, like Mark Twain's, greatly exaggerated. I argued that mainframes would decline in importance except in the rôle of corporate data servers. This was based on an argument about the relative processing power of machines great and small that has been long outdated by progress according to Moore's Law[1] and the relative decline in mainframe prices. I also pointed to certain applications – such as running ATM networks – where the channel capacity provided by mainframes made them indispensable and where processing power was not the key requirement. This seems to be the situation now.

In closing, having got so many predictions wrong in the past, I will hazard but one. I suspect that within a few years (or less) a new language will take the industry

---

[1] Moore's Law states that processing power doubles about every 1.5 years. It should hold true until at least 2006.

by storm. It may have some syntactic similarities with Java, but otherwise it may look remarkably like Eiffel.

⊟ 10.5 Summary

E-commerce is the killer application for OT. It implies BPR. It needs CBD techniques and sound application and component architecture.

Every application can be developed using object-oriented methods. We briefly covered GUIs, simulation, GIS, concurrent systems, expert systems, blackboard systems and neural nets. We looked in more detail at agent-based systems, noting that object-oriented methods can be used to model agents provided that rulesets can be embedded in objects and that agents are a suitable metaphor for modelling business processes. Finally, I revisited some past predictions and made some new ones.

⊟ 10.6 Bibliographical notes

There are too many books on the web, GUIs, AI and expert systems to mention here. Peuquet and Marble (1990) is a first-rate introduction to geographic information systems and includes some seminal papers in that area. Foster and Taylor (1990) give a gentle introduction to the concepts of parallel programming in general, and the ideas behind Strand in particular. Harland and Drummond (1991) discuss the architectural support for object-oriented programming provided by the Rekursiv machine and its systems programming language, Lingo. (Graham and Jones, 1988) reflects some of my own views on expert systems and is quite a good bibliographical source, though now out of print. Feigenbaum *et al.* (1988) report on several live applications of AI and their benefits. Tello (1989) looks at some of the object-oriented AI programming systems. (Englemore and Morgan, 1988) is a comprehensive source book on blackboard systems. The essential reference on neural nets is by Rummelhart and McClelland (1986), while Aleksander and Morton (1990) give a tutorial introduction to the topic. The AI notion of frames is explained in (Winston, 1984) and very lucidly in (Shadbolt, 1989).

A useful early work on DAI is (Huhns, 1987). An excellent introduction to the topic of multi-agent systems is given by Ferber (1995). Müller and Dieng (2000) discuss how to deal with conflicts between multiple agents. An excellent and very easy to read account of how to build intelligent agents using Java is provided by Bigus and Bigus (1998). Source code for simple search, inference and learning algorithms is usefully included on an accompanying CD-ROM.

Some of the applications mentioned in this chapter are covered, though with the exception of GUIs not in great detail, by Winblad *et al.* (1990). Khoshafian and

Abnous (1990) discuss the issue of object-oriented UIs in some detail, and describe many of the interface applications and products. Pinson and Weiner (1990) describe six of the applications in detail and include useful remarks on the suitability of the various languages used and on project management issues. Taylor (1992) discusses 18 applications of object-orientation. Khoshafian *et al.* (1992) describe an object-oriented approach to office automation with detailed information on multimedia, client-server, network, GUI and groupware technologies. Turner (1984) provides a popular exposition of Martin Löf's intuitionistic type theory which is also briefly described in (Graham and Jones, 1988) which also covers AI and uncertainty in some detail. Love (1992) talks obliquely, but from direct experience, about several important commercial applications.

A

Fuzzy objects: inheritance under uncertainty

It is the nature of all greatness not to be exact.
Edmund Burke (Speech on American Taxation)

This appendix is included to support some of the remarks made in Chapters 6 and 7, because the material presented here is not easily accessible in the literature. It is not essential to read the appendix to understand the remainder of the book, and those readers without a background in expert systems, fuzzy set theory or mathematics may find it slightly heavy going.

In Chapter 6 we saw that there was a number of strategies available for dealing with conflicts in the inheritance of values and defaults when multiple inheritance is supported. This technical appendix describes one of the more unusual of these techniques that arises when the data are uncertain or the inheritance links themselves cannot be asserted with complete certainty. This problem either does not arise with the inheritance of methods or, if it does, it needs a very complex method for dealing with the propagation of certainty factors attached to the output variables returned by methods. We thus will restrict ourselves to examining the inheritance of attributes. The partial inheritance of methods, represented by a certainty factor, is taken to mean the possibility that the object can carry out the operation. This clearly has little value for a programmer but may be of immense utility in describing systems in contexts such as enterprise modelling and business process re-engineering.

This appendix describes a computational method of representing uncertain knowledge which was developed as a generalization of the frame notion introduced by Minsky (1981) and others and the object concepts of object-oriented programming. Since the generalization uses, in an intrinsic way, the theory of fuzzy sets due to Zadeh (1965), it is natural to designate the generalized objects *fuzzy objects*. These structures were first introduced, in an AI context, by Graham and Jones (1987) under the name fuzzy frames. Recently, some other, more restricted, notions of fuzzy objects have appeared, such as the one due to Yazici *et al.* (1992).

To begin with, we shall review briefly the AI version of objects – the theory of frames – and the, perhaps less familiar, machinery we will require from fuzzy set theory. At the end of the appendix we explore some of the intriguing questions which the theory raises, some of its problems and suggest topics for further research. In doing this there is cause to compare this approach with the fuzzy quantifiers of Zadeh (1982) and nonmonotonic logic (McDermott and Doyle, 1980; Reiter, 1985). It is suggested that there are important links to current issues in semantic data modelling and object-oriented databases. It is also suggested that fuzzy objects offer a unified framework for the representation of both certain and uncertain knowledge about objects, and, in a sense to be explained, generalize fuzzy relations and, *a fortiori*, relations.

⊟ A.1 Representing knowledge about objects in AI

In terms of knowledge engineering, there are many ways to represent knowledge; as rules, by logic, in procedures, etc. Each of these formalisms is usually better at expressing one particularly suitable type of knowledge. For example rules are good at describing knowledge about causality, logic at expressing relationships, and there is no better way to describe knowledge about calculating a cube root, say, than as a procedure. On the other hand, describing a bowl of fruit or a beautiful stained glass window in the form of rules would be hopelessly tedious to say the least. See (Brachman and Levesque, 1985), (Shadbolt, 1989) or (Graham and Jones, 1988) for more complete treatments of knowledge representation. The forms of AI knowledge representation which seem to best capture knowledge about objects and their properties (such as bowls of fruit) are generally referred to as semantic networks and frames. We will concentrate on these object-like representations.

Often knowledge is uncertain, and usually some additional mechanism has to be introduced in expert systems to model the uncertainty. This can be done by assigning certainty factors or probabilities to rules in rule-based approaches or to their atomic clauses, or through the use of some truth maintenance procedure, depending on the type of uncertainty involved. Shastri (1988) observes that: 'an agent cannot maintain complete knowledge about any but the most trivial environment, and therefore, he must be capable of reasoning with incomplete and uncertain information'.

In frame-based or object-oriented systems, uncertainty often arises as a side effect of multiple inheritance. Here we concentrate on the kinds of uncertainty which can be readily modelled with fuzzy sets, but, in principle, the arguments should apply to stochastic problems equally well.

A.1.1 Semantic networks and frames

I must perforce state my philosophical position *vis-à-vis* the notion of a 'frame'. I unrepentantly regard frames as data structures, rather than as models of human cognition of some sort. Further, there is little or no distinction made here between frames and structurally equivalent notions such as semantic networks. This puts this exposition at odds with many workers in AI such as, for example, Brachman who are concerned with the logical adequacy of the theory rather than the mostly practical issues which motivate this work. It also distances me from those who, likes Hayes (1985), would reduce frames to some sort of first order logic. For me, the whole point of frames is to facilitate higher order constructs of the sort found in, *inter alia*, object-oriented databases and semantic data models.

A semantic network consists of a set of nodes and a set of ordered pairs of nodes called 'links', together with an interpretation of the meaning of these. I will restrict myself to describing this interpretation using a descriptive semantics; that is, a set of statements describing the interpretation. Terminal links are called 'slots' if they represent properties (predicates) rather than objects or classes of objects. A frame is a semantic net representing an object (or a stereotype of that object) and will consist of a number of slots and a number of outbound links. Consider, for clarification, the frame for a toy brick shown in Figure A.1 in the form of a network.

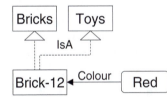

Figure A.1 A frame represented as a semantic network.

It may also be represented in a tabular form as follows.

```
Brick-12
IsA:     Brick,
         Toy
Colour:  Red
```

A collection of frames, or objects, forming a semantic network will be referred to in this appendix as an **object-base**. In the above example, there are implicitly frames for Brick and Toy.

Figure A.2 illustrates the inheritance of properties into slots as shown also in the form of two frames as follows.

```
Brick                           Toy
AKO:    Block,Commodity         AKO: Commodity
Shape:  Cuboid
```

Frames can inherit properties through IsA or AKO links, so that Brick-12 inherits the Shape slot's value from Brick in this case, as well as those properties of toys, commodities and blocks which offer no contradiction. IsA is used to stand for membership and AKO to stand for inclusion. Touretzky (1986) has argued that attempts to make the distinction between IsA and AKO founder when systems permit multiple inheritance. This exposition ignores, to some extent, the controversy surrounding the various usages of IsA and AKO links (Brachman, 1983).

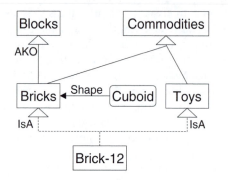

Figure A.2 Multiple inheritance of properties.

Winston (1984) introduces sub-slots (facets) to permit default values, demons and perspectives. This extension to the theory of fuzzy objects is not discussed herein but there seems to be no obstacle to such a development.

A.1.2 Property inheritance

Inheritance provides computer systems with a method of reasoning with implicit facts. Various frame-based languages have been implemented; FRL, KRL, KEE, Leonardo and others as described in Chapter 3. Most of these systems, however, suffer from various problems. They usually have no formal semantics, they are not good at reasoning about exceptions (nonmonotonic logic) and they cannot handle partial inheritance, either in the sense of partially inheriting a property or of inheriting a combination of partially true properties. Other authors have discussed partial inheritance, but from a completely different point of view. An example is (Khan and Jain, 1986). The programme of this appendix is to remedy all these defects within a single unified framework.

Touretzky (1986) points out that nonmonotonic or default logics, while possessing a formal semantics, are hopelessly general for practical purposes because they do not have the facility of inheritance systems to reason with implicit data.

A sort of duality is being asserted here between logics that add extra operators, such as L and N in modal logics and M in nonmonotonic logics, and those that expand the truth space, such as many-valued, fuzzy and probability logics. An example of the latter, which is exploited in this appendix, is fuzzy logic with Zadeh's fuzzy quantification given the Sigma-Count interpretation of his test-score semantics (Zadeh, 1982; Kandel, 1986).

Shastri (1988) has argued cogently that frame systems need to be able to support what he calls 'evidential reasoning'. The solution proposed by Shastri avoids the need to deal with both non-monotonicity and fuzzy truth values. His approach involves a frequency count semantics. I, however, have taken the view that fuzzy truth values have a certain utility and feel that there may be a place for both approaches.

It will be shown, informally, later how the mechanisms of fuzzy objects can be used to overcome some of the problems of nonmonotonic reasoning which often arise in inheritance systems or through polymorphism connascence.

Fuzzy objects also provide a computationally efficient means of modelling truth maintenance systems or possible worlds, without the introduction of modal operators.

A certain amount of the machinery of fuzzy logic will be required, and this is introduced as briefly as possible. For the reader with no previous knowledge of fuzzy sets, (Graham and Jones, 1988) provides an explanation of all the concepts used here.

A.2 Basic concepts of fuzzy set theory

The concept of a fuzzy set is due to Zadeh (1965) and involves the relaxation of the restriction on a set's characteristic function that it be two-valued. This section gives a very fast summary of the techniques from fuzzy set theory which we will require later in this appendix. This is merely to fix terminology, and is not intended as a tutorial. Fuller explanations can be obtained from (Graham and Jones, 1988) or in some cases from (Kandel, 1986).

A.2.1 Fuzzy sets

A fuzzy set is a function $f{:}X \longrightarrow I$ whose codomain is the unit interval, A. It may be interpreted as a linguistic value over the variable represented by the domain. For example, if the domain, X, represents wealth (over an arbitrary monetary scale) we can introduce fuzzy sets to stand for the imprecise linguistic terms 'rich', 'comfortable' and 'poor' as illustrated in the diagram in Figure A.3. The unit interval (vertical axis) is used to represent the degree of truth, so that 'poor' is fully true for wealth zero but falls off as wealth increases until eventually a point is reached when it is entirely untrue; has zero truth. Of course, we could envisage other terms such as 'monstrously rich' or 'totally impoverished', but this is not an essay on social policy. Fuzzy sets are conveniently represented pictorially in this way. They may also be represented as vectors of truth values.

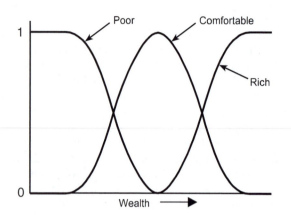

Figure A.3 Fuzzy term set for the variable 'wealth'.

There are several fuzzy logics. In the standard one, which is the one adopted here, the operations of the propositional calculus are defined for fuzzy predicates as follows.

$$f \text{ AND } g = \min(f,g)$$
$$f \text{ OR } g = \max(f,g)$$
$$\text{NOT } f = 1 - f$$

Implication is then defined in the usual way, by:

$$(f \Rightarrow g) = (\text{NOT } f) \text{ OR } g = \max(1-f, g)$$

Given a term set of permissible linguistic values, it is possible to extend it using the propositional operators and operations known as **hedges**. As examples the hedges 'very' and 'quite' are often defined by:

$$\text{VERY } f = f^2; \quad \text{QUITE } f = \sqrt{f}$$

Thus, expressions such as 'very rich or not very poor' receive an interpretation as a fuzzy set. This has evident utility in knowledge representation, and this has been explored in many other works.

A.2.2 Rules of inference

Given these basic definitions it is possible to approach the problem of representing inexact inferences with fuzzy sets. The two kinds of statements we may wish to use are assertions of the form X is A and rules of the form:

If X is [not] A [and/or X' is ...] then Y is B

X, X' and Y stand for objects and A and B stand for fuzzy sets.

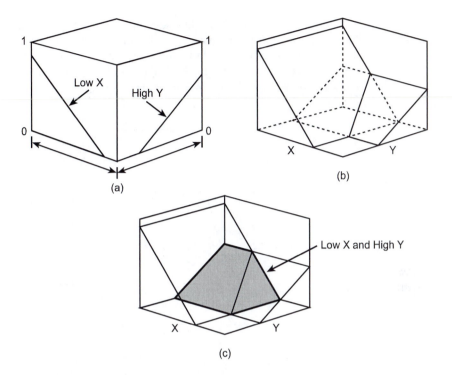

Figure A.4 (a) Fuzzy sets over two different domains; (b) the extension in the Cartesian product of two fuzzy sets; (c) the intersection of two fuzzy sets.

Simple syllogisms such as *modus ponens*:

> X is A
> <u>If X is A then Y is B</u>
> Y is B

are handled as follows. The extension in the Cartesian product of all linguistic variables appearing as assertions is computed and their intersection E taken. The extension and intersection of two fuzzy sets are illustrated in Figure A.4. This fuzzy set is interpreted as an elastic constraint on the solution. Next, taking the consequent clause of each rule separately, the current scalar value of the variable X is used to determine the truth level of the antecedent fuzzy set, so that the fuzzy set B is effectively truncated at this level. The resultant, truncated fuzzy set is formed by union with the constraint set E. This rule will be used in this appendix, although others have been suggested.

For a simple example of fuzzy inference, consider the rule

> If X is A then Y is B.

The fuzzy sets A and B are illustrated in Figure A.5. If the input is the value x from the domain X then the first step in the inference is to determine the truth value of x; its compatibility with A. In Figure A.5(a) this is seen to be 0.6. Therefore, the fuzzy set B is truncated at this level. The output from the inference is this truncated fuzzy set, shown as the shaded area in Figure A.5(b).

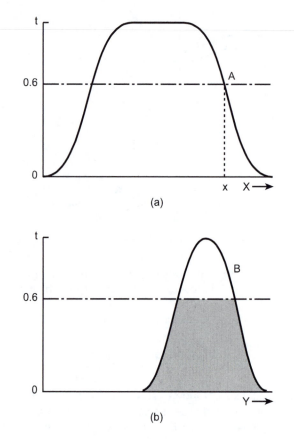

Figure A.5 (a) The value x has a compatibility (or truth value) of 0.8 with the fuzzy set A. **(b)** The fuzzy set B is truncated at the truth level of x.

A.2.3 Defuzzification

In case it is not convenient to work with fuzzy sets as output values, the result may be 'defuzzified' to return a scalar value. There are a number of ways this can be accomplished. We will need to know about two. The 'mean of maxima' (or maximum) method involves returning the scalar in the domain of the resultant fuzzy set which maps to the arithmetic mean of its maxima. The 'centre of moments' (or moments) method returns the average of all domain values weighted by their truth in the output fuzzy set; in other words, the centre of gravity of a notional cardboard cut-out of the graph of the fuzzy set. The appropriateness of these methods in different applications is discussed extensively by Graham and Jones (1988). Basically, the moments rule is best for control applications where a smooth variation in output is desired, and the mean-of-maxima rule for decision support applications where discrete jumps between output states are preferable. Figure A.6 illustrates that different scalar values will be returned by these two rules for any non-symmetric fuzzy set.

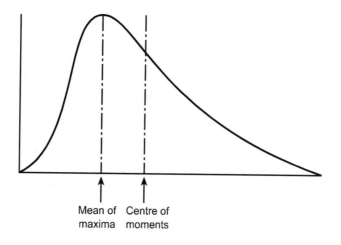

Mean of   Centre of
maxima   moments

Figure A.6 Two methods of defuzzification.

If a fuzzy set is required as output, but some regularity in its form is desirable, then a method known as linguistic approximation may be invoked. This involves the predefinition of an allowed **term set** of fuzzy sets over the domain, such as the one given in Figure A.3. In the case of fuzzy numbers (fuzzy subsets of the real line) an example term set might be {tiny,small,medium,large,huge}. The term set may be extended by fuzzy set operations (e.g. to include 'not very small'). Linguistic approximation returns the term 'closest' to the resultant fuzzy set, according to some stated measure of distance.

A.2.4 Fuzzy quantifiers

Fuzzy quantifiers are represented by words such as 'most', 'almost all', 'some' and so on, as opposed to the crisp quantifiers 'for all' and 'there exists'. They often occur implicitly in natural language. Thus, 'birds fly' may be interpreted as 'most birds can fly'. Zadeh (1982) introduces rules of inference and a formal semantics for such statements. His test-score semantics interprets quantifiers as elastic constraints on a family of fuzzy relations, which are regarded as entities. This structure is viewed as a test which scores according to the compatibility of the quantifier with the objects in the world (the database). A typical rule of inference for this system is

Q1 A are B
Q2 (A and B) are C
Q1 * Q2 A are (B and C)

where the Q's are fuzzy quantifiers, interpreted as fuzzy numbers, and * stands for the product of fuzzy numbers. For example, this justifies the syllogism:

Most (about 90%) birds can fly
Most (about 90%) flying birds have feathers
At least many (about 81%) birds have feathers

Of course, there are other rules of inference. The exact meaning of the test scores depends on the measure used for the cardinality of a fuzzy set. The usual one is the Sigma-count measure, which is to say the arithmetic sum of the grades of membership (the integral in the continuous case). More details may be found in (Kandel, 1986).

This completes the presentation of the minimal set of concepts from fuzzy set theory which we shall require in this appendix.

A.3 Fuzzy objects

We now come to the main results of this appendix. First, the notion of an object is extended to that of a fuzzy object, in two ways; first, by allowing attributes to contain fuzzy sets as values, in addition to text, list and numeric variables or other objects.[1] Second, inheritance through AKO and IsA attributes is allowed to be partial. Later we will see how to generalize in a third dimension by allowing instances to contain more than one set of attribute values, to facilitate the representation of possible worlds or time-variant objects.

To explain the advantages and mechanics of fuzzy objects it is preferable to use an example, rather than to develop the formal mathematics. Consider the following problem. You are an Aardvark customer faced with the problem of estimating the safety implications following from the purchase of various leisure items. Objects give us a way of representing knowledge about and data concerning key abstractions or concepts in the domain. The most natural way to analyse the problem (remembering that we are thinking of building a computerized adviser here) is to

---

[1] This is not necessarily a real extension, since fuzzy sets form an abstract data type. It is only an extension if this data type is regarded as primitive.

```
┌─────────────────────────────────┐   ┌─────────────────────────────────┐
│ Vehicle                         │   │ Toy                             │
├─────────────────────────────────┤   ├─────────────────────────────────┤
│ AKO       : Commodity           │   │ AKO       : Commodity           │
│ Uses      : (travel, pleasure) [list] │ │ Uses      : (pleasure) [list]   │
│ Keeper    : undefined [text]    │   │ Keeper    : child [text]        │
│ Necessity : high [fuzz]         │   │ Necessity : low [fuzz]          │
│ Safety    : high [fuzz]         │   │ Safety    : undefined [fuzz]    │
│ Utility   : high [fuzz]         │   │ Utility   : high [fuzz]         │
│ Cost      : high [fuzz]         │   │ Cost      : low [fuzz]          │
├─────────────────────────────────┤   ├─────────────────────────────────┤
│ Methods                         │   │                                 │
├─────────────────────────────────┤   └─────────────────────────────────┘
│ Rules                           │
│    Contro rules                 │
│     nherit by maxima            │
│    Defuzzify by maxima          │
└─────────────────────────────────┘
```

```
┌─────────────────────────────────┐   ┌─────────────────────────────────┐
│ Dinghy                          │   │ Hang-glider                     │
├─────────────────────────────────┤   ├─────────────────────────────────┤
│ AKO    : Vehicle [0.4],         │   │ AKO    : Vehicle [0.05],        │
│           Toy [0.6]             │   │           Toy [0.7]             │
│           Dangerous object [0.1]│   │           Dangerous object [0.9]│
│ Safety : undefined [fuzz]       │   │ Safety : undefined [fuzz]       │
│ Cost   : undefined [fuzz]       │   │ Cost   : undefined [fuzz]       │
│ Draft  : 3 [reel];              │   │                                 │
│          IfNeeded = depth-calc  │   └─────────────────────────────────┘
├─────────────────────────────────┤
│ depth-ca c                      │
└─────────────────────────────────┘
```

```
┌─────────────────────────────────┐   ┌─────────────────────────────────┐
│ Car                             │   │ Toy-car                         │
├─────────────────────────────────┤   ├─────────────────────────────────┤
│ AKO    : Vehicle [0.9],         │   │ AKO    : Vehicle [0.3],         │
│           Toy [0.6]             │   │           Toy [0.9]             │
│           Dangerous object [0.1]│   │ Safety : undiefined [fuzz]      │
│ Safety : undefined [fuzz]       │   │ Cost   : undiefined [fuzz]      │
│ Cost   : undefined [fuzz]       │   │                                 │
└─────────────────────────────────┘   └─────────────────────────────────┘
```

```
┌─────────────────────────────────┐   ┌─────────────────────────────────┐
│ Book                            │   │ Magazine                        │
├─────────────────────────────────┤   ├─────────────────────────────────┤
│ AKO    : Dangerous-object,      │   │ AKO    : Book [0.5],            │
│           Toy [0.6],            │   │           Toy [0.3             │
│ Cost   : undefined [fuzz]       │   │           Borrowed object [0.5]│
│ Safety : undefined [fuzz]       │   │ Safety : undefined [fuzz]       │
│ Adult  : No [text]              │   │ Cost   : undefined [fuzz]       │
└─────────────────────────────────┘   └─────────────────────────────────┘
```

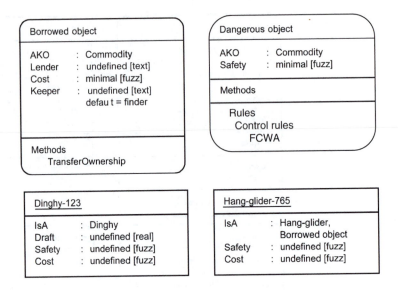

Figure A.7 Some fuzzy objects.

list the physical objects involved. Suppose they include a dinghy and a hang-glider among a number of others. These objects are types of more general objects, and have associated with them various attributes, methods and rules. The methods are not relevant to this discussion. Figure A.7 shows how we can represent this knowledge about some objects interesting in this context using fuzzy objects. Note that the instances are distinguished from the classes by the use if IsA: instead of AKO: attributes, and by icons with sharp corners. The rounded rectangle notation for fuzzy classes merely renders the UML stereotype <<fuzzy>> for convenience of presentation. AKO is short for Superclasses. We will now consider nine of these objects, in each case annotating them with explanation of a rudimentary syntactic convention, on the way to a solution of the problem. The most general object is referred to as a commodity.

One can divide the figure among essential and accidental classes and instances. The first six (on the preceding page) are essential. Notice, incidentally, the syntactic provision for defaults and backward chaining demons (IfNeeded procedures). Forward chaining (IfUpdated) demons would be dealt with similarly. The way the rules compartments of the icons are interpreted will become clear later.

First, consider the concept of a vehicle. Our general knowledge about the attributes of vehicles can be summarized in the structure shown in Figure A.8.

Here the Superclasses attribute points to another object, in this case the most general one possible. This time we use the UML stereotype. Vehicle, along with the other structures illustrated, is a fuzzy object in two respects. First, the degree of property inheritance from the object(s) in the Superclasses attribute may be specified as a number between 0 and 1 in square brackets after the name. In this case no value is given and the default value of [1.00] is assumed. Secondly, the other attributes may contain fuzzy sets (vectors of truth values) as values. The bracketed expressions indicate the type of the value; either [fuzz], [real], [list], [text] or some user defined abstract data type. The fuzzy set, high, used in the Vehicle object may be represented as in Figure A.9. Note that, since this is a class, the value (such as high) represent defaults.

Vehicles <<fuzzy>>
Superclasses: Commodities
Uses (text,0,n) : (travel,pleasure) Keeper (text,0,1) Necessity (fuzz,1,1) : high Safety (fuzz,1,1) : high Utility (fuzz,1,1): high Cost (fuzz,1,1): high

Figure A.8 The fuzzy class or type of vehicles.

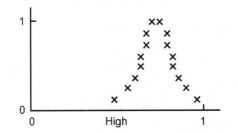

Figure A.9 A fuzzy set representing 'high' on an arbitrary interval scale.

We may assume certain attribute values for the general commodity by including an object for it. Let us assume here only that Commodity has known values of high for Safety and Utility.

If it is normal to assume that something purchased is safe then the Toy object will inherit the value 'high' for Safety, since the attribute contains 'undefined', the uniform fuzzy set on the interval scale, which is equal to 1 everywhere. The other attributes are unaltered. Inheritance occurs based on the immediately superior object only, and then only when the 'child' has an undefined value. In some applications, it may be preferable to allow inheritance into even those attributes which contain defined values. In such a case the inheritance mechanism is modified in such a way that the intersection (minimum) of the fuzzy sets in the parent and child is taken. This corresponds to what could be designated: 'the Fuzzy Closed World Assumption' (FCWA). That is, if the values assigned to attributes represent immutable knowledge about the state of the world and the constraints it imposes, then we would not wish to permit a contradictory reassignment that ignored the influence of the value in a parent. This is an interesting variant of overriding, which emphasizes the sharing of information, and compromise, between parent and child objects. The repository for this control information is the *rules* compartment of the object, where the declarative semantics are encapsulated.

Two more objects representing general classes of objects must now be discussed. They are the accidental objects: Borrowed-object and Dangerous-object.

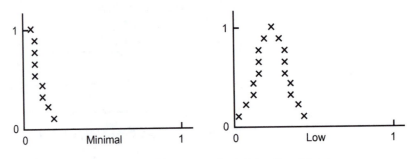

Figure A.10 Fuzzy sets for 'minimal' and 'low'.

Here we may wish to consider the sad possibility that a borrowed object, such as a book, may pass from *meum* to *tuum* without the transition being too noticeable.[2] Thus, in the case of the borrowed Magazine object, only 0.5 of the ownership properties of Borrowed-object may be inherited. In particular, the inheritance mechanism attaches a 0.5 certainty factor to the Lender and Keeper values (if they are known). The mechanism for fuzzy attributes is that the fuzzy sets (*minimal* in this case) are truncated at the 0.5 level. Returning to the mainstream of our argument, two new fuzzy sets have been introduced, so their definition is given in Figure A.10, pictorially as before.

Now we come to the objects describing fairly specific items in the scheme. For example, we have Dinghy and Hang-glider. We could of course consider further crisp attributes such the wing-span of a hang-glider.

We now have to understand how the undefined attributes in the lowest level objects (representing instances) for Dinghy-123 and Hang-glider-765 may be filled. Notice first that we have a non-fuzzy attribute for Draft, and multiple inheritance from higher levels. Let us look at the Safety attribute of Dinghy first.

---

[2] In other words, be (politely) stolen!

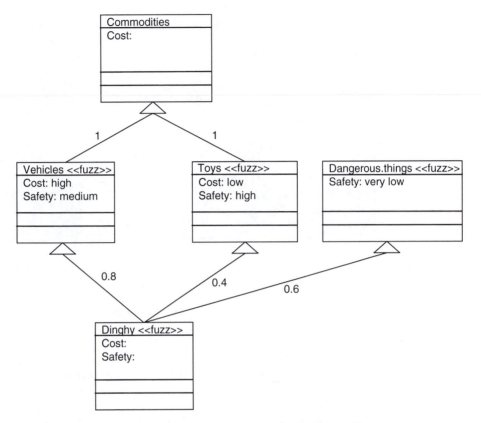

Figure A.11 Partial inheritance network for Hang-glider-765.

Since a dinghy is a vehicle the Safety: attribute inherits 'high', but as this is only true to the extent 0.4 the fuzzy set is truncated at this level. It also inherits the value 'minimal' from Dangerous-object, but only to degree 0.1. The inheritance path from Commodity via Toy gives the value 'high' in degree 0.6. These fuzzy sets are combined with the union operator as shown in the diagram in Figure A.12(b). If this were the final result of some reasoning process the resultant fuzzy set would be defuzzified (in this case with the mean-of-maxima operation) to give a truth or possibility value for the term 'safe'. Alternatively, linguistic approximation could be applied to return a word corresponding to a normal, convex fuzzy set[3] approximating the returned value. In a different application, the moments defuzzification method might be applied. This is a control decision in the same category as the fuzzy closed world assumption, and, I feel, should be left to the discretion of the user or systems

---

[3] That is, a fuzzy set which attains the value of 1 somewhere (normal) and which has only one peak (convex). The fuzzy sets of Figures A.3, A.5(a), A.6, A.8 and A.9 all have both these properties.

designer and encapsulated locally within the rules window. Figure A.12(b) shows the fuzzy set for the dinghy's cost. In the absence of evidence to the contrary, Dinghy-123 inherits both these values.

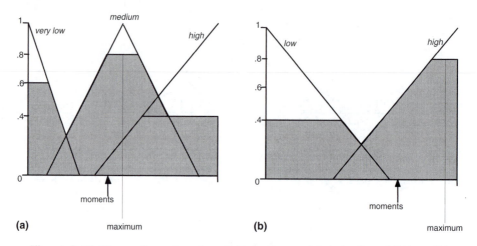

Figure A.12 The mathematics of partial inheritance: **(a)** derivation of Safety; **(b)** derivation of Cost.

Cost here is being interpreted as the cost that one might be willing to bear, and thus the cost of a dinghy purchased just for fun ought, normally, to be low. The case of the safety attribute of Hang-glider is a little more interesting. The diagrams in Figure A.13(a) illustrate the text.

Here, the Safety attribute inherits the union of the fuzzy set minimal from Dangerous-object [0.9] and high from both vehicle [0.05] and Commodity (via Toy) [0.7]. Applying the operation of union or disjunction to these three fuzzy sets (we of course exclude 'undefined' from this process) to represent the view that AKO attributes are *alternative* viewpoints from which the object may be viewed, we arrive at a resultant fuzzy set. Defuzzification then gives a value close to 0 (or the linguistic approximation 'minimal').

Thus the system is able to deduce correctly that a hang-glider is a very dangerous toy along with the unsurprising conclusion that it doesn't cost much to borrow one in the case of Hang-glider-765.

The choice of the maximum operator here may be regarded as problematical because of the difficulty in assigning a definite semantics to the disjunction operation, OR, in normal speech. However, the system proposed here should allow for this by the provision of a control parameter, or rules, which would allow users to specify the alternative minimum operation to deal with applications wherein the natural interpretation of the combination of values is different and perhaps represents the possibilistic view that only evidence receiving support from all sources should be inherited. This is what the rules in the icon for the vehicle object in Figure A.7 refer to. This discussion also indicates the need to extend the number of rule types within the rules box of the object. This is dealt with in Section A.6.

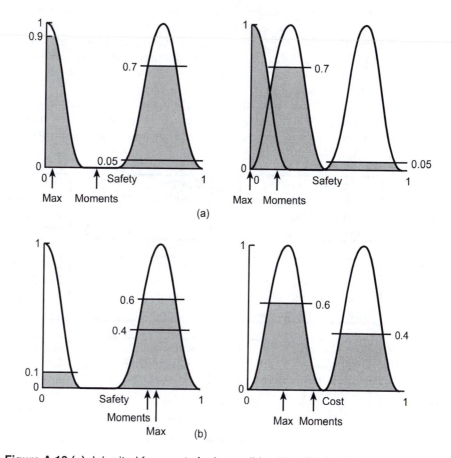

Figure A.13 (a) Inherited fuzzy sets for hang-glider-765; **(b)** inherited fuzzy sets for dinghy-123.

Clearly, the reason we have adopted the view that a hang-glider is only a vehicle to a small extent is that one usually thinks of a vehicle as a safe-ish means of getting from A to B and, indeed, back again. This is not independent from our assumptions about dangerous objects. This warns of a possible design problem for fuzzy object-bases. However, there is a further problem. If, as is quite reasonable, a survey showed that most people actually gave a higher value, say 0.95, to the 'toyness' of a hang-glider then the result would be quite different under the maximum rule of inference, and quite counter-intuitive. Hang-gliders would be highly safe. The apparently counter-intuitive nature of this result – which, incidentally, only has noticeable, serious consequences under the moments rule – could be due to the incompleteness of this example.

It is worth remarking that all object-oriented, frame and multiple inheritance systems pose a similar dilemma. A property, such as dangerousness, can be associated with an individual either by inheritance or by explicit inclusion in the object's descriptor. A way round this problem is suggested in Section A.7. Currently, the topic of design criteria for fuzzy and indeed crisp semantic models is a research issue. What is required is analogous to the theory of normal forms in database design theory.

To put matters right temporarily, let us now explore an example which does conform to intuition more closely than the one chosen above to explicate the syntax and semantics. The type declarations have been dropped as they are always clear from context.

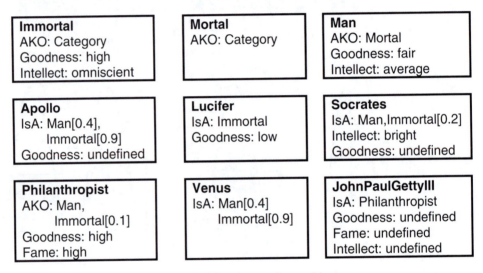

Figure A.14 Some more fuzzy objects.

In Figure A.14 the inheritance mechanism enables us to infer that John Paul Getty III is a nice chap who'll be remembered for quite a while, because philanthropists are usually famous. Apollo, on the other hand, inherits average intelligence as the epitome of manliness and omniscience from his godliness. We know from our Homer that Apollo was in fact only wise on occasion, and this is reflected in the returned fuzzy set for his intellect, whose linguistic approximation is something like 'bright' if we use the moments rule. Apollo's goodness is also reduced by his manliness. In the absence of a richer structure or, in other words, more knowledge and information, we can only deduce average intelligence for John Paul Getty III, although he might be remembered by posterity as brighter due to the magnifying effect of a degree of immortality (in the sense of living in memory here) on intelligence. Clearly, this kind of object base has considerable application to computerized models of common-sense reasoning. Zadeh (1985) refers to the type of reasoning implied here as that of 'usuality', while Touretzky (1986) (erroneously) calls it 'normative' reasoning (he means 'what is normal').

This example, of course, raises many of the usual questions about inheritance that we find in crisp systems. In addition, we are led to ask what would happen in a more complex object-base. In particular, in certain applications it might be necessary to consider that the inheritance of god-like properties by offspring and offspring of offspring should be subject to attenuation but not to complete exception (e.g. Leda, Europa, etc.). In that case, we would want to invoke the fuzzy closed world assumption to 'visit the sins of the fathers upon the children unto the third and fourth generation'. The other question raised here, as compared with the previous example, is the evident comparability of the categories represented by the AKO links. This suggests that well-designed object-bases should evince this property. I will have more to say on the soundness of designs later.

For some reason, it is apparent that the moments method of defuzzification is the more appropriate one in the example deductions discussed here. This is because we were dealing with the usuality of properties which are subject to combination in reaching a 'balanced view', rather than ones which contribute to either/or decision making. There could be problems if we had mixed objectives in our use of the object-base. We would at least have to type the AKO links – using the rules window – were the two strategies to be required over the same object-base.

I have thus presented, via a couple of very simple examples, the basic theory of fuzzy objects and explained its logic of inheritance. I have concentrated on attributes but operations can have inheritable possibilities attached and rules in SOMA can be fuzzy rules of the sort found in languages such as REVEAL (Graham and Jones, 1988). I now want to justify these efforts by presenting a more practical example.

A.4   An application

Consider the problem faced in allocating a marketing budget among the various activities which could lead to higher sales of a product. It is part of the folk-lore of marketing that different types of product will benefit from different budget allocations. Suppose that the methods at our disposal are:

Advertising	Promotion	Sales Training	Packaging	Direct Mail

Now, suppose that we compare the allocation ideal for breakfast cereals with that for package software. Advertising, promotions and packaging are clearly all useful, but there isn't much point in direct mailing to cereal consumers, and the degree of training required by the sales force isn't usually considered to be high. In such a situation, we might well represent the allocation of resources in the following matrix of percentages.[4]

	Adverts	Promotion	Sales training	Packaging	Direct mail
Breakfast cereal	30	50	5	15	0
Package software	10	5	15	20	50

In the case where knowledge is expressed inexactly we can readily replace these numbers by fuzzy numbers as follows.

	Adverts	Promotion	Sales Training	Packaging	Direct Mail
Breakfast Cereal	about a third	about half	hardly any	a little	none
Package software	less than a little	hardly any	a little	about a fifth	about half

Here we have two fuzzy relations, for Breakfast-cereal and Package-software. Presumably they can be regarded as part of a larger database of products; in fact product classes. Viewing them as classes prompts us to write them down as fuzzy objects and ask about inheritance through AKO links. To see that inheritance (of the attributes under consideration) may be partial, consider the fuzzy object representing the class of commodities called Vending-Machine. A vending machine may be viewed as office furniture, catering equipment or even as packaged food depending on the marketing approach taken. Fuzzy objects give a natural way to build a description of this problem and suggest an implementation which is able to combine evidence and reason with exceptions.

Figure A.15 shows how the combined partial inheritance of fuzzy (i.e. linguistically expressed) allocations from general classes of products may be used to infer an allocation for specific types of product. All attributes are fuzzy and undefined attributes are left blank. The fuzzy set which is returned into the DirectMail attribute may be defuzzified and linguistically approximated, to indicate that investment in this area of about a third of the budget will be likely to produce the best results. This result is based purely on the fact that vending machines share features with catering equipment, office furniture and packaged food about which more is known. As it happens, in this example, the moments and maximum methods of defuzzification will give approximately the same result.

---

[4] Warning to marketing executives: These figures are not meant to represent a truly effective strategy.

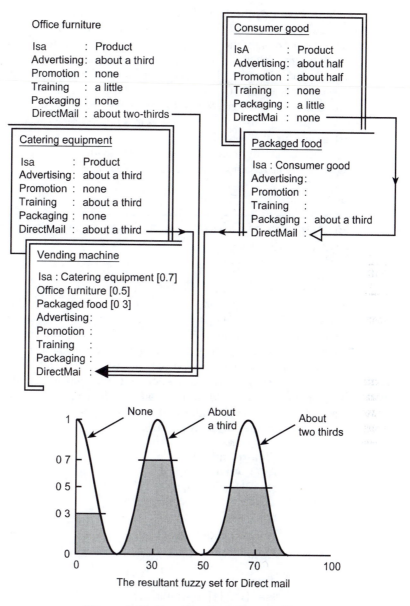

Office furniture

Isa   : Product
Advertising: about a third
Promotion : none
Training   : a little
Packaging : none
DirectMail : about two-thirds

Consumer good

IsA   : Product
Advertising: about half
Promotion : about half
Training   : none
Packaging : a little
DirectMai : none

Catering equipment

Isa   : Product
Advertising: about a third
Promotion : none
Training   : about a third
Packaging : none
DirectMail : about a third

Packaged food

Isa : Consumer good
Advertising:
Promotion :
Training   :
Packaging : about a third
DirectMail :

Vending machine

Isa : Catering equipment [0.7]
Office furniture [0.5]
Packaged food [0 3]
Advertising:
Promotion :
Training   :
Packaging :
DirectMai :

None   About
                   a third   About
                                          two thirds

1

0 7

0 5

0 3

0

0   30   50   70   100

The resultant fuzzy set for Direct mail

Figure A.15 How to sell vending machines.

Another possible practical application is to 'dotted line' relationships in organizations, where the responsibilities of certain specialists to technically related parts of an organization may override or mingle with those of the formal reporting hierarchy. One application of such an object-base is to assist with the decision as to whom should be consulted when the specialist is asked to work overseas for a year. Another concerns the construction of formal models of the sort of loose-tight properties of organizations referred to by Peters and Waterman (1982).

It is my belief that there are a tremendous number of opportunities for the application of fuzzy objects. Among the most promising are enterprise and strategic business modelling. Of course, it may be argued that these applications can be addressed by other technologies, but none that I can think of offer simultaneously the advantages of naturality of expression in a unified representational formalism to the extent that fuzzy objects do.

Let us briefly compare this system with a couple of other methods of representing uncertain statements about objects.

A.5 Fuzzy objects, fuzzy quantifiers and nonmonotonic logics

We can now explore the application of fuzzy objects to one of the classical problems in inheritance, using non-standard quantifiers instead of nonmonotonic logic. Touretzky discusses (and dismisses) this approach by reference to the work of Altham (1971), but seems to be unaware of Zadeh's more encouraging results for the representation of fuzzy quantifiers and their inference properties.

As we have seen, Zadeh's theory of dispositions and fuzzy quantifiers and test score semantics lets us express one of the classical motivating problems of nonmonotonic logic as 'Most birds can fly'. It is a part of the folk-lore of fuzzy sets that this can be neatly expressed with fuzzy inheritance; thus a fuzzy objects approach is indicated. Here is the object-base:

Flying-animal
AKO: Animal
Can-fly: true [fuzz]

Bird
AKO: Flying-animal [0.9]
Wings: 2

Penguin
AKO: Bird
Can-fly: false [fuzz]

Tweety
IsA: Bird [1], Penguin [1]
Can-fly: ?

The fuzzy sets involved are illustrated in Figure A.16. The answer is that Tweety is a bird and can't fly. So far this is the same result as that suggested in McDermott and Doyle (1980) – but we can do better: Penguins do sort of fly (they make fluttering movements when diving or running) and the fuzzy set shown in

Figure A.17 preserves this information in a way. Another approach to this problem would be to use analogical reasoning, but this is often a very complex approach.

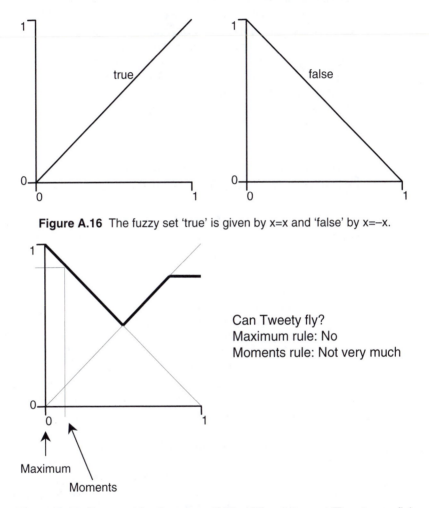

Figure A.16 The fuzzy set 'true' is given by x=x and 'false' by x=−x.

Can Tweety fly?
Maximum rule: No
Moments rule: Not very much

Maximum

Moments

Figure A.17 Fuzzy set for the compatibility of the statement 'Tweety can fly'.

A rather obvious generalization springs to mind at this point. The numerical factor representing the degree of inheritance could be replaced by a linguistic variable (a fuzzy set or fuzzy number). This would mean that the truncation of inherited fuzzy sets would itself be fuzzy. We could call such objects 'ultrafuzzy objects' or '2-fuzzy objects'. However, finding a formal semantics then becomes much harder, and I suspect that the practical value of such a theory would be severely limited by its complexity. In fact, this generalization would correspond much more closely to the interpretation of fuzzy quantifiers given in Section A.2.4. where fuzzy quantifiers are represented as fuzzy numbers. The inheritance mechanism of 2-fuzzy objects could indeed be modified to exploit the inference rules of approximate reasoning (e.g. the intersection-product syllogism given in A.2.4). This is certainly worthy of further investigation.

It is useful to interpret a fuzzy AKO link as a most/some type fuzzy quantifier. In the hang-glider/toy example this is also a natural interpretation. AKO links may be used (or mis-used) for a variety of conflicting purposes. A good design theory would force us to state the interpretation of the inheritance links and not mix them up. An alternative is to permit fuzzy objects to have a number of 'typed' inheritance links. Then inheritance could take place through a manifold of different networks.

A.6 Business policy and fuzzy models

Business policy is set and followed in an uncertain world. The sources and kinds of uncertainty are manifold. They include:

- Lack of understanding.
- Conceptual error, uncertainty in judgement, lack of evidence, unreliable sources of data and information or lack of certainty in evidence. These and the imprecision of natural language and sensory apparatus all lead to variation in degrees of belief. A definition may be linguistic, and the possible data values will then have to be selected from a set of linguistic descriptors. For example, in a determination of a patient's clinical symptoms, the degree of pain present can only be described in terms such as 'slight pain', 'severe pain', 'very severe pain' and so on.
- Conflicting or complementary sources of facts.
- Hidden variables producing apparent randomness.
- The existence of exceptions.
- The energy required to obtain certain data.
- Random events leading to variation in the degree of likelihood.
- Variation in the degree of possibility or necessity.
- Instrumental or experimental error, faulty sensory equipment leading to variation in the degree of precision. This is, of course, the standard situation in scientific measurement, and is managed on the assumption that errors of observation are normally distributed about the true value of the observed variable.
- The abundance of irrelevant data leading to variation in the degree of relevance.
- Variation in the extent to which a proposition holds.
- Variation in the degree of truth or provability of a proposition.
- Variation in the degree of the mandate for performing some action.

■ Variation in the degree of compulsion or duty.

To arrive at a decision in the presence of absolute certainty with respect to all the relevant facts and considerations is a luxury rarely afforded to human beings. Assumptions must be made about data that are not available, about events which may or may not have occurred, and about consequences likely to flow from a given decision.

Many of these assumptions may be made unconsciously or subconsciously. Some may be made explicitly, with whatever degree of justification may be adduced. Mathematics may be prayed in aid of some assumptions made on statistical bases. Otherwise, rules of thumb and accrued experience serve as a guide.

Traditionally, systems analysts are taught to 'prefer a fact to an opinion' and to remove all inexactitude from specifications. This is a good principle but can be taken too far. Zadeh's Principle of Incompatibility (Zadeh, 1973) states that:

> As the complexity of a system increases, our ability to make precise and yet significant statements about its behaviour diminishes until a threshold is reached beyond which precision and significance (or relevance) become almost mutually exclusive characteristics.

Zadeh's original motivation came from attempts to construct numerical controllers for complex electronic equipment. This was recognized as a difficult problem because, partly due to the Law Of Requisite Variety (Ashby, 1956), as the controlled equipment became complex the controller became so even more rapidly. So much so that the controllers were either ineffectual or so complex as to defy the understanding of their designers. Zadeh formulated this in his Principle.

One way round the contradiction is to represent vague, imprecise human knowledge directly rather than mediating with some artificial representation such as a precise formula. In the context of automatic control, it turns out that a human operator formulates a control policy as 'when the gauge shows hot, I have to turn this knob down a little bit' rather than as 'when the temperature increases beyond 98.4 the input is reduced by 4.7%'. This is the approach taken by fuzzy set theory. It can be applied as readily to business policy as to industrial controllers.

Here is an example of the policy adopted by the product manager of a fast-moving consumer good such as washing powder; the same one used already in Chapter 5. It is expressed particularly succinctly but represents a fairly accurate picture of how such prices are set in practice.

1. OUR PRICE SHOULD BE LOW
2. OUR PRICE SHOULD BE ABOUT 2*DIRECT.COSTS
3. IF THE OPPOSITION.PRICE IS NOT VERY HIGH THEN OUR PRICE SHOULD BE NEAR THE OPPOSITION.PRICE

There are several things to note about this policy. First, it is expressed in vague terms and yet would be perfectly understandable to any other product manager as a basis for action. More remarkably perhaps, this is executable code in a language called REVEAL. This is possible because REVEAL uses fuzzy sets to implement the linguistic terms such as LOW. It is worth studying exactly how this code is implemented.

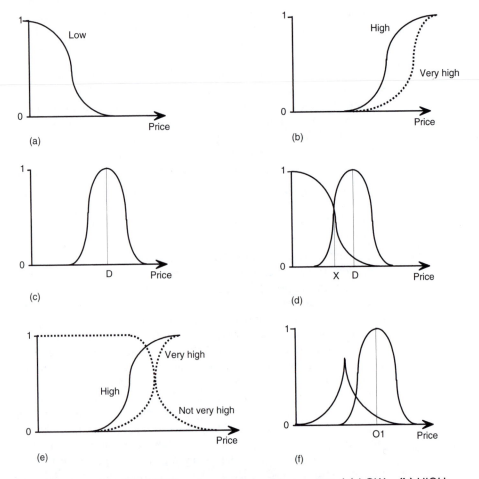

Figure A.18 LOW, HIGH and some derived fuzzy sets: **(a)** LOW; **(b)** HIGH; **(c)** About D; **(d)** LOW and About D; **(e)** Not Very HIGH = 1 − HIGH^2; **(f)** (LOW and About D) and Near O1.

First, two fuzzy sets called LOW and HIGH are defined as vectors over the scale of relevant prices for washing powders. These are illustrated in Figure A.18(a) and (b). 'Very' is an operator that takes the square of every point of the curve representing the fuzzy set. The result VERY HIGH is shown in A.18(b) too. The words OUR, SHOULD and THE are declared as noise words. BE is a synonym for IS and NEAR means the same as ABOUT.

Statement 1 in the policy means that the price should be as compatible as possible with LOW; i.e. the price ought to be zero. This contradicts the assertion that it should be twice direct costs; a result of the need to turn a profit based on experience. The remarkable thing is that the fuzzy policy will automatically resolve this contradiction by taking that price that gives the maximum truth value for the intersection of the fuzzy sets. This is labelled X in Figure A.18(d). The peaked intersection now represents an elastic constraint, or feasible region, for price. Figure A.18(c) shows the fuzzy set ABOUT 2*DIRECT.COSTS.

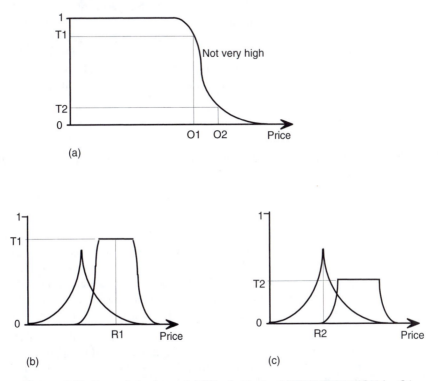

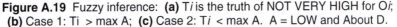

Figure A.19 Fuzzy inference: **(a)** T*i* is the truth of NOT VERY HIGH for O*i*; **(b)** Case 1: T*i* > max A; **(c)** Case 2: T*i* < max A. A = LOW and About D.

Rule 3 must now be interpreted. We take an actual value for opposition O and compute how true NOT VERY HIGH is for it. This truth value is T. The fuzzy inference rule is interpreted as truncating the output fuzzy set NEAR OPPOSITION at the level T. We now arrive at the result by taking the union of LOW AND ABOUT D with this truncated set. D stands for 2*DIRECT.COSTS here. Finally, if we want an actual value for PRICE rather than a fuzzy set, we must defuzzify. In this case we choose the mean of maxima method to do this. Figure A.19(b) and (c) illustrate that there are two cases. As the value of T exceeds the maximum truth in the feasible region there is a sudden jump in output from R2 to R1. This models exactly what happens in real life; decision output is discontinuous. In process control, smooth output is required and the centre of moments defuzzification rule would be used.

The purpose of this example is to show how fuzzy rules, used to capture business policy, can be made to provide quite precise, although perhaps non-linear and complex, models of behaviour. In SOMA, rulesets are embedded in objects and can be inherited. Business policy can be modelled in this way and fuzzy rulesets are permitted. One may either create a special purpose "policy" object to which all other objects refer or distribute the policy to the pertinent objects. Which is best will depend on the application.

The use of fuzzy rules, and indeed of rules in general, is optional in SOMA. They need not be used and may only be used rarely. It is my belief and experience, however, that when they are needed they provide a very powerful modelling technique that helps build a common, shared understanding between users and developers.

A.7   Control rules for fuzzy multiple inheritance systems

Let us summarize the control régimes available within the theory of fuzzy objects. These are global rules only if stated within the rules window of the most general object, if there is one. Otherwise, they may be subject to local variations.

(1) **The default régime**: If an attribute is filled, don't inherit into it. If it isn't then combine the truncated inherited attributes with the maximum operator. For non-fuzzy variables the maximum of the certainty factors represented by the AKO values is attached to the inherited value. Multiple inheritance of non-fuzzy values may result in multi-valued attributes (lists).

Different fuzzy logics may be used according to the application at hand. The maximum operator may then be replaced with the appropriate t-conorm. The maximum (or conorm) operator may be replaced for individual AKO attributes by the minimum (or corresponding norm). The choice of maximum corresponds to regarding conflicting values as alternative viewpoints. The choice of minimum corresponds to maximal caution and the view that the conflicting sources complement each other.

(2) **The Fuzzy Closed World Assumption**: Inherit all defined values and perform a union. Some theory of attenuation may be added. The control strategy precludes exceptions, but this is sometimes what is required. For example, when we reason that dogs have four legs because they are mammals and that humans are an exception, having only two, we are plumping for Naive Physics in contradistinction to a mature Biology. Humans (normally) do have four legs; it is merely that two of them have become adapted to other purposes. From such a viewpoint, we want an

inheritance mechanism that propagates the mammality in despite of the human exception; that takes account of both factors.

Each régime bifurcates because one of the maximum or moments methods of defuzzification must needs be selected, unless linguistic approximation is employed. This gives the system designer a choice from at least 24 control régimes. It also suggests the need for some experimental work.

Thus, the array of permissible control régimes can be characterized by the following decisions.

1. Should defined attributes inherit?
2. Should multiple inheritances be combined with union or intersection?
3. Which fuzzy logic is appropriate?
4. Which defuzzification method is to be used?

☐ A.8   Design theory for fuzzy objects

In this section, I examine some of the problems that arise in the design of fuzzy object systems, and suggest some design guidelines.

Fuzzy objects are not alone in raising general problems in terms of multiple attribute or property inheritance. Touretzky (1986) lists the analogous problems with crisp inheritance systems and suggests some very reasonable ways round them in terms of a lattice-theoretic semantics. I suspect that it is possible to use Touretzky's hierarchical distance ordering to provide attenuation of inheritance for fuzzy objects.

As a parenthetical remark at this point, it is worth observing that Touretzky's semantics generate the truth tables of Kleene 3-valued logic rather than the Lukasiewitz logic, the multi-valued logic which corresponds to fuzzy logic (Giles, 1976). Lukasiewitz motivation for the uncertain term was contingent statements (about the future); indeterminate values. The motivation behind Touretzky's system is the presence of links which indicate that no conclusion may be drawn (or value inherited). Other three-valued logics (that of Bochvar, say) offer interpretations in terms of meaninglessness. The difference therefore between my approach and that of the mainstream, symbolic processing movement as represented by Touretzky here is this: conflict in inheritance is not to be interpreted as undecidability but as possibility; as potentiality.

A.8.1   Completeness of design

It is not just on theoretical grounds that this approach offers some benefits. There are some problems that Touretzky's approach does not address. The problem that the hang-glider is safe because toys are (because the typical commodity is) could be viewed as one of conflict resolution. Perhaps we could decompose the link using an additional class object such as Dangerous-toy in such circumstances. Using an inferential distance ordering approach assumes that this has not only already been done, but that all possible such decompositions have been explicated in the object-base. Otherwise, a slight perturbation of the design could result in totally different behaviour under inheritance. What is therefore required is a procedure which determines whether an object-base is 'complete' in this sense. We need to develop a design theory for general object-bases. This would appear to be a very difficult problem, since the recognition of a 'good' expansion is clearly a question of relevance. The absence of such a theory forces one to adopt some method of default reasoning under Reiter's closed world assumption (not the fuzzy version mentioned above).

The analogous question of completeness hangs over all attempts to structure knowledge and data. Even in conventional Entity-Relationship data models it is recognized that a sound design is achieved only by the exercise of great skill. Decomposition is assisted by a theory of normal forms, but completeness can rarely be assured when the model is of a real, dynamic system.

Furthermore, because of the fact that Dangerous-toy is evidently one of the accidental objects we were warned of in Section 9.2, warning bells should be ringing.

A.8.2 Objects versus attributes

A major problem in the area of design criteria arises when we have to decide whether the degree to which an object (whether instance or class) has a property is determined by inheritance or by attribute filling (which in turn can result from inheritance). Thus, the two objects:

Object-1 <<fuzzy>>
AKO: ? Property-A:degree [fuzz]

Object-2 <<fuzzy>>
AKO:Object-with-property-A [degree]

are equivalent in all except syntax. The problem is to decide when to choose between the alternative formulations. I will call such objects **tautological**. They are a particularly nasty kind of accidental object.

This is nothing more than the class-attribute problem of database design. Making the choice correctly remains a matter of skill and judgement. The analysis of judgements described in Chapter 6 may help, but is only a guide to good practice in distinguishing accidental from essential abstractions. As a step towards a solution of the problem, the status of such 'tautological objects' is discussed below.

This problem also raises the question of the status of the two kinds of fuzziness: the fuzziness subsisting in the way classes (or instances and classes) are related, and the fuzziness inherent in predicates of description (attributes). It is necessary to ask if we are committing the unforgivable sin of mixing different kinds of uncertainties. This is clearly a danger with poor designs. On the other hand, it may be argued that more expressive power results from allowing the programmer to mix both forms as convenient.

A.8.3 Tautological objects and maximal decomposition

What, we may ask, is the status of tautological objects like the one below?

Dangerous_objects <<fuzzy>>
Superclasses: Objects Danger: not less than high [fuzz]

These objects are recognizable as having only one non-AKO attribute with a meaning predicate and value corresponding exactly to the object's name. The AKO attribute also contributes nothing new. The specification of the object asserts that a dangerous object is an object which has the property of being dangerous to the degree 'high' or more.

In crisp systems we would automatically disallow such perversions. But, in the hang-glider example above, if we disallow all tautological objects on principle, then the only way the low value for safety can ever get into the attribute is if we put it there. This could accord with intuition, because there is really no *a priori* reason (at least not within the confines of our given object-base) why we should think a hang-glider dangerous; it just **is**. This is a convenient way of resolving the problem, which incidentally begs the same question for the design of crisp object systems. On the other hand it is sometimes unnatural not to include such objects: An elephant is a grey object; a grey object is a drab object. Once again, this issue of the difference between the essential and the accidental comes to the fore.

One interesting angle on this problem is that the presence of a tautological object in a design invariably indicates the presence of a personal construct of the kind used by Kelly grids, e.g. Danger-Safety, so that the presence of tautological objects in a design naturally results from using the methods of knowledge elicitation derived from Kelly grids.

Another, useful point of view is suggested by the discussion of judgement analysis and the recognition of universals given in Chapter 6.

Other structures which one would naturally disallow in a theory of non-redundant (or normal) forms for object-bases include cycles. In the crisp case, the problem raised by the example discussed immediately below does not arise, since a loop of the type below always represents equality and the network may be collapsed. In the case of fuzzy objects it is harder to decide whether there is a need for such relationships.

For example, the phrase 'Most men are avaricious' may be represented by fuzzy objects in the form:

Men <<fuzzy>>		Greedy.men <<fuzzy>>
AKO:Greedy-men [0.8]		AKO:Men [1]

This pair of fuzzy objects contains an irreducible cycle. Crisp inheritance systems usually demand acyclicity. This is certainly computationally convenient, but no theory exists to say that it is strictly necessary for coherent inheritance, except for the collapse argument given above. The problem just pointed out is, however, special to the fuzzy case; because, for fuzzy objects the cycles do not collapse. One way to remove the problem is to disallow the cycle and expand the network to include a new object representing 'avaricious entity' (e.g. a petrol hungry car). Then, a greedy man is avaricious [1] (or has the attribute avaricious filled with 'high') and a man [1], and a man is avaricious [0.8] and there are no cycles. In doing this we have broken the no tautologies rule, though. Thus, there seems to be a trade-off between cycles and the use of tautological objects.

The intimate relationship between acyclicity in a design and the presence of tautological objects suggests the following design rules.

DR1   Tautological objects should be introduced to break cycles.

DR2   Tautological objects should be used to prevent users asserting a property for an object explicitly. This has the effect of preventing update anomalies where two objects would inherit the same value from the tautological object but may be assigned different values by the user.

DR3   Otherwise, tautological objects should be avoided.

There is one other problem with the hang-glider example worth a mention. Regarding the problem of determining safety as one of conflict resolution in the presence of fuzzy inheritance means that one could look for a mechanism which would recognize the presence of 'very bimodal' distributions in returned fuzzy sets and then prompt the user for a decision. The difficulty with this approach is centred on that of finding a universally acceptable measure of distance between fuzzy sets. It would, however, be worth exploring on an experimental basis.

This completes the exposition of the design theory for fuzzy objects. I should now like to offer some insight into the intuitions that led to the notion and in doing so suggest the place of the theory within knowledge representation as a whole.

A.9   The relationship of fuzzy objects to other concepts

In this final section, I suggest that fuzzy objects are a natural generalization of both relations and objects. The argument is informal, but assumes a mathematical background. It may be omitted without interfering with the main thread of the argument given above.

A.9.1 Fuzzy objects as a generalization of fuzzy relations

The first observation to make is that fuzzy relations generalize relations.

A relation is a subset of some Cartesian product of sets. It can also be regarded as a function from that product into the truth set of classical logic $2=\{0,1\}$. A fuzzy relation is such a function where the codomain is the truth lattice of a multi-valued logic; in the case we consider, the unit interval fulfils this rôle. Of course, a tabular (extensional) representation is also possible.

Now, it is well known (at least in mathematics) that there is a bijective correspondence between functions $A \times B \longrightarrow I$ and functions $A \longrightarrow I^B$. This also holds for n-dimensional Cartesian products. The correspondence is given by assigning to every function $f(a,b)$ the function which takes a point a to the function (fuzzy set):

$$g : B \longrightarrow I: b \longmapsto f(a,b).$$

This proves that, in tabular representation, the form

Loves:	Person1	Person2	Degree
	John	Mary	0.9
	Mary	John	0.2
	Jill	Mary	0.4

corresponds to the form

Loves:	Person	Possibility distribution
	John	$\pi 1$
	Jill	$\pi 2$
	Mary	$\pi 3$

The possibility distributions are fuzzy sets (not illustrated here). For example, $\pi 1$ shows the degree to which John loves each other person in the universe of discourse. Its truth value for Mary is 0.9.

Thus, the syntax we use in fuzzy objects (ignoring the AKO attributes for a moment) corresponds to an adequate syntax for fuzzy relations.

The next point to notice is that relations may form a category with arrows that preserve some desired properties of relations, such as projections or joins or both. Zadeh's extension principle (see (Kandel, 1986)) implies that, with a suitable notion of property-preserving arrow, fuzzy relations also may form a category. The exact definition of the arrows is not important for our argument – it would be if we wished to proceed to formal proofs. There is an obvious embedding functor from relations to fuzzy relations:

$$\text{(Rel)} \longrightarrow \text{(FuzRel)}$$

This gives an exact meaning to the statement that fuzzy relations (fuzzy relational databases) generalize relations (relational databases).

If we now add the inheritance structure to a fuzzy relation we have fuzzy objects (classes) as a generalization of fuzzy relations.

A.9.2 Fuzzy objects as a generalization of objects

In a similar way class objects (regarded as sets of instances) also generalize relations.

Apart from first normal form and object identity, which in any case can be system generated in a relational system, the key differences between objects and relations are that objects do not require atomic values of attributes – there may be sub-attributes (facets), methods, list valued entries, and (because of inheritance) we cannot predict in advance the number of attributes in the data dictionary definition of an object. The first relaxation is equivalent to saying that the underlying logic is no longer first order (as with fuzzy relations). The second says that we are working in a potentially (countably) infinite Cartesian product. Intuitively, this corresponds to the assertion that an object may be assigned *any* attribute in the world; blueness, hunger, pointedness, etc. Real objects only have a few relevant attributes, but in the object model they MIGHT inherit anything. Instances are only an exception to this rule when we restrict to single inheritance, since, although instances inherit *all* their parent class properties, they may belong to potentially all classes which may be defined.

Having said this, instance objects are normally thought of as representing single objects. This is the reason we sometimes talk about sets of objects or classes. An n-tuple in a relation corresponds to one filling of a class by an instance; each filling corresponds to a real thing. Of course, there is absolutely no reason why instances themselves should not be multi-valued. There are at least two interpretations of this: (1) each 'filling' corresponds to a 'possible world'; (2) each filling corresponds to a state on some world line. This provides a start on generalizing objects, or fuzzy objects, to contain temporal modelling capabilities. This will not be explored further here.

Regarding classes as abstract data types lets us view them as algebras. Thus, mappings which preserve the algebraic structure, the methods, may exist. Looked at in this way, object sets, classes, may form a category – the arrows preserving the object composition structures (and possibly having something to do with inheritance). Thus again we get the embedding functor:

$$(\text{Rel}) \longrightarrow (\text{Class})$$

which takes relations to objects with no (non-attribute) methods; that is, none other than the standard get and put methods.

The practical application of this idea, on its own, is that truth maintenance systems and temporal logic systems acquire a very coherent implementation framework, and many of the techniques of relational database theory can be mapped across to this framework.

Adding the ability for objects to hold fuzzy sets as attribute values shows that fuzzy objects can be viewed as a generalization of objects.

Obviously, the idea has only been sketched here, and much further work remains to be done.

A.9.3 Fuzzy objects as a pushout

Having two functors in the category of categories, as described, naturally leads to the question: What is their pushout? If we could construct it, we would have the universal generalization of both objects and fuzzy relations. I conjecture at this point that fuzzy objects are a very reasonable candidate for this pushout and thus that fuzzy objects generalize all object knowledge representations.

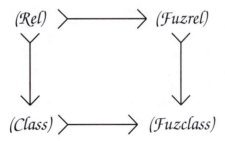

Figure A.20 A conjectured pushout in the category of categories.

If this result or even a much weaker version of it (that the diagram of Figure A.20 commutes) could be established, then we would have a step towards a unified theory covering the following issues in knowledge representation.

■   The relational model of data.

- Object-orientation and inheritance systems.
- Fuzzy relations and fuzzy information retrieval.
- Nonmonotonic reasoning.
- Temporal reasoning, possible worlds and modal logic systems.

This is a bold claim. The arguments above are tentative. However, at the very least, it is worthy of further exploration. I hope that researchers will take up some of these ideas as lines of research.

A.10   Summary

This appendix informally defined the syntax and semantics of fuzzy objects and the corresponding fuzzy extension to SOMA. These extensions may easily be incorporated to standard notations such as UML in the future and I have tried to illustrate how current UML may be used as it stands.

Fuzzy objects in SOMA can have fuzzy attribute values which can be inherited. The theory of how to do this under multiple inheritance was described. Fuzzy objects may also inherit both crisp and fuzzy attribute values *partially*; that is, with a defined certainty value. The appendix showed how these numbers could be combined with inherited fuzzy sets to model the partial inheritance of partial properties. The partial inheritance of methods, represented by a certainty factor, is taken to mean the possibility that the object can carry out the operation. Rules can be fuzzy rules.

Several candidate applications were suggested. Fuzzy objects may be of immense utility in describing systems in contexts such as enterprise modelling and business process re-engineering. Among the most difficult of the other applications which suggest themselves is the application to the interpretation of natural language statements. It is to be hoped that other, more academic, researchers will take this up as a research topic. My interest is in the practical issues. Additionally, I have suggested a line of research for mathematicians interested in database theory and the abstract algebra of relations. I hope that this too will be taken up and solved by the academic community.

The design and methodological issues surrounding fuzzy objects were also explored. A number of unsolved problems in this area were suggested as topics for further research. In general, I believe that this research must be predicated on applications. There is a clear resonance between the issues dealt with here and the current interest in object-oriented databases.

The theory described is readily implementable. This makes it possible to move on to the stage of implementation and applications.

⊟ A.11 Bibliographical notes

A partial and rudimentary version of this theory appeared as (Graham and Jones, 1987) and a fuller one in (Graham and Jones, 1988). The latter is a reasonable guide to the vast literature on fuzzy sets and systems. The classic reference on that subject is (Dubois and Prade, 1980). (Kandel, 1986) is a sound introduction to the basic mathematics, while (Graham and Jones, 1988) is more oriented towards applications and covers fuzzy rule-based systems, including REVEAL, in detail. The journals *Fuzzy Sets and Systems* and *The Journal of Approximate Reasoning* are good sources of current research material on both theory and applications.

Other, all different, definitions of fuzzy objects or fuzzy inheritance may be found in the work of Dubois *et al.* (1991), Baldwin and Martin (1996), Cross (1996), Nguyen and Van Le (1996) and Van Gyseghem and De Caluwe (1996).

Recent research on the topic of this chapter has been rare, but (Pedrycz and Sosnowski, 1998) is an interesting and quite orthogonal contribution. Lu and Zhou (2000) describe a notion of selective inheritance among fuzzy objects. Cross and Firat (2000) discuss another definition of fuzzy object, with some similarity to the one in this chapter, and show how it may be applied to geographic information systems with powerful consequences.

The literature on AI frame systems is also quite vast. (Winston, 1984) and (Lenat and Guha, 1990) give the theoretical view, while (Shadbolt, 1989) is an informed but gentle introduction.

B

Seminal analysis and design methods

I have called this principle, by which each slight variation, if useful, is preserved, by the term of Natural Selection. We will now discuss in a little more detail the struggle for existence.

Charles Darwin (*The Origin of Species*)

This appendix is provided for those with an interest in the genesis of current methods for object-oriented design, analysis and requirements modelling. It records the precursors of UML as well as the very many contributions from methodologists that have influenced modern methods and, in some cases, continue to do so.

B.1 Early object-oriented design methods and notations

There have been many object-oriented design methods, the oldest of which was probably due to Grady Booch whose original papers (1982, 1986) set out what was chiefly a design method for Ada, but coined the term. From this point of view object-oriented design is based on the principle of encapsulation, rather than either the composition of functions (as with traditional methods) or a fully object-oriented approach embracing inheritance. This encapsulation can be readily implemented using Ada packages or Modula-2 modules, whereas inheritance and polymorphism are unnatural constructs in these hierarchically structured languages. Message passing can, however, be simulated easily using function or procedure calls which implement the constructor and access operations of an object. Booch later published a much extended and improved method that was not closely tied to Ada and which influenced parts of UML strongly. It is discussed separately below.

BOOCH86   Booch's original method begins with a data-flow analysis which is then used to help identify objects by looking for both concrete and abstract objects in the problem space that will be found from the bubbles and data stores in the data flow diagram (DFD). Next, methods are obtained from the process bubbles of the DFD. An alternative but complementary approach is Abbott's (1983) textual analysis described in Chapter 6. This technique can be automated, as some of the tools developed to support HOOD and Saeki *et al.* (1989) showed. Most of the methods descended from Booch's work used some form of textual analysis of this sort. Booch's notation represents objects as blobs or 'clouds' as shown in Figure B.1. Arrows indicate which objects use the services (or methods) of other objects, thus defining client-server(or usage) relationships and message handling.

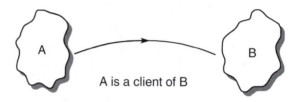

Figure B.1 Booch notation for the client-server relationship between objects.

Groups of objects are partitioned into 'subsystems' of manageable size corresponding to the levels or layers of a DFD as pictured in Figure B.2(a). Classes are identified with Ada packages and drawn as shown in Figure B.2(b). Booch did not see any need to denote attributes in his notation as all access to the object's interface is via a method, or operation; although Ada itself permits access to the data structures within a package specification. The shaded area represents the implementation of the package or package body, and an unshaded rectangle (or parallelogram for generics) denotes the specification. The unshaded ovals represent a package's name or type declaration and the unshaded rectangles each denote a method.

The icons shown in Figure B.2(b) and B.3 have become known as Gradygrams and influenced the module notation in UML. Booch distinguishes between two kinds of client-server relationship between objects as illustrated in Figure B.3. If the arrow starts from the shaded rectangle that represents the body of the object A then the implementation of A depends on the services offered by B. If the arrow originates from the type declaration oval then only the specification (or interface) of A depends on B. This reflects the concern with design rather than analysis.

Sommerville (1989) uses Ada as an all-purpose design language. This is a common approach for authors of method-based code generators who use an Ada-like program description language (PDL) as an intermediate stage between pictorial or textual design and actual code. In Ada, classes are identified with abstract data types and correspond to packages that, in the argot of Ada programmers, export limited private or private types. Instances correspond to instances of private or limited private types or packages that serve as abstract state machines. Methods correspond to subprograms exported from a package specification. As a rule of thumb, if a single instance of a class is required it should be defined directly as a package, but if a number of instantiations are needed it should be defined as a class. If the object's state need be accessed by other objects, it should be defined as an instantiation of a class. Inheritance is difficult in Ada but a limited form can be implemented through derived types or generic packages.

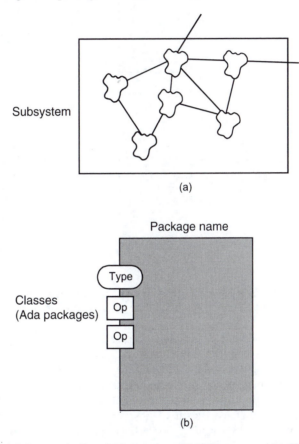

Subsystem

(a)

Package name

Classes
(Ada packages)

Type

Op

Op

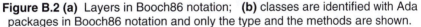

(b)

Figure B.2 (a) Layers in Booch86 notation; **(b)** classes are identified with Ada packages in Booch86 notation and only the type and the methods are shown.

Booch appeared to undergo something of a conversion since this early work. His later work (1991) showed a broadened perspective on object-oriented design, no longer tied to any specific language such as Ada. His revised notation and method supported implementation in Smalltalk, CLOS, C++, Ada or most object-based or object-oriented languages. He also evolved quite general guidelines on object recognition and the management of object-oriented design and programming projects. We discuss his revised method in a separate subsection below.

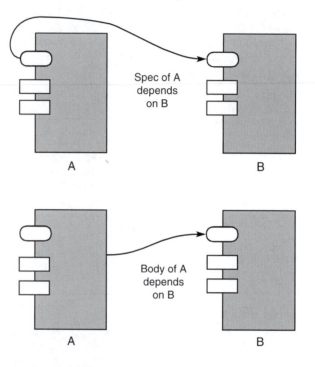

Figure B.3 Booch86 notation distinguishes between clients that use the specification or interface of servers and those which use their implementation.

Following Booch's pioneering work a number of specifically design-oriented methods emerged which were closely coupled to systems developments using the Ada language, such as GOOD, HOOD and MOOD. We will look at two of these. Several other design methods and notational conventions, which were not tied to Ada, followed close on the heels of the Ada methods. We will look fairly closely at two: OOSD and Booch's 1991 work. Three others are discussed briefly. These are OODLE, JSD and a borderline analysis/design technique: RDD/CRC. Other methods and notations, not discussed, include a widely used one due to J.A. Buhr (1984), which was used in the team*work*/Ada CASE tool and in the Texel method, and which influenced methods such as OODLE.

GOOD　The General Object-Oriented Design (GOOD) method was developed at NASA by Seidewitz and Stark (1986). It covered both requirements specification and design of Ada projects. The method proceeded, as with Booch's, from a preliminary layered set of data flow diagrams to an identification of the objects involved. One looks in the DFDs for externals, data stores, control interfaces and control stores.

Classes are discovered by examining the flow of data and control. Examination of the main processes leads to an abstract model of the system's function, and by tracing the incoming and outgoing flows attached to these processes a set of layered diagrams can be constructed. These diagrams emphasize control and data relationships among entities. Thus the entities and entity groupings become the objects and the original data transformations become their methods. As with Booch's method and other Ada derived methods, this approach enforces a top-down seniority hierarchy among objects, based on how objects use each other.

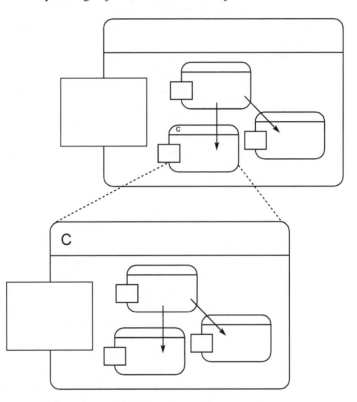

Figure B.4 HOOD decomposition of objects with use and inclusion relationships. The arrows may be interpreted as 'uses' and the enclosure of a package in the diagram denotes that it is part of the enclosing object.

HOOD   The notion of a seniority hierarchy is picked up by another method, HOOD. The 'H' in HOOD in fact stands for Hierarchical – the reader will be able to infer what the 'OOD' stands for. This method was also very much directed at Ada development and was developed at the European Space Agency. It was directly influenced by GOOD and also drew on the Abstract Machines method of Matra Espace and techniques originated at CISI Ingénière, both French companies. Like GOOD, it emphasized composition (part-of) hierarchies, but had nothing whatsoever to say about classification (inheritance) hierarchies. In HOOD, objects are either 'passive' or 'active'. Passive objects can only use the services of other passive objects but active ones can use any object's services. HOOD is a top-down method that proceeds by decomposing a top level object and then further decomposing the resultant objects. In effect then there are two hierarchies in HOOD: the compositional hierarchy and the usage hierarchy. The usage hierarchy may, in fact, be a network.

Diagrammatically, HOOD follows a Booch-style, Gradygram notation. A typical notation is shown in Figure B.4, which also indicates how the inclusion or composition hierarchy is denoted by icon inclusion. Seniority or usage relationships are shown by arrows with the arrowheads pointing at the more junior partner as in Figure B.5(a). Figure B.5(b) gives a notation for the 'implemented by' link which is shown as a dotted line. The parent operation 'start' is implemented by the operation 'begin' of the child object A which delivers all the functionality expected of 'start'. The 'implemented by' link is a very useful decomposition technique that influenced SOMA wrappers.

The HOOD method used a number of steps to decompose each object, starting with a basic design step which might involve diagramming techniques from other structured analysis and design methods. The concepts so derived are mapped onto objects and external interfaces. This step breaks down into stating the problem, usually as text, and then analysing and structuring the data. The Abbott idea of using nouns and verbs to identify objects and methods mentioned earlier is supported. As an example of how conventional techniques were used in identifying objects, consider how to map concepts from the conventional Yourdon structured design method. Context diagrams give hardware objects and external interfaces. DFDs give abstract data types and data pools. The information model also gives data types. State transition diagrams give active objects and object-based control structures.

The next step is to produce an informal solution strategy. This breaks down into a number of tasks: an outline in natural language, rough HOOD diagrams and a description of the current level of abstraction. The third step is to formalize the solution strategy. This is done in stages by identifying and describing the objects and their operations, grouping them and producing HOOD diagrams showing parent–child relationships and operations (the composition hierarchy), usage (client-server or seniority) hierarchies, 'implemented by' links, dataflows and exceptions. Lastly, any design decisions must be justified. It was also recommended that one recorded links to the original requirements specification for future traceability.

A note on terminology is necessary at this point. HOOD calls methods 'operations' and 'implemented by' links refer to the need of operations in parent objects to call operations in a child object.

Now the solution strategy is formalized the next step is to formalize the solution itself. This consists in refining the object definition skeleton (ODS) of parent objects by defining types, constants and data, refining the ODS of terminal objects by

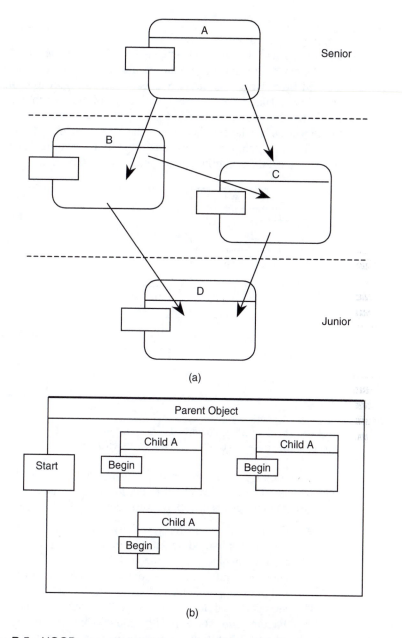

(a)

(b)

Figure B.5 HOOD use relationships and implemented_by links: **(a)** the seniority hierarchy with use relationships; **(b)** the parent method START is said to be 'implemented by' the method BEGIN of CHILD_A which supplies the functionality of START. Implemented_by links in HOOD are shown by a dotted arrow. Other usage relationships are not shown on this diagram.

defining their internals and operation control structure (OPCS), checking for inconsistencies, producing documentation and generating and testing Ada code.

As noted already, usage relationships are indicated by arrows. Exceptions are denoted by a bar across the arrow, as shown in Figure B.6, but are not dealt with explicitly. That is, the direction of flow of the exception is not shown (it is implicitly the reverse of the use arrow) and the exception is dealt with in relation to the object as a whole rather than attached to a parameter or data flow. In this example, if the temperature exceeds some limit, or a breakdown in the temperature sensor occurs, the exception 'overheated' can be raised.

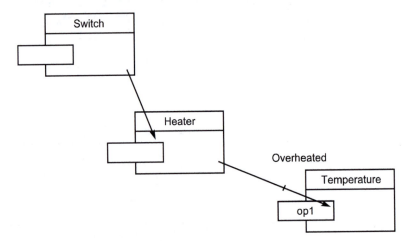

Figure B.6 Exception flow in HOOD. The exception OVERHEATED is raised by the object TEMPERATURE and processed by HEATER.

Data flows can also be recorded using the notation illustrated in Figure B.7 which is based on structure charts (Yourdon and Constantine, 1979).

Common criticisms of HOOD were identified by Hodgson (1990) as follows:

- There is no support for genericity, inheritance or polymorphism. Generics are commonly used by Ada programmers and so this is a serious deficiency even for an object-based method.
- There is insufficient separation of the definition of an object from its use and little support for reusability.
- The graphical formalism is both incomplete and inconsistent. HOOD diagrams do not explicitly show which operations are used by which objects, what flows are defined on each operation, how exceptions are propagated and what data are encapsulated by objects. The notation depicts subprograms as objects and control structure is also shown as a subprogram that passes control to a task. The parent object is depicted with the same notation as the child.

■ There are difficulties with the strict parent–child seniority hierarchy. In real-time systems, events and exceptions may affect the execution of a deeply nested subobject and it is inefficient to pass control through many enclosing objects.

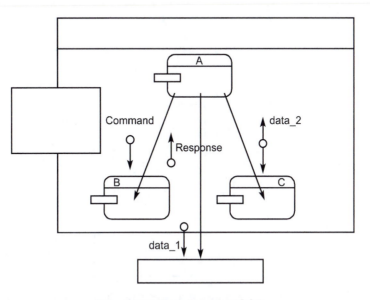

Figure B.7 Data flows in HOOD.

Additionally, many people feel that HOOD, while appropriate for many real-time military applications, was less so for commercial ones. The lack of support for inheritance makes it object-based rather than object-oriented. Thus, reuse was supported but not extensibility. The rôle of data structure (entity attributes) is played down in favour of concentration on functional abstraction. In the next section we will examine a notation which partially meets some of these shortcomings.

OOSD   Some of the criticisms listed above are dealt with in another design method, Object-Oriented Structured Design (OOSD), introduced by Wasserman, Pircher and Muller (1990). OOSD was, strictly speaking, not a method but a notation to which methodological rules can be added. This notation was probably the closest of all the methods discussed so far to the spirit of object-orientation in that it supported inheritance as well as abstraction. Although it was much closer to object-oriented principles, it still bore the marks of the influence of Ada. It also provided a more gradual transition for developers familiar with structured design, on which it is partly based.

OOSD was a non-proprietary notation for architectural design that combined top-down structured and object-oriented design. It aimed at supporting general object-oriented goals such as reuse, modularity, extensibility and the representation of inheritance and abstraction. It also aimed to support visual representation of interfaces among design components, code generation, language independence, communication between designers and users, and a variety of approaches. Ambitious aims!

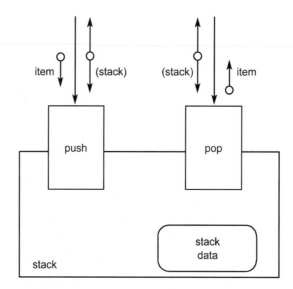

Figure B.8 An OOSD object representing a stack.

OOSD once again uses a notation derived from Booch's but it is also influenced by structure charts (Yourdon and Constantine, 1979) and its support for concurrency is based on Hoare's (1974) notion of monitors. Classes are shown as rectangles with smaller superimposed rectangles denoting their methods. Attributes are not explicitly mentioned in the OOSD literature but the ostensibly private storage pool could be used for this notational purpose. Attributes are also implicit in data flows which are indicated by arrows originating in unfilled circles. These flows are enumerated explicitly, as illustrated in Figure B.8, in a similar notation to that of structure charts. In OOSD angle brackets denote indirection or parameters as usual.

Client-server relationships are shown by thicker arrows between objects. If one of these arrows has an output data flow as in Figure B.9 this indicates that the client object (save_state) instantiates the object.

Unlike HOOD, OOSD declares exceptions explicitly. The notational convention is diamond-shaped areas overlapping the object body. The exception parameter passing is shown in the same notation as that for data flows but with filled diamonds at the arrow butts.

Hidden operations are catered for in the manner shown in Figure B.11 where 'is full' is used by the externally visible push method.

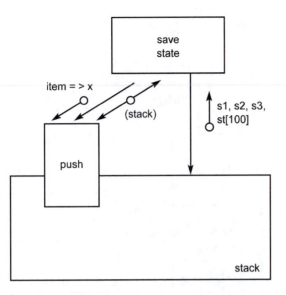
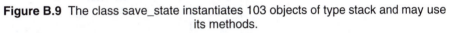

Figure B.9 The class save_state instantiates 103 objects of type stack and may use its methods.

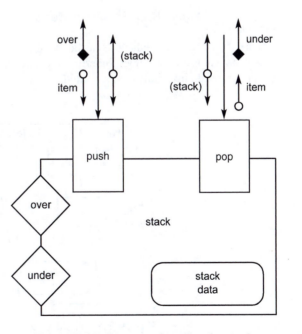

Figure B.10 Exception handling for stack.

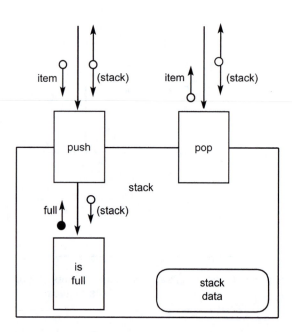

Figure B.11 Showing hidden operations in OOSD.

Generic classes are dealt with in the same way but the rectangular class body outline is drawn as a dotted line. Inheritance between classes is indicated by a dotted arrow and multiple inheritance is permitted.

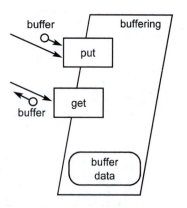

Figure B.12 A buffering monitor.

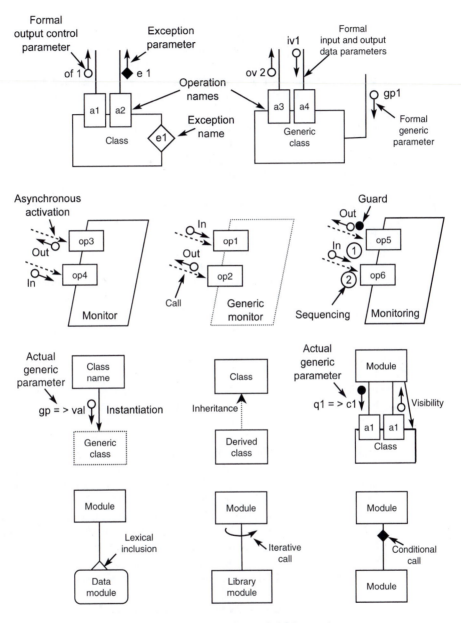

Figure B.13 The complete OOSD notation.

Concurrent or asynchronous processes are catered for by monitors which are shown as parallelograms, as shown in Figure B.12. This notion of a monitor is rather like that of a class but its data are shared out among its various methods. In the case illustrated, more than one process (as with network interrupts) may put or get data. These operations need exclusive access to the hidden buffer data.

The entire set of OOSD symbols is shown in Figure B.13. The reader requiring a deeper understanding may consult the paper by Wasserman *et al.* (1990), from which this summary is largely taken, for a very clear, detailed exposition.

OOSD was not intended so much as a method as a notation to support object-oriented design methods in general. The user of OOSD can add design rules according to the particular method in use. Where these design rules are explicit, this may be formalized easily, but where vague rules, such as HOOD's insistence that objects should have 'a low fan out', are involved the designer's judgement is required – pending perhaps the use of expert systems technology for this purpose.

OOSD was meant to be language independent and is not tied to Ada or any other language. This means that some of the notions of OOSD may not be explicitly supported by the target language. Implementing classes is a lot easier in C++ than in FORTRAN, although possible in both. Again, languages such as FORTRAN with no support for concurrency make it harder to implement designs that include monitors. Equally, some of the detail of languages is not captured by OOSD. For example, there is no equivalent to Ada's limited private types or C++'s virtual functions or friends. Another important point to note is that OOSD is a notation for architectural design rather than detailed, physical design. This means that it offers little help with the physical clustering of files on disks, the most suitable hardware, meeting service levels or the optimal use of memory.

Other notable points for OOSD were its ready acceptance by developers already familiar with structured design and its suitability for real-time systems because of the monitor concept. The arrows in an OOSD diagram, for example, are interpreted exactly as in a structure chart. It makes a distinction between the definition of an object and later reference to it by other objects. This means that the notation does not require all the details of an object to be displayed each time it is used. The protocol for overriding methods in multiple inheritance is also significant. If a method may be inherited in two ways, it must be named to make clear which way is preferred, or overridden. For example, in the domain of geometry, the class of geometrical objects may have subclasses 'regular figure' and 'solid'. A regular solid is in both these classes. Now, all geometric objects have a method called 'invariant rotation', but for general solids this is a far less complicated method than for regular figures. Thus regular solids must inherit a method designated as 'regular figure invariant rotation' or override with its own method, according to the requirements of the problem. In OOSD, methods may be added to a subclass or overridden. They may not be dropped.

OOSD was one of the more advanced hybrid, low level object-oriented design notations of the first generation.

JSD AND KISS   Jackson System Development (JSD) (Jackson, 1983) was an object-based rather than object-oriented method. JSD models are decomposed in terms of events or actions and their time dependencies. Within these events the JSD approach first defines objects. The next step constructs a specification in terms of communicating sequential processes that can access each other's state – violating thus the principle of information hiding.

A number of similarities between JSD and object-oriented design methods can be identified. JSD contains useful techniques for entity and method identification in its modelling stage. Also, the time ordering analysis technique of JSD may be regarded as a means of documenting classes. JSD and object-oriented design use the concept of objects similarly though their terminologies are different. JSD can give guidance on which objects and operations are likely to be relevant to a problem. This is especially so where the time ordering of events is important. Otherwise, the links are fairly tenuous.

Jackson has declared his concern with the problem we discussed in Chapter 1; that inheritance violates encapsulation and therefore reusability. Jackson's ideas have certainly been and remain extremely influential on the development of other object-oriented methods.

Object-oriented versions of JSD emerged and attempts were made to create object-oriented extensions of conventional methods that use JSD-style Entity Life History (ELH) techniques such as SSADM-4 where, for example, Effect Correspondence diagrams are suggested as a means of showing visibility. The more extreme suggestions even claimed that inheritance is nothing more than a one-to-many relationship and can thus be accommodated within SSADM data modelling techniques. An object-oriented SSADM was defined by Robinson and Berrisford (1994).

The KISS object-oriented analysis and design method (Kristen, 1995) makes use of textual analysis and ideas from JSD, especially its entity life histories based on regular grammars. Its ELHs are constructed using an innovative kit of 'dominoes' as an alternative to the usual diagramming techniques. KISS may have been influenced by the SSADM-like MERODE, which also emphasizes ELHs.

All the methods dealt with so far were extremely weak in the area of semantic data modelling, and none of the diagramming techniques, except KISS, allowed for detailed description of attributes.

BOOCH91 AND BOOCH93

Booch's (1991) revised design method and notation consisted of four major activities and six notations. The first steps deal with the static aspects of the system, both logical and physical. The dynamics are dealt with using the existing techniques of state transition and timing diagrams. Schematically, this may be shown as:

Logical structure
Class diagrams
Object diagrams

Physical structure
Module diagrams
Process diagrams

Dynamics of classes
State transition diagrams

Dynamics of instances
Timing diagrams

Booch suggested that Abbott-style linguistic interpretation, conventional structured analysis techniques and object-oriented analysis were all suitable precursors to object-oriented design, but warned that developers using structured analysis must resist 'the urge to fall back into the abyss of the structured design mindset': good advice to this day.

Both classes and instances are shown as formless blobs in the manner of Figure B.1, but classes have a dotted outline. If these blobs have shadows, as in Figure B.1, this indicates that they denote free subprograms, which some languages permit.

A fairly rich notation for the relationships between classes is added, which uses different kinds of line to indicate usage, inheritance and other relationships. Figure B.14 shows these symbols. Booch recommended a form of layering, so that classes are organized into 'categories' containing several related classes. These layers are shown as rectangles. Arrows between these rectangles denote visibility or usage relationships.

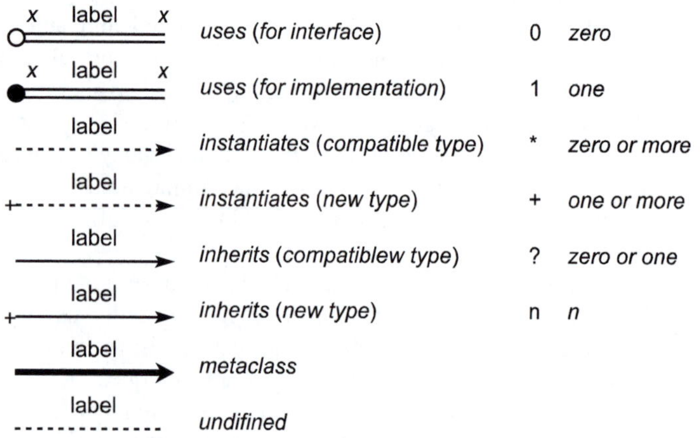

x label *x* ⊶════════ uses (*for interface*)	0 zero
x label *x* ●════════ uses (*for implementation*)	1 one
label ┄┄┄┄┄┄➤ instantiates (*compatible type*)	* zero or more
label +┄┄┄┄┄┄➤ instantiates (*new type*)	+ one or more
label ────────➤ inherits (*compatiblew type*)	? zero or one
label +───────➤ inherits (*new type*)	n *n*
label ━━━━━━━➤ metaclass	
label ┄┄┄┄┄┄ undifined	

Figure B.14 Booch91 class diagram relational icons.

Each class, in Booch's method, is described by filling a standard template which includes identity, attributes, methods and the following extra design information.

Documentation (text)
Visibility (exported/private/imported)
Multiplicity (0/1/n)
Superclasses
Used classes
Generic parameters
Interface implementation (public/protected/private)
State transition diagram
Concurrency (sequential/blocking/active)
Persistence (static/dynamic)

Space complexity (text)

Note that there are some data semantics present but no process semantics, although the state transition diagram associated with each class can represent this information. Some items, such as concurrency and space complexity, are related to quite low level physical design.

Class and object diagrams and their associated templates describe the logical, static design of a system. The physical design may differ from the logical. For example, data may be clustered for efficient access, or processes clustered according to related usage to prevent thrashing. To enforce this distinction, which is not made in his earlier work, Booch distinguished between classes and modules; the latter corresponding to program segments, which could be separately compiled functions in C++ or complex Ada packages. The notation for modules was based on the earlier Gradygram notation shown in Figure B.2(b). Process diagrams, which are really simple block diagrams, show the communication relationships between physical devices and processors.

The dynamics of a system must also be described. This is accomplished in two ways. The state transition diagrams show the dynamics of classes, which is a technique shared with several of the object-oriented analysis methods discussed in this appendix. The instance level dynamics are shown by timing diagrams borrowed from the field of hardware design. These timing diagrams show the methods of each instance commencing and terminating in relation to each other, as shown in Figure B.15.

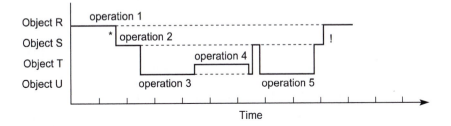

Figure B.15 A timing diagram as used in Booch91. The asterisk indicates the creation of an instance and the shriek its destruction.

Timing diagrams may only be manageable for reasonably small systems, depending on the complexity of interaction among processes. The Objectory method offered a similar method for handling the dynamics of instances. Birtwistle (1979) uses activity diagrams in his DEMOS.

Booch's method was one of the best worked out design methods at the time, and was superior to GOOD and HOOD in not being tied to Ada and in having a much more general notion of structure. These richer semantic properties of the method meant that the it overlapped the territory of the analyst as well as that of the designer. This is justified by the incremental approach to software engineering which Booch advocates; for, in prototyping, analysis and design are often closely interwoven. The main weakness of Booch's method, and it had this in common with other object-oriented design methods, is that the global dynamics were tagged on almost as an afterthought. Further, there was no serious attempt to deal with business rules and other such process-semantic aspects of specification. Having said that, Booch93 was the best design method for C++ (and of course Ada) programmers and in my opinion was in this respect slightly superior to many of its descendent, UML-based epigones.

One of the central problems of software engineering is that of coping with complexity. Object-oriented design methods address precisely this issue. Waterfall models and other bureaucratic or 'cookbook' approaches to system building fail to recognize that managing complexity requires great flexibility. Risk-driven and incremental approaches recognize the need for sound but adaptive methods. Booch recommended what he calls 'round-trip gestalt design'. That is, a process of incremental complete designs at different levels of abstraction and refinement, proceeding neither strictly top-down nor bottom-up. This process proceeds roughly in the following order.

- Identify classes and instances
- Define their semantics
- Find relationships among them
- Implement the design as a prototype
- Examine the system for cohesion and consistency
- Redefine classes, instances, semantics and structures on the basis of what has been learnt

The process stops when it is believed that all the key abstractions and functions have been defined and is highly non-linear. Defining an object's methods and interface may affect the protocol of another object or a classification structure. Equally, discovering a structure may lead to the perception of new objects. Lastly, we should note the obvious: there is never a best or optimal design. Different designers will produce different models and they may be equally suitable for their purpose.

This method stressed that identifying objects and their classes is a logical design decision independent of their organization into modules, which is a physical design decision.

Booch's method distinguished client-server, seniority or use relationships and containment or parent–child relationships. At the class level, containment has two senses: classification (the concept is contained) and composition (the thing is contained). The Booch design method makes the distinction but gives no guidance on how these two kinds of structure are interrelated. Use relationships define the control structure of a system, or its message passing topology.

Booch distinguishes three rôles for objects. **Actors** or active objects can initiate behaviour in other objects but not be acted upon and **servers** can only be operated upon by other objects. **Agents** do both. In my view the client-server relationship is better viewed as a relative notion. An object can be a server in one respect but an actor in others. This usage has no connexion with the actor systems discussed in Chapter 3.

In this method, and in general, there is a trade-off between use and containment structures. Containing an object (say having it as an attribute value) reduces the number of objects which are visible to the enclosing object. Obversely, containment restricts the easy use of an object by other parts of the system and may compromise its reuse potential. This observation points to an important design decision. The granularity of objects is one of the key design decisions and, as has been remarked, beginners tend to get it wrong. They tend to make the granularity too fine.

The Booch method underwent further development and an improved version appeared in 1993. The emphasis was shifted entirely towards C++ compared to the earlier approach. Many notational improvements were included, some to take account of C++ features and some to recognize the contributions of other methodologists, but the method remained essentially the same. The method effectively disappeared when Booch became one of the original two authors of UML.

OODLE AND RECURSIVE DESIGN

The Shlaer-Mellor approach to object-oriented analysis is described in Section B.2. In this section we examine two of its design-oriented components. Like most other methods Shlaer-Mellor notation has been superseded by UML, but its methodological precepts remain. It is especially notable for introducing the distinction between translational (recursive) as opposed to elaborational approaches.

OODLE (Object-Oriented Design LanguagE) is a design-specific component of the Shlaer-Mellor method whose approach to object-oriented analysis is described in the next chapter. It prescribes four types of diagram interrelated by a layering scheme to help with documentation and potential automated support. The notation is said to be language independent though there is a small hint of Ada in the notation and the support for friends is reminiscent of C++. The diagram types are as follows.

- **Dependency diagrams** show usage (client-server) and friend relationships between classes.
- **Class diagrams** show the external view of a class in a manner similar to Buhr (1984).
- **Class structure charts** show the structure of the methods of a class and the flow of data and control.
- **Inheritance diagrams** depict inheritance.

Figure B.16 shows all three notations in outline. In the dependency diagram single arrows denote messages while double ones show friendship violations of encapsulation. In the class diagram, the top box is the class name and the other inner rectangles are its methods. Hexagons drawn outside the icon and connected to a method show parameters passing. If drawn inside the icon they depict hidden data structures. In class structure charts, rectangles denote methods and hexagons parameters passing between them in much the manner of OOSD. OODLE is a much richer notation than these simplified diagrams indicate, with support for the representation of such things as polymorphism, exceptions and so on.

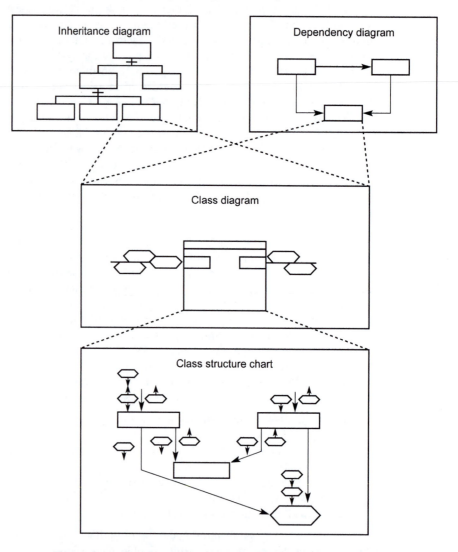

Figure B.16 Simplified OODLE diagrams and their relationships.

Several problems have motivated the idea of recursive design. Often classes do not fit together well. Also, despite the fact that reuse is based on external interfaces only, different styles of implementation across different objects lead to maintenance difficulties. Design therefore should be recursive rather than iterative. It should also be done using a method with precise semantics whenever possible. Recursive design is an abstract, general design principle rather than a design process in itself.

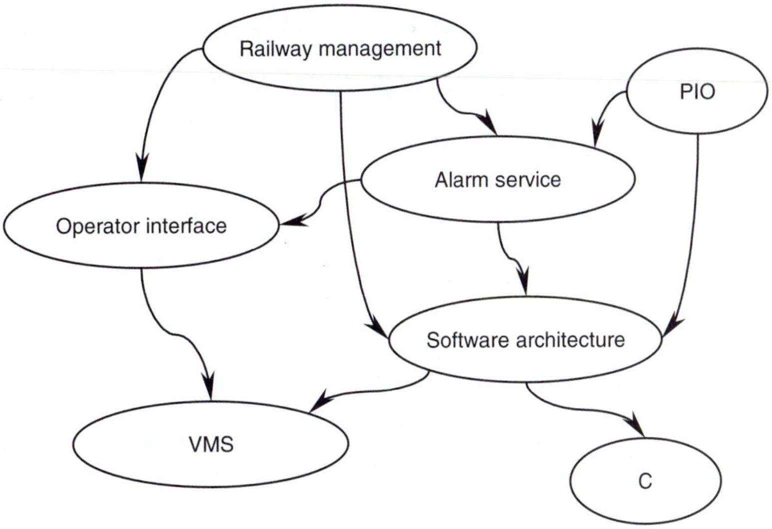

Figure B.17 A typical Shlaer-Mellor domain chart.

The basic idea, and a good idea it is too, is that the performance and maintainability of a system should be addressed by applying a set of general rules across all code modules rather than by low level tinkering to tune systems. The latter approach makes every component into a special case. There is wisdom in this and it contrasts with much existing practice in object-oriented projects and is at odds with the elaborational approaches of Booch and vanilla-flavoured UML-based methods. However, it could be objected that when reuse is really carried out, new developments are exactly special cases. Recursive development requires that the application is separated from various reusable domains at different levels and that formal bridging techniques are constructible between domains at different levels. For example, we might construct a standard bridging technique between low level UI designs and a particular operating system. The key domain is the 'architecture domain' which insulates application domains from particular implementations as illustrated in Figure B.17. Curiously, this is exactly what the designers of NeXtStep and Taligent were trying to do at the operating system level. HOOD offers such a bridge, but only to one architecture: that of Ada tasking. This is not general enough for most purposes.

Lastly, recursive development can be contrasted with iterative development as shown in Table B.1.

From this it may be deduced that the time for all stages of iterative development is proportional to the complexity of the requirement, whereas for recursive development design and code costs are fixed and, after an initially higher investment, reuse benefits accrue to each successive project.

Table B.1 Iterative versus recursive design.

Iterative	Recursive
FOR EACH requirement DO	FOR EACH requirement DO
analyse	analyse
design	execute analysis model (test)
code	END DO
execute code (test)	define design rules
END DO	test rules
integrate software	apply rules to 'generate' code

The term 'generated' here could refer to code hand-generated from the rules, but it is hard to see the argument other than as supporting the CASE approach. In my opinion, recursive design principles could just as readily be applied to conventional development. The Shlaer-Mellor method emphasized evolution over revolutionary object-oriented approaches.

CRC AND RDD

A responsibility-driven approach to analysis and design using Class, Responsibility and Collaboration (CRC) cards, due to Beck and Cunningham (1989) and described fully in (Wirfs-Brock *et al.,* 1990) is useful for documenting object-oriented designs and also for teaching the basic concepts. This technique is also known as RDD (Responsibility Driven Design). It has the singular advantage of using nothing more expensive than a box of index cards as a CASE tool, although originally the idea was to use a hypertext system. Cardboard was found to be more effective in practice.

The CRC approach assumes the existence of a written requirements specification and proceeds by using an Abbott-like textual analysis to name the key objects. For each object representing a class, a card is prepared containing the class name, and lists of superclasses and members. Next, a further textual analysis finds the 'responsibilities' or methods required by the class. These methods are further refined by examining three kinds of structure: classification, composition and, novelly, analogy structures. The use structure is determined as a list of classes which each class 'collaborates' with, and these are added to the cards. Once again the composition structures are examined to identify usage, along with 'has-knowledge-of' and 'depends-on' relationships. Collaboration helps with granularity as classes with no collaborations are factored out at this stage. The structures are now analysed to differentiate between abstract and concrete classes and a set-theoretic notation used to picture shared methods. The classes are also organized into layers, or subsystems, which are assigned contractual relationships with other subsystems and lists of delegated tasks. Lastly, all the components, classes, methods, subsystems and contracts are designed in detail.

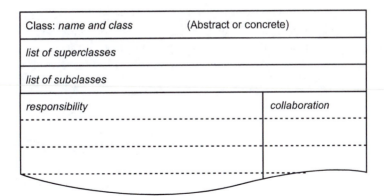

(a)

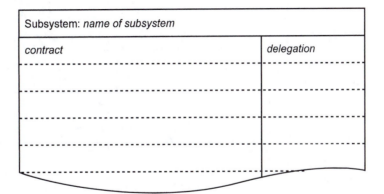

(b)

Figure B.18 CRC class and subsystem cards.

This approach emphasizes responsibilities, or methods, over attributes, or data, to help defer as many implementation decisions as possible, but it still acknowledges the existence of attributes. It is usable at both the design and analysis levels and, notation aside, can be regarded as a valuable set of guidelines which may be added to other object-oriented analysis approaches. Alone, it gives scant help in identifying objects or describing overall control structures. The contracts can be used to define pre- and post-conditions, which helps with some of the control structure, but there is little to support business rules and functional semantics.

Formally, responsibilities are divided into attributes that represent **responsibilities for knowing**, or the state of the object, and **responsibilities for doing**, or the operations the object can perform. **Collaborations** are requests to a server to help fulfil a client responsibility and constitute visibility or usage relationships at a detailed level. General associations are not well handled by CRC. A **contract** is the set of messages that a client can send to a server and constitutes the high level usage relationship. Contracts are sometimes used to group related responsibilities.

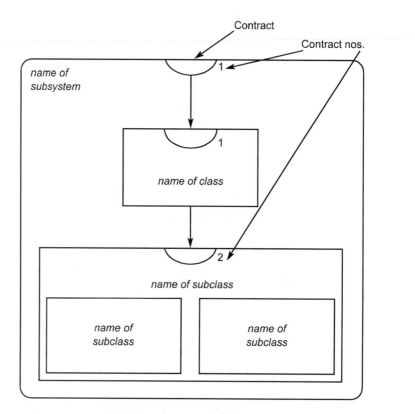

Figure B.19 An example collaboration graph.

Figure B.18 shows a typical CRC card and a subsystem card. Listing the members or subclasses is not a good idea since it compromises encapsulation and thereby reuse. Collaborations may be shown graphically by a collaboration graph using the notation shown in Figure B.19. The method uses these graphs to extract coherent subsystems based on containment and contractual groupings. For anything but trivial systems these graphs become very cluttered indeed and while the idea is good it is not easy to apply in practice. Other methods of layering and grouping must be found.

The method requires a written requirements statement as input and proceeds through the following steps.

1. Identify objects (from the nouns in the specification) and organize them into classification structures
2. Find responsibilities (from the verbs in the specification)
3. Assign responsibilities to classes
4. Examine the structures to refine responsibilities
5. Find collaborations
6. Discard classes without collaborations
7. Refine the structures
8. Group responsibilities into contracts
9. Use collaborations to define subsystems
10. Fill in the details

Many users of RDD use walkthroughs to validate their model and discover the global dynamics of the system; something that few other methods do well, incidentally.

RDD is a simplistic but very practical method. Much of its notation is poor and it does not cover all the issues. It is usually used as a precursor to the use of other notations. It is a useful pedagogical tool as it does get people to understand the behavioural emphasis of object technology quite quickly. An enhancement of the CRC technique in the context of requirements capture and analysis was exposed in Chapter 7.

⊟ B.2 Early object-oriented analysis methods and notations

Analysis methods arrived later than those for object-oriented design and I have retained the chronological ordering in this presentation.

SHLAER-MELLOR OOSA
The very first book with object-oriented analysis in its title was due to the late Sally Shlaer and Steve Mellor (Shlaer and Mellor, 1988), but the method could not really be regarded as object-oriented for several reasons, including the complete absence of any notion of inheritance. As described in their book it was little more than an object-based extension of data modelling. However, a later book by Shlaer and Mellor (1992) introduced inheritance (entity subtyping) and the idea that methods could be discovered by modelling the life cycles of entities with STDs. Their stance on object identity is still suspect, though, because they regard identifiers as sets of attributes or keys. Further, normalization rules (rules of attribution) are applied to objects, regarding them as little more than relational tables.

The first step in Shlaer and Mellor's method is the definition of objects and their attributes. The entity modelling notation is descended from the Ward/Mellor notation. Emphasis is placed next on defining object life histories, using Moore-style state transition diagrams and the corresponding tables. These are then used to define operations. The notation for the state models is also fairly standard. Global dynamics are handled by co-ordinating object life cycles annotated in Object Communication Models which show events (or equivalently messages) passing between entities. Relationships are also given life-cycle models.

This method proceeds by creating an information (or data) model showing objects, attributes and relationships. Next, a state model describes the states of objects and transitions between states. Finally, a DFD defines the process model. The method is influenced strongly by relational design; objects are in first normal form and object identity is not a natural feature of designs. Users of the method tend to be users who have migrated from the Ward/Mellor approach and the applications I have heard of seem to have a real-time or process control flavour rather than a commercial DP flavour, but this may be an historical accident. It is a complex method covering analysis and design which has had a controversial history but which was fairly popular. The design aspects of this method and its notation were discussed in the last section and need not be revisited here.

A novel idea is the definition of reusable domains, as already illustrated in Figure B.17, which helps impose a layered approach to software engineering and encourage reuse. This method is supported by several CASE tools and still quite widely used.

COAD

Another approach that owed a lot to the tradition of Entity-Relationship modelling was published by Coad and Yourdon (1990, 1991, 1991a) and is primarily interesting as the first widely published account of a simple, reasonably complete, practical, object-oriented analysis (*qua* analysis) method and supporting notation, suitable for commercial projects. Coad and Yourdon introduced a less clumsy notation than that found in Booch, Shlaer-Mellor or most of the design-oriented approaches. They shifted the agenda very much to analysis as opposed to design. Ada data structures, decomposition into modules or other language level constructs play no part in their method, which was remarkable for its simplicity though incomplete in some areas.

One of the most notable features of the Shlaer-Mellor and Coad-Yourdon notations was the explicitness of attributes. We have already seen how this violates the traditional object-oriented principle that objects are specified by their methods alone. However, we also saw that attributes can be identified with standard methods that access their state, such as 'put salary' and 'get salary'. The complexity of the data structures present in most commercial systems leads to the need to make attributes explicit.

There were two editions of the analysis book by Coad and Yourdon published within a year of each other. Later, Yourdon disassociated himself from the method and developed another method (Yourdon *et al.*, 1995) called Mainstream Objects, which had many similarities to SOMA. As a result the Coad-Yourdon method became known simply as Coad.

Coad suggested that analysis proceeds in five stages which he labelled:

- *Subjects*: The problem area is decomposed into 'subjects' which corresponds to the notion of 'levels' or 'layers' in data flow diagrams and to Booch's subsystems or class categories. These subjects should be of a manageable size in that they contain only about five to nine objects.
- *Objects*: Next, the objects are identified in detail by searching for business entities in much the same way as a data analysis would be performed. Coad and Yourdon give little additional guidance on how to perform this task.
- *Structures*: Two completely different structures are identified, classification structures and composition structures. This is where inheritance is dealt with as the classification structures are merely specialization/generalization trees. Coad says little about how these trees are processed or interact
- *Attributes*: As in conventional data analysis, attributes are detailed and modality and multiplicity relationships specified using a version of Extended Relational Analysis (ERA). In this there is a departure from some other object-oriented design methods which only specify methods.
- *Services*: This is the Coad word for operations. Each object type must be equipped with methods for creating and deleting instances, getting and putting values and with special methods characterizing the object's behaviour.

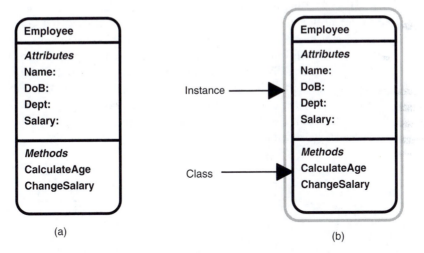

Figure B.20 (a) Coad-Yourdon notation for a general object; **(b)** the revised notation drew a grey outline around objects that might have instances.

Coad's (1991a) object-oriented design added to these five activities (or layers as he calls them) four components. Principally, his OOD consists in refining the products of OOA into what they call the Problem Domain Component of the design (by adding new solution space classes) and adding three new components called the Human Interaction (HIC), Task Management (TMC) and Data Management Components (DMC). These components allow design-specific issues – such as threads of control, specific processors, package software and so on – to be included in the OOA diagrams. Great emphasis is laid on the similarity of notation for analysis and design and the way this smoothes the transitions so sharply felt in traditional methods. This work on OOD addressed some criticisms which were made of the OOA method. For example, trigger and terminate constraints are introduced for Services. However, no real distinction between logical and physical design is made. Also, Coad is evidently aware of the oft levelled critique that his OOA can't handle dynamics. Hence, perhaps, we find on page 151: 'simulation of the behavioural dynamics being modelled. Inbound and outbound Message Connections may be highlighted, based on the selection of a Service or Services. Alternatively, threads of execution can be displayed – one at a time, or all together, using different line patterns for each thread – once they have been defined'. It is not made clear whether this requires every single message instance to be enumerated or how completeness can be checked.

The diagrammatic notation defined by Coad and Yourdon shows an object type as a triple icon, as shown in Figure B.20(a).

A low cost tool called OOATool was produced for sale by Coad's company, Object International. It was later superseded by the *Together* family of CASE tools.

The possibility of message passing between objects is shown in the same way as the original Booch notation, by arrows. In this area, Booch is in some ways actually a lot clearer than Coad and I preferred his terminology of clients and servers. His later notation, shown in Figure B.14, was definitely superior. Coad, like Booch, actually permits analysts to enumerate messages. In using the method the present author found that this is useful at a first attempt at analysis, but that it results in a dreadful mess when things get complex. In fact the resultant spaghetti is redundant because the method names show which messages will be processed if passed. All we need show is visibility; whether a message *may* be passed.

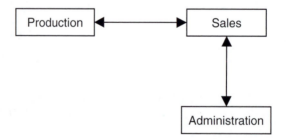

Figure B.21 Subjects are groups of, ideally, between five and nine objects or possibly coherent classification or composition structures.

In the second edition of his book, Coad caved in to criticisms that he had failed to distinguish classes and instances in the first. He drew a grey outline around the class icon to indicate its typical instance, if it has any instances, as shown in Figure 20(b). Messages are regarded as being sent to instances and end on the outer box. The usage structure is also muddled, since these arrows show actual implementation message passing rather than client-server relationships between classes.

Layering into 'subjects' is a process that takes place at various stages of analysis and can be used for an initial decomposition at the start or to organize the model after objects have been identified or refined. A similar process is usually associated with data flow diagrams. Subjects are represented by square boxes and message passing by arrows as though the layers were objects. However, in this method subjects are arbitrary decompositions to aid understanding and have no clear semantics. Worse, it is possible to have messages or even inheritance links crossing the boundary of a subject, though this is ill-advised. Some subjects arise quite naturally, as objects are assembled into classification or composition structures.

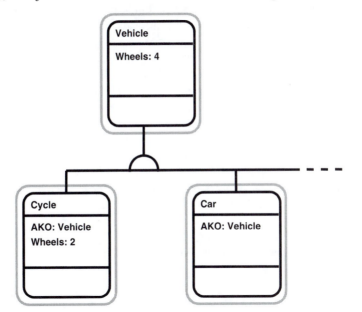

Figure B.22 Inheritance hierarchy in Coad notation.

Coad proposed the notation shown in Figure B.22 for inheritance hierarchies and that in B.23 for composition. The arrowhead denotes composition.

Regarding these structures as subjects, messages sent to the subject are normally regarded as being sent to the top of a composition structure and the bottoms of a classification structure. However, there will always be applications where this is not the case. Messages and relationships are shown only between instances. A problem introduced with the second edition is a distinction between three kinds of composition: part-whole, container-contents and collection-members. This represents a fundamental misunderstanding about semantic primitives. The last two are merely extra structures, not special cases of composition. Such structures may be used but should not be confused with composition structures. There may indeed be other important structures in a particular application. For example, a database concerned with anthropological research might well employ kinship as a fundamental structure.

When defining attributes, exactly the same considerations apply as in any data modelling exercise. The analyst is able to take advantage of inheritance and assume that unspecified elements are inherited where this makes sense. Multiple inheritance of attributes, or of methods, is not supported by the 1990 version. In the second edition, multiple inheritance is notationally permitted, but there is nothing to help with conflict resolution short of annotating every single attribute and method with such instructions as may be necessary. This leads me to assert that even the revised method did not genuinely support multiple inheritance. It is necessary at this stage to record the exception handling and parameter passing behaviour of the object. This must be textual as there is no notational support for exceptions.

One of Coad's most useful suggestions concerned the use of standard object and method description templates. The approach was based on the formal specification language, Ina Jo (Wing and Nixon, 1989), but any program template style will help enforce a communicable style of documentation and assist in making both object and method specifications complete. The template must name the object and list the attribute and method names in the interface just as in the diagrammatic notation. However, it must also indicate features of the attributes, such as whether they are always or only occasionally derivable, annotate the object with the designer's intentions and remarks on traceability, criticality, sizing constraints and so on. For each method the template specifies its purpose in the form of English or structured English statements. Of course, the text may be annotated with diagrams when this is helpful. Fundamentally, each method is specified in the same way that analysts have always specified system components. The only difference is that these details will be hidden within the object and only accessed via their interfaces.

Coad is weakest when it comes to specifying the dynamics of systems, but a state transition approach is suggested for object dynamics though no notation for this is defined. There is no explicit support for specifying business rules.

Defining the data semantics was usually not addressed by early object-oriented design methods such as HOOD and OOSD. This reflects the latter's concern with really quite low level programming abstractions and their genesis in real-time applications where complex data management problems either do not arise or are dealt with separately. Further, object-oriented programming languages have not been noted for their handling of persistent objects, and some authorities (e.g. Wegner, 1987) even go so far as to say that persistent objects contradict the very spirit of object-orientation, while others such as Meyer insist that it is fundamental to the approach. An analysis method aimed at commercial systems must, however, worry about these issues.

There were certain other defects in the Coad approach. Under the influence of the relational database movement, it insisted that attributes should be 'atomic'. This is wrong. Object-orientation is about modelling complex objects which need not be atomic. It also talks about keys rather than object identity and about normalization, although these issues are dismissed as 'deferred to design'.

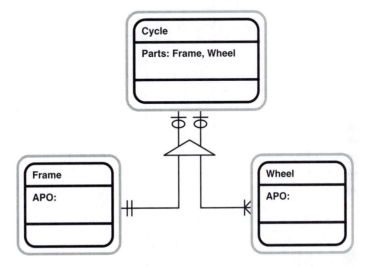

Figure B.23 Composition hierarchy in Coad notation.

Figure B.24 shows most of the features of the Coad-Yourdon notation as it appears in the second edition of their analysis book. In this diagram, which represents an analysis of vehicle registrations, there are two layers, one composition structure and several classification structures. The heavy arrows represent message passing.

The method was not perfect but it was simple and properly object-oriented. Contrast it now with a notation of considerable richness and complexity that was considerably defective in terms of OO purity: OMT.

OMT
The Object Modelling Technique (OMT) became one of the most popular object-oriented analysis methods. It originated from the work of Michael Blaha, Bill Premerlani and James Rumbaugh and their colleagues at General Electric (Rumbaugh *et al.*, 1991). It is an approach with strong roots in traditional structured methods and offered a rich but complicated and detailed notation. The complexity was partly paid for by the ability of some of the tools that supported it to generate code headers automatically. UML is essentially based on the OMT notation, albeit with influences and contributions from other methods' notations.

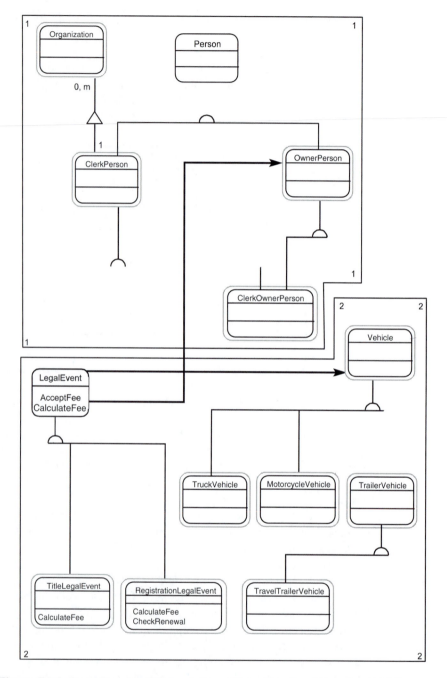

Figure B.24 Coad-Yourdon OOA notation. (From Coad and Yourdon (1991). Reprinted by kind permission of Prentice Hall, Upper Saddle River, NJ.)

OMT contained a rudimentary micro-process which broke down into three main phases or activities: analysis, system design and object design. **Analysis** assumes that a requirements specification exists (or at least provides no techniques thereto) and proceeds by building three separate models using three different notations. The first to be built is the Object Model (OM) which consists of class diagrams and a data dictionary. The notation was fundamentally that of ER modelling with operations and other annotations added to the entity icons. Next, for every object a Dynamic Model (DM) is built consisting of STDs drawn in an extended Harel notation and global event flow diagrams. The third step was not used by every practitioner and then only at the highest level of abstraction by most of those who do. This is the Functional Model (FM). The FM was indistinguishable from a DFD to all intents and purposes. Operations discovered in both the DM and FM are then added to the OM and a walkthrough performed, after which an Analysis Report including all the above deliverables is produced.

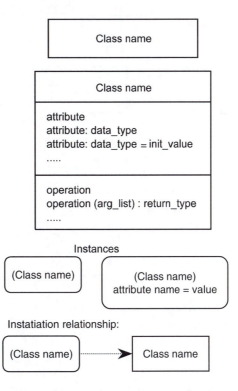

Figure B.25 Classes and instances in OMT.

The basic Object Modelling notation is shown in Figures B.25 to B.29. It was a richer notation than Coad's. Note in Figure B.25 that attributes are typed and operations given argument lists and return types and that instances have round corners and bracketed names. Figure B.26 shows that associations with attributes are expanded into first-class objects. Associations are annotated with rôles and may have qualifiers. For example, if Class-1 is Directory, Class-2 is File and the qualifier is Filename in Figure B.25 then it is the filename which specifies the uniqueness of a file within a directory. The one-to-many relationship between Directory and File is thus effectively reduced to one-to-one.

Association:

Qualified association:

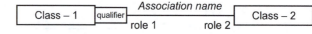

Multiplicity of associations:

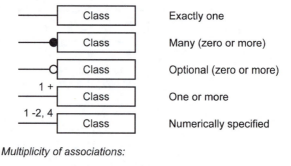

Multiplicity of associations:

Figure B.26 Associations in OMT.

Classification structures are shown as in Figure B.28 from which it can be seen that the notation is richer than that of Coad in expressing exclusivity and optionality. Composition structures are shown as in Figure B.29. A particularly strong, though not really object-oriented, feature of OMT was the ability to represent recursive composites as in Figure B.30. Figure B.31 is included to give an idea of just how complex this notation was; and we haven't finished yet. The Dynamic Model notation, based on Harel (1987) state charts, is even richer.

Figure B.32 shows a global event trace for the activity of making a phone call. An object of interest, the phone line in this case, is placed at the centre and a sequence of events traced as shown. There could be several such sequences. From an analysis of this external behaviour an internal state model of phone line is built as shown in Figure B.33. The notation used is based on Harel state charts and explained further by Figure B.34. Events, which may occur with attributes, cause actions that may be guarded by conditional statements (pre-conditions). On completion of the action the object enters the target state. When a state is entered the 'do' activity is performed. Actions are instantaneous but activities take time. When the system leaves the state the activity ceases. With the Harel notation, states can have substates and exist concurrently. The entire DM notation, in all its complexity, is shown in Figure B.35.

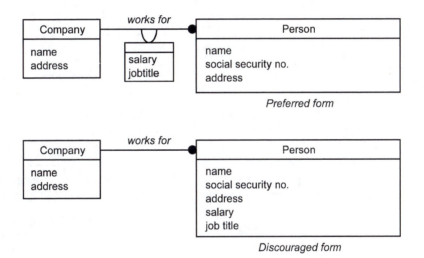

Figure B.27 Associations are expanded into objects in preference to adding attributes to existing objects.

The final modelling stage is the production of the FM. This is not always done and most practitioners only used it at a high level, roughly as a conventional analyst would use context diagrams (level zero DFDs). As we shall see when we discuss Ptech, this attitude to process (or architectural) modelling is common. In fact the notation is hardly distinguishable from a DFD notation. It is illustrated completely in Figure B.36. Having completed the three (or two) models the operations discovered are copied to the OM and we can move on to system and object design.

System Design proceeds by organizing the objects into subsystems, identifying concurrency from the DM, allocating subsystems to processors or tasks, deciding on whether data are to be stored in files, memory or a database management system, deciding on the use of peripherals and global resources, deciding on control structures, setting boundary conditions (start/end/fail) and setting trade-off priorities. This too is documented in a Design Document.

Object Design involves converting the information in the DM and FM to OM operations. The remaining steps are to:

1. design algorithms;
2. optimize access paths;
3. implement control;
4. adjust structures;
5. design attribute details;
6. package structures into modules;
7. write a Design Report, including a detailed OM, DM and FM.

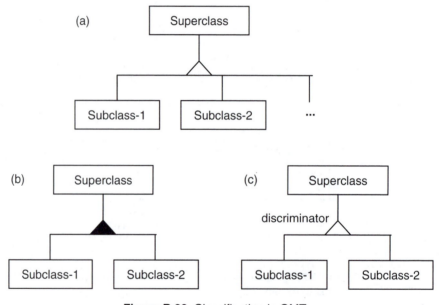

Figure B.28 Classification in OMT.

OMT was intended to be a method for both analysis and design but although it contained a fairly complete method for analysis it tends only to give heuristics for design. OMT covers more issues than most other methods but it remains incomplete in some areas and it is very complex to learn and use the notations. The omissions included the ability to model business rules at a high level or control rules at all.

I think history will regard OMT as popular because it addressed the concerns of OO developers in the early 1990s, who were typically writing C++ front-ends to relational databases. OMT let them do this in pictures but never really challenged them to learn anything new or really understand object technology. As if to confirm this, Rumbaugh *et al.* (1991) give some sound heuristics for implementing object-oriented designs in relational databases and in conventional languages.

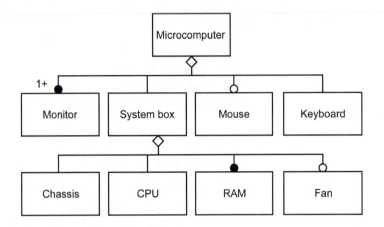

Figure B.29 An OMT composition (aggregation) structure for PC assemblies.

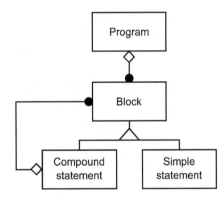

Figure B.30 Recursive composition structure showing how programs are built up.

MARTIN-ODELL AND PTECH

Ptech, from Associative Design Technology, was a proprietary set of methods and tools covering both analysis and design. It had some features in common with object-oriented approaches. The Ptech CASE tool also generated code for C++ and Ontos.

The ideas behind Ptech are based on the metaphor of process engineering as the production of systems by assembling reusable components; an approach that of course separates analysis and logical design from implementation. The emphasis is therefore on what is done rather than how it is done. In that sense Ptech is process-oriented rather than strictly object-oriented, although the approaches have many features in common. Ptech combines this process-driven view with the abstraction features of more data-centred, object-oriented design and some ideas from set theory and artificial intelligence.

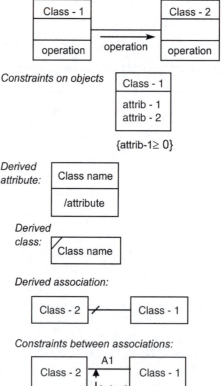

Figure B.31 More notation for the OMT Object Model.

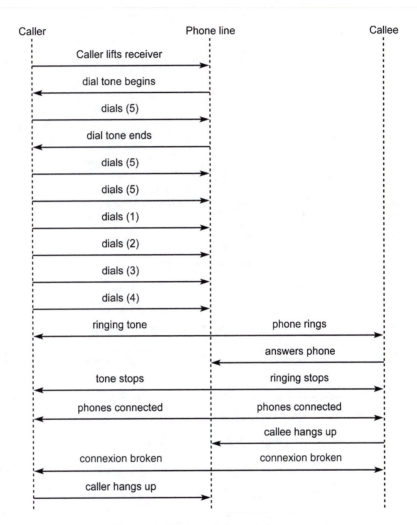

Figure B.32 An event trace diagram.

Edwards (1989), the author of Ptech, stresses the need for a formal basis for any object-oriented method and criticizes what he calls 'naive' methods of object-oriented analysis such as Coad-Yourdon or OMT. The emphasis, in Ptech, is on prototyping throughout. Edwards also thought that executable specifications are prerequisites for reverse engineering and maintenance, and I agree.

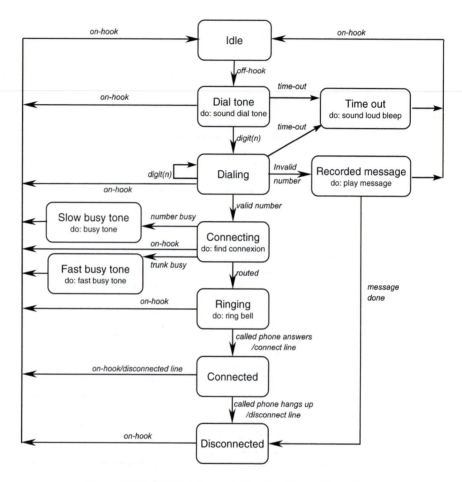

Figure B.33 OMT state model for the Phone_line object.

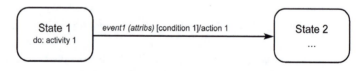

Figure B.34 OMT State Transition Diagram notation.

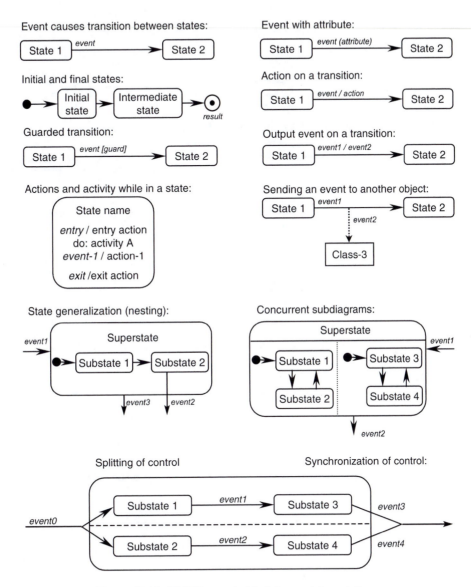

Figure B.35 OMT Dynamic Model complete notation.

Process:

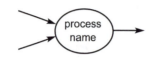

Dataflow between processes:

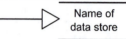

Data store or file object:

Name of
data store

Dataflow that results in a datastore:

Actor objects (as source or sink of data):

Control flow:

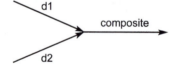

Access of data store value:

Update of data store value:

Access and update of data store value:

Composition of data value:

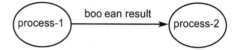

Dup ication of data value:

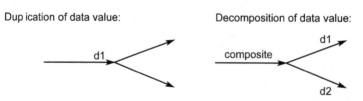

Decomposition of data value:

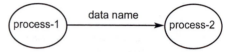

Figure B.36 OMT Functional Model complete notation.

Ptech was the basis for much of the Martin-Odell method described in a book by James Martin and Jim Odell (1992). The latter was the main source of the activity diagram notation of UML.

The Ptech notational system consists of three types of diagram: concept diagrams (broadly equivalent to extended entity-relationship diagrams in the general Bachman style) called object schemata or concept schemata, event diagrams or schemata (which fulfil the rôle of state transition diagrams) and activity/function diagrams (with much the same purpose as DFDs). The first two diagramming notations are supported by formal languages: the class calculus and the event calculus. Figure B.37 summarizes the main architectural components of the method.

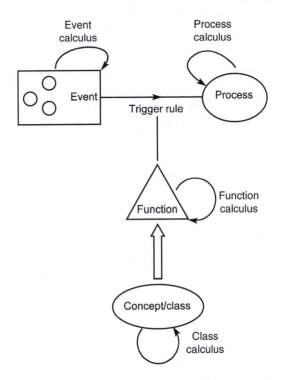

Figure B.37 The Ptech process engineering metaphor.

Concept diagrams show the static aspects of processes and event diagrams their dynamics. It is possible to illustrate how instances are created and terminated and how they move in and out of classes using a combined concept and event diagram. The activity diagrams give a high level functional view broadly analogous to that given by a data flow diagram. Concepts are regarded as sets and set theory is used to describe concepts using simple set operations such as union, intersection and difference.

Inheritance is shown by inclusion of icons as in Figure B.38, and non-exhaustive partitions by an extra bar. Thus, in this figure, a token can be either a slug, a 5 pence piece, a 10p or a 50p, and nothing else. These four subtypes *partition* the token concept. The last three form a partition of the coin concept. A value can be represented by a coin or something else as yet unspecified. This is represented by the double line at the bottom of the class outline. Ptech shows events with round cornered boxes. The other notation shown in Figure B.39 is Ptech's version of data semantics (the function calculus) and need not concern us here. This figure and Figures B.40 and B.41 refer to a fragment of the design of a vending machine.

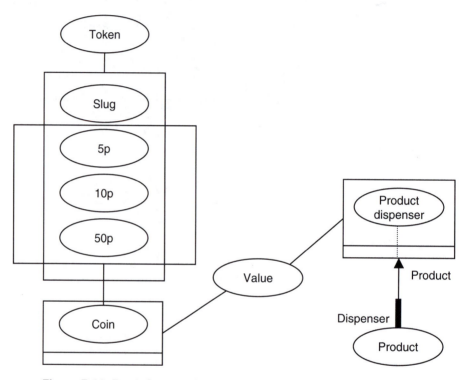

Figure B.38 Ptech Concept Schema showing inheritance and partitioning inheritance.

Events are n-place concepts – i.e. objects with n attributes – which have definite pre- and post-conditions. The post-conditions imply that every process has a definite goal. With events, the set-theoretic class calculus is paralleled by a function calculus based on the lambda calculus. This permits the definition of triggers and business rules. Figure B.39 illustrates an event diagram from the vending machine design. The rectangles represent events and arrows terminating in circles represent trigger rules or pre-conditions. The triangles represent post-conditions or decision processes which evaluate to true or false, depending on the outcome of the preceding processes (the incoming arrows).

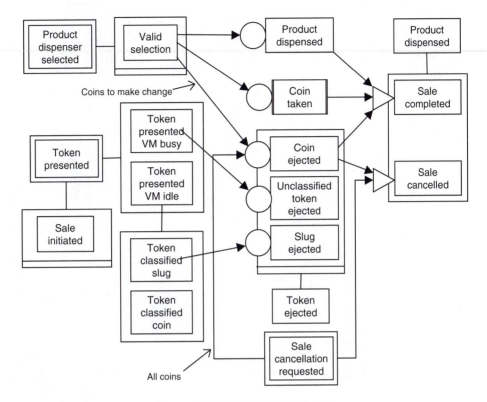

Figure B.39 Ptech event schema.

The Ptech event modelling notation is, broadly speaking, a finite state machine notation with enriched semantics to deal with constraints, pre-conditions and the like. This is undoubtedly a useful notation but the recommended notation for matching these diagrams to the object model, which involves drawing rough outlines round event icons and linking them to class icons in a separate object diagram with arrows, is extremely messy. The main flaw in the approach is summed up in the remark: 'Operation reusability is a key factor in OO specification and implementation'. I disagree and think that type reusability is the key and this is why integrating the object and behaviour models is so critical. Ptech event diagrams are especially useful in grasping the control structure of a system. They add something essential and lacking in many object-oriented approaches. However, regarding concepts as sets violates the spirit of object-orientation, because concepts with methods are much more than sets; they are algebras at least. Ptech focuses much more on events than objects. This is both its strength and its weakness, since true object-oriented methods focus on reusable objects but are usually weak in global

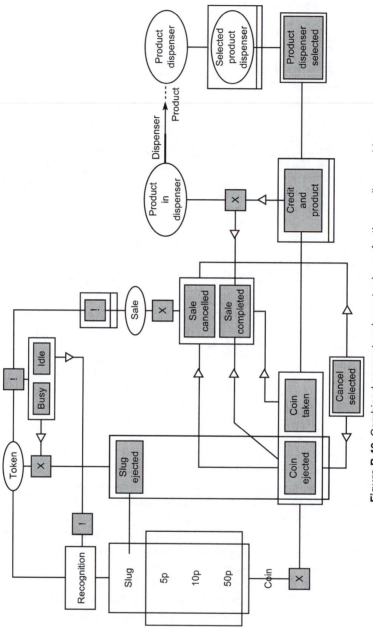

Figure B.40 Combined concept and event schema for the vending machine.

dynamic modelling. However, in Ptech events are objects too and they can participate in classification structures. The Ptech behavioural model is well thought out and simpler to comprehend but not as detailed as that of OMT.

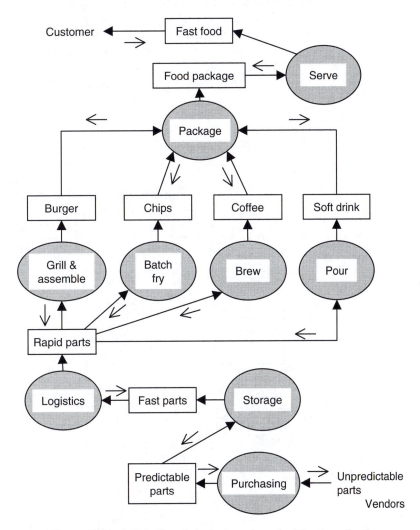

Figure B.41 Activity/function diagram for a fast food application.

Ptech concept and event diagrams can be combined as shown in Figure B.40. Here double boxes represent events external to the system. An ! means creation, and an X means termination. Note the similarity to ! and * in Booch timing diagrams.

The final diagram type in Ptech is the activity/function schema or Object Flow Diagrams, which are introduced to give 'a high level functional view'. As with the object flow models of OMT, I expect that few practitioners made much use of this technique as it provided nothing more than top-down modular decomposition and a more object-oriented levelling approach is more appropriate.

Figure B.41 shows such a schema describing process flow of control in a fast food restaurant. The circles are processes and the rectangles are the products of these processes. The arrows represent data flows or dependencies.

In methodological terms, Ptech consists of four main activities: object structure analysis, object behaviour analysis, object structure design and object behaviour design.

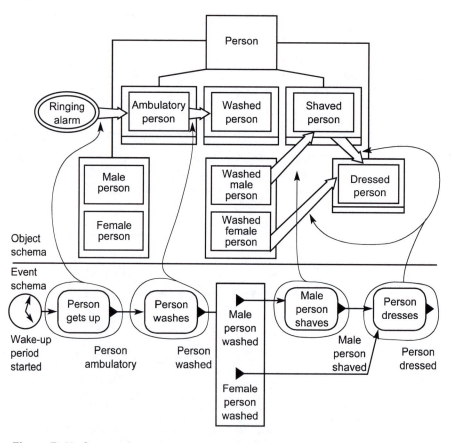

Figure B.42 Cross-referencing event and object (concept) schemata. (Reprinted from Martin and Odell (1992) by kind permission of the authors.)

Object Structure Analysis (OSA) involves building concept schemata showing classes, associations, classification and composition. Object Behaviour Analysis uses event schemata and shows state transitions, event types, trigger rules, control conditions and operations. Object Structure Design adds implementation-dependent aspects to OSA and Object Behaviour Design adds the details of the methods. The behavioural model has sufficient expressive power to denote pre-conditions but not, so far as I can tell, invariance conditions.

Business rules can be expressed as pre-conditions and a declarative syntax is permitted, albeit allowing single rules rather than full rulesets. This would require the specification of a procedural process. The notational convention for tying the behavioural aspects to the structural ones, which we are told by Martin and Odell is 'very important', is clumsy as exemplified by Figure B.42.

We have only been able to scratch the surface of the Martin-Odell approach in this brief exposition. It was a very rich and expressive notation and method. In fact, the worst thing that can be said is that it was, as a theory and as a tool, horrendously complicated. It takes an expert to use it well.

For details of the original method the reader should refer to Martin and Odell (1992) which contains some deep insight into how object-orientation contributes to business or enterprise modelling. The contribution here is that business rules and constraints should not be left as an afterthought, as they are in most extant object-oriented analysis techniques, nor should they be 'buried in multiple COBOL programs'. In other words, object technology should support adaptable businesses.

The Ptech method was used successfully in the UK National Health Service for modelling in clinical health care, although sufficient cause was found to make modifications and extensions (Fowler and Capey, 1991). The application is not a traditional data processing one but concerned the technical domain of storing and retrieving information on patients' treatments. At the start of the project several piecemeal systems already existed in domains such as transplant surgery, diabetes, and so on. It was desired to construct a process model to unite these separate systems. The methods background was that SSADM and later IE had been used.

Teams were small and, most interestingly, consisted typically of one or two analysts and one or two clinicians (doctors, nurses, etc.). The clinicians were given training in the analysis technique and, in time, became the best analysts. This was only made possible because an object-oriented approach makes direct models of the real-world medical domain. That project was the basis for several of Martin Fowler's analysis patterns (Fowler, 1997). The event notation illustrated in Figures B.40 and B.42 was the basis for the UML activity diagrams discussed in Chapter 8. Also, Jim Odell's work on the set-theoretic foundations of class diagrams has been widely influential (Martin and Odell, 1996, 1998; Graham, 1998).

DEFRAY   Desfray (1992) describes the Class-Relationship method for object-oriented analysis and design marketed by a French company, Softeam, in the context of C++ projects for which it is specifically designed. The method is notable for its use of a notation derived from Chen Entity-Relationship models and therefore potential compatibility with Merise, the structured method widely used in France. It is also notable for paying attention to formal methods through the use of Eiffel-like assertions. A CASE tool, Objecteering, was sold.

The Class-Relationship method has three separate models for each system: an object/entity model, a state transition model and a data flow model. As with other approaches such as OMT, it is often difficult to see the utility of the data flow model and models of message passing are richer than DFDs. Be this as it may, this was a respectable way of doing object-oriented analysis and easily stood comparison with OMT. Some improvements, such as a further refinement of the notion of 'abstract relation', are still possible and the data flow model specifies the linking of processes and contains a notion of events and their ordering. The Entity-Relationship and state-transition notations are simpler and more natural and the ability to use assertions addresses a fundamental deficiency of most other methods (the exceptions being BON, Ptech and SOMA). The sequence of techniques is similar to OMT: build the data/class model, find the assertions, use the dynamic model to deal with events and the sequencing of methods and finally use the DFDs if required. The concept of encapsulation is emphasized far more than in OMT. Desfray suggests that the state transition model could be improved by the introduction of specific states and a mechanism for state synthesis.

In terms of what the method covers, the Entity-Relationship models include full support for inheritance in addition to all familiar data modelling constructs. While relationships can be regarded as objects, Desfray makes an important distinction between classes and relationships. 'Relationships never possess methods. Their unique function is to connect classes.' A little thought shows that this is a valid distinction and one not made in earlier work on the subject; although in contrast OMT specifically permits 'link operations' I have never found a valid use for them. This helps with the distinction between attributes and classes. A relation is a directed link between two classes that allows a class to know about the other class's instances. Bi-directional relationships are discouraged. He also states that 'a relationship is part of the definition of the concept that a class represents'. The next innovation is the introduction of inheritable class invariants corresponding to a limited form of business rules. Classes are regarded as being formed from a composition or aggregation of their attributes, regarded as object types. A general rule in entity modelling is that the only authorized attributes are those that belong to a base class. This helps avoid confusion arising from merging domains or from multiple inheritance; an element is not allowed to be part of two classes in this method. Classes are organized into *schemata* corresponding to Coad-Yourdon subject areas but in common with that approach these schemata appear to lack the semantics of classes, as messages may not be sent to them. 'A schema is the representation of a domain. It is composed of a group of classes. It constitutes the specification of a particular domain. A class belongs to one and only one schema. An application is thus partitioned into schemata.' (p. 86) 'The Class-Relationship method permits [mutual] usage relationships (message passing) between classes but forbids them between schemata.' (p. 91) – provided, that is, that the classes are part of the same schema. Ameliorating this situation, certain classes may be declared as 'interface classes' for the schema. Schemata also possess invariants defined as the union of all the invariants of contained classes plus 'some general clauses'. (p. 93) To clarify this, mutual usage is defined as follows: if classes C1 and C2 can use each other's services the relationship is mutual. The latter can only happen within a schema. However, if schema S2 can use S1 then S1 is forbidden from using S2. Desfray gives guidelines for eliminating schema level mutual relationships. There are three categories of usage relationship between classes:

1. *Operational* usage: C1 uses C2 only to allow a method of C1 to execute to completion.
2. *Context* usage: C1 uses C2 as a parameter of a method of C1.
3. *Characteristic* usage: C1 uses C2 when C1 inherits from C2. Schema S1 has a usage link with another schema S2 when at least one of S1's classes uses at least one of S2's. S1 classes can only access the interface classes of S2 and not its 'body' classes. This brings schemata quite close to the 'wrappers' of SOMA. In addition, schemata may have inheritance links between them.

The most important innovation is the use of assertions, although these are restricted to pre-conditions and post-conditions. Guarantees and so on are not mentioned, which only affects the applicability of the method to systems where parallelism is important. Class invariants are supported, however.

OSA

OSA (Object-Oriented Systems Analysis) is an approach developed at Hewlett Packard and similar to OMT in that the method follows the conventional tripartite division of analysis into three separate (but related) activities with a notation for each. It differs in being a slightly simpler notation and in a number of other ways. It is described by Embley *et al.* (1992).

OSA begins with an entity-relationship notation (the Object Relationship Model or ORM) which permits the description of attributes, classification and aggregation structures and data semantics in the form of associations. More general constraints are merely written on the diagrams in note form next to the object they relate to and thus constraints have no relation to inheritance. The claimed advantage of this approach is that it does not constrain the analyst. However, (Embley *et al.*, 1992) says that 'Since notes do not constrain object classes or relationship sets, an ORM diagram has the same meaning with, or without them.' (*punctuation as original*). Thus, it appears that information is lost by the final model. The complete set of notations available within the ORM is shown as Figure B.43.

A state transition notation allows the analyst to describe the behaviour of each object. This Object Behaviour Model (OBM) defines the methods for the object, but the ORM may not be extended to include them. Triggers, real-time constraints, exceptions and events are all handled within the OBM and it is here that the similarity with OMT is most apparent, although the emphasis is on modelling the internal behaviour of the objects rather than the interactions between objects. Figure B.44 illustrates the OBM notations.

Finally, message passing is described in a dataflow-like Object Interaction Model (OIM). The advantage over OMT is that this model deals more evidently with message passing than with atemporal data flows but it could be argued, by those who support such views, that logical data flows are not catered for at all. In some sense the OIM combines data flow and state transitions. Figure B.45 shows the permissible OIM notations.

Good levelling facilities allow the analyst to move between high and low level views of a system. Views are classified as *dominant* or *independent* according to whether the high level view is the name of an existing class or one with separate identity respectively.

Decomposition rules are given for both ORMs and OBMs and it is claimed that the ability to structure all modelling constructs consistently with high level views is a unique feature of OSA. A lot of this notation seems unnecessarily complex from some points of view, but the ideas are undoubtedly useful. Each of the ORM, OBM and OIM can be levelled in this way and the notation in indicated in Figure B.46. In (Embley *et al.*, 1992) detailed diagrams contain a great deal of supplementary annotation of such things as constraints, exceptions and transition priorities.

The OIM notation is perhaps the most useful insofar as it differs from other OOA methods. However, it would not be easily grafted onto other approaches as the analyst is able to link messages to the internal states and transitions of each object. Some of the things one would do in the OMT dynamic model are done here in the OSA approach.

OSA was 'model driven' in the sense that a model is constructed rather than asking analysts to follow a fixed series of steps – characterized as a 'method driven' approach. As with Ptech and OMT, it remains unclear how the three independent analysis results are to be combined into a single object model although some attention is paid to consistency and conformance between diagrams. It is claimed that OSA makes no distinction between classes and attributes and that this helps enforce consistency. This is a hard claim to accept given the immense philosophical significance of the object/attribute problem. OSA permits multiple inheritance notationally but, in common with Coad-Yourdon, omits any treatment of conflict resolution.

The appendix to (Embley *et al.*, 1992) sets out a logical formalism for the ORM component of OSA. A small worry is that presenting an object-oriented model in a first order language seems to throw away one of the chief simplicities of object-orientation: the ability to express complex structures directly in higher order terms.

OSA was a reasonably complete method which bears comparison with OMT and had, in my view, a slightly better notation. However, the popularity of OMT and the lack of OSA CASE tools precluded it from great success.

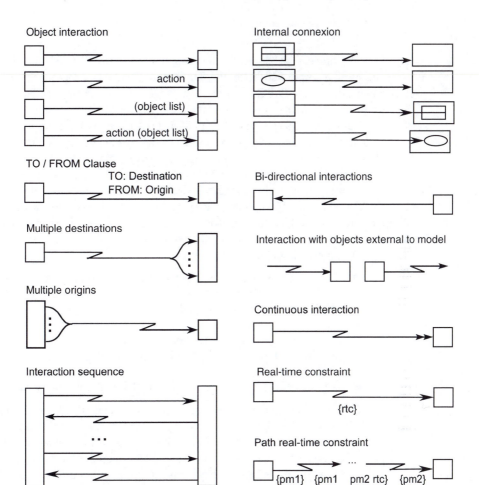

Figure B.45 OSA object interaction model.

SYSTEMS ENGINEERING OO

LBMS Systems Engineering (OO) or SEOO was a method developed at the British company LBMS. It had four aspects:

1. work breakdown structures and techniques;
2. a Shared Object Modelling method;
3. specific GUI design techniques (Redmond-Pyle and Moore, 1995);
4. relational database linkages.

A method is viewed as a process model plus techniques with their rules and end-products. The proposed life cycle is a rapid development one and emphasis is placed on ending stages with something executable that can be evaluated by users.

The process has several points in common with OPEN (Graham *et al.*, 1997b) and was incorporated with the latter and Catalysis process patterns in a joint submission to the OMG in 1999. SEOO was one of the first methods to distinguish shared (i.e. domain), application and interface objects.

Cameron (1992) argued that in structured methods for data processing systems data modelling has proved to be a highly effective technique for analysis and design. However, much of the semantic richness available to the analyst is lost in the representation. Further, he claimed that in rejecting process–data separation many object-oriented analysis approaches lose the benefits of data modelling and proposed the Shared Object Modelling technique as a direct successor to data modelling. The technique is intended to object-oriented yet retain the advantages of data modelling, and be well suited to commercial data processing applications.

Data modelling is successful because:

- Data analysis is used as a modelling tool. Analysts use data models as a basis for understanding functionality. The data model is stable relative to the information requirement that it supports.
- Processing components, either whole subsystems or individual transactions, interact via the shared data described by the data model and held in the database. To isolate and stabilize most of the important system interfaces so early is a huge benefit.
- There is a direct route from a data model to a preliminary database design.

On this view, data modelling should be generalized to a form of object modelling and the split between persistent data and all processing replaced by a split between shared objects and the other objects. Object-orientation provides a more powerful modelling medium than data. The shared objects similarly form the important interfaces between subsystems. There is still a direct route, albeit slightly longer, from shared object model to database design.

It is the instances (analogously the data) that are shared, not just the classes (analogously the data definitions). Sharing, possibly across many systems, imposes a discipline on the range of methods a shared object should support. Processing specific to a particular application should be excluded. Otherwise the class definition of widely used objects, for example Customers, would be continually under review as applications are added and modified. Creating separate subtypes of Customer for each application doesn't help, because it is the individual objects that are shared, and they cannot change their type for each application. Application-specific functionality is modelled outside the shared object model, in terms of other objects (e.g. user interface objects) which use services provided by shared objects.

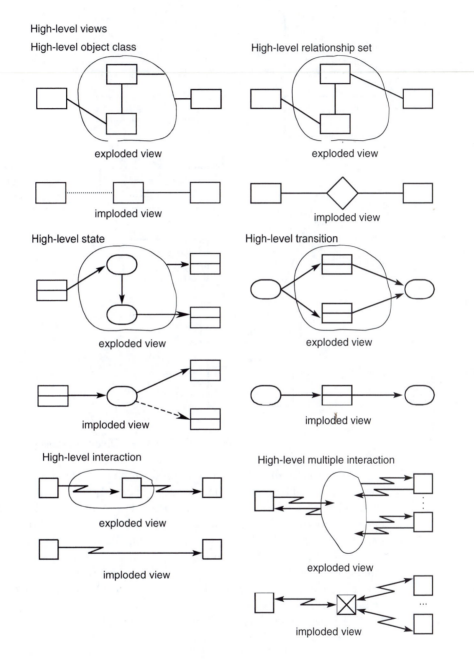

Figure B.46 Levelling in OSA.

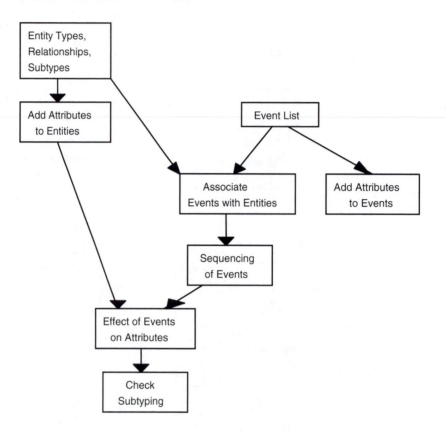

Figure B.47 Shared Object Modelling.

One benefit of a system developed around a shared object model is that applications can be relatively independent, in exactly the way that several programs can independently interact with a database. One application can be extended with new or modified objects, or have objects removed, with minimal effect on other applications, provided that the shared object interfaces are not changed.

Few of the widely known object-oriented analysis and design methods placed importance on the distinction between shared and other objects. Yet it seems a prerequisite for the success of an object-oriented analysis method in business computing.

The diagram in Figure B.47 and the key in Table B.2 describe the Shared Object Modelling technique in more detail. The high level of integration is important. The individual parts have equivalents in most structured methods. A data model is equivalent to a view of the object model. The dynamic behaviour of the objects is another useful view of the object model. These descriptions are developed as views of an integrated whole rather than as separate models to be integrated later, if at all.

This integration distinguishes shared object modelling from structured methods, and even to an extent from, say, the OMT approach.

Table B.2 Key to Figure B.47.

Entity Types, Relationships and Sub-types: Very similar to a data model (entity-relationship model) but interpreted as the static view of the shared object model. The term 'entity' is retained for objects and classes in the shared object model.

Add Attributes to Entities: Attributes are interpreted as queries on entities. (Following Meyer (1989) queries are methods, in his terminology 'routines', that return values but do not affect the state.)

Event List: An analysis of the dynamics of the business area. An event is something that happens in the business area that causes a change of state to an entity. (In Meyer's terms, a 'command'. Actually it is a little more complicated as one event can affect more than one entity.)

Associate Events with Entities: A cross-reference.

Add Attributes to Events: Each event may have values associated. For example, an amount and a date both describe a financial transaction.

Sequencing of Events: A description of the possible orderings of events. A subset of the Harel (1987) notation is used. Violations of these constraints are treated as errors.

Effect of Events on Attributes: Defines the semantics of the events (commands) by specifying their effect on the attributes (queries). This is usually done informally and often selectively, because most of the effects are obvious.

Check Subtyping: Check that the substitutability rule for subtyping is obeyed by the events and the sequencing constraints. Review the type hierarchy in the shared object model. (Substitutability means that a client of objects of type A should be satisfied with objects of a subtype of A.)

GUI modelling is regarded as a special kind of analysis activity. Context diagrams and something rather similar to use cases are used to define tasks and output. Further design principles (such as IBM's CUA, 1991) are applied. The window design is separated from user object design, resulting in a three-layer model in which there are windows using the services of user objects in the next layer that in turn use the services of shared objects.

For relational database interfaces a mechanism akin to database views is used to overcome the problems associated with joins; 'many short-lived objects implement one long-lived object'.

Systems Engineering OO is a hybrid method which is important for its contribution of a layered, shared object model and emphasis on evolutionary migration from existing technologies.

BON

BON (Better Object Notation) is described in Nerson (1992) and is one of very few methods to take the importance of business rules and class invariants seriously. It derives from the Eiffel school of thought and therefore the inclusion of assertions is less surprising. It was developed under European ESPRIT II funding and is influenced by Booch, Coad-Yourdon, Page-Jones and Constantine, Shlaer-Mellor, OMT, OOSD, CRC and work on object-oriented Z (Duke *et al.*, 1991) making BON a true hybrid. Emphasis is placed on such issues as the continuity of analysis and design, scalability, reversibility, traceability, static and dynamic models and component management. The activities within BON are:

1. *Define the system boundary.* This involves identifying external events.
2. *Identify candidate classes.* BON classes are defined by attributes, operations, constraints and relationships with other classes. No specific object identification techniques are included.
3. *Group classes into clusters.* Clusters are subsystems or UML-style packages that have no clear semantics but are definitely not regarded as objects. They are used to group cohesive sets of classes.
4. *Define candidate classes in terms of questions, commands and constraints.* Analysts must ask: 'What data can be asked for?'. Questions become attributes or Eiffel 'functions'. Commands are operations and constraints are either assertions or class invariants. Class invariants may be thought of as rules and all constraints as describing the knowledge maintained by the objects. Analysts must ask whether objects behave similarly to tease out classification structures. Associations are recorded in a rather odd textual manner.
5. *Define the behaviour of each class in terms of events, object communication protocols and object creation charts.* Events can be external or internal. Internal events are usually time related and lead to the discovery of communication protocols and assertions related to global system control. The notation for describing classes includes special symbols for depicting inward and outbound data flows. Pre- and post-conditions and class invariants are written in a formal logic notation. An example class invariant stating that corporate customers should not be given weekend discounts is expressed as:

   ```
   client.is_corporate ⇒ ∀ l∈documents • ¬l.discount.weekend_rate
   ```

   which could perhaps be more readily expressed in structured English. Object creation charts show which classes create instances of other classes.
6. *Define class features, invariants and contractual relationships.* Class features may correspond to internal events. Static and dynamic relationships are shown on separate charts using an unusual and fairly idiosyncratic notation.
7. *Refine the class descriptions.* Here reuse opportunities are sought.
8. *Develop classification structures.*

9. *Complete and review the architecture.*

Class indexing is used to aid future retrieval from libraries using a standard header template. BON has several strengths not found in many other methods such as the emphasis on component management and rules. However, I find the notation unappealing. It will be of great interest, however, to Eiffel developers since it supports that language's constructs directly while remaining language independent.

BON is close in spirit to SOMA, described in the next section. A CASE environment based on a PCTE-compliant repository and called EiffelCase is available. There are two tools, a drawing tool and a component management system. Some of the BON notation is illustrated in Figures B.48 and B.49.

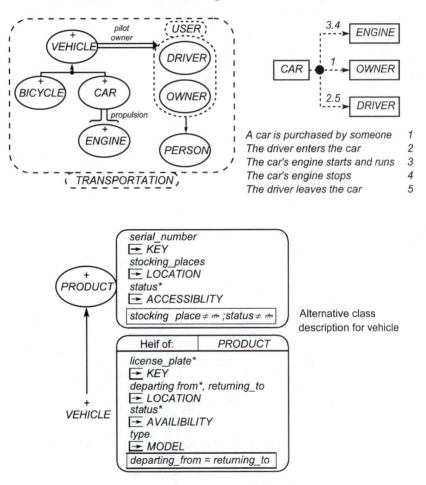

Figure B.48 Fragments of the BON notation.

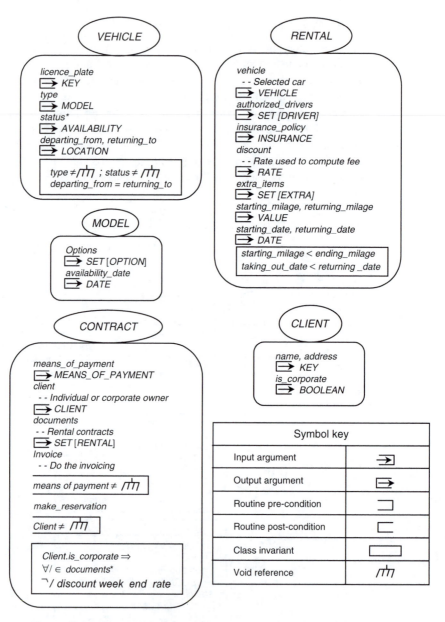

Figure B.49 Class descriptions for a car rental system in BON notation.

In the static model shown in Figure B.48 (top left) clusters are represented as dashed rounded rectangles and are tagged with a name. Classes are represented as a name inside an ellipse, with optional annotations:

- deferred classes are topped with a star sign;
- non-deferred descendant classes are topped with a plus sign;
- reused classes have an underlined name.

Inheritance relationships are represented with a single line ending in an arrowhead oriented from the descendant to the parent. Client–server relationships are represented by a double line ending in an arrowhead in the case of an association, and with an open curly brace in the case of aggregation. The double line may be tagged with class feature names involved in the client–server collaboration. Relationships are defined between classes and can be extended to clusters.

In the dynamic model (top right) objects are represented by rectangles. A shadow is used to indicate multiple instances. Communication is represented by dashed lines, labelled with sequence numbers referred to in textual scenarios.

Obviously, most of this can be rewritten in UML.

FUSION The Fusion Method (Coleman and Hayes, 1991; Coleman *et al.*, 1994) is a hybrid method developed by a team led by Derek Coleman at Hewlett–Packard Laboratories in the UK. HP did a survey of methods in use within HP and generally extant in 1990, resulting in a set of requirements for an object-oriented analysis and design method. The chief requirement identified was for a model of usage with a simple notation. No method met all HP's needs. OMT gives a process for analysis but only heuristics for design.

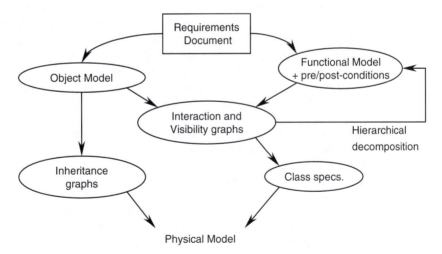

Figure B.50 Fusion process model.

Fusion was constructed by borrowing ideas from other methods. It is still being developed in this way. The main influences have been OMT's notation, RDD's interaction modelling, ideas from Booch91 on visibility and some ideas from the Z and VDM schools of formal methods. The use case idea from Objectory is incorporated too. The Fusion process model is illustrated in Figure B.50.

The dynamic model of OMT (and that of other methods such as Shlaer-Mellor) was not found to be useful in practice and is not used. This is an encouraging if remarkable finding compared to the conventional wisdom, which makes me suspect that excessive emphasis on state models is the result of telecomms and real-time application backgrounds. Data flow diagrams are not used for the functional model because they are too operational. Pre- and post-conditions are used instead, though I have sometimes found that these are hard for users to understand. Methods are not introduced until the design stage. Concurrency is not supported and so there are no invariance conditions in the method yet. Because these assertions are not attached to classes they cannot be inherited.

One tricky problem for some practitioners of object-oriented analysis is to know when to stop doing analysis. It is claimed that Fusion helps with this problem. Visibility is introduced at design time. Interactions define which objects need which methods – again at design time. CRC is used for the interaction model although contracts are not used. This can be done in rôle play sessions.

OBA

OBA or Object Behaviour Analysis is described by Rubin and Goldberg (1992). OBA is a method that starts by eliciting scripts from interviews or documents which are similar to use cases and developing a context model. Next, the participants and their responsibilities are identified and initiators distinguished. Modified CRC cards are used to record the details of objects and discover classification and usage structures and other associations, though aggregation is not emphasized. Finally, Harel state-transition models are developed for each object.

OBA has more to say about requirements capture than most other methods but is not particularly remarkable in other areas. The approach to requirements capture outlined in Chapter 7 incorporates some of these ideas.

SYNTROPY

Syntropy was an influential method developed by Steve Cook, John Daniels and their colleagues at Object Designers Limited (Cook and Daniels, 1994). The method claimed to be notation independent but used the popular OMT notation by default. The emphasis is on a behaviour-oriented approach making much of the notion of behavioural specialization (classification). Some of the mechanisms of Syntropy were taken from Booch91. The major contributions of Syntropy included the use of formal type specification techniques and state diagrams, the distinguishing of classes and types and the distinction between 'essential' (i.e. real-world) models and analysis models. Syntropy influenced Catalysis strongly because of its formal methods emphasis and it has been said that Catalysis did for UML what Syntropy did for OMT.

MOSES

Henderson-Sellers gave this name to the method outlined in his (1992) book and other publications. The notation was influenced by Page-Jones' Uniform Object

Notation but was simpler. The method is a hybrid method for object-oriented analysis based on earlier published work from several authors and emphasizes the need to incorporate existing structured methods where possible. I think this is indicative of a current trend towards such hybrid methods. Like most other methods, there is scant help on identifying objects. Notation is provided for all the important structural features of an object-oriented system. Rules are not supported. The most important new contribution was the 'fountain' life-cycle model, wherein deliverables bubble up and shower down on you rather than spinning out of the vortex of a spiral model. Showing classification and other associations on the same diagram, as other methods do, is (correctly) discouraged. The case studies described in (Henderson-Sellers, 1992) confused me a little. For example, a bibliography object is decomposed into objects with names like 'sort' and 'quit' which the text had taught me to think of as methods if I understood it correctly. The only time I would reason otherwise is if I were trying to reuse components from an existing function library. The method included guidelines for implementation in various object-oriented languages. This method was extended and refined as MOSES but superseded by the work on OPEN (Graham *et al.*, 1997b; Henderson-Sellers *et al.*, 1998).

MOSES (Henderson-Sellers and Edwards, 1994) stands for Methodology for Object-Oriented Software Engineering of Systems and was also based on an extension of the Uniform Object Notation, though it is claimed that other notations are permissible. It provided a comprehensive life-cycle model and emphasized the continuum of representation, project management guidelines and extensibility. The fountain model is incorporated in this work.

TEXEL   Texel was an object-oriented analysis and design method with strong roots in the Ada development world, although it is claimed that C++ developments can also be supported and inheritance is not neglected as in HOOD. The version described here was extended to include a detail waterfall-like process model and utilization of use cases with the notation reworked in a mixture of Booch93, OMT and UML (Texel and Williams, 1997). The method is supported by P.P. Texel and Co. of New Jersey and the originator Putnam Texel. The company also provide training and can call on a large number of case studies. Although most of these are military or real-time applications it is claimed that MIS applications are equally well supported.

The activities within the original Texel are as follows. First, nominate candidate object types (called object classes), attributes, etc. This may take as input a written specification, system documents (such as DFDs and data dictionaries) or domain expert interviews. Every noun, verb, etc. is written down uncritically at this stage. No specific interviewing or object identification techniques are recommended. 'Disposition keys' are added to each phrase showing whether it is thought that the entry is a class, attributes, duplicate, descendant, process and so on. This process converts the 'Candidate Object Class List' to the 'Disposition List'. The next product is the 'Baseline Object Class List' which represents the likely list of classes at this stage. Traceability is emphasized throughout. From the BOCL, an ER diagram similar to a Shlaer-Mellor Information Structure Diagram (entity model) is produced showing associations but not aggregation. The ER notation is semantically incomplete, showing multiplicity and modality but not exclusivity or partitioning. The diagram is refined by adding attributes, aggregation, trace correlations and system boundaries. There are no specific techniques for class or attribute placement (see Monarchi, 1992). Finite state machines are used for behaviour placement later; that is, after the production of the Overview Object Class Analysis Diagram (OOCAD) and the derivative Object Class Analysis Diagram (OCAD).

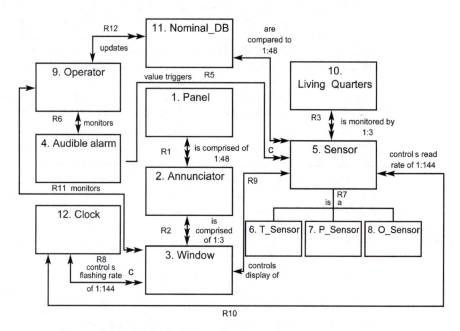

Figure B.51 OOCAD diagram for a sealed environment monitor.

Figures B.51 and B.52 illustrate the OOCAD and OCAD for a sealed environment monitor (SEM). Two documents, the Object Class Specification (OCSD) and the Relationship Specification (RSD), are then produced, ending the static phase of analysis. The first documents the classes of the OCAD. The second documents the links in this diagram descriptively. These are partially illustrated in Figures B.53 and B.54 using the same example of a SEM.

Phase I of the Texel method is illustrated schematically in Figure B.55. Phase II of analysis results in state models for each class. This activity takes a similar approach to that of Shlaer and Mellor (1991). The purpose is to identify events and methods for each object. This of course doesn't help much for objects without significant state which occur commonly in business models, which is one of the reasons why methods such as Fusion eschew state models. The Texel solution is to produce a bogus state for the offending objects though in practice it is admitted that they may be just written down.

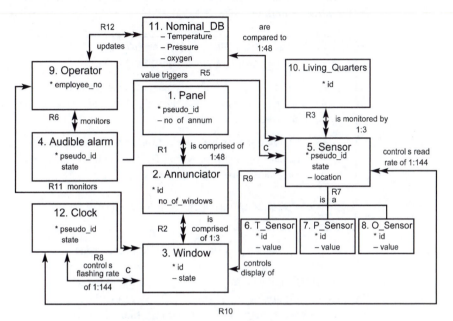

Figure B.52 Corresponding OCAD diagram.

---

4. Audible_Alarm

Audible_Alarm (Pseudo_Id,State)
Description: The Audible_Alarm is a device that will notify the HCC Operator when the value of one of the environmental conditions deviates from the normal value by 3% or more.

There is only one Audible_Alarm associated with the HCC SEM.

The Audible_Alarm is turned on by the SEM and turned off by the Operator.

4.1 Audible_Alarm.Pseudo_ID

Description: .....

Figure B.53 Part of an OCSD – Audible_Alarm.

One of the best features of the method is that the Object Class Communication Model (OCCM) produced at this stage permits message and event flow to be analysed. A distinction is thus made between internal events (identified first) and external events. Messages are shown explicitly, however, so that the notation may not scale up to really complex commercial systems. Figure B.56 shows the OCCM for the SEM example.

R5.   Sensor (TRIGGERS) Audible_Alarm (Mc:1)

            Audible_Alarm (IS TRIGGERED BY) Sensor

            The severity of the deviation between the actual value read by a sensor and its counterpart in the Nominal_DB dictates whether or not the alarm should sound.

            Condition: If the deviation between the value read by a Sensor and the nominal value in the Nominal_DB is 3% or higher then, and only then, is the Audible_Alarm sounded.

R6.   Operators (MONITORS) Audible_Alarm (1:1)

            ......

Figure B.54 Part of an RSD.

The final analysis step is the production of state models for each class as illustrated in Figure B.57. Figure B.58 shows just how complex these state models can become even for straightforward things like windows.

Multiple inheritance is forbidden. Complex constraints and rules are not representable non-procedurally and assertions are not part of the design stage.

Design proceeds via an informal strategy similar to that of Booch. Classes that will become the objects (Ada packages) of the design are defined and linked by an outline main algorithm. Inheritance is flattened away using variant discriminated record types in preference to generics. Ada structure charts conceptually similar to those of Buhr are used to represent the design graphically and then an Ada PDL is produced or generated.

Throughout the process great emphasis is placed on producing traceability matrices linking requirements to analysis and design products. I find this disturbing because the whole point of object-oriented analysis and design is surely that traceability is incremental and traces should be reconstructed dynamically by linked steps.

Texel has separate ER, STD and message flow models. Its real-time roots are evidenced by the centrality of the use of STDs where normally it is not permitted to define operations prior to obtaining a state model. It is closely related to the Shlaer-Mellor approach and draws on Booch. Like most methods, it does not cover all aspects of the OMG reference model and there is nothing on object identification, component management, metrics or testing – except for the use of CRUD-like requirement/object matrices that are further annotated with events. Group and view concepts are very limited except for a concept similar to Coad's Subjects. The process model is latent and no specific iteration or prototyping management techniques are visible in the documentation.

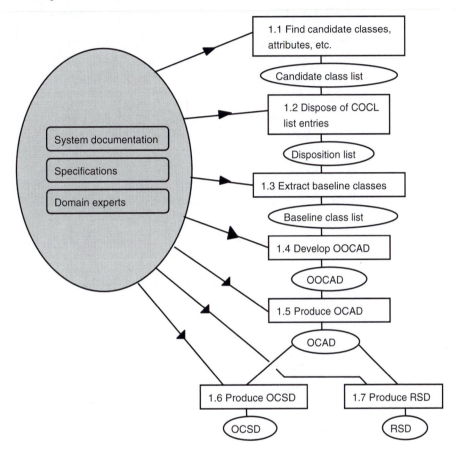

Figure B.55 Texel analysis process, Phase I.

The main problem with this method is that it is difficult to see how it would be useful in designing for a language dissimilar to Ada such as Smalltalk, Eiffel or an object-oriented 4GL.[1] The second problem applies to business systems where one suspects that methods deriving from domains such as telecommunications, real-time, military and the like are less suitable than those derived from the semantic data modelling tradition.

---

[1] C++ can be written in an Ada-like way but this is not necessarily the right way. As the saying goes, you can write FORTRAN in any language.

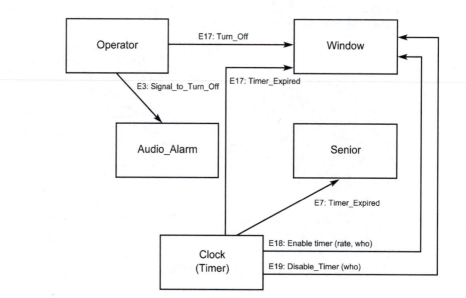

Figure B.56 Example OCCM.

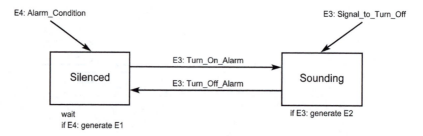

Figure B.57 Texel state model for Audible_Alarm.

OORASS

OORASS (Object-Oriented Rôle Analysis, Synthesis and Structuring) was developed by Reenskaug and others (1981, 1996) at Taskon AS in Norway. It covers analysis and design and is unusual in emphasizing the rôles played by objects and addressing several areas in an evolutionary life cycle.

Analysis starts with the discovery of **areas of concern** which are effectively high level business functions and the unit for forming coherent subsystems. Next, each area is modelled using collaborating agents and objects which may take on various **rôles**. The rôles are obtained from all the objects with the same position within the structure of an area of concern.

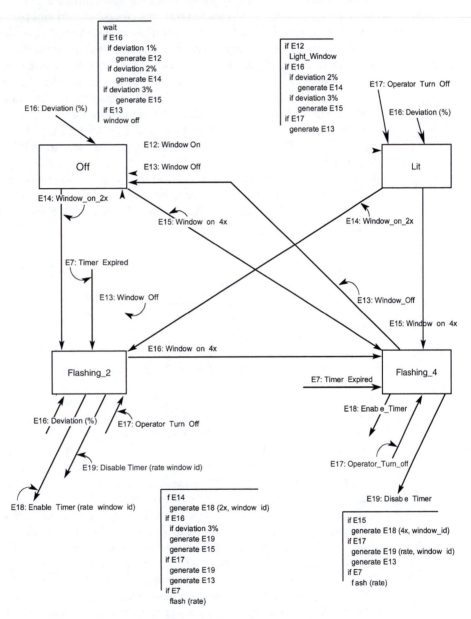

Figure B.58 Texel state model for Window.

Rôles are interpreted in a similar way to the rôles of the agents of Objectory but the idea is extended to the internals of a system rather than restricted to external agents. Different objects may adopt different rôles in different contexts. Rôles have resource requirements (references to servers), competence (things they know), duties and rights (operations). Rôle X may 'know about' rôle Y; that is, contain a reference enabling messages to be sent. These client-server links are refined by **port** symbols as shown in Figure B.59. The single circle port indicates that rôle X knows about zero to one instances of rôle Y. The double circle port says that Y knows about zero to many instances of X. No port symbol indicates that the rôle at that end of the link does not know about the other rôle. This introduces the multiplicity semantics of entity modelling into usage diagrams and may be useful for high level requirements capture in a similar way to the manner in which use cases in OOSE are used with inheritance.

Each port symbol may have associated to it a set of operations called a **contract** that defines what the visible rôle has to be able to offer. OORASS is neutral on the notation to be used for object representation. The notion of rôles is related to UML interfaces.

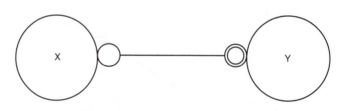

Figure B.59 OORASS rôle diagram.

Analysis is regarded as a top-down, but not hierarchical, process and there are analogies with the layering approach of SOMA in this respect, though rôle models are not decomposed as such. The modelling is complete when the analysts fully understand the area of concern and the model is stable. If not, or if the area does decompose, the analyst should redefine the area and repeat the activity.

Types, or object types, are synthesized from rôles and this defines the visible behaviour of some objects. Rôle **synthesis** creates new objects by inheriting behaviour from simpler ones. Such synthesis influenced the notion of template instantiation in Catalysis. Terminologically, OORASS defines classes as the implementation of types and allows type networks to differ from class networks. Multiple inheritance is permitted. Structuring uses a meta-model to specify the run-time behaviour of objects as they are bound to each other during instantiation. This capability is remarkably absent from most other object-oriented analysis methods. More formally, synthesis begins with an area of concern and looks for events and responses. These map onto messages and operations. Candidate objects are identified, though no formal techniques are proposed within OORASS, and then

CRC cards are used to identify and assign operations and collaborations. Next, message sequence diagrams are drawn followed by rôle diagrams. Last, the message sequences are used to identify the contracts with constraints and invariants.

The advantage of this approach is that analysts are allowed to construct simple rôle models representing object interaction and then combine them in a uniform way to create larger models. This is claimed to enhance the reusability of the products of analysis and design and is similar in philosophy to use cases. It addresses a major weakness of many other methods in specifically addressing the run-time dynamics of systems at the analysis level.

OORASS is supported by a CASE tool called OORAM, also available from Taskon. The method is aimed at building systems emphasizing message passing and distribution. It contains many powerful and interesting modelling ideas that have yet to be fully incorporated into mainstream methods.

OTHER METHODS

ADM3 (Firesmith, 1993) is an extension of an earlier Ada-oriented method, ASTS, with an emphasis on real-time system development. It consists of notations for state modelling, control modelling and time modelling and uses ideas from semantic networks. It is a complex method reminiscent in some respects of both Booch91 and OMT. ADM also influenced the development of OPEN and OML.

Frame-Object Analysis or FOA (Andleigh and Gretzinger, 1992) is a method deriving from conceptual modelling in advanced database and artificial intelligence work and emphasizes the use of semantic nets. It covers quite a lot of the life cycle from requirements to testing and is unusual in emphasizing business rules. In this method a frame is a major component of an information system identified with a semantic net consisting of objects and associations. Effectively frames are subsystems or layers and are collections of objects. Each object has identity, attributes and operations. Frame diagrams are used to depict containment, classification, associations, data flow, sequencing and state transitions and it is far from clear how one is to avoid confusing classification and composition or state transitions with data flow. The strength of FOA is its emphasis on business rules and the use of database constraints and triggers to represent them, though there is little additional notational support for this. The method is most suitable for database system construction where C++ is to be used as the development language and an advanced relational system as the storage manager.

CGI Yourdon was the name given to a version of the original DFD-centred Yourdon methods family maintained by CGI. They proposed an object-oriented extension to the Yourdon structured methods (Marden, 1990) and offer training in it. A very similar approach is described in (Sully, 1993). The approach relies heavily on the use of DFD notation to describe the internal behaviour of objects. The approach derives objects from DFDs, ERDs or STDs if such conventional models have been built. This is useful for people already steeped in the Yourdon philosophy but strange in that most other object-oriented methods play down the significance of data flow and no other method uses data flow to record the description of objects themselves. The external view of an object is represented with a Gradygram notation showing the identity of the object and its visible operations. Inheritance and associations are represented with Chen-style diagrams and usage (object dependency) diagrams are also drawn where appropriate with a style similar to HOOD seniority diagrams. Internally, the structure of the object is represented as a traditional DFD, with dotted lines showing control flows. Where there are control transformations, these are represented using STDs, decision tables or state tables. In contrast with most well-known OOA methods, this does help distinguish objects with complex significant states but I am not convinced that the emphasis on DFDs is otherwise very helpful. Other methods tend to use DFDs only for context modelling.

Page-Jones and Weiss (1989) developed the Synthesis approach to OOA/D. Later, Page-Jones *et al.* (1990) introduced what they called a **Uniform Object Notation** in the context of a general approach to object-oriented analysis and design, with much in common with conventional software engineering practice. The notation is similar to several other object-oriented analysis and design notations discussed in this book, with clear influences from Booch and Structured Design. Even more recently, Page-Jones (1992) generalized Constantine's classic notion that good design minimizes coupling and maximizes cohesion by defining connascence and three different kinds of encapsulation. Level 0 encapsulation represents the idea that a line of code encapsulates a certain abstraction. Level 1 is the encapsulation of procedures into modules and level 2 is the encapsulation of object-oriented programming. Two elements of a system are connascent if they share the same history and future or, more exactly, if changes to one may necessitate changes to the other. Good design should eliminate unnecessary connascence and minimize connascence across encapsulation boundaries and maximize it within them. For level 0 and level 1 encapsulation this reduces to the principle of coupling and cohesion. As pointed out in Chapter 1, inheritance compromises reuse. The connascence principle tells us that inheritance should be restricted to visible features or that there should be two separate hierarchies for inheriting the implementation and the interface, as suggested in Chapter 3. It would also discourage the use of friends in C++. Page-Jones classifies several kinds of connascence as name, type, value, position, algorithm, meaning and polymorphism. Polymorphism connascence is particularly interesting for object-oriented design and is closely related to the problems of nonmonotonic logic. For example, if FLY is an operation of BIRD and PENGUIN is a subclass of BIRD then FLY may sometimes fail and sometimes succeed. This causes maintenance problems should the system be changed. I think that rules, as described in the next section, may be used to avoid this problem, as may the fuzzification of objects and inheritance discussed in Appendix A. The principle of connascence is a profound contribution and should be adopted by every object-oriented designer.

Berard (1993) offers a reasonably comprehensive object-oriented life-cycle model reminiscent in some respects of MOSES. Again a semantic net influence is present in the form of Berard's Object and Class Specifications. These consists of a 'Precise and Concise Description' (a sort of executive summary for the object), various graphical representations including semantic networks and state transition diagrams, lists of required and suffered operations, constants and exceptions. The notation is detailed and more in tune with the mind-set of a designer than that of an analyst in my opinion. There is no provision for rules.

SOMA (Graham 1991a, 1994a, 1995) had its own notation based on ERA and Coad, but this is no longer of interest. Its chief innovations were the use of chainable rulesets encapsulated in classes, its task-centred approach to requirements engineering and business process modelling and its contract-driven life-cycle model. These have been retained in the presentation in this volume, so no more need be said here.

OPEN (Firesmith *et al.*, 1997; Graham *et al.*, 1997b; Henderson-Sellers *et al.*, 1998) was a combination of the methods of the authors referenced and several other methodologists around the world. It too has been covered adequately in the body of this book.

Mainstream Objects (Yourdon *et al.*, 1995) was another Fusion-like method with a similar approach and notation to SOMA and many interesting contributions on process.

OOSE (Object-Oriented Software Engineering) (Jacobson *et al.*, 1992) was a method for object-oriented analysis and design derived from Jacobson's **Objectory** (from Object Factory). Objectory was a proprietary method and OOSE a simplified version which was said to be inadequate for use in production. Objectory was unusual among OO methods in attempting to address the entire software development life cycle. It was originally derived from experience in building telephone exchange systems at L.M. Ericsson using block design techniques and is one of the oldest object-oriented methods. It has its other roots in object-oriented programming and data modelling. Many of its ideas, notably use cases and testing, ended up as part of UML and/or RUP.

Other methods abounded. COOSD is a method developed by Aksit who are based at the University of Twente in Holland. It is based on composition in the style of the functional data model. The key novel ideas are those of rôle participation and abstract communication types. ORCA (OO Requirements Capture and Analysis) uses Frameworks and DONT diagrams. Space does not permit an exhaustive coverage of these ideas, but it is certain the emerging hybrid methods will pick up and synthesize them as the field matures. Other methods that cannot be covered in detail include ALEX-OBJ, MOOD, OSDL, OSMOSYS and SYS_P_O. Several other methods are mentioned in the Bibliographical notes below. By 1994 there were probably well over 50 more or less complete object-oriented methods in existence. This was clearly an unsustainable situation, especially as none of them were complete and many merely represented opinions on what is important at various points in the life cycle. Users had to synthesize a complete method from fragments of the published ones. The UML notation emerged in this context and resolved thus half of the problem. But we must remember that method is more than notation. The process of synthesizing a good method is still going on – and this book is a contribution to the debate.

⊟ B.3   Bibliographical notes

Booch's early papers (1982, 1886) have been mentioned extensively in the foregoing and were very influential. His later book (Booch, 1991) was probably the most profound and comprehensive view of early object-oriented design you are likely to find. It contained a large number of insights and heuristics about what constitutes a good design, how to apprehend objects and how to use and manage the technology. Wasserman *et al.* (1990) describe OOSD fully and compare it with HOOD, GOOD and MOOD. A good source of information on HOOD is by Robinson (1992) which contains the complete HOOD Version 3.0 manual, an excellent tutorial and a version of the paper by Hodgson quoted at the start of this chapter. The HOOD Version 3.1 manual was published by Prentice Hall.

OODLE and recursive development are described in (Shlaer and Mellor, 1992). The CRC cards approach is well described in (Wirfs-Brock *et al.*, 1990) which contains two useful worked examples. Lorenz (1993) presents a method and notation which has much in common with the approach of Wirfs-Brock *et al.* but covers more issues, though in less depth.

The 1993 revision of the Booch method contained a number of significant additions and improvements, including a slightly greater emphasis on analysis, a much simplified and improved set of relational icons compared with those illustrated in Figure B.14, increased compatibility with other notations and methods (notably OMT and Objectory) and a cut-down version of the notation – known as 'Booch Lite'. Interestingly, the second edition of Booch's book concentrated almost exclusively on the C++ language rather than the five languages that he used for illustrative purposes in the first.

Many of the object-oriented methods surveyed represented opinions rather than mature methods. Hybrid methods based on synthesized ideas from these suggestions, conventional methods, AI and semantic modelling are still emerging, now uniformly using UML.

A huge number of sources appeared in the 1990s claiming to offer object-oriented design and analysis methods, although few bore close examination as complete methods; (Coad and Yourdon, 1990, 1991 and 1991a), (Desfray, 1992), (Embley *et al.*, 1992), (Jacobson *et al.*, 1992), (Martin and Odell, 1992), (Rumbaugh *et al.*, 1991), and (Shlaer and Mellor, 1988, 1992) are among the exceptions and have been discussed extensively in this chapter. BON is described in (Nerson, 1992), OBA in (Rubin and Goldberg, 1992). Without particularly endorsing or criticizing any of their methods, I should also mention the suggestions of Ackroyd and Daum (1991), Alabiso (1988), Bailin (1989), de Champeaux *et al.* (1993), Colbert (1994), Davis (1993), Dillon and Tan (1993), Gorman and Choobineh (1989), Halliday and Weibel (1993), Ilvari (1991), Kappel (1991), Kilov and Ross (1994), Lee and Carver (1991), Lieberherr *et al.* (1988), McGregor and Sykes (1992), Page-Jones *et al.* (1990), Ward (1989) and Wilson (1990). Dedene (1994) describes his MERODE method. The methods of Wirfs-Brock *et al.* (1990) and Lorenz (1993) mentioned in Chapter 7 both use CRC cards as a prime modelling technique. Lorenz also contains a notion of use cases.

Winblad *et al.* (1990) give a survey with a different emphasis from that given herein, and no suggestions for extensions to the methods described. Wilkie (1993) surveys several methods, including the OSMOSYS method developed by Winter Partners. A really first-rate survey and classification of over 20 methods was given by Monarchi and Puhr (1992). (Henderson-Sellers and Edwards, 1994) updates (Henderson-Sellers, 1992), provides a survey of several methods and describes MOSES.

Berard (1993) offers many insights and clarifications along with a detailed discussion of the application of Constantine's ideas on cohesion and coupling to object-oriented systems, though I prefer the briefer treatment of Page-Jones (1992).

C

UML notation summary

A limited vocabulary, but one with which you can make numerous combinations, is better than thirty thousand words that only hamper the action of the mind.

Paul Valéry

This appendix illustrates most of the UML notation set. I have omitted a few rarely used and dysfunctional elements. Explanations and examples for most of the symbology will be found in Chapters 6 to 8. As we go to press, it represents UML Version 1.3 accurately, and I am assured that Version 1.4 contains no substantive notational changes. However, Version 2.0 may involve a substantial revision.

C.1 Object modelling symbols

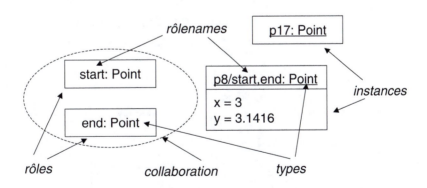

Figure C.1 Instances, rôles and collaborations.

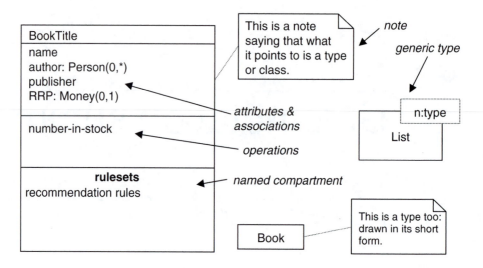

Figure C.2 Classes and types.

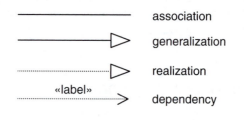

Figure C.3 Dependency symbols.

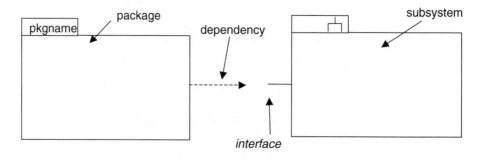

Figure C.4 Packages and subsystems.

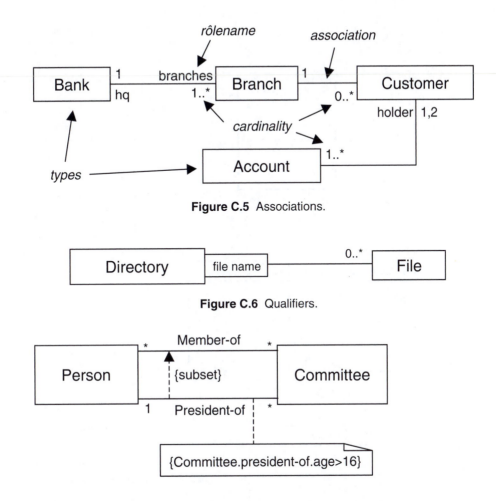

Figure C.5 Associations.

Figure C.6 Qualifiers.

Figure C.7 Unencapsulated constraints. Some constraints are pre-defined in UML, such as {ordered} and {or} – see Figure 6.7(a).

Figure C.8 Visual stereotypes for classes.

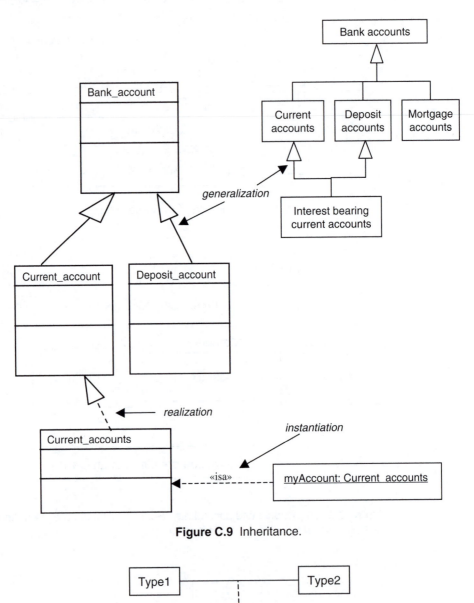

Figure C.9 Inheritance.

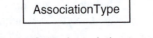

Figure C.10 Association types.

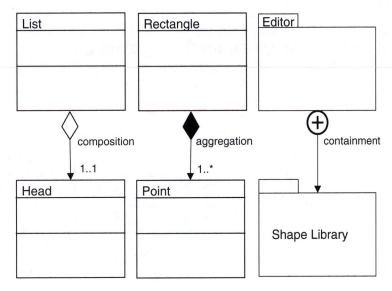

Figure C.11 Aggregation.

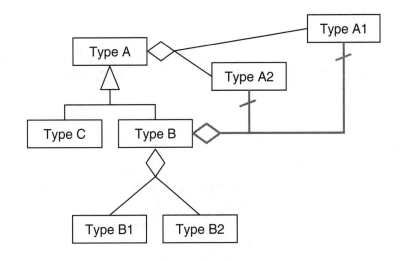

Figure C.12 Derived dependencies.

+ public   – private   # protected

Figure C.13 Visibility symbols for packages and class features.

▤ C.2 Action (use case) modelling symbols

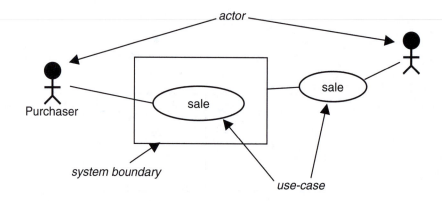

Figure C.14 Actors and use cases. The dependencies of Figure C.3 may also connect use case icons.

▤ C.3 Sequence and collaboration diagram symbols

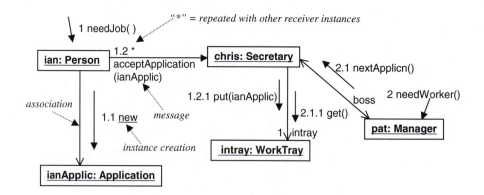

Figure C.15 Collaboration diagram notation.

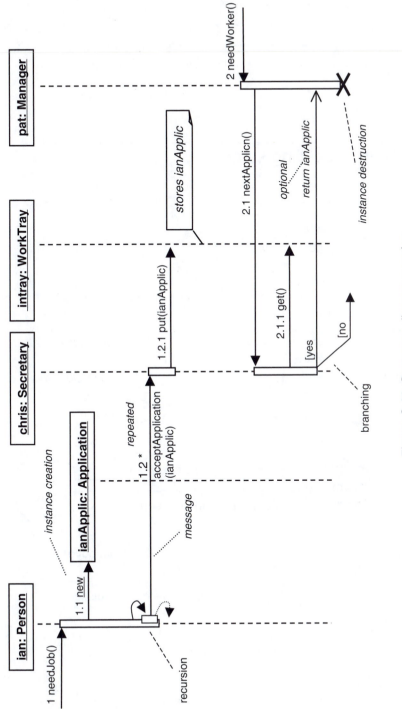

Figure C.16 Sequence diagram notation.

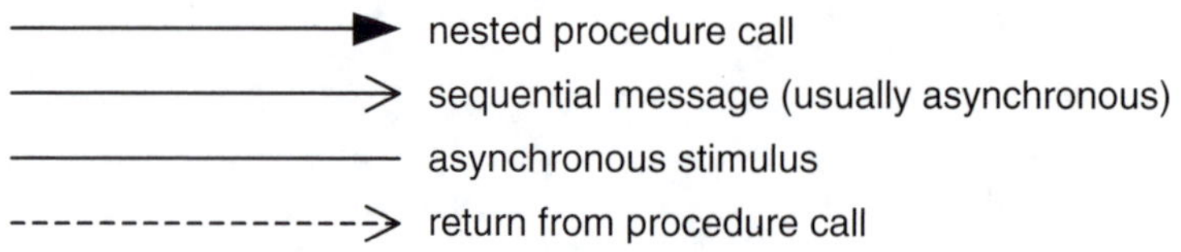

nested procedure call

sequential message (usually asynchronous)

asynchronous stimulus

return from procedure call

Figure C.17 Message types.

⊟ C.4 State modelling symbols

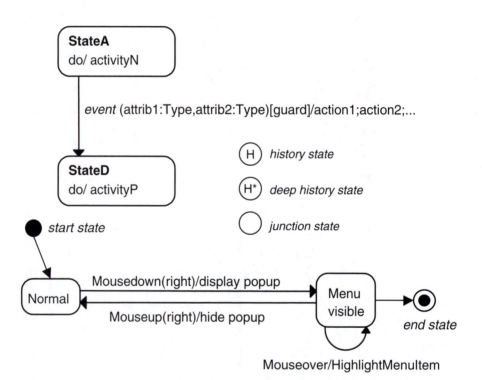

Figure C.18 State chart notation.

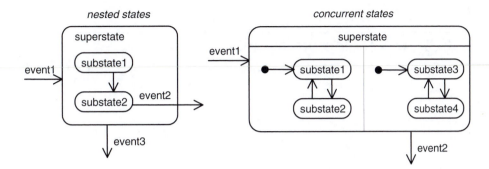

Figure C.19 Nested and concurrent states.

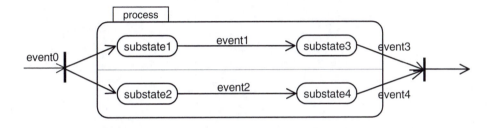

Figure C.20 Concurrent event bifurcation and synchronization.

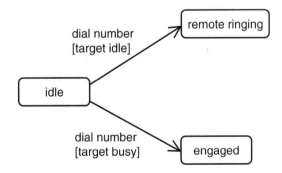

Figure C.21 Guarded transitions.

⊟C.5 Action diagram symbols

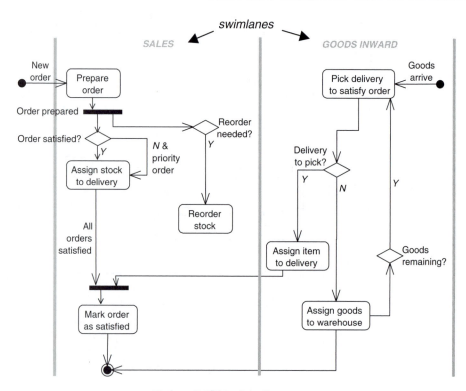

Figure C.22 Action diagrams.

⊟C.6 Implementation and component modelling symbols

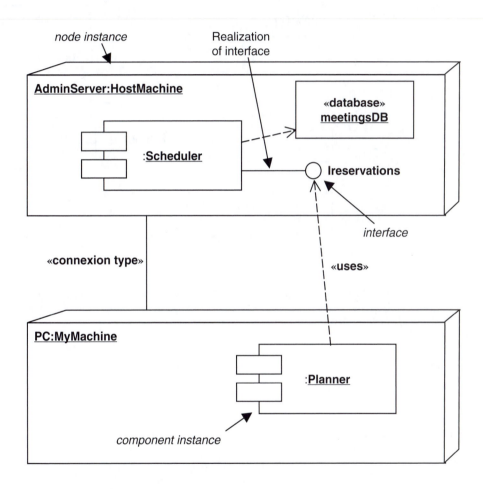

Figure C.23 Nodes and interfaces.

C.7 Collaborations and patterns

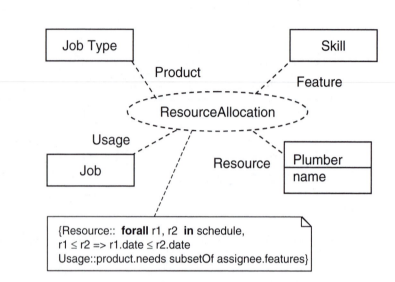

Figure C.24 Collaborations. This notation is also used to represent patterns. The dependency symbols of Figure C.3 may be used to connect patterns and collaborations.

C.8 Real-time notation

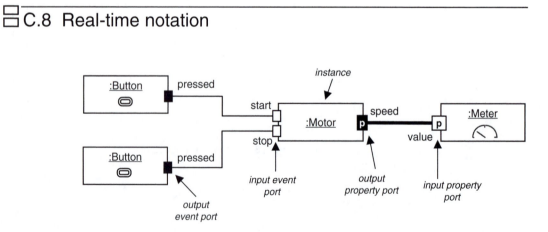

Figure C.25 Ports and connectors.

GLOSSARY OF TERMS

Italicized words in a definition may be found as entries in the glossary. Acronyms are expanded in the Subject Index.

@pre
> Indicates the value of an attribute prior to an action. Part of OCL.

Abstract class/type
> Either the same as *metaclass* or more usually a class/type with no instances; that is, there must be subclasses/subtypes. The opposite of a *concrete* class/type. Sometimes, a class representing an abstract concept.

Abstract data type (ADT)
> An abstraction, similar to a class, that describes a set of objects in terms of an encapsulated or hidden data structure and operations on that structure.

Abstract type
> The same as *abstract class*, but with no implementation. A type designed to supply common behaviour to a set of subtypes, or *abstract data type*.

Abstraction
> 'The act of separating in thought' (OED) – representing the essential features of something without including background or inessential detail.

Access operations/methods (or accessors)
> Operations/methods which access the state of an object but do not modify it.

Accidental object
> An object defined solely by its properties. See *essential object* and *tautological object*.

Action
> Something that happens and causes a change to the state of the world: a task, activity, use case, etc.

Active object
> An object which can initiate message passing.
> **OR:** An object that provides services to others, can be copied as a surrogate and needs concurrency control. Passive objects on the other hand may be physically distributed when their services are required.
> **OR:** An object whose methods are activated by a change in its state; a *demon*.

Activity
> An action within a *project* with definite, usable deliverables.

Actor
> An object which suffers no operations but only operates on other objects (Booch).
> **OR:** An object with an address and a current state that may communicate with other objects only by message passing. Actors can change their local state, create new actors and send messages. Actor systems replace inheritance with delegation (Hewitt).
> **OR:** A user of a system adopting a rôle with respect to that system (Jacobson).

Ad hoc polymorphism
Giving different operations on different types the same name without their semantics being related.

ADT (see *abstract data type*).

Agent
An object which performs some operation at the request of another object and may in turn operate upon another object.
OR: A person, organizational unit, program or device acting within a business or system, and which can communicate with other agents.
OR: In Eiffel, a construct to allow Lisp-like late binding.

Agent communication language (ACL)
A language used by heterogeneous, mobile, intelligent agents to exchange data, plans, etc.

Agent Object Model (AOM)
A model of a business process expressed in term of agents and *conversations* among them.

Aggregation
The same as *composition*. In UML, an instance level association that is transitive and antisymmetric: giving it the semantics of containment rather than whole-part. Multiple composition is permitted.

AKO
A Kind Of. The inheritance relationship between classes and their superclasses: *generalization*.

Alexandrian form
A standard way of writing down patterns.

Algorithm
A procedure which is guaranteed to terminate in a finite time.

Anthropomorphism
Modelling objects as if they exhibited people-like characteristics.

Anti-pattern
A standard but incorrect or damaging solution to a recurring problem, named to help people discuss it easily. See also *pattern*.

APO
A Part Of. The *composition* relationship between parts and wholes.

Applet
A program that runs in a browser and which is not stored on the client machine it runs on but is downloaded when needed.

Application framework
A collection of objects designed to solve a particular class of problem. The classes are specialized to deal with specific applications. A common example is an application framework for graphical user interface development.

Application object
An object that is relevant to a particular application rather than of reusable significance within a domain.

Applicator
An operation that applies one of its arguments (a reference to a function) to the other arguments.

Assertions

Statements of the form 'A is B' in rule-based languages. Also called 'facts'.
OR: In formal languages a general term for *pre-conditions*, *post-conditions* or *invariance-conditions*.

Association

A mapping or pair of mappings between two types/classes indicating that message passing could possibly occur between them.

Association set

A named set of typed *associations* between use cases equivalent to a sequence diagram with concurrency.

Association type/class

A type/class introduction to describe details of an association.

Atomic

Not reducible to more detailed terms or structure.

Atomic task

A task or *use case* that, if decomposed further, would require the use of terms not in the *domain ontology*: normally described in a single sentence.

Attribute

A static, or printable, property of an object. It cannot exist independently of the object although its values can. Attributes may take other objects as values making attributes equivalent to associations. See *instance variable* and *association*.

Backward chaining

A method of search, or inference, with starts with a conclusion and follows a chain of rules backwards to find plausible reasons or causes for the conclusion.

Base class

A class from which the behaviour of other classes is inherited. A *superclass*.

Behaviour sharing

A form of *polymorphism*, when several entities have the same interface. This is achieved by inheritance or *operator overloading*.

Behaviour

The set of methods of an object defines its behaviour.

Blackboard system

A system where objects register interest in a 'blackboard' object that controls the agenda for and progress with problem solving.

Blocking send

A message that suspends the sender's behaviour until a response is received from the server.

BNF

Backus-Naür Form: a notation for describing programming language syntax.

Boundary objects (see *interface objects*)

Browser

A tool to help programmers navigate visually through the classification structures of a system, following the inheritance links.
OR: A tool for browsing the web.

Business Object Model (BOM)

A UML model comprising types and actions that make sense to the business; possibly in the form of an executable specification.

Business object

A object in a requirements analysis or specification that is mentioned in business process and task descriptions (Graham);

OR: Something representable by an icon that makes sense to users (Sims);

OR: A commonly used software component that occurs in the domain terminology.

Business rule

An if/then statement about the types, attributes and operations in a *Business Object Model*.

Caching

Storing replicated data on a tier separate from the actual database and ensuring synchronization between the two.

Cardinality constraints

Invariants that specify the range of the number of objects that an association may point to; e.g. there may be between zero and one values for a DateOfBirth attribute.

Cartooning

Representing real-world agents in the *Business Object Model*; often as intelligent *agents*.

Chunk

Something held in activated memory as a unit.

Class

An abstraction of a set of instances that specifies the common static and behavioural characteristics of its instances, including the public and private nature of the state and behaviour. A class is a template from which object instances are created.

Class card

A paper representation of an object with a standard layout, used to support rôle-playing, walkthroughs and validation of object models. See also *CRC card*.

Class inheritance

The inheritance of features and their implementation by a class from its superclass(es); as opposed to *interface inheritance*.

Class invariant

A statement about the attributes and/or operations of a class that relates them.

Class method (class operation)

A method/operation which is inherited by all subclasses of the class it belongs to and which defines the behaviour of the collective of instances rather than individual ones. The values of class variables may be inherited by subclasses and overridden.

Class variable (class attribute)

An attribute which is inherited by all subclasses of the class it belongs to and which defines the state of the collective of instances rather than individual ones. The values of class variables may be inherited by subclasses and overridden.

Class-based programming

The same as object-oriented programming.

Classification, AKO or IsA structure

A tree or network structure based on the semantic primitives of inclusion (AKindOf) and membership (IsA) which indicates that inheritance may implement specialization or generalization. Objects may participate in more than one such structure, giving rise to multiple inheritance. Strictly, classification is the relationship between instances and their class.

Classless inheritance (see *delegation*).

Class-oriented (or -based)
Object-based systems in which every instance belongs to a class, but classes may not have superclasses.

Client
An object which uses the services of another, server, object. That is, clients can send messages to servers.

Collaboration
The relationship of clients to servers via usage or message passing.

Component
A properly specified object with attributes, operations, invariants and collaborators;
OR: A binary unit of independent production, acquisition and deployment with contractually specified interfaces and explicit context dependencies only (Szyperski);
OR: A unit of executable deployment that plays a part in a component kit.

Component kit
A set of components together with defined protocols for connecting them together.

Composition (or A-Part-Of) structure
A (usually) tree structured set of links based on the semantic primitive 'part-of' which indicates that certain objects may be assembled from collections of other objects. In nature, objects may participate in more than one such structure. In UML, composition is a restricted form of UML aggregation in which instances that are parts are created and destroyed by the whole; multiple wholes are disallowed.

Concrete class
A class that may have instances.

Constrained genericity (see *genericity*).

Constructor operations
Methods which create and initialize the state of an object.

Container class
A class that defines a data structure for collecting instances of other types; e.g. lists, bags, sets, queues and stacks.

Contract
The set of messages that a client can send to a server which defines its responsibilities. Sometimes (in CRC) a coherent subset of this set.

Controller objects
Objects that serve as centres of the logic of a system, calling and managing other objects. They should be avoided.

Conversation
A goal-directed interaction between agents in a business with a standard recursive structure that includes up to six actions or use cases.

CRC (Class, Responsibility and Collaboration) cards
A *class card* with a standard layout used to help discuss designs.

Data semantics
Specification of the meaning of data and their relationships; specifically the multiplicity and modality of relationships, inheritance and composition. These relationships include integrity constraints.

Data type
A *type* but with no operations.

Database trigger (see *trigger*).

Deadlock

A condition where processing halts while two operations wait for each other to complete; and which will go on forever unless interrupted.

Declarative semantics

The same as *functional semantics*.

Deferred class

A class with any feature provided only as a specification: its implementation to be provided by some subclass. In a Java interface all features are deferred. Eiffel provides more flexibility by allowing individual features to be deferred.

Deferred inheritance

Use of deferred classes.

Delegation

In *actor* or *prototype* languages, the passing of responsibility to carry out a method to another object. A form of classless inheritance.

Demon or **dæmon**

An object or procedure which is activated by a change of state; a data-driven procedure. The same as a *trigger*.

Deontic logic

The logic of duty or obligation.

Dependencies

Relationships between objects other than association, composition and inheritance.

Derived class

A refinement or specialization of an existing class.

Derived dependencies/associations

Dependencies or associations between objects that arise because of inherited features.

Destructor operations

Methods which destroy objects and reclaim their space.

Dialectics

A form of argument based on the resolution of contradictory components, or the view that everything is constantly transformed by the resolution of internal contradictions. The unity and conflict of opposites.

Domain objects

Objects significant beyond one application that may be reusable.

Domain ontology (see *ontology*).

Dynamic binding

The allocation of storage at run time rather than compile time. The same as *late binding* and the opposite of *static* (or *early*) *binding*.

Dynamic classification

Allowing instances to migrate from one class to another (forbidden in object-oriented programming languages).

Early binding

The same as *static binding* and the opposite of *late* (or *dynamic*) *binding*.

Effect

A post-condition that is conjoined with all other operation post-conditions of a type.

Elaborational methods

These proceed by adding detail to a single object model as development continues. See also *Translational methods*.

Empiricism

The philosophical position that perception, rather than objective reality, is primary to all knowledge. Empiricism and certain philosophical positions derived from it, such as that of Kant, Logical Positivism and Pragmatism, has been the dominant philosophy in Western science since Bacon.

Encapsulation

The scoping of unrestricted reference to an object. Objects may examine or change their own state, but its accessor methods prevent other objects from making inappropriate requests or updates. Closely related to the concept of *information hiding*.

Epistemology

The science or theory of knowledge.

Essential objects

Objects known by more than just the values of their attributes.

External agent

An agent that is outside the current business area.

Facet

A feature of a feature of an object.

Factory object

Instances that take responsibility for creating and deleting other instances of classes.

Fan-in and fan-out

The fan-in of an object with respect to a *structure* is the number of clients from which control is passed to the object. Its fan-out is the number of servers that it uses or points at via this structure.

Feature

An attribute, operation, invariant or ruleset belonging to a type.

Forces

Influences to be considered and balanced when using a *pattern*.

Forward chaining

A method of search, or inference, which starts with one or more facts and follows a chain of rules forwards to find one or more consequences of the facts.

Frame

A data structure used in artificial intelligence similar to an object. Frames have *slots* which may contain data and procedures.

Framework (see *model framework* and *application framework*).

Framework substitution

Filling in the placeholders in a model framework template with the names of types.

Friend

In C++, a method of an object with privileged access to the private implementation of another object.

Functional semantics

The specification of the meaning of the procedural and control aspects of an object. In particular, the specification of rules for triggers, conflict resolution, handling exceptions, control régimes and general business rules.

Fuzzy inheritance

Inheriting attributes with an attached certainty factor. In the case of multiple inheritance, these are combined using an inference rule.

Fuzzy object

An object which may contain or inherit attribute values which are fuzzy sets, and which may inherit any attribute with an attached certainty factor, thus modelling partial inheritance.

Fuzzy quantifier

A term such as *some*, *a few* or *most* which quantifies an expression inexactly.

Fuzzy ruleset

A ruleset whose terms include fuzzy-valued variables and which is processed using a fuzzy forward chaining algorithm.

Fuzzy set

A generalization of a set where membership may be partial. The set of tall men is a fuzzy set.

Garbage collection

The process of reclaiming the core storage occupied by objects no longer in use or reachable from the current task image.

Generalization

The opposite of *specialization*. *vb.* Moving 'up' a *classification structure*. *n.sing.* A more general class than some other which inherits from it.

Generic classes/types

Classes/types that can have a variable type specified by a parameter, such as a list.

Generic package

An ADA package that includes generic parameters.

Genericity

The ability to parametrize classes or types; a special case of *polymorphism*. *Constrained genericity* requires the parameters to have specific operations, otherwise it is said to be *unconstrained*.

Guarantee

A statement that a server must maintain as true throughout the execution of an operation (see also *rely clause* and *invariance condition*).

Guard

A precondition of a transition in a state-transition diagram.

Hairies and conscripts model

A model of reuse management and knowledge circulation that combines a fixed reuse team with temporary secondment of project developers.

Hedge

A term in fuzzy logic that modifies a term in the term set, such as VERY or FAIRLY.

Identity

An object (instance, class, type or rôle) has unique identity throughout its life.

Idiom

A *pattern* relevant only to a particular programming language.

Impedance mismatch

The waste of programmer effort involved in translating between objects and database tables.

Implementation

The private or hidden features of an object.

Inference

The process of inferring new data from existing data using a set of *rules* or *invariants*.

Inference régime

The logic used to process a *ruleset*, often FOPC with backward or forward chaining.

Inferential distance ordering

The partial ordering of an inheritance network according to the number of superclasses through which a value is inherited. The distance is the number of steps in the inheritance chain. For example, in the inference 'Fido has hair because Fido is a dog and dogs are mammals (and mammals have hair)', the distance is 2.

Information hiding

The principle which states that the state and implementation of an object or module should be private to that object or module and only accessible via its public interface. Closely related to *encapsulation*.

Inheritance

The relationship between classes whereby one class inherits all or part of the description of another more general class, and instances inherit all the properties and methods of the classes they belong to.

Inspections

Structured meetings to find defects in deliverables.

Instance method/operation

A method/operation that acts on individual instances rather than their entire class/type – as opposed to *class method/operation*.

Instance variable/attribute

A data holding attribute contained within an instance that describe the state of that instance. Only the declaration of an instance variable, not its value, may be inherited by subclasses. See also *attribute* and *class variable*.

Instance

A particular object or individual example of a class.

Instantiation

The creation of a data item representing a variable or a class – giving a value to something.

Intelligent agent

An object with reasoning ability, either in the world (person, organization, etc.) or in a system (a class with *rulesets* and a *inference régime*).

Interface

The visible methods of an object together with any invariants on the object.

Interface inheritance

The inheritance of features without their implementation by a class or interface.

Interface objects

Objects concerned with the interface to a system. Also called *boundary objects*.

Invariance condition

A condition that remains true all the time that a method is executing, generalizing *guarantee* and *rely*.

Invariant (see *class invariant*).

IsA

The classification (inheritance) relationship between instances and their classes; as in: 'Jane Gray IsA PERSON'. See *classification*.

Iterator

A method that permits all parts of an object to be visited.

Late binding – the same as *dynamic binding*.

Locational transparency

Being able to use an object without being aware of its location in a distributed system.

Long transactions

Transactions that may not be aborted when deadlock occurs and must be versioned.

Manipulator

A value in an expression that causes side effects. Usually implemented as references to other methods and often used as the operator argument of an *applicator*.

Mapping

A single-valued, directional association.

Marshalling

Lining up the parameters of a method into a format suitable for transmission across an object request broker.

Member function

A function declared within a class with access to its internal state.

Membership function

The characteristic function of a set, or in particular a fuzzy set, which takes values between 0 and 1. A value of 0 indicates that a member of the domain of the membership function is not in the set and 1 indicates full membership. With fuzzy sets, such as the set of tall men, a member can have a partial membership. For example, a man 5'11" high might be given the value 0.6 in the set 'tall'. For all practical purposes, a membership function is the same thing as a fuzzy set.

Message

A request for an object to carry out one of its operations.

Message passing

The philosophy that objects only interact by sending messages to each other that request some operations to be performed.

Metaclass

In languages like Smalltalk, a class whose instances are classes, as opposed to an *abstract class* that has no instances, only subclasses. Sometimes used loosely as a synonym for abstract class. See also *superclass*.

Method

A procedure or function which an object can perform. Strictly the implementation of an operation in some language, but used loosely to mean the same as *operation*.

Mixin

An abstract class containing a package of methods which can be inherited by (mixed into) any class. Normally mixins are associated with CLOS.

Modal logic

The logic of possibility which introduces two extra operators to ordinary first order logic, L (meaning 'it is possible that') and N (meaning 'it is necessary that'), along with new rules to manipulate them.

Model framework

A related group of packages in which you can substitute concrete things for its abstract placeholders. Typically, a framework represents a reusable pattern.

Model template (same as *model framework*).

Modes

States of a system, usually its user interface, that prevent certain actions from being performed while the state persists. For example, modal dialogue boxes may prevent edit operations from being used.

Monomorphism

The opposite of Polymorphism, where a message may have only one, system-wide, interpretation.

Multiple classification

Allowing an instance to belong to more than one class (forbidden in object-oriented programming languages).

Multiple inheritance

Inheritance where a more specialized object can inherit its description from more than one more general class and where contradictions may result.

Nonmonotonic logic

A type of formal logic in which theorems can be retracted (unproved) in the light of new facts. Most logic is *monotonic* in the sense that adding new facts always increases the number of provable theorems.

Object

Anything with unique identity throughout its life. Either an object-type or one of its instances. A class or an instance of a class. Note that other books use the term *object* solely to refer to instances. This book follows the Smalltalk philosophy where 'everything is an object'.

Object identity

The rule that objects have unique identity throughout their existence.

Object request broker

Middleware that supports the locational transparency of distributed object invocations, usually complying with the CORBA standard.

Object-based

Systems are object-based when they allow objects to encapsulate both data and methods and which enforce object identity.

Object-oriented

Object-oriented systems are *object-based*, class-based, support inheritance between classes and superclasses and allow objects to send messages to themselves.

Object-relational databases

Relational databases with a front-end that makes them appear to be object-oriented databases.

Object-type

This is the standard OMG term. It means an entity type equipped with *operations* which encapsulate its data structure. Usually referred to as a *class*, though strictly classes are implementations of object-type. Sometimes abbreviated to *object*.

OCL

The Object Constraint Language defined within UML: a language based on formal logic.

Ontology

The science or study of Being. Also the conceptual model underpinning a domain of knowledge; hence domain ontology.

Operation

A procedure that an object knows how to perform and which gives access to the object's data. Operations are implemented as *methods*.

Operator overloading

A special case of *polymorphism*; attaching more than one meaning to the same operator symbol. 'Overloading' is also sometimes used to indicate using the same name for different objects.

Overloading

Giving two different responsibilities to two different things with the same name.

Overriding

The ability to change the definition of an inherited method or attribute in a subclass.

Package

An Ada construct that combines a set of declarations into a single program unit which can be used to create an abstract data type.

Partial inheritance (see *fuzzy inheritance*).

Passive objects (see *active objects*).

Pattern

A standard solution to a recurring problem, named to help people discuss it easily and to think about design.

Persistence

The property of objects to persist in terms of identity, state and description through time, regardless of the computer session which created or uses them. Objects stored, ready for use, on secondary storage.

Phenomenology

A school of thought within modern philosophy which asserts the active rôle of the subject in perception, characterized by the slogan: there is no object without a subject. The term is either used exactly to refer to the idealist positions of Brentano and Husserl and their existentialist followers such as Heidegger and Sartre, or more loosely to include Hegel and some modern materialists.

Polymorphism

Literally: many-formedness. The ability of an object or operator to refer to instances of different classes at run time. Thus, polymorphic messages may be interpreted differently when received by different objects or in different contexts.

Power types

Types whose instances are themselves types.

Pre-conditions and post-conditions

Logical statements that must evaluate to true before a method may commence or after it has completed, respectively.

Private parts/operations/methods/attributes/features

Those parts of an object, methods or attributes, which may not be accessed by other objects, only by subclasses or instances.

Programme

A set of *projects*.

Project

A set of activities that completes in less than six months with a team of six or fewer people and delivers a useful system. Part of a *programme*.

Protected parts/operations/methods/attributes/features

A feature is protected if only subclasses have access to it.

Protocol

The set of public operations of an object.

Prototype

A mock-up or experimental version of a computer system used to discover more about requirements or design;

OR: An instance that acts like a class in that its properties can be acquired by other instances (see also *delegation*).

Public interface

That part of an object, methods or attributes, which may be accessed by other objects. The public part of an object constitutes its interface.

Pushout

In the mathematical theory of categories, the universal object standing at the terminal corner of a square of arrows. Universal here means that any other object in that place could be factored through the universal one. This formalizes the notion of 'the object most easily constructed' or the 'best' or 'most natural' object. For example, Cartesian products are universal with respect to their projections.

Qualifier

A term that qualifies another; a *hedge* in fuzzy set theory.

Quantification

In logic, setting limits on how many things an expression applies to. Classical logic has two quantifiers, *there exists* (written $\exists$) and *for all* (written $\forall$).

Referential integrity

A property of relational databases where if a relation R contains a foreign key whose values are taken from the primary key values of a relation S then every occurrence of the foreign key in R must either match a primary key value in R or be null. R and S may be the same relation. More generally, a property of a pair of weak semi-inverse associations between objects that says that if you traverse both then the intersection of the images of the starting values will contain those values.

Referential transparency

Programming where every expression or variable has the same value within a given scope; all variables are local.

Refinement

A set of *Catalysis* techniques that add detail to a model while retaining traceability, often using inheritance or aggregation.

Reflection

A facility to extend a model 'at run time' such as the use of *power types*.

Rely clause

A pre-condition that must remain true throughout the execution of the operation it refers to. Should it be violated, the specification does not state what clients can expect as a result. The server is not responsible for maintaining the condition (see also *guarantee* and *invariance condition*).

Responsibility

Some thing that an object can be regarded as knowing about (an *attribute*) or knowing how to do (an *operation*).

Retrieval

A function that determines the value of an abstract attribute in an interface from the actual implementation.

Rule

A rule or constraint that specifies some relationship between two or more attributes and/or operations within an object. Occasionally rules specify the conflict resolution strategy that objects will adopt when there is, for example, a conflict arising from multiple inheritance.

Ruleset

A set of If ... then ... statements or *invariants* together with a named inference régime. Rules are regarded as independent and their order does not matter. Rule-based languages are non-procedural in this sense.

RUP workflow (see *workflow*).

Scenario

A specific occurrence of an action, task, use case, etc. A concrete story about some business process.

Schema evolution

Changing the definition of what types of things are stored in a database.

Script

A stereotypical, generic and essential description of an action (task, use case, activity, etc.).

Selector operation

A method which can access but not alter the state of an object.

Selector

A method that evaluates the current state of an object.

Self-recursion

Being able to send messages to oneself.

Self-reference

The same as self-recursion; being able to refer to oneself in a method.

Server

An object which suffers operations but may not act upon other objects. It may only send messages to other objects as a result of a request from them, unless it is also a client of other servers. See *client*.

Set abstraction

Considering concrete instances as belonging to a class defined by abstract properties or predicates.

Signature

The interface of an object minus its invariants: its name, attributes and methods.

Slot

The word used in AI frame systems for attributes. Note that attributes of frames can contain methods. An instance variable in CLOS.

Software integrated circuits (software ICs)

Pluggable components.

Specialization

The opposite of *generalization*. *vb.* Going 'down' a *classification structure*. *n. sing.* A more restricted class than some other which it inherits from.

Static binding

The opposite of dynamic binding. Values are bound to variables, or methods to messages, at compile time. Also called *early binding*.

Static typing

Fixing the types of objects at compile time.

Stative types

Types that represent the states of an object or objects.

Stereotype

A label used to characterize the rôle a class or type can play.

Strong typing

The property of a programming language which ensures that all expressions are guaranteed to be type consistent – usually achieved by *static typing*.

Structure

A set of dependencies of the same type on a UML class, type or use case diagram: usually one of inheritance, aggregation, association or usage.

Subclass

A class which has an AKO link to a more general class; as in: 'a DOG is AKindOf MAMMAL'.

Subject (area)

In Coad-Yourdon object-oriented analysis, the same as a *level*.

Substitutability

The principle that states that all messages sent to a class should be understood by all its specializations; so that it can be substituted for them.

Subsystem

A general term like *level, subject* or *subject area* referring to a subdivision of a system description to make it more understandable or tractable.

Superclass

A class which has one or more members which are (more specialized) classes themselves. A *base class*.

Syllogism

A logical or other process whereby two unlinked terms are linked by an intermediate term. A relationship between particular, individual and universal, in any order. The classical example is the deductive syllogism: 'All men are mortal (universal). Gaius is a man (particular). Therefore, Gaius is mortal (individual).'

Task association set

A named set of associations between use cases or actions; equivalent to a sequence diagram with concurrency.

Tautology

A statement which is true by definition, such as 'red roses are red'. Tautological objects have no features other than those which define them, such as RedThings.

Template (see *generic type* and *model template*).

t-norm

A generalization of the various kinds of 'and' operation in fuzzy logics. *t-conorms* generalize 'or' operations similarly. A typical non-standard t-conorm is the probabilistic sum: $a+b+a*b$.

Translational methods

Methods that proceed by transforming object models into new forms as development continues.

Trigger

A *demon*. A rule which fires in response to a change of state.

Type

A set together with operations defined on this set. See *abstract data type*.

UML

The Unified Modelling Language for object-oriented analysis and design adopted as a standard by the OMG and used throughout this book.

UML-RT

An extension of UML to deal with real-time systems.

Unconstrained genericity (see *genericity*).

Use (or usage) structure

The structure of relationships between clients and servers connected by message passing.

Use case

A behaviourally related **sequence** of transactions in a dialogue with a system whose task it is to yield a result of measurable value to *actors* who **use** the system.

Virtual functions

Functions with no implementation (see also *deferred methods*).

Virtual machine

Software that simulates a hardware instruction set on other hardware.

Visibility

The ability of one object to be a server to others.

Weak typing

The opposite of strong typing. Type errors may occur at run time.

Worker

A rôle adopted by a project team member (in RUP).

Workflow

An activity in a project(in RUP).

Wrapper

A partition of a diagram with only a few objects treated as a composite object communicating with other layers.

XP

A rapid application development method emphasizing automated testing and short cycles (eXtreme Programming);

OR: Xeroderma Pigmentosum, a rare but debilitating skin affliction.

REFERENCES AND
BIBLIOGRAPHY

Abadi, M. and Cardelli, L. (1996) *A Theory of Objects*, Berlin: Springer-Verlag

Abbott, R.J. (1983) Program Design by Informal English Descriptions, *Communications of the ACM* **26**(11), 882–894

Abrial, J.R. (1974) Data Semantics. In Klimbie and Koffeman (Eds.) *Data Base Management*, Amsterdam: North-Holland

Ackroyd, M. and Daum, D. (1991) Graphical notation for object-oriented design and programming, *Journal Of Object-Oriented Programming* **3**(5), 18–28

Adams, G. and Corriveau, J-P. (1994) Capturing Object Interactions. In Magnusson, Meyer, Nerson and Perrot (1994)

Agha, G. (1986) *Actors: A Model of Concurrent Computation in Distributed Systems*, Cambridge MA: MIT Press

Agha, G. and Hewitt, C. (1987) *Actors: A Conceptual Foundation for Concurrent Object-Oriented Programming*. In Shriver, B. and Wegner, P. (Eds.) (1987)

Agha, G., Wegner, P. and Yonezawa, A. (Eds.) (1993) *Research Directions in Concurrent Object-Oriented Programming*, MIT Press

Agha, S. (1989) *Hypertext Systems*, M.Sc. Thesis, City University, London

Agrawal R. and Gehani, N. (1989) ODE: the language and the data model, *Proc. ACM SIGMOD Conf. on the Management of Data*, Portland, Oregon

Ahad, R. and Dedo, D. (1992) OpenODB from Hewlett-Packard: a commercial object-oriented database management system. *Journal of Object-Oriented Programming*. **4**(9), 31–35

Ahmed, S. *et al.* (1992) Object-oriented database management systems for engineering: a comparison, *Journal Of Object-Oriented Programming* **5**(3), 27–44

Akscyn, R.M. and McCracken, D.L. (1984) The ZOG Approach to Database Management. In *Proceedings of the Trends and Applications Conference: Making Database Work*, Gartherburg, Maryland

Akscyn, R.M., McCracken, D.L. and Yoder, E.A. (1988) KMS: A Distributed Hypermedia System for Managing Knowledge in Organisations, *Communications of the ACM*, **31**(7), 820–835

Alabiso, B. (1988) Transformation of data flow analysis models to object-oriented design. In Meyrowitz (1988)

Albano, A. *et al.* (1988) The Type System of Galileo. In Atkinson, M.P., Buneman, O.P. and Morrison, R. (Eds.) *Data Types and Persistence*, Berlin: Springer-Verlag, 101–119

Albrecht, A.J. (1979) Measuring application developement productivity, *Proceedings of the Joint SHARE/GUIDE/IBM Application Development Symposium*, Oct. 1979, 34–43

Albrecht, A.J. and Gaffney, J.E. (1983) Software Function, Source Lines of Code and Development Effort Prediction: A Software Science Validation, *IEEE Transactions on Software Engineering*, **9**(6), 639–647

Aleksander, I. and Morton, H. (1990) *An Introduction to Neural Computing*, Chapman & Hall

Alencar, A.J. and Goguen, J.A. (1991) OOZE: An object-oriented Z environment. In America, P. (Ed.) Proc. of ECOOP'91, *Lecture Notes in Computer Science 512*, Berlin: Springer

Alexander, C. (1964) *Notes on the Synthesis of Form*, Harvard: University Press

Alexander, C. (1979) *The Timeless Way of Building*, Oxford: University Press

Alexander, C., Ishikawa, S. and Silverstein, M. (1977) *A Pattern Language*, Oxford: University Press

Alexander, C. (1996) *A Foreshadowing of 21st Century Art*, New York: Oxford University Press

Alexander, C. (1999) The Origins of Pattern Theory: The Future of the Theory and the Generation of a Living World, *IEEE Software* September/October, 71–82

Alpert, S., Brown, K. and Woolf, B.R. (1998) *The Design Patterns Smalltalk Companion,* Reading MA: Addison-Wesley

Allen, P. and Frost, S. (1998*) Component-Based development for Enterprise Systems: Applying the SELECT Perspective*, Cambridge: University Press/SIGS

Altham, J.E.J. (1971) *The Logic of Plurality*, Methuen

Ambler, S. (1998) *Process Patterns*, Cambridge, England: The University Press

Ambler, S. (1999) *More Process Patterns*, Cambridge, England: The University Press

Andersen, B. (1992) *Ellie: a general, fine-grained, first-class, object based language*, *Journal Of Object-Oriented Programming* **5**(2) 35–41

Anderson, J.A., McDonald, J., Holland, L. and Scranage, E. (1989) Automated Object-Oriented Requirements Analysis and Design, *Proceedings of the 6th Washington ADA Symposium*, 265–272

Anderson, J.R. (1976) *Language, Memory and Thought*, Laurence Erlbaum

Andleigh, P.K. and Gretzinger, M.R. (1992) *Distributed Object-Oriented Data-Systems Design*, Englewood Cliffs NJ: Prentice Hall

Andrews, T. and Harris, C. (1990) Combining Language and Database Advances in an Object-Oriented Development. In Zdonik and Maier (1990)

Aoyama, M. (1993) Concurrent Development Process Model, *IEEE Software*, July 1993, 46–55

Apple (1988) *The MacApp Interim Manual*, Cupertino CA: Apple Computer Inc.

Apple Computer Inc. (1987) *Apple Human Interface Guidelines: The Apple Desktop Interface*, Cupertino, CA: Addison-Wesley

Arranga, E.C. and Coyle, F.P. (1996) *Object-Oriented COBOL*, New York: SIGS Books

Arthur, L.J. (1985) *Measuring Programmer Productivity and Software Quality*, New York: Wiley

Ashby, W.R. (1956) *An Introduction to Cybernetics*, London: Chapman & Hall

Ashby, W.R. (1960) *Design for a Brain*, 2nd Edition, London: Chapman & Hall

Atkinson, M.P. and Buneman, O.P. (1988) Types and Persistence in Database Programming Languages, *ACM Computing Surveys* **19**(2), 105–190

Atkinson, M.P., Bancilhon, F., DeWitt, D., Dittrich, K., Maier, D. and Zdonik, S. (1989) The Object-Oriented Database System Manifesto, *Deductive and Object-Oriented Databases*, Amsterdam: Elsevier 1990; also in *Proceedings of the First International Conference on Deductive and Object-Oriented Databases*, Kyoto, Japan, December 4–6, 1989, 40–57

Attwood, T. (1991) At last! A distributed database for Windows 3.0, *Object Magazine* **1**(1) 36–57

Austin, J.L. (1962) *How to Do Things with Words*, Cambridge MA: Harvard University Press

Bachman, C. (1977) The rôle concept in data models. In *Proceedings of the 3rd International Conference on Very Large Databases*, IEEE, New York, 464–476

Baecker, R.M. and Buxton, W.A.S. (Eds.) (1987) *Readings in Human Computer Interaction: A multi-disciplinary approach*, San Mateo CA: Morgan Kaufmann

Bailin, S.C. (1989) An object-oriented requirements specification method, *Comm. ACM* **32**(5), 608–623

Baldwin, J.F. and Martin, T.P. (1996) Fuzzy classes in object-oriented logic programming, *Proc. 5th IEEE International Conf. on Fuzzy Systems*, New Orleans LA, 1358–1365

Bancilhon, F., Delobel, C. and Kanillakis, P. (Eds.) (1991) *Building an Object-Oriented Database System: The Story of O₂*, Morgan-Kaufmann

Banker, R.D., Kauffman, R.J. and Zweig, D. (1993) Repository Evaluation of Software Reuse, *IEEE Trans. on Software Engineering* **19**(4)

Bapat, S. (1994) *Object-Oriented Networks: Models for architecture, operations and management*, Englewood Cliffs NJ: Prentice Hall

Barfield, L. (1993) *The User Interface: Concepts & Design*, Wokingham: Addison-Wesley

Barker, R. (1990) *CASE*METHOD: Entity Relationship Modelling*, Wokingham: Addison-Wesley

Barr, A. and Feigenbaum, E. (1981) *The Handbook of Artificial Intelligence* (3 vols.), Pitman

Basden, A. (1990a) Towards a Methodology for Building Expert Systems I, *Codex* **2**(1) 15–19, Uxbridge: Creative Logic Ltd

Basden, A. (1990b) Towards a Methodology for Building Expert Systems II, *Codex* **2**(2) 19–23, Uxbridge: Creative Logic Ltd

Bass, L., Clements, P. and Kazman, R. (1998) *Software Architecture in Practice*, Reading MA: Addison-Wesley

Bassett, P.G. (1997) *Framing Software Reuse*, Upper Saddle River NJ: Prentice Hall

Beck, K. (1993) A Short Introduction to Pattern Languages, *Smalltalk Report* February

Beck, K. (1997) *Smalltalk Best Practice Patterns*, Upper Saddle River NJ: Prentice Hall

Beck, K. (2000) *Extreme Programming Explained: embrace change*, Reading MA: Addison-Wesley

Beck, K. and Cunningham, W. (1989) A Laboratory for Teaching Object-Oriented Thinking. In Meyrowitz (1989)

Beck, K. and Fowler, M. (2000) *Planning Extreme Programming*, Reading MA: Addison-Wesley

Beech, D. (1987) Groundwork for an Object-Oriented Database Model. In Shriver and Wegner (1987)

Beech, D. (1992) Relational versus Object DBMS, lecture notes, Object World, July 1992, San Francisco.

Belcher, K. (1991) Object-orientation: The COBOL approach, *Object Magazine* **1**(1) 74–83

Bell, D.A., Shao, J. and Hull, M.E.C. (1990) Integrated Deductive Database System Implementation: A Systematic Study, *Computer Journal* **33**(1), 40–48

Bellman, R. and Zadeh, L.A. (1970) Decision Making in a Fuzzy Environment, *Management Science* **17**(4), 141–164

Berard, E.V. (1993) *Essays on Object-Oriented Software Engineering – Volume 1*, Englewood Cliffs NJ: Prentice Hall

Berliner, H. (1981) The B* Tree Search Algorithm: A Best-first Proof Procedure. In Webber, B.L. and Nilsson, N.J. (Eds.) *Readings in Artificial Intelligence*, Tioga Publishing Company.

Beyer, H. and Holtzblatt, K. (1997) *Contextual Design: Defining Customer-Centred Systems*, New York: Morgan Kaufmann

Bezivin, J. amd Meyer, B. (1991) *TOOLS4: Proceedings of the fourth international conference on the Technology of Object-Oriented Languages and Systems*, Englewood Cliffs NJ: Prentice Hall

Bezivin, J., Hullot, J-M., Cointe, P. and Leiberman, H. (Eds.) (1987) *ECOOP'87 European Conference on object-oriented programming*, Lecture Notes in Computer Science 276, Berlin: Springer Verlag

Biggerstaff, T. and Richter, C. (1989) Re-usability Framework, Assessment and Directions, *Tutorial: Software Reuse – Emerging Technology*, IEEE Computer Society, EH0278-2, 3–11

Bigus, J.P. and Bigus, J. (1998) *Constructing Intelligent Agents with JAVA*, New York: Wiley

Birrel, N.D. and Ould, M.A. (1985) *A Practical Handbook for Software Development*, Cambridge: University Press

Birtwistle, G.M. (1979) *Discrete Event Modelling On Simula*, London: MacMillan

Blaauw, G.A. (1970) Hardware Requirements for the Fourth Generation. In Greunberger, F. (Ed.) *Fourth Generation Computers*, Englewood Cliffs N.J: Prentice Hall

Black, A., Hutchinson, N., Jul, E. and Levy, H. (1986) Object Structure in the Emerald System. In Meyrowitz (1986), 78–87

Blaha, M. and Premerlani, W. (1998) *Object-Oriented Modelling and Design for Database Applications*, Upper Saddle River NJ: Prentice Hall

Blair, G., Gallagher, J., Hutchison, D. and Shepherd, D. (1991) *Object-Oriented Languages, Systems and Applications*, London: Pitman

Blum, A. (1992) *Neural Networks in C++: An object-oriented framework for building connectionist systems*, New York: Wiley

Blum, B.I. (1996) *Beyond Programming: To a New Era of Design*, New York: Oxford University Press

Blum, B.I. (1998) *Software Engineering: A Holistic Approach*, New York: Oxford University Press

Boar, B. (1984) *Application Prototyping: A Requirements Definition Strategy for the 80s*, New York: Wiley

Bobrow, D. G. and Stefik, M. (1983) *The LOOPS Manual*, Xerox Corporation

Bobrow, D. G. and Winograd, T. (1977) An Overview of KRL, A Knowledge Representation Language, *Cognitive Science* **1**(1), 3–46. Also in Brachman and Levesque (1985)

Bobrow, D., Kahn, K., Kiczales, G., Masiuter, L., Stefik, M. and Zdybel, F. (1986) CommonLOOPS: Merging Lisp and object-oriented programming. In Meyrowitz (1986), 17–29

Bodkin, T. and Graham, I.M. (1989) Case Studies of Expert Systems Development using Microcomputer Software Packages, *Expert Systems* **6**(1), 12–16.

Boehm, B.W. (1981) *Software Engineering Economics*, Englewood Cliffs NJ: Prentice Hall

Booch, G. (1982) Object-Oriented Design, *Ada Letters* **1**(3), 64–76

Booch, G. (1986) Object-Oriented Development, *IEEE Trans. on Software Eng.*, Vol SE-12(2), 211–221

Booch, G. (1987a) *Software Engineering with ADA* (2nd Edition), Benjamin Cummings

Booch, G. (1987b) *Software Components with ADA*, Benjamin Cummings

Booch, G. (1990) On the Concepts of Object-Oriented Design. In Ng, P.A. and Yeh, R.T. (Eds.) *Modern Software Engineering: Foundations and Current Perspectives*, Van Nostrand, New York, 165–204

Booch, G. (1991) *Object Oriented Design with Applications*, Benjamin/Cummings

Booch, G. (1994) *Object Oriented Design with Applications*, 2nd Edition, CA: Benjamin/Cummings

Booch, G. (1999) Software Architecture and the UML, keynote presentation to *UML World*

Booch, G., Rumbaugh, J. and Jacobson, I. (1999) *The Unified Modelling Language User Guide*, Reading MA: Addison-Wesley

Boose, J.H. (1986) *Expertise Transfer for Expert Systems Design*, Amsterdam: Elsevier

Boose, J.H. and Bradshaw, J.M. (1988) Expertise Transfer and Complex Problems: Using AQUINAS as Knowledge Acquisition Workbench for Knowledge Based Systems. In Boose, J.H. and Gaines, B.R. (Eds.) *Knowledge Acquisition Tools for Expert Systems*, Academic Press

Boose, J.H. and Gaines, B.R. (Eds.) (1988) *Knowledge Acquisition for Knowledge Based Systems*, Academic Press

Borenstein, N.S. (1990) *Multimedia Applications Development with the Andrew Toolkit*, Englewood Cliffs NJ: Prentice Hall

Borenstein, N.S. (1991) *Programming as if People Mattered: Friendly Programs, Software Engineering, and Other Noble Delusions*, Princeton NJ: Princeton University Press

Borning, A. and Ingalls, D. (1982) A type declaration and inference system for Smalltalk. In *Proc. of 9th Annual ACM Symposium on Principles of Programming Languages* (Albuquerque, NMex, Jan) New York: ACM, 133–141

Bosch, J. (2000) *Design and Use of Software Architectures*, Harlow, England: Addison-Wesley

Brachman, R.J. (1983) What IS-A is and isn't: an analysis of taxonomic links in semantic networks, *IEEE Computer* **16**(10), 30–36

Brachman, R.J. and Levesque, H.J. (1985) *Readings in Knowledge Representation*, Morgan Kaufmann

Bradley, N. (2000) *The XSL Companion*, Harlow, England: Addison-Wesley

Braithwaite, R.B. (1953) *Scientific Explanation*, Cambridge: University Press

Braune, R. and Foshay, W.R. (1983) Towards a practical model of cognitive information processing, task analysis and schema acquisition for complex problem solving situations, *Instructional Science* **12**, 121–145

Bretl, R., Maier, D., Otis, A., Penney, J. *et al.* (1989) *The GemStone Data Management System*. In Kim, W. and Lochovsky, F.H. (Eds.) (1989)

Brice, A. (1993) Using models in analysis, *Computing* 27th May 1993, p. 41

Brodie, M.L. and Mylopoulos, J. (Eds.) (1986) *On Knowledge Base Management Systems*, Berlin: Springer-Verlag

Brodie, M.L., Mylopoulos, J. and Schmidt, J.W. (Eds.) (1984) *On Conceptual Modelling*, Berlin: Springer-Verlag

Brooks, F. (1975) *The Mythical Man Month*, Reading MA: Addison-Wesley

Brooks, F. (1986) No Silver Bullet: Essence and Accidents of Software Engineering. In H.-J. Kluger (Ed.) *Information Processing '86*, Amsterdam: Elsevier

Brown, A.W. (1991) *Object-Oriented Databases and their Applications to Software Engineering*, London: McGraw Hill

Brown, R.G. (1992) Adding business rules to data models, *Data Base Newsletter* **20**(6)

Brown, W. (1993) Object-Oriented Testing, Proceedings of Object Technology 93, BCS OOPS Group annual conference

Brown, W., Malveau, R., McCormick, H. and Mowbray, T. (1998) *AntiPatterns: Refactoring Software Architectures and Project in Crisis*, New York: Wiley

Browne, D. (1994) *STUDIO: STructured User interface Design for Interaction Optimisation*, London: Prentice Hall

Bruce, T.A. (1992) Simplicity and complexity in the Zachman framework, *Database Newsletter* **20**(3), 3–11

Brynjolfsson, E. (1993) The productivity paradox in information technology, *Communications of the ACM* **36**(12), 67–77

Buchanan, B. and Shortliffe, E. (1984) *Rule-Based Expert Systems: The MYCIN Experiments of the Stanford Heuristic Programming Project*, Reading MA: Addison-Wesley

Budd, T. (1998) *Understanding Object-Oriented Programming with JAVA*, Reading MA: Addison-Wesley

Buhr, R.J.A. (1984) *System Design with Ada*, Englewood Cliffs NJ: Prentice Hall

Buhr, R.J.A.and Casselman, R.S. (1996) *Use Case Maps for Object-Oriented Systems*, Englewood Cliffs NJ: Prentice Hall

Bulman, D.(1991) Refining candidate objects, *Computer Language* Jan. 1991, 30–39

Burstall, R.M., McQueen, D.B. and Sannella, D.T. (1980) HOPE: An experimental applicative language, Internal Report CSR-62-80, University of Edinburgh

Buschmann, F., Meunier, R., Rohnert, H., Sommerlad, P. and Stal, M. (1996) *Pattern-oriented Software Architecture: A System of Patterns*, Chichester, England: Wiley

Bush, V. (1945) As We May Think, *Atlantic Monthly* **176**(1), 101–108

Butler, A. and Chamberlain, G. (1988) The ARIES Club: Experience Of Expert Systems In Insurance and Investment. In Moralee, D.S. (Ed.) *Research And Development In Expert Systems IV*, Cambridge University Press

Cain, B. and Coplien, J.O. (1993) A rôle-based empirical process modeling environment, *Proc. 2nd Int. Conf. on Software Process*, Berlin

Cameron, J. (1992) Ingredients for a New Object-Oriented Method: Development process, shared object modelling and GUI design will integrate OT and MIS, *Object Magazine* **2(4)**, 64–67

Cant, S.N., Jeffrey, D.R. and Henderson-Sellers, B. (1992) A conceptual model of cognitve complexity of elements of the programming process, *Inf. Software Technology* (to appear)

Card, D.N. and Glass, R.L. (1990) *Measuring Software Design Quality*, Englewood Cliffs NJ: Prentice Hall

Card, S.K., Moran, T.P. and Newell, A. (1983) *The Psychology of Human Computer Interaction*, Hillsdale NJ: Lawrence Erlbaum

Cardelli, L. and Wegner, P. (1985) On Understanding Types, Data Abstraction and Polymorphism, *ACM Computing Surveys* **17**(4), 471–522

Cardenas, A. and McLeod, D. (Eds.) (1990) *Research Foundations on Object-Oriented Databases*, Englewood Cliffs NJ: Prentice Hall

Carey, J., Carlson, B. and Graser, T. (2000) *San Francisco Design Patterns*, Reading MA: Addison-Wesley

Carmichael, A. (1994) *Approaches to Object-Oriented Analysis and Design*, London: Gower Press

Carrington, D., Duke, D., Duke, R., King, P., Rose, G. and Smith, G. (1990) Object-Z: An object-oriented extension to Z. In *Formal Description Techniques II*, Amsterdam: North-Holland

Carroll, J.M. (1995) *Scenario-Based Design*, Chichester, England: Wiley

Cato, J. (2000) User Centred Interface Design, Harlow, England: Addison-Wesley

Cattell, R.G.G. (1991) *Object Data Management: Object-Oriented and Extended Relational Database Systems*, Reading MA: Addison-Wesley

Cattell, R.G.G. and Skeen, J. (1990) Engineering Database Benchmark, Technical Report, Sun Microsystems, Mountain View CA

Cattell, R. (Ed.) (1994) *The Object Database Standard: ODMG-93,* San Mateo, CA: Morgan Kaufmann Publishers

Champeaux, D. de (1997) *Object-Oriented Development Process and Metrics*, Upper Saddle River NJ: Prentice Hall

Champeaux, D. de, Lea, D. and Faure, P. (1993) *Object-Oriented System Development*, Reading MA: Addison-Wesley

Chan, A., Dayal, U. Fox, S. and Ries, D. (1983) Supporting a Semantic Data Model in a Distributed Database System. In *Proceedings of the 9th International Conference on Very Large Databases*, Very Large Database Endowment, Saratoga, CA, 354–363

Charniak, E. and McDermott, D. (1985) *Introduction to Artificial Intelligence*, Reading MA: Addison-Wesley

Chaudhri, A.B. and Osmon, P. (1996) A Comparative Evaluation of the Major Commercial Object and Object-Relational DBMSs, Technical Report, London, England: City University

Checkland, P. (1981) *Systems Thinking, Systems Practice*, Chichester: Wiley

Checkland, P. and Scholes, J. (1991) *Soft Systems Methodology in Action*, Chichester, England: Wiley

Cheesman, J. and Daniels, J. (2000) *Component Modeling with UML*, Harlow, England: Addison-Wesley

Chen, P. (1976) The Entity-Relationship Model: Toward a Unified View of Data, *ACM Transactions on Database Systems* **1**(1), 9–36

Cheng, J. and Jones, C. (1990) On the usability of logics which handle partial functions. In Morgan, C and Woodcock, J. (Eds) *Proc. 3rd Refinement Workshop*, Berlin: Springer.

Chidamber, S.R. and Kemerer, C.F. (1991) Towards a metrics suite for object-oriented design. In Paepcke, A. (Ed.) *OOPSLA'91 ACM Conference on Object-Oriented Programming Systems, Languages and Applications*, Reading MA: Addison-Wesley

Chidamber, S.R. and Kemerer, C.F. (1993) A metrics suite for object-oriented design, CISR Working Paper 249, MIT Sloan School of Management, Cambridge MA

Chidamber, S.R. and Kemerer, C.F. (1994) A metrics suite for object-oriented design, *IEEE Trans. Software Engineering* **20**, 476–493

Chomsky, N. (1980) *Rules and Representations*, Oxford: Basil Blackwell

Chorafas, D.N. and Steinmann, H. (1993) *Object-Oriented Databases: An Introduction*, Englewood Cliffs NJ: Prentice Hall

Clausewitz, C. von (1968) *On War*, Rapoport translation of 1908, Harmondsworth: Penguin Books

Coad, P. (1992) Object-Oriented Patterns, *Comms. ACM* **35**(9), 152–158

Coad, P., LeFebvre, E. and DeLuca, J. (1999) *Java Modeling in Color with UML*, Upper Saddle River NJ: Prentice Hall

Coad, P. and Nicola, J. (1993) *Object-Oriented Programming*, Englewood Cliffs NJ:Yourdon Press/Prentice Hall

Coad, P., North, D. and Mayfield, M. (1997) *Object Models: Strategies, Patterns and Applications*, Upper Saddle River NJ:Prentice Hall

Coad, P. and Yourdon, E. (1990) *Object-Oriented Analysis*, 1st Edition, Englewood Cliffs NJ:Yourdon Press/Prentice Hall

Coad, P. and Yourdon, E. (1991a) *Object-Oriented Analysis*, 2nd Edition, Englewood Cliffs NJ:Yourdon Press/Prentice Hall

Coad, P. and Yourdon, E. (1991b) *Object-Oriented Design*, Englewood Cliffs NJ:Yourdon Press/Prentice Hall

Cockburn, A. (1997) Using goal-based use cases, *J. Object-Oriented Programming* **10**(5)

Codd, E.F. (1976) A Relational Model of Data for Large Shared Data Banks, *Comm. of the ACM* **13**(6), 377–387

Codd, E.F. (1985) Is Your Relational Database Management System Really Relational?, Oracle Users' Conference, San Diego, California

Colbert, E. (1994) The OOSD Method: Requirements analysis with object-oriented software development. In Carmichael (1994)

Coleman, D. and Hayes, F. (1991) Lessons from Hewlett-Packard's experience of using object-oriented technology. In Bezivin and Meyer (1991)

Coleman, D., Arnold, P., Bodoff, S., Dollin, C., Gilchrist, H., Hayes, F. and Jeremaes, P. (1994) *Object-Oriented Development: The Fusion Method*, Hemel Hempstead, England: Prentice Hall

Collins, H.M. (1990) *Artificial Experts: Social knowledge and intelligent machines*, Cambridge MA, MIT Press

Comer, D.E. (1999) *Computer Networks and Internets*, 2nd Edition, Upper Saddle River NJ: Prentice Hall

Connell, J.L and Shafer, L.B. (1989) *Structured Rapid Prototyping: An Evolutionary Approach*, Yourdon Press

Constantine, L.L. (1995) Essential modeling: use cases for user interfaces, *Interactions* (ACM), **2**(2)

Constantine, L.L. and Lockwood, L. (1999) *Software for Use: Models and Methods of Usage-Centred Design*, Reading MA: Addison-Wesley

Cook, S. (Ed.) (1989) *ECOOP'89 European Conference on Object-Oriented Programming*, Cambridge University Press

Cook, S. (1994) Analysis, Design, Programming: What's the Difference? In O'Callaghan, A.J. and Leigh, M. (Eds.) *Object Technology Transfer*, Henley-on-Thames: Alfred Waller

Cook, S. and Daniels, J. (1992) Essential techniques for object-oriented design, *Proceedings of OOPS-59*, London: BCS OOPS Group

Cook, S. and Daniels, J. (1994) *Designing Object Systems*, Hemel Hempstead, England: Prentice Hall

Cook, W. (1989) A Denotational Semantics of Inheritance and its Correctness. In Meyrowitz (1989)

Cooper, J.W. (2000) *Java Design Patterns*, Reading MA: Addison-Wesley

Coplien, J.O. (1992) *Advanced C++: Programming Styles and Idioms*, Reading MA: Addison-Wesley

Coplien, J.O. (1995) A Generative Development-Process Pattern Language. In Coplien and Schmidt (1995)

Coplien, J. O. (1999) Reevaluating the Architectural Metaphor: Toward Piecemeal Growth, *IEEE Software* September/October, 40–44.

Coplien, J.O. and Schmidt, D. (Eds) (1995) *Pattern Languages of Program Design*, Reading NJ:Addison-Wesley

Costello, J. (1992) The shape of screens to come, *Computer Weekly*, 27 August 1992

Coutaz, J. (1987) *PAC, an Object-Oriented Model for Implementing User Interfaces*, Laboratoire de Genie Informatique, University de Grenoble, BP 68

Cox, B.J. (1986) *Object-Oriented Programming – An Evolutionary Approach*, Reading MA: Addison-Wesley

Cox, B.J. and Novobilski, A. (1991) *Object-Oriented Programming – An Evolutionary Approach*, 2nd Edition, Reading MA: Addison-Wesley

Cox, E. (1994) *The Fuzzy Systems Handbook: A practitioner's guide to building, using and maintaining fuzzy systems*, Boston: Academic Press

Cross, V. (1996) A unifying framework for the fuzzy object model, *Proc. 5th IEEE International Conf. on Fuzzy Systems*, New Orleans LA, 1358–1365

Cross, V. and Firat, A. (2000) Fuzzy objects for geographic information system, *Fuzzy Sets and Systems* **113**(1), 19–36

D'Souza, D.F. (1992) Dynamic Modelling of Object-Oriented Systems, *Proceedings of OOP'93/C++ World, Munchen 1993*, New York: SIGS Publications

D'Souza, D.F. (1997) Framework and Component Based Design, Tutorial Notes, Object Expo Europe '97

D'Souza, D.F. and Wills, A.C. (1999) *Objects, Components and Frameworks with UML: The Catalysis Approach*, Reading MA: Addison-Wesley

Dadam, P. (1988) *Research and Development Trends in Relational Databases (NF2 Relations)*, IBM Scientic Centre, Heidelberg

Dahl, O.J. (1987) Object-Oriented Specification. In Shriver and Wegner (1987), 561–576

Dahl, O.J. and Nygaard, K. (1966) SIMULA – An Algol-based Simulation Language, *Comm. of the ACM* **9**, 671–678

Dahl, O.J., Myrhaug, B. and Nygaard, K. (1968) *SIMULA 67 Common Base Language*, Norwegian Computing Centre, Oslo

Dalton, R. (1992) Predicting the Cost of a Sale, *Software Management*, March 1992

Danforth, S. and Tomlinson, C. (1988) Type Theories and Object-Oriented Programming, *ACM Computing Surveys* **20**(1), 29–72

Daniels, J. and Cook, S. (1993) Strategies for sharing objects in distributed systems, *JOOP*, **5**(8), 27–36

Daniels, J. (2000) Component contracts, keynote lecture at TOOLS Europe.

Daniels, P.J. (1986) The user modelling function of an intelligent interface for document retrieval systems. In Brookes, B.C. (Ed.) (1986) *IRFIS 6: Intelligent Information Systems for the Information Society*, Amsterdam: North Holland, 162–176

Date, C.J. (1981) *An Introduction to Database Systems*, 3rd Edition, Reading MA: Addison-Wesley

Date, C.J. (1983) *An Introduction to Database Systems*, Volume II, Reading MA: Addison-Wesley

Davenport, T.H. (1993) *Process Innovation: Reengineering work through information technology*, Harvard: Business School Press

Davenport, T.H. and Short, J.E. (1990) The New Industrial Engineering: Information Technology and Business Process Redesign, *Sloan Management Review*, Summer 1990, 11–27

Davis, A.M. (1993) *Software Requirements: Objects, Functions and States, Revision*, Englewood Cliffs NJ: Prentice Hall

Davis, R. and Lenat, D.B. (1982) *Knowledge Based Systems in Artificial Intelligence*, NY: McGraw Hill

Dedene, G. (1994) M.E.R.O.D.E. and the practical realization of object-oriented business models. In Carmichael (1994)

Deitel, H.M. and Deitel, P.J. (1994) *C++ How to Program*, Englewood Cliffs NJ: Prentice Hall

Delobel, C., Lécluse, C. and Richard, P. (1995*) Databases: From Relational to Object-Oriented Systems*, International Thompson Publishing

DeMarco, T. (1982) *Controlling Software Projects*, Yourdon Press

Demers, A.J. and Donahue, J.E. (1979) Revised report on Russell. TR79-389, Dept. of Computer Science, Cornell University, Ithaca NY

Desfray, P. (1992) *Ingénerie des objets: Approche classe-relation application à C++*. Paris: Editions Masson.

Devlin, K. (1991) *Logic and Information*, Cambridge: University Press

Diaper, D. (1993) CSCW: Psychology, sociology ... and computing, *Computer Bulletin*, February 1993, 22–25

Diaper, D. and Sanger, C. (Eds.) (1993) *CSCW in Practice: An introduction and case studies*, London: Springer-Verlag

Dick, K. and Swett, A. (1995) Objectivity/DB. *Object Magazine* **5**(5), 82–84

Dietrich, W.C., Nackman, L.R. and Gracer, F. (1989) Saving a Legacy with Objects. In Meyrowitz (1989)

Dillon, T. and Tan, P.L. (1993) *Object-Oriented Conceptual Modeling*, Sydney NSW: Prentice Hall

Dorfman, L. (1990) Object-Oriented Assembly Language, Pennsylvania: Windcrest

Dorfman, M. and Thayer, R.H. (1990) *Standards, Guidelines and Examples on System and Software Requirements Engineering*, Los Alamitos, CA: IEEE Computer Society Press

Douglass, B.P. (1998) *Real-Time UML*, Reading MA: Addison-Wesley

Dreyfus, H.L. and Dreyfus, S.E. (1986) *Mind over Machine: The power of human intuition and expertise in the era of the computer*, Oxford: Basil Blackwell

Dubois, D. and Prade, H. (1980) *Fuzzy Sets and Systems: Theory and Applications*, Academic Press

Dubois, D., Prade, H. and Rossazza, J.P (1991) Vagueness, typicality and uncertainty in class hierarchies, *J. of Intelligent Systems* **6**, 167–183

Duda, R., Hart, P. *et al.*, (1976) *Development of the PROSPECTOR consultation system for mineral exploration*, SRI report projects 5822 and 6415, Menlo Park CA: SRI International

Dugundji, J. (1966) *Topology*, Boston MA: Allyn and Bacon

Duke, R., King, P., Rose, G. and Smith, G. (1991) *The Object-Z Specification, Version 1*, Software Verification Research Centre, University of Queensland Technical Report 91–1

Durham, A. (1992a) *IT Horizons* **1**(3)

Durham, A. (1992b) BETA: The pattern language, *Object Magazine* **2**(4) 82–83

Durr, E. (1992) VDM++: A formal specification language for object-oriented designs. In DeWilde and Vandewalle (Eds.) *IEEE CompEuro 92 Proceedings*, IEEE Press

Eason, K.D. (1989) Tools for participation: How managers and users can influence design. In Knight, K. (Ed) *Participation in Systems Development*, London: Kogan Page

Eastlake, J.J. (1987) *A Structured Approach to Computer Strategy*, Chichester: Ellis Horwood

Eckel, B. (1989) *Using C++*, Osborne-McGraw Hill

Edwards, J. (1989) Lessons learned in more than ten years of practical application of the Object-Oriented Paradigm, *Proceedings of CASExpo-Europe*, London

Edwards, J.S. (1991) *Building Knowledge Based Systems*, London: Pitman

Ege, R., Singh, M. and Meyer, B. (Eds.) (1993) *TOOLS8: Proceedings of the eighth international conference on the Technology of Object-Oriented Languages and Systems*, New York: Prentice Hall

Ehn, P. (1988) *Work-oriented Design of Computer Artifacts*, Arbetslivscentrum, Stockholm

Ehn, P., Mollervd, B. and Sjogren, D. (1990) Playing in reality: a paradigm case, *Scand. J. Inf. Systems* **2**, 101–120

Ehn, P. and Kyng, M. (1991) Cardboard computers: mocking up hands-on-the future. In Greenbaum, J. and Kyng, M. (Eds) *Design at Work: Co-operative Design of Computer Systems*, Hillsdale NJ: Lawrence Erlbaum

Eliëns, A. (1992) An object-oriented approach to distributed problem solving. In Bramer, M.A. and Milne, R.W. (Eds.) *Research and Development in Expert Systems IX*, Cambridge University Press

Ellis, M.A. and Stroustrup, B. (1990) *The Annotated C++ Reference Manual*, Reading MA: Addison-Wesley

Elmasri, R. and Navathe, S.B. (1989) *Fundamentals of Database Systems*, Benjamin/Cummings

Elmore, P., Shaw, G.M. and Zdonik, S.B. (1989) The ENCORE object-oriented data model, Technical Report, Brown University

Embley, D.W., Kurtz, B.D. and Woodfield, S.N. (1992) *Object-Oriented Systems Analysis: A Model-Driven Approach*, Englewood Cliffs: Yourdon Press

Emmerich, W. and Schäfer, W. (1993) Dedicated object management system benchmarks for software engineering applications. *Proc. Software Engineering Environments*, 130–142, Reading, England

Englebart, D. (1963) A Conceptual Framework for the Augmentation of Man's Intellect. In Howerton, P.W. and Weeks, D.C. (Eds.) *Vistas in Information Handling*, Vol 1, Spartan Books, Washington

Englebart, D. and English, W.K. (1968) A Research Centre for Augmenting Human Intellect. In *Proceedings of the 1968 AFIPS Conference*, AFIPS Press – Montale NJ, 395–410

Englemore, D. and Morgan, A. (Eds.) (1988) *Blackboard Systems*, Wokingham, England: Addison-Wesley

Ericsson, K.A. and Simon, H.A. (1984) *Protocol Analysis: Verbal Reports as Data*, Bradford Books

Ersavas, T. (1999) Squeak as a development platform, *Proc. OOPSLA '99*, Reading MA: Addison-Wesley

Ewald, A. and Roy, M. (1993) Why OT is good for system integration, *Object Magazine* **2**(5), 60–63

Fagan, M. (1974) Design and Code Inspections and Process Control in the Development of Programs, IBM Report IBM-SDD-TR-21-572

Farhoodi, F. (1994) CADDIE: an advanced tool for organizational design and process modelling. In *Software Assistance for Business Re-Engineering*, Chichester: Wiley

Feigenbaum, E. McCorduck and Nii, H.P. (1988) *The Rise of the Expert Company*, London: Macmillan

Ferber, J. (1995) *Les Systèmes Multi-Agents: Vers une intelligence collective*, Paris: InterEditions

Fichman, R.G. and Kemerer, C.F. (1993) Adoption of Software Engineering Process Innovations: The Case of Object-Orientation, *Sloan Management Review*, Winter 1993, 7–22

Fiedler, S.P. (1989) Object-Oriented Unit Testing, *Hewlett-Packard Journal*, April 1989, 69–74

Firesmith, D.G. (1993) *Object-Oriented Requirements Analysis and Design: A Software Engineering Approach*, Chichester: Wiley

Firesmith, D.G., Henderson-Sellers, B. and Graham, I.M. (1997) *OPEN Modeling Language Reference Manual*, NY: SIGS Books, Cambridge University Press

Fishman, D.H., *et al.* (1989) *Overview of the IRIS DBMS*. In Kim, W. and Lochovsky, F.H. (Eds.) (1989)

Flanagan, D. (1996) *Java in a Nutshell*, Bonn: O'Reilly & Associates

Flores, F. (1997) The leaders of the future. In Denning, P.J. and Metcalfe, R.M. (Eds.) *Beyond Calculation: The next 50 years of computing*, New York: Copernicus

Foley, J., Kim, W., Kovavavics, S. and Murray, K. (1989) Defining Interfaces at a High Level of Abstraction, *IEEE Software* **6**(1), 25–32

Forgy, C.L. (1981) The OPS5 User's Manual, Tech Rep CMU-CS-81-135 Computer Science Dept, Carnegie-Mellon University.

Forsythe, R. (Ed.) (1989a) *Expert Systems: Principles and Case Studies* (2nd Edition), London: Chapman & Hall

Forsythe, R. (Ed.) (1989b) *Machine Learning*, London: Chapman & Hall

Foster, I. and Taylor, S. (1990) *Strand: New Concepts in Parallel Programming*, Englewood Cliffs NJ: Prentice Hall

Fowler, M. (1996) *Analysis Patterns*, Harlow, England: Addison-Wesley

Fowler, M. (1997) *UML Distilled,* 2nd Edition, Harlow, England: Addison-Wesley

Fowler, M. (2000) *Refactoring*, Reading MA: Addison-Wesley

Fowler, M. and Capey, A. (1991) The use of object-oriented analysis to define a generic model for health care, *Proceedings of SCOOP Europe*, London 1991

Friedman, J. (1993) New Options for Object Databases, *Object Magazine* **2**(6)

Futatsugi, K., Goguen, J., Jouannaud, J-P. and Meseguer, J. (1985) Principles of OBJ2, *Proceedings of the 12th Annual Symposium on Principles of Programming Languages*, ACM, New York, 52–66

Gabriel, R.P (1996) *Patterns of Software*, Oxford: University Press

Gaines, B. and Shaw, M. (1992) Documents as Expert Systems. In Bramer, M. and Milne, R. (Eds.) *Research and Development in Expert Systems IX*, Cambridge University Press

Galitz, W. (1981) *Human Factors in Office Automation*, Atlanta, GA: Life Office Management Association

Gamma, E. (1992) *Object-Oriented Software Development Based on ET++: Design Patterns, Class Library, Tools* (in German). Berlin: Springer-Verlag

Gamma, E., Helm, R. Johnson, R. and Vlissedes, J. (1995) *Design Patterns: Elements of Reusable Object-Oriented Software*, Reading MA: Addison-Wesley

Gane, C. (1990) *Computer-Aided Software Engineering: The Methodologies, the Products and the Future*, Englewood Cliffs NJ: Prentice Hall

Gardner, K., Rush, A., Crist, M., Konitzer, R. and Teegarden, B. (1998) *Cognitive Patterns*, Cambridge: University Press

Gause, D. and Weinberg, G. (1989) *Exploring Requirements*, New York NY: Dorset House

Gilb, T. and Graham, D. (1993) *Software Inspection*, Wokingham: Addison-Wesley

Giles, R. (1976) Lukasiewitz Logic and Fuzzy Theory, *Int. J. Man–Machine Studies* **8**

Gjessing, S. and Nygaard, K. (Eds.) (1988) *ECOOP'88 European Conference on Object-Oriented Programming*, Lecture Notes in Computer Science 276, Berlin: Springer Verlag

Glass, G. and Schuchert, B. (1996) *The STL Primer*, Upper Saddle River NJ: Prentice Hall

Goguen, J. and Meseguer, J. (1986) EQLog: Equality, Types and Geric Modules for Logic Programming. In DeGroot, D. and Lindstrom, G. (Eds.) *Logic Programming*, Englewood Cliffs NJ: Prentice Hall

Goguen, J. and Meseguer, J. (1987) Unifying Functional, Object-Oriented and Relational Programming with Logical Semantics. In Shriver and Wegner (1987)

Gohil, N. (1988) Object-Oriented Database Management, Unpublished Bachelor's thesis, Imperial College of Science and Technology

Goldberg, A. (1984) *Smalltalk-80: The Interactive Programming Environment*, Reading MA: Addison-Wesley

Goldberg, A. and Robson, D. (1983) *Smalltalk-80: The Language and its Implementation*, Reading MA: Addison-Wesley

Goldberg, A. and Rubin, K. (1995) *Succeeding with Objects*, Reading MA: Addison-Wesley

Goldberg, D.E. (1989) *Genetic Algorithms in Search, Optimization and Machine Learning*, Reading MA: Addison-Wesley

Goldfarb, C.F. and Prescod, P. (1998) *The XML Handbook*, Upper Saddle River, NJ: Prentice Hall

Goodall, A. (1994) The year of the agent, *AI Watch* **3**(8), 1–10

Goodwin, M. (1989) *User Interfaces in C++ and Object-Oriented Programming*, Cambridge MA: MIT Press

Gorman, K. and Choobineh, J. (1989) The Object-Oriented Entity-Relationship Model (OOERM), *J. Man. Info. Systems* **33**(9), 41–65

Gosling, A., Joy, B. and Steele, G. (1996) *The Java Language Specification*, Reading MA: Addison-Wesley

Graham, I.M. (1987) Expert Systems find an Ideal Setting, *Banking Technology*, July 1987, 17–24

Graham, I.M. (1991a) *Object-Oriented Methods,* 1st Edition, Wokingham, England: Addison-Wesley

Graham, I.M. (1991b) Fuzzy Logic in Commercial Expert System Shells: Results and Prospects, *Fuzzy Sets and Systems* **40**(3) 451–472

Graham, I.M. (1991c) Corrigendum to Fuzzy Logic in Commercial expert systems – Results and Prospects, *Fuzzy Sets and Systems* **43**, 337–338

Graham, I.M. (1991d) Structured Prototyping for Requirements Specification in Conventional IT and Expert Systems, *Computing and Control Engineering Engineering Journal*, **2**(2) 82–89.

Graham, I.M. (1992a) A Method for Integrating Object Technology with Rules, *Proceedings of Advanced Information Systems 92*, Oxford, Learned Information

Graham, I.M. (1992b) Interoperation: Combining object-oriented applications with conventional IT, *Object Magazine* **2**(4), 36–37

Graham, I.M. (1992c) Interoperation: combining objects, *Object Magazine* **2**(4) 36–37

Graham, I.M. (1993a) Migration strategies column, *Object Magazine* **2**(5)–**3**(5).

Graham, I.M. (1993b) Migration using SOMA: A Semantically Rich Method of Object-Oriented Analysis, *Journal of Object-Oriented Programming* **5**(9), Feb. 1993

Graham, I.M. (1993c) On the Impossibility of Artificial Intelligence, *BCS Expert Systems Newsletter*

Graham, I.M. (1994a) *Object-Oriented Methods*, 2nd Edition, Wokingham: Addison-Wesley

Graham, I.M. (1994b) Beyond the Use Case: Combining task analysis and scripts in object-oriented requirements capture and business process re-engineering. In Magnusson, Meyer, Nerson and Perrot (1994)

Graham, I.M. (1994c) SOMA: Combining object-oriented analysis with rules and task analysis. In Carmichael (1994)

Graham, I.M. (1994d) On the Impossibility of Artificial Intelligence, *BCS Specialist Group in Expert Systems Newsletter*, Summer 1994

Graham, I.M. (1994e) Getting to number one with object technology, *Object Manager*, October 1994, 13–16

Graham, I.M. (1995) *Migrating to Object Technology*, Wokingham: Addison-Wesley

Graham, I.M. (1996) Task scripts, use cases and scenarios in object-oriented analysis, *Object-Oriented Systems* **3**(3), 1996, 123–142

Graham, I.M. (1998) *Requirements Engineering and Rapid Development: An Object-Oriented Approach*, Harlow, England: Addison-Wesley

Graham, I.M. and Jones, P.L.K. (1987) A Theory of Fuzzy Frames. In Moralee, D.S. (Ed.) *Research and Development in Expert Systems IV*, Cambridge University Press

Graham, I.M. and Jones, P.L.K. (1988) *Expert Systems: Knowledge, Uncertainty and Decision*, London: Chapman & Hall

Graham, I.M. and Milne, R.M. (Eds.) (1991) *Research and Development in Expert Systems X*, Cambridge University Press

Graham, I.M., Bischof, J. and Henderson-Sellers, B. (1997a) Associations considered a bad thing, *J. Object-Oriented Programming*, **9**(9)

Graham, I.M., Henderson-Sellers, B. and Yanoussi, H. (1997b) *The OPEN Process Specification*, Harlow, England: Addison-Wesley

Graham, I.M. and O'Callaghan, A. (1997) Migration Strategies, Tutorial Notes: Object World London.

Grand, M. (1998) *Patterns in Java – Volume 1*, New York: John Wiley

Grass, J.E. (1991) Design Archaeology for Object-Oriented Redesign in C++. In Korson *et al.* (1991)

Gray, P.M.D. (1984) *Logic, Algebra and Databases*, Chichester: Ellis Horwood

Gray, P.D. and Mohamed, R. (1990) *Smalltalk-80: A Practical Introduction*, London: Pitman

Gray, P.M.D. and Kemp, G.J.L. (1990) An OODB with entity-based persistence: a protein modelling application. In Addis, T.R. and Muir, R.M. (Eds.) *Research and Development in Expert Systems VII*, Cambridge University Press

Gray, P.M.D., Krishnarao, G.K. and Paton, N.W. (1992) *Object-Oriented Databases: A Semantic Data Model Approach,* Englewood Cliffs NJ: Prentice Hall

Greenberg, S. (1991) *Computer-supported Cooperative Work and Groupware*, New York: Academic Press

Gregory, R. (1983) Xanadu: Hypertext from the Future, *Dr. Dobbs Journal* **75**, 28–35

Grossmann, R. (1984) *Phenomenonology and Existentialism: An Introduction*, London: Routledge & Kegan Paul

Grotehen, T. (1995) Notes on a meeting with Grady Booch 1995.07.27 (unpublished communication)

Guilfoyle, C. and Warner, E. (1994) *Intelligent Agents: The New Revolution in Software*, Ovum Ltd

Gupta, R. and Horowitz, E (1991) *Object-Oriented Databases with Applications to CASE, Networks and VSLI CAD*, Englewood Cliffs NJ: Prentice Hall

Guttag, J., Horning, J.J. and Wing, J.M. (1985) *Larch in Five Easy Pieces*, Palo Alto CA: Digital Systems Research Centre

Haack, S. (1978) *Philosophy of Logics*, Cambridge: University Press

Halasz, F.G. (1988) Reflections on NoteCards: Seven Issues for the Next Generation of Hypermedia Systems, *Comm. of the ACM*, **31**(7), 836–852

Halliday, S. and Weibel, M. (1993) *Object-Oriented Software Engineering*, Englewood Cliffs NJ: Prentice Hall

Halmos, P. (1950) *Measure Theory*, New York: Van Nostrand

Halstead, M.H. (1977) *Elements of Software Science*, Amsterdam: North-Holland

Hammer, M. (1990) Reengineering Work: Don't Automate, Obliterate, *Harvard Business Review*, July–August, 104–112

Hammer M. and Champy, J. (1993) *Re-engineering the Corporation: A manifesto for the business revolution*, NY: Harper Collins

Hammer, M. and McLeod, D. (1978) The semantic data model: a modelling mechanism for database applications, *Proc. ACM SIGMOD*

Hammer, M. and McLeod, D. (1981) Database description with SDM: a semantic database model, *ACM Trans. on Database Systems* **6,** 351–386

Hansen, T.L. (1990) *The C++ Answer Book*, Reading MA: Addison-Wesley

Harel, D., (1987) Statecharts: A Visual Formalism for Complex Systems. In *Science of Computer Programming* **8**, 231–274, North Holland.

Harland, D.M. (1988) Rekursiv: *Object-Oriented Architecture*, Chichester: Wiley

Harland, D.M. and Drummond, B. (1991) REKURSIV – Object-Oriented Hardware. In Blair *et al.* (1991)

Harmon, P. and Taylor, D.A. (1993) *Objects in Action: Commercial applications of object-oriented technologies*, Reading MA: Addison-Wesley

Harrison, W. and Ossher, H. (1993) Subject-oriented programming, *Proc. OOPSLA'93*, 411–28, Reading MA: ACM Press

Hart, A. (1989) *Knowledge Acquisition for Expert Systems*, 2nd Edition, London: Kogan Page

Hayes, I. (Ed.) (1987) *Specification Case Studies*, Englewood Cliffs NJ: Prentice Hall

Hayes, P.J. (1985) The Logic of Frames. In Brachman and Levesque (1985)

Hayes-Roth, F., Waterman, D.A. and Lenat, D.B. (1983) *Building Expert Systems*, Reading MA: Addison-Wesley

Heeg, G., Magnusson, B. and Meyer, B. (Eds.) (1992) *TOOLS7: Proceedings of the seventh international conference on the Technology of Object-Oriented Languages and Systems*, New York: Prentice Hall

Heitz, M. (1988) HOOD: A Hierarchical Object-Oriented Design Method, *Proceedings of the 3rd German ADA Users Congress*, Munich, 12-1 – 12-9

Hekmatpour, S. (1987) Experience with Evolutionary Prototyping in a Large Software Project, *ACM Software Engineering Notes* **12**(1), 38–41

Hempel, C.G. (1966) *Philosophy of Natural Science*, Englewood Cliffs NJ: Prentice Hall.

Henderson-Sellers, B. (1992) *A BOOK of Object-Oriented Knowledge*, Sydney, Aus: Prentice Hall

Henderson-Sellers, B. (1993) The economics of reusing library classes, *JOOP* **6**(4), 43–50

Henderson-Sellers, B. (1996) *Object-Oriented Metrics: Measures of Complexity*, Sydney: Prentice Hall

Henderson-Sellers, B. (1998) OPEN relationships – associations, mappings, dependencies and uses, *Journal of Object-Oriented Programming* **10**(9), 49–57

Henderson-Sellers, B. and Constantine, L.L. (1991) Object-Oriented Development and Functional Decomposition, *Journal Of Object-Oriented Programming* **3**(9), 11–17

Henderson-Sellers, B. and Edwards, J.M. (1990) The Object-Oriented Systems Life Cycle, *Communications of the ACM* **33**(9), 143–159

Henderson-Sellers, B. and Edwards, J. (1994) *BOOK TWO of Object-Oriented Knowledge: The working object*, Sydney, Aus: Prentice Hall

Henderson-Sellers, B. and Pant, Y.R. (1993) Adopting the reuse mindset throughout the lifecycle, *Object Magazine* **3**(4), 73–75

Henderson-Sellers, B., Constantine, L.L. and Graham, I.M. (1996) Coupling and cohesion: towards a valid metrics suite for object-oriented analysis and design, *Object-Oriented Systems* **3**(3), 143–158

Henderson-Sellers, B., Simons, A. and Yanoussi, H. (1998) *The OPEN Toolbox of Techniques*, Harlow, England: Addison-Wesley

Henderson-Sellers, B., and Unhelkar, B. (2000) *OPEN Modelling with UML*, Harlow, England: Addison-Wesley

Hewitt, C. and de Jong, P. (1984) Open Systems. In Brodie *et al.* (1984)

Hickman, F.R., Killen, J., Land, L. *et al.* (1989) *Analysis for Knowledge-based Systems*, Chichester: Ellis Horwood

Hill, R.D. (1986) Supporting concurrency, communication and synchronization in human computer interaction – The Sassafras UIMS, *ACM Transaction on Graphics* **5**(3), 179–210

Hill, R.D. and Hermman, M. (1989) The structure of TUBE – A tool for implementing advanced interfaces, *Proceedings of Eurographics '89*, Amsterdam: North-Holland

Hillside Group (2000) http://www.hillside.net/patterns/, 15 June 2000

Hoare, C.A.R. (1974) Monitors: an operating system structuring concept, *Comms. ACM* **17**(10), 549–557

Hodgson, R. (1990) *Finding, Building and Reusing Objects*, Proceedings of Object Oriented Design, Unicom Seminars, Uxbridge

Hodgson, R. (1991) The X Model: A process model for object-oriented software development. In *Proc. of Toulouse'91* (Toulouse, France) 713–728

Hollowell, G. (1993) *Handbook of Object-Oriented Standards: The object model*, Reading MA: Addison-Wesley

Holsapple, C.W. and Whinston, A.B. (1986) *Manager's Guide to Expert Systems using Guru*, Dow Jones–Irwin

HOOD Working Group (1989) *HOOD Reference Manual*, Issue 3.0, European Space Agency, Noordwijk, Netherlands

Hood, R., Kennedy, K. and Muller, H. (1987) Efficient Recompilation of Module Interfaces in a Software Development Environment. In Henderson, P. (Ed.) *Proceedings of the ACM SIGSOFT/SIGPLAN Software Engineering Symposium on Practical Software Development Environments*, ACM Press, 180–189

Hook, J. (1984) Understanding Russell – A First Attempt. In Goos, G. and Hartmanis, J. (Eds.) *Semantics of Data Types*, Berlin: Springer-Verlag

Horty, J.F., Thomason, R.H. and Touretzky, D.S. (1990) A Skeptical Theory of Inheritance in Nonmonotonic Semantic Networks, *Artificial Intelligence* **42**, 311–348

Hu, D. (1989) *C/C++ Expert Systems*, Cambridge MA: MIT Press

Huhns, M.N. (1987) *Distributed Artificial Intelligence*, London: Pitman

Hull, R. and King, R. (1987) Semantic Database Modelling: Survey, Applications and Research Issues, *ACM Computing Surveys* **19**(3), 201–260

Humphrey, W.S. (1989) *Managing the Software Process*, Reading MA: Addison-Wesley

Hutchison, D. and Walpole, J. (1991) Distributed Systems and Objects. In Blair *et al.* (1991)

IBM (1991a) *Common User Access: Guide to User Interface Design*, Cary, NC: International Business Machines.

IBM (1991b) *Common User Access: Advanced Interface Design Reference*, Cary, NC: International Business Machines.

IBM (1992) *Object-Oriented Interface Design: CUA guidelines*, New York: QUE

IEL (1986) *Crystal User Manual*, Richmond, England: Intelligent Environments Limited

Ilvari, J. (1991) Object-Oriented Information Systems Analysis: A framework for object identification, *Trans. of the IEEE*, 205–218

Ince, D. (1991) *Object-Oriented Software Engineering with C++*, London: McGraw-Hill

Ingalls, D.H.H. (1978) *The Smalltalk-76 Programming System: Design and Implementation*, Fifth Annual ACM Symposium on Principles of Programming Languages, Tucson, Arizona

Ishikawa, Y. and Tokoro, M. (1987) Orient84/K: An Object-Oriented Concurrent Programming Language for Knowledge Representation. In Yonezawa and Tokoro (1987), 159–198

Jackson, M.A. (1983) *System Development*, Chichester, England: Prentice Hall

Jackson, M.A. (1995) *Software Requirements and Specifications*, Harlow, England: Addison-Wesley

Jackson, M.A. (1998) A Discipline of Description, *Requirements Engineering* **3**(2), 73–78

Jackson, M.A. (2001) *Problem Frames and Methods*, Harlow, England: Addison-Wesley

Jackson, P. (1986) *Introduction to Expert Systems*, Wokingham: Addison-Wesley

Jacobs, S. (1992) What is Business Process Automation?, *Expert Systems Applications*, August 1992, 5–10

Jacobson, I., Booch, G. and Rumbaugh, J. (1999) *The Unified Software Development Process*, Reading MA: Addison-Wesley

Jacobson, I., Christerson, M. Jonsson, P. and Overgaard, G. (1992) *Object-Oriented Software Engineering: A Use Case Driven Approach*, Wokingham: Addison-Wesley

Jacobson, I., Ericsson, M. and Jacobson, A. (1995) *The Object Advantage: Business Process Re-engineering with Object Technology*, Wokingham, England: Addison-Wesley

Jagannathan, D. *et al.* (1988) SIM: A database system based on the semantic data model, *Proc. ACM SIGMOD 88 Conf.*, 46–55

Jeffcoate, J., Hales, K. and Downes, V, (1989) *Object-Oriented Systems: The Commercial Benefits*, Ovum Ltd, London, ISBN 0-903969-42-4

Jeffries, R.E., Anderson, A. and Hendrickson, C. (2000) *Extreme Programming Installed*, Reading MA: Addison-Wesley

Johnson, P. (1992) *Human Computer Interaction: Psychology, Task Analysis and software engineering*, London: McGraw-Hill

Johnson, R.E. and Foote, B. (1988) Designing Reusable Classes, *Journal Of Object-Oriented Programming* **1**(2)

Jones, C. (1986) *Systematic Software Development using VDM*, Englewood Cliffs NJ: Prentice Hall

Jones, C. (1994) *Assessment and Control of Software Risks*, Englewood Cliffs NJ: Yourdon Press

Jones, C.B. (1980) *Software Development: A rigorous approach*, Englewood Cliffs, NJ: Prentice Hall

Jones, P.L.K. (1999) *Practical Rapid Development*, Harlow, England: Addison-Wesley

Jones, T.C. (1986) *Programming Productivity*, New York: McGraw-Hill

Jones, T.C. (1988) A short history of function points and feature points, ACI Computer Services

Jungclaus, R. (1993) *Modeling of Dynamic Object Systems*, Weisbaden: Vieweg

Kaehler, T. and Krasner, G. (1983) LOOM: Large Object-Oriented Memory for Smalltalk-80 Systems. In Krasner, G. (Ed.) *Smalltalk-80: Bits of History, Words of Advice*, Reading MA: Addison-Wesley

Kandel, A. (1986) *Fuzzy Mathematical Techniques with Applications*, Reading MA: Addison-Wesley

Kapor M. (1991) A Software Design Manifesto: Time for a Change, *Dr. Dobb's Journal* **172**, January, 62–68.

Kappel, G. (1991) Using an object-oriented diagram technique for the design of information systems. In H.G. Sol and K.M. van Hee (Eds.) *Dynamic Modelling of Information Systems*, Amsterdam: Elsevier

Kay, A. and Goldberg, A (1977) *Personal Dynamic Media*, IEEE Computer 1977 – originally a 1976 Xerox technical report.

Keen, P.G.W. and Knapp, E.M. (1995) *Business Process Investment: Getting the right process right*, Harvard: Business School Press

Keene, S. (1989) *Object-Oriented Programming in Common Lisp*, Reading MA: Addison-Wesley

Kelly, G.A. (1955) *The Psychology of Personal Constructs*, New York: W.W. Norton

Kendall, E.A., Malkoun, M.T. and Chong, J. (1997) The application of object-oriented analysis to agent-based systems, *J. of Object-Oriented Programming*, **9**(9), 56–65

Khan, N.A. and Jain, R. (1986) Explaining Uncertainty in a Distributed Expert System. In Kowalik, J.S. (Ed.) *Coupling Symbolic and Numerical Computing in Expert Systems*, Amsterdam: North Holland

Khoshafian, S. and Abnous, R. (1990) *Object Orientation: Concepts, Languages, Databases, User Interfaces*, New York: Wiley

Khoshafian, S., Baker, A.B., Abnous, R. and Shepherd, K. (1992) *Object-Oriented Multi-Media Information Management in Client/Server Architectures*, New York: Wiley

Kiczales, G. (1994) Why are black boxes so hard to reuse? *Notes from OOPSLA '94*

Kiczales, G., des Rivières, J. and Bobrow, D.G. (1991) *The Art of the Metaobject Protocol*, Boston MA: MIT Press

Kiczales, G. and Lopes, C. (1999) Aspect-Oriented Programming with AspectJ, *Proc. OOPSLA '99*, Reading MA: Addison-Wesley

Kilov, H. and Ross, J. (1994) *Information Modeling: An object-oriented approach*, Englewood Cliffs NJ: Prentice Hall

Kim, W. (1990) *Introduction to Object-Oriented Databases*, Cambridge MA: MIT Press

Kim, W. and Lochovsky, F.H. (Eds.) (1989) *Object-oriented Concepts, Databases and Applications*, Reading MA: Addison-Wesley

Kim, W., Ballou, N., Chou, H.T. *et al.* (1989) *Features of the ORION object-oriented database*. In Kim and Lochovsky (Eds.) (1989)

King, R. (1989) My Cat is Object-Oriented. In Kim and Lochovsky (1989)

Kirkerud, B. (1989) *Object-Oriented Programming with SIMULA*, Wokingham: Addison-Wesley

Kitagawa, H. and Kunii, T. (1989) *The unnormalized relational data model for office form processor design*, Berlin: Springer-Verlag

Kleppe, A. and Warmer J. (2000) Making UML activity diagrams object-oriented, *Proc. Tools Europe 2000*, Upper Saddle River NJ: Prentice Hall

Knudsen, J.L., Lofgren, M., Lehrmann-Madsen, O. and Magnusson, B. (Eds.) (1994) *Object-Oriented Environments: The Mjølner approach*, Hemel Hempstead, England: Prentice Hall

Korson, T. and McGregor, J.D. (1993) Technical Criteria for the Specification and Evaluation of object-oriented Libraries, *Proceedings of Object Expo Europe 1993*, New York: SIGS Publications, 33–36

Korson, T., Vaishnavi, V. and Meyer, B. (Eds.) (1991) *TOOLS5: Proc. Fifth International Conference on the Technology of Object-Oriented Languages and Systems*, New York: Prentice Hall

Kosko, B. (1991) *Neural Networks and Fuzzy Systems: A dynamical systems approach to machine intelligence*, Englewood Cliffs, NJ: Prentice Hall

Kosko, B. (1993) *Fuzzy Thinking: The new science of fuzzy logic*, New York: Hyperion

Koza, J.R. (1992) *Genetic Programming: On the programming of computers by means of natural selection*, Cambridge MA: MIT Press

Kristen, G. (1995) *Object-Orientation: The KISS Method*, Wokingham, England: Addison-Wesley

Kristensen, B.B., Madsen, O.L., Moller-Pedersen, B. and Nygaard, K. (1987) The BETA Programming Language. In Shriver and Wegner (1987), 7–48

Krutchen, P. (1995) The 4+1 View of Software Architecture, *IEEE Software* November, 42–50.

Kruchten, P. (1999) *The Rational Unified Process*, Reading MA: Addison-Wesley

Kurtz, B., Woodfield, S. and Embley, D. (1991) *Object-Oriented Systems Analysis and Specification: A Model Driven Approach*, Englewood Cliffs NJ: Prentice Hall

LaLonde, W.R. and Pugh, J.R. (1990) *Inside Smalltalk: Volume I*, Englewood Cliffs NJ: Prentice Hall

LaLonde, W.R. and Pugh, J.R. (1991) *Inside Smalltalk: Volume II*, Englewood Cliffs NJ: Prentice Hall

Lang, K. and Perlmutter, B. (1986) Oaklisp: An object-oriented Scheme with First Class Types. In Meyrowitz (1986), 30–37

Lano, K. and Haughton, H. (1992) Reasoning and Refinement in object-oriented specification languages, *Proc. of ECOOP'92*, Berlin: Springer

Lano, K. and Haughton, H. (Eds.) (1994) *Object-Oriented Specification Case Studies*, Englewood Cliffs, NJ: Prentice Hall.

Laranjeira, L.A. (1990) Software Size Estimation of Object-Oriented Systems, *IEEE Transactions on Software Engineering* **16**(5), 510–522

Larman, C. (1998) *Applying UML and Patterns*, Upper Saddle River NJ: Prentice Hall

Laurel, B. (Ed.) (1990) *The Art of Computer Interface Design*, Reading, MA: Addison-Wesley

Lausen, G. and Vossen, G. (1998) *Models and Languages of Object-Oriented Databases*, Harlow, England: Addison-Wesley

Lea, D. (1994) Christopher Alexander: An Introduction for object-oriented designers, *ACM SIGSOFT* **19**(1), 39–46

Leathers, B. (1990) Cognos and Eiffel: A Cautionary Tale, *Hotline on Object-Oriented Technology* **1**(9), 1–8

Lécluse, C., Richard, P. and Velez, F. (1988) O_2, an object-oriented data model. In Zdonik and Maier (1990)

Lee, G. (1993) *Object-Oriented GUI Application Development*, Englewood Cliffs, NJ: Prentice Hall

Lee, S. and Carver, D.L. (1991) Object-Oriented Analysis and Specification: A knowledge based approach, *Journal Of Object-Oriented Programming* **3**(9), 35–43

Lieberherr, K., Holland, I., Lee,G. and Riel, A. (1988) Object-oriented programming: an objective sense of style, *IEEE Computer*, **21**(6)

Leffingwell, D. and Widrig, D. (2000) *Managing Software Requirements: a unified approach*, Reading, MA: Addison-Wesley

Lektorsky, V.A. (1984) *Subject, Object, Cognition*, Moscow: Progress Publishers

Lemay, L. and Perkins, C.L. (1997) *Teach Yourself Java in 21 days*, 2nd Edition, Indiana: Sams.net

Lenat, D.B. and Guha, R.V. (1990) *Building Large Knowledge Based Systems: Representation and Inference in the Cyc Project*, Reading MA: Addison-Wesley

Lenin, V.I. (1964) The State and Revolution, *Collected Works Vol 25*, Moscow: Progress Publishers

Lenzerini, M., Nardi, D. and Simi, M. (Eds.) (1991) *Inheritance Hierarchies in Knowledge Representation and Programming Languages*, Chichester, England: Wiley

Lewis, E. (Ed.) (1995) *Object-Oriented Application Frameworks*, Greenwich, CT: Manning

Lientz, B.P. and Swanson, E.B. (1979) *Software Maintenance: A User/Management Tug of War*, Data Management, April 1979, 26–30

Linnemann, V. (1987) Non First Normal Form Relations and Recursive Queries: An SQL-Based Approach, IEEE Conference on Data Engineering, 591–598

Lippman, S.B. and Lajoie, J. (1998) *C++ Primer*, 3rd Edition, Reading: Addison-Wesley

Liskov, B., Snyder, A., Atkinson, R. and Schaffert (1977) Abstraction Mechanisms in CLU, *Communications of the ACM*, **20**(8)

Liu, C. (1996) *Smalltalk, Objects and Design*, Greenwich MA: Manning

Lloyd, D. (1990) LISP is no Impediment!, *Systems International*, Jan 1990, 43–45

Londeix, B. (1987) *Cost Estimation for Software Development*, Wokingham: Addison-Wesley

Loosely, C. (1992) Separation and integration in the Zachman framework, *Database Newsletter* **20**(1), 3–9

Lorenz, M. (1993) *Object-Oriented Software Development: A Practical Guide*, Englewood Cliffs NJ: Prentice Hall

Lorenz, M. and Kidd, J. (1994) *Object-Oriented Software Metrics*, Englewood Cliffs NJ: Prentice Hall

Love, T. (1992) *Object Lessons*, New York: SIGS Books

Lu and Zhou (2000) *Selective Inheritance in Fuzzy Object Modelling*, unpublished manuscript

Macaulay, L.A. (1996) *Requirements Engineering*, London: Springer

Machiavelli, N. (1961) *The Prince*, translation by G. Bull, Harmondsworth: Penguin Books

Mackenzie, K.D. (1991) *The Organizational Hologram: The effective management of organizational change*, Boston: Kluwer Academic

MacLane, S. (1971) *Categories for the Working Mathematician*, New York: Springer

MacLean, R., Stepney, S., Smith, S., Tordoff, N., Gradwell, D. and Hoverd, T. (1994) *Analysing Systems: Determining Requirements for Object-Oriented Development*, Hemel Hempstead, England: Prentice Hall

MacLennan, B.J. (1982) *Values and Objects in Programming Languages*, SIGPLAN Notices **17**(12), 70–79

MacQueen, D. (1986) Using dependent types to express modular structure. In *Proc. of 13th Annual ACM Symposium on Principles of Programming Languages* (St. Petersburg Beach, Fla, Jan) New York: ACM, 277–286

Madsen O.L. and Moller-Pedersen, B. (1988) *What object-oriented programming may be – and what it does not have to be*. In Gjessing and Nygaard (1988)

Madsen O.L., Moller-Pedersen, B. and Nygaard, K. (1993) *Object-Oriented Programming in the BETA Programming Language*, Wokingham, England: Addison-Wesley

Magnusson, B., Meyer, B., Nerson, J-M. and Perrot, J-F. (Eds.) (1994) *TOOLS 13*, Hemel Hemstead, England: Prentice Hall

Maiden, N.A.M. and Rugg, G. (1996) ACRE: selecting methods for requirements acquisition, *IEE Software Engineering Journal*, May, 183–192

Maiden, N.A.M. and Sutcliffe, A.G. (1994) Requirements critiquing using domain abstractions, *Proc. of IEEE Conference on Requirements Engineering*, IEEE Computer Society Press, 184–193

Maiden, N.A.M., Cisse, M., Perez, H. and Manuel, D. (1998) *CREWS Validation Frames: Patterns for Validating Systems Requirements*, Centre for Human Computer Interface Design, City University, London

Maiden, N.A.M., Minocha, S., Manning, K. and Ryan, M. (1997) *SAVRE: Systematic Scenario Generation and Use*, Centre for HCI Design, City University, London

Maier D. and Stein J. (1987) Development and Implementation of an Object-Oriented DBMS. In Shriver and Wegner (1987)

Mak, V.W. (1992) Connection: an inter-component communication paradigm for configurable distributed systems. In *Proc. of Int. Workshop on Configurable Distributed Systems*, London

Malan, R., Letsinger, R. and Coleman, D. (1996) *Object-Oriented Development at Work*, Upper Saddle River NJ: Prentice Hall

Mandrioli, D. and Meyer, B. (1992) *Advances in Object-Oriented Software Engineering*, Englewood Cliffs NJ: Prentice Hall

Manola, F. and Dayal, U. (1986) PDM: An Object-Oriented Data Model, *International Workshop on Object-Oriented Database Systems*, California

Marcuse, H. (1941) *Reason and Revolution: Hegel and the Rise of Social Theory*, London: Oxford University Press

Marcuse, H. (1955) *Reason and Revolution*, Oxford: University Press.

Marden, R.J. (1990) Object-Oriented System Development: Notation and Method (unpublished manuscript)

Martin, J. and Odell, J.J. (1992) *Object-Oriented Analysis And Design*, Englewood Cliffs NJ: Prentice Hall

Martin, J. and Odell, J.J. (1995) *Object-Oriented Methods: A Foundation*, Englewood Cliffs NJ: Prentice Hall

Martin, J. and Odell, J.J. (1996) *Object-Oriented Methods:Pragmatic Considerations)*, Englewood Cliffs NJ: Prentice Hall

Martin, J. and Odell, J.J. (1998) *Object-Oriented Methods: A Foundation (UML Edition)*, Englewood Cliffs NJ: Prentice Hall

Martin-Löf, P. (1975) An Intuitionistic Theory of Types: Predicative Part. In Rose, H.E. and Shepherdson, J.C. (Eds.) (1975) *Logic Colloquium 1973*, Amsterdam: North-Holland, 73–118

Martin-Löf, P. (1982) Constructive Mathematics and Computer Programming. In *Logic, Methodology and Philosophy of Science VI* (Proceedings of the 6th International Congress, Hanover 1979), Amsterdam: North-Holland, 153–175

Marx, G. (1992) *Computerworld*, 20 April 1992

Marx, K. (1961) *Capital*, Vol. I, Afterword to the second German edition, translated by Moore and Aveling, Moscow: Foreign Languages Publishing House

Masiero, P. and Germano, F.S.R. (1988) JSD as an Object-Oriented Design Method, *Software Engineering Notes* **13**(3), 22–23

Matthews, D. (1983) Programming Language Design with Polymorphism. PhD Dissertation, Computer Lab., University of Cambridge, England

McCabe, F.G. (1992) *Logic and Objects*, Englewood Cliffs NJ: Prentice Hall

McCabe, T.J. (1976) A complexity measure, *IEEE Trans. on Software Engineering*, **2**(4), 308–320

McCarthy, J. (1960) Recursive Functions of Symbolic Expressions and their Computation by Machine, Part I, *Comm. of the ACM* **3**(4)

McCauley, C. (1999) CORBA at Irish Life, *Proc. Enterprise CORBA*, London: ELM Ltd

McCawley, J.D. (1981) *Everything that Linguists have always wanted to know about Logic (but were ashamed to ask)*, Oxford: Basil Blackwell.

McDermott, D. and Doyle, J. (1980) Nonmonotonic Logic I, *Artificial Intelligence* **13**(1,2)

McGraw, G. (1998) *Securing Java*, New York: Wiley

McGregor, J.D. and Sykes, D.A. (1992) *Object-Oriented Software Development: Engineering Software for Reuse*, New York: Van Nostrand

McInnes, S.T. (1988) *The Generic Relational Model*, PhD Thesis, Department of Computer Science, University of Strathclyde, Glasgow

McLarty, C. (1992) *Elementary Categories, Elementary Toposes*, Oxford University Press

Meersman, R.A., Kent, W. and Khosla, S. (Eds.) (1991) Object-Oriented Databases: Analysis, Design and Construction (DS-4), *Proceedings of the IFIP TC2/WG2.6 Working Conference*, Windermere, England, July 1990, Berlin, Springer-Verlag

Meira, S. and Cavalcanti, A. (1992) Modular object-oriented Z specifications. In *Z Users Meeting 1990*, Workshops in Computing, Berlin: Springer

Menzies, T., Edwards, J.M. and Ng, K. (1992) The case of the mysterious missing reusable libraries. In Meyer, B. and Potter, J. (Eds.) (1992) *TOOLS 9*, Sydney: Prentice Hall

Meyer, B. (1988) *Object-oriented Software Construction*, Englewood Cliffs NJ: Prentice Hall

Meyer, B. (1990) *Eiffel: The Language and the Environment*, Englewood Cliffs NJ: Prentice Hall

Meyer, B. (Ed.) (1993) Special Issue: Concurrent Object-Oriented Programming, *Comms. ACM*, **36**(9)

Meyer, B. (1994) *Reusable Software: The Base Object-Oriented Component Libraries*, Hemel Hempstead, England: Prentice Hall

Meyer, B. (1995) *Object Success*, Hemel Hempstead, England: Prentice Hall

Meyer, B. (1997) *Object-oriented Software Construction*, 2nd Edition, Upper Saddle River NJ: Prentice Hall

Meyer, B. and Mandrioli, D. (Eds.) (1992) *Advances in Object-Oriented Software Engineering*, Englewood Cliffs NJ: Prentice Hall

Meyer, B. and Nerson, J-M. (Eds.) (1993) *Object-Oriented Applications*, Englewood Cliffs NJ: Prentice Hall

Meyrowitz, N. (Ed.) (1986) *OOPSLA'86 ACM Conference on Object-Oriented Programming Systems, Languages and Applications*, ACM SIGPLAN Notices **21** (11)

Meyrowitz, N. (Ed.) (1987) *OOPSLA'87 ACM Conference on Object-Oriented Programming Systems, Languages and Applications*, ACM SIGPLAN Notices **22** (12)

Meyrowitz, N. (Ed.) (1988) *OOPSLA'88 ACM Conference on Object-Oriented Programming Systems, Languages and Applications*, ACM SIGPLAN Notices **23** (11)

Meyrowitz, N. (Ed.) (1989) *OOPSLA'89 ACM Conference on Object-Oriented Programming Systems, Languages and Applications*, Reading MA: Addison-Wesley

Meyrowitz, N. (Ed.) (1990) *OOPSLA'90 ACM Conference on Object-Oriented Programming Systems, Languages and Applications*, Reading, MA: Addison-Wesley

Michaels, W.I. (1992) Re-designing customer driven IS processes, *Database Newsletter* **20**(6), 1–12

Microsoft (1992) *The Windows Interface: An Application Design Guide*, Seattle: Microsoft Corp.

Miller, A.V. (1969) *Hegel's Science of Logic* (translation), London: George, Allen and Unwin

Miller, G.A. (1956) The magical number seven, plus or minus two: some limits on our capacity for processing informatiom, *Psychological Review* **63**, 81–97

Milner, R. (1978) A Theory of Type Polymorphism in Programming, *J. Comput. Syst. Sci.* **17**, 348–375

Minsky, M.L. (1981) A Framework for Representing Knowledge. In Haugeland (Ed.), *Mind Design*, MIT Press

Minsky, M.L (1985) *The Society of Mind*, London: Heinemann

Minsky, M.L. and Papert, S. (1969) *Perceptrons*, MIT Press.

Mitchell, J. and Plotkin, G. (1985) Abstract types have existential type. In *Proc. of 12th Annual ACM Symposium on Principles of Programming Languages* (New Orleans, LA, Jan) New York: ACM, 37–51

Mock, M. (1990) DoubleVision: A Foundation for Scientific Visualization. In Pinson and Wiener (1990)

Monarchi, D.E. and Puhr, G.I. (1992) A Research Typology for Object-Oriented Analysis and Design, Comms, ACM **35**(9), 35–47

Moon, D. (1986) Object-Oriented Programming with Flavors. In Meyrowitz (1986), 1–8

Moon, D. (1989) The Common Lisp object-oriented programming Language Standard. In Kim and Lochovsky (1989)

Monday, P., Carey, J. and Dangler, M. (2000) *San Francisco Component Framework*, Reading MA: Addison-Wesley

Moran, T.P. (1981) The Command Language Grammar: A representation for the user interface of interactive computer systems, *IJMMS* **15**, 3–50

Morgan, G. (1997) *Images of Organization*, Thousands Oaks, CA: Sage

Mowbray, T. and Malveau, R. (1997) *CORBA Design Patterns*, New York: Wiley

Mowbray, T. and Zahavi, R. (1995) *The Essential CORBA*, New York: Wiley

Mullender, S. (Ed.) (1989) *Distributed Systems*, Reading MA: Addison-Wesley

Müller, H.J. and Dieng, R. (Eds.) (2000) *Computational Conflicts*, Heidelberg: Springer

Mullin, M. (1989) *Object-Oriented Program Design*, Wokingham: Addison-Wesley

Mumford, E. (1986) *Designing Systems for Business Success: The ETHICS Method*, Manchester: Business School

Musser, D.R. and Saini, A. (1996) *STL Tutorial and Refererence Guide*, Reading MA: Addison-Wesley

Myers, B.A. (1991) GARNET, *IEEE Software* **8**(2)

Myers, G.J. (1979) *The Art of Software Testing*, New York: Wiley

Naur, P. and Randell, B. (Eds.) (1969) *Software Engineering: Report on a Conference Sponsored by the NATO Science Committee 7–11 October 1968, Garmisch, Germany*: NATO Science Committee

Nelson, T.H. (1980) Replacing the Printed Word: A Complete Literary System. In Lavington, S.H. (Ed.) *Information Processing 80*, Amsterdam: North Holland, 1013–1023

Nelson, T.H. (1981) *Literary Machines*, Nelson, Swathmore PA

Nerson, J. (1992) Applying Object-Oriented Analysis and Design, *Comms. ACM* **35**(9), 63–74

Newell, A. and Simon, H.A. (1963) GPS: A Program that Simulates Human Thought. In Feigenbaum, E.A. and Feldman, J.A. (Eds.), *Computers and Thought*, McGraw Hill

NeXT Computers Inc. (1991) *The NeXTSTEP Environment: Concepts*, NeXT Computers Inc.

NeXT Computers Inc. (1992) *NeXTSTEP User Interface Guidelines: Release 3*, Reading MA: Addison-Wesley

Nguyen, G.T. and Rieu, D. (1989) Schema Evolution in Object-Oriented Database Systems, *Data & Knowledge Engineering* **4**(1), 43–68

Nguyen, Q. and Van Le, T. (1996) A fuzzy dynamic multiple inheritance model in object-oriented simulation, *Proc. European Simulation Multiconference*, Budapest, Hungary, 624–628

Nierstrasz, O. and Tsichritzis, D.E. (1989) Integrated Office Systems. In Kim and Lochovsky (1989)

Nierstrasz, O., Gibbs, S. and Tsichritzis, D.E. (1992) Component-oriented software development, *Comms. ACM* **35**(9), 160–165

Nordström, B., Petersson, K. and Smith, J.M. (1990) *Programming in Martin-Löf's Type Theory*, Oxford: University Press

Nori, K.V., Amman, U., Jensen, K., Nageli, H. and Jacobi, C. (1991) Pascal-P implementation notes. In Barron, D. *Pascal: The Language and its Implementation*, New York: Wiley

Norman, D.A. (1988) *The Psychology of Everyday Things*, New York: Doubleday

Norman, D.A. and Draper, S.W. (1986) *User Centred System Design*, Hillsdale NJ: Lawrence Erlbaum

O'Callaghan, A.J. (1994) Object Technology Skills: What, Why and How. In O'Callaghan, A.J. and Leigh, M. (Eds.) *Object Technology Transfer*, Henley-on-Thames:Alfred Waller

O'Callaghan, A. (1997a) Object-oriented reverse engineering, *Application Development Adviser* **1**(1), 35–39

O'Callaghan, A. (1997b) Realizing the reality, *Application Development Adviser* **1**(2), 30–33

O'Callaghan, A. (1998) A plethora of patterns, *Application Development Adviser* **1**(3), 32–33

O'Callaghan, A.J. (1999) Migrating Large-Scale Legacy Systems to Component-based and Object Technology: The Evolution of a Pattern Language. *Communications of the AIS*, **2**(3). http://cais.isworld.org/

O'Callaghan, A.J. (2000a) Getting what you want, *Application Development Advisor* **3**(5), 64–67

O'Callaghan, A.J. (2000b) Patterns for an Architectural Praxis, *Proc. European Pattern Languages of Program Design*, Irsee, Germany

Object Management Group (1992) *Common Object Request Broker Architecture*, Framington MA: Object Management Group

O'Connor, P. (1991) A knowledge based trading system that management can trust, *Expert Systems User*, July

O'Sullivan, J. (1999) XML Messaging at Chase Manhattan Bank Global Markets, *Proc. OT'99*, Oxford, England

Odell, J.J. (1994) Six different kinds of composition, *J. of Object-Oriented Programming* **5**(8), 10–15

ODI (1992) *ObjectStore Release 2.0 User Guide and Reference Manual*, Object Design Inc., 1 New England Executive Park, Burlington MA

Open Software Foundation (1990) *OSF/Motif: Style Guide*, Englewood Cliffs NJ: Prentice Hall

Otte, R., Patrick, P. and Roy, M. (1996) *Understanding CORBA*, Upper Saddle River NJ: Prentice Hall

Ousterhout, J.K. (1994) *Tcl and the Tk Toolkit*, Reading MA: Addison-Wesley

Ovum Ltd (1992) *Workflow Management Software: The Business Opportunity*, London: Ovum

Paepcke, A. (Ed.) (1991) *OOPSLA'91 ACM Conference on Object-Oriented Programming Systems, Languages and Applications*, Reading MA: Addison-Wesley

Page-Jones, M. (1992) Comparing Techniques by means of Encapsulation and Connascence, *Comms. ACM* **35**(9), 147–151

Page-Jones, M., Constantine, L.L. and Weiss, S. (1990) Modelling object-oriented systems: The Uniform Object Notation, *Computer Language* (Oct. 1990), 70–87

Page-Jones and Weiss, S. (1989) Synthesis: An object-oriented analysis and design method, *American Programmer* **2**(7) 64–67

Parnas, D. (1972) On the Criteria to be Used in Decomposing Systems into Modules, *Comm. ACM* **15**(2), 1053–58

Parsaye, K., Chignell, M., Khoshafian, S. and Wong, H. (1989) *Intelligent Databases: Object-Oriented, Deductive Hypermedia Technologies*, New York: Wiley

Parson, J. and Wand, Y. (1995) Using objects for systems analysis, *Communications of the ACM*, **40**(12), 104–110

Peckham, J. and Maryanski, J. (1988) Semantic Data Models, *ACM Computing Surveys* **20**(3), 153–189

Pedrycz, and Sosnowski, (1998) Fuzzy object-oriented system design, *Fuzzy Sets and Systems* **99**(2), 121–134

Perry, D.E. and Kaiser, G.E. (1990) Adequate testing and object-oriented programming, *Journal Of Object-Oriented Programming* **3**(5) 13–19

Perry, D.E and Wolf, A.L. (1992) Foundations for the Study of Software Architecture, *Software Engineering Notes* **17**(4), 40–52

Peters, T. (1987) *Thriving on Chaos: Handbook for a Management Revoloution*, New York: Alfred Knopf

Peters, T. (1992) *Liberation Management: Necessary Disorganization for the Nanosecond Nineties*, London: Macmillan

Peters, T.J. and Waterman, R.H. (1982) *In Search of Excellence*, New York: Harper & Row

Peterson, J.L. (1981) *Petri Net Theory and the Modelling of Systems*, Englewood Cliffs, NJ: Prentice Hall

Petri, C.A. (1962) *Kommunikation mit Automaten*, Ph.D dissertation, University of Bonn

Peuquet, D.J. and Marble, D.F. (Eds.) (1990) *Introductory readings in Geographic Information Systems*, London: Taylor and Francis

Pinson, L.J. and Weiner, R.S. (1988) *An Introduction to Object-Oriented Programming and C++*, Reading MA: Addison-Wesley

Pinson, L.J. and Weiner, R.S. (1990) Object-Oriented Design of a Branch Path Analyzer for C-Language Software Systems. In Pinson and Wiener (1990)

Pinson, L.J. and Weiner, R.S. (Eds.) (1990) *Applications of Object-Oriented Programming*, Reading MA: Addison-Wesley

Pohl, I. (1994) *C++ for C Programmers*, 2nd Edition, Benjamin/Cummings

Pohl, I. (1996) *C++ Distilled*, Reading MA: Addison-Wesley

Pohl, K. (1993) The three dimensions of requirements engineering. In Rolland, C., Bodart, F. and Cauvet, C. (Eds) *Proc. CAISE'93*, Paris: Springer, 175–292

Pohl, K., Jarke, M. and Weidenhaupt, K. (1997) The use of scenarios during systems development – the current state of practice, submitted to *ICRE*

Porter, M. (1980) *Competitive Strategy: Techniques for analyzing industries and competitors*, New York: The Free Press

Potter, J. and Takoro, M. (Eds.) (1992) *TOOLS6: Proceedings of the sixth international conference on the Technology of Object-Oriented Languages and Systems*, New York: Prentice Hall

Pountain, D. (1988) Rekursiv: An object-oriented CPU, *Byte* **13**(11), 341–349

Pountain, D. (1989) Occam II, *Byte* **14**(10), 279–84

Pree, W. (1995) *Design Patterns for Object-Oriented Software Development*, Reading MA: Addison-Wesley

Prieto-Diaz, R. (1993) Status Report: Software Reusability, *IEEE Software*, May 1993, 61–66

Prieto-Diaz, R. and Freeman, P. (1987) Classifying Software for Reuseability, *IEEE Software* **4**(1), 6–16

Putnam, L.H. (1978) A General Empirical Solution to the Macro Software Sizing and Estimating Problem, *IEEE Trans. on Software Engineering*, July 1978, 345–361

Quillian, M.R. (1967) Word Concepts: A Theory and Simulation of some Basic Semantic Capabilities, *Behavioural Science* **12**, 410–430

Quinlan, J.R. (1979) Discovering Rules from Large Collections of Examples: A case study. In Michie, D. (Ed.) *Expert Systems in the Microelectronics Age*, Edinburgh University Press

Raghavan, R. (1990) Building Interactive Graphical Applications Using C++. In Pinson and Weiner (1990)

Rational (1997) *UML Notation Guide*, Internet: www.rational.com

Rawlings, R. (1991) Some Numbers from an Object-Oriented Development, *Object-Oriented Software Engineering*, BCS ITEXT

Reason, J.T. (1990) *Human Error*, Cambridge: University Press

Redmond-Pyle, D. and Graham, I.M. (1992) Object-Oriented Methods In Europe, paper presented at Data Management'92, Bristol University

Redmond-Pyle, D. and Moore, A. (1995) *Graphical User Interface Design and Evaluation*, London: Prentice Hall

Reenskaug, T.M.H. (1981) User-oriented Descriptions of Smalltalk Systems, *Byte* Aug 1981, 149–166

Reenskaug, T., Wold P. and Lehne A. (1996) *Working with Objects: The OOram Software Engineering Method*, Englewood Cliffs NJ: Prentice Hall

Reisig, W. (1986) *Petri Nets: An introduction*, Berlin: Springer

Reisner, P. (1981) Formal Grammars and Human Factors Design of an Interactive Graphics System, *IEEE Trans. on Software Engineering* **5**, 229–240

Reiss, S.P. (1991) Tools for Object-Oriented Redesign. In Korson *et al.* (1991)

Reiter, R. (1985) On Reasoning by Default. In Brachman and Levesque (1985)

Rentsch, T. (1982) *Object-oriented Programming*, SIGPLAN Notices **17**(9), 51–79

Riecken, D. (1994) Special Issue on Intelligent Agents, *Comms ACM*, July

Rising, L. (Ed.) (1998) *The Patterns Handbook*, New York: Cambridge University Press.

Roach, S.S. (1991) Services under siege: The restructuring imperative, *Harvard Business Review*, Sept–Oct 1991, 82–92

Roberts, R.B. and Goldstein, I.P. (1977) The FRL manual, AI Memo. No. 409, MIT Artificial Intelligence Laboratory

Robinson, J.A. (1965) A machine-oriented logic based on the resolution principle, *Proc. of the ACM* **12**

Robinson, K. and Berrisford, G. (1994) *Object-Oriented SSADM*, Englewood Cliffs NJ: Prentice Hall

Robinson, P. (Ed.) (1992) *Object-Oriented Design*, London: Chapman & Hall

Rosenberg, J. and Koch, D. (Eds.) (1990) *Persistent Object Systems*, Berlin: Springer-Verlag

Rosene, F. (1995) A Software Development Environment called STEP. In *Proc. ACM Conference on Software Tools*

Ross, J. And Kilov, H. (1994) *Information Modelling: An object-oriented approach*, Englewood Cliffs, NJ: Prentice Hall

Royce, W. (1998) *Software Project Management: A Unified Framework*, Reading MA: Addison-Wesley

Royce, W.W. (1970) Managing the development of large scale software system, *Proc. IEEE WESCON*, 1–9

Rubin, K. and Goldberg, A. (1992) Object Behaviour Analysis, *Comms. of the ACM* **35**(9), Sept 1992, 48–62

Rumbaugh, J. (1993) Forceful Functions: How to do numerical computation, *Object Magazine* **6**(6), 18–24

Rumbaugh, J., Blaha, M., Premerlani, W. *et al.* (1991) *Object-Oriented Modelling and Design*, Englewood Cliffs NJ: Prentice Hall

Rumbaugh, J., Booch, G. and Jacobson, I. (1999) *The Unified Modelling Language Reference Manual*, Reading MA: Addison-Wesley

Rumbaugh, J. and Selic, B. (1998) Using UML for Modeling Complex Real-time Systems, http://www.objectime.com/otl/technical/umlr t_overview.pdf, 15 June 2000

Rummelhart, D.E. and McClelland, J.L. (1986) *Parallel Distributed Processing: Explorations in the Microstructure of Cognition* (2 vols.), Cambridge MA: MIT Press

Rush, G. (1985) The fast way to define system requirements, *Computerworld*, 7 October

Russell, S. and Norvig, P. (1995) *Artificial Intelligence: A Modern Approach*, Englewood Cliffs NJ: Prentice Hall

Saeki, M., Horai, H. and Enomoto, H. (1989) Software Development Process from Natural Language Specification, *Proceedings of the 11th International Conference on Software Engineering*, New York: IEEE Computer Society

Sakkinen, M. (1988) Comments on 'the Law of Demeter' and C++, *SIGPLAN Notices* **23**(12), p. 38

Schaffert, C., Cooper, T., Bullis, B., Kilian, M. and Wilpot, C. (1986) An Introduction to Trellis/Owl. In Meyrowitz (1986), 9–16

Schank, R.C. and Abelson, R.P. (1977) *Scripts, Plans, Goals and Understanding*, Lawrence Erlbaum Associates

Scharenberg, M.E. and Dunsmore, H.E. (1991) Evolution of classes and objects during object-oriented design and programming, *Journal Of Object-Oriented Programming* **3**(9), 30–34

Schlageter, G., Unland, R., *et al* (1988) OOPS: An Object-Oriented Programming System with Integrated Data Management Facility, *Proc. IEEE 4th Int. Conf. on Data Engineering*, Los Angeles, 118–125

Schmid H.A. and Swenson, J.R. (1975) On the Semantics of the Relational Data Model, *Proc. 1975 ACM SIGMOD International Conference on Management of Data*

Schmucker, K. (1986) *Object-Oriented Programming for the Macintosh*, Hayden Book Company

Schneiderman, B. (1987) *Designing the User Interface: Strategies for effective human computer interaction*, Reading MA: Addison-Wesley

Schreiber, G., Wielinger, R. and Breuker, J. (Eds.) (1993) KADS: *A Principled Approach to Knowledge Based System Development*, London: Academic Press

Scott Gordon, V. and Bieman, J.M. (1993) Reported effects of rapid prototyping on industrial software quality, *Software Quality Journal* **2**, 93–108

Scott, A.C., Clayton, J.E. and Gibson, E.L. (1991) *A Practical Approach to Knowledge Acquisition*, Reading MA: Addison-Wesley

Searle, J. R. (1969) *Speech Acts*, Cambridge: University Press

Seidewitz, E. and Stark, M. (1986) *General Object-oriented Software Development*, Software Engineering Letters 86–002

Selic, B., Gullekson, G. and Ward, P.T. (1994) *Real-time Object-Oriented Modelling*, New York: Wiley

Senge, P.M. (1990) *The Fifth Discipline: The Art And Practice Of The Learning Organization*, New York: Doubleday; London: Random House

Servio Logic (1989) *Programming in OPAL*, Beaverton OR: Servio Logic Devmt. Corp.

Shadbolt, N. (1989) Knowledge Representation in Man and Machine. In Forsythe, R., *Expert Systems: Principles and Case Studies*, 2nd Edition, Chapman & Hall

Shafer, D. and Taylor, D.A. (1993) *Transforming the Enterprise through COOPERATION: An object-oriented solution*, Englewood Cliffs, NJ: Prentice Hall

Sharble, R.S. and Cohen, S. (1994) The object-oriented brewery: a comparison of two OO development methods, *ACM Sigsoft* **18**(2)

Shastri, L. (1988) *Semantic Networks: An Evidential Formalization and its Connectionist Realization*, London: Pitman

Shaw, M. (1990) Prospects for an Engineering Discipline of Software, *IEEE Software* **7**(6), 15–24

Shaw, M., DeLine, R., Klein, D.V., Ross, T.L., Young, D.M. and Zelesnik, G. (1995) Abstractions for Software Architecture and Tools to Support Them, *IEEE Trans. on Software Eng.*, **21**(4), 314–315

Shaw, M. and Gaines, B. (1992) On the Relationship between Repertory Grid and Term Subsumption Knowledge Structures: Theory, Practice and Tools. In Bramer, M. and Milne, R. (Eds.) *Research and Development in Expert Systems IX*, Cambridge University Press

Shaw, M. and Garlan, D. (1996) *Software Architecture: Perspectives on an Emerging Discipline*, Englewood Cliffs NJ: Prentice Hall.

Shelton, R.E. (1993) An Object-Oriented Method for Enterprise Modeling: OOEM, *Proceedings of OOP'93, Munich*, 61–70, New York: SIGS Publications

Shipman, D. (1981) The Functional Data Model and the Data Language DAPLEX, *ACM TODS* **6**(1)

Shlaer, S. and Mellor, S.J. (1988) *Object-Oriented Systems Analysis – Modelling the World in Data*, Englewood Cliffs NJ: Yourdon Press

Shlaer, S. and Mellor, S.J. (1992) *Object-Lifecycles: Modelling the World in States*, Yourdon Press

Shneiderman, B. (1987) User Interface Design for the Hyperties Electronic Encyclopedia, *Proceedings of the Hypertext '87 Workshop*, University of North Carolina at Chapel Hill

Short, J.E. and Venkatramen, N. (1992) Beyond business process redesign: Redefining Baxter's Business Network, *Sloan Management Review*, Fall 1992, 7–17

Shortliffe, E.H. (1976) *Computer Based Medical Consultations: MYCIN*, American Elsevier.

Shriver, B. and Wegner, P. (Eds.) (1987) *Research Directions in Object-oriented Programming*, Cambridge MA: MIT Press

Simon, H.A. (1965) *The Shape of Automation for Men and Management*, publisher unknown

Simon, H.A. (1981) *The Sciences of the Artificial*, 2nd Edition, Cambridge MA: MIT Press

Simons, A. and Graham, I. (1999) 30 things that go wrong in object modelling with UML 1.3. In Kilov, Rumpe and Simmonds (Eds.), *Behavioral Specifications of Businesses and Systems*, Kluwer Academic Publishers

Sims, O. (1994) *Business Objects: Delivering Cooperative Objects for Client-Server*, London: McGraw-Hill

Skarra, A.H. and Zdonik, S.B (1986) The Management of Changing Types in an Object-Oriented Database. In Meyrowitz (1986)

Smith, J.M. and Smith, D.C.P. (1977) Database abstractions – aggregation and generalization, *ACM Trans. on Databaser Systems* **2**, 105–133

Smith, M.D. and Robson, D.J. (1992) A framework for testing object-oriented programs, *JOOP* **5**(3), 45–53

Snyder, A. (1987) *Inheritance and the Development of Encapsulated Software Systems*. In Shriver and Wegner (1987)

Software Futures (1994) Objects and Software Reuse: Dead on arrival at your company, *Software Futures* **3**(3)

Soley, R.M. (Ed.) (1990) *Object Management Architecture Guide*, Framington MA: Object Management Group

Sommerville, I. (1989) *Software Engineering*, 3rd Edition, Wokingham: Addison-Wesley

Sowa, J.F. (1984) *Conceptual Structures: Information processing in mind and machine*, Reading MA: Addison-Wesley

Sowa, J.F. and Zachman, J.A. (1992) Extending and formalizing the framework for information systems architecture, *IBM Systems Journal* **31**(3), 590–616

Stapleton, J. (1997) *Dynamic Systems Development Method: The Method in Practice*, Harlow, England: Addison-Wesley

Stephenson, N. (1992) *Snow Crash*, Harmondsworth: Penguin Books

Stern, R. (1990) *Hegel, Kant and the Structure of the Object*, London: Routledge

Stoecklin, S.E., Adams, E.J. and Smith, S. (1988) Object-Oriented Analysis, *Proceedings of the 5th Washington ADA Symposium*, ACM, New York, 133–138

Stonebraker, M.R. and Rowe, L.A. (Eds.) (1987) *The Postgres Papers*, Research memo. UCB/ERL M86/85, University of California, Berkeley

Stonebraker, M.R., Rowe, L.A., Lindsay, B., Gray, P., Carey, Brodie, M.L., Bernstein, P. and Beech, D. (1990) The Third Generation Database System Manifesto, *Proceedings of the 1990 SIGMOD Conference*, ACM

Stout, L. (1991) A survey of fuzzy set and topos theory, *Fuzzy Sets and Systems* **42**(1), 3–14

Stroustrup, B. (1986) *The C++ Programming Language*, Reading MA: Addison-Wesley

Stroustrup, B. (1988) What is Object-Oriented Programming?, *IEEE Software*, May 1988, 10–20

Stroustrup, B. (1994) *The Design and Evolution of C++*, Reading MA: Addison-Wesley

Stroustrup, B. (1997) *The C++ Programming Language*, 3rd Edition, Reading MA: Addison-Wesley

Stroustrup, B. (2000) Interview in *Application Development Adviser*

Suchman, L.A. (1987) *Plans and Situated Actions: The problem of human–machine communication*, Cambridge, Cambridge University Press

Sully, P. (1993) *Modelling the World with Objects*, Englewood Cliffs NJ: Prentice Hall

Sun Microsystems Inc. (1989) *Open Look: Graphical User Interface Functional Specification,* Reading MA: Addison-Wesley

Swaffield, G.E. (1990) Development of a Structured Method for Knowledge Elicitation, PhD Thesis, Thames Polytechnic, London

Swatman, P.A. and Swatman, P.M.C. (1992) Formal specification: an analytic tool for (management) information systems, *J. of Information Systems*, **2**(2), 121–160

Symbolics (1988) *Statice*, Cambridge MA: Symbolics Inc.

Symons, G. (1989) *Software Sizing and Estimating: Mk II Function Point Analysis*, Chichester: Wiley

Szyperski, C. (1998) *Component Software: Beyond Object-Oriented Programming*, Harlow, England: Addison-Wesley

Szyperski, C., Omohundro, S. and Murer, S. (1994) Engineering a programming language – the type and class system of Sather, *Lecture Notes in Computer Science 782*, Berlin: Springer

Tanenbaum, A.S. and Renesse, R. van (1985) Distributed Operating Systems, *ACM Computing Surveys* **17**(4), 419–470

Taylor, D. (1992a) *Object-Oriented Information Systems: Planning and Implementation*, New York: Wiley

Taylor, D. (1992b) *Object-Oriented Technology: A Manager's Guide,* Reading MA: Addison-Wesley

Taylor, D. (1997) *Object-Oriented Technology: A Manager's Guide,* 2nd Edition, Reading MA: Addison-Wesley

Taylor, D.A. (1995) *Business Engineering with Object Technology*, New York: John Wiley & Sons

Tello, E.R. (1989) *Object-oriented Programming for Artificial Intelligence: A Guide to Tools and System Design*, Reading MA: Addison-Wesley

Ten Dyke, R.P. and Kunz, J.C. (1989) *Object-Oriented Programming*, IBM Systems Journal **28**(3)

Teorey, T.J., Yang, D.Q. and Fry, J.P. (1986) A Logical Design Methodology for Relational Databases Using the Extended Entity-Relationship Model, *ACM Computing Surveys 18(2)*, 197–222

Tesler, L. (1981) The Smalltalk Environment, *BYTE* Aug 1981, 90–147

Texel, P.T. and Williams, C.B. (1997) *Use Cases Combined with Booch/OMT/UML: Process and Products*, Upper Saddle River NJ: Prentice Hall

Thimbleby, H. (1990) *User Interface Design*, New York: ACM Press (Addison-Wesley)

Tognazzini, B. (1992) *TOG on Interface*, Reading MA: Addison-Wesley

Tomlinson, C. and Scheevel, M. (1989) Concurrent Object-Oriented Programming Languages. In Kim and Lochovsky (1989)

Topper, A. (1995) *Object-Oriented Development in COBOL*, New York: McGraw-Hill

Touretzky, D.S. (1986) *The Mathematics of Inheritance Systems*, London: Pitman

Turner, D.A. (1985) Miranda: A Non-Strict Functional Language with Polymorphic Types. In Jouannaud, J-P. (Ed.) *Functional Programming Languages and Computer Architectures*, Berlin: Springer Lecture Notes in Computer Science 201, 1–16

Turner, R. (1984) *Logics for Artificial Intelligence*, Chichester: Ellis Horwood

Ullman, J.D. (1981) *Principles of Database Systems*, Maryland: Computer Science Press

Ullman, J.D. (1989a) *Principles of Database and Knowledge-base Systems*, Volume I, Computer Science Press

Ullman, J.D. (1989b) *Principles of Database and Knowledge-base Systems*, Volume II – The New Technologies, Computer Science Press

Ungar, D. and Smith, R.B. (1987) Self: The power of simplicity. In Meyrowitz (1987)

Van Gyseghem, N. and De Caluwe, R. (1996) Overview of the UFO database model, *Proc. 4th European congress on Intelligent Techniques and Soft Computing (EUFIT)*, Aachen, Germany, 858–862

Van Harmelen, M. (2000) *Object Modelling and User Interface Design*, Harlow, England: Addison-Wesley van Rijsbergen, C.J. (1993) The State of Information Retrieval: Logic and information, *Computer Bulletin*, February 1993, 18–20

Vlissides, J., Kerth, N. and Coplien, J.O. (Eds.) (1996) *Pattern Languages of Program Design 2*, Reading MA: Addison-Wesley

Waldén, K. and Nerson, J-M. (1995) *Seamless Object-Oriented Software Architecture*, NY: Prentice Hall

Wand, Y. (1989) A Proposal for a Formal Model of Objects. In Kim, W. and Lochovsky, F.H. (Eds.) (1989) *Object-oriented Concepts, Databases and Applications*, Reading MA: Addison-Wesley

Ward, P. (1989) How to Integrate Object-Orientation with Structured Analysis and Design, *IEEE Software* **6**, March 1989

Warmer, J. and Kleppe, A. (1999) *The Object Constraint Language*, Reading MA: Addison-Wesley

Wasserman, A.I., Pircher, P.A. and Muller, R.J. (1990) The Object-oriented Structured Design Notation for Software Design Representation, *IEEE Computer*, March 1990, 50–62

Webster, J. (1996) *Shaping Women's Work: Gender, Employment and Information Technology*, London: Longman Sociology

Wegner, P. (1987) The object-oriented classification paradigm. In Shriver, B. and Wegner, P. (Eds.) *Research Directions in Object-Oriented Programming*, Cambridge: University Press

Wegner, P. and Zdonik, S. (1988) Inheritance as an Incremental Modification Mechanism, Proc. ECOOP'88, *Lecture Notes in Computer Science 322*, p. 55–77, New York: Springer

Weiner, N. (1948) *Cybernetics*, Cambridge MA: MIT Press

Weiner, R. and Pinson, L. (1990) *The C++ Workbook*, Reading MA: Addison-Wesley

Weiser, S.P. and Lochovsky, F.H. (1989) OZ+: An object-oriented database system. In Kim and Lochovsky (1989)

Weiskamp, K. and Fleming, B. (1990) *The Complete C++ Primer*, Academic Press

Wellman, F. (1992) *Software Costing: An objective approach to estimating and controlling the cost of computer software*, London: Prentice Hall

Weyuker, E. (1988) Evaluating software complexity measures, *IEEE Trans. on Software Engineering* **14**(9), 1357–1365

Whitewater Group (1989) *Actor Language Manual*, Evanston IL: The Whitewater Group Inc.

Whitmire, S.A. (1997) *Object-Oriented Design Measurement*, New York: Wiley

Wieringa, R.J. (1996) *Requirements Engineering*, Chichester, England: Wiley

Wilkie, F.G. (1993) *Object-Oriented Software Engineering: A Guide from Concepts to Practice*, Wokingham: Addison-Wesley

Wills, A.C. (1991) Specification in Fresco. In Stepney, Barden and Cooper (Eds.) *Object-Orientation in Z*, Berlin: Springer

Wills, A.C. (1996) Frameworks and CBD. In Patel, D., Sun, Y. and Patel, S. (Eds.) *Proc. OO Info. Systems*, Berlin: Springer

Wills, A.C. (2001) *Understanding and Using Catalysis*, Harlow, England: Addison-Wesley (provisional title)

Wilson, D. (1990) Class diagrams: A tool for design, documentation and teaching, *Journal of Object-Oriented Programming* **3**(9), 38–44

Wilson, P. (1990) *Computer Supported Cooperative Work*, Oxford: Intellect Books

Winblad, A.L., Edwards, S.D. and King, D.R. (1990) *Object-Oriented Software*, Reading MA: Addison-Wesley

Winder, R. (1993) *Developing C++ Software*, 2nd Edition, Chichester: Wiley

Winder, R. (2000) *Developing Java Software*, 2nd Edition, Chichester: Wiley

Wing, J.M. amd Nixon, M.R. (1989) Extending Ina Jo with Temporal Logic, *IEEE Transactions on Software Engineering*, Feb. 1989

Winograd , T. (Ed.) (1996) *Bringing Design to Software*, Reading MA: Addison-Wesley

Winograd, T. and Flores, F. (1986) *Understanding Computers and Cognition*, Reading MA: Addison-Wesley

Winston, P.H. (1984) *Artificial Intelligence* (2nd Edition), Reading MA: Addison-Wesley

Wirfs-Brock, R. and McKean, A. (1996) *Responsibility-Driven Design*, unpublished tutorial notes

Wirfs-Brock, R., Wilkerson, B. and Wiener, L. (1990) *Designing Object-Oriented Software*, Englewood Cliffs NJ: Prentice Hall

Wirth, N. (1976) *Algorithms + Data = Programs*, Englewood Cliffs, NJ: Prentice Hall

Witt, B.I., Baker, F.T. and Merritt, E.W. (1994) *Software Architecture and Design – Principles, Models and Methods*, New York: Van Nostrand Rheinhold

Woods, W.A. (1985) What's in a Link. In Brachman and Levesque (1985)

Woolfe, R. (1991) Managing and redesigning business processes to achieve dramatic performance improvements, *European Business Journal*, 1991

WWISA (World Wide Institute of Software Architects) (2000) www.wwisa.org/ 14 June 2000

Wu, C.T. (1990) Development of a Visual Database Interface: An Object-Oriented Approach. In Pinson and Weiner (1990)

Wulf, W.A., London, R.L. and Shaw, M. (1976) An Introduction to the Construction and Verification of Alphard Programs, *IEEE Trans. on Software Engineering*, SE-2

Xephon (1992) *The Mainframe Market Monitor*, Newbury, England: Xephon

Yazici, A., George, R., Buckles, B.P. *et al.* (1992) A survey of conceptual and logical data models for uncertainty management. In Zadeh, L. and Kacprzyk, J. (Eds.) *Fuzzy Logic for the Management of Uncertainty*, New York: Wiley

Yokote, Y. and Tokoro, M. (1987) Concurrent Programming in ConcurrentSmalltalk. In Yonezawa and Tokoro (1987), 129–158

Yonezawa, A. and Tokoro, M. (Eds.) (1987) *Object-Oriented Concurrent Programming*, Cambidge MA: MIT Press

Young, J.Z. (1986) *Philosophy and the Brain*, Oxford University Press

Young, R.M., Green, T.R.G. and Simon, T. (1989) Programmable User Models for Predictive Evaluation of Interface Designs. In Bice. K. and Lewis, C. (Eds.) *Human Factors in Computer Systems – CHI'89*, Reading MA: Addison-Wesley

Yourdon, E. (1992) *The Decline and Fall of the American Programmer*, Englewood Cliffs NJ: Prentice Hall

Yourdon, E. (1994) *Object-Oriented Systems Design*, Englewood Cliffs NJ: Prentice Hall

Yourdon, E. and Constantine, L.L. (1979) *Structured Design: Fundamentals of a Discipline of Computer Program and Systems Design*, Englewood Cliffs NJ: Prentice Hall

Yourdon, E., Whitehead, K., Thomann, J., Oppel, K. and Nevermann, P. (1995) *Mainstream Objects: An Analysis and Design Approach for Business*, Englewood Cliffs NJ: Prentice Hall

Yuan, G. (1995) A depth-first process model for object-oriented development with improved OOA/OOD notations, *Report on Object-Oriented Analysis and Design* **2**(1), 23–37

Zachman, J.A. (1987) A framework for information systems architecture, *IBM Systems Journal* **26**(3), 276–292

Zadeh, L.A. (1965) Fuzzy Sets, *Information and Control* **8**

Zadeh, L.A. (1971) Similarity relations and fuzzy orderings, *Information Sciences* **3**, 177–200

Zadeh, L.A. (1973) Outline of a New Approach to the Analysis of Complex Systems and Decision Processes, *IEEE Trans. Systems Man. and Cybernetics*, SMC-3, 28–44

Zadeh, L.A. (1982) A Computational Approach to Fuzzy Quantifiers in Natural Languages, University of California (Berkeley) Memo. UCB-ERL M82-36

Zadeh, L.A. (1985) Syllogistic Reasoning in Fuzzy Logic and its Application to Usuality and Reasoning with Dispositions, *IEEE Transactions* SMC-**15**(6)

Zamir, S. (1999) *Handbook of Object Technology*, Boca Raton FL: CRC Press

Zdonik, S.B. and Maier, D. (Eds.) (1990) *Readings in Object-Oriented Database Systems*, Morgan Kaufmann

Zdonik, S.B. and Wegner, P. (1985a) *A Database Approach to Languages, Libraries and Environments*, Technical Report CS-85-10, Department of Computer Science, Brown University

Zdonik, S.B. and Wegner, P. (1985b) *Language and Methodology for Object-Oriented Database Environments*, Technical Report CS-85-19, Department of Computer Science, Brown University

NAME INDEX

SUBJECT INDEX

– (*see* private)
(*see* protected)
$ (*see* class)
/ (*see* derived)
@pre, 263
+ (*see* public)
−>includes, 263
×, 251
1NF (*see* first normal form)
4+1 model of architecture, 333, 334, 335, 338
4GLs, 473, 616
80/20 rule, 456

A

Aardvark, 28-29, 32, 55–56, 166, 185, 187, 219, 278, 596, 634
ABCL/1, 101
ABEL, 73
abstract classes, 19, 35, 352, 548
abstract data types, 15, 18, 52 95, 186, 194
ABSTRACT FACTORY, 354
Abstract Windows Toolkit – Java (AWT), 83, 357
abstraction, 17, 21, 26, 305
Acceptance Test Plan, 510–11, 532
access or accessor methods, 15, 19, 94, 119
accidental and essential objects, 200, 307, 316, 655
ACCOUNTABILITY, 346

ACLs (*see* agent communication languages)
Act 3, 101, 589
action model metrics, 548
Action Technologies Workbench, 433
actions, 261, 367
activated memory, 556
activation diagrams, 422
active objects, 131, 612, 668
active rôle of the subject in perception, 383
Active X, 7, 84, 128, 132
activities, 483, 486, 488–89, 492–94, 496, 505, 508, 512–13, 519–20, 522, 528, 530, 536
activity diagrams, 239, 398, 405, 459, 711
activity/function diagrams, 705
actor languages and systems, 4, 17, 101, 110, 588, 599
Actor, 100, 585
actors – Booch, 680
actors, 4, 247, 261, 400, 417, 614
ad hoc polymorphism, 24, 78
ad hoc queries, 119, 206, 226
Ada 83, 85
Ada 95, 86, 102
Ada packages, 679, 730
Ada, 4–5, 24, 35, 80–81, 86, 104–105, 110, 128, 236, 615, 663–64, 666–67, 671

Adabas Entire, 189–90, 193
ADAM, 212, 221
Adaplex, 163, 183, 184
ADAPTER, 343, 358
Adaptive, 55
ADAPTOR pattern language, 336, 349–351, 358
adjoint functors 282–83, 292
ADLs (*see* Architectural Description Languages)
ADM3, 735
adoption strategies, 62
AESOP, 326
AGCS, 343
agent communication languages, 593, 605, 607–609, 613
agent co-ordination, 612
Agent Object Model (AOM), 401, 423, 549, 614
agent-based systems, 593
agents, 6, 96, 260–61, 330–31, 378, 382–83, 388, 400, 402, 408, 414, 417, 423, 549, 605–606
architecture of, 609
as objects, 401, 611
basic, 607
communication between, 400
data retrieval, 608
design of, 608
heterogeneous, 608
in Booch, 680
in Eiffel, 82